Under the General Editorship of

JOSEPH W. TOWLE

Washington University

Houghton Mifflin
Adviser in Management

Edited by

DALTON E. McFARLAND

Professor of Management, Michigan State University

HOUGHTON MIFFLIN COMPANY · BOSTON

CURRENT ISSUES AND
EMERGING CONCEPTS
IN MANAGEMENT

Readings from the Academy
of Management / Volume II

NEW YORK · ATLANTA · GENEVA, ILL. · DALLAS · PALO ALTO

General Editor's Introduction

This second volume of readings from the publications of the Academy of Management follows the first collection by four years. During this period the *Journal of the Academy of Management,* which was established in 1958 with Professor Paul M. Dauten, Jr. of the University of Illinois as its first Editor, has been successfully published. The *Proceedings* of the annual meetings have continued to appear. After completing his three-year term as Editor of the *Journal,* Professor Dauten served as Editor of the first edition of *Current Issues and Emerging Concepts in Management.* Now another Editor, Professor Dalton E. McFarland of Michigan State University, who directed the affairs of the *Journal* from 1961 through 1963, has been invited to select and edit the readings for Volume II.

Professor McFarland is especially well qualified for this task. In addition to his experience as Editor of the *Journal,* he is the author of several management textbooks and monographs and has served at Michigan State University since 1952. He has been Professor and Chairman of the Department of Management at Michigan State University since 1960. Among numerous professional affiliations, Professor McFarland has made many notable contributions to the growth and progress of the Academy of Management during recent years. He has served as a member of several Academy committees, as Chairman of the Research and Publications Committee, and in 1964 he was Vice President. It is a "pleasant coincidence" that he is President of the Academy at the time when this second volume of readings is published under his editorship.

The frequently quoted purpose of the Academy of Management is, ". . . to foster the search for truth and the general advancement of learning through free discussion and research in the field of management." During recent years the national and regional meetings, as well as the publications of the Academy, have provided professors and other theorists with one of the largest and most active forums for the free discussion of management theory and practice. These opportunities for the exchange of ideas and for the publication of new concepts and research in management are most valuable, particularly when the impact of computer technology, new mathematical models, and contributions from the behavioral sciences are accelerating the evolutionary processes almost to the point of revolutionizing management theory. If a unified theory of management is to evolve, modern theories of organization and administration must be screened, tested, and integrated with the proven fundamentals of management, developed and practiced throughout the history of man. This emerging integration of concepts and theories, apparent in this volume, appears to offer a most promising opportunity for the Academy of Management and, indeed, for all who teach and practice business administration.

This edition offers, in relatively brief and inexpensive form, carefully selected articles with part introductions and headnotes which help to bring about an overall unity while making it easier for each instructor to use the material according to his particular course organization and requirements. The level of difficulty and range of coverage suggest that the book would be appropriate for seminars and courses in graduate schools of business administration while also serving as a useful supplementary text for introductory undergraduate management courses. It should interest business executives who endeavor to keep abreast of trends and developments in management science and thought. Its convenient size and broad coverage of subjects in the areas of organization, administration and operations research, for example, should make it appealing to participants in executive development programs. Since only two articles in Volume II appeared also in Volume I, professors conducting seminars in management at the graduate level might well decide to use both Volume I and II of *Current Issues and Emerging Concepts in Management* with students seeking broader coverage and deeper insight into the history and development of management thought. Because these volumes contribute significantly to the literature in the field, Houghton Mifflin Company has welcomed the opportunity to publish them for the Academy.

JOSEPH W. TOWLE
Washington University

Preface

The widespread acceptance of the first edition of *Current Issues and Emerging Concepts in Management* has encouraged the Academy of Management and the publisher to bring out a second volume of readings from Academy publications. This new volume benefits from three additional years of publication of the *Academy of Management Journal*. In addition, it makes possible the presentation of valuable material omitted from the previous collection because of space limitations.

Like its predecessor, this book is intended as supplementary material for university management courses, and as an overview for the use of managers in business enterprises. That such hopes are justified is indicated by the large number of requests by professors of management and company training directors for permission to reproduce for classroom use many of the articles contained herein.

Whereas the first volume emphasized history and philosophy of management, and management as science and art, the second emphasizes theoretical problems in management, organization, and executive behavior. The four sections of the present volume center on issues of great controversy and importance in management:

Part   I — The emerging theory of management
Part II — Organization theory
Part III — Executive behavior in the business enterprise
Part IV — Problems of international management

This classification of articles within this scheme is admittedly arbitrary, but it serves to relate several important selections in a logical overall framework.

Wherever possible, the articles included were based on the authors' research. They deal with crucial substantive problems now engaging the attention of a wide variety of scholars and teachers, representing not only management, but other basic disciplines as well. The selections reflect the changing, dynamic character of management, and indicate some of the unfinished business now facing the management researcher. For the student of management, they indicate not only current issues and concepts, but also the challenges that lie ahead in the search for better knowledge.

The editor of this volume wishes to acknowledge, with deep appreciation, the work of the authors of the selections included, for it was their willingness to entrust an infant journal with their careful work that made this collection possible. Professor Joseph W. Towle of Washington University, and Mr. Hugh E. Joyce of the Houghton Mifflin Company furnished many valuable ideas and provided constant encouragement and assistance along the way, and to them goes the credit for originally conceiving this series. To my assistant, Mr. Edward Johnson, and my typist, Miss Sonja Carlson, I express my appreciation for their continuing interest, hard work, and meticulous attention to detail. To Mrs. Russell McAllen I express my thanks for so adeptly managing the office in which most of the work took place.

DALTON E. McFARLAND
Michigan State University

Table of Contents

PART ONE

Emerging Management Theory

Introduction

1. The Management Theory Jungle — *Harold Koontz*   7
2. Management Theory: Functional and Evolutionary — *Waino W. Suojanen*   24
3. The Tactics of Jungle Warfare — *Lyndall F. Urwick*   37
4. Transcend the Current Debate on Administrative Theory — *Paul J. Gordon*   53
5. The Next Development in Management Science: A General Theory: — *William C. Frederick*   68
6. An Inquiry into the American System of Industrial Management — *William Gomberg*   77
7. Managers' Theories of Management — *Dale Yoder, Raymond E. Miles, Lawrence McKibbin, Robert E. Boynton, and George W. England*   84
8. Processes vis-a-vis Systems: Toward a Model of the Enterprise and Administration — *Wendell French*   94
9. Basic Frameworks for Decisions — *Charles Z. Wilson and Marcus Alexis*   108
10. Two Approaches to Computer Simulation — *Kalman J. Cohen*   126

PART TWO

Emerging Organization Theory

Introduction

11. Organization as a Separate Branch of Management — *Alvin Brown*   138
12. Organization Theory: An Overview and an Appraisal — *William G. Scott*   151
13. Recent Breakthroughs in Methods of Research on Organizations — *Albert H. Rubenstein*   174

14. Organizational Constructs: An Approach to Understanding   185
    Organization — *William B. Wolf*

15. Decentralization of Authority in a Bureaucracy —   195
    Bernard H. Baum

16. Management Science and Group Behavior: Work Unit   204
    Cohesiveness — *Robert T. Golembiewski*

17. The Application of Queuing Theory to the Span of Control —   218
    Lawrence S. Hill

18. Decisions and Research in Staff Utilization — *Alan C. Filley*   237

19. The PERT System: An Appraisal of Program Evaluation Review   251
    Technique — *Daniel D. Roman*

20. Toward a Behavioral Science Theory of Wages —   264
    David W. Belcher

21. A Behavioral Approach to Wage Administration: Work Flow   282
    and Structural Design — *Robert T. Golembiewski*

22. Managerial Authority in the Employment Relationship —   295
    Stanley Young

PART THREE

Studies of Executive Behavior

Introduction

23. Creative Leadership: Human vs. Metal Brains — *Stanley Stark*   308

24. Uncertainty, Expectations, and Foundations of the Theory of   318
    Planning — *Milton H. Spencer*

25. Entrepreneurial Prototype in Bank Management: A Compara-   329
    tive Study of Branch Bank Managers — *William D. Litzinger*

26. Criteria for the Determination of Compensation and Organiza-   340
    tional Status for Managerial Jobs — *Robert J. House, Leon E.
    Peters, Hugh M. Stephenson, and James E. McElwain*

27. The Authoritarian Cultural Lag in Business — *Eugene Emerson*   357
    Jennings

28. Rationality and Executive Motivation — *Richard F. Ericson*   372

29. The Situation and the Opportunistic Executive — *Stanley E. Bryan*   392

30. Logical Analysis and Executive Performance — *M. C. Branch*   416

31. Not By Loyalty Alone — *William R. Gall*   422

32. Business and the Social System: End of the Brumaire —   431
    Clarence C. Walton

33. Value Perspectives in Management Decision —   444
    Wilmar F. Bernthal

PART FOUR

Problems of International Management

Introduction

34. Management and Organization in Japanese Industry —   455
    Joseph N. Froomkin

35. The Universality of American Management Philosophy —   462
    Richard R. Gonzalez and Claude McMillan, Jr.

36. Cross-Cultural Perspectives on Management Principles —   472
    Winston Oberg

37. Managerial Motivation in Soviet and Czechloslovak Industries: 490
    A Comparison — Barry M. Richman

CURRENT ISSUES AND EMERGING

CONCEPTS IN MANAGEMENT

Readings From The Academy

of Management / Volume II

PART ONE

The fact that management theory is evolving at an ever more rapid pace is due in no small measure to the burgeoning of the behavioral and mathematical sciences as scholars extend their research into various spheres of application in the world of business. It is significant that the effort to cast a general theory of business enterprise has not yet been fruitful. Since the publication of Veblen's *The Theory of Business Enterprise* in 1904,[1] only a few comprehensive theoretical works have appeared. A satisfactory general theory, in the sense of "grand theory" seems still beyond reach.

Perhaps theory will not always be so elusive. Recently, several books have attempted systematic treatments of empirical and other research data at a conceptual level high enough to justify the use of the term "theory," if not grand theory. For the most part, these theoretical developments have come from research in the fields of economics of the firm, operations research, computer and mathematical applications, organization theories, and behavioral explanations of executive behavior. In

[1] Thorstein Veblen, *The Theory of Business Enterprise*, Charles Scribner's & Sons, 1904.

Emerging Management Theory

1963, Cyert and March presented A Behavioral Theory of the Firm,[2] based on empirical studies of decision-making within the firm. The impact of computer technology and quantitative analysis techniques are clearly apparent in this volume, as are its orientations in economic analysis. Published in 1964, Joseph McGuire's Theories of Business Behavior[3] surveys emerging theory based on research in psychology, sociology, economics, mathematics, and cultural anthropology. These more recent contributions will no doubt spur further efforts to develop a systematic theory of business enterprise.

It could be argued that a general theory of management will be necessary before a theory of business enterprise can be complete. Yet theoretical developments in management are no farther along than theories of business enterprise. Comprehensive theoretical analysis in management research is rare. Management scholars borrow and apply concepts rather

[2] Richard M. Cyert and James G. March, A Behavioral Theory of the Firm, Englewood Cliffs, N.J., Prentice-Hall, Inc., 1963.

[3] Joseph W. McGuire, Theories of Business Behavior, Englewood Cliffs, N.J., Prentice-Hall, Inc., 1964.

than delineate their own. Management research is still largely at descriptive levels, and researchers give inadequate attention to the assumptions and beliefs on which research is based. Borrowing and applying the concepts, findings, and methodologies of other disciplines is no doubt desirable, but management research cannot afford to restrict itself to being merely a testing ground for other disciplines. Until management research springs from the demands of an increasingly comprehensive and rigorous body of coherent management theory, the management discipline remains without solid foundation.

Confusion still beclouds our theoretical horizons. Management appears to be a discipline of broad scope comprehending wide-ranging research interests, but its aims and directions are uncertain. Its identity is vague, its boundaries undefined. Worst of all, conceptual clarity is seriously lacking. Business administration and management, for example, are often treated as synonymous from a theoretical point of view. Organization is not clearly distinguished from management. Deans, scholars, and writers of various persuasions too frequently assume the interchangeability of these terms. Clarity and precision in the use of basic concepts, recommended by several authors in this section, would go far toward sharpening the theoretical basis of both management and business administration. But it is all too easy to slip from a discussion of management or organization into a morass of problems and opinions about business administration generally, or to move back and forth from management to organization without recognizing the differences between them.

Another difficulty in management theory is the confusion that surrounds the relationships of the supporting and ancillary disciplines. Such disciplines are important for two reasons, the first being that they provide an infusion of subject matter that substantiates and supports management subject matter, enriches its insights, and clarifies its assumptions. The second reason is that the methodologies employed by the supporting disciplines are important tools for theoretical and applied research in management. But there is much confusion between the subject matter and the research tools. To say that using star-shaped communication nets leads to certain predictable behavior patterns under given conditions is important to the social psychologist who uses experimentation to establish this knowledge and build his discipline. Yet this means little within the discipline of management until a managment researcher (and theorist) fits the finding into a management framework and tests it by further research. He may then find that the use of the same set of behavioral research tools, adapted to his own frame of reference, provides a valuable instrument for improving our knowledge of the business enterprise. He must keep clearly in mind that he has used both a substantive finding and a set of methods.

Behavioral and mathematical tools and methodologies have thus been mistaken for the management processes themselves. The result is undue eclecticism in the field of management. Although behavioral and mathematical ideologies promise great discoveries and rewards, the refinement and verification of theoretical considerations within management have lagged.

Some encouraging progress can be noted on the management theory scene, however. More and more scholars are working on theoretical problems, or considering research where gaps exist, rather than letting theory evolve naturalistically from scattered, impulsive research efforts. More replication studies are beginning to appear. A recent book, *Toward a Unified Theory of Management*,[4] analyzes the current state of management theory. It summarizes the main theoretical streams of thought now current, and describes some of the forces acting for and against a unified theory of management, as discussed by participants in a management symposium in 1962.

Despite deviations from the rigors of a true discipline, management today has achieved a measure of eminence as a basic field of study in collegiate schools of business administration. No doubt this is partly due to the fact that almost everyone thinks he can talk and write knowledgeably about it. Yet, for management scholars, this emerging role represents a challenge as well as an accomplishment, for progress to date is but a reflection of the unfinished tasks ahead. It is fitting that, from time to time, teachers and researchers audit the attainments and deficiencies of their work. Hence this volume emphasizes where possible the products of research within schools of business administration.

The first four articles in this section may be considered as a unit. The paper on "The Management Theory Jungle," appearing in late 1961, aroused strong controversy, with reactions both for and against its main thesis that serious divergencies among theoretical schools of thought in management need to be brought into closer harmony. However one may disagree with the article's assertions and implications, it seems clear that, as the paper suggests, management scholars must reevaluate and redirect the theoretical bases upon which the field of management appears to rest. That the jungle problem is more than one of taxonomy, classifications, typologies, or semantics is indicated in the papers by Professors Suojanen, Urwick, and Gordon. These thoughtful reactions to the jungle concept serve to amplify and interpret the problem more fully.

The article by William C. Frederick on a general theory of management shows the eventual sweep and elegance that theory may ultimately attain. The author is generally optimistic about the possibilities for a general theory, and suggests some of its outer horizons. The Gomberg

4 Harold Koontz (Ed.), *Toward a Unified Theory of Management*, New York, McGraw-Hill Book Company, Inc., 1964.

article, too, indicates the breadth of vision of theoretical frontiers, and suggests by analogy some broad goals and a specific research approach for testing the conceptual framework advanced. Research methods for testing attitudes that underlie the theories of management held by managers are presented in the Yoder article. By means of an experimental game, the authors examined managerial decisions along a series of scales for five areas of theory. The scaling for each area ranged from early, historical applications to the most recent advanced theory. The executive responses revealed similarities and differences in personal patterns of management theory held by the executives.

In the final three articles, we see applications of the behavioral and mathematical points of view which are directed toward basic but specific problems of managerial behavior. Professor French develops a model of the business enterprise which integrates the concepts of process and system with certain other constructs, to build a model of the enterprise, which in turn makes possible a model of the administrator's job.

Crucial to management theory is the matter of how within given frameworks decision-making occurs. Professors Wilson and Alexis contrast "open" and "closed" decision frameworks. This article argues for open systems, with greater recognition for conscious and unconscious cognitive processes in which search locates feasible alternatives, as compared to closed systems in which rational choices are made among known sets of alternatives. The future of "open" decision models is bright, since they bring greater flexibility into the process of problem-solving.

In the final article Professor Kalman J. Cohen compares the "synthesis" and "analysis" approaches to computer simulation. The various types of simulation are analyzed, together with the varying types of empirical information required by the different approaches.

1

The Management Theory Jungle*

Harold Koontz

University of California, Los Angeles

With the publication of this landmark article on the confusion of theoretical approaches in the field of management, Professor Koontz introduced the jungle concept into the vocabulary of management specialists. His descriptions aroused much healthy controversy, and resulted in calling attention to the need for greater rigor in theoretical analysis. He cites the difficulties that block understanding among management theorists and suggests ways in which the jungle may give way to clearer and more fruitful theory. By more sharply defining concepts, by clarifying semantic difficulties, by testing fundamental propositions — in short, by following the precepts of science — management may become much more of a science than many now think possible.

Although students of management would readily agree that there have been problems of management since the dawn of organized life, most would also agree that systematic examination of management, with few exceptions, is the product of the present century and more especially of the past two decades. Moreover, until recent years almost all of those who have attempted to analyze the management process and look for some theoretical underpinnings to help improve research, teaching, and practice were alert and perceptive practitioners of the art who reflected on the many years of experience. Thus, at least in looking at *general* management as an intellectually based art, the earliest meaningful writing came from such experienced practitioners as Fayol, Mooney, Alvin Brown, Sheldon, Barnard, and Urwick. Certainly not even the most academic worshipper of empirical research can overlook the empiricism involved in

* Taken from the *Journal of the Academy of Management*, vol. 4, no. 3, December, 1961, pp. 174–188.

distilling fundamentals from decades of experience by such discerning practitioners as these. Admittedly done without questionnaires, controlled interviews, or mathematics, observations by such men can hardly be accurately regarded as *a priori* or "armchair."

The noteworthy absence of academic writing and research in the formative years of modern management theory is now more than atoned for by a deluge of research and writing from the academic halls. What is interesting and perhaps nothing more than a sign of the unsophisticated adolescence of management theory is how the current flood has brought with it a wave of great differences and apparent confusion. From the orderly analysis of management at the shop-room level by Frederick Taylor and the reflective distillation of experience from the general management point of view by Henri Fayol, we now see these and other early beginnings overgrown and entangled by a jungle of approaches and approachers to management theory.

There are the behavioralists, born of the Hawthorne experiments and the awakened interest in human relations during the 1930's and 1940's, who see management as a complex of interpersonal relationships and the basis of management theory the tentative tenets of the new and undeveloped science of psychology. There are also those who see management theory as simply a manifestation of the institutional and cultural aspects of sociology. Still others, observing that the central core of management is decision-making, branch in all directions from this core to encompass everything in organization life. Then, there are mathematicians who think of management primarily as an exercise in logical relationships expressed in symbols and the omnipresent and ever revered model. But the entanglement of growth reaches its ultimate when the study of management is regarded as a study of one of a number of systems and subsystems, with an understandable tendency for the researcher to be dissatisfied until he has encompassed the entire physical and cultural universe as a management system.

With the recent discovery of an ages-old problem area by social, physical, and biological scientists, and with the supersonic increase in interest by all types of enterprise managers, the apparent impenetrability of the present thicket which we call management theory is not difficult to comprehend. One can hardly be surprised that psychologists, sociologists, anthropologists, sociometricists, economists, mathematicians, physicists, biologists, political scientists, business administration scholars, and even practicing managers, should hop on this interesting, challenging, and profitable bandwagon.

This welling of interest from every academic and practicing corner should not upset anyone concerned with seeing the frontiers of knowledge pushed back and the intellectual base of practice broadened. But what is rather upsetting to the practitioner and the observer, who see great social potential from improved management, is that the variety of approaches to management theory has led to a kind of confused and destructive jungle warfare. Particularly among academic disciplines and their disciples, the primary interests of many would-be cult leaders seem to be to carve out a distinct (and hence "original") approach to management. And to defend this originality, and thereby gain a place in posterity (or at least to gain a publication which will justify academic status or promotion), it seems to have become too much the current style to downgrade, and sometimes misrepresent, what anyone else has said, or thought, or done.

In order to cut through this jungle and bring to light some of the issues and problems involved in the present management theory area so that the tremendous interest, intelligence, and research results may become more meaningful, it is my purpose here to classify the various "schools" of management theory, to identify briefly what I believe to be the major source of differences, and to offer some suggestions for disentangling the jungle. It is hoped that a movement for clarification can be started so at least we in the field will not be a group of blind men identifying the same elephant with our widely varying and sometimes viciously argumentative theses.

The Major "Schools" of Management Theory

In attempting to classify the major schools of management theory into six main groups, I am aware that I may overlook certain approaches and cannot deal with all the nuances of each approach. But it does seem that most of the approaches to management theory can be classified in one of these so-called "schools."

The Management Process School

This approach to management theory perceives management as a process of getting things done through and with people operating in organized groups. It aims to analyze the process, to establish a conceptual framework for it, to identify principles underlying it, and to build up a theory of management from them. It regards management as a universal process, regardless of the type of enterprise, or the level in a given enterprise, although recognizing, obviously, that the environment of management differs widely between enterprises and levels. It looks upon management theory as a way of organizing experience so that practice can be improved through research, empirical testing of principles, and teaching of fundamentals involved in the management process.[1]

Often referred to, especially by its critics, as the "traditional" or "universalist" school, this school can be said to have been fathered by Henri Fayol, although many of his offspring did not know of their parent, since Fayol's work was eclipsed by the bright light of his contemporary, Frederick Taylor, and clouded by the lack of a widely available English translation until 1949. Other than Fayol, most of the early contributors to this school dealt only with the organization portion of the management process, largely because of their greater experience with this facet of management and the simple fact that planning and control, as well as the function of staffing, were given little attention by managers before 1940.

This school bases its approach to management theory on several fundamental beliefs:

    (1) that managing is a process and can best be dissected intellectually by analyzing the functions of the manager;

    (2) that long experience with management in a variety of enterprise situations can be grounds for distillation of certain fundamental truths or generalizations — usually referred to as principles — which have a clarifying and predictive value in the understanding and improvement of managing;

    (3) that these fundamental truths can become focal points for useful research both to ascertain their validity and to improve their meaning and applicability in practice;

    (4) that such truths can furnish elements, at least until disproved, and certainly until sharpened, of a useful theory of management;

    (5) that managing is an art, but one like medicine or engineering, which can be improved by reliance on the light and understanding of principles;

    (6) that principles in management, like principles in the biological and physical sciences, are nonetheless true even if a prescribed treatment or design by a practitioner in a given case situation chooses to ignore a principle and the costs involved, or attempts to do something else to offset the costs incurred (this is, of course, not new in medicine, engineering, or any other art, for art is the creative task of compromising fundamentals to attain a desired result); and

---

[1] It is interesting that one of the scholars strongly oriented to human relations and behavioral approaches to management has recently noted that "theory can be viewed as a way of organizing experience" and that "once initial sense is made out of experienced environment, the way is cleared for an even more adequate organization of this experience." See Robert Dubin in "Psyche, Sensitivity, and Social Structure," critical comment in Robert Tannenbaum, I. R. Weschler, and Fred Massarik, *Leadership and Organization: A Behavioral Science Approach* (New York: McGraw-Hill Book Co., 1961), p. 401.

(7) that, while the totality of culture and of the physical and biological universe has varying effects on the manager's environment and subjects, as indeed they do in every other field of science and art, the theory of management does not need to encompass the field of all knowledge in order for it to serve as a scientific or theoretical foundation.

The basic approach of this school, then, is to look, first, to the functions of managers. As a second step in this approach, many of us have taken the functions of managers and further dissected them by distilling what we see as fundamental truths in the understandably complicated practice of management. I have found it useful to classify my analysis of these functions around the essentials involved in the following questions:

(1) What is the nature of the function?
(2) What is the purpose of the function?
(3) What explains the structure of the function?
(4) What explains the process of the function?

Perhaps there are other more useful approaches, but I have found that I can place everything pertaining to management (even some of the rather remote research and concepts) in this framework.

Also, purely to make the area of management theory intellectually manageable, those who subscribe to this school do not usually attempt to include in the theory the entire areas of sociology, economics, biology, psychology, physics, chemistry, or others. This is done not because these other areas of knowledge are unimportant and have no bearing on management, but merely because no real progress has ever been made in science or art without significant partitioning of knowledge. Yet, anyone would be foolish not to realize that a function which deals with people in their various activities of producing and marketing anything from money to religion and education is completely independent of the physical, biological, and cultural universe in which we live. And, are there not such relationships in other "compartments" of knowledge and theory?

The Empirical School

A second approach to management I refer to as the "empirical" school. In this, I include those scholars who identify management as a study of experience, sometimes with intent to draw generalizations but usually merely as a means of teaching experience and transferring it to the practitioner or student. Typical of this school are those who see management or "policy" as the study and analysis of cases and those with such approaches as Ernest Dale's "comparative approach."[2]

2 *The Great Organizers* (New York: McGraw-Hill Book Co., 1960), pp. 11–28.

This approach seems to be based upon the premise that, if we study the experience of successful managers, or the mistakes made in management, or if we attempt to solve management problems, we will somehow understand and learn to apply the most effective kinds of management techniques. This approach, as often applied, assumes that, by finding out what worked or did not work in individual circumstances, the student or the practitioner will be able to do the same in comparable situations.

No one can deny the importance of studying experience through such study, or of analyzing the "how-it-was-done" of management. But management, unlike law, is not a science based on precedent, and situations in the future exactly comparable to the past are exceedingly unlikely to occur. Indeed, there is a positive danger of relying too much on past experience and on undistilled history of managerial problem-solving for the simple reason that a technique or approach found "right" in the past may not fit a situation of the future.

Those advocating the empirical approach are likely to say that what they really do in analyzing cases or history is to draw from certain generalizations which can be applied as useful guides to thought or action in future case situations. As a matter of fact, Ernest Dale, after claiming to find "so little practical value" from the principles enunciated by the "universalists," curiously drew certain "generalizations" or "criteria" from his valuable study of a number of great practitioners of management.[3] There is some question as to whether Dale's "comparative" approach is not really the same as the "universalist" approach he decries, except with a different distiller of basic truths.

By the emphasis of the empirical school on study of experience, it does appear that the research and thought so engendered may assist in hastening the day for verification of principles. It is also possible that the proponents of this school may come up with a more useful framework of principles than that of the management process school. But, to the extent that the empirical school draws generalizations from its research, and it would seem to be a necessity to do so unless its members are satisfied to exchange meaningless and structureless experience, this approach tends to be and do the same as the management process school.

The Human Behavior School

This approach to the analysis of management is based on the central thesis that, since managing involves getting things done with and through people, the study of management must be centered on interpersonal relations. Variously called the "human relations," "leadership," or "behavioral

3 *Ibid.*, pp. 11, 26–28, 62–68.

sciences" approach, this school brings to bear "existing and newly developed theories, methods, and techniques of the relevant social sciences upon the study of inter- and intrapersonal phenomena, ranging fully from the personality dynamics of individuals at one extreme to the relations of cultures at the other."[4] In other words, this school concentrates on the "people" part of management and rests on the principle that, where people work together as groups in order to accomplish objectives, "people should understand people."

The scholars in this school have a heavy orientation to psychology and social psychology. Their primary focus is the individual as a socio-psychological being and what motivates him. The members of this school vary from those who see it as a portion of the manager's job, a tool to help him understand and get the best from people by meeting their needs and responding to their motivations, to those who see the psychological behavior of individuals and groups as the total of management.

In this school are those who emphasize human relations as an art that the manager should advantageously understand and practice. There are those who focus attention on the manager as a leader and sometimes equate management to leadership, thus, in effect, tending to treat all group activities as "managed" situations. There are those who see the study of group dynamics and interpersonal relationships as simply a study of socio-psychological relationships and seem, therefore, merely to be attaching the term "management" to the field of social psychology.

That management must deal with human behavior can hardly be denied. That the study of human interactions, whether in the environment of management or in unmanaged situations, is important and useful one could not dispute. And it would be a serious mistake to regard good leadership as unimportant to good managership. But whether the field of human behavior is the equivalent of the field of management is quite another thing. Perhaps it is like calling the study of the human body the field of cardiology.

The Social System School

Closely related to the human behavior school and often confused or intertwined with it is one which might be labeled the social system school. This includes those researchers who look upon management as a social system, that is, a system of cultural interrelationships. Sometimes, as in the case of March and Simon,[5] the system is limited to formal organizations, using the term "organization" as equivalent to enterprise, rather than the authority-activity concept used most often in management. In other

---

[4] R. Tannenbaum, I. R. Weschler, and F. Massarik, *Leadership and Organization* (New York: McGraw-Hill Book Co., 1961), p. 9.
[5] *Organizations* (New York: John Wiley & Sons, Inc., 1958).

cases, the approach is not to distinguish the formal organization, but rather to encompass any kind of system of human relationships.

Heavily sociological in flavor, this approach to management does essentially what any study of sociology does. It identifies the nature of the cultural relationships of various social groups and attempts to show these as a related, and usually an integrated, system.

Perhaps the spiritual father of this ardent and vocal school of management theorists is Chester Barnard.[6] In searching for an answer to fundamental explanations underlying the managing process, this thoughtful business executive developed a theory of cooperation grounded in the needs of the individual to solve, through cooperation, the biological, physical, and social limitations of himself and his environment. Barnard then carved from the total of cooperative systems so engendered one set of interrelationships which he defines as "formal organization." His formal organization concept, quite unlike that usually held by management practitioners, is any cooperative system in which there are persons able to communicate with each other and who are willing to contribute action toward a conscious common purpose.

The Barnard concept of cooperative systems pervades the work of many contributors to the social system school of management. For example, Herbert Simon at one time defined the subject of organization theory and the nature of human organizations as "systems of interdependent activity, encompassing at least several primary groups and usually characterized, at the level of consciousness of participants, by a high degree of rational direction of behavior toward ends that are objects of common knowledge."[7] Simon and others have subsequently seemed to have expanded this concept of social systems to include any cooperative and purposeful group interrelationship or behavior.

This school has made many noteworthy contributions to management. The recognition of organized enterprise as a social organism, subject to all the pressures and conflicts of the cultural environment, has been helpful to the management theorist and the practitioner alike. Among some of the more helpful aspects are the awareness of the institutional foundations of organization authority, the influence of informal organization, and such social factors as those Wight Bakke has called the "bonds of organization."[8] Likewise, many of Barnard's helpful insights, such as his

[6] *The Functions of the Executive* (Cambridge, Mass.: Harvard University Press, 1938).

[7] "Comments on the Theory of Organizations," 46 *American Political Science Review*, No. 4 (December, 1952), p. 1130.

[8] *Bonds of Organization* (New York: Harper & Brothers, 1950). These "bonds" or "devices" of organization are identified by Bakke as (1) the functional specifications system (a system of teamwork arising from job specifications and arrangements for association); (2) the status system (a vertical hierarchy of authority); (3) the communications system; (4) the reward and penalty system; and (5) the organization charter (ideas and means which give character and individuality to the organization, or enterprise).

economy of incentives and his theory of opportunism, have brought the power of sociological understanding into the realm of management practice.

Basic sociology, analysis of concepts of social behavior, and the study of group behavior in the framework of social systems do have great value in the field of management. But one may well ask the question whether this *is* management. Is the field of management coterminous with the field of sociology? Or is sociology an important underpinning like language, psychology, physiology, mathematics, and other fields of knowledge? Must management be defined in terms of the universe of knowledge?

The Decision Theory School

Another approach to management theory, undertaken by a growing and scholarly group, might be referred to as the decision theory school. This group concentrates on rational approach to decision — the selection from among possible alternatives of a course of action or of an idea. The approach of this school may be to deal with the decision itself, or to the persons or organizational group making the decision, or to an analysis of the decision process. Some limit themselves fairly much to the economic rationale of the decision, while others regard anything which happens in an enterprise the subject of their analysis, and still others expand decision theory to cover the psychological and sociological aspect and environment of decisions and decision-makers.

The decision-making school is apparently an outgrowth of the theory of consumer's choice with which economists have been concerned since the days of Jeremy Bentham early in the nineteenth century. It has arisen out of such economic problems and analyses as utility maximization, indifference curves, marginal utility, and economic behavior under risks and uncertainties. It is, therefore, no surprise that one finds most of the members of this school to be economic theorists. It is likewise no surprise to find the content of this school to be heavily oriented to model construction and mathematics.

The decision theory school has tended to expand its horizon considerably beyond the process of evaluating alternatives. That point has become for many only a springboard for examination of the entire sphere of human activity, including the nature of the organization structure, psychological and social reactions of individuals and groups, the development of basic information for decisions, an analysis of values and particularly value considerations with respect to goals, communications networks, and incentives. As one would expect, when the decision theorists study the small, but central, area of decision *making*, they are led by this keyhole look at management to consider the entire field of enterprise operation and its environment. The result is that decision theory becomes no longer a neat and narrow concentration on decision, but rather a broad view of the enterprise as a social system.

There are those who believe that, since management is characterized by its concentration on decisions, the future development of management theory will tend to use the decision as its central focus and the rest of management theory will be hung on this structural center. This may occur and certainly the study of the decision, the decision process, and the decision maker can be extended to cover the entire field of management as anyone might conceive it. Nevertheless, one wonders whether this focus cannot also be used to build around it the entire area of human knowledge. For, as most decision theorists recognize, the problem of choice is individual, as well as organizational, and most of what has been said that is pure decision theory can be applied to the existence and thinking of a Robinson Crusoe.

The Mathematical School

Although mathematical methods can be used by any school of management theory, and have been, I have chosen to group under a school those theorists who see management as a system of mathematical models and processes. Perhaps the most widely known group I arbitrarily so lump are the operations researchers or operations analysts, who have sometimes anointed themselves with the rather pretentious name of "management scientists." The abiding belief of this group is that, if management, or organization, or planning, or decision-making is a logical process, it can be expressed in terms of mathematical symbols and relationships. The central approach of this school is the model, for it is through these devices that the problem is expressed in its basic relationship and in terms of selected goals or objectives.

There can be no doubt of the great usefulness of mathematical approaches to any field of inquiry. It forces upon the researcher the definition of a problem or problem area, it conveniently allows the insertion of symbols for unknown data, and its logical methodology, developed by years of scientific application and abstraction, furnishes a powerful tool for solving or simplifying complex phenomena.

But it is hard to see mathematics as a truly separate school of management theory, any more than it is a separate "school" in physics, chemistry, engineering, or medicine. I only deal with it here as such because there has appeared to have developed a kind of cult around mathematical analysts who have subsumed to themselves the area of management.

In pointing out that mathematics is a tool, rather than a school, it is not my intention to underestimate the impact of mathematics on the science and practice of management. By bringing to this immensely important and complex field the tools and techniques of the physical sciences, the mathematicians have already made an immense contribution to orderly thinking. They have forced on people in management the means and desirability of seeing many problems more clearly, they have pressed on scholars and practitioners the need for establishing goals and measures of effectiveness, they have been extremely helpful in getting the management area seen as a logical system of relationships, and they have caused people in management to review and occasionally reorganize information sources and systems so that mathematics can be given sensible quantitative meaning. But with all this meaningful contribution and the greater sharpness and sophistication of planning which is resulting, I cannot see that mathematics is management theory any more than it is astronomy.

The Major Sources of Mental Entanglement in the Jungle

In outlining the various schools, or approaches, of management theory, it becomes clear that these intellectual cults are not drawing greatly different inferences from the physical and cultural environment surrounding us. Why, then, have there been so many differences between them and why such a struggle, particularly among our academic brethren, to obtain a place in the sun by denying the approaches of others? Like the widely differing and often contentious denominations of the Christian religion, all have essentially the same goals and deal with essentially the same world.

While there are many sources of the mental entanglement in the management theory jungle, the major ones are the following:

The Semantics Jungle

As is so often true when intelligent men argue about basic problems, some of the trouble lies in the meaning of key words. The semantics problem is particularly severe in the field of management. There is even a difference in the meaning of the word "management." Most people would agree that it means getting things done through and with people, but is it people in formal organizations, or in all group activities? Is it governing, leading, or teaching?

Perhaps the greatest single semantics confusion lies in the word "organization." Most members of the management process school use it to define the activity-authority structure of an enterprise and certainly most practitioners believe that they are "organizing" when they establish a framework of activity groupings and authority relationships. In this case, organization represents the formal framework within an enterprise that furnishes the environment in which people perform. Yet a large number of "organization" theorists conceive of organization as the sum total of human relationships in any group activity; they thus seem to make it equivalent to *social* structure. And some use "organization" to mean "enterprise."

If the meaning of organization cannot be clarified and a standard use of the term adopted by management theorists, understanding and criticism should not be based on this difference. It hardly seems to me to be accurate for March and Simon, for example, to criticize the organization theories of the management process, or "universalist," school for not considering the management planning function as part of organizing, when they have chosen to treat it separately. Nor should those who choose to treat the training, selecting, guiding or leading of people under staffing and direction be criticized for a tendency to view the employee as an "inert instrument" or a "given rather than a variable."[9] Such accusations, proceeding from false premises, are clearly erroneous.

Other semantic entanglements might be mentioned. By some, decision-making is regarded as a process of choosing from among alternatives; by others, the total managerial task and environment. Leadership is often made synonymous with managership and is analytically separated by others. Communications may mean everything from a written or oral report to a vast network of formal and informal relationships. Human relations to some implies a psychiatric manipulation of people, but to others the study and art of understanding people and interpersonal relationships.

Differences in Definition of Management as a Body of Knowledge

As was indicated in the discussion of semantics, "management" has far from a standard meaning, although most agree that it at least involves getting things done through and with people. But, does it mean the dealing with all human relationships? Is a street peddler a manager? Is a parent a manager? Is a leader of a disorganized mob a manager? Does the field of management equal the fields of sociology and social psychology combined? Is it the equivalent of the entire system of social relationships?

While I recognize that sharp lines cannot be drawn in management any more than they are in medicine or engineering, there surely can be a sharper distinction drawn than at present. With the plethora of management writing and experts, calling almost everything under the sun "management," can one expect management theory to be regarded as very useful or scientific to the practitioner?

The *a priori* Assumption

Confusion in management theory has also been heightened by the tendency for many newcomers in the field to cast aside significant observa-

[9] March, J. G., and H. A. Simon, *Organizations* (New York: John Wiley & Sons, Inc., 1958), pp. 29–33.

tions and analyses of the past on the grounds that they are *a priori* in nature. This is an often-met accusation made by those who wish to cast aside the work of Fayol, Mooney, Brown, Urwick, Gulick, and others who are branded as "universalists." To make the assumption that the distilled experiences of men such as these represent *a priori* reasoning is to forget that experience in and with managing *is* empirical. While the conclusions of perceptive and experienced practitioners of the art of management are not infallible, they represent an experience which is certainly real and not "armchair." No one could deny, I feel sure, that the ultimate test of the accuracy of management theory must be practice, and management theory and science must be developed from reality.

The Misunderstanding of Principles

Those who feel that they gain caste or a clean slate for advancing a particular notion or approach often delight in casting away anything which smacks of management principles. Some have referred to them as platitudes, forgetting that a platitude is still a truism and a truth does not become worthless because it is familiar. (As Robert Frost has written, "Most of the changes we think we see in life are merely truths going in or out of favor.") Others cast away principles of Fayol and other practitioners, only to draw apparently different generalizations from their study of management; but many of the generalizations so discovered are often the same fundamental truths in different words that certain criticized "universalists" have discovered.

One of the favorite tricks of the managerial theory trade is to disprove a whole framework of principles by reference to one principle which the observer sees disregarded in practice. Thus, many critics of the universalists point to the well-known cases of dual subordination in organized enterprise, coming to the erroneous conclusion that there is no substance to the principle of unity of command. But this does not prove that there is no cost to the enterprise by designing around, or disregarding, the principle of unity of command; nor does it prove that there were not other advantages which offset the costs, as there often are in cases of establishing functional authorities in organization.

Perhaps the almost hackneyed stand-by for those who would disprove the validity of all principles by referring to a single one is the misunderstanding around the principle of span of management (or span of control). The usual source of authority quoted by those who criticize is Sir Ian Hamilton, who never intended to state a universal principle, but rather to make a personal observation in a book of reflections on his Army experience, and who did say, offhand, that he found it wise to limit his span to 3 to 6 subordinates. No modern universalist relies on this single observation, and, indeed, few can or will state an absolute or universal numerical ceiling. Since Sir Ian was not a management theorist and did not intend to be, let us hope that the ghost of his innocent remark may be laid to deserved rest!

What concerns those who feel that a recognition of fundamental truths, or generalizations, may help in the diagnosis and study of management, and who know from managerial experience that such truths or principles do serve an extremely valuable use, is the tendency for some researchers to prove the wrong things through either misstatement and misapplication of principles. A classic case of such misunderstanding and misapplication is in Chris Argyris' interesting book on *Personality and Organization*.[10] This author, who in this book and his other works has made many noteworthy contributions to management, concludes that "formal organization principles make demands on relatively healthy individuals that are incongruent with their needs," and that "frustration, conflict, failure, and short-time perspective are predicted as results of this basic incongruency."[11] This startling conclusion — the exact opposite of what "good" formal organization based on "sound" organization principles should cause, is explained when one notes that, of four "principles" Argyris quotes, one is not an organization principle at all but the economic principle of specialization and three other "principles" are quoted incorrectly.[12] With such a postulate, and with no attempt to recognize, correctly or incorrectly, any other organization and management principles, Argyris has simply proved that wrong principles badly applied will lead to frustration; and every management practitioner knows this to be true!

The Inability or Unwillingness of Management Theorists to Understand Each Other

What has been said above leads one to the conclusion that much of the management theory jungle is caused by the unwillingness or inability of the management theorists to understand each other. Doubting that it is inability, because one must assume that a person interested in management theory is able to comprehend, at least in concept and framework, the approaches of the various "schools," I can only come to the conclusion that the roadblock to understanding is unwillingness.

Perhaps this unwillingness comes from the professional "walls" developed by learned disciplines. Perhaps the unwillingness stems from a fear that someone or some new discovery will encroach on professional and academic status. Perhaps it is fear of professional or intellectual obsolescence. But whatever the cause, it seems that these walls will not be torn down until it is realized that they exist, until all cultists are willing to look

[10] New York: Harper & Brothers, 1957.
[11] *Ibid.*, p .74.
[12] *Ibid.*, pp. 58–66.

at the approach and content of other schools, and until, through exchange and understanding of ideas some order may be brought from the present chaos.

Disentangling the Management Theory Jungle

It is important that steps be taken to disentangle the management theory jungle. Perhaps it is too soon and we must expect more years of wandering through a thicket of approaches, semantics, thrusts, and counter-thrusts. But in any field as important to society where the many blunders of an unscientifically based managerial art can be so costly, I hope that this will not be long.

There do appear to be some things that can be done. Clearly, meeting what I see to be the major sources of the entanglement should remove much of it. The following considerations are important:

1. *The Need for Definition of a Body of Knowledge.* Certainly, if a field of knowledge is not to get bogged down in a quagmire of misunderstandings, the first need is for definition of the field. Not that it need be defined in sharp, detailed, and inflexible lines, but rather along lines which will give it fairly specific content. Because management is reality, life, practice, my suggestion would be that it be defined in the light of the able and discerning practitioner's frame of reference. A science unrelated to the art for which it is to serve is not likely to be a very productive one.

Although the study of management in various enterprises, in various countries, and at various levels made by many persons, including myself, may neither be representative nor adequate, I have come to the conclusion that management is the art of getting things done through and with people in *formally organized groups*, the art of creating an environment in such an organized group where people can perform as individuals and yet cooperate toward attainment of group goals, the art of removing blocks to such performance, the art of optimizing efficiency in effectively reaching goals. If this kind of definition of the field is unsatisfactory, I suggest at least an agreement that the area should be defined to reflect the field of the practitioner and that further research and study of practice be done to this end.

In defining the field, too, it seems to me imperative to draw some limits for purposes of analysis and research. If we are to call the entire cultural, biological, and physical universe the field of management, we can no more make progress than could have been done if chemistry or geology had not carved out a fairly specific area and had, instead, studied all knowledge.

In defining the body of knowledge, too, care must be taken to distinguish between tools and content. Thus mathematics, operations research, accounting, economic theory, sociometry, and psychology, to mention a few, are significant *tools* of management but are not, in themselves, a part of the *content* of the field. This is not to mean that they are unimportant or that the practicing manager should not have them available to him, nor does it mean that they may not be the means of pushing back the frontiers of knowledge of management. But they should not be confused with the basic content of the field.

This is not to say that fruitful study should not continue on the underlying disciplines affecting management. Certainly knowledge of sociology, social systems, psychology, economics, political science, mathematics, and other areas, pointed toward contributing to the field of management, should be continued and encouraged. And significant findings in these and other fields of knowledge might well cast important light on, or change concepts in, the field of management. This has certainly happened in other sciences and in every other art based upon significant science.

2. *Integration of Management and Other Disciplines.* If recognition of the proper content of the field were made, I believe that the present crossfire of misunderstanding might tend to disappear. Management would be regarded as a specific discipline and other disciplines would be looked upon as important bases of the field. Under these circumstances, the allied and underlying disciplines would be welcomed by the business and public administration schools, as well as by practitioners, as loyal and helpful associates. Integration of management and other disciplines would then not be difficult.

3. *The Clarification of Management Semantics.* While I would expect the need for clarification and uniformity of management semantics would largely be satisfied by definition of the field as a body of knowledge, semantics problems might require more special attention. There are not too many places where semantics are important enough to cause difficulty. Here again, I would suggest the adoption of the semantics of the intelligent practitioners, unless words are used by them so inexactly as to require special clarification. At least, we should not complicate an already complex field by developing a scientific or academic jargon which would build a language barrier between the theorist and the practitioner.

Perhaps the most expeditious way out of this problem is to establish a commission representing academic societies immediately concerned and associations of practicing managers. This would not seem to be difficult to do. And even if it were, the results would be worth the efforts.

4. *Willingness to Distill and Test Fundamentals.* Certainly, the test of maturity and usefulness of a science is the sharpness and validity of the principles underlying it. No science, now regarded as mature, started out with a complete statement of incontrovertibly valid principles. Even the oldest sciences, such as physics, keep revising their underlying laws and discovering new principles. Yet any science has proceeded, and more than that has been useful, for centuries on the basis of generalizations, some laws, some principles, and some hypotheses.

One of the understandable sources of inferiority of the social sciences is the recognition that they are inexact sciences. On the other hand, even the so-called exact sciences are subject to a great deal of inexactness, have principles which are not completely proved, and use art in the design of practical systems and components. The often-encountered defeatist attitude of the social sciences, of which management is one, overlooks the fact that management may be explained, practice may be improved, and the goals of research may be more meaningful if we encourage attempts at perceptive distillation of experience by stating principles (or generalizations) and placing them in a logical framework. As two scientists recently said on this subject:

> "The reason for this defeatist point of view regarding the social sciences may be traceable to a basic misunderstanding of the nature of scientific endeavor. What matters is not whether or to what extent inexactitudes in procedures and predictive capability can eventually be removed . . . : rather it is *objectivity*, i.e., the intersubjectivity of findings independent of any one person's intuitive judgment, which distinguishes science from intuitive guesswork however brilliant. . . . But once a new fact or a new idea has been conjectured, no matter how intuitive a foundation, it must be capable of objective test and confirmation by anyone. And it is this crucial standard of scientific objectivity rather than any purported criterion of exactitude to which the social sciences must conform."[13]

In approaching the clarification of management theory, then, we should not forget a few criteria:

(1) The theory should deal with an area of knowledge and inquiry that is "manageable"; no great advances in knowledge were made so long as man contemplated the whole universe;

(2) The theory should be *useful* in improving practice and the task and person of the practitioner should not be overlooked;

(3) The theory should not be lost in semantics, especially useless jargon not understandable to the practitioner;

(4) The theory should give direction and efficiency to research and teaching; and

(5) The theory must recognize that it is part of a larger universe of knowledge and theory.

[13] Helmer, O., and N. Rescher, "On the Epistemology of the Inexact Sciences," (Santa Monica, California: The Rand Corporation, P-1513, 1958), pp. 4–5.

2

Management Theory:
Functional and Evolutionary*

Waino W. Suojanen

Florida State University

Professor Suojanen invades the management theory jungle with the proposition that the boundaries of management can be defined more clearly by means of a biological analogy rather than by an analogy to physics. This article traces the functional and evolutionary approaches to management theory that are suggested by functional and evolutionary approaches to biological science. The author argues that conflicts between functional and evolutionary theories arise from the fact that functional theory is based on a static, hierarchical value system, whereas values in American society have changed from the impacts of freedom, democracy, science and changing technology. This framework makes possible a critique of the bureaucratic theory of Max Weber upon which the functional school has based much of its thought. The analysis suggests the means by which evolutionary theories of management may offer better explanations of managerial behavior, and better solutions to management problems. The article adds further classification and analysis to the jungle concept introduced by Professor Koontz.

During recent years, scholars from many different disciplines have been engaged in a continuing controversy as to which concepts are relevant, and which irrelevant, to the theory of management. Today it is almost impossible to find two people who share more than a very general agreement as to what should be included, and what excluded, in the definition and study of management theory. Disagreement and controversy have almost

* Taken from the *Journal of the Academy of Management*, vol. 6, no. 1, March, 1963, pp. 7–17.

reached the point where any theoretical light that has been generated has been overwhelmed by emotional heat.

The attack on the "principles" or "management process" school, whose origins trace to Frederick W. Taylor, Henri Fayol, and Max Weber, has been vigorous. As one persuasive scholar has indicated, a legion of critics has advanced to the assault — each suggesting in one way or another that his approach is superior to that of the "principles" school.[1] The fair-minded must, however, admit that the "principles" do possess certain operational merit and theoretical value. Just as the principles of classical physics are still indispensable for many purposes, although the theory of relativity has shown that they now have only limited validity, a certain validity also adheres to many of the principles of management.

On the other hand, the more ardent defenders of the universalistic approach to management have not been without fault in this controversy. While it appears that the critics of the traditional — or Newtonian — school of management have not yet developed anything equivalent to Einstein's theory of relativity, the objective requirements of scholarship do indicate that the "functional" school cannot continue to ignore or brush aside the mounting research data of the quantitative, behavioral and social sciences.[2]

It is the intent of this paper to suggest that the weeds in the "management jungle" may be eradicated — and order brought to the discipline — by defining the field with a greater degree of precision than has been the case in the past. In the opinion of the writer, a giant stride toward the delimitation of the field of management theory can be achieved by going beyond the analogy to physics to an even more pertinent analogy drawn from the field of biology.

Some years ago, biologists were preoccupied with a controversy which, in many respects, was almost the exact parallel of the current "management jungle." It was resolved, to the satisfaction of the many battling factions, by settling on a definition of the field.[3]

Biological Classification

This definition of the field resulted in a classification which recognized that biology is neither a unified nor a uniform science. Beyond the level of pure description, it has been subdivided into the two quite different

[1] Harold Koontz, "The Management Theory Jungle," *Journal of the Academy of Management*, December, 1961. p. 175. The writer is indebted to Harold Koontz and LCdr. Robert J. Massey for comments and criticism.

[2] In subsequent discussion, the term "functional" will be used to refer to the early "scientific management" or "universalistic" school depicted by (F) in Figure 2.1 on page 35.

[3] Ernst Mayr, "Cause and Effect in Biology," *Science*, November 10, 1961, p. 1501. Much of the analogy in this paper is drawn from the Mayr article.

areas of functional and evolutionary biology. Though individual research effort is usually concentrated in one of these areas, a biologist must also possess knowledge and understanding of the other, or risk a charge of narrow-minded specialization.

Functional biology. Functional biology is concerned with the operation and interaction of a single, essentially static, biological component. The component may range all the way from a whole individual to a single cell, or a single part of a cell.

The question that the functional biologist always endeavors to answer is "How?" The principal technique that he utilizes in order to answer this question is the experiment through which he seeks to isolate the variable or phenomenon under study from the complexities of the organism.

Evolutionary Biology. In contrast to his functionally oriented colleague, the evolutionary biologist always seeks the answer to the question "Why?" In evolutionary biology there are no *absolute phenomena.* All events are space-bound and time-bound. This means that a full understanding of the structure or function of an organism can be acquired only against its historical background.

The evolutionary biologist seeks the reasons for the diversity of the organic world as well as the ways by which it has come into being. He tries to understand the factors that have caused all of the changes in plant and animal life over periods of time. He studies the steps by which all of the almost unbelievable adaptations, so characteristic of every part of the organic world, have occurred. Seldom if ever can the evolutionary biologist, in his research, approach the ideal of the controlled physical or chemical experiment because "any living cell carries with it the experiences of a billion years of experimentation by its ancestors."

From Biology to Management

In recent years, many scholars have implicitly utilized the functional and evolutionary approaches in an attempt to bring some order to the management theory jungle. Koch has pointed out that

> Studies of organization and control tend to cluster around opposite poles, with the comparative approach falling somewhere in between. Traditional or formal theory deals with authority as the key to administration and with downward paths of authority delegation as indicated at the beginning of this review. The behavioral science theory of organization advocates the decision premise viewpoint in contrast to hierarchical status and maintains that the path of authority is upward. . . . To the forward-thinking practitioner of organization and control, it is not so important to adhere strictly to *universal* traditions, nor to achieve rigorously the *logical positivism* of the behavioral scientists. What is

important is to face up to and solve the organizational problems of growth in response to change.[4]

Thompson has suggested that the conflict between the opposite poles of organization theory arises from a science-hierarchy incompatibility. More specifically

> Modern organization has evolved from earlier forms by incorporating advancing specialization. In an earlier period, organizations could depend much more on the "line of command." The superior could tell others what to do because he could master the knowledge and techniques necessary to do so intelligently. As science and technology developed, the superior lost to experts the *ability* to command in one field after another, but he retained the *right* as part of his role.[5]

Both Koch and Thompson argue that authority and its downward delegation in the hierarchy — as conceived in the functional theory of organization — appears to be in conflict with the evolutionary theory of organization, in which the flow of authority is *upward*. Students and practitioners of management have both commented on this apparent paradox. The functional-evolutionary classification provides a framework within which both of these opposing points of view may be reconciled and the semantic difficulties dispelled.

Both Koch and Thompson imply that their comments apply to present-day organizations in which the participants are, in the main, citizens of the United States. As a result, their analyses are best understood against the background of American culture and its underlying system of values. The impasse between the functional and evolutionary theories of management, at both the theoretical and the applied levels, stems from the fact that the functional theory is based on a static, hierarchical system of values, whereas the values of the American society have been considerably mediated by the twin impacts of freedom and democracy as well as science and technology. The ambivalence that now characterizes both management theory and administrative practice may well be responsible for the attempt to apply the principles of the functional theory to the values of an ever freer, increasingly technological society.

Functional Management

The organizational model of functional management traces back to Max Weber and the theory of rational authority. Weber assumed the legitimacy of rational authority to be "the *power* to make decisions which are *obeyed*

---

[4] Edward G. Koch, "Three Approaches to Organization," *Harvard Business Review*, March–April, 1961, p. 162.

[5] Victor A. Thompson, *Modern Organization*, (New York: Alfred A. Knopf, 1961), pp. 12–13.

without question by others as a basis for action." This idea — that authority is delegated downward — is as old as the institution of hierarchy. For countless generations "the few had been born to command and the many had been born to obey."

The democratic and technological revolutions had not caused noticeable changes in the structure of the organizations that man creates to accomplish his tasks, although they had already wrought enormous changes in the nature of society itself, when Weber developed his theory of bureaucracy. From his coign of vantage in the stream of history, Weber's theory was a brilliant piece of analysis and synthesis. Without question, his rational bureaucracy was a far better method for structuring the enterprise than its predecessor forms. However, we contend his theory was out-dated even while it was being enunciated.

What Weber failed to recognize — and considering his cultural background it is easy to understand this — was the impact that science and technology would have on management. In the period between the decay of feudalism and the development of his theory, values of freedom, democracy, and the dignity of the individual were rising into ascendance in the Western world. At the same time, scientific inquiry and the spirit of innovation were giving birth to an equal emphasis on such complementary values as rationality, progress, and academic freedom. The theory of bureaucracy, in this respect, was functional to its very core. Its principal assumption — the downward delegation of authority — derived its legitimacy from the ordered and static world of feudalism.

If the organization is viewed from the timeless or static perspective of Weber and the functional school — one which in essence accepts the legitimacy of hierarchy — then authority and its downward delegation provides a sufficient condition from which to construct a theory of management. Such a theory provides an adequate explanation having considerable predictive value because authority and its downward delegation are assumed to be constant and immutable. By virtue of this assumption, the functional theorist is able to develop other broad basic principles, such as unity of command, span of control, and management by exception, that are both logically consistent and empirically demonstrable. The matter of empirical demonstration is vitally important, because the functional theorist can point to existing organizations and to actual managers as living proof that here indeed is "how" the process of administration actually takes place in the real world.

Empirical demonstration of the applicability of the functional theory to an actual organization is best exemplified by the tactical military unit. In order to accomplish its mission — that of victory in combat — the tactical military unit must be organized under a *crisis-oriented* philosophy. This philosophy includes the downward delegation of authority, an inviolable

chain of command, a narrow span of control and a high degree of specialization of labor.

The "principles," on which the organization of the crisis-oriented, tactical
military unit are based, correspond, virtually one-for-one, with those of the
Weberian bureaucratic model. This is not merely coincidental — both
forms of organization have their origins in the ordered, hierarchical world of
feudalism. After all, the soldier had had to face and solve the problems
of coordinating the activities of large numbers of people in an earlier and
more conscious fashion than either the businessman or the civil servant.

During the first three decades of the twentieth century very few scholars
were inclined to quarrel with the assumptions of the functional theory.
Until the results of the Hawthorne studies were publicized, the bulk of
research effort in the behavioral sciences had been devoted to the study
of deviant, rather than normal, behavior. The social sciences had not yet
advanced to the point where they could offer alternatives to the assumptions of the functional theory. The interest of quantitative scientists in
problems of management had to wait until they had been recruited to
serve their governments during World War II.

Perhaps most important of all, the static model of the functional theory
provided sufficient guidance in an era when "the public be damned" attitude was still characteristic of much top-management thinking. If this was
the way in which the customer who furnished the revenues of the organization was regarded, it is easy to understand why the attitude of management toward employees was even more authoritarian. The functional
theory of management was practical. Since most businessmen and civil
servants are not inclined to question that which works, the functional
theory became representative of nonmilitary philosophy as a natural consequence of its success in the military organization.

Functional Management and Structural Modifications

At the time that Weber developed the model of rational bureaucracy,
the pure functional model of organization had already begun to undergo
a considerable modification. As Thompson points out, in a simpler day
and age "the superior could tell others what to do because he could master
the knowledge and techniques necessary to do so intelligently." As science
and technology expanded and the individual line superior could no longer
master the necessary knowledge and techniques, the need for change became peremptory. In order to meet this need, the "line and staff" form
of organization was created.

The staff was initially assimilated into the structure of the military organization under the organizational fiction that it served only to advise
and counsel. Command continued as the province of the line: "the commander alone is responsible for what his unit does or fails to do — he

cannot delegate this responsibility." Despite this fiction, with the accelera-
tion of technology, the staff tended to make more and more decisions
previously considered to be the prerogatives of the line alone.

The impact of science and technology had two important effects on the
organization of the tactical military unit. The principal functions of the
commander — personnel, intelligence, operations and logistics — were assigned to assistant chiefs of staff. When added together and coordinated
by the chief of staff, these functional tasks represented the totality of the
commander's task, although the commander still retained individual responsibility. In addition, a special staff was created to advise both the
commander and the general staff. The special staff officer was an expert
in some particular field of knowledge — as new areas of technology rose in
prominence to the point where they had an impact on military operations,
more special staff positions were created.

The traditional form of military organization, as modified by the general
staff–special staff construct, has proven adequate to serve the needs of
tactical military units to the present day. This has not, however, turned
out to be the case at the departmental level of the American armed services.
As the writer has pointed out previously, the trend at the top level of the
military organization has brought into prominence the functions of both
the military comptroller and the military research and development manager.[6] Both of these developments represent a belated recognition on the
part of the military organization of the importance of the scientific-
technological revolution in the world at large.

The worlds of business and public administration have never accepted the
general-staff concept as a basic feature of organization. In the crisis-
oriented military organization, each mission is different and the planning
required must usually be performed on an emergency basis in a short period
of time. The contrary is true of the *routine-oriented* business or government. Once the product or service line of the organization has been
determined, and the company has become operational, the emergencies
that arise are usually of such nature that they can easily be handled by
line executives without resort to a general staff. Problems requiring technical knowledge beyond that possessed by the line executive may require
the assistance of (special) staff personnel. However, as in the tactical
military organization, the organizational fiction that only the line has the
power to decide is maintained.

From a dynamic point of view, the transition from line-and-staff organization to the committee is a simple and logical step. However, the contrary
has always been the case in the functional theory, which tends to view the

---

[6] Waino W. Suojanen, "Military Organization and the General Staff," *Journal of the
Academy of Management*, August, 1961, p. 116.

committee as intrusive rather than inclusive to organization structure. Used as a decision-making body, the committee violates at least two of the principles of functional theory — those of the downward delegations of authority and of the unity of command. The functional theory accepts the committee because of its ubiquity. This acceptance is halfhearted, however, because a device violating one or more functional principles can never achieve genuine respectability. The efforts of the functional theorists to overcome this ambivalence are usually couched in terms that discuss the dangers of committee, while at the same time commenting that they are being increasingly employed within the framework of management because of the democratic nature of modern society.

Functional theory has had extreme difficulty in accepting "human relations" as a fundamental aspect of the management framework. The peripheral role that "human relations" has always occupied in the functional structure is due to the diametrically opposed ways in which the two theories view authority. At least implicity, if never explicitly, the "human relations" school views authority as "the *right* to make decisions which are *accepted* by others as the basis for action." This is quite different from the functional theory, discussed earlier, in which authority is defined as "the *power* to make decisions which are obeyed without question by others." The incompatibility between the two is so obvious that it need not be belabored. From the viewpoint of our analogy, it is easy to understand why "human relations" as such has fallen into disrepute in organizations structured around the functional theory. As long as attempts are made to place the flesh of the evolutionary theory on the skeleton of the functional theory, many objective observers will continue to regard "human relations" merely as another technique for manipulating men.

The Antecedents of Evolutionary Management

Koontz has classified the critics of the functional theory into (1) the empirical school, (2) the human behavior school, (3) the social system school, (4) the decision theory school, and (5) the mathematical school.[7] In a sense, the term "critic" may be too strong — nonetheless, the record indicates that there has been very little love lost between the pioneers of the functional school and the more recent settlers in the management jungle.

In numerous instances, as Koontz indicates, the deductive assumptions of these schools have been incompatible with the basic framework of the functional theory. Nevertheless, many of the generalizations are based on unimpeachable experimental evidence. To ignore these results constitutes

[7] Koontz, *op. cit.*, pp. 177–182.

a rejection of the scientific method itself. Management theory has not yet advanced to the point where the discipline can afford to reject the concept that research increases the sum total of human knowledge.

The warfare between those scholars more oriented toward functional theory and those with a stronger predilection toward evolutionary theory has been further aggravated by semantic confusion and an unwillingness to understand opposing points of view. This has created a "dog in the manger" attitude among some evolutionary theorists which has caused them to ignore, and indeed to attempt to replace entirely, almost all aspects of the functional theory. This state of affairs has not been improved by the stouthearted rejoinder of the functionalists that the principles of organization are enduring in nature and universal in application. Rather, this has tended to make evolutionary theorists even less sympathetic to the plea that there might be an embryo, if not a baby, in the functionalists' bath water.

The argument is not enough that principles of organization constitute the true basis for an objectively scientific theory of management, though developed from personal experience, observations of effective managers, and buttressed by the comments of authorities who have made contributions to this important field. The evolutionary theorist can argue with equal plausibility that principles developed from personal experience, personal observation, and resort to authority may not only be "wrong" but may also lead to "bad application" because they have not been derived in accord with accepted scientific method.

Behavioral, quantitative and social scientists, on their part, have not developed an evolutionary theory of management — comparable with functional management in terms of the biological analogy — because of the prevailing, positivist bias against values and value judgments. Because of this refusal to recognize that human institutions are not only time-and-space-bound but also *culture-bound*, logical positivism has prevented the development of a model of the management world comparable to that established by evolutionary biologists to explain the reasons for change in the animal and vegetable worlds.

Further Classification and Future Evolution

The functional theory provides an optimal solution to the problem of structuring the crisis-oriented organization.[8] The mission of this type of organization requires an almost completely authoritarian structure. In this respect, the instant obedience which its top leadership must command is historically traceable to a nondemocratic hierarchical structure.

[8] Examples of organizations falling into this category are tactical military units, law enforcement agencies, and fire departments.

The functional theory provides a satisfactory, although not necessarily optimal, solution to the problem of structuring the routine-oriented organization. The degree to which the theory provides guidance and explains success is noticeably less here than in the case of the crisis-oriented organization, because of the conflict between its assumptions and the values of the democratic revolution. However, in the absence of an operational, evolutionary theory applicable to the routine-oriented organization, the functional theory has continued to reign supreme into an age of ascendant democracy and science.

The functional theory provides optimal solutions in the crisis-oriented organization — where the values of participants must be ignored. It provides satisfactory guidance in the routine-oriented organization where only the values of the democratic revolution are violated. However, it fails abjectly in the *knowledge-oriented* organization, where it collides head-on with both the values of democracy and the traditions of individual autonomy in the sciences and professions.

In the real world, however, the functional theory has provided the foundation upon which most scientific and professional organizations have been structured. Scientific and professional methodology tends to value independent, individual work more highly, and to place relatively less emphasis on cooperative relationships. In actual practice, personal and group relations, of the kind critical to success at the level of the organization, occupy a peripheral role in the methods of the sciences and the traditions of the professions. Because these values have never become articulated to the point of suggesting the type of organization best suited to this kind of collaborative endeavor, managers, lacking any other form of guidance, have had to turn to the functional theory.

In the functional theory, the legitimacy of authority depends mainly on hierarchical position or the power over men. In the truly evolutionary organization the basis of authority, or better yet influence, is individual reputation as determined by professional achievement. Functional theory emphasizes the delegation of authority; the relevant consideration in evolutionary theory is the autonomy of the individual. Individual autonomy, or freedom, is equally determined by professional achievement. In essence, tradition operates so as to reinforce freedom as a value in terms of a democratic society.

The evolutionary theory offers the solution to the problems of structuring the knowledge-oriented organization. Wherever the primary mission of the organization is that of the discovery, preservation, application, and dissemination of knowledge — as opposed to combat or production — the evolutionary theory provides a much more relevant frame of reference. Included in this category are not only research and development laboratories, but such diverse associations as medical groups, partnerships of attorneys, educational faculties, consulting organizations, auditing firms, legislative bodies, regulatory agencies, advisory councils, managing authorities, many types of committees, and the boards of directors of all kinds of organizations.

The central characteristics shared in common by these organizations and segments of organizations are colleague authority and committee structure. The functional theory speaks of the "well-understood dangers" of the committee (and colleague authority); in contrast, the success of the evolutionary theory is directly related to the extent to which these concepts are utilized in determining policy and establishing objectives. This should not be construed as a criticism of the functional theory *per se*, but rather as a recognition that in the study of management (as in biology) there is both unity and diversity.

The geometrical relationship between the functional and the evolutionary theories of management is developed in more detail in Figure 2.1. Hopefully, this approach defines the field of management with a greater degree of precision than has been the case in the past. By the same token, the caution expressed in the following "quotation" should be kept in mind:

> Management therefore is destined to retain its autonomy, which means that to be known and understood, management mechanisms will still have to be studied and formulated in their own right and full diversity. And this explains why in management so many generalizations must stop far short of the vast inclusiveness of laws of physics, hence, why the range of validity of each must be determined empirically. It is this inherent feature of management nature, rather than backwardness or extravagance, then, which necessitates testing over a far wider spectrum of variables, such as species, cell types, stages, environments, and so forth, than would seem necessary or even pardonable in most of physics. It sanctions the usage of repeating management experiments with appropriate variations: with change of objects, agents, dosage, timing, methods of observation, measurement, recording, and the like.[9]

In summary, the preceding discussion suggests that management theory can profit by drawing on the system of classification that brought peace to the ranks of the biologists. This *modus vivendi* indicates, by analogy, some of the issues which have been responsible for the current controversy in management theory. Given agreement on the classification premises, management theory becomes an open-ended function of three factors: (1) the orientation of the organization, (2) the participants in the organization, and (3) the cultural environment.

---

[9] Paul Weiss, "Experience and Experiment in Biology," *Science*, May 11, 1962, p. 470. The writer has taken the liberty of substituting "management" for "biology" or "biological" wherever these words appear in the original.

Until now, the task of developing valid generalizations has shown substantial progress only for the crisis-oriented organization, with its implied authoritarian social structure. The questions to be answered in the future are those having to do with routine-oriented and knowledge-oriented organizations, particularly the latter. Prevailing concepts about bureaucracy and rational authority will undoubtedly undergo considerable modification as the theory is advanced. Under the assumption that there is a place for all, the management theory jungle may hopefully be transformed into an orchard, or at least an orderly tree farm, in which theorists of many different persuasions will be able to plant and prune in harmony, thereby advancing the state of the art on all relevant fronts.

Figure 2.1

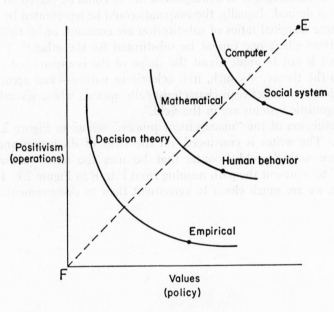

Vertical axis – Sharing of authority

Explanation of Figure 2.1

The ordinate measures the degree of positivism (quantification) present in the theory of management. The decision theory and mathematical categories of management appear above the 45-degree line. The writer has added a "computer" theory there, partly because it makes the chart symmetrical and partly because such a school exists, i.e., at the Carnegie Institute of Technology.

The abscissa measures the degree to which values must be considered in formulating various management theories. The empirical, human-behavior, and social-system schools appear below the 45-degree line because they place more emphasis on values than on measurement.

The isoquants (contour lines), representing the vertical axis, measure the degree to which authority is shared, or the change from downward to upward delegation of authority. In essence, as one moves from the origin F (functional theory) upward toward the summit E (evolutionary theory), each variable increases. Simply stated, this means that an evolutionary theory is more quantitative in orientation, more cognizant of the relevance of values, and more inclined to view upward delegation of authority as progress rather than retrogression, as opposed to a functional theory based on the static and hierarchical view of society.

Each of the categories of management theory could be placed on a single isoquant if desired. Equally, the isoquants could be represented by straight lines where marginal ratios of substitution are constant, or by right angles in situations where one cannot be substituted for the other.[10] The issue at present is not to argue about the shape of the isoquants but to bring order to the theory. As such, it is eclectic in nature — and according to the dictionary: "eclecticism characteristically appears where several powerful antagonistic systems are in the field."

The omission of the "management process" school in Figure 2.1 is deliberate. The writer is convinced, on the basis of discussion and correspondence with Harold Koontz, that he uses the term "management process" to represent the path running from F to E in Figure 2.1. If this is the case, we are much closer to agreement than to disagreement.

---

[10] For further explanation, see George J. Stigler, *The Theory of Price*, (New York: The Macmillan Company, 1949), pp. 67–72.

3

The Tactics of Jungle Warfare*

Lyndall F. Urwick

Longueville, N.S.W., Australia

Colonel Lyndall F. Urwick is an eminent British authority on management who has had a distinguished military career followed by extensive management consulting. He finds Professors Koontz and Suojanen in agreement in their description of confusion in management theory, and takes a skillful "outsider's look" at conflicts within the management discipline He concurs with Professor Suojanen's strategy of making the theory jungle a more orderly place where theorists can all do better work. The author comprehensively surveys the rise to prominence of the behavioral science and mathematical approaches. He questions the functional analysis and biological analogy propounded by Professor Suojanen, attacking the implication that the theories of behavioral scientists are evolutionary and hence destined to supersede functional theories of management. He concludes that we are not yet warranted in abandoning the attempt to achieve a unified, integrated theory of management.

Professor Harold Koontz' paper on *The Management Theory Jungle*[1] called attention to a tendency in the academic study of management in the U.S.A. which has troubled outside observers for some years. "Inky warfare" is both an occupational disease and the favourite hobby of some professors. Through practice they become extremely skilled at the gentle art of verbal in-fighting. For an outsider who, having been prevented by the demands of more lethal warfare from proceeding beyond a first degree, is not even a passable academic, to venture into the area of hostilities is

---

* Taken from the *Journal of the Academy of Management*, vol. 6, no. 4, December, 1963, pp. 316–329.

[1] Harold Koontz, "The Management Theory Jungle," *Journal of the Academy of Management*, December 1961, p. 175.

therefore a hazardous step. But, on the other hand, an outside view may be helpful.

Perhaps a good starting point is Von Clausewitz' famous distinction between tactics and strategy . . . "The Art of War divides itself into tactics and strategy. The former occupies itself with the form of the separate combat, the latter with its use."[2]

That there is a combat, both Professor Koontz and Professor Suojanen are agreed. To quote the latter "Today it is almost impossible to find two people who share more than a very general agreement as to what should be included, and what excluded, in the definition and study of management theory. Disagreement and controversy have almost reached the point where any theoretical light that has been generated has been overwhelmed by emotional heat."[3]

It has certain obvious roots. Perhaps the principal of these is the fact that the United States is a very large country. In the last half-century this continent has developed academic apparatus for the study of management at a speed and on a scale which are, as far as the writer is aware, unparalleled in the history of education anywhere in the world. Inevitably much of the communication between individuals is in written, and often published, form. It is difficult, if not often impossible, for the holders of opposing views to meet personally and learn to laugh with and at each other as human beings. The temptation to score "debating points" is frequently irresistible.

The danger of such a situation has been emphasized by David Lilienthal: "making decisions from papers has a dehumanizing effect. Much of man's inhumanity to man is explained by it."[4] In the British Infantry Division with which the writer served in World War I one of the standing orders to the General Staff was "Never enter into an argument on paper. Go and see the man."[5]

From one point of view this particular combat is extremely comic. Here are two groups of people, one of which has been engaged quite seriously in trying to teach rising generations the art of managing for the last half-century. And the art of managing is primarily and fundamentally the art of arranging for human cooperation in the pursuit of objectives. The other group is drawn from what are described broadly as "the behavioural sciences." That is to say it specializes in knowledge about human behaviour.

[2] General Carl von Clausewitz, *On War*, English Translation by Colonel J. J. Graham, London, Kegan Paul, 1940, Bk. II, Cp. 2, V. I. p. 94.

[3] Waino W. Suojanen, "Management Theory: Functional & Evolutionary," *Journal of the Academy of Management*, vol. 6, no. 1, March 1963, p. 7.

[4] David E. Lilienthal, *TVA–Democracy on the March*, Penguin Books, London, 1944, p. 126.

[5] 11th British Division, Standing Orders, Office Orders, 1917. Ms. copy in the author's possession.

And here are two of them faced with what is, after all, a fairly elementary management problem — how to arrange for reasonable cooperation between people of the same occupation, of the same level of education and intellectual ability, of the same nationality — putting up about as big a "black" in elementary human relations as it is possible to imagine.

Of course they are not unique. In 1959, in the University of Cambridge, England, Sir Charles Snow delivered the Rede Lecture on the subject of "The Two Cultures and the Scientific Revolution."[6] This moved Dr. F. R. Leavis to entitle his Richmond Lecture, delivered in the Hall of Downing College in the same University in 1962, "The Significance of C. P. Snow."[7] It was about as barbed an attack on the thinking of a not uneminent colleague as the writer has ever read. In a sense the combat between the established teachers of management and the behavioural scientists is merely an extension to the management field of the sharper conflict between those educated in science and those educated in the humanities which was the theme of Snow's lecture, as of Dr. Leavis' retort.

As it is incumbent on anyone discussing such a subject publicly to declare his "interest" the writer would add that he secured his university degree in Modern History. Subsequently he had some brief instruction from the late Sidney and Beatrice Webb on the application of scientific method to sociological enquiry. Since 1934 he has been a management consultant.

But while the tactics of the combat, its form, is not without interest and amusement, its strategy, its use, is more questionable. Those who are likely to laugh longest at it are those, and they are a considerable number, perhaps more than the "behavioural scientists" realize, perhaps more than anyone in the United States realizes, who still think that "there's not much in all this management stuff anyway." They do not believe that human government can be made the subject of knowledge, whether exact or less exact. It's just a power struggle, a matter of experience and political agility. And the spectacle of the American universities, who have led the world in the study of the subject, sharply divided on what the subject is about, will cause this group of reactionaries immense satisfaction. There is a very real danger of yet another instance of "What is truth? said jesting Pilate; and would not stay for an answer."[8]

It is therefore constructive and helpful to find Professor Suojanen making suggestions designed to reduce "the management theory jungle" to an orderly tree farm, in which theorists of many different persuasions will be

[6] C. P. Snow, *The Two Cultures and the Scientific Revolution*, Cambridge (England), The University Press, 1959.

[7] F. R. Leavis, *The Significance of C. P. Snow*, full text printed in *The Spectator*, London, March 9, 1962.

[8] Francis Bacon, *Essays*, 1621, "Of Truth."

able to plant and prune in harmony, thereby advancing the state of the art on all relevant fronts."[9] His strategy is correct. It is essential that at least "the emotional heat" should be turned off discussion of the subject. But his article fails to suggest to the writer that he has any conception of the causes of this "emotional heat." "Emotional heat" is not an abstraction. The phrase means that some human being, a person, feels hot and hurt and angry because of what some other person has written or said or done.

He will no doubt agree with the writer that the initiative has come from the "behavioural scientists." For the last fifty years the universities of the United States have been steadily building up Departments or Faculties of Business Administration; today there are some 500 of them. They have developed from various angles, administratively speaking. Some of them have hived off from existing faculties of engineering, economics or, more rarely, political science. Some have tended to replace the older subject of Commerce, which may perhaps be defined as teaching the business leaders of tomorrow the bad practices of yesterday. Some have been started up quite independently by a combination of younger men from various faculties.

The heads of these departments have had a difficult row to hoe. On the one side they have had to face up to the scepticism of their colleagues in charge of established subjects. They have been "upstarts," newcomers in the academic fold. On the other hand they have had to make headway against a widespread tendency among businessmen to fail to understand what university education is about, to demand professional training in techniques rather than basic study of theory, the pursuit of knowledge of immediate practical utility rather than of knowledge for its own sake. Thirdly, and perhaps most important of all, they have been discovering that management is a field of study in which it is particularly difficult to train and keep competent instructors because of the competing claims of business which can afford to pay much higher salaries than can the universities for young men of real initiative and ability. It is no accident that proportionately fewer third degrees are taken by students in business management than by those in any other subject.

Management is also a difficult subject to teach. In the first place it is new as a recognized discipline and was, at the beginning, uncertain as to its pattern and content. In the second place managing is a practical art. The activity is in itself a synoptic or integrating function. It is engaged in uniting the contributions of quite a large variety of specialized bodies of knowledge and special skills in the service of a common objective. And the disciplines which underlie these special skills belong to different categories of knowledge, which, traditionally, are assigned to independent faculties in University organization.

[9] *Op. cit. N.* (3), p. 16.

Thus the body of knowledge known generically as management includes a large contribution from

1. Engineering and its underlying body of physical sciences such as mathematics, physics, mechanics and so on. This has enabled it to attain a much higher degree of precision in analyzing and measuring the tasks, especially the tasks using mechanical help, which it asks individuals to perform. It has issued in the applied body of knowledge usually described as Production or Industrial Engineering.

2. Individual Physiology and Psychology and the underlying sciences in the biological group on which they are based. While Psychology is a much newer recruit to the body of inductive discipline than the physical sciences — till within the last decades of the XIX Century it was usually regarded as a branch of speculative philosophy — it is, of course, an extremely interesting and challenging development. Interest in it was also stimulated by the two World Wars which occurred in the first half of the XX Century, both by the possibilities which it uncovered of greater accuracy in the assignment of individuals to tasks and by its contribution, through the special branch of medicine known as psycho-pathology, to the problem of dealing with the special neuroses developed by the strains of war. But, since it was a young science and its methodologies not wholly reliable, it had to be supplemented by reliance on practical experience and responsible judgment. These two elements in combination have been built up into the body of knowledge usually known as Personnel Management. Its function is to assist the manager to greater accuracy in adjusting each individual to the task he/she may be asked to perform.

3. Economics and the sciences underlying economic theory and practice, such as Statistical Method, Accounting, Commercial Geography and Law. These have enabled management to attain greater precision in the task of arranging and correlating the different tasks which members of a group are called upon to perform and in developing the methodologies of functions other than production and personnel, such as transportation, marketing and so on. They have issued in a number of applied bodies of knowledge such as Cost Accounting, Management Accounting and Organization and Methods.

4. Political Science and the more modern studies underlying it such as Sociology, Social Psychology and Anthropology. In addition a great deal of special study has been devoted to what is described broadly as "The Industrial Problem," i.e., the failure of employers and managers on the one side and of employed persons, represented by trade unions, on the other, to arrive at any agreed view as to the purpose and organization of economic life. The writer's own instructors, Sidney and Beatrice Webb, produced, of course, a shelf-full of weighty volumes on this and kindred subjects. These contributed to the manager's understanding of the behaviour of human beings in groups, just as 2. contributes to his understanding of the

behaviour of the individual as an isolated individual. They tend to correct one of the cardinal weaknesses of orthodox economics, namely that it is strongly biased towards the assumption that the relations between the individual and the institution in which he works should be regarded purely from the standpoint of his reactions as an individual. The influence on those reactions of social conditioning should be ignored. Their difficulty lies, of course, in the fact that their content is extremely close to what are commonly described as ideologies, the theories which men hold as to political and social organization. Men cling to these theories with passionate conviction; currently conflicting ideas on the subject are the foundation of what is known as the "cold war." They are the most common basis of what are described as "value judgments."

But the manager is concerned most of his time with the reactions of human beings *in groups,* though he should be equally concerned with the reactions of individuals as isolated individuals. And at the present time there is virtually no technique known to man for forming concepts as to group behaviour other than observation of the behaviour of persons as individuals. If therefore Psychology, regarded as the study of individual behaviour, is as yet a long way from being an exact science, the prospect of an exact science of group psychology is much more remote. At the same time managers are compelled by practical necessity every day to numerous actions based on their estimate of what group reactions are likely to be. And such estimates are particularly prone to bias due to the social and political background of the individual.

Nevertheless a considerable volume of effort has been devoted to building up techniques in this area under such titles as Publicity, Marketing, Consumer Studies, Public-Customer-Stockholder- & Industrial Relations, Group Dynamics and the like. Much research has centered around terms such as Leadership, Morale and Entrepreneurship.

In addition to the difficulty of unifying these very different disciplines — different in origin, in outlook, in methodology, in degree of development — into a single balanced course covering three or four years of undergraduate study, heads of departments of business administration have been faced by a limiting time factor. The generations pass quickly. The undergraduate they are teaching today may be an up-and-coming young president of an industrial undertaking within ten to fifteen years of leaving the university. Attractive though it may be to the academic mind to contemplate the gradual evolution of more exact knowledge, the student who is going out into practical life will probably never again have such an opportunity of continuous whole-time study. The kind of outlook on life which he takes with him from the university determines the mental equipment with which he will probably face the gravest practical problems, involving often the lives of many thousands of his fellow-citizens, within ten to fifteen years.

It is no use teaching him what exact science may be able to do in 20 to 30 years' time. It is much more important to teach him a healthy scepticism as to premature conclusions which seem to carry the authority of science. For nothing is more dangerous than scientific knowledge which claims complete accuracy prematurely. The bio-chemist Professor J. B. S. Haldane has made the point neatly. "A hundred and fifty years ago one of Napoleon's armies was put on a cheap and portable diet drawn up by the best physiologists of that day. Some essential ingredients were left out with disastrous results." But in World War I British politicians took the advice of some very competent biochemists "and rationing was a success."[10]

About twenty years ago, in the midst of all these preoccupations, heads of schools of business administration were faced with a rather sudden outbreak of claims by "behavioural scientists," chiefly sociologists and social psychologists, that they should play a larger part in the teaching of management. Curiously enough this "take-over bid," and it was of the nature of a "take-over bid," really originated in a variety of influences which were not strictly sociological.

Some of it stemmed from the work of Elton Mayo and the group associated with him in the famous Hawthorne experiments. Elton Mayo was not himself a sociologist. He was by training and inclination a psychiatrist. He was pre-eminently a clinician with a genius for helping unhappy people. His devotion to "any human being who needed help"[11] was his most pronounced characteristic. In his earlier clinical work he seems to have thought that most social problems were basically individual. But his experience at Hawthorne convinced him that many of the stresses and strains to be encountered in modern industry are social in origin.

He did not think, however, that Sociology as it was being taught in the United States in the first half of this century was likely to provide a remedy. "The so-called social sciences do not seem to equip students with a single skill that is usable in ordinary human situations. Sociology is highly developed, but mainly as an exercise in the acquisition of scholarship. Students are taught to write books about each other's books. . . . The equivalent of the clinic, or indeed of the laboratory, are still to seek. . . . The social sciences are impressed by the achievement (of the physical sciences); but the unfortunate effect has been to encourage too much jerry-building of imposing facades in the social area. . . . Those graduates of brilliant

[10] J. B. S. Haldane, "Science and Politics" in *Possible Worlds*, London, Chatto and Windus, 1928, p. 186.

[11] Personal statement to the author by T. N. Whitehead who worked with Mayo at Hawthorne.

achievement who lead the procession out of the universities are not well equipped for the task of bringing order into social chaos."[12]

Obviously the sociologists were going to take up the cudgels. One relatively impartial observer has suggested that "attention might be drawn to some of critics" own failings. They have subjected the putative motivation and the level of professional integrity of the human relations researchers to a form of unfriendly public scrutiny which must be quite rare in the literature of the social sciences."[13] One of Mayo's own colleagues, whose findings accord fairly closely with those with which Professor Suojanen appears to agree, has commented "To have to admit that this war was waged by intellectuals and academics and by men called political and social scientists makes me still blush with shame for my 'reference group.' That men who called themselves 'scientists' should understand so little the nature of scientific questions and evidence appalled me"[14]

Sociology itself, quite apart from its bearing on management, was somewhat rent by faction. One fairly recent book identifies two of the warring "schools" as "The Grand Theorists" and "The Abstracted Empiricists."[15]

Another influence was the possibility of using mathematical theory, greatly encouraged by the development of the computer, to short-circuit the necessarily more prolonged evolution of exact knowledge in the sciences of individual and social psychology. Much of the most recent work in the management field consists of somewhat elaborate exercises in the application of statistical method. Two difficulties present themselves:

1. Men grow and change. Whatever results may be obtained from statistics bearing on a group of human beings on Monday will no longer be absolutely valid on Tuesday, even with the same group of human beings. They will be different human beings. There is some danger that the ardent pursuit of statistical method may lead management into much the same error which Veblen attributed to the orthodox economists. . . . "The hedonistic conception of man is that of a lightning calculator of pleasures and pains, who oscillates like a homogeneous globule of desire of happiness under the impulse of stimuli that shift him about the area, but leave him intact . . . Spiritually the hedonistic man is not a prime mover. He is not the seat of a process of living."[16]

[12] Elton Mayo, *The Social Problems of an Industrial Civilization with an appendix on the Political Problem*, London, Routledge & Kegan Paul, 1949, p. 19.

[13] Henry A. Landsberger — *Hawthorne Revisited*, Ithaca, New York, Cornell University, 1958, pp. 50, 51.

[14] F. J. Roethlisberger, Foreword to the paperback edition of Mayo's *Human Problems of an Industrial Civilization*, New York, Viking Press.

[15] C. Wright Mills, *The Sociological Imagination*, New York, Oxford University Press, 1959, cpp. 2 & 3.

[16] Thorstein Veblen, "Economics and Evolution" in *The Place of Science in Modern Civilization*, New York, 1919, p. 73.

2. Much of this mathematical proof is based on questionnaires addressed to workers and/or managers. The writer's father used to tell a story which illustrates the limitations involved. An acquaintance of his, a former Indian administrator, had written an elaborate book on famine in India. It was a weighty tome in two volumes containing hundreds of statistical tables. Another Indian administrator spoke slightingly of it. The writer's father, being an amiable person, pointed out its apparent authority. "My dear fellow," came the reply, "every figure in that book is based on statements made by the ryot or Indian peasant. The ryot, when asked a question by a British official, invariably lies."[17]

These comments are not advanced in any spirit of controversy, but merely to illustrate the kind of difficulties which faced the heads of established university faculties of business administration when approached, and it was sometimes reproached, with the "take-over bid" by the behavioural scientists. A "take-over bid" is a delicate matter to negotiate in the most favourable circumstances. It is no more than an amusing accident that one of the standard books on the subject in Great Britain should have been written by two authors named Bull and Vice.[18] "Bull," of course, is a British Army colloquialism for the over-elaboration of "spit and polish"; vice is a well-recognized term. Recently in Great Britain the Board of Directors of the largest chemical corporation attempted to "take over" the largest corporation making artificial silk. The attempt having failed, the Directors of the silk company held a thanksgiving service in one of London's most famous churches. In any such operation, human emotions at their most sensitive are inevitably involved.

These considerations point up some of the difficulties in Professor Suojanen's "olive branch" — difficulties which he has not, perhaps, sufficiently considered.

From the practical point of view it appears to the writer an essential preliminary precaution if a negotiation of this kind is in prospect, and he is assuming with Professor Suojanen, "values of freedom, democracy and the dignity of the individual," that the parties to controversy should avoid calling each other names. New bodies of knowledge need, of course, new technical terms for precise communications between peers. But in constructing these technical languages care is necessary if terms are to be avoided which, in popular usage, carry a defamatory implication when ap-

---

[17] Author's recollection. If, for instance, the technique of "sampling" where human beings are concerned or the technique of questioning, were wholly reliable, why should the United States continue the very expensive procedure of holding Presidential and other elections to political office? The statistical results of a sample, properly selected and controlled, would be equally effective. The activities of "pollsters" to date do not suggest that either of these techniques is wholly reliable.

[18] George Bull and Anthony Vice, *Bid for Power*, London, Elek Books, Ltd., 1958.

plied to the work of others. Professor Herbert Simon, for example, has applied the terms "classical" and "traditional," (and he has printed them in quotation marks) to the work of many of his predecessors.[19] In the climate of American popular opinion, with its rejection of the past, love of novelty and optimism as to the speed of progress, these epithets are freely translated into "obsolete" and "out-of-date." He is compounding with the notorious denial of the values of scholarship — Henry Ford's "History is bunk."[20]

Professor Suojanen tends to fall into this tactical error. On the first page of his paper he describes the work of many earlier management theorists as the "principles" or "management process" school, the universalistic approach, the traditional — or Newtonian — school of management and the "functional" school.[21] The latter is his final choice in pursuit of the biological analogy which is the subject of his paper.

Many students of management would question whether the analogy with biology is viable. As has been pointed out above, management is not a single discipline. It is the body of knowledge bearing on the art of managing which draws on many disciplines. Managing has been defined as "getting things done with and through people." And while knowledge about people is, of course, an essential component of the art, it is also necessary for the manager to have some knowledge of the things, that is, of the objectives of the undertaking, whatever it is.

On this basis the "discipline" of an established kind which most nearly resembles management is medicine. And biology is only one of the many "sciences" on which medicine draws in training practitioners. The analogy with biology does, however, allow Professor Suojanen to suggest that the views of the earlier management theorists are *functional*, while those of the behavioural scientists are *evolutionary*.

The last epithet assumes that the future is with "the behavioural scientists." This assumption is in its very nature open to the Scottish verdict "not proven."

As for *functional* as descriptive of the ideas of earlier management theorists it is, on Professor Suojanen's own showing, misleading. For, later on in his paper, he identifies these earlier theories with hierarchy and authority. It is true that F. W. Taylor emphasized "functional foremanship." But what he meant by that phrase was exactly the opposite of the theories to which Professor Suojanen applies the epithet "functional." In fact, he was very close to Professor Suojanen who would discard military experience as "crisis-oriented." Taylor wrote "throughout the whole field

---

[19] James G. March & Herbert A. Simon, *Organizations*, New York, John Wiley & Sons, 1958, Cp. 2, pp. 12–33.

[20] Henry Ford, Libel Suit v. The Chicago Tribune, July 1919.

[21] F. W. Taylor, *Scientific Management*, New York, Harper & Brothers, 1947; *Shop Management* (1903) p. 99.

of management the military type of organization should be abandoned, and what may be called 'the functional type' substituted in its place."[22]

It is a feature of Taylor's philosophy with which many later theorists, including the writer, have disagreed. They feel that Taylor overlooked a very simple principle, namely that the more you specialize functions, the more ample and intricate must be your machinery for coordinating actions, assuming of course, that the object of the exercise is to secure cooperative action from a larger or smaller group of people. But it is surely to make confusion worse confounded to employ the epithet "functional" in the exactly opposite meaning to that which it has hitherto been used in the literature of management.

To be sure the terminology, the semantics, of management are in a sorry state of confusion, as the writer has pointed out elsewhere.[23] He has had it demonstrated to him on a number of occasions that any serious attempt to resolve these misunderstandings would be a challenge to that freedom of the individual which is at the core of American political philosophy. But if "freedom" is translated as the right of any individual to affix any label to any object which he pleases, an enormous amount of intellectual luggage is bound to be sent to the wrong address. Words become inevitably bludgeons or beatitudes instead of instruments of communication.

To quote J. B. S. Haldane once again, "Mechanics became a science when physicists had decided what they meant by such words as weight, velocity and force, *but not till then*."[24] It may be, for the reasons stated, impossible to initiate any serious effort to clean up this confusion. But so long as it persists there is a special obligation on all those who value management as a subject to avoid epithets liable to generate "emotional heat."

A second claim by the "behavioural scientists" which has a similar effect, is that they have a peculiar responsibility for the maintenance of the intellectual standards of science. Here again Professor Suojanen in discussing the loss of love between what the writer would call the "practical" (Koontz' "Management Process") School and "the more recent settlers in the management jungle" asserts "To ignore the results (of the latter) constitutes a rejection of the scientific method itself. Management, the discipline can (not) afford to reject the concept that research increases the sum total of human knowledge."[25]

Let us turn back to F. W. Taylor again. On this subject he remarked "There is another type of scientific investigation which has been referred

[22] *Ibid.*

[23] Lyndall F. Urwick "The Problem of Management Semantics," *California Management Review*, Vol. II No. 2, Spring 1960, pp. 77–83. Quotation from Haldane *Ibid.* p. 77, Note 2.v. also *Op. Cit.* N. (10) p. 185. Italics added.

[24] *Ibid.*

[25] Suojanen *Op. Cit.* N. (3) p. 13.

to several times in this paper, and which should receive special attention, namely the accurate study of the motives which influence men."[26] It is the writer's conviction that, were Taylor alive today, he would welcome many of the researches of "the behavioural scientists." And the writer knows of no instance of any sincere and authoritative worker in the management field who does not so welcome them.

What they do reject, where they have practical responsibilities, is that they should attempt to teach "principles" founded on inadequate or irrelevant measurement, or which are at odds with the facts of situation after situation, in which they were not involved personally, but which they have encountered in real life. If the writer is correct in using the medical analogy with management, medicine does just that. No research work, no treatment however well supported by laboratory experiments, is accepted and incorporated into general medical teaching and practice, until it has been through the fire of "clinical experience." And any enthusiasm for "results" which leads to light-heartedness or carelessness in this respect is properly regarded as quasi-criminal. Recent press controversy about "thalidomide babies" is an illustration. Human lives and human happiness are at stake. So they are in management.

As for the generalization that "research increases the sum total of human knowledge" that is only true in the sense that all genuine research at least increases the area in which men are aware of their ignorance. And that is a gain. But that *all* the research work that is at present being carried out in any country adds positively to the "sum total of human knowledge" is not a tenable proposition. Quite a large proportion of the research work undertaken leads to "dead ends." The writer has never seen figures on this subject. It is not the kind of figure which research institutions and workers are anxious to publicize. But the broad fact is well-known to all serious workers in the sciences.

A third assumption inherent in Professor Suojanen's exposition is that there are only two kinds of knowledge, (1) Knowledge like that developed by the physical sciences and, (2) Knowledge developed from "personal experience, personal observation and resort to authority." This is a very large assumption. It rules out completely all those 'disciplines' which preceded the modern scientific age such as philosophy, history, political science, and the whole of man's recorded experience of administrative problems.

Moreover, it is an assumption which is bound to cause "emotional heat" in any "knowledge-oriented" undertaking, because it challenges the "colleague authority" of quite a large number of established "disciplines." It is an assumption with which it is extremely dangerous to initiate negotiations for a "take-over bid." To quote Professor Suojanen himself "In the truly

[26] Taylor *Op. Cit. N.* (21) "The Principles of Scientific Management" (1911) p. 119.

evolutionary organization the basis of authority, or better yet, influence, is individual reputation as determined by professional achievement." Does he not appreciate that this assumption calls in question as no-knowledge the whole of the professional achievement of those among his colleagues who do not adhere to the methodologies developed by that group of "behavioural scientists" described by a fellow-sociologist as "the abstracted empiricists?"[27]

Finally, on the subject of assumptions, Professor Suojanen quotes, apparently with approval, the dictum that "the behavioural science theory of organization advocates the decision premise viewpoint."[28] In the opinion of many students of management this premise is not only untenable, but is distorting the study of management. It is an attractive, but extremely dangerous oversimplification. And it is misleading students who are unaware of its ambiguous character all over the world. For instance, "management is a decision-making process."[29] Its use in management has been analogous to saying "man is a two-legged animal" and thus confining the study of human anatomy, physiology and psychology exclusively to the legs.

It is attractive because it is flattering to managers. As Mary Parker Follett has observed: "I have seen an executive feel a little self-important over a decision he had made, when that decision had really come to him ready-made. An executive decision is a moment in a process. The growth of a decision, the accumulation of authority, not the final step, is what we need most to study."[30]

It is dangerous because it represents the process of management as consisting almost exclusively of this momentary act and therefore, even when the growth leading up to it is studied, of placing much too much emphasis on the processes by which those concerned in carrying out decisions participate in making them. This derives from our preoccupaton with the *forms* of political democracy, and our identification of democracy itself with the forms to which we are accustomed. The writer is just as concerned as is Professor Suojanen with the values of democracy. But he believes that those values can be most effectively preserved, by giving to all those concerned in any activity a satisfying sense of participation in the activity as a whole rather than by copying political models as to the forms and procedures for recording decisions.

It also ignores all that part of the management process which is concerned with communicating downwards. Professor Suojanen may be pleased to know that the writer agrees with him that, at an earlier stage,

[27] V. N. (15).

[28] *Op. cit.* N. (3) quoting from Edward G. Koch "Three Approaches to Organization," *Harvard Business Review*, March–April 1961, p. 162.

[29] Australian Institute of Management, Melbourne Division, *Management Diary*, V. 3 No. 4 June 1963 "Decision Making by Management," p. 1.

[30] M. P. Follett, "The Illusion of Final Authority" in *Freedom and Coordination*, London, Pitmans, 1949, p. 1.

students of management, including the writer himself, have placed too much emphasis on *authority* as the key to organization theory. He concurs with the late Chester Barnard that authority is accorded to a communication by the recipient. That is to say, it moves upwards. What moves downwards is communication. "The need of a definite system of communication creates the first task of the organizer and is the immediate origin of executive organization."[31] Barnard has some trenchant things to say about the difficulties of democratic process on the political model where what men are aiming at is integrated action.[32]

Finally come Professor Suojanen's proposals for resolving these difficulties. These are briefly that we should abandon the attempt at an integated theory of management altogether. We should regard management as an "open-ended function of three factors: (1) the orientation of the organization: (2) the participants in the organization, and (3) the cultural environment."[33] With regard to (1) he proposes to classify human institutions into three groups. a. Those that are crisis-oriented, b. Those that are routine-oriented, and c. Those that are knowledge-oriented.

This seems to the writer a very curious proposition to originate with an advocate of the "behavioural and social sciences." Because if these sciences have an integrating principle it is that they deal with man and his behaviour. In fact it is to deny the possibility of any coherent theory of human behaviour at all. We can only hope for a theory of man as a soldier (crisis-oriented), of man as a business executive (routine-oriented) and of the same man as a member of a Board of Directors (knowledge-oriented). Moreover, if the writer follows the argument correctly, we shall have to have separate studies of human behaviour in all these contexts for every different national and social environment — for American man and Russian man and Chinese man.

When the formal study of management was first proposed, rather more than half-a-century ago, and it was first proposed in connection with business undertakings, there was a chorus of criticism from men of different trades, "my business is different." Because managing had always been learned empirically, by experience, men were unable to distinguish between knowledge-of-acquaintance with a particular trade and knowledge about managing *per se*. The man who made boots was quite unable to convince himself that he could learn anything from the man who made boats.

That has passed and it is being increasingly accepted that the body of knowledge described as Management is equally applicable not only to any

[31] Chester I. Barnard, *"The Functions of the Executive,"* Cambridge, Mass., Harvard University Press, 1938, p. 217.

[32] Chester I. Barnard, *Organization and Management:Selected Papers,* Cambridge, Mass., Harvard University Press, 1949, "Dilemmas of Leadership in the Democratic Process," pp. 24–50.

[33] Suojanen *Op. Cit. N.* (3) p. 15.

kind of business undertaking, but to voluntary and governmental and charitable institutions, indeed, to any form of organized human coopera-tion for a defined objective. There are, of course, difficulties in applying it to men of different cultural and racial backgrounds, because of differing traditions and ideals.

But they are difficulties which the Western countries will fail to over-come at their peril. As Sir Charles Snow has observed "In all non-indus-trialized countries, people are not eating better than at the subsistence level. . . . Whatever else in the world we know survives to the year 2000, that won't. . . . The West has got to help in this transformation. The trouble is, the West with its divided culture finds it hard to grasp just how big and, above all, just how fast, the transformation must be."[34] The U.S.A. has set the industrialized countries a noble example in the energy and generosity with which they have set to work to tackle this problem.

It is an unprofitable, indeed a dangerous, moment for professors of man-agement in the United States to be deeply divided as to what they do know and have got to teach. All human institutions today are or should be crisis-oriented. All should have a sufficient substratum of agreed routine to enable them to go forward with the immense tasks which face them without expending too much effort on reconciling differences of theory. All should be knowledge-oriented because the world is living in the middle of the biggest technological revolution in human history, and the Army, the Business or the University which is not prepared to be adaptable is useless.

To the writer it seems strange that Professor Suojanen should be seeking for a new basis of classification when American democratic theory and practice have already offered the world an analysis of the processes of gov-ernment which goes far to reconcile the divergent "schools," if they would once agree to a few common definitions and a system of classification. The well-established distinction between the "political or legislative, executive and judicial" aspects of government can go far to assimilate the views of different theorists if they will once accept it.

For decisions of a "political" character the writer would agree with Pro-fessor Suojanen that a committee form of organization is probably the most appropriate. But at whatever decisions a committee may arrive about policy it cannot, as a committee, communicate them. If the members present attempt to do so individually there will be as many different ver-sions of what the committee has decided as there are members. If the at-tempt is made to reduce the decision to an agreed form of writing, usually described as a "minute," the probability is that the document, in trying to satisfy everyone, will end by being understandable only to those present at

[34] C. P. Snow *Op. Cit. N.* (6) pp. 39–40.

the discussion. Moreover, if the members of the committee are also the persons who carry out its decisions, the chances are that their action will be imperfectly coordinated because of differences in timing.

There is therefore an executive function of government, embodied in the United States in the Presidency, which deals with *action*. But because any individual who deals with action may be oppressive or mistaken in the treatment of individuals, there is also a judicial function of government to see that this does not happen.

Admittedly the judicial function has been very imperfectly developed in systems of business government, though some recent legislation is a step in that direction. And probably a great deal of the friction in business between managers and workers can be traced to the absence of machinery for this purpose.

But if theorists would once agree to say which of these aspects of management they were talking about, progress would follow. And the writer suggests that these are the right lines on which to seek a solution. In the meanwhile "the tactics of jungle warfare" have generated a great deal of "emotional heat," and have created adverse conditions for a "take-over bid" by any one of the parties. Perhaps if they could agree that scientific method involves certain systematic steps — definition, analysis, measurement, hypothesis, experiment, proof — and come to a mutual decision to arrive at agreement on steps 1. and 2. before discussing each other's work under headings 3. and 4., they might find the outskirts of the jungle cleared and the possibility that some border skirmish would set it alight proportionately reduced.

A recent book by a member of the behavioural science group observed "Work groups which have high peer group loyalty and common goals appear to be effective in achieving their goals."[35] From the small sample of teachers of management in the United States known personally to the writer, it would seem to him unthinkable that *both* those conditions should not be achieved quite quickly.

---

[35] Rensis Likert, *New Patterns of Management*, New York, McGraw-Hill Book Company, 1931, p. 30.

4

Transcend the Current Debate on Administrative Theory*

Paul J. Gordon

Indiana University

This article protests the classificatory emphasis in the preceding articles on management theory and elsewhere, and suggests a less compartmentalized scheme for analyzing the main schools of thought in management. Whereas Urwick alluded to military as well as business administration, Gordon includes a much broader sphere of administration — in hospital, religious, public, educational, and other types of institutions. He compares four approaches; traditional, behavioral, decisional, and ecological, surveying them with considerable detachment. He suggests that these areas constitute a four-pronged approach, a multi-faceted framework for a complex problem, with better possibilities for identifying and measuring the relevant variables.

Far too much of the recent literature on administrative theories has been dedicated to scuffling over which of several schemes of classification of a complex terrain might be better. The battle, if one is to be conducted and useful, should be on grounds other than classification alone. One system is better or worse than another only because it has more use in achieving the purposes intended. This gets down to whether it helps or hinders insight, verification and communication.

What is far more important for the practicing executive is the recognition that any particular approach to administration carries a number of assumptions, recognized or not, that can lead to both intended and unintended consequences.[1] Currently competing approaches can be classed

---

* Taken from the *Journal of the Academy of Management*, vol. 6, no. 4, December, 1963, pp. 290–302.

[1] This would apply to the practicing professor, researcher, consultant and writer as well.

in a manner to help thoughtful executives consider the uses and limits of each.

At least four approaches to administration can be distinguished in America today. The distinctions are not as compartmentalized as any scheme for analytical purposes might suggest. Each is really a perspective or a relative emphasis more than a separate school of thought. At different times among people of various backgrounds one perspective or another has been in the ascendency; others have been relatively subordinated. Brief elaboration may provide perspective and a framework for fitting together theories, research and practice useful for continued study and improvement. For convenience, we shall use the labels: *traditional; behavioral; decisional* and *ecological.*[2]

Traditional

The approach that has recently been called traditional represents the accumulation that has passed along from: the *mother sciences; rationalized views of administration,* frequently of European origin; and, the *scientific management movement,* with its development attributed at least partly to North Americans.

Mother Science Emphasis

During the period and among institutions and individuals when the *mother sciences* constituted the dominant perspective, the activity of organizations was seen as principally economic in the case of business, political in the case of government and social for institutions such as hospitals. Early teaching in business administration was heavily influenced by the ideas of classical economists. The movement for better teaching and practice in public administration made relatively little headway until the overpowering preoccupation with political theory and law were eased. Writings on hospital administration only recently emphasize administration more than medicine and technology. Literature for practitioners early in this century was heavily influenced by principles and analogies drawn from various branches of engineering. Only gradually was fuller recognition given to economic, political, social, technological and moral aspects of administration and behavior that cut across organizations.

In fields such as business administration, public administration, educational administration, military administration, church administration, institutional and hospital administration and international administration, in general, policy and program were conceived to be uppermost. Policy was

---

[2] The term "traditional" is meant in no slighting sense. Both the traditional approach and the newer decisional one are based on a necessary rational core. The traditional has simply been around longer.

seen as the province of boards and chief executives. Administration was viewed more as a kind of housekeeping, record-keeping, maintenance of physical plant and routine supervision. Policy and administration were conceived to be related but separate entities, each treated at the correct level of hierarchy in larger organizations. Only later did writers describe policy and administration as joined and reciprocal, each setting premises and limits for the other. Eventually, the term administration came to cover both.

Broad Rational Emphasis

The *rational view of administration,* as represented by Henri Fayol, Luther Gulick and Lyndall Urwick, was a break with the mother science approach.[3] Administration was perceived as a separate and recognizable field of human activity. Administration was perceived as what administrators do. What they do was seen as a function — called administration — and composed of highly interrelated sub-functions such as planning, organizing and controlling. These people were concerned with the total task of administration applied to the total unit of organization. They were concerned with administration at all levels of sizeable organizations in all kinds of enterprise.

They sought to develop universal theories and principles that would explain and prescribe guides for planning, organization and control in any kind of administrative situation. Although not always specified, it was assumed that wise administrators would know enough to adapt these guides to particular situations. Emphasis was more at the top policy level of the organization with the subdivision and specialization of work in a rational way below. Administration was perceived as based on principles that could be deduced and applied in a rational, orderly and systematic way. Many of the currently discussed theories and principles of administration can be traced to the writings of Fayol, Gulick, Urwick, and their colleagues and predecessors.

Early Scientific Management

The *scientific management movement,* as represented by Frederick W. Taylor, Frank and Lillian Gilbreth, Henry L. Gantt and others, was also concerned with rational study and improvement in administration. These people were advocates of knowing what work had to be done and getting it done in the most effective and efficient manner. They were concerned with division and specialization of work; the measurement of work and effort; and, the efficient and humane expenditure of effort. More recent focus on the individual in the work situation and his relationships with

[3] Deliberate choice to hold footnotes to a minimum should make this paper more readable, especially for an audience well equipped to supply those that pertain.

members of a group has suggested shortcomings in the earlier scientific management activities. In practice, the emphasis of the scientific management movement may have been more on the physiological than on the psychological and sociological aspects of behavior in the work situation. The writings of the pioneers for a scientific management movement, however, indicate interest in broader aspects of the well-being of people at work.

In contrast to the rational view of administration as posited by Fayol and others, a great part of the experimentation and writing of the scientific management group was more at the shop level. Emphasis was on engineering the most efficient arrangement of means to ends to get work done at the foreman and worker level. Applications were especially in manufacturing and construction. Many of the current uses of job analysis, motion and time study, work flow and plant layout, work simplification, process charting, production scheduling and the like had their beginning in the scientific management movement. These are residuals of a larger concept.

Traditional Summarized

According to the traditional view, the task of administration is that of planning relationships among the work, the people and the workplace; establishing organizational relationships with suitable authority and responsibility so that work can be directed; then measuring and controlling to be sure that specifications are met. That is, rationalizing and engineering an efficient means to ends relationship.

The anatomy of administration, that is the framework for exposition and analysis, is made up of certain administrative functions. These have been most elaborately articulated as planning, organizing, staffing, directing, coordinating, reporting and budgeting. For these, the perceptions and semantics among writers have varied. Some of the recent literature has amended this functional outline with the inclusion of more emphasis on motivation, communication and leadership; and, by conceiving of these activities as sub-processes that combine to make up a larger and integrative process of administration.

The goals of administration are to promote effectiveness, (achieving desired organizational objectives), and efficiency, (doing so without waste). The ways of dividing work at each level of organization involve combinations of decisions on the basis of: major work functions to be performed by the organization, (for example, in business — marketing, production and finance); the processes involved, (for example, the stages of refining oil in continuous-flow equipment); professional groupings, (for example, economists in one organizational unit); and, the products, the clientele or the area most to be developed or served. The criteria to be used in designing and regulating organizations for the accomplishment of work are certain well-established "principles" such as unity of command (one boss), span of control (not too many subordinates), and homogeneous assignment (like activities put together). These are founded on concepts of authority and responsibility arranged in a hierarchy from top to bottom of an organization.

The traditional view, compared with those that follow, is more work-centered. Administration is treated more as a technical problem to be solved on a highly rationalized and programmed basis with formal arrangements and guide-lines. The ends are frequently taken as given; means are to be engineered to produce desired outcomes with maximum efficiency. Fundamental ideas include those of hierarchy, authority, function, specialization, measurement and efficiency. The influences that have shaped the traditional view are more those of classical economics, engineering and law.

Behavioral

Following the traditional approach with its work-centered emphasis, increasing but not always approving attention was directed to the emerging behavioral approach. In contrast, the emphasis of the behavioral approach was more on the people and the way that live people behave in live organizations. Through their writings the behavioralists have frequently appeared as opponents of rationalization. Likewise, they have often been questioned as critics who cast doubts on an established order but provide no firm edifice in its stead. (The objective view may be neither as black nor as white as one might suppose in reading the extremist positions of either school.)

Argument Over Evidence

Advocates of the behavioral approach, still somewhat in formative stages and less neatly classified, have claimed not only that the traditionalists have neglected many aspects of administration; but further, that the traditional propositions were frequently wrong. The behavioralists complained that the traditional approach prematurely generalized in order to formulate principles too often based on personalized experienced and limited evidence. The experience, they contended, was not sufficiently perceptive of behavior in live organizations and not adequately verified. Misconceptions, they argued, were conveyed through preoccupation with abstraction, rationalization and technique. These, they said, caused trouble through focusing on the physiological and mechanical attributes of men and machines while ignoring observable evidence of how people really behave. Such a mental set, they suggested, might lead the traditionalist into the hazard of wanting to bend reality to fit into his own mentally conceived model of the real world. (Modernists of various sorts are not entirely free of this hazard.)

In contrast, the behavioralists sought to compile as proof for their contentions empirical studies, characteristically more inductive than deductive. Many of the earlier studies were limited in the number of cases examined. Occasionally the implications were misinterpreted, especially through premature effort to find answers to meet operational problems. Fairly early in the behavioral approach, evidence was developed with which to refute some of the traditional propositions. Yet there appeared no systematic body of theory and evidence fully to replace the old with the new.

The traditionalists countered with charges that the behavioralists were gnawing away at existing beliefs without offering any substantive additions or replacements. They claimed that really perceptive behavioralists might recognize that wise administrators in practice took note of phenomena not detailed in the traditional principles. The traditionalists intimated that the behavioralists were making unwarranted claims for new discoveries. The behavioralists countered that their contribution was one of opening for public inspection their use of evidence and research methods to arrive at findings and conclusions.

Hallmarks of Behavioralists

One of the essential characteristics of the behavioral approach is the insistence on observable and verifiable phenomena that may serve at least in part as evidence for anything to be recognized as knowledge, principle or finding. For example, instead of asking about a man's traits (abstractions not easily to be observed and verified), the behavioralist is more likely to ask — what does he do — what does he say — what does he not do — what does he not say?

If one recognized the foregoing as the hallmark of the behavioralist, one will also perceive that various social scientists do not necessarily equate on a one to one basis with the behavioralist approach. Psychologists, sociologists, anthropologists, political scientists, biologists, economists and even mathematicians outside the conventional view of so-called social sciences may or may not be behavioralists.

Whether they are behavioralists or not can best be judged by the evidence of how they themselves behave in pursuing and disseminating knowledge. Some behavioralists might consider their research more "pure" under conditions of controlled laboratory experimentation. But, one may well use a behavioralist approach, even to some extent clinical and experimental methods, without insisting on "pure" science at every point. It seems only a matter of common sense to declare that the call for completely aseptic research technique and conclusions completely validated on a mathematical basis in fields such as administration is one way to stifle any progress at all.

Early behavioral contributions, publicized under what came to be the much-abused "human relations" label, were sometimes fragmentary, inconclusive and preoccupied with the plight of the misunderstood man at the lowest end of the hierarchical totem pole. Also, the legitimate concern with non-rational aspects of behavior led to preoccupation in some instances with psychotic behavior, hardly one of the cornerstones on which to build administration. Some behavioralists viewed the task of organizing, for example, as that of establishing relationships among individuals, groups and somewhat ominous things called formal organizations and bureaucracies.

More recently there has been more concern with what may be called normal behavior at all levels of organization. Increasingly, misinterpretations of earlier findings have been corrected through the work of the behavioralists themselves and through others. The swing in favor of the totally permissive and supportive climate with rule only by consent and emphasis only on rewards (never on penalties) may have been overdone. Insofar as there is any consensus, behavioralists currently seem to view the goals of administration as those of facilitating suitable combinations of support and constraint in order to achieve whatever degree of conformity and coordination may be essential for accomplishing the main activities of the enterprise.

Behavioral Summarized

Organization is viewed primarily as a social system — one that develops interactions, conflicts and cohesions not always within the power of the administrator to understand and control. Organizational decisions are perceived to involve various combinations of individuals, groups, social structures, bureaucracies and institutions. Administration is infused with individual and group feelings, sentiments, perceptions, identifications, motivations, inducements and sometimes culturally patterned responses and interactions. Questions of influence, the distribution and control of power and reconciliation of diverse interests both internal and external in relation to the organization are also involved. These are further conditioned by the development of informal patterns of leadership and group interaction that do not show on the official organizational chart but may either advance or hinder the achievement of official purposes.

According to the behavioral view, the task of administration is to choose those arrangements, broadly speaking, that are most likely to evoke a system of cooperative relationships among the people who are to achieve the mission of the organization. In contrast to other approaches, the behavioral view centers more on the people, their interactions and cooperation. It emphasizes, more than the traditional approach, the development of insight and understanding based on empirical investigation. It challenges administrators and students to understand non-rational as well as rational and informal as well as formal aspects of organizational behavior. The contribution of psychology and sociology to this approach are generally recognized; less often cited are those of political science and anthropology.

Decisional

The perspective taken in the more recently stressed decisional approach is that the task of administration is that of decision-making. The organization is viewed as a decision-making unit and the administrator as a decision-maker. Rational analysis of utilities desired and the outcomes, probabilities, risks and uncertainties related to each set of alternatives under postulated conditions is characteristic of current developments. The design of models and the testing of quantitative techniques are further indicative of the nature of the effort that is going forward in trying to advance a "new science of managerial decision-making."[4]

Concepts and Tools

Differences in relation to other approaches are founded on the relative emphasis accorded decision as such and on the greater use of new and powerful tools for quantitative analysis. One of the recognized operational utilities of the decisional approach, as a way of conceiving of administration, is that it provides a better integrating device than some of the earlier approaches. One of the current limitations, at least as used by some proponents, is the relative omission of the qualitative and non-rational factors that are recognized to be present in some of the most crucial executive decisions. To include within the view of decision-making only the aspects that can be readily quantified and programmed may cut the most important parts. This many others have noted.

Nevertheless, this approach has barely begun and the universal requirement to make decisions or see that they are made provides a nexus for the integration of many approaches. The decision emphasis, more than some of the others, seems to get one up to the point of commitment involving subsequent action. Action as such cannot be cut altogether from the view of the executive task.

As with the earlier approaches, there is no fixed point in time that can be cited as the precise starting point of the decisional approach. Neither is it nicely segmented conceptually and semantically from the others or within itself. In the market place today, one may find material of recent

---

[4] Since the wording is the title of the Herbert A. Simon, (Harper and Brothers, 1960) book, the exception to the no-footnoting guide is in order.

publication treating decision as: an exercise in "common sense," sound thinking and logic; an integrated process of problem solving; and the application of "scientific method" in thinking through administrative issues. Recent material on learning theory, information theory, innovative behavior and heuristic programming can be related to both the behavioral and the decisional approaches. Decisions, of course, cut across the other approaches as well. Some writers have a scheme of thought that subordinates other aspects of administration to decision-making. Others view decision as no more than a momentary phenomenon among interdependent processes of thought and action.

Systems and Processes

The conceptualization that is involved here is one that some have viewed as a systems approach. That is, provided that we reject the older image of systems as a bundle of office procedures. The newer view relates administrative systems to unified arrangements of interdependent factors such as the solar system. The total input and output and processing of information and action by men and machines, for example, can be conceptualized as the integration of many sub-systems into a larger total system not unrelated to the decisional view.

The concept of administration as a process, which is at the core of the decisional approach, provides a framework for analyzing dynamic relationships among several variables. The concept of a process, decisional or any other kind, has not been the unique contribution of the decisionalist. The traditionalists have described planning, organizing and the like as a series of interdependent processes all adding up to a larger concept of an administrative process. The behavioralists have examined interaction, communication and learning as processes and the process of fusing people and organizations. But the concept has been more fully and widely characteristic of contributions by the decisionalists.

Once administration is conceptualized as decision-making, then the processes of making decisions assume major importance. The decisional (systems) view of administration is more sharply concerned than the earlier ones with the establishment of relationships among objectives, strategies and competition — whether political, social, economic or technological — internal to the organization or external.

Decisional Summarized

The goal is achieving objectives under competitive conditions. The function of administration is to facilitate the flow of information and the making of appropriate decisions. Persons faced with decisions must choose among combinations of ends, means, strategies, tactics, and information inputs and outputs. The anatomy of decision-making includes, not necessarily in this classification and sequence, but by some name: information, objectives, strategies, alternatives, probabilities and consequences.

This approach is decision and systems centered: information, including that about competitive forces, is regarded as a central problem. Certain aspects are more highly analytical, frequently involving quantitative expression. What we have summarized as the decisional approach is currently close to what has been included under the recently popular term — managerial sciences. That term, however, embraces some of the other approaches.

Mathematics, statistics, econometrics, engineering and quantitative programming techniques have already provided the basis for important contributions to this approach. The economic and marketing environment of the firm, for example, in business, and the theory of games as applied to decision-making in war-time and peace-time have been prominent. Political science, which includes concern with relative power position, representation of diverse and competing interests and ultimate accountability, is still relatively untapped as an important well-spring of administrative theory. The last observation fits equally well the ecological approach.

Ecological

The ecological approach is concerned with relationships among: the organization; its internal and external environment; and, whatever forces regulate interdependent adaptation, innovation and change. The term is taken from biology. Ecology is that branch of biology that deals with mutual relations between organisms and their environments.[5]

Adaptive Behavior

In the case of business, one might center attention on the relationship between the economic and marketing environment and the internal productive, distributive, financial and managerial capacities of the individual firm. The scope might be confined to one activity or extended to encompass an industry. In public administration, a focus of continuing interest is the relationship between the environment in which any governmental program must operate and the internal views, resources and administration of the agency. The importance of examining the reciprocal activity of simultaneously adapting to environment and effecting innovation in new environments should be self-evident in international administration.

The ecological view, as defined here, is that the task of administration is to build and strengthen organizations that will have the capacity to re-

[5] Since compartmentalization is usually somewhat artificial at best, readers will recognize that the "life sciences" approaches to "systems" could fit here but is not divorced from "systems" as treated technologically and sociologically.

spond to changing environment and to create opportunities for growth. Growth here does not have to mean increased size. It could mean diminished size with greater strength, competitive ability and return on the investment. The latter would fit most clearly the case of business.

The goals of administration are survival and strengthening of the integrity and resources of the organization as a corporate unit amid the pressures of external, internal and organizational change. The administrator would seek the optimum mix between frequent organizational changes that might harm desirable relationships, on the one hand, and undue concern for stability in relationships that might lead to atrophy, on the other.

Ecological Summarized

This view is more eclectic than those already cited (it borrows from all of them) and more heuristic (ready for readjustment of ends, means and behavior anywhere along the line in the light of new discovery). To put the matter less abstractly, here we have an approach that starts with the grass roots, (the customer for business administration, the voter for public administration or the patient for hospital administration), and then adds the necessary operational elements. It borrows along the way from the so-called principles of the traditionalists, the cooperative ideas of the behavioralists and the competitive strategies of the decisionalists. According to this view, administration functions as a catalyst in order to facilitate the direction and rate of growth and change most suitable for a viable organization.

The ecological approach, as defined, is growth-centered; regards viability as the key issue; and, is environmentally — even culturally and cross-culturally oriented. The last point especially has significance in a world increasingly sensitive to the international aspects of almost every major human endeavor. The basic underlying studies on which one might draw more fully in developing this approach would include, as a minimum, biology and anthropology. Viewed as an issue of responsiveness, political science is also relevant.

Multiple Approach

The foregoing adds up to a multiple approach to a complex matter. The approach is at least four-pronged, with the four major headings serving as a convenience to house many more detailed considerations. The practical implications for continuing education, research, and practice are several.

First of all, it avoids getting caught up in the current debate on administrative theory — trapped within one set of assumptions or another without profit and without a larger view of the possible consequences. It should be evident that each of the four major approaches has a special perspective founded on certain assumptions and leading to certain possible consequences. The executive who views primarily the work with little regard for the other aspects may lose sight of the objectives and the social consequences of his activity. The executive who views more exclusively the people and social interaction may be entirely too preoccupied with internal cooperation and lose sight of the ultimate decisions, the competition, and the kind of profit and capital that his organization is supposed to build. The executives who are preoccupied with the fascinating game of making decisions may lose sight of the action and the follow-up necessary to assure the result. Others can be so involved in the attention to adaptive behavior that they fail to assess and strengthen the character and the integrity of the enterprise for which they are responsible. So the whole relationship involving assumptions, perspectives, and consequences is worthy of examination. There are other uses as well.

The framework provides a fairly easy way to join in an educational setting the contributions of: the traditionalists who have dealt with processes such as planning, organizing and controlling; the behavioralists who have analyzed various processes of social and political interaction; the decisionalists who have emphasized different perceptions of decision processes; and, the ecologists who have stressed processes of adaptation and accommodation between organisms and environments. The content of an executive or graduate program might be cut in different ways. Yet, the probabilities are that increasingly all four views will have to be clearly presented, appraised and synthesized if the better programs are to set the stage for continued learning.

The framework should facilitate evaluation and use of research findings. Ideally, researcher and practitioner should share a concern to discover and verify the existence of similarities, differences and patterns under stated conditions with stated probabilities. The aim of research generally is to establish bases for prediction and therefore bases for better decisions for the future. The framework set forth has the flexibility and the "openness" in no way to close off advance of knowledge in the field; yet it can be treated as "closed" in order to establish commitment and assure delivery in executive work. As others have said, the need is for material that is both theoretically connected and empirically tested.

Finally, administration has come to mean taking decisions and actions to achieve organizational objectives. More than others, the administrator is *responsible for setting the character of the organization, the goals for the future and the direction and rate of change that may anticipate or mold future conditions. What most distinguishes administration is responsibility — responsibility to see that decisions and actions necessary to achieve organizational objectives are taken — and, responsibility for strengthening the total resources on which the future of the organization must be built.* Ultimately, the administrator is responsible for integrating the activities of a total unit of organization in relation to its total environment over time. How can such responsibilities be discharged except through applying the best of the old and the new to the aspects of administration that are environmental, organizational and personal as a minimum?

An Academic Epilogue

In these pages, we have presented four viewpoints, each of which is an important and yet only a partial perspective. One does not have to make a forced choice and then cast the others aside. The distinguishing features have been emphasized in order to highlight the perspectives and contributions of each. Entering into any new field of study, one of the important guides is to learn the orientation of the field. Orientations change from time to time. At any particular point, however, knowing the orientation will help in recognizing what issues are considered important, what kinds of data are accumulated and what methods of analysis are used.

Building a Useful Framework

One important aspect of building a conceptual framework for administration is the idea of a number of variables related differently under differing circumstances. Precisely what the key variables may be, what their relative importance may be and how they may be related under different circumstances are not settled matters. Nor can they be conceived as settled and remain settled in this kind of a field. So, if one is not sure what the key variables may be and not sure of their relative importance, postulations must be made, subject to continuing discovery, learning and correction.

The idea that there are such variables, however, is fundamental. They provide the substance of administration without which processes, techniques and viewpoints in a vacuum can be sterile. The differences in relative importance among the variables under differing circumstances are also important. They account, at least in part, for significant differences in business, public and institutional administration in different settings. As a beginning, one can say that some of the key variables will be those in the external environment in which the organization conducts its activities and those represented in the internal programs of the organization itself. Further, one may include the external and internal attributes of organizational behavior and the techniques for qualitative and quantitative analysis. In addition, there can be little question that administrators themselves may be among the key variables in any administrative situation.

Another important aspect of building a conceptual framework is to provide for the inclusion of values, especially those related to the choices of ends and means for the organization and behavior for members. While advocating one set of values or another may not represent an addition to scientific knowledge, the analysis of values among organizations and their apparent relation, if any, to decisions and actions is highly important. Persons responsible for administration and the preparation of administrators cannot put aside, as unscientific, questions related to values.

The different purposes for which organizations are established and the different purposes conceived and advanced, consciously or not, by their members are but one of several factors related to value. Others include the estimate of worth attached to economic, social and political philosophies and the moral and ethical standards of administrators themselves. These also account for significant differences in administration among diverse institutional, national and international settings. In brief, in purposive organizations, purposes are important. They must be part of the conceptual apparatus of the administrator and part of the study of administration.

A third important aspect of building a conceptual framework is to decide on some unifying concept that will help in picturing the ways in which substantive aspects and value aspects may be combined and related for effective administration. For this purpose, the concepts of a series of sub-processes of decision and action joined into a larger process of administration provides a framework as satisfactory as any other, provided its utilities and limitations are recognized.[6]

The process concept is a mental tool for conceptualizing how to put the parts of administration together. The idea of sub-processes joined into a larger process of administration has the utility of providing the structural aspect of the framework so that it can be visualized, so that it can be communicated, so that the parts can be related to the whole and so that the contributions of many related fields can be brought into focus within one framework.

The utility of the process concept in administration is similar to that of the "scientific method" in the physical and biological sciences. It has been said that the unity of all science is in the method. The emphasis on method permits the transfer of learning from one substantive field to another in the sciences. The emphasis on process provides a sorting rack that permits comparative studies and therefore the transfer of learning and the accumulation of knowledge in administration. Once understood and retained, the process concept also helps the practitioner put his knowledge to use. In both instances, there is more accord on the need for a central unifying concept than there is in delineating the parts and agreeing that things actually get done that way.

[6] The conceptualization of "processes" used here, it should be said explicitly, is not solely linear but closer to a general systems network (both open and closed and heuristic on occasion).

Provisional Working Theory

A final aspect of building a conceptual framework for administration is to define the major orientation or point of view. For the purposes of this discussion, each of the four broad approaches, (traditional, behavioral, decisional and ecological), is perceived as incorporating sub-processes all of which, combined and fused, join into the larger process of administration. As with evaluative work in the field of anthropology, we have chosen to establish a framework which is in itself subject to continued testing, refinement and possible future replacement. The framework permits the incorporation and comparison of many approaches as well as the joining of values, substance, and processes.

It points the way to a synthesis that transcends the currently competing approaches while at the same time building on the significant contributions of each. It permits the degree of structure necessary to give order to a field to be studied and mastered while at the same time avoiding orthodoxy. In effect, this whole approach constitutes a provisional working theory of administration.

5

The Next Development in Management Science: A General Theory[*]

William C. Frederick

University of Pittsburgh

Taking an imaginative and far-reaching approach, Professor Frederick is optimistic about the possibilities for the construction of a general theory of management. The evolution of this theory centers on five major components whose contributions are traced. Like Gordon, the author attempts to extract the best from the several contending approaches, finding the emergent theory in a synthesis or integration of the substantiated concepts developed by the five approaches.

Within perhaps five years — certainly not more than ten years hence — a general theory of management will be evolved, stated, and generally accepted in management circles. Given the state of management knowledge, the invention is almost inevitable. The exact time and place of this invention are not yet discernible, nor is it particularly important that we know them. But it will be important to recognize the development when it occurs, for it will have startling and far-reaching effects in the field of management.

The larger issue which underlies this prediction is the nature of invention. In one sense, this prediction is a case study of how inventions occur. As we all know, inventions consist of the combination of previously existing elements or ideas into new and unique patterns. The automobile, for example, was a combination of a buggy and a steam engine, later replaced by the internal combustion engine. The airplane is simply a com-

* Taken from the *Journal of the Academy of Management*, vol. 6, no. 3, September, 1963, pp. 212–219.

bination of a glider (which is a modified kite) and an engine. Even such simple devices as the bow and arrow illustrate the same principle, for it is a combination of a spear (which in turn is a combination of a stick and a sharp piece of stone or bone) and a bow, the latter having had other uses in primitive societies. These combinations or "inventions" as we call them, occur — either deliberately or by accident — when someone develops a new insight or sees a new possibility in elements already in use.

Someone — an academician? a practitioner? a consultant? — toiling in the vineyards of management thought will develop such a new insight within the next few years, and he will bring forth a new intellectual harvest in which all students of management may rejoice.

But, for the moment, let us simply recognize that there is now no general theory of management and ask ourselves what this means. It means there is no general agreement about what management is. It means, further, there is no coherent and consistent body of scientific principles which can constitute the basis for a management science. It means also there are no clear-cut grounds for declaring management to be a profession as is true of doctors, lawyers, and others. Finally, it means there are only the sketchiest guide lines for collegiate business schools in educating for management and for company training directors in encouraging executive development. After a half century of management science this seems disappointing and frustrating. But it is, unfortunately, true.

However, in spite of the lack of *general* understanding, researchers have made separate and piece-meal advances over the years, and it is from these advances that the general theory will be constructed. Five major components of the general theory of management can be discerned. Each of them will be discussed briefly to see what contributions they will make to the evolution of the general theory.

The first of these components is what might be called classical management principles. These are the major ideas and concepts as evolved out of and through Taylor, Gantt, the Gilbreths, Fayol, and others in that particular tradition. They find modern expression in such books as that by Professors Koontz and O'Donnell, *Principles of Management.*[1] We shall cite three principal contributions.

In the first place, Taylor and his followers have given us the first approximation of the meaning of management. However, some management students would emphasize that this is *only* an approximation of the meaning of management. A criticism of the classical concept of management is that it is too imbued with notions of authority and power. The concepts

[1] Harold Koontz and Cyril O'Donnell, *Principles of Management,* 2nd edition, New York: McGraw-Hill, 1959.

of authority and power are laced throughout the analysis of management principles by such authors as Koontz and O'Donnell, and there is some reason now to doubt the validity of the role played by authority and power in the management process. But nevertheless it is fair to say that a major contribution of the Taylor school has been that it has given us a first approximation of the meaning of management.

A second contribution of the classical management school is that it has spelled out and analyzed some of the basic management functions. These functions are (1) planning, which emphasizes that management is a rational process of problem solving; (2) organizing, which delineates the types of organizations that management may utilize and the peculiar problems that develop around these organizational structures; (3) staffing, which declares that management is a human process; (4) directing, which emphasizes the importance of leadership in the management process; and (5) controlling, which reminds us of the necessity of self-correcting devices as a part of the management process. The classical management school has aided us greatly by giving us a detailed description of these basic functions of the managerial process.

The third contribution of this school is that it made the first breakthrough in developing a set of management principles. It thus provided us with a theoretical basis on which a science of management could be built up. Although in some respects the classical management principles are today as archaic as Adam Smith's economic principles are, it would be a mistake to underemphasize this contribution which the classical management school has made. Crude though it was, it was at least a beginning, and we badly needed pioneers who would boldly conceptualize in the early days of management thought.

The second major component of the general theory consists of the contributions made by the human relations school. Mayo, Roethlisberger, and Dickson come readily to mind, though many others were to follow their lead.[2] Needless to say, the human relations school has taken modern management by storm. It is generally unfashionable today to oppose human relations study and techniques. Any manager today who is known to be unfamiliar with or opposed to the idea of human relations in industry is

---

[2] Elton Mayo, *The Human Problems of an Industrial Civilization*, New York: The Macmillan Company, 1933; and *The Social Problems of an Industrial Civilization*, Boston: Division of Research, Graduate School of Business, Harvard University, 1945. F. J. Roethlisberger and William J. Dickson, *Management and the Worker: Technical vs Social Organization in an Industrial Plant*, Boston: Harvard University, Graduate School of Business Administration, Bureau of Business Research, 1934, and *Management and the Worker: An Account of a Research Program Conducted by the Western Electric Company, Hawthorne Works, Chicago*, Cambridge, Mass.: Harvard University Press, 1939.

considered to be slightly outmoded and encrusted with tradition, lacking in foresight.[3]

The great contribution of this group of thinkers has been to demonstrate that the management environment is a human and social environment. This contribution has great and far-reaching implications for the managerial process and for all managers who participate in it. They have also demonstrated that the factory is a social organization. They have pointed out that the social values a worker holds are important to his work performance. It has also been established as a tenet of management science that the informal organizational structure of the work situation is relevant and a powerful force, and that a manager disregards the informal organization at his own peril. The human relations group has also emphasized that motivation is a function of the total environment of the worker and that the worker brings certain social and cultural values with him that affect the manner in which he performs his work. Finally, this school has pointed out that a careful treatment of workers is important to the productive process.

Before turning now to the third major component of the general theory of management, it is worth pointing out that the first two components — classical management principles and the human relations school — are developments whose beginnings antedate World War II, while each of the remaining components have received the attention of those interested in management science mainly since the Second World War. We shall discover as we discuss the remaining components that less and less of a tangible nature is known about them; and as will be pointed out later, it is precisely this underdevelopment of the remaining components that today is delaying the emergence of a general theory of management.

The third major component of the general theory of management is known today as decision theory. The contributors to decision theory are many today, and it is difficult to single out any one person for more credit than others. However, among those who have been active in the field are Herbert Simon, Irwin Bross, J. F. McClosky, W. W. Cooper, A. Charnes, Franklin Lindsay, Robert Luce, Howard Raiffa, H. McDonald, J. D. Williams, and many others.[4]

Included in decision theory are a number of theoretical developments and mathematical techniques that have evolved since World War II. Most

[3] For two statements expressing some measure of scepticism about the enthusiastic reception given human relations see Malcolm P. McNair, "Thinking Ahead: What Price Human Relations?" *Harvard Business Review*, March–April, 1957, pp. 15–39; and Donald R. Schoen, "Human Relations: Boon or Bogle?" *Harvard Business Review*, November–December, 1957, pp. 41–47.

[4] For representative works, see Herbert A. Simon, *Administrative Behavior: A Study of Decision-making Processes in Administrative Organization*, New York: Macmillan,

of these developments, it is true, trace their lineage back prior to World War II into the body of mathematics and statistical theory. However, there has been a great flowering of these techniques and the invention of several new procedures that were not known before the second World War. Among those procedures that have played a prominent role are statistical decision theory; several types of mathematical programming, including linear programming, quadratic programming and dynamic programming; information theory; communication theory, including an emphasis on semantics, linguistics and small group communication processes; inventory theory; transportation distribution theory; and a number of others.

This body of decision theory which is at present somewhat amorphous and ill-defined has nevertheless already provided us with several important contributions to management science. In the first place it has demonstrated more than ever before that management basically is a rational process of solving problems, or rather that the management process is capable of being a rational procedure for solving problems. Decision theory does not declare that perfect rationality characterizes managerial processes but it does provide us with both an insight and possible procedures by which management decision making is primarily a function of available information, and it emphasizes the key role, the strategic role, that information plays in making management decisions. Thirdly, it has enabled us to delineate more clearly the components of decision making — the means, ends, and values which characterize the decision-making process. Fourth, decision theory has enabled us to outline the various steps and procedures that are required in rational decision making by providing us with maps or structures of actual decision processes. Fifth, decision theory has led to a reduction of the role that intuition plays in making management decisions. Sixth, since the emergence of decision theory and its application there has been a greater reliance on statistical and mathematical methodology as a procedure for reaching management decisions. Seventh, there has been likewise a reduction of the time and energy spent on routine processes and decisions, with a greater reliance now on management's ability to recognize those situations where new techniques can be utilized. And finally, there has been a freeing of management for the more imaginative tasks of forward planning, implementation of policy, and a revision of the organization to take advantage of some of the new management techniques.

1947, and *The New Science of Management Decision*, New York: Harper, 1960; Irwin D. Bross, *Design for Decision*, New York: Macmillan, 1953; Franklin A. Lindsay, *New Techniques for Management Decision Making*, New York: McGraw-Hill, 1958; and Donald Davidson and Patrick Suppes, *Decision Making: An Experimental Approach*, Stanford, California: Stanford University Press, 1957.

Behavioral science is the fourth major component of the evolving general theory of management. This element is distinct from, though related to, the contributions of the human relations school. In a sense, it is a dramatic extension of the contributions of the human relations school, but in its deeper implications it goes much further than Mayo and his group had pushed social science in their day.[5]

The contributions made by behavioral science to management science have been slight so far, although most will agree that there is a great deal of potential development for the future. Many authors who deal with the subject are themselves rather vague about the possibilities for management.[6] The vagueness is related to the relatively underdeveloped character of behavioral science and of the efforts to link it up with management and administration.

As these relationships are more clearly delineated by further study and research, it is quite likely that what we call management science will actually tend to become behavioral science in the future. That is, the major subject matter of management science will be drawn largely from the behavioral sciences and the contributions that they can make to our understanding of the management and administrative process. Already we are witnessing the inroads made upon business school faculties by psychologists, and cultural anthropologists. As they team up with production specialists, mathematicians, statisticians, and programmers, the study of management will take on more of the tenor and tone of behavioral science.

To be more specific, though, relative to behavioral science, one of its big contributions will be in the area of organizational theory. We are now learning that the classical management theory of organization is sadly lacking in psychological and sociological reality. The sinews that bind an enterprise together are not yet well defined but it is becoming increasingly clear that the social dynamics of interaction between individuals and groups, as they are shaped by the culture in which they live, play a key role in organizing the efforts of persons and workers. Psychology, sociology and cultural anthropology will have much to say and to contribute to an understanding of these organizational relationships. Furthermore, since the management environment is now increasingly understood as a human environment there will be much greater attention paid to group interactions and group dynamics and, once again, the behavioral scientists will have things of importance to say. Behavioral science will also have much to contribute in

[5] Representative of the behavioral science group are Chris Argyris, *Personality and Organization*, New York: Harpers, 1957, and *Understanding Organizational Behavior*, Homewood, Illinois: Dorsey Press, 1960; and Rensis Likert, *New Patterns of Management*, New York: McGraw-Hill, 1961.

[6] Maneck S. Wadia, "Management Education and the Behavioral Sciences," *Advanced Management*, September, 1961, pp. 7–10.

the area of communications and semantics which, it is now recognized, are becoming more prominent parts of the management process.

The fifth major component of the general theory of management is value theory. Reduced to more commonly accepted terminology this refers to the theory of business responsibility or the social responsibilities of business enterprise. It is considerably broader than the term "business ethics" commonly implies. It embraces the ethical implications of business enterprise but goes beyond that. Value theory has yet to make its major contributions to management science. There are few names for us to mention in this field for it is a very underdeveloped field of inquiry. Outstanding contributors are Peter Drucker, Richard Eells, Clarence Walton and C. West Churchman.[7]

As value theory evolves it will be its major task to provide a set of values which will (1) define management as a science and not simply subjective art; (2) define the ends and goals of business enterprise and management (so far all we have asked of science is that it help define the means of achieving culturally prescribed ends and goals; (3) define the social and public responsibilities of management and business; and (4) integrate the diverse themes found in management principles, human relations, decision theory, and behavioral science. The major function of value theory will be to integrate the other major components and weave their themes into a coherent body of management theory.

This is obviously a key and strategic role that we are assigning to value theory. The lag we witness in the development of value theory, however, is the primary reason why a general theory of management has not yet been developed. It seems significant that of all the figures in the history of management thought, Mary Parker Follett came closest to stating a general theory of management; and she has been the only one with a relatively well developed and consistently thought out general value theory.[8]

So, if these major components are woven together we shall have the emergence of a general theory of management. Its major characteristics will be four. First, it will be scientific in character and it will emphasize that management is a science and not simply a subjective art. Second, it will be mathematical in character, as evidenced by decision theory. Third, it will draw heavily on the behavioral and social sciences. And fourth, it will be philosophical in orientation for it must deal with issues of values and ethics.

[7] For two recent attempts to grapple with value theory see Richard Eells and Clarence Walton, *Conceptual Foundations of Business*, Homewood, Illinois: R. D. Irwin, 1961; and C. West Churchman, *Prediction and Optimal Decision: Philosophical Issues of a Science of Values*, Englewood Cliffs, N.J.: Prentice-Hall, 1961.

[8] *Cf. Dynamic Administration: The Collected Papers of Mary Parker Follett*, edited by Henry C. Metcalf and L. Urwick, New York: Harper, 1942.

In considering the consequences of the emergence of a general theory of management, one casts about in one's mind for a possible analogy from some other field of inquiry. The work of John Maynard Keynes, *The General Theory of Employment, Interest and Money*, might be such an analogy.[9] This theory was evolved during the Great Depression and was published in 1936. It is safe to say that economics was never the same after the publication of Keynes' *General Theory*. There are not many respectable economists in the nation or, for that matter, in the entire Western world, who do not subscribe to the basic tenets of the Keynesian economics. It is true that there are many variations upon the basic theme but there is a chorus, albeit a sometimes discordant chorus of voices, that sings out the strains of the Keynesian economics. The same thing might be true of the field of management. It is doubtful, once the general theory has evolved, that management will ever be the same again.

More specifically, two major consequences will follow the emergence of a general theory of management. First of all, the general theory will unify management knowledge. This development, in turn, will enable us to define the profession of management in clear-cut terms. It will enable us to define the management process and to delineate its various parts. And, it will enable us to define the subject matter for management education. In the second place, the general theory will push management toward becoming a science and therefore will result in easier and more certain definition and resolution of the problems facing management.

Now that we have predicted the invention of a general theory of management, discussed its major components, and suggested what its consequences may be, we shall now return to the nature of invention which, as noted earlier, is the larger issue underlying this discussion.

Four points should be obvious. First, to say that "necessity is the mother of invention" is an over-simple and incomplete explanation of the inventive process. We have "needed" a general explanation (or theory) of management for a long time. But we have had to await the emergence and development of certain important component parts — especially behavioral and social science, the application of mathematics to management processes (and also the computer technology), and value theory.

Before an invention can occur we need the elements to combine. It takes more than individual "genius." Our needs and "necessities" arise out of and are defined by what it is possible to attain — and we attain through inventions and discoveries. Therefore, it might make more sense to say that "invention is the mother of necessity."

Second, all of us, when confronted by a new and unique and ingenious gadget, say to ourselves, "Why didn't I think of that?" In the inventive

[9] John Maynard Keynes, *The General Theory of Employment, Interest and Money*, London: Macmillan, 1936.

process, things always seem easy and uncomplicated by using hindsight. What is the significance, then, of predicting an invention such as we have done here by using foresight?

It can only mean that there exists a rich proliferation of elements and ideas capable of being combined into a new discovery. This should be comforting and encouraging to those interested in the managment profession. It indicates that management science has come far and that it is on the verge of a major new break-through.

Third, we might ask ourselves, have we witnessed the birth of the general theory of management in this article? After all, we have outlined the major components of the theory and have suggested the ways in which those components might be integrated through value theory and have even speculated about the consequences that might flow from the development of such a theory. Is not this the beginning of the general theory of management? The answer is clearly no. Our insights here are only an anticipation of the general theory. The history of invention shows quite clearly that nearly every major invention and discovery has been preceded by a number of anticipations and hesitant starts toward the development of the full product. This was certainly true of Keynes' *General Theory*. Historians of economic thought have traced elements of Keynesianism far back into the literature of economics and political science.

Fourth, the history of invention shows clearly that new inventions and new ideas change the world in which they occur. John Dewey was correct when he said:

> "Let us admit the case of the conservative: if we once start thinking no one can guarantee what will be the outcome, except that many objects, ends and institutions will be surely doomed. Every thinker puts some portion of an apparently stable world in peril, and no one can wholly predict what will emerge in its place."[10]

The power and force of ideas are great. Much that is familiar in the world of management will be changed. It is true that one cannot wholly predict the shape of things to come after the emergence of a general theory of management — but the chances are great that it will be a better world in which to live and work.

---

[10] John Dewey, *Characters and Events*, edited by Joseph Ratner, New York: Holt, 1929, quoted on page 1.

6

An Inquiry into the American System
of Industrial Management*

William Gomberg

Wharton School of Finance and Commerce

Can all management be incorporated in a single model? Like Koontz, Urwick, Suojanen, and Gordon, Professor Gomberg sees a management theory jungle, albeit a different one than the others. He argues that an integrative framework is needed into which we can fit first-hand observations, clinical and case material and mathematical models. The key concept he advances is "clinical reality" as a foundation for empirical research that would test the management theory as advanced in leading textbooks.

American corporations constitute a unique form of industrial government. Their managers are made up of groups of people whose decisions shape the allocation and use of America's resources. They act in a pluralistic economy where it is assumed that they are subject to no particular national plan except in cases of dire national emergencies. To some extent their freedom to act is circumscribed by a political government, but part of their residual skill consists in preserving maximum freedom to act in a democratic society and maintain political acceptability therein. What are the sets of principles that influence their decisions? We are, of course, referring to general management.

The function performed by the generalist in management includes that of containing within one system all of the functional specialists: for example, the marketing man who wants to promise today's orders for tomorrow's delivery, the production man who wants to lump all orders to fit a minimum-cost production pattern irrespective of the delivery requirements, the

* Taken and adapted from the *Journal of the Academy of Management*, vol. 4, no. 2, August, 1961, pp. 123–128.

financial man who is interested in minimizing investment costs and the plant engineer who is anxious to buy the latest automated equipment. In addition he must understand how to maintain political acceptability in a democratic society.

The President's Commission on National Goals agrees that we must maintain a substantial growth in productivity.[1] Its members split on whether the goal should be 3.4% or 4% or 5%. How does the management at the micro-decision level tie in with a national objective of sustained economic growth at the macro-level — or are these national objectives just meaningless rhetoric? We rely for the allocation of our national resources upon the decisions of a decentralized system of autonomous institutions, the business corporations. Are they in any way directed by a sense of national purpose?

Businessmen talk about management as a profession. They talk of management as trustees on behalf of stockholders, laborers, customers, distributors, suppliers and the public at large; that is, some of the time. Is there a set of principles that governs these decisions? The textbooks say yes and attempt to outline and describe a set of precepts.

Businessmen talk one way in their idealistic moments and a different way in the conversation at their clubs. On some occasions, at university commencements for example, the fundamental guiding precepts of the emerging profession of business are extolled. On more cynical occasions, managers themselves will denigrate the study of management and talk of purely intuitive instincts. They describe steering the enterprise by the seat of their pants.

Which of these two pictures describes reality? Is the businessman merely catering to a public relations need when he talks in terms of the professional requirements of business at the top level or is he indulging a pseudo-cynicism when he both glorifies and derides his function simultaneously?

Robert Gordon asked some of these questions and came to inconclusive answers. His book *Business Leadership in the Large Corporation*[2] was based upon his observations of business behavior during the 1930's. He stated then that "despite the mounting literature on corporate management, we still know surprisingly little about how and by whom in the large corporation prices are set, investment decisions are made, key executives and directors are chosen." Since the publication of the Gordon book, we have seen the explosive growth of the large corporation, first in its adaptation to the post-war economy and then its integration into a cold-war economy.

[1] *New York Times*, November 28, 1960, pp. 21, 22.
[2] Gordon, Robert, *Business Leadership in the Large Corporation.* The Brookings Institution, Washington, D.C., 1945, p. 12. (Recently reprinted in a paperback edition by the University of California Press.)

The system of decentralized decision-making which it represents is both defended and attacked from many quarters. The challenge from industrial systems abroad is obvious. Within the country itself, influential voices, like Galbraith,[3] have raised questions whether or not the allocation of resources should continue to be left to what is implied to be an irresponsible management. Galbraith's attack is a continuation of the assault of other intellectuals upon the basic competence of management to be trusted with the allocation of resources. The very same questions are raised by Arthur Schlesinger, Jr.[4]

On the other hand, other academic observers like Adolf Berle[5] have talked about the growing sense of trusteeship of the corporation and the growth of what he calls the corporate conscience. All of this, however, has been in the realm of speculation with an occasional example to fortify an intuitive insight. What is needed is a comprehensive look at what is actually happening.

If private decentralized management is to rise to these attacks, it must begin with a careful examination of what is taking place at the corporate level. We may well begin with an examination of the internal structure of function.

Four complimentary approaches to general management receive emphasis. They are:

(1) The presentation of management as a set of self-contained, abstract, functional principles such as planning, organization, control, etc.

(2) The presentation of clinical cases and problems without any attempt to distill an abstract set of principles. It relies upon the indoctrination of a set of miscellaneous intuitive artistic insights.

(3) The treatment of management as an application of insights from the behavioral disciplines such as anthropology, psychology, sociology, etc.

(4) The structuring of mathematical and simulation models first as a specialized functional tool of general management and then an extension as a completely self-contained system.

An analysis of each of these exclusive approaches indicates a combination of virtues and limitations.

The presentation of management as a set of self-contained abstract principles employs the method of logical sequence. The observer is able to organize his thinking around a set of rules and principles that will guide his organizational behavior. This is the original method evolved by the

[3] Galbraith, John, *The Affluent Society*, Boston, Houghton-Mifflin Co., 1958.

[4] Schlesinger, Arthur M. Jr., *The Vital Center*, Boston, Houghton-Mifflin Company, 1949.

[5] Berle, Adolf, *20th Century Capitalism; Power Without Property*, New York, Harcourt, Brace and Company, 1959.

pioneer management thinkers, beginning with Taylor's publication of *Shop Management,* and *Principles of Scientific Management.*

Its limitations are that the observer without a background of experience upon which to draw comes away with a skeleton upon which he is unable to hang concrete data. Confinement to this approach alone runs the risk of steeping the observer in meaningless platitudes.

The case method has the virtue of bringing before the observer a plethora of data and business events that fill the void of the observer's inexperience. On the other hand, the case method leaves the observer's capacity for abstraction relatively unsatisfied. His cases become a set of disconnected models which he tries on the future reality that he faces like so many beds of Procrustes. Each case is unique and therefore we may assume that there are no principles of general management.

The treatment of management as a set of applications of the insights from the behavioral disciplines such as anthropology, psychology, sociology, etc., has the virtue that it breaks out of the superficialities and blind alleys into which management was led by the indiscriminate human relations enthusiasm. It seeks to bring the rigor of its research tools into the business environment and substitute them for the anecdote and homily.

However, an exclusive preoccupation with the behavioral studies tends to displace the focus of the observer. He must remain a student of the business clinic rather than seek to abstract data from the clinic which will fit the intellectual model of the behavioral specialist.

The mathematical approach to management confined itself for some time to the refinement of the functional specialties. For example, the use of mathematics has revolutionized inventory control and the routing, scheduling and dispatching of work. These applications of mathematics are refinements of older rule-of-thumb methods.

Another group of men are convinced that the computer is a creative device that will make, eventually, the entire hierarchy of business decisions. A business corporation will be portrayed as a huge mathematical model. Copernican-like breakthroughs are announced for the future. To what extent does this philosophy find any possibility of realism in the present business climate?

The management generalist starts with the business institution itself as the basis of his conceptual scheme and attempts to build his theory systematically with the institution itself as the basic point of departure in a *systems* analysis.

This means that the study of general management must consist both of a descriptive clinical phase and complex analytic phase. The management generalist cannot permit himself the luxury of complex analytic mathematical models built upon a few "self-evident propositions." He must carefully investigate and describe the different models that have been evolved out of experience and fit them into a conceptual scheme. The artificial distinction between analytic and descriptive methodology is rejected by him. He cannot analyze in a vacuum and his field is replete with rich clinical material. What is needed is a detailed clinical study of operating management to consist of:

a. An examination of the nature of the governing process of private enterprise to determine the criteria for business decisions.

b. Identification of the criteria and mechanisms to coordinate decisions and their associated implementing activities.

c. Analysis of the process of accommodation of the managerial decisions within the firm and with other institutions in the larger society.

d. The impact of the corporation on the private life of the participants in the corporate executive structure.

To be sure there is no paucity of writings on the subject of general management. The problem is to correlate what is written with what actually takes place. Frank Gilbreth had observed that workingmen use a number of different methods when they work at their jobs without being aware of the difference. They pursue one method when they work and still another when they teach. Is the same true about members of management? Do they act one way when they operate and another way when they describe what they are doing?

Can all of management be encompassed within a single model? A common complaint is that management principles express non-operational platitudes. An old epigram says that what is everybody's property is nobody's property. Principles designed to explain all managerial behavior ranging from the operation of a small retail establishment to the operation of a gigantic multi-industry organization really explains nothing. Is not the time ripe for a new approach? Has it become necessary to develop a number of functional types of management which will describe the different behaviors that arise under different sets of circumstances? Can a series of categories be defined with the accent on differences rather than sameness that will achieve for management the same kind of useful conceptual pattern that Professor Hoxie developed to explain differences among trade unions? It is indeed strange that the trade union movement, a secondary response to managerial intiative, has received much deeper theoretical treatment to explain differences in behavior than management, the central institution of any industrial society.

These questions arise in educational circles and great debates are carried on over what constitutes a proper education in management. This debate can only begin to get rational answers when it is disclosed what actually happens at the management levels in the corporation. What is needed is first hand observation within a systematic frame of reference. There is no shortage of homilies on managerial principles. There is no shortage of case histories recorded in splendid isolation. There is no shortage of proposed mathematical models. What is missing is the integration of all of these materials and a comparison of their implications with clinical reality.

How real are the concepts of organizing, planning and control as described in typical textbooks? To what extent are the new sophisticated techniques the playtoys of an intellectual staff that serve the prestige needs of the corporation vs. actual generators of decisions?

Methods of Approach

The following research approach is outlined more to suggest a beginning than to delineate a final plan. Extensive changes in the methodology outlined below may arise in the course of the pursuit of the investigation.

The focus of attention would be a number of key decisions in the area of planning, controlling and organizing. We would try to concentrate on decisions that were five years old or more to minimize the impact of any current emotional trauma on the participants. Interviews would be scheduled with the top executive officer of about twenty key corporations. An attempt would be made to solicit aid in identifying a number of key decisions arrived at after staff recommendations. We would particularly concentrate on those decisions that arose out of conflicting subordinate recommendations. An attempt would be made to isolate those factors that entered into the thinking of the chief executive as he made his selection from a number of alternative contradictory recommendations from his staff and subordinate officers. An attempt would be made by a means of depth interviews with the top executive and his staff and subordinate officers to determine what happened. Reviews of the available minutes of any of the meetings that were held in the course of estimating this policy would likewise be undertaken.

A hypothesis would be that the data collected would support a functional classification for management similar in form to the equivalent functional classification developed by Hoxie for unions. Hoxie found unionism to be not a single social movement but an imperfect fusion of several, no one of which could be adequately accounted for in purely economic terms. His analysis of unionism was characterized by emphasis upon function, the distinction of fundamental types, and a pluralistic causal interpretation. The types listed by Hoxie follow:

Business unionism — its outlook is that of the craft or trade, its aims are narrowly economic. Its principle purpose is collective bargaining.

Uplift unionism accepts the existing social order. Its mission is the diffusion of leisure class culture and bourgeois virtues among the workers. Mutual insurance is its main function and homiletics its preoccupation. A typical example is the now defunct women's trade union league.

Revolutionary unionism avowedly aims at the revolutionary overthrow of the existing social order. It is divided into the socialistic and quasi-anarchistic elements.

Predatory unionism practices secret rather than open violence. It is lawless but it professes no far-reaching philosophy. It aims at nothing but the immediate advantage of its own membership.

Hold-up unionism — its most-brilliant successes come from illicit alliances with employers to organize joint monopolies.

Dependent unionism — where the union is dependent upon others for its basic strength.

Company unionism or office workers' unions in union offices represent an example of this class.

Just as the trade unions fall into these categories it is anticipated that managements will fall into types. Cutting through all types and influencing their development will be the following influences:

(1) The socio-cultural factor of the environment from which the owners are drawn, as against the managers in a specific legal environment.

(2) The influence of firm size and technology upon the behavior of the management.

(3) The characteristic of the industry and technology that lead to dominance by some one functional group, e.g., is the management finance-influenced, production-oriented, or sales-dominated principally? An interesting question is, how did this initial picture continue after the basic cause leading to its dominance ceased?

It is our hope that we shall be able to develop a variety of functional types of management that will be as fruitful in explaining and predicting managerial behavior as was Hoxie in explaining trade union behavior.

7

Managers' Theories of Management*

Dale Yoder, Raymond E. Miles, Lawrence McKibbin and Robert E. Boynton

Stanford University

and George W. England

University of Minnesota

This article details the development and use of a management game designed to investigate the patterns of management theory used by managers in action situations. The key to understanding the true nature of managers' theories of management involves a thorough understanding of the attitudes and values of managers. This falls, generally, within Professor Frederick's fifth area of theory described in the preceding article. This paper reports the evolution of the game and the development of the various scales for each of several theory areas. The game has been put through a large number of experimental administrations, and the scores on the scales represented in individual and group profiles.

This statement describes the purpose, rationale and development of the *What's Your Theory?* game and related experiments in the identification of managers' patterns of management theory. The statement has been prepared to answer inquiries about the game and to explain its meaning, use, implications and availability.[1]

The *What's Your Theory?* game developed out of conferences and discussions in which managers and students of management were invited to

---

* Taken from the *Journal of the Academy of Management,* vol. 6, no. 3, September, 1963, pp. 204–211.

[1] The point of view described here has been developed and is shared by the authors as members of a research group in the Stanford University Graduate School of Business, Division of Industrial Relations.

participate in and contribute to a series of studies of manager attitudes. The studies adopt a common concept of "attitudes," assuming that attitudes modify perceptions of various referents or values and are behaviorally relevant as predispositions toward action or behavior, so that significant clues to manager and organizational effectiveness may be found in distinctive patterns of manager attitudes.

The intention to investigate attitudes of managers was in part generated by the demonstrated usefulness of similar investigations of employee and supervisor attitudes, investigations that have provided useful insights and added understanding with respect to behavior in working organizations. It seems reasonable that if understanding of employee and supervisor attitudes has helped to explain and predict individual and group behavior in employment, attention to the attitudes of managers can become a source of similarly valuable insights.[2]

Preliminary designs for manager attitude studies recognized that attitudes likely to be significant in manager careers and organizational effectiveness represent several distinctive levels or strata. Current plans contemplate studies of at least three levels, as suggested in the accompanying Figure 7.1. In the figure, these levels are designated as (1) attitudes toward a system or hierarchy of life values, which may be described as the personal *philosophy* of the manager; (2) attitudes toward *theories of management*, that is, explanations of the behavior of organizations and their members; and (3) attitudes toward *management policies* — the intentions and courses of action selected and adopted by management for its guidance in organizing and administration.[3]

The *What's Your Theory?* game and related experiments have been concerned with the second of these three levels. The game developed in efforts to help managers identify and distinguish their attitudes toward management theory. An underlying assumption holds that managment is at least in part a rational process; that managers see their problems and their decisions as involving a variety of cause-and-effect relationships. They regard organizational behavior as explainable and understandable. They interpret problems and consider or review manager decisions and actions in terms of these assumed relationships, which include the impacts of organizations on individuals and of individuals on organizations. These more or less widely accepted and plausible explanations of the interaction of individuals, groups and the working environment are major theories of management. The explanations (theories), with varying degrees of accep-

[2] See "Selected Bibliography on Manager Attitudes Toward Management Theory" (Mimeographed), Division of Industrial Relations, Stanford University Graduate School of Business, 1962.

[3] For more on this background, see Dale Yoder, "Management Theories as Managers See Them," *Personnel*, vol. 39, no. 4, July–August, 1962, pp. 25–30, and "Management Policy for the Future," *Personnel Administration*, vol. 25, no. 5, September–October, 1962, pp. 11–14.

Figure 7.1

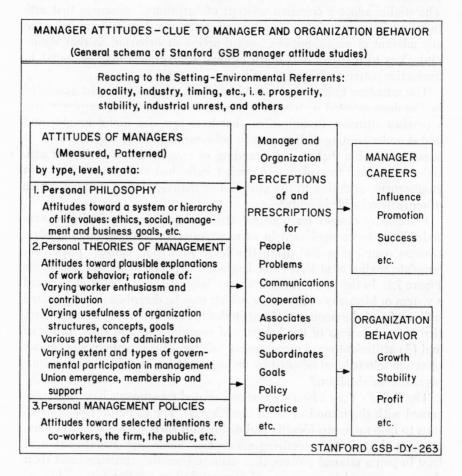

MANAGER ATTITUDES – CLUE TO MANAGER AND ORGANIZATION BEHAVIOR

(General schema of Stanford GSB manager attitude studies)

Reacting to the Setting – Environmental Referrents: locality, industry, timing, etc., i. e. prosperity, stability, industrial unrest, and others

ATTITUDES OF MANAGERS
(Measured, Patterned)
by type, level, strata:

1. Personal PHILOSOPHY

   Attitudes toward a system or hierarchy of life values: ethics, social, management and business goals, etc.

2. Personal THEORIES OF MANAGEMENT

   Attitudes toward plausible explanations of work behavior; rationale of:
   Varying worker enthusiasm and contribution
   Varying usefulness of organization structures, concepts, goals
   Various patterns of administration
   Varying extent and types of governmental participation in management
   Union emergence, membership and support

3. Personal MANAGEMENT POLICIES

   Attitudes toward selected intentions re co-workers, the firm, the public, etc.

Manager and Organization
PERCEPTIONS
of and
PRESCRIPTIONS
for
People
Problems
Communications
Cooperation
Associates
Superiors
Subordinates
Goals
Policy
Practice
etc.

MANAGER CAREERS

Influence
Promotion
Success
etc.

ORGANIZATION BEHAVIOR

Growth
Stability
Profit
etc.

STANFORD GSB–DY–263

tance or rejection, presumably influence the actions and decision of those who hold positions of power in these organizations. In short, managers' theories shape organizational policies and programs as well as manager careers.

Some managerial problems, for example, involve questions about how associates and assistants are motivated in their work. Answers represent theories of work. Some manager decisions raise questions about the impact of various structural variations in working organizations on group effort and contribution. Other decisions must lean heavily on theories of administrative behavior and practice. Some problems may seem to a manager to be traceable to various forms and degrees of governmental influence in management; others may be explained in part as expressing the viewpoints and activities of unions and their members. Many problems may appear to managers as generated in economic processes both within the organization and in its environmental relationships.

Individual managers vary in the degree to which they accept or reject various explanations or theories. Thus, Manager A may accept with little qualification the explanation that unionization of employees and demands for collective bargaining are largely the result of agitation by demagogues. Manager B, on the other hand, may view union activity as essentially a labor marketing or pricing process. Manager C may hold yet another theory of unions and regard the interpretations advanced by Managers A and B as unacceptable.

The *What's Your Theory?* game was designed to discover just such differences in acceptance of management theories. Six dimensions or areas of theory have been defined as justifying distinction in a central core of relevant explanations; experience to date has sought to identify and appraise degrees of acceptance in five of these areas.

Preliminary studies sought to discover rather precisely the explanations traditionally and currently advanced by managers. In part, this phase of the study encouraged managers and students of management to state and explain their explanations. What, for example, is the explanation for wide variation in worker productivity, contribution and job enthusiasm? Why do employees join and support unions? On what basis do societies impose regulatory laws on business and management?

At the same time, in this stage of the studies, the writings of managers and their spokesmen and interpreters were combed for answers to similar questions.

From these sources, a catalog of explanations was developed. Each viewpoint was summarized in a brief paraphrase from the literature of management. Language was modified, on the basis of experiment, to facilitate easy comprehension and similarity of interpretation. Items were classified in five of the major theory areas, which were defined as follows:

1. WORK — explanations of the varying interest, effort and effectiveness with which workers accept and perform their assignments.
2. ORGANIZATION — explanations of organizational impact in terms of concept, structure and the organizing process.
3. ADMINISTRATION — explanations of manager influence and effectiveness in terms of manager characteristics, decisions and overt behavior.
4. ROLE OF GOVERNMENT — explanations of public participation in management in terms of assumed responsibilities and obligations of government.
5. UNIONS — explanations of the emergence and persistence of employee collective bargaining associations.

The Theory Scales. To facilitate exploration of manager attitudes toward management theory, these brief statements of theory for each major area were arranged in a series that outlined the sequence of their emergence and development. Each such series thus arrayed statements from one extreme that describes early, historic explanations to another in which the most recently advanced theory is described. In the center of this array, statements expressed a view that has gained traditional acceptance and continues to hold extensive support.

This arrangement created something approximating a continuum of ordered positions ranging from the historic to the ultra modern for each of the theory areas. To test the usefulness of this concept of theory continua as well as to discover the effectiveness of individual items, fourteen items for each of five theory areas were submitted — in random sequence — to a panel of management theorists. Extremes of each range were briefly defined for panel members, who were asked to order or position each item in a sequence from one extreme to the other. The ranges of explanations in each area were defined as follows:

1. WORK: from (a) the degree of worker acceptance of an obligation to take orders to (z) possible satisfactions for a hierarchy of personal needs.
2. ORGANIZATION: from (a) structures designed simply to extend the owners' control to (z) those designed to fuse and achieve the multiple goals of participants.
3. ADMINISTRATION: from (a) charisma — personal magnetism to (z) highly specialized knowledge and skill with professional responsibility.
4. ROLE OF GOVERNMENT: from (a) government as the persistent protector of private property rights to (z) governmental responsibility for the security and welfare of individual citizens.
5. UNIONS: from (a) unions as the product of agitation by malcontents to (z) unions as member attempts to satisfy personal needs in the distinctive setting of industrialized employment.

The measured success of the panel in verifying the positions for which each item was intended provided a basis for selecting the most discriminating items and, at the same time, confirmed the acceptability and usefulness of the continuum concept.

Thereafter, nine items with demonstrated validity were arranged to provide an experimental "long-form" scale for each theory area. In subsequent discussions with managers, they were asked to select the item or items in each scale that best or most nearly expressed their personal preference among explanations.

One version of these long-form scales ordered the items from one extreme to the other. A second presented the items in random order. Participants playing the game were asked to eliminate the three items they considered least appropriate and to mark with a "plus" the three they found most satisfactory as expressing their views.

At the same time, for parallel experiments, short-form scales were prepared for each theory area (see Figure 7.2). Each scale in the short form includes three items, one representing each of the poles and the third the mid-point of the range. Participants choose one or more items in each area as representing the best expression of their views.

Figure 7.2   Short Form Questionnaire. What's Your Theory?
STANFORD-GSB-DY-629

Explanation: This exercise is designed to help you recognize your own *position* with respect to five central areas of management theory.

Directions: Examine the statements in each book below separately. Then, *in each block*, select and check (√) the single statement or combination of statements that most nearly expresses your viewpoint. For example, you might check only statement 1 in the first block, statements 1 and 2 in the second, etc.

Tentative explanations of *workers' job interest, effort and enthusiasm.*
WORK

_____1. Personal conscience and interest can never assure a fair day's work from most workers; only required performance standards can do that.

_____2. For most employees, what they do in their work is less important to them than what they earn.

_____3. Most workers only perform at their best when assured an opportunity to help determine the content or procedure of their jobs.

Tentative explanations of the *effectiveness of working organizations.*
ORGANIZATIONS

_____1. For efficiency in working organizations, owners must make most major decisions and, through managers, tell all workers what to do.

_____2. The key to effective organization is mainly the assignment of well-defined tasks to competent specialists.

_____3. A major factor in organizational effectiveness is clear recognition that worker-members are the basic source of the organization's authority.

Tentative explanations of the *varying effectiveness of manager-administrators.*
ADMINISTRATORS

_____1. A manager's success is largely determined by his unique ability to gain and hold the personal loyalty of his associates.

_____2. Successful managers solve most of their problems and make most of their decisions by logically developed rules and regulations.

_____3. A distinctive mark of modern successful managers in their dedication to the study and continued improvement of managerial theory and practice.

Continued on page 90

Figure 7.2   Continued

Tentative explanations of *varying degrees of government participation in management.*

GOVERNMENT

_____1. In free societies, government should generally support managers' views to assure the long-term protection of individual initiative.

_____2. Government regulation of employment should do little more than to maintain a balance of power between employers and employees.

_____3. Government agencies should set an example in developing the most advanced, up-to-date, "model" employment relationships.

Tentative explanations of the *emergence, growth, and activities of unions.*

UNIONS

_____1. Unions would decline in influence and possibly disappear altogether without leadership by the leftist, radical fringe.

_____2. Underlying practically all member support of union programs is the members' expectation that their unions will get them higher wages.

_____3. Members join unions to find satisfactions for various human needs otherwise usually unsatisfied in modern, large-scale working organizations.

The decision to allow managers freedom to accept more than one item in each scale followed from experience indicating that few managers find any one item satisfactory as defining their interpretation and explanation. For the same reason, a procedure in which managers rank items in each scale in the order of their acceptability was discontinued after several experimental administrations. Managers prefer a procedure that selects something like a "position" on the continuum, rather than acceptance of any single statement. Manager A, for example, may prefer a combination of two or three items in each area; his attitude combines at least partial acceptance of these plausible explanations.

This method of administration has proved useful, also, in indicating the sharpness or certainty with which each manager selects his position. If he chooses items distributed throughout the continuum, that selection is regarded as indicating a measure of uncertainty or indecisiveness.

Experimental administrations. More than 2,000 public and private managers have "played the game," using these scales, in management seminars and conferences. In addition, several hundred managers have contributed to the studies by participation in intra-firm management development programs in which the scales have served as the starting point for discussions of management theory. The scales have also been used in similar discussions with several hundred students in at least four universities.

Continued on page 92

Results or scores on the scales have generally been represented in the form of five- or seven-step profiles, in which items are weighed according to their positions in the scale continua. To score the long forms, one procedure designates — as a measure of theory position — the central of the three selected items after they have been ordered. For subsequent and more detailed analysis, procedure calculates a score as the sum of the weights for the three selected items. For the short form, scores range from 1 to 5 (the extremes), with a midpoint (3) and two transitional or mediatory positions (2 and 4).

In conferences and seminars, group profiles have been developed and compared with those of other groups of managers (See Figure 7.3).

In one early administration, the two long forms of the scales — one with items ordered and the other with the same items in random sequence — were submitted to a group of more than 250 managers. One half used the ordered-item form; the other half used the form with items disordered. Analysis of responses indicates that this variation in form occasioned no significant differences in resulting patterns or profiles for the two subgroups.

Throughout these experimental administrations, the scales have proved interesting to many managers in part because they point to similarities and differences in personal patterns of management theory. Managers have found the game interesting and helpful in discovering and identifying their personal views (and those of associates) with respect to explanations of individual and group behavior in working organizations. Discussion of these patterns frequently encourages managers to review and reconsider their theory positions and supporting evidence.

At the same time, managers who have played the game frequently comment on the possible implications of differences in individual theory positions, as disclosed by the scales, as factors in intra-management communications. Theory positions are presumably reflected in the manager's perception of problems and in his prescription of solutions. Differences in position may, for this reason, complicate communication and collaboration.

It should be clearly understood, when the scales are used for this purpose, that scores carry no simple implication of correctness or superiority; there are no universally correct answers or profiles. Some positions are more extensively supported than others in terms of experience and research in particular industries and cultural settings; similarly, for specific times and places, some theoretical positions have been generally discredited. It may reasonably be assumed that some positions are more appropriate than others in cultural settings that involve varying stages of economic and cultural development. Thus, for example, theory appropriate for the management of an electronics firm in Minnesota may not be realistic for an organization that directs agricultural workers in India.

Continuing studies. In current studies, detailed information on a number of classification variables, including industry, location, numbers and types of workers and others, is being related to theory patterns, as is personal data with respect to age, sex, education, and other characteristics of managers who play the game. Data from experimental administrations are being subjected to comprehensive statistical analysis to discover the acceptability of individual items, inter-correlations among scale scores, and the impact of minor variations in form and administrative procedure.

Figure 7.3   Examples of group profiles (Note that numbers are small. They are examples, not norms).

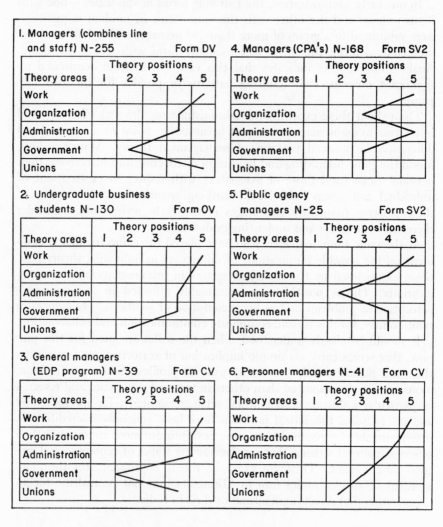

Further studies in process or in planning stages will seek to relate the similarity or compatibility of theory patterns in small groups of managers to (1) the influence individual managers exert on their colleagues, (2) intra-management communication and cooperation, and (3) possible contributions of management development programs. As noted, the significance of uncertainty or indecision — as indicated by the range of items selected by a manager in each continuum — also deserves thorough probing. A supplemental questionnaire that may provide more detailed data on the manager's understanding of theory offers promise of assistance in evaluating these diverse positions. A contemplated verification study will compare individual theory profiles of managers with their preferences in management policy and with their day-to-day decisions as described and evaluated by colleagues. A contemplated simulation study is being designed to compare predicted behavior with a sequence of management decisions.

Meanwhile, an economics scale has been prepared to round out the coverage of central management theory, and scales for the measurement of manager attitudes in the other two levels described in Figure 7.1 — philosophy and policy — are being readied for experimental administration. The combination of measured attitudes in these three levels — theory, philosophy and management policy — in a test of the total model that will relate these attitudes to manager careers and organizational effectiveness is a major objective in the ongoing series of studies.

8

Processes Vis-A-Vis Systems:
Toward a Model of the Enterprise and Administration*

Wendell French

University of Washington

The process elements of management theory have come under attack in recent years, probably because they are so closely associated with forces generated by the scientific management school of thought with its emphasis on functionalism. Professor French presents a rigorous and careful definition of process and a skilfully developed concept of system. He then links these concepts together to build a model of the business enterprise. This model is a goal-oriented network of systems and process model that makes possible the more accurate specification of managerial roles.

The central thesis of this paper is that the enterprise can usefully be described as a man-directed, dynamic network of processes and facilitating systems, and that a useful model of the administrator's job logically follows from this description. We shall first contrast the concepts of "process" and "system" and then integrate these concepts with certain other constructs toward building (a) a model of the enterprise and (b) a model of the administrator's job.[1,2]

* Taken and adapted from the *Journal of the Academy of Management*, vol. 6, no. 1, March, 1963, pp. 46–57.

[1] Our use of the word "enterprise" will be consistent with Barnard's use of the term. See Chester I. Barnard, *The Functions of the Executive* (Cambridge, Massachusetts: Harvard University Press, 1938), pp. 65–67. "The organization" will be used synonymously with "enterprise." In addition, we shall use the terms "administration" and "management" synonymously.

[2] In such model building, perhaps we can avoid the "jungle warfare" which Koontz

The Construct of "Process"

A Definition of "Process." The word "process" is used extensively in the literature of many disciplines. For example, authors in management theory write about "the decision-making process," "the planning process," "the collective bargaining process," "the management process," and "the administrative process." Authors in the physical sciences talk about chemical, biological, and physical processes. In the social sciences there are references to social, psychological, and economic processes.

Processes are also seen as impinging upon and interacting with one another. In ecology, for example, there are descriptions of the interaction between living organisms and the environment,[3] and in psychology there is reference to biological and social processes interacting through the human personality.[4] In the field of management, processes are seen as being in a state of interdependence.[5]

Typically, authors use the word "process" without definition, which suggests that there may be a commonly held meaning attached to the word which is generally consistent with dictionary definitions. Occasionally, however, authors desire more precision in the use of the word. For example, Newman and Summer define process as ". . . a series as actions that lead to the accomplishment of objectives."[6] Argyris defines process as ". . . any course or sequence of behavior accomplishing a necessary purpose."[7] According to Guest: "process" denotes progressive action or a series of acts performed by persons in the course of moving the organization from one state to another."[8] Lundberg defines process as ". . . a

perceives as being prevalent among management theorists. There is no intention of denying the usefulness of other models, nor of claiming any ubiquitous utility in what is proposed. Different models have different uses. See Harold Koontz, "The Management Theory Jungle," Journal of the Academy of Management, 4:174–188 (December, 1961).

[3] See John H. Storey, The Web of Life (New York: The Devin-Adair Company, 1954).

[4] See Gardner Murphy, Personality: A Bio-Social Approach to Origins and Structure (New York: Harper and Brothers, 1947), pp. 1–37. For other references on the interactions of processes, See Kurt Lewin, Field Theory in Social Science (New York: Harper and Brothers, 1951), p. 57; Harold J. Leavitt, "Management According to Task: Organizational Differentiation," Management International (January–February, 1962), p. 22; and Chester I. Barnard, op. cit., p. 6.

[5] See E. Wight Bakke and Chris Argyris, Organizational Structure and Dynamics (New Haven: Yale University, Labor and Management Center, 1954), pp. 10, 26; and M. E. Salveson, "An Analysis of Decisions," Management Science, 4:212 (April, 1958).

[6] William H. Newman and Charles E. Summer, Jr., The Process of Management (Englewood Cliffs, N.J.: Prentice-Hall, 1961), p. 9.

[7] Chris Argyris, Organization of a Bank (New Haven: Yale University Labor and Management Center, 1954), p. 9.

[8] Robert H. Guest, Organizational Change: The Effect of Successful Leadership (Homewood, Illinois, The Dorsey Press and Richard D. Irwin, Inc., 1962), pp. 139–149.

sequence of events which collectively yield a specified product or state and which together exhibit a particular function."[9]

The following definition of "process" is consistent with the above definitions, but lends itself more directly to the purposes of this paper: *a process is a flow of interrelated events moving toward some goal, purpose, or end.* In this definition, "flow" implies movement through time in the direction of a consequence. "Interrelated" denotes interaction within the process, and events which are highly relevant one to another. "Events" are changes or happenings that occur at one point or period, of time, and may be any of an infinite number of phenomena. "Goal" suggests a human objective, while "purpose" suggests either human objectives or objectives in a metaphysical sense. "End" implies some conclusion or consequence which may not necessarily be sought or planned by man. Thus, a process may or may not have man-intended (or human-oriented) consequences.[10]

Examples of Characteristics of "Processes." A familiar process in nature is erosion. Here is seen a flow of events including the occurrence of rain, the flow of water, and fluctuations in temperature, resulting in the washing away of tillable soil. An example of a process from management is the "staffing process," a flow of events which results in the continuous filling of positions within the organization. This flow is comprised of such elements as advertising, interviews, decisions to hire, transfers, and promotions. (It should be pointed out at the outset that "process" does not preclude system." Man-directed processes always involve systematization, as will be elaborated upon later.)

Processes have certain characteristics which are obvious and others that are not so apparent. Unless the most minute processes have been identified (which is doubtful), all processes will contain a number of sub-processes. Similarly, a given process will constitute a segment of a broader process unless the most universal process has been identified (which is also questionable).

An example of a process which is at once a sub-process and a process containing sub-processes is tree growth. This process can be sub-divided into the interrelated processes of plant food assimilation and distribution, photosynthesis, pollination, etc. But at a higher level of abstraction, the tree can be perceived as a part of the life-process of a forest in which there are interacting processes of tree growth, moisture distribution, soil-building, animal growth, food growth, erosion, aging, decay, combustion, and others.

Using our example from management, the staffing process may be seen as a network of sub-processes, including the recruiting process, the inter-

[9] Craig C. Lundberg, "Administrative Decisions: A Scheme for Analysis," *Journal of the Academy of Management*, 5:168 (August, 1962).

[10] It is not implied that the word "process" automatically denotes these phenomena. The word "process" simply seems to be the best label to summarize these conditions. Hopefully, for the purpose of this paper, the word "process" will conjure the intended picture.

viewing process, etc. In turn, the staffing process is, itself, one of several interacting sub-processes within a broader management process. Thus, a process may be narrow or broad, simple or abstract, depending upon the particular frame of reference or focus of the perceiver.

The "length" of process is defined in terms of some goal, purpose, or end. For example, the employment of college students can be considered the culmination of the college placement process. But these events may also be considered early events in the staffing process of each employing organization. Thus, any given process will be a continuation of one or more other processes, and its dimensions are defined in terms of the relevance of events to a particular consequence.

Another important characteristic of a process, which is probably not so obvious, is that a process will usually, if not always, contain elements which are simultaneously components of one or more other processes. For example, the process of the decay of a plant will also be a component of a soil-building process. The staffing process, while an intra-enterprise process, has at the same time components pertaining to the broader life or career processes of the individuals involved. Similarly, the staffing process overlaps other processes within the organization. For example, a decision to offer a particular initial salary is a component of the financial management process as well as a component of the staffing process.[11]

Along with other characteristics of processes, this phenomenon of mutuality of process components is a particularly useful concept in building a model of the administrator's job, as we shall see later. Examined next, however, will be the concept of "system" and certain other constructs.

"System" Defined and Contrasted with "Process"

A Definition of "System." The concept of "system" has been defined and utilized by many authors. The construct has been utilized, for example, in cybernetics,[12] biology and physics,[13] psychology,[14] sociology,[15] management,[16] and in a variety of other basic and applied fields.[17]

---

11 For references on the interrelatedness of events, see especially George A. Kelly, *The Psychology of Personal Constructs*, Vol. 1 (New York: W. W. Norton and Company, 1955), p. 6; John H. Storer, *op. cit.*; and Chester I. Barnard, *op. cit.*, pp. 78–79.

12 See, for example, Stafford Beer, *Cybernetics and Management* (New York: John Wiley and Sons, 1959).

13 See Ludwig von Bertalanffy, "The Theory of Open Systems in Physics and Biology," *Science*, 111:23 ff. (January 13, 1950).

14 See Floyd Allport, *Theories of Perception and the Concept of Structure* (New York: John Wiley and Sons, 1955), pp. 469 ff.; and George A. Kelly, *op. cit.*, p. 57.

15 See Talcott Parsons, Robert F. Bales, and Edward A. Shils, *Working Papers in the Theory of Action*, (Glencoe, Illinois: The Free Press, 1953). These authors also use the word "process" extensively.

16 See Richard A. Johnson, Fremont E. Kast, and James E. Rosenzweig, *The Theory and Management of Systems* (New York: McGraw-Hill Book Company, 1963); Stanford L. Optner, *Systems Analysis for Business Management* (Englewood Cliffs, N.J.: Prentice-Hall, 1960); Chester I. Barnard, *op. cit.*, pp. 77; Robert V. Presthus, "Toward

The definition of system which follows will be consistent with the construct as it has evolved in the literature, but traditional usage will be enlarged to include the concept of "process," and the relationship between "system" and "process." Thus, *a system is a particular linking of elements which has a facilitating effect, or an intended facilitating effect, on the carrying out of a process.*

In this definition, "particular" suggests that System₁ is different in some respects from System₂, although both may be contributing to the carrying out of similar processes. The "elements" of a system may be components such as devices, raw materials, techniques, procedures, plans, and people. "Facilitating effect" suggests that systems are ordinarily designed (or they evolve) as a means of carrying out or regularizing processes. "Intended" suggests (a) that mistakes can be made in the design of a system so that it works at cross-purposes with intended consequences or in opposition to the survival of an organism or organization, and (b) that a system can be in a static condition. The reader will also note that this definition, since it incorporates the concept of process, includes the important idea that a system is goal, consequence, or end oriented. And finally, in the context of the above definition, "carrying out" means unfolding or progressive development.

Some Examples and Characteristics of Systems. Stafford Beer provides useful examples of systems:

> ". . . It is legitimate to call a pair of scissors a system. But the expanded system of a woman cutting with a pair of scissors is also itself a genuine system. In turn, however, the woman-with-scissors system is part of a larger manufacturing system — and so on."[18]

Thus, the definition of a system is always an arbitrary matter, as is the definition of a process. It should be noted, however, that a system can be static (the scissors), whereas, by definition, a process is always dynamic (the cloth-cutting process).

The current weapon-system concept relative to missiles development, as described by Optner, provides a further example of systems and related subsystems:

A Theory of Organizational Behavior," *Administrative Science Quarterly*, 3:50 (June, 1958); and William G. Scott, "Organization Theory: An Overview and An Appraisal," *Journal of the Academy of Management*, 4:15–20 (April, 1961).

[17] Robert M. Gagne, et al., *Psychological Principles in System Development* (New York: Holt, Rinehart, and Winston, 1962); and Roy R. Grinker, ed., *Toward a Unified Theory of Human Behavior* (New York: Basic Books, 1956). The contributors to both books also use the word "process" a good deal. See also Allen Newell and Herbert A. Simon, "The Logic Theory Machine," *IRE Transactions On Information Theory* (New York: Institute of Radio Engineers, 1956), p. 61. Newell and Simon subsume "process" within their complex information-processing system.

[18] Stafford Beer, *op. cit.*, p. 9.

". . . the nose cone is conceived as a subsystem; propulsion and guidance are subsystems; and the missile, its ground support equipment, material and personnel are the system."[19]

In this example can be seen a particular linking of devices, materials, and people held in readiness to facilitate a process — namely, the process of delivering a projectile on a target. Other systems might also be used to facilitate the same process. For example, the atomic submarine with its Polaris missiles, electronic devices, men, procedures, equipment, and supplies form another integrated system to accomplish the same purpose. Similarly, a supersonic bomber with its ground support, crew, weaponry, and other components constitute yet another system designed to facilitate this same process.

This same concept of systems may also be seen in the familiar examples of forests and trees. A given forest is a particular linking of plant and animal life, non-living organic material, atmosphere, moisture, streams, and so forth, all of which facilitate the processes described earlier. The tree itself is a system — a particular, integrated linking of elements including roots, sap, trunk, leaves and cells which carry out the process of tree growth. The leaf itself can be considered another system (or subsystem) employed to facilitate the process of photosynthesis — i.e., the utilization of sunlight to convert carbohydrates to sugar from carbon dioxide and water.

Using an example from management, the employment process in a given firm is facilitated by a particular linkage of people and employment devices and procedures, such as application blanks, a battery of tests and a series of interviews. In all likelihood, the employment systems of different firms will differ, although some of the major components may be identical — e.g., the test battery.

Optner provides some additional important characteristics of systems by differentiating between "structured" and "incompletely structured" systems. A structural system has highly regulated inputs, is essentially free from disturbance, and has outputs within highly predictable limits. Examples are hydraulic and electrical systems. In contrast, an incompletely structured system has inputs which are variable in terms of quality and quantity; it is subject to considerable disturbance, and has relatively unpredictable outputs. An example would be industrial enterprise, or any system involving people.[20]

---

[19] Stanford L. Optner, *op. cit.*, p. 4. To Optner, a system consists of inputs (energy, materials, information), a processor (the machine or human mechanism doing the work), and outputs (the product). The system may also include a feedback mechanism. Of course, these are the characteristics of a system in operation — in its dynamic state. In a static state the system might include all of these elements with the exception of the outputs.

[20] *Ibid.*, pp. 3–9. Beer labels a company an "exceedingly complex" and "probabilistic" system. Stafford Beer, *op. cit.*, pp. 9–18. In addition, any human organization would be

It would appear that the less structured a system, the more that unsystematized processes must be inferred. Or to say it another way, the non-structured part of a system implies process.

The above definition and characteristics of "systems" vis-a-vis "processes" will be employed below in developing a model of the organization and of the manager's job. First, however, Fayol's classification scheme and the concept of "organizational resources" will be examined as to their mutual compatability and as to their relevance to the concept of "process."

Fayol's Constructs

Dating from the early 1900's and the writings of Fayol, authors in the field of management theory have stressed certain managerial activities common to the manager's job, i.e., "planning, organization, command, co-ordination, control. . . ."[21] Koontz and O'Donnell call these activities "functions."[22] Newman labels these activities "processes" as does Catheryn Seckler-Hudson.[23]

These authors and others since Fayol have slightly modified the above categories to suit their purposes.[24] In general, however, management theorists of the "Fayol School" have retained Fayol's classification scheme with only minor modifications, and this scheme will be a major ingredient in the model of the manager's job to be discussed below.[25] Within the scope of this paper, reference will be made to Fayol's categories as "administrative processes."

The Concept of Organizational Resources

Another classification scheme relative to the manager's job has had wide acceptance, particularly among economists. This classification scheme dif-

---

a bio-social-physical system since all organizations utilize physical devices, machines, or artifacts of some kind.

[21] Henri Fayol, *General and Industrial Management*, Constance Storrs, trans. (London: Sir Isaac Pitman and Sons, 1961), p. 3.

[22] Harold Koontz and Cyril O'Donnell, *Principles of Management*, 2nd ed. (New York: McGraw-Hill Book Company, 1959), p. 35.

[23] William H. Newman, *Administrative Action* (New York: Prentice-Hall, 1950), pp. 5–6; and Catheryn Seckler-Hudson, "Major Processes of Organization and Management," in Harold Koontz and Cyril O'Donnell, *Readings in Management* (New York: McGraw-Hill Book Company, 1959), pp. 22.

[24] For example, Terry refers to planning, organizing, directing, leading, coordinating, and controlling. Newman refers to planning, organizing, assembling resources, directing, and controlling. Le Breton and Henning refer to planning, organizing, staffing, directing, coordinating, and controlling. See George R. Terry, *Principles of Management* (Homewood, Illinois: Richard D. Irwin, Inc., 1953), p. 5; William H. Newman, *op. cit.*, p. 6; and Preston P. Le Breton and Dale A. Henning, *Planning Theory* (Englewood Cliffs, New Jersey: Prentice-Hall, Inc., 1961), pp. 3–4.

[25] The "Fayol school" has also been labeled "the management process school," the "traditional school," and the "universalist school." See Harold Koontz, *op. cit.*, pp. 175–176.

ferentiates between productive factors — e.g., labor, money, materials — which the manager utilizes in the proper proportions in attempting to maximize profits.[26]

Although there has been criticism of this classification scheme by those who prefer to stress that management has to do with "getting things done through people,"[27] a number of authors of the "Fayol school" find the resource classification scheme compatible with the constructs of administrative processes. For example, according to Terry, "Management is the activity which plans, organizes, and controls the operations of the basic elements of men, materials, machines, methods, money, and markets . . ."[28] Newman makes a similar statement when he suggests: "The work of executives may be divided into subject fields, such as sales, production, or finance. It may also be divided into administrative processes; for example, planning, directing, and controlling."[29]

Such an integration was implicit even in Fayol's writings. After discussing the six activities (or functions) of industrial undertakings — technical, commercial, financial, security, accounting, and managerial — he stated: "To organize means building up the dual structure, material and human, of the undertaking . . . To . . . co-ordinate means building together, unifying and harmonizing all activity and effort."[30] Further:

> ". . . To govern is to conduct the undertaking towards its objective
> by seeking to derive optimum advantage from all available resources
> and to assure the smooth working of the six essential functions."[31]

Thus, Fayol seems to suggest an integration of resources and functions.

Bakke, in particular, has made considerable use of the "resource" concept in recent years. Writing in the fields of industrial relations and management theory, he refers to ". . . human, material, capital, ideational, and natural . . ." resources and to the necessity for their integration.[32]

Using a similar classification scheme, it appears useful to categorize the resources of the enterprise in the following way: human resources, financial

---

[26] See Paul A. Samuelson, *Economics*, 5th ed. (New York: McGraw-Hill Book Company, 1961), p. 5.
[27] Koontz and O'Donnell, *op. cit.*, pp. 3, 45–46.
[28] George R. Terry, *op. cit.*, p. 8.
[29] William H. Newman, *op. cit.*, pp. 5–6.
[30] Henri Fayol, *op. cit.*, p. 6.
[31] *Ibid.*, p. 6.
[32] E. Wight Bakke, "The Concept of Social Organization," in Mason Haire, ed., *Modern Organization Theory* (New York: John Wiley and Sons, 1959), p. 37; and E. Wight Bakke, *The Human Resources Function* (Champaign, Ill.: Institute of Labor and Industrial Relations, University of Illinois, Lecture Series No. 21), pp. 3–5. Bakke also utilizes the term "process" extensively. See his "The Concept of Social Organization," *op. cit.*, pp. 59–73; and *The Fusion Process* (New Haven: Yale University, Labor and Management Center, 1953).

resources, material (including capital equipment), markets[33] and all of the accumulated ideas and knowledge pertaining to these resources, including the methods and techniques of science. These resources may be equated with the following sub-processes, which, for want of a better term, we shall call "resource procurement and utilization processes," or as a way of abbreviating further, "operational processes": (a) personnel management, (b) financial management, (c) materials and production management, (d) marketing management, and (e) research, development, and engineering management.

Toward a Model of the Enterprise

Within the framework of the concepts described above, the following definition of the organization can now be suggested: *An enterprise is an essentially-man-directed and multiple-goal-oriented network of interacting administrative and operational processes and corresponding facilitating systems, and is immersed in a broader network of processes and systems with which it interacts.*

This definition recognizes several important characteristics of organizations which, although set forth as theoretical propositions, in the author's opinion reflect the facts of enterprise life:

1. The "management" people in the enterprise are simultaneously designers, managers, and components of systems. The so-called "rank-and-file" members of the enterprise, while perhaps not participating in the design of systems nor in the direction of human components of systems, nevertheless, may be acting as "managers" of segments of systems. (The above definition does not deny the authority network of the enterprise, nor the concept of the enterprise as a socio-technical system.)

2. An organization is "essentially-man-directed" in that human planning and direction, whether efficient or not, are major characteristics of organization. The organization is only *essentially* man-directed, however, since the nature of the organization is also a function of a network of external environmental processes over which managers may have little or no control. In addition, since an organization is an "incompletely structured" system, by definition it is implied that there are some unsystematized processes in existence, some of which may not be man-directed, at least at a conscious level. It follows that some processes may be flowing in a direction contrary to enterprise goals, i.e., that some may be anti-goal oriented.

3. As is well recognized, the organization is probably always directed

---

[33] Markets have characteristics different from the other resources, of course. For example, markets are necessarily located in the external environment. See Talcott Parsons, "Suggestions for a Sociological Approach to the Theory of Organization — I," *Administrative Science Quarterly*, 1:62 (June, 1956).

toward attaining multiple goals. Multiple goals increase the complexity of the network of organizational processes and systems.

4. There can be no organization without a network of systems. Systems are essential for channeling processes in the direction of, and toward the fulfillment of, enterprise goals.

5. The organization is a complex network of interdependent flows of events having to do with human planning, organizing, directing, coordinating, and controlling of the procurement and utilization of various human and non-human resources. Thus, we can conceptualize two major types of processes: (a) *administrative processes*, i.e., planning, organizing, directing, coordinating, and controlling; and (b) *operational processes*, i.e., personnel management, financial management, materials and production management, marketing management, and research, development, and engineering management.[34] The first category is essentially a category including activities common to all management jobs. The second category, while roughly the rationale for the departmentalization of many industrial firms, includes processes which by definition cannot be completely departmentalized.[35]

6. Not only do these administrative and operational processes interact and impinge upon each other — e.g., the flows of events pertaining to financial resources impinge on and interact with flows of events pertaining to human resources — but the systems designed to facilitate these various processes impinge upon and interact with each other.

7. While individual executives and departments may be assigned to focus on, or specialize in the administration of specific processes, no executive or department, if the assumptions described below are true, can possibly have exclusive authority for the management of one of these processes on an organization-wide basis. The chief executive (or executive committee) will typically manage all of these processes within an enterprise, however, in the sense that the chief executive will usually have authority over all subordinate executives and employees.

8. Since a given organizational process will have some elements in common with other processes, *systems designed to facilitate major processes are likely to have components which are also components of the other systems.* This is not so likely to be true in the case of subsystems.

[34] It would not be accurate to visualize these processes in two-dimensional space with the administrative processes described by horizontal lines and the operational processes by vertical lines, if such pictorial representation is equated with organization charts and departmentalization. These categories are not mutually exclusive ways of subdividing enterprise activities.

[35] There are, of course, many other ways to cut up the total "pie." Bakke and Argyris, for example, identify "work flow," "authority," "reward and penalty," "perpetuation," "identification," "communication," and "evaluation," as "essential organizational processes." See Bakke and Argyris, *op. cit.*, pp. 10–11.

9. Any given organization will process a unique fabric of processes and systems. It is highly unlikely that the flows of events described above and the quality and quantity of the available resources external to and within any two organizations will be identical.

10. This fabric of interacting processes and facilitating systems which is the organization cannot adequately be visualized in three-dimensional space since it is an "n-dimensional" matter. However, simple illustrations showing the mutual components of a few interdependent systems can be drawn.

Toward a Model of the Manager's Job

Assuming these characteristics of the enterprise, what, then, is the nature of the job of the manager? A number of observations seem to follow logically. It would seem that it is the task of management (not necessarily in this order) to:

1. Define the goals of the organization (and redefine them as the situation requires).

2. Assemble the human and non-human resources necessary to obtain these goals.

3. Visualize the internal processes essential to attaining enterprise goals.

4. Understand the network of external processes and systems which impinge upon the organization and its attainment of goals.

5. Design, direct, coordinate, and control internal systems in order to facilitate and/or regularize the internal processes which have been visualized. (It would seem that processes must be visualized before systems can be designed to facilitate or control them.)

6. Recognize the overlap of broad systems, identify overlapping components, and plan the network of systems so that such overlapping will produce a minimum of undesirable disturbance.

7. Recognize that a given manager will simultaneously be a component in a wide array of systems, and design systems to minimize intra- and inter-person conflict and inefficiency.

8. Define (a) the segments of processes and systems over which different individuals are given authority, and (b) the components which are managed mutually with other managers.

9. Install a new system only after careful planning of how it will be linked into the existing network of interdependent and impinging systems.

10. Identify non-planned processes to ascertain to what degree systematization would be useful, or, if these processes conflict with goal-attainment, the degree to which they can be contained or eliminated. If uncontrollable, identify their possible impact on risk-taking and goal-attainment.

11. Ascertain the degree of structuring, particularly in the area of inter-personal processes and sub-processes, which will optimize the attainment of enterprise goals. It is likely that a number of enterprise sub-processes such as interviewing, participation, management development, etc., re-quire a minimum of systematizing and that over-systematizing in these and other areas defeats organizational purposes.[36] Similarly, the manager needs to anticipate to what degree systematization of various processes will increase or decrease flexibility in meeting internal and external demands for change.

In general, then, it would seem that *the task of the administrator is to define enterprise goals, assemble resources, visualize the processes essential to the attainment of these goals, and to design the network of facilitating systems.* It is implied, of course, that the administrator will be an active component in certain systems in this network.

Perhaps the following illustration about forest management will serve to point up the above definition of the administrator's job (this illustra-tion applies "process" and "systems" terminology to descriptions of forest management provided by colleagues):

> The management of forest typically involves many goals — for ex-ample, the production of tree and plant products, the furnishing of creational areas, water supply and conservation, soil conservation, wild-life production and protection, grass for the grazing of domesticated animals, and streams for the production and conservation of fish life. Thus, the management of a forest requires systematic manipulation and control of a highly complex network of interacting processes, including tree, plant, animal, fish, bird, insect, fungus, and virus growth, and other processes involving fire and erosion. All must be maintained or controlled in some kind of equilibrium which will op-timize the attainment of multiple goals.
>
> The interdependence of trees, low vegetation, and deer presents a typical forest-management problem. If the tree growth in the forest is too dense, shrubs and grasses will be choked out, and the deer, dependent upon these for food, will be unable to survive. On the other hand, if trees are selectively cut and conditions become more favorable for the growth of shrubs and other low vegetation, the deer population will rapidly multiply. Eventually, unless checked in some way, the deer may exceed the food supply provided by grasses and shrubs, and before starving, will eat the young tree growth necessary for replenishing the timber crop. Thus, it becomes the task of forest management to devise systems to control various impinging processes

[36] The accumulated knowledge from such fields as non-directive counseling and psycho-therapy suggests that personality maturation and growth of initiative and capa-bility can be stifled by an over-structuring of certain flows of events.

and to maintain a dynamic equilibrium appropriate to the attainment of the pre-established multiple goals. Not only does the forest manager design systems, but through decision making and other behavior he becomes simultaneously an active component in a wide variety of systems in this interdependent and dynamic network.

This, then, is the manager's job. When subordinates are added to the picture — with the concomitant complexities — the model still applies.

The Utility of the Process-System Approach

The "process-system" approach toward a model of the organization and of the manager's job seems to have utility in explaining, clarifying, or analyzing certain enterprise phenomena. For example, the approach may be used to clarify or analyze concepts about authority. Since the broad processes (and systems) which comprise the organization are interdependent and have mutual components, no one manager, unless he is the chief executive, can completely preempt the management of any general administrative process (i.e., planning, controlling, etc.,) or any operational process (i.e., financial management, personnel management, etc.) on an enterprise-wide basis. This does not mean that an executive may not be assigned general responsibility over the management of one of these processes — indeed, this may be the wisest course of action — but it does mean that he is dependent upon the cooperation of other managers who will also have authority over certain mutually-held components within this assigned process. Furthermore, he will be dependent upon the effective management of the processes which precede and follow his arbitrary segment of responsibility.

The "process-system" approach also serves to focus attention on the question of efficiency of flows of events across traditional departmental lines and between organizations, thus permitting improvements in the design of facilitating systems. The many advantages of the flow concept have been discussed by Forrester,[37] Brewer,[38] Drucker,[39] Chapple and Sayles,[40] and others.

In addition, this approach sheds some light on the conditions which seem to differentiate successful vs. unsuccessful personnel systems. For

[37] Jay W. Forrester, "Industrial Dynamics," *Harvard Business Review*, 36:37–52 (July–August, 1958). See also Jay W. Forrester, *Industrial Dynamics* (New York: John Wiley and Sons, 1961).

[38] Stanley H. Brewer, *Rhocrematics: A Scientific Approach to the Management of Material Flows* (Seattle: University of Washington, Management Series No. 2, 1960). See also Stanley H. Brewer and James Rosenzweig, "Rhocrematics and Organizational Adjustments," *California Management Review*, 3:52–71 (Spring, 1961).

[39] Peter F. Drucker, "The Economy's Dark Continent," *Fortune*, April, 1962, pp. 103–265.

[40] Eliot D. Chapple and Leonard R. Sayles, *The Measure of Management* (New York: The Macmillan Company, 1961).

example, an analysis of the literature of incentive systems reveals that successful systems feature considerable management attention to the prevailing fabric or enterprise processes and systems, while a conspicuous ingredient in many unsuccessful incentive systems is lack of attention to existing impinging and overlapping systems and processes.[41] In short, the installation of systems without planning for possible adjustments in prevailing systems and processes is likely to result in undesirable disturbances within the enterprise.

The "process-system" approach may also provide a framework for determining the extent to which event-flows relative to the utilization of human and other resources can be productively systematized, and to what degree. Finally, by focusing on *both* processes and systems, a wider range of enterprise characteristics and phenomena may be examined.

Conclusion

The concept of "process" has been discussed and contrasted with "system." Both have been integrated with concepts relating to general administrative processes and enterprise resources toward the development of models of the enterprise and of the administrator's job. These models seem to have utility in explaining certain intra-enterprise phenomena, and may be useful in further analysis of the enterprise and the role of the administrator.

[41] For examples of case descriptions of successful and unsuccessful applications of incentive systems see Thomas Q. Gilson and Myron J. Lefcowitz, "A Plant-Wide Productivity Bonus in a Small Factory: Study of an Unsuccessful Case," *Industrial and Labor Relations Review*, 10:284–296 (January, 1959); and Joseph N. Scanlon, "Profit Sharing Under Collective Bargaining: Three Case Studies," *Industrial and Labor Relations Review*, 2:58–74 (October, 1948). Katzell also emphasizes the importance of the "surrounding circumstances or parameters." See Raymond A. Katzell, "Contrasting Systems of Work Organization," *American Psychologist*, 17:105 (February, 1962).

9

Basic Frameworks for Decisions*

Charles Z. Wilson

DePaul University

and Marcus Alexis

University of Rochester

Decision theory has always loomed large within management theory. Indeed, some theorists see little else significant in management or in organization theory. Developments in behavioral science and applied mathematics have spurred a burgeoning interest in decision-making. The authors of this article present a broad view of a number of frameworks and decision concepts and models. Open and closed decision models are described. The effectiveness of these models in explaining decision behavior is analyzed. This article illustrates in relatively nontechnical terms the application of these two types of models to various decision situations.

Introduction

Decision making has been an integral part of the management literature for more than half a century. But because of an immoderate emphasis on decision-making as an hierarchical "right," explorations of the behavioral aspects of the decision process(es) were at a minimum for much of this time. It was not until the early 50's that developments in decision theory gained a noticeable momentum. During this period we witnessed, on the one hand, the emergence of more powerful and sophisticated tools

* Taken and adapted from the *Journal of the Academy of Management*, vol. 5, no. 2, August, 1962, pp. 150–164. At the time of this study, the authors were Ford Faculty Fellows at Carnegie Institute of Technology and Harvard University, respectively. They wish to acknowledge the assistance of the Behavioral Theory of The Firm project at the Graduate School of Industrial Administration, Carnegie Institute of Technology.

of mathematics and statistics, and, on the other hand, a revitalization of the social sciences. Together these developments forged the intellectual setting from which many of the current contributions to decision theory evolve.[1]

Unfortunately, however, the bulk of the literature on decision theory is developed along rigorous lines and spanned across several disciplines requiring more than a modest amount of mathematics, statistics, psychology, sociology and economics. Much of these materials are incomprehensible to the non-specialist and in many cases pose a formidable challenge for the specialist. The purpose of this paper is to present a panoramic view of frameworks and related decision concepts underlying the wide range of decision models now in use. For the purposes of this paper, the discussion is anchored to two general types of framework. We have designated one type of framework as "closed." This is the classical decision situation where a decision maker faces a known set of alternatives and selects one or several of such courses of action by a "rational selection" process.[2] The second general type of framework is designated as "open." It parallels the "adaptive" or "learning" model.[3] This particular kind of framework is designed to facilitate a more complex view of the decision process. The act of choice spans many dimensions of behavior, rational as well as nonrational aspects.

"Open" and "closed" decision models, of course, are not mutually exclusive. One of the contentions of this paper is that both general types of decision models result from the same set of basic decision elements. Differences between the types stem mainly from the recognition and degree of emphasis accorded certain of the elements.

Decision Elements

Of major interest to students of decision theory is the "complete" decision model. For a decision model to be "complete," that is, universally applicable, it must be able to prescribe behavior in the most complex as well as simplest cases. It must be capable of reflecting all dimensions of

---

[1] There are several interesting summaries of developments in social science fields. See Ward Edwards, "The Theory of Decision Making," *Psychological Review*, 51, September, 1954, pp. 380–471; William J. Gore and Fred S. Silander, "A Bibliographical Essay on Decision Making," *Administrative Science Quarterly*, 4, June, 1959, pp. 97–121.

For a survey of quantitative developments, see Robert Schlaifer, *Probability and Statistics for Business Decisions*, (New York: McGraw-Hill, 1959); Herman Chernoff and Lincoln E. Moses, *Elementary Decision Theory*, (New York: John Wiley & Sons, 1959) and R. M. Thrall, C. H. Coombs and R. L. Davis, *Decision Processes*, (New York: John Wiley & Sons, 1954).

[2] Herbert A. Simon, "Some Strategic Considerations in the Construction of Social Science Models," *Mathematical Thinking in the Social Sciences*, Paul F. Lazarsfeld, (ed.) (Glencoe: The Free Press, 1954).

[3] Kenneth J. Arrow, "Utilities, Attitudes, Choice: A Review Article," *Econometrica*, 26, January, 1958, pp. 1–23.

choice situations. Needless to say, the search for the "complete" model is a shifting goal and perhaps will continue to elude dynamic, aspiring researchers. The persistent research nevertheless has been rewarding. As a by-product of attempts to define and outline the "complete" model, we have come to recognize at least six elements common to all decisions: (1) the state of nature; (2) the decision maker; (3) the goals or ends to be served; (4) the relevant alternatives and the set of actions from which a choice will be made; (5) a relation which produces an ordering of alternatives in some arrangement; and (6) the choice itself, the selection of one or some combination of alternatives.

The state of nature refers to those aspects of the decision maker's environment which affect his choice. Included herein are the relationships between choices and outcomes. These relationships may be random, that is, probabilistic. It is also possible for the relationships not to be known by the decision maker.

The individual or group making a choice is referred to as the decision maker. The decision maker is influenced not only by facts of the choice situation; he is also a product of his environment — the total set of social, political and economic forces around him.

By goals or ends are meant those objectives which the decision maker seeks to attain. In some choice situations the goals are clearly defined and operative. In others, such as the sequential choice situation, where choices are influenced by past choice(s) and outcome(s), goals are not always identifiable, operational or stable.

Alternatives, ordering of relations, and choice will not be discussed here because of the depth of coverage given in the sections immediately following.

By specifying the nature of these elements or in some cases according them mere recognition, it is possible to define a range of frameworks.

"Closed" Decision Models

Organizations are goal-oriented systems. That is, they are designed to improve the planning, problem-solving and decision-making abilities of individuals in pursuit of common goals. Therefore, it is not surprising that the most commonly used and accepted analytical framework for choice behavior or decision-making in organizations is the "closed" decision model.

At the center of this framework is a concept of rationality rooted in the consciousness of individual choice behavior. Usually an individual is faced in a given situation with a number of choices or several possible courses of action. Each course of action is likely to lead to a unique consequence or to one of several possible consequences. We call an individual rational if he takes into account the possible consequences of actions open to him, if he is aware of a certain preference ordering and considers it, and if, in the light of such knowledge, he chooses that course of action which, in his estimation, leads to the best or most preferred consequence. In terms of six elements common to all decision models, the ideal rational man makes a choice(s) on the basis of:

(1) A known set of relevant alternatives with corresponding outcomes.
(2) An established rule or relation which produces an ordering of the alternatives.
(3) Maximizing something such as money rewards, income, physical goods or some form of utility.

Many of the widely accepted decision models in management science assume a kind of administrative rationality similar to that prescribed for the ideal rational man.[4] Such models are structured in "closed" frameworks. They are "closed" because of the minimal weight given to the environment of the decision maker, and the complexity of the act of choice as such.

Linear programming problems are particularly interesting examples of rational choice or "closed" decision-making. Consider this simple production decision. Company T has two products, A and B, which can be produced in two different departments, I and II. The departments have different production capacities and unit profit per item of production. The decision is to select that combination of products A and B which best utilizes the total available capacity. Let's suppose that the following is given:

X_a, X_b — are possible quantities of product A and B
2.00, 2.50 — are unit profits (dollars) for product A and B
.50, 1.0 — are percentages of capacity required to produce a unit of product A and B in department I
.80, .50 — are percentages of capacity required to produce a unit of product A and B in department II

Then the model for our decision consists of an objective function

(1) profit $= 2.00X_a + 2.50X_b$

to be maximized subject to

(2) Dept. I: $.50X_a + 1.00X_b \leq 100\%$
    Dept. II: $.80X_a + .50X_b \leq 100\%$

and

(3) $X_a > 0$ and $X_b > 0$.

4 David W. Miller and Martin K. Starr, Executive Decisions and Operations Research, (Englewood Cliffs: Prentice-Hall, 1960); also C. West Churchman, Russell L. Ackoff, and E. Leonard Arnoff, Operations Research, (New York: John H. Wiley & Sons, 1957).

That is, the production of any one of the departments must not exceed its full capacity but always be positive.

The goals or ends to be served are represented by profits. In other words, profits are a substitute for the whole structure of organization goals.

The decision maker can identify all feasible alternatives. The objective function combined with the constrained set of production possibilities makes possible the generation of a complete set of feasible solutions. The growth of computer operations and effective information systems has greatly enhanced this particular aspect of "closed" models.

Finally, problem solving algorithms such as the simplex method not only generate but also order feasible solutions and hence assure the selection of an "optimal" course of action.[5] Linear programming applications, in general, use restricted but very powerful "closed" models.

Games of strategy (Game Theory) are also structured in "closed" frameworks.[6] There are (1) clearly defined goal; (2) a number of alternatives open at each phase of the situation and; (3) players or participants who can estimate the consequences of their choices. The latter implies taking into consideration that outcomes are determined not only by one's own choice but also by choices of others. Thus, we have a "rational routine": identify alternatives, order, and select "best" course of action in light of predetermined goals.

There are countless other examples of "closed" models. Organizational decision making in general is concerned with sets of problems that can be framed in the typical "closed" choice situation. Limited resources, if not other factors, will act as ultimate restraints. "Closed" models, therefore, have enjoyed an increasing popularity. Recent developments have served to broaden the applicability of "closed" decision models by giving extensive attention to several states of nature often ignored. The remainder of this section will be devoted to a discussion of the impact of these developments on those decision elements emphasized in "closed" frameworks.

Alternatives: Action-Outcome Relations

One way that different states of nature affect decision models is through the correspondence between alternatives (choices) and the possible outcome (consequences). There exist three knowledge states of choice-outcome relations.[7]

---

[5] There are other algorithms but the simplex approach is most widely used. See George B. Dantzig, "Maximization of a Linear Function of Variables Subject to Linear Inequalities," *Activity Analysis of Production and Allocation*, T. C. Koopmans (ed.) (New York: John Wiley & Sons, 1951).

[6] Anatol Rapoport, *Fights, Games and Debates*, (Ann Arbor: University of Michigan Press, 1960), Chapter 6.

[7] James G. March and Herbert A. Simon, *Organizations*, (New York: John Wiley & Sons, 1959), p. 137.

(a) *Certainty:* It is assumed that there is complete and accurate knowledge of the consequence of each choice.
(b) *Uncertainty:* The consequences of each choice cannot be defined by a correspondence relationship even within a probabilistic framework.
(c) *Risk:* It is assumed that accurate knowledge about the probability distribution of the consequence of each alternative exists.

Certainty implies a state of awareness on the part of decision makers that seldom exists. The emphasis on certainty or deterministic foundations in decision-making is a holdover from the early associations of social and physical sciences. Some contended that the laws of the physical sciences and the related deterministic methodology might be extended to social behavior.[8] But the contemporary revolution in both social and physical sciences has done much to minimize this view.

Genuine uncertainty is untenable in "closed" decision models. A basic premise in all "closed" decision models is that alternatives and consequences as well as goals are given. Thus, at least equal probabilistic measures can be assigned to possible outcomes of a given course of action. The current developments in subjective probability have done much to eliminate states of genuine uncertainty.

It is fair to say that models of risk dominate the kinds of foundations assumed in decision theory. The likelihood of each of the possible outcomes resulting from a particular course of action can generally be stated in either an objective or subjective probabilistic frame of reference. This is true if *all* outcomes for a given course of action cannot be specified independently. The U.S. Department of Commerce cannot, for example, list all of the consequences of a $5 billion decline in new plant expenditure. But it is nevertheless feasible for government economists to determine within a probabilistic framework the likelihood of certain major consequences.

Certainty and uncertainty may be thought of as limiting cases of risk.

Objective Probability: Objective probability is fashioned from the regularity of *en masse* behavior. Its operational meaning flows from the Law of Large Numbers which asserts: the probability of any specified departure from the expected relative frequency of an event becomes smaller and smaller as the number of events considered becomes larger and larger. Stating this differently, given a large number of events and the relative frequency with which each event takes place, a stated probability of a particular event becomes more reliable as the number of events considered are increased.

---

[8] Rashevsky, for example, illustrates how much of the methodology of physical sciences is applicable to social behavior. See James S. Coleman, "An Expository Analysis of Rashevsky's Social Behavior Models," Lazarsfeld, *op. cit.*, pp. 105–165.

We may define the objective or *a priori* probability of an event as the relative frequency with which an event would take place, given a large but finite number of observations. More generally, the probability of an event E, denoted by $P(E)$, can be represented by the ratio:

$$\frac{\text{number of possible outcomes of E}}{\text{total number of possible experiment outcomes}}.$$

Experiment is assumed to be any set of observed phenomena. The total number of outcomes in this case is finite and countable and the number of outcomes of E are less than or equal to the total number of outcomes. In all cases where E is not the only possible outcome, a sufficiently large number of outcome observations will show E to be less than the total and hence $P(E)$ to be less than 1.

$P(E)$ is the probability measure of a simple event, one which is not related to the occurrence of any other event. If A denotes a choice and a_1, a_2, a_3 . . . a_n denote a set of outcomes, $P(a_1|A)$, $P(a_2|A)$, $P(a_3|A)$ . . . $P(a_n|A)$ are compound events; more specifically, they are *conditional probability* measures of a_1, a_2, a_3 . . . a_n when A is chosen. The values of $P(a_1|A)$, $P(a_2|A)$, $P(a_3|A)$ . . . $P(a_n|A)$ may be determined experimentally as in coin tossing or by empirically derived frequency distributions. *Extensive* experience is a basic requirement for "good" objective probability measures. One, for example, could toss a die six times to determine the probability or likelihood of the number two occurring. Suppose one observes that two (2) occurs $\frac{1}{3}$ of the time; i.e., $P(X = 2) = \frac{1}{3}$ where X is a number on the die. This is an objective measure of the relative frequency of the number two occurring in a toss of the die but it is *not* the probability of two (2). We identify the probability of an event with the relative frequency over a *large number* of tosses. If an unbiased die is tossed a sufficiently large number of times, the relative frequency and, hence, the probability of a two (2) is $\frac{1}{6}$; $P(X = 2) = \frac{1}{6}$.

Also, care must be exercised to insure the selection of the "right" statistical model. Contrary to popular beliefs, the normal distribution does not always work well as a generalized theoretical framework for estimating probability measures.[9] In many cases, getting the "right" theoretical framework poses an extremely difficult problem. Selecting the statistical model may be as important an operation in obtaining objective probabilistic measures as acquiring sufficient experience.

Reasonably accurate frequency distributions are available for many types of "closed" decision models. Electric power companies, for example, have years of experience to serve as a basis for estimating the probabilities of

[9] The central-limit theorem tells us that a population with finite variance and mean has the property that the distribution of sample means drawn from it approaches the normal distribution. But this is only true if the variance is finite!

generating outages. Likewise, commercial airlines would have little difficulty in estimating the probability of "no-show" reservations.

In recent years, there has been a growing concern about non-recurring decisions. How does one construct a probabilistic foundation when decisions are unique? To the extent that there are unique elements in United States–Cuba relations, it is impossible to assign objective probability measures to the success or failure of particular actions. To date no uniformly acceptable solution method has been devised.

Equally as important, but more hopeful of solution, is the problem of convincing decision makers to use available data. The availability of objective probability measures is no assurance that they will be used in the decision process. The decision maker and experimenter are often different persons and the decision maker may not base his action on objective probabilities developed by the experimenter. If the "staff man" informs the line manager that an alternative T will result in outcome t_1 20% of the time or $P(t_1/T) = .20$, does the superior accept this estimate or adjust it upward (downward)?

Subjective Probability: Subjective probability has a long history, dating back to Jacob Bernoulli in the 17th Century. Renewed interest in the subject has been generated because of the probabilistic base of many decision models and the recognition that decision makers are not always completely informed. Unlike its objective relation, subjective probability is heavily behavioral in its approach.[10] The decision maker is not assumed to maximize on the basis of objective probabilities. He interprets action-outcome likelihoods in terms of personal perceptions. Unless very well informed, his estimates are likely to be different than the objective probabilities. Some experimental evidence strongly suggests a linear correspondence between subjective and objective probability but this does not necessarily mean that decision makers using subjective probability estimates behave *as if* they were acting on the basis of objective probability data. For one thing, behavior is related not only to the estimate of probability but to the subjective value of the expected outcome.

Evidence suggests that the decision maker acts on the basis of some combination of the following:

(1) degrees of belief in relative frequency basis of objective probability
(2) perceptions of objective probability
(3) evaluation of the importance of the situation
(4) revocability of the decision

Subjective probabilities may depart from objective measures because of any one of the factors.

[10] Leonard J. Savage, *The Foundation of Statistics*, (New York: John Wiley & Sons, 1954).

The objective probability that an unbiased coin will fall heads on any toss is equal to the probability that it will fall tails. Thus they are both equal to one-half. An observer who is not familiar with the laws of probability might conclude that after a series of heads the coin is more likely to fall heads than tails on succeeding trials. In other words, the observer's limited experience of coin tossing leads him to "believe" that the probability of heads is greater than that of tails. The future actions of the individual may be affected by this perceptive estimate regardless of how objective or reliable given probability measures may be.

Any model which seeks to predict decision behavior must recognize the likely discrepancy between personalistic (subjective) and objective probabilities.

Utility: Ordering of Alternatives

Another way of broadening the "closed" decision model to reflect a more "complete" set of elements is through the preference ordering of alternatives by the decision maker. The ordering of alternatives is an operation defined in the domain of the individual's value system. Early writers on utility discussed the ordering of alternatives as an ordinal ranking process (first, second, etc.). To this extent, a range of social or environmental forces shaping the individual's values are brought to bear indirectly in "closed" decision models.

Decision models today require that utility theory be developed beyond the ordinal stage. Each outcome must have an assigned, interval-scaled value. Structuring utility functions with such properties is not always feasible. Except where money or some easily measurable commodity can be taken as equivalent to measures of utility or at least related in an ascertainable manner, the determination of utilities, or even proof of their existence, is a most difficult matter.[11]

Contemporary utility theory starts with a set of human behavior axioms consistent with the generally prescribed concept of rationality in decision choice models. Each axiom is assumed to be testable.[12] That is, the axioms are stated such that the experimenter can assign operational meanings and relations to terms using the disciplines of logic and measure theory.

To date, several axiomatic systems for a theory of utility have been developed. Some are more "complete" than others. A "complete" axiomatic system must include what is known as the closure axiom. This axiom asserts that a person always prefers one of two outcomes or else is indifferent.

The one axiom common to all systems of rational behavior and subject to the most attention is the transitivity axiom. This axiom reads: If A is

[11] C. West Churchman, *Prediction and Optimal Decision*, Englewood Cliffs: Prentice-Hall, Inc., 1961), Chapter 8.
[12] Churchman, *ibid.*

preferred to B, and B is preferred to C, then A is preferred to C. Without transitivity, we could not "link" the many sub-preference systems of an individual.

Developing the Utility Index: The discussions on utility theory seem to indicate the following are necessary for the construction of a utility index:

   (a) a set of mutually exclusive independent events
   (b) an axiomatic system permitting the assignment of numerical values
       to each outcome
   (c) a probability measure of each outcome possibility
   (d) the assumption that the decision maker is a maximizer
   (e) a willingness to gamble on the part of the decision maker

To construct a utility index, we must be able to derive an interval scale which satisfies the requirement that none of the empirically determined relations are disturbed. This is accomplished if the ratio of two pairs of measures taken on different scales will always be the same. A linear transformation satisfies this requirement.[13] Consider the following example.

A university research team is interested in measuring the subjective value of money to each of a group of students. To measure these subjective values (utilities), the researchers construct an experiment (a choice situation) in which the student is given the alternative of a specified but uncertain (risky) cash prize and of a certain (non-risky) cash prize. To distinguish between the risky and non-risky prizes, the former is referred to as an expected prize and the other as cash reward.

The expected prize is always some probability combination of zero and $1,000. The cash reward varies. A utility value of 100 is arbitrarily assigned to $1,000 and a ultility value of zero to zero dollars. The utility of any cash reward is found by multiplying the probability of $1,000 by 100.

By now it is clear that the expected prize is nothing more than a gamble with a payoff of either zero or $1,000. Each gamble is independent of all other gambles and income is stated in numerical terms. Thus we have all the necessary requirements for the construction of an interval scale.

The scale is constructed by finding gambles and cash prizes to which students are indifferent. If a student is indifferent between a gamble involving a 50–50 chance of zero or $1,000 and a cash income of $400, we say *that the utility of $400 is equal* to $\frac{1}{2}(0) + \frac{1}{2}(100)$ or 50. The student may then be found to be indifferent between a cash income of $600 and a gamble in which the probability of zero is .25 and of $1,000 is .75. The interval scale value of $600 is then equal to $\frac{1}{2}(0) + \frac{3}{4}(100)$ or 75.

This procedure is continued for a large number of cash rewards and expected prizes involving $1,000 and zero. From the data collected, it is

[13] Anatol Rapoport, *op. cit.*, pp. 124–128.

possible to express the preference of each student as a mathematical function of money and utility. Utility functions so constructed are not interpersonally comparable. In general it is not possible to construct a function for the students as a group. An exception, of course, would be possible only if all the students had the same subjective valuation of money; that is, they had the same interval scale. This is highly unlikely.

It is easy to generalize from the gamble about the students to ones involving different sums. All that is required for an interval scale is a method by which utility can be expressed as a linear transformation.

Stochastic Choice: Ordinarily if individuals do order all alternatives, they will not be able to assign consistent utility to the same alternatives in repetitive situations without some error. This is particularly true if A is only slightly preferred to B. Instead of asserting absolutely that A is preferred to B, it would be more realistic to say, for example, that A is preferred to B "95% of the time." Or B may be preferred to A "5% of the time." In general such probabilistic preferences would give a more plausible interpretation of "indifferent" or "preferred." By weakening the "consistency requirement" in the axiomatic framework of preference orderings, extensive empirical testing would be more meaningful.[14]

With either one of the above approaches to preference ordering, there are serious obstacles to empirically deriving utility indexes.

Experiments that have been conducted to date indicate the need for an unusually high degree of sophistication in research methods.[15] This complicates the task of enlarging the collection of empirically derived utility functions. Thus it appears that for times to come, the underlying assumptions and valuations of the decision maker in choice situations will remain beyond our reach.

Optimization or Suboptimization?

The decision maker may act as if he is maximizing in "closed" decision models. But his decisions may not *in fact* be "optimal" for the organization. In organizational decision making, the decision maker may be restricted by the hierarchical arrangement of the organizations and the flows of information through channels. The "closed" decision model for most organizational decision-making postures may therefore depart from the popularized concept of "maximizing" behavior.

Suboptimization is more typical of organizational decision-making. The decision maker acts on the basis of the decision framework and information

[14] Herbert A. Simon, "Theories of Decision-Making in Economics and Behavioral Science," *American Economic Review*, 49, No. 3, June 1959, p. 262.
[15] See, for example, Donald Davidson, Patrick Suppes and Sidney Siegel, *Decision Making: An Experimental Approach*, (Stanford: University Press, 1957).

available to his particular unit or department in the hierarchy. He makes decisions from a "local" point of view.

Such decisions may be optimal for any given department, but less than optimal for the organization as a whole. The organization is affected by the total set of effects; a department may not be. Decisions beneficial to one department may create difficulties elsewhere in the organization which are much greater than the benefits received by the decision maker's department.

A company may decide to charge divisions for the use made of warehousing to assure economic utilization of facilities. The division managers have the alternative of using outside space if it is less costly. If the divisions are charged on the basis of the number of square feet occupied, it is easy for the decision maker to compare the cost of using company facilities versus independent warehouses. If company warehouses are partially empty and a division uses outside warehousing because it is less costly, the decision may well be "best" from the point of view of the division's income statement, but this is not the case for the company as a whole. The additional cost of storing in company facilities would have been zero and company profits would have been higher.

Summarizing the discussion on "closed" decision models, we find that the applicability of such models can be increased by modifying certain of the basic assumptions and relations such as action-outcome sequences and preference orderings under different states of nature. Undoubtedly these modifications tend to broaden and add some realism to "closed" decision models, but even after such revisions, the theoretical foundations of "closed" models are inadequate to serve as points of departure for a general understanding of the human decision processes. The decision processes are far more dynamic than those depicted by the scheme of a "closed" model.

Goals are not defined in as clear-cut a manner as choice-decision models hypothesize. Goal-striving behavior occurs within a range of structure of goals. The selection of a particular goal or goal structure is itself a decision. Moreover, information is generally inadequate to identify all alternatives, and relevant alternatives are not necessarily stable; they may change with successive decisions.

There is serious doubt as to the ability of the "closed" decision model to stimulate complex choice behavior, although it may do very well for simple choices.

"Open" Decision Models

In "closed" models a few dimensions of the decision environment are selected and admitted into the decision process; action-outcome relations, utility and so on. The decision maker is assumed to be a logical, methodical maximizer. In contrast, the "open" decision model parallels an "open system." Like the open system, it is continually influenced by its total environment. And, of course, it also influences the environment. Decisions shape as well as mirror environment. Contrary to main elements of "closed" decision models, it does not assume that the decision maker can recognize all goals and feasible alternatives. A more realistic view of the decision maker is emphasized. He is a complex mixture of many elements — his culture, his personality, and his aspirations.

Behavioral Foundations of "Open" Decision Model

The "open" decision model accents the individual's ability to control his behavior. For the most part, human behavior is learned and not controlled by biological forces shaped by "inborn" dimensions. This means that behavior is the outcome of conscious and unconscious "selective processes" and therefore must reflect the limitations of human cognition and the complexity of man's total environment.

Human Cognition: Between the stimulus or "cue" and the ultimate action which follows, lies a filtering system or image.[16] The image is a construct of relationships, experiences, values and emotions. It is characterized by an internal capacity to grow from within as well as from the retention of external experiences. This point is illustrated by man's capacity to create, from series of unrelated events, ideas that become the sources of monumental essays, names, symphonies or organizations.[17]

The image is the key element in cognitive behavior. It contains not only what is, but what might be. Man not only knows, but knows that he knows.[18] The decision maker's decision reflects his perceptions of people, roles, and organizations in addition to his own values and emotions. Even the most intelligent of us act on the basis of images including more than the objective facts of the decision situation.

But despite man's power to behave "rationally," that is to say, his ability to select and order his responses to stimuli, he is bounded by a limited perspective. He possesses limited computational skills and, therefore, does not always make the best use of available information. Often he is inclined to deal with simplified models of real situations.[19]

Thus, the assumptions of "closed" decision models loses meaning in the context of an "open" system. An individual cannot weigh *all* alternatives. and still further, if the decision maker does not possess the ability to recog-

[16] Kenneth E. Boulding, *The Image*, (Ann Arbor: University of Michigan Press, 1956).

[17] Boulding, *op. cit.*, pp. 25–27.

[18] Boulding, *ibid.*

[19] Simon, Herbert A., *Models of Man*, (New York: John Wiley & Sons, Inc., 1957), p. 197.

nize and weigh the many choices that may be available, how does he "maximize" in the sense prescribed by "closed" decision models?

Role Behavior: If each individual's decision is the result of a personalized selection process, how then does an organization, or for that matter society, channel such personal-centered behavior toward group defined ends? The answer lies in the make-up of the image. It is true that the image is a nondescript framework of experiences, values and expectations. But it is also characterized by order. Some experiences and expectations are collected and "stored" as single entities. Such programs of experiences and expectations become the basis for standardized responses to recurring stimuli. The whole collection of experiences and expectations, some developed from recurring and others from nonrecurring situations, are said to form premises for individual decisions.

Thus, to the extent that the organization is able to plant dominating premises, it is able to control and unify the behavior of participants. Organization structures provide status systems with roles defined. These become premises for individual decisions and hence behavior. The organization likewise provides experiences and information through training and communication. These, too, are premises for decisions and can become powerful means of influencing individuals toward organizational goals.[20] The role system, however, is perhaps the most discussed method of standardizing individual behavior.

For society as a whole, we also get individual behavior that is generally structured by premises reflecting experiences and expectations associated with roles. Public approval is often dependent on the way one acts and his role. For some roles — motherhood, fatherhood, doctor, etc., there are well-defined sets of standardized behaviors or norms that must be adhered to by the "acting" individuals. Fathers are expected to be the breadwinners in the American family; they are expected to assume financial responsibility. The laws of society frequently reflect the expectations as to how one is to act in a role. Fathers may be jailed for nonsupport. Creditors may sue husbands for debts incurred by their wives. Every person acts out at least one role for which there is an expected pattern. It may be his role as a citizen, soldier, teacher, student, corporate officer or public official.

Decisions in "Open" Models

The single-choice "open" decision model in some ways resembles a dynamic means-ends or "closed" scheme. That is, the decision is made within the framework of a predetermined goal and established alternative. But the comparison ends there. Consider the model in Figure 9.1. See over.

---

[20] Simon, Herbert A., *Administrative Behavior*, 2nd edition (New York: The Macmillan Company, 1957), pp. 123–25.

Figure 9.1   A single choice "open" model.

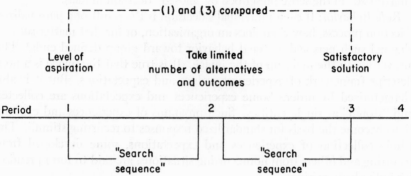

The decision maker passes through three time periods:

Period 1: The individual starts out with an idealized goal structure. He defines one or more action goals as a "first approximation" of the "ideal goal" in the structure. The action goal(s) may be considered as representative of the decision maker's *Aspiration Level*.[21]

Period 2: The individual engages in search activity and defines a limited number of outcomes and alternatives. He does not attempt to establish the relations rigorously. His analysis proceeds from loosely defined rules of approximation. The limited alternatives defined establish a starting point for further search toward a solution.

Period 3: Search among the limited alternatives is undertaken to find a "satisfactory" as contrasted with an "optimal" solution. "Satisfactory" is defined in terms of the aspiration level or action goals.

A number of differences between "closed" and "open" decision models which are not always apparent are highlighted:

(1) predetermined goals are replaced by some unidentified structure which is approximated by an aspiration level.
(2) all alternatives and outcomes are not predetermined; neither are the relationships between specific alternatives and outcomes always defined.
(3) the ordering of all alternatives is replaced by a search routine which considers fewer than all alternatives.
(4) the individual does not maximize but seeks to find a solution to "satisfy" an aspiration level.

Even in a single choice situation, the "open" model offers a "deeper" description of the choice process than "closed" decision models. If choices are defined in a stochastic context, this model can be predictive.

[21] Kurt Lewin, *et al.*, "Level of Aspiration," *Personality and the Behavior Disorders*, vol. 1, J. Mcv. Hunt (ed.) (New York: Ronald Press, 1944).

The Multiple-Choice "Open" Model

The multiple choice "open" model is a more ambitious attempt to emphasize cognition processes in decision making. The model is a hierarchy of "single decisions"; each successive decision is an attempt to improve the outcome in light of new information gained in the previous decisions. It provides a highly realistic simulation of human problem-solving.

The key element in the multiple-choice "open" model is the attainment discrepancy or the difference between the levels of aspiration and achievement. In most cases, some attainment discrepancy is almost certain because of the decision maker's inability to equate with any degree of precision a given outcome with his aspiration level. Generally an outcome

Figure 9.2   The multiple choice "open" decision model.

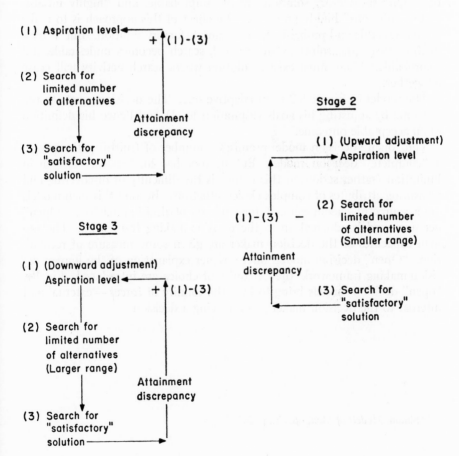

can only be identified with a region about the aspiration level. A given outcome is satisfactory (unsatisfactory) or successful (unsuccessful) according to the magnitude of the attainment discrepancy. In our model, only significant discrepancies (plus or minus) are considered.

The attainment discrepancy controls the *modus operandi* for reaching a stable solution in "open" models. The size and direction of the discrepancy induce adjustments in both the level of aspiration and search activity.[22]

In Figure 9.2, it is explicitly assumed that a "plus" discrepancy increases the level of aspiration and decreases the range of search for solutions. A "negative" discrepancy decreases the level of aspirations and broadens the range of search. These behavioral attributes are specifically defined to assure "bound" properties in the model. This means that the range of fluctuations is restricted. The decision and aspiration level fluctuates between positions of minimum and maximum potential. Lewin *et al.* introduce "bound" properties in a similar model by making the attainment of "highly satisfactory solution" highly improbable, and "highly unsatisfactory solutions" highly probable. The effect of this approach is to make search desirable and probable given an unsatisfactory solution. But as reasonably satisfactory solutions are reached, search becomes undesirable and improbable. There must exist a solution where search activity will cease altogether.

The model in Figure 9.2 is an adaptive one. The decision reacts to the outcome by adjusting his goals (aspiration level) and hence his definition of an acceptable outcome.

The "open" decision model promises a number of fruitful paths toward a "complete" decision model. But it, too, has limitations. The main limitation (rather serious at this point) is the difficulty of discovering and measuring attributes of complex choice situations. Beyond this such models are a source of encouragement for students of decision-making. "Open" decision models add realism to the decision-making framework. The human capacities of the decision maker are given some measure of recognition. "Open" decision models offer a richer explanation of the human decision-making framework; the dynamics of choice are introduced. Finally, "open" decision models bring to bear the totality of forces — external and internal to the decision maker — influencing a decision.

[22] Simon, *Models of Man, op. cit.*, p. 253.

Conclusions

There is a growing disenchantment with "closed" decision models in economic and management science circles.[23] A serious reconsideration of decisions that confront the organization decision maker and the required decision foundations appears to be in order. At this point there is evidence that the most vital decisions are non-recurring. "Search" is required to find feasible alternatives. And often this "search" must not be constrained by the bounds of some preferred solution. Problem solving requires a flexible and dynamic framework. Organizations grow and thus have growing aspirations; so must their problems and what constitute acceptable solutions. The future of "open" decision models, in light of these straws in the wind, seems highly promising.

[23] See, for example, Charles Hitch, "Uncertainties in Operations Research," *Journal of Operations Research*, vol. 8, no. 4, July–August, 1960, pp. 437–45 and Kenneth J. Arrow, "Decision Theory and Operations Research," *Journal of Operations Research*, vol. 5, no. 6, December, 1957, pp. 765–74.

10

Two Approaches to Computer Simulation*

Kalman J. Cohen

Carnegie Institute of Technology

Underlying the search for better management theory is the need for more effective research tools and methodologies. Computer simulation provides a method of studying complex systems. By manipulating a simulation model of a system on the computer, a considerable amount of useful information about the real system to which it corresponds can be derived. This article analyzes the use of computer simulation for synthesis (using deductive logic) and analysis (using inductive logic).

Simulation

Simulation is a technique for studying the behavior of complex systems. The usefulness of this technique has been widely demonstrated in increasing our understanding of a wide range of phenomena from such fields as economics, psychology, business and industry, engineering, physics, chemistry, and military strategy, tactics, and logistics.

In exploring the behavior of complex systems, scientists and engineers frequently utilize intellectual constructs known as "models." A formal model of a complex system is an abstract representation of the real system, defined or characterized by a set of explicitly stated assumptions. Since any model is necessarily a simplification of the real system to which it corresponds, to prevent the model from being "over-simplified," it is useful to specify in advance the types of applications for which the model is intended, thus indicating the areas where considerable amounts of realistic detail are required.

A simulation model is one particular kind of formal model. The explicit

* Taken and adapted from the *Journal of the Academy of Management*, vol. 4, no. 1, April, 1961, pp. 43–49. This paper was presented at the Twentieth Annual Meeting of the Academy of Management in St. Louis, Missouri, on December 28, 1960.

assumptions which characterize a simulation model describe the dynamic processes determining the behavior of the complex system being studied. To simulate a complex system, we first formulate a simulation model of the system, and then we sequentially carry out the dynamic processes which are specified by the explicit assumptions of the model. If the simulation model is properly formulated, relative to the types of questions it is intended to answer, then simulation can provide a considerable amount of useful information about the corresponding real system.

A variety of mechanisms can be used in constructing simulation models. They can be classified under three broad headings: physical simulation models, analog simulation models, and mathematical simulation models.

Physical simulation models are scaled reproductions of the corresponding system. Since physical simulation models usually portray reality on a greatly reduced scale, they can also be thought of as miniaturized reconstructions of complex systems. Some examples of physical simulation models are scale model airplanes in wind tunnels, scale model ships in flood basins, military maneuvers, and pilot production plants. While there are some types of applications for which physical simulation models are extremely useful, such models are in general more expensive to construct and more awkward to manipulate than analog or mathematical simulation models.

Both analog and physical simulation models are endowed with an air of concreteness, since they are fabricated from such components as human beings and hardware items. However, these two types of simulation models differ considerably in the manner by which they portray reality. Rather than trying to be a conveniently scaled copy of a complex system, an analog simulation model is intended to be merely an analogy of the corresponding system. Webster defines "analogy" as "a relation of likeness, between two things or *of* one thing *to* or *with* another, consisting in the resemblance not of the things themselves but of two or more attributes, circumstances, or effects"[2] While the actual appearance of an analog simulation model is usually very different from that of the corresponding complex system, the components comprising the analog simulation model are interconnected in ways which are analogous to the interrelations among the corresponding components in the real system. Some examples of analog simulation models are an electronic analog of an oil pipeline network, a hydraulic analog of the circular flow of money in an economic system, and a mechanical analog of a production and distribution system.

In contrast to the concreteness of both physical and analog simulation models, mathematical simulation models are composed entirely of abstract

[2] *Webster's New Collegiate Dictionary*, Springfield, Massachusetts; G. and C. Merriam Co., 1956, p. 32.

symbols. In a mathematical simulation model, a set of mathematical relations is used to characterize the dynamic processes present in the real dynamic system. In simulating a mathematical model, computational procedures are used to trace numerically the implications of these mathematical relations. Various kinds of calculating devices can be used in simulating a mathematical model. For very simple models, a human using only a pencil and paper might be adequate. As the models become more complex, a human simulating the model might find it advantageous to use some mechanical computational aids such as a desk calculator, adding machine, slide rule, or table of logarithms. Most of the interesting mathematical simulation models which have been formulated are so complex that they call for the use of an electronic computer, of either the analog or the digital type. However, no matter what type of computer is used to simulate a mathematical model, its function is simply that of carrying out in numerical terms the dynamic processes embodied in the formal assumptions of the model.

Computer Models

The term "computer model" is used to refer to a mathematical model which is intended to be simulated on an electronic digital computer. Computer models are the most widely used and versatile type of simulation model. The potential applicability of computer models is limitless, for any mathematical model, no matter how large and how complex, can in principle be simulated by an appropriate electronic digital computer. However, in practice economic considerations limit the comprehensiveness of computer models, since even the largest and fastest electronic computer has neither infinite storage capacity nor infinitesimal operating speeds, and the costs of computing time are often substantial. To a greater extent than is true of other types of simulation models, computer models have demonstrated their usefulness for studying the behavior of complex systems in such diverse areas as the physical sciences, the social sciences, engineering, management, and the military.

The greatest single advantage of computer models in comparison with other types of either simulation or non-simulation models is the relative ease with which considerable amounts of realism, together with the concomitant complexity, can be embodied in the models. While adding complexity will always increase the expense and difficulty of deriving the implications of a computer model, in principle it is always possible (if not necessarily practical) to simulate a computer model, no matter how complex it might be. In contrast, adding complexity to non-computer models will not only increase the expense and difficulty of deriving the implications of the model, but it will often lead to models which even in principle cannot be made to yield any conclusions.

In comparison with other types of simulation models, computer models possess four additional advantages. First, because modern electronic digital computers operate at extremely high speeds, it is usually much faster to derive interesting consequences from computer models than from other types of simulation models. Second, because of the great accuracy of electronic digital computers, it is not very likely that arithmetical or other simple errors will occur and cause erroneous inferences to be drawn from the model. Third, the results of a computer model are completely reproducible. If the same computer program is run several times using the same input data, exactly the same output will be produced every time. Finally, a computer model can more easily assume a modular character than can other types of simulation models. It is extremely convenient to be able to formulate a complex model in terms of several component submodels, to deal with each component separately at first, and then to integrate them into a complete model.

In comparing computer models with conventional mathematical models, it is necessary to consider the extent to which the different models describe the corresponding real system. If a direct mathematical solution can be obtained for a formal mathematical model, considerably more information about the behavior of the corresponding system is thereby obtained than would be provided by using simulation procedures on the same model. Furthermore, it is usually less expensive to solve a model mathematically whenever it is possible than to trace its solution numerically through simulation techniques. However, it is often the case that a direct mathematical solution cannot be obtained for a computer model. In this situation, the researcher must decide whether it is better to utilize computer simulation techniques to obtain "less general" and "more expensive" results for a complex, realistic, and meaningful model, or else to simplify the model until it can be solved mathematically, thus obtaining "more general" and "less expensive" results for a simple, unrealistic, and possibly inapplicable model. Increasingly, the practical answer to this strategic question is turning out to favor computer simulation models, because of the extremely large amounts of relevant and realistic detail which can be incorporated in them. The trend towards the use of computer models should accelerate as researchers gain more experience and greater ability in working effectively with them, and as electronic digital computers become larger, faster, and less expensive.

Synthesis and Analysis

Now that we have discussed the general concept of simulation and the importance of electronic computers in current simulation studies, we are ready to consider the two different approaches which can be taken in using computer models to explore the behavior of complex systems. In another paper,[3] we have applied the labels "analysis" and "synthesis" to these two approaches. This usage is suggested by the primary definitions of these terms given by Webster: "analysis" is "separation of anything into constituent parts or elements; also an examination of anything to distinguish its component parts or elements, separately or in their relation to the whole";[4] "synthesis" is "composition or combination of parts, elements, etc., so as to form a whole; also, the whole thus formed."[5] The basis for the distinction between analysis and synthesis rests upon the types of fundamental questions the researcher is trying to answer and the kinds of empirical knowledge he possesses.

Most operations research simulation studies have used computers as tools of synthesis. In a computer model intended for synthesis, all of the individual structural relations are assumed known to a high degree of accuracy. However, what is not known is how the component relations will interact as a complete system.[6] In this situation, the question in which the researcher is primarily interested is what will be the behavior of the over-all system? Although the entire system response is determined once the characteristics of all the structural relations have been specified, in practice the forms of the underlying relations are frequently so complex and the number of variables contained in them is frequently so large that no mathematical techniques are known which will enable us to derive the over-all system behavior as a set of closed mathematical formulas. When this is the case, the operating characteristics of all the components of the system can be represented by a computer program, and an electronic computer can be used to simulate the behavior of the over-all system. The output from the computer is then assumed to correspond to the time paths which would be traced by the real system.

When computer simulation is used as a tool of analysis, the situation is almost exactly the opposite of that pictured above. The over-all behavior of the system is observable and known, but the characteristics of the individual components comprising the system are not completely understood.[7] In this situation, the researcher is interested in discovering the structural relations which underlie the system. One way of testing whether he has is to try to formulate a model specifying the actions of each indi-

---

[3] Kalman J. Cohen and Richard M. Cyert, "Computer Models in Dynamic Economics," *The Quarterly Journal of Economics*, vol. 75, no. 1 (February, 1961).

[4] Webster's *New Collegiate Dictionary, op. cit.*, p. 32.

[5] *Ibid.*, p. 862.

[6] The complete system may in fact have never been observed, and the researcher may even hope that it never will be, as, for example, when the model represents an air battle between two Great Powers. In this connection, see R. H. Adams and J. L. Jenkins, "Simulation of Air Operations with the Air Battle Model," (abstract), *Bulletin of the Operations Research Society of America*, Vol. 7, Supplement 2 (1959), pp. B–96f.

[7] This is frequently the case in economics. For a specific example, see Kalman J. Cohen, *Computer Models of the Shoe, Leather, Hide Sequence*, Englewood Cliffs, New Jersey: Prentice-Hall, Inc., 1960.

vidual component, and then to manipulate the model to see whether the resulting system corresponds to observed behavior. If the forms of the separate equations of the model are reasonably simple and if the number of individual variables involved is reasonably small, then traditional mathematical methods may suffice for this purpose. Frequently, however, it will be impossible to derive a set of closed mathematical formulas which embody the consequences of the model, but when this is the case, it is always possible to use computer simulation as a technique for manipulating the formal model.

In summary, when computer models are used for purposes of synthesis, it is assumed that we satisfactorily know the individual behavior of the underlying components of a complex system, and that our primary interest is in discovering the unknown behavior of the complete system. When computer models are used for purposes of analysis, on the other hand, it is assumed that we satisfactorily know the over-all behavior of the complete system, and that we are mainly interested in inferring the unknown behavior of the individual parts of the system.

The use of computer models for synthesis is an example of pure deductive logic. The operating characteristics of the individual components are essentially the postulates of a formal deductive system, the programmed interactions of the components with each other are the rules of inference, and the over-all patterns of behavior traced by the complete system are the derived theorems. In any formal deductive system, once we agree that the postulates and the rules of inference are empirically true, we necessarily agree to accept all theorems derived from them as also being empirically true. Hence, when a computer model is used as a tool of synthesis, the problem of empirical validation of the model should primarily be focused on the level of the detailed actions and interactions of the individual components.

The use of computer models for analysis is an example of pure inductive logic, i.e., of empirical inference. Although the underlying operating characteristics of the system's components are tentatively treated as postulates, the fundamental interactions of the components as rules of inference, and the over-all system behavior as theorems of a formal deductive system, empirical testing is carried out at the level of the theorems, i.e., with regard to the behavior of the complete system. If the over-all system behavior is in fact found to be in serious disagreement with the "theorems" derived from the model, we then must infer that the formal model is in some way an inadequate representation of the world. However, when the time paths generated by the computer model correspond closely to the observed behavior of the complete system, then the underlying model must be regarded as confirmed by the available evidence.[8]

[8] Strictly speaking, it would be more accurate to say "not refuted" than "confirmed" in this case, for it is always possible that more than one model could be found which

In practice, some computer simulation studies seem to be blends of both the synthesis and the analysis approaches.[9] This will occur most frequently when we have fragmentary but incomplete empirical knowledge of both the complete system and its individual parts. In this circumstance, the researcher can obtain the greatest benefit from computer models if he goes through an iterative process of alternately using simulation as a tool of analysis and as a procedure for synthesis, obtaining successive refinements in his knowledge of the behavior of the underlying components and the over-all system at each stage.

It is useful to draw a sharp distinction between analysis and synthesis, the two approaches to computer simulation, in order to establish the criteria whereby some important methodological questions can be answered. A conscientious researcher, in trying to exploit the full potential which computer simulation techniques can offer in studying the behavior of complex systems, must find answers to such questions as how should the functional forms in a computer model be specified, how should the parameters of a computer model be estimated, and how should a computer model be validated? The manner in which these questions should be answered will differ depending on whether the computer model is being used for purposes of analysis or of synthesis.[10] These methodological problems are relatively more important when computer simulation is used as a tool of analysis than when it is used as a technique for synthesis. Even in the latter case, however, they are probably worthy of more explicit consideration than has usually been accorded them by researchers. It is all too easy to assume that we in fact adequately know the individual behavior of the components in particular systems. Even though this may be true at a gross level, overlooking some of the more subtle interactions of the

---

would yield the same complete system behavior. This problem is not unique to the use of computer simulation as a tool of analysis, but it essentially arises in all empirical sciences. For a general philosophical discussion of this problem, see Bertrand Russell, *Human Knowledge: Its Scope and Limits*, New York: Simon and Schuster, 1948, pp. 421–507.

[9] For example, see Jay W. Forrester, "Industrial Dynamics — A Major Breakthrough for Decision Makers," *Harvard Business Review*, vol. 36, no. 4 (July–August, 1958), pp. 37–66; Alan J. Rowe, "A Research Approach in Management Controls," *Management Control Systems*, Donald G. Malcolm, Alan J. Rowe, and Lorimer F .McConnell, eds., New York: John Wiley and Sons, Inc., 1960, pp. 273–299; and Joel M. Kibbee, "Management Control Simulation," *ibid.*, pp. 300–320.

[10] For a discussion of the methodological problems which arise from the use of computer models as a tool of analysis, see Cohen and Cyert, *op. cit.* In contrast, considerations of the methodological problems present when computer models are used for purposes of synthesis are presented in R. W. Conway, B. M. Johnson, and W. L. Maxwell, "Some Problems of Digital Systems Simulation," *Management Science*, vol. 6, no. 1 (October, 1959); and in John W. Wester, Jr., "Experience in Complex Simulation," (abstract), *Bulletin of the Operations Research Society of America*, vol. 7, Supplement 2 (1959), pp. B–95f.

individual components can introduce serious errors into the resulting over-all system behavior. For example, when the individual structural equations of the model contain stochastic terms, we might correctly identify the marginal distributions from which each random element is drawn, and yet go seriously astray by incorrectly assuming that these stochastic terms are independently distributed and non-serially correlated. Even though computer simulation is used strictly for purposes of synthesis, it is prudent to check our assumed knowledge of the individual components' behavior by trying empirically to validate the over-all system behavior for at least one case.[11]

[11] One example where such an attempt was made is Hebron E. Adams and Richard E. Forrester, "Carmonette: A Computer Combat Simulation," (abstract), *Bulletin of the Operations Research Society of America*, vol. 7, Supplement 2 (1959), pp. B–98f.

PART TWO

This Part includes selections on important problems in organization theory. The first six (articles 11 through 16) present clarification of concepts and terminology, and a review of the current state of organization theory and research methodologies. The remaining six articles (17 through 22) focus our attention on a wider range of substantive problems subsumed under organization theory.

Just as the terms management and business administration are erroneously used as synonyms, organization is often loosely equated with management. Researchers studying organizations often represent their findings and conclusions as management postulates. A further source of confusion about organization is its linkage with the word behavior. Thus researchers refer to organizational behavior, which can mean either behavior *in* an organization, or behavior *of* an organization. Distinctions such as these are important, and the first article in this section goes far toward clarifying them. The author, Mr. Alvin Brown, argues for greater precision and clarity in the use of the term organization, and suggests the way in which it is linked to the concept of management. And Mr. Brown's hopes for recognition of organization as a major subject for study, research, and teaching have, increasingly, become a reality.

Emerging Organization

Theory

With growing attention coming from practitioners and researchers, organization theory inevitably changes. Professor Scott's article traces some of the changing views reflected in organization theory. The evolutionary changes are classified, for purposes of discussion, into three groupings of theories: classical, neo-classical, and modern. The purpose of this scheme of classification is not to expunge earlier doctrines, but rather to indicate time continuities, to crystallize comparisons, and to draw out the basic elements common to all theoretical orientations. Professor Rubenstein also notes the importance of change, not only through the impact of a diversity of disciplinary fields interested in organization, but also through an increasing diversity of research methodologies employed by researchers. He suggests a number of ways in which research may be classified in terms of research methods.

More depth in the analysis of research methodologies is suggested by a reading of Professor Wolf's article on organization constructs. He points to the multi-dimensional nature of such constructs, and to their utility in going beyond cause and effect reasoning to involved interrelationships in explaining complex organizational behavior. Bernard Baum, through the concept of decentralization, examines the problem of authority in a case study of the Federal Civil Service. He views the organization as a system composed of related components, and as Wolf suggests, finds value in exploring the interrelationships of mutually interdependent variables. This article illustrates how case study research methods can be used in examining how concepts are related to on-going situations.

Utilizing concepts of small-group behavior, Professor Golembiewski undertakes a microcosmic scrutiny of important structural components of business organizations. He focuses on the element of cohesiveness as a strategic concept in small-group analysis. He examines both formal and informal aspects of small-group structure in work settings. After reviewing significant findings on cohesiveness research, he concludes that this research reveals a mixed picture of incomplete analytical development and demonstrated theoretical importance.

The span of control concept has long been a source of controversy in management and human relations thinking. Lawrence S. Hill moves the debate from a mere reliance on the verbalization of concepts in this "landmark article" which applies to the span-of-control problem. This application of queuing theory generated many opinions, pro and con. An interchange of arguments between author and critics is included at the end of this article. Like span of control, staff concepts also have long been debated. Professor Filley presents the results of research which explored the relationships between the growth rates of companies and the growth rates of their staffs. He concludes that the geometric increase in staff growth predicted by "traditional" theory is not found. He questions the assumptions underlying any postulated linear relationship between line and staff growth.

An increasing number of organization theorists are concerned with work flow as the basis for organization design. For example, Chapple and Sayles used work flow measurements in an analysis of organizational problems, concluding that organizations should be designed from the bottom up, rather than from the top down.[1] Numerous authorities have recommended job enlargement programs to remedy the defects inherent in excessive task specialization, and to replace interest factors deleted from overly specialized jobs.[2] While PERT is essentially a planning and control tool, matching work flow against stages in time, it also has many implications for systems analysis and organization design, therefore it may serve to open up new areas of research on organization theory.

A key aspect of the business organization is the way in which it utilizes a reward and punishment system calculated to influence the be-

---

[1] Eliot Chapple and Leonard R. Sayles, *The Measure of Management*, New York: The Macmillan Company, 1960.

[2] John Logemann, "Job Enlargement Boosts Production," *Nation's Business*, December, 1954, pp. 34–38.

havior of its members. Professor David W. Belcher applies theories of motivation, pulling these behavioral findings together to fill the gaps left in the explanations of wage determination advanced by general economists and labor economists. Stimulated by this approach, Golembiewski again utilizes the work flow analysis described previously in selection 16. He extends Belcher's analysis by inquiring into behavioral factors associated with the flow of work and structural design in organizations. He also shows how these points of view lead in the direction of relatively unorthodox structural designs. He finds two advantages in the unorthodox structuring: (1) an easing of the measurement of performance, and (2) an encouragement of the development of informal groups responsible for the total flow of work.

In the final article of this section, Professor Stanley Young elaborates on the authority aspects of the employer-employee relationship, treated by most organization theorists as a critical factor in the structure of organizations. This article is essentially a rational analysis of the exchange relationship between an employer and an employee.

11

Organization As
a Separate Branch of Management*

Alvin Brown

Vice-President, Emeritus, Johns-Manville Corporation

> *This provocative article, first presented in an address before the Academy of Management in 1949, recognizes the importance of organization as a discipline for serious study. The author meticulously develops a careful definition of organization and points the way to greater clarity of definition and classification. The relationships between the two concepts of organization and management are explained and clarified. The need for a better taxonomy is set forth sharply.*

Of a subject talked about as much as organization, it seems strange to have to plead that it is a subject. But I think that plea needs to be made. I fear we assume too readily that what has a name, has therefore a being. This name, organization, implies a body of knowledge. Where is that body of knowledge? Where does it exist? Has it a being? I have to doubt it. Presently I shall try to satisfy you of my reasons for that doubt.

Lest you think while I am doing so, however, that my anxiety is about mere form, let me assure you it is not. Classification for its own sake can be a delightful pastime, but not one to be intruded upon others. To classify is not my purpose. My concern is about lack of classification as a cause of lack of understanding. I am concerned about what we lose because of that lack of understanding. What we lose seems sufficiently deplorable to be worth your thought. Of this also I shall try to satisfy you.

---

* Taken and adapted from the *Annual Proceedings of the Academy of Management*, December 30, 1949.

In talking about organization, it will be impossible to avoid talking also about management. I hope I shall do so with restraint, because I do not profess any insight into management as a body of knowledge. In speaking of management in relation to organization, I do not know, indeed, whether I speak of a broader but inclusive subject, or of a different subject. I do not know whether I turn to a wider field of knowledge or to a separate one. And this lack of understanding seems plainly to come from lack of classification or lack of definition.

Perhaps this barrier to my understanding will be plainer by an example from another field of knowledge.

Philosophy as an Example

For a long time I had almost no concept of the scope of philosophy. When, in my rambling reading, I ran into accredited philosophers, they never seemed to speak of the same things. It was as though one man were to say, "I am very fond of curry"; and another man to reply, "Oh, but I should think you would prefer a *cold* shower."

Then, in a moment of inspiration, I consulted the encyclopedia, and the puzzle cleared up measurably. I read first of all that "philosophy is a general term whose meaning and scope have varied very considerably" through the ages. Then I found that philosophy comprises psychology, epistemology, and ontology; not to mention logic, ethics, and aesthetics. I found, in other words that philosophy is a congeries of subjects. Doubtless these subjects are related. Doubtless there is some synthesizing concept that binds them together as philosophy. Nevertheless I had been unable to conceive philosophy until I knew its subdivisions. It was only by conceiving its parts — by seeing them as separate branches — that I gained a key to the scope of philosophy itself.

Concept of Management

When I turn to management, I have the same difficulty, without, alas, the same ready source of enlightenment.

The encyclopedia is a great work. I am in debt to it in many ways. When my children were young the encyclopedia solved many a problem for me. But suppose one of my sons had asked me, What does management mean? Doubtless, with half a thought, I would have said, Son go look it up in the encyclopedia. And if he had? He would have found two kinds of management: scientific and farm. He would have learned the importance of using the right size of shovel and the need of rotating crops.

Well, certainly, these things are important; and certainly also I exaggerate somewhat. And I apologize to Mr. Taylor's memory if it is necessary. But, nevertheless, it is true that the encyclopedia gives no answer to anybody who wants to know about industrial management.

If I go to The Management Index of the American Management Association, I see that management functions comprise personnel, office management, finance, production, marketing, packaging, and insurance. I ask myself if this list of functions is a characteristic action of a thing, and therefore not a separate thing. So I conclude that these functions are intended to define the scope of management.

When I turn to the catalogue of a school of business, I find a department of management and industrial relations. This department offers, among others, courses in planning factory layout and equipment, techniques of time and motion study and work simplification, purchasing and storekeeping, and analysis and interpretation of business costs. Since I have never heard these subjects ascribed to industrial relations, I must conclude that they are regarded as part of the concept of management. On the other hand, there is a separate department for marketing, which presumably excludes that subject from the scope of management.

Then again, the author of a recent article on the meaning of management[1] tells me the subject should be divided into seven phases: economic, administrative, engineering, anatomical, physiological, psychological, and sociological. Cost accounting for example belongs to the administrative phase; incentive plans to the economic phase.

From these conspectuses, one ought to believe that management comprehends a wide range of subject. Were it not for some important omissions, one ought to believe that it comprises the entire range of knowledge employed in industrial enterprise. In either case, one is left with the feeling that the only way to know the scope of management is to know all its subdivisions.

If I go to the dictionary, I get no more light, because management, as a word, seems to have at least two meanings. It can refer to the means of accomplishing an end: the things done or provided for by a manager. In that sense, it may well include such things as production and marketing, for those are things that a manager does or provides for.

On the other hand, the word can refer to the art or faculty of managing. In that sense, it could be a concept quite apart from the things that are done by a manager. This concept would exclude what may be called the objective branches of industrial knowledge: the specialized subjects such as engineering, production, marketing, and finance. It would regard management as something outside these objective aims; perhaps as the tactic by which they are sought, or the *influence* that procures them. My words halt when I try to express this distinction, but I am sure the con-

---

[1] E. H. Anderson, *Harvard Business Review*, V, XXVII, pp. 678–92.

cept is valid. From this viewpoint, management would, I think, imply much the same as what we mean by leadership.

To me, this second concept of management has a strong appeal. I am simply unable to comprehend a subject that embraces everything. I am unable to grasp a subject if it can include both the book written by my friend, Professor Schell, and a book about, say, the principles of accounting. To regard management as the omnibus of all industrial knowledge is, for me at least, to deprive it of meaning.

Value of Classification

Please do not think I am trying to add to the knowledge of management. Quite the contrary. I am only asking questions about it in a forum where such questions may hope to be answered. I am not bringing coals to Newcastle; I have come to Newcastle for coals. And I do so because of the plight in which I find my own especial object of interest, which is organization.

Some people, I suppose, might doubt the usefulness of classification. They might, I suppose, dismiss my questions as a needless search for fine distinctions. I am sure you will not do so. I am sure you will agree that definition is the first step to understanding. As with philosophy, so with management, I do not see how it can be understood unless it is defined.

Organization and Management

But, as I said, I do not ask the question for its own sake. I ask it because of its bearing upon the concept of organization. I ask it because the existence of organization, as something more than a name, seems to depend upon the answer.

How often in industrial literature do we find the term, organization and management! How often do we find them, that is, linked together as though they were reciprocal or complementary ideas. In industrial literature, the association is as ubiquitous as that of ham and eggs.

It may not be too wide off my subject to glance at the union of ham and eggs. They are often said to have an affinity. I should be inclined to doubt that, if it refers to their natures. As I see it, the alliance of ham and eggs, if not a marriage of mere convenience, is at least one that is distinguished by its outward felicity rather than by any inward communion. Perhaps I make my point sufficiently clear if I say that the two associates are quite different things — and that some people may prefer to have them separately.

The union of organization and management in industrial literature, on the contrary, seems to deny them any separate entity. It seems to say that organization is management and management is organization. If it does not go quite that far, it implies at least that the two subjects are inseparable: that they were not put together, like ham and eggs, but that they both came out of the same egg to begin with.

Thus, in the titles of texts you find the two words joined as often as they are separate. Nor does their separate use as titles indicate separation of subject. A book called management will, likely enough, treat of organization. A book called organization will often treat of many things that seem little related to the definition of the word.

The collected papers of Mary Parker Follett[2] give a perfect example of this fusion. The volume is called "Dynamic Administration." Miss Follett herself is quoted as saying, "I am studying business management." And the writer of the foreword says she searched for "the true principles of organization."

Whether there is a causal relationship with literature, I do not know; but college courses show the same coalition. I have looked at the catalogues of seven business schools. Two offer courses called organization and management. Two, and probably three, offer courses named management that actually include organization. One has a course named organization that includes management. The last uses neither title, but deals with both in a course called administrative practices.

Thus, it is plain enough that organization and management are mingled, both in writing and in teaching. Is this a natural fusion, or is it confusion? I think the question is important. I think it is important to the understanding of both subjects. And the answer should depend upon whether we can define the nature and scope of organization.

The Word, Organization

This brings us face to face with the doubt I expressed at the outset. Organization is a name, but is it a concept? Does it have a meaning with relation to industrial enterprise?

From the encyclopedia we get no more help in trying to answer this question than we did in the case of management. The only listing in its index is "Organization (of labour): see Trade Unions." All that we learn from that is that organization, whatever it be, is not the exclusive property of industry. Beyond this reference to trade unions, the encyclopedia is mute.

If we go to the dictionary, we get too much help. The meaning of the word is too broad to solve the problem. In the first place, it has both a dynamic and a static meaning: it can mean either the act of organizing or the state of being organized. This double meaning leaves us often to wonder, when we hear the word used, whether the reference is to organization as a process or to organization as a condition. It is the same as if,

[2] Mary Parker Follett, *Dynamic Administration*, New York, Harper & Brothers, 1940.

when speaking of education, you were not sure whether it meant the principles and practice of teaching and learning or the literate level of the population at large.

I sometimes wonder if this was not the trap that snared those who suppose that knowledge of organization can be gained by the case method. This method assumes, you know, that, to do the right thing, all you have to know is what other men do. Thus, if other men, in their enterprises, have a department of statistics, you should have one, too. And if other enterprises do not have a department of organization, you should not have one either. This notion of organization is limited, in other words, to existing patterns; to organization as a condition rather than as a process. It encourages men to be content with what is, and not to spend their time seeking what might be better. I am sure I say this without offense to anyone present, because the proper case-method man would be abroad observing how managers manage rather than here seeking how managers might manage better.

Well, you will not be surprised when I say that organization can be a useful concept to industrial enterprise only if it is regarded as a process. In the words of the dictionary, it is the process of arranging or constituting in interdependent parts, each having a special function or relation with respect to the whole.

But the trouble with this definition is that the process can be applied in many directions. We can speak of organizing productive processes, in the sense of designing the layout of equipment and the flow of work. We can speak of organizing our work, in the sense of scheduling and systematizing it. All these uses of the word are appropriate, and all of them are useful to industry. I suspect they are sometimes intended by people who use the term, organization and management.

Nevertheless, most men, in speaking of industrial organization, are probably thinking of the means of concerting human effort. And even so limited, we still need two meanings: one to refer to the process; the other to the body of knowledge upon which the process relies.

Organization of Human Effort

If there is any difficulty about limiting this subject to the concert of human effort, I suggest it is a difficulty with words and not with ideas. Certainly the layout of equipment and the flow of work are a subject — a concept — distinct from the integration of men and their duties. What more evidence of this do we need than that men can be expert in one of these fields with no particular need of knowledge in the other? Only in using the same kind of systematic approach have they any likeness. They are no more to be related because they both organize than two activities would be related because they both compute.

This means, of course, that the single word, organization, is a defective title when we are only talking about organizing human effort. I wish there were a more explicit single word for it. Perhaps someone, some day, will apply such a title, and, what is more necessary, gain acceptance of its use. Failing that, I can name it only by definition. Restricting the dictionary definition, it would be the process of arranging men as parts of an enterprise, allotting their functions, and defining their relations. It seems the same thing to say that, in this use, organization would define the responsibilities of members of enterprise and the relations among them.

To define the responsibilities of the members of an enterprise is, of course, to apportion among them all the things that must be done to realize the aims of the enterprise. The act applies intelligence and fore-thought to this apportionment instead of leaving it to chance or individual choice. Intelligence relies upon the principles and experience that can be laid up in a body of knowledge. The result of apportionment is a structure of jobs. The result, indeed, is the structure of the enterprise, since an enterprise without an apportionment of duties would be a form-less thing, difficult to imagine.

But to define individual jobs is only half the process. The jobs alone are no more than the unassembled parts of a machine. They must be placed in relationship to each other. The persons who will perform the jobs will have relations with each other. To organize this human effort, we just define these relations. This definition must be a part of the con-cept of organization, and a part of its body of knowledge.

In dealing with these relationships, the case method is especially inade-quate. Given the time, it is not too difficult to find out what departments existing enterprises have, and what the individual responsibilities are. These are reasonably objective things. Relationships are much less tangi-ble. I doubt whether the case student can expose the relationships in an enterprise, even if this were to tell him what they ought to be.

That, however, is a digression. We were looking for a subject. We were looking to see whether organization — of human effort — is a con-cept as well as a name. Have we not now identified one? When we say that organization defines jobs and the relations among them, do we not express the concept of a process and of a related body of knowledge that is distinct from all other branches of industrial knowledge? Even though it may not now be a subject, is it not possible for it to be one?

A Limited Concept

I think industrial enterprise — or any human enterprise, for that matter — has three concerns. One, certainly, is personnel. Another is administra-tion, by which I mean all the things that have to be done to carry out the purpose of the enterprise. The third is organization. In the sense in which I have defined it — the sense, indeed, in which, as a need, it makes itself manifest to anyone who studies enterprise — it is a subject, an activity, a science, separate and apart from both personnel and administration.

It is true that both personnel and administration can be divided into other subjects, while organization, though it has two parts, is single and compact in itself. It may be, then, that I have unduly narrowed the classification of the other subjects. With that question I am not greatly concerned. I gladly resign it to others more qualified than I. My only concern is to show that organization is a separate and unique subject.

Personnel comprises, of course, such subjects as employee selection, the terms of employment, incentives, employee relations, and working conditions. Most of these activities relate to employees in the aggregate. Organization decides what human effort is needed: the personnel activities supply and maintain it. They differ as much in their functions, the one from the other, as the writing of a play differs from casting it.

Administration employs an even larger number of activities. The American Management Association ascribed seven functions to management, of which all but personnel are plainly administrative activities. And, of course, there are others. These are things to be done in carrying on the work of the enterprise, and they cannot be done until organization has prescribed jobs and relationships and until personnel has supplied people. That seems enough to satisfy us that organization, as a subject and as an activity, is distinct from administration. They are as different as writing a play and acting it.

This limited concept of organization has sometimes been assailed as neglecting the human element. My concern for the human element is in even worse condition than my concept of management, but, whatever it is, it has these days been personified and deified; and to neglect it is the ultimate heresy. Nevertheless, I must take the risk of saying that I regard this accusation against organization as a soft impeachment, not to say a testimony of integrity. For why should organization go adventuring beyond its own domain?

It is true that organization may touch on personnel or on administration at some points. Thus, in defining the relations among members of an enterprise, organization must express the need and duty of supervision. In doing so, however, organization is scarcely called upon to say in what manner supervision should be exercised: whether, for example, it should be urbane or peremptory. I suppose the job of doing that belongs to administration. Or, it may be, to management.

Proximity of frontiers, however, does not make two subjects one. If it did, cost accounting would be the same as time study, and advertising the same thing as personal salesmanship.

Surely we can decide that the process of organizing human effort in an industrial enterprise is a separate branch of industrial knowledge and a distinct kind of industrial activity.

Organization vs. Management

And yet, perhaps I have still not shown that organization is a subject separate from management. Though organization emerges as a subject apart from the other objective concerns of industrial enterprise, is there some reason to think it too closely allied to management to be viewed separately?

All I can say to that is that I have never heard a reason given. The association is taken for granted; no need to explain it seems to have occurred to anyone.

If there is no apparent reason, there is, on the other hand, a cause that is plain enough when one looks at the evolution of industrial enterprise. The cause is that *every* function was management until it was discovered to be a separable function. In the same sense, government is just government until it is specialized as legislative, executive, and judicial.

In its beginnings, industry specialized the more obvious functions. It was easy to sort out functions such as production and sales. They were naked segments of the stream of administration. Each was a compact job that general management could delegate and supervise. And there were also some collateral jobs that plainly invited specialization: accounting, legal advice, corporate formalities.

Taylor, of course, first showed how to specialize phases of a function that previously had been regarded as single. He did so, it is true, for the production function and not for general management; but the lesson for general management was plain enough to read.

Delegation of functions such as production and sales had still left to management all the phases of administration that affected two or more of these primary functions. When enterprise grew larger, the burden of these common phases of administration grew intolerable. Under the spur of necessity, general management began to apply Taylor's lesson. This created a new type of function. This type of function ran, you might say, at right angles to the primary functions, because it affected all of them. Organization now employed a weft as well as a warp.

Thus, many of the phases of finance had to await this discovery before they were specialized. The urgency of the personnel problem had to force itself upon many managers before it was specialized. Relations with the public, with government, and with stockholders are even more recent specialties. All these functions relieved general management of phases of administration that bore upon the primary functions. It seems clear that this specialization did not so much wait upon the willingness of managers to divest themselves of duties as upon their ability to conceive of these duties as separate fields of endeavor. Some matters, such, for example, as financial analysis of operations, are still waiting to be born because they have not been identified as separable functions.

It is worth adding, too, that, having been forced to this kind of specialization because they could not do the whole job themselves, managers found that a specialist did the job better than they would have done it even if they had had the time.

Organization, as a separate function, is in this prenatal stage today. A case study three years ago by the National Industrial Conference Board found the function of organization planning in only three of 24 large companies. Perhaps we should be surprised that there *are* three, rather than that so many ignore it. Many managers talk glibly of the importance of organization, but their actions do not show that they regard it as a separate subject.

I think this historical descent of functions explains why organization is thought to be close to management. It is close to management only because it *is* close; only because, in other words, it has not been emancipated. Personnel problems were close to management before they were recognized as a function. What characteristic of organization makes it closer to management than personnel? None, I am sure, except that it is not conceived as a separate activity.

To rescue organization from its plight, then, it scarcely seems important to decide whether it is a part of management or not. If it is a part of management, it should plainly be a separate branch. Recognition as a separate branch is all that it needs. Let it reside in any community so long as it has its own house.

The Price of Amorphism

For anyone who thinks all this is mere academic fussiness, let me compute the price of the present amorphous condition of organization. Where industry finds a specialty, it will specialize. It specializes in labor relations, in public relations, in industrial engineering, and in many another subject no more important than organization. Need I undertake to prove that specialization is good? I am sure there is no doubt about that. Can it be that organization is the one subject where specialization offers no advantage? That would be hard to believe.

And so what happens for the lack of specialization? Organization suffers. The common respect in which the name is held is, in large part, a respect for the name alone. Most managers practice organization by intuition, not by principle. Intuition can be as reliable here as it is in most cases. In dealing with organization, managers will fly by the seat of their pants as they will in no other industrial activity. Indeed, it concedes too much to say that they deal with organization. It would be closer to the truth to say that they have a confiding faith that organization will take care of itself. Were that not so, they would not leave so much of it to people who are specialists in many things but not in organization.

No one who watches the practice of industrial organization — or the lack of it — can believe that many managers see the extent of the problem.

I do not so much refer to the primary functions — what you might call the standard table of departments. Here the case method, if it deters an enterprise from rising above the general level, at least enables it to follow the fashion. Of course, I might suggest that since problems are not uniform among enterprises, uniformity of departments is evidence that organization is not too well served. But I will not press this point. I wish the other needs of organization were as well served.

For, ordinarily, the manager's thought of organization stops at the department boundary. Within departments, organization is commonly left to the department head. That department head has a specialty to pursue. If he has found time to master organization, he is an exception. How many specialists find time — or inclination — to become traffic or tax experts? About as many find time to become experts in organization.

No one expects the department head to be his own lawyer or to buy his own insurance or to keep his own accounts. He commonly has help in evaluating his jobs and in setting his job standards. Often he is advised about his office methods and his office equipment. His expenditures are made by somebody else and somebody else sees that there is cash to make those expenditures. In his contacts with the public, he is guided by someone else so that his company will speak with one voice instead of many. The need of uniformity requires someone to prescribe his office hours and to regulate the vacations, holidays, and sick leave of his people. Auditors will see whether his work conforms to established practices. His stationery, forms, and supplies will be bought for him by a common purchasing agent. If he needs to travel, a traffic man will buy his transportation. This guidance and this help enable him to concentrate on his own specialty, whatever it is. Only when it comes to organization is he abandoned to the primitive ways of enterprise. Only when it comes to organization is he left to chart his own way, without compass or rudder, on an unmarked sea.

I wish this were the end of the invoice. But the larger part of the price is yet to be counted. This is the price paid for the imperfect practice of relationships. All members of an enterprise need to practice these, and few are taught to do so. Since good administration depends upon proper relationships, the lack of them leaves administration with one of its props missing.

Let us suppose an example. A State law requires insuring employees against accident and illness; and it gives the option of insuring with a State agency or with an insurance company. The insurance company will charge $20,000 less than the State. The insurance man, whose duty is to buy insurance at the least cost, would use the insurance company. The employee relations man, however, for reasons I need not detail but which we may concede are weighty, wants to use the State fund. The question presented, of course, is whether the personnel reasons are worth $20,000.

The issue is primarily for the insurance man. The cost of using the State fund is reasonable if the employee relations reasons are worth $20,000. He will inquire into those reasons and make up his mind. And here is the organizational test. Will he submit to the judgment of the personnel man? Or will he form his own judgment? Will he, in other words, use his own judgment or subordinate it to another's? The process of his mind may be difficult to detect, but the principle of organization is clear. If he lets another's judgment substitute for his own, he defaults in the performance of his responsibility.

Examples, I am afraid, tend to confine, not expand, our understanding of a matter. They are exposed to being understood as definitive of the matter, instead of merely illustrative. That is the trouble with cases when they are not grounded in principle. Please do not let my little example persuade you that the play of relationships is narrow. Consider how many miscarriages of responsibilty the same ignorance of principle can cause among the many members of an enterprise and over long periods of operation. Consider the other principles of which ignorance can produce a like effect. The cumulative result is serious enough to be viewed with alarm.

Application of principle insures right administration. Neglect of principle can cause wrong administration. We cannot suppose that the difference between right and wrong administration is without a serious effect upon the results of enterprise.

In brief, the price of neglect of organization is wasted effort and faulty administration. With all the unearned increments of intuition and luck, the price is still high.

The Hope of Organization

I am afraid the improvement of organization rests on dead center. Neglected as a function by industrial enterprise, literature and the schools ignore it as a subject. Ignored as a subject by literature and the schools, industrial enterprise neglects it as a function.

One who is persuaded of the importance of organization can only hope that somewhere, somehow, this deadlock will be broken. His most reasonable hope ought to rest upon the students in business schools, for they are the industrial managers of tomorrow. Were they aware of organization as an industrial factor, one could hope for the best. But how can we hope when they are encouraged to believe that it is only an episode in management? A rich variety of courses beckons them during their period of schooling. They see the spotlight on labor problems, on personnel administration, on job analysis, on office methods, on production layout, on work simplification, on many another special department of industrial knowledge. But organization is disguised as an addendum to management. In this obscurity, what reason have they to suppose that organization is worth a special thought?

These claims for organization are modest. There is no need to ask any pre-eminence for it. There is no need to puff it up above other subjects. All it needs is to *be* a subject. All it needs is to be recognized, studied, taught, and practiced *as* a subject. All it needs is to be allowed to come of age; to be cut loose from the apron strings of management.

My hope, in other words, is to see more written about organization as such. My hope is to see an end to the loose use of the name and the loose concept of the subject. My hope is to see someone fill that grievous gap in the encyclopedia — and, for that matter, to fill the management gap as well. My hope is to see schools teach organization — as such. When these things come, we may reasonably hope that industrial enterprise will see organization as a function.

When these things do come, industrial enterprise will be the better for them.

12

Organization Theory:
An Overview and an Appraisal*

William G. Scott

DePaul University

Organization is treated as a logical evolution in management thought. Classical, neo-classical and modern theories are described and related to the emerging theory of management. This framework makes possible not only a comparative treatment, but also a substantial analysis of the present state of theoretical development in organization theory. The author asserts that modern organization theory is contributing to the advancement of knowledge, but that it needs a framework and a basis for integrating concepts into a common perception of organization.

Man is intent on drawing himself into a web of collectivized patterns. "Modern man has learned to accommodate himself to a world increasingly organized. The trend toward ever more explicit and consciously drawn relationships is profound and sweeping; it is marked by depth no less than by extension."[1] This comment by Seidenberg nicely summarizes the pervasive influence of organization in many forms of human activity.

Some of the reasons for intense organizational activity are found in the fundamental transitions which revolutionized our society, changing it from a rural culture, to a culture based on technology, industry, and the city. From these changes, a way of life emerged characterized by the *proximity* and *dependency* of people on each other. Proximity and dependency, as conditions of social life, harbor the threats of human conflict, capricious antisocial behavior, instability of human relationships, and

---

* Taken and adapted from *The Journal of the Academy of Management*, vol. 4, no. 1, April, 1961, pp. 7–26.
[1] Roderick Seidenberg, *Post Historic Man* (Boston: Beacon Press, 1951), p. 1.

uncertainty about the nature of the social structure with its concomitant roles.

Of course, these threats to social integrity are present to some degree in all societies, ranging from the primitive to the modern. But, these threats become dangerous when the harmonious functioning of a society rests on the maintenance of a highly intricate, delicately balanced form of human collaboration. The civilization we have created depends on the preservation of a precarious balance. Hence, disrupting forces impinging on this shaky form of collaboration must be eliminated or minimized.

Traditionally, organization is viewed as a vehicle for accomplishing goals and objectives. While this approach is useful, it tends to obscure the inner workings and internal purposes of organization itself. Another fruitful way of treating organization is as a mechanism having the ultimate purpose of offsetting those forces which undermine human collaboration. In this sense, organization tends to minimize conflict, and to lessen the significance of individual behavior which deviates from values that the organization has established as worthwhile. Further, organization increases stability in human relationships by reducing uncertainty regarding the nature of the system's structure and the human roles which are inherent to it. Corollary to this point, organization enhances the predictability of human action, because it limits the number of behavioral alternatives available to an individual. As Presthus points out:

> Organization is defined as a system of structural interpersonal relations . . . individuals are differentiated in terms of authority, status, and role with the result that personal interaction is prescribed. . . . Anticipated reactions tend to occur, while ambiguity and spontaneity are decreased.[2]

In addition to all of this, organization has built-in safeguards. Besides prescribing acceptable forms of behavior for those who elect to submit to it, organization is also able to counterbalance the influence of human action which transcends its established patterns.[3]

Few segments of society have engaged in organizing more intensively than business.[4] The reason is clear. Business depends on what organization

---

[2] Robert V. Presthus, "Toward a Theory of Organizational Behavior," *Administrative Science Quarterly*, June, 1958, p. 50.

[3] Regulation and predictability of human behavior are matters of degree varying with different organizations on something of a continuum. At one extreme are bureaucratic type organizations with tight bonds of regulation. At the other extreme are voluntary associations, and informal organizations with relatively loose bonds of regulation.

This point has an interesting sidelight. A bureaucracy with tight controls and a high degree of predictability of human action appears to be unable to distinguish between destructive and creative deviations from established values. Thus the only thing which is safeguarded is the *status quo*.

[4] The monolithic institutions of the military and government are other cases of organizational preoccupation.

offers. Business needs a system of relationships among functions; it needs stability, continuity, and predictability in its internal activities and external contacts. Business also appears to need harmonious relationships among the people and processes which make it up. Put another way, a business organization has to be free, relatively, from destructive tendencies which may be caused by divergent interests.

As a foundation for meeting these needs rests administrative science. A major element of this science is organization theory, which provides the grounds for management activities in a number of significant areas of business endeavor. Organization theory, however, is not a homogeneous science based on generally accepted principles. Various theories of organization have been, and are being evolved. For example, something called "modern organization theory" has recently emerged, raising the wrath of some traditionalists, but also capturing the imagination of a rather elite *avant-garde*.

The thesis of this paper is that modern organization theory, when stripped of its irrelevancies, redundancies, and "speech defects," is a logical and vital evolution in management thought. In order for this thesis to be supported, the reader must endure a review and appraisal of more traditional forms of organization theory which may seem elementary to him.

In any event, three theories of organization are having considerable influence on management thought and practice. They are arbitrarily labeled in this paper as the classical, the neo-classical, and the modern. Each of these is fairly distinct; but they are not unrelated. Also, these theories are on-going, being actively supported by several schools of management thought.

The Classical Doctrine

For lack of a better method of identification, it will be said that the classical doctrine deals almost exclusively with the *anatomy of formal organization*. This doctrine can be traced back to Frederick W. Taylor's interest in functional foremanship and planning staffs. But most students of management thoughts would agree that in the United States, the first systematic approach to organization, and the first comprehensive attempt to find organizational universals, is dated 1931 when Mooney and Reiley published *Onward Industry*.[5] Subsequently, numerous books, following the classical vein, have appeared. Two of the more recent are Brech's, *Organization*[6] and Allen's, *Management and Organization*.[7]

[5] James D. Mooney and Alan C. Reiley, *Onward Industry* (New York: Harper and Brothers, 1931). Later published by James D. Mooney under the title *Principles of Organization*.

[6] E. F. L. Brech, *Organization* (London: Longmans, Green and Company, 1957).

[7] Louis A. Allen, *Management and Organization* (New York: McGraw-Hill Book Company, 1958).

Classical organization theory is built around four key pillars. They are the division of labor, the scalar and functional processes, structure, and span of control. Given these major elements just about all of classical organization theory can be derived.

(1) *The division of labor* is without doubt the cornerstone among the four elements.[8] From it the other elements flow as corollaries. For example, *scalar* and *functional* growth requires specialization and departmentalization of functions. Organization *structure* is naturally dependent upon the direction which specialization of activities travels in company development. Finally, *span of control* problems result from the number of specialized functions under the jurisdiction of a manager.

(2) *The scalar and functional processes* deal with the vertical and horizontal growth of the organization, respectively.[9] The scalar process refers to the growth of the chain of command, the delegation of authority and responsibility, unity of command, and the obligation to report.

The division of the organization into specialized parts and the regrouping of the parts into compatible units are matters pertaining to the functional process. This process focuses on the horizontal evolution of the line and staff in a formal organization.

(3) *Structure* is the logical relationships of functions in an organization, arranged to accomplish the objectives of the company efficiently. Structure implies system and pattern. Classical organization theory usually works with two basic structures, the line and the staff. However, such activities as committee and liaison functions fall quite readily into the purview of structural considerations. Again, structure is the vehicle for introducing logical and consistent relationships among the diverse functions which comprise the organization.[10]

(4) *The span of control* concept relates to the number of subordinates a manager can effectively supervise. Graicunas has been credited with first elaborating the point that there are numerical limitations to the subordinates one man can control.[11] In a recent statement on the subject, Brech points out, "span" refers to ". . . the number of persons, themselves carrying managerial and supervisory responsibilities, for whom the senior manager retains his over-embracing responsibility of direction and planning,

---

[8] Usually the division of labor is treated under a topical heading of departmentation, see for example: Harold Koontz and Cyril O'Donnell, *Principles of Management* (New York: McGraw-Hill Book Company, 1959), Chapter 7.

[9] These processes are discussed at length in Ralph Currier Davis, *The Fundamentals of Top Management* (New York: Harper and Brothers, 1951), Chapter 7.

[10] For a discussion of structure see: William H. Newman, *Administrative Action* (Englewood Cliffs: Prentice-Hall, Incorporated, 1951), Chapter 16.

[11] V. A. Graicunas, "Relationships in Organization," *Papers on the Science of Administration* (New York: Columbia University, 1937).

co-ordination, motivation, and control."[12] Regardless of interpretation, span of control has significance, in part, for the shape of the organization which evolves through growth. Wide span yields a flat structure; short span results in a tall structure. Further, the span concept directs attention to the complexity of human and functional interrelationships in an organzation.

It would not be fair to say that the classical school is unaware of the day-to-day administrative problems of the organization. Paramount among these problems are those stemming from human interactions. But the interplay of individual personality, informal groups, intraorganizational conflict, and the decision-making processes in the formal structure appears largely to be neglected by classical organization theory. Additionally, the classical theory overlooks the contributions of the behavioral sciences by failing to incorporate them in its doctrine in any systematic way. In summary, classical organization theory has relevant insights into the nature of organization, but the value of this theory is limited by its narrow concentration on the formal anatomy of organization.

Neoclassical Theory of Organization

The neoclassical theory of organization embarked on the task of compensating for some of the deficiencies in classical doctrine. The neoclassical school is commonly identified with the human relations movement. Generally, the neoclassical approach takes the postulates of the classical school, regarding the pillars of organization as givens. But these postulates are regarded as modified by people, acting independently or within the context of the informal organization.

One of the main contributions of the neoclassical school is the introduction of behavioral sciences in an integrated fashion into the theory of organization. Through the use of these sciences, the human relationists demonstrate how the pillars of the classical doctrine are affected by the impact of human actions. Further, the neoclassical approach includes a systematic treatment of the informal organization, showing its influence on the formal structure.

Thus the neoclassical approach to organization theory gives evidence of accepting classical doctrine, but superimposing on it modifications resulting from individual behavior, and the influence of the informal group. The inspiration of the neoclassical school were the Hawthorne studies.[13] Current examples of the neoclassical approach are found in human rela-

[12] Brech, *op. cit.*, p. 78.
[13] See: F. J. Roethlisberger and William J. Dickson, *Management and the Worker* (Cambridge: Harvard University Press, 1939).

tions books like Gardner and Moore, *Human Relations in Industry*,[14] and Davis, *Human Relations in Business*.[15] To a more limited extent, work in industrial sociology also reflects a neoclassical point of view.[16]

It would be useful to look briefly at some of the contributions made to organization theory by the neoclassicists. First to be considered are modifications of the pillars of classical doctrine; second is the informal organization.

Examples of the Neoclassical Approach to the Pillars of Formal Organization Theory

(1) The *division of labor* has been a long standing subject of comment in the field of human relations. Very early in the history of industrial psychology study was made of industrial fatigue and monotony caused by the specialization of the work.[17] Later, attention shifted to the isolation of the worker, and his feeling of anonymity resulting from insignificant jobs which contributed negligibly to the final product.[18]

Also, specialization influences the work of management. As an organization expands, the need concomitantly arises for managerial motivation and coordination of the activities of others. Both motivation and coordination in turn relate to executive leadership. Thus, in part, stemming from the growth of industrial specialization, the neoclassical school has developed a large body of theory relating to motivation, coordination, and leadership. Much of this theory is derived from the social sciences.

(2) Two aspects of the *scalar and functional* processes which have been treated with some degree of intensity by the neoclassical school are the delegation of authority and responsibility, and gaps in or overlapping of functional jurisdictions. The classical theory assumes something of perfection in the delegation and functionalization processes. The neoclassical school points out that human problems are caused by imperfections in the way these processes are handled.

For example, too much or insufficient delegation may render an executive incapable of action. The failure to delegate authority and responsibility equally may result in frustration for the delegatee. Overlapping of authorities often causes clashes in personality. Gaps in authority cause

[14] Burleigh B. Gardner and David G. Moore, *Human Relations in Industry* (Homewood: Richard D. Irwin, 1955).

[15] Keith Davis, *Human Relations in Business* (New York: McGraw-Hill Book Company, 1957).

[16] For example see: Delbert C. Miller and William H. Form, *Industrial Sociology* (New York: Harper and Brothers, 1951).

[17] See: Hugo Munsterberg, *Psychology and Industrial Efficiency* (Boston: Houghton Mifflin Company, 1913).

[18] Probably the classic work is: Elton Mayo, *The Human Problems of an Industrial Civilization* (Cambridge: Harvard University, 1946, first printed 1933).

failures in getting jobs done, with one party blaming the other for short-comings in performance.[19]

The neoclassical school says that the scalar and functional processes are theoretically valid, but tend to deteriorate in practice. The ways in which they break down are described, and some of the human causes are pointed out. In addition the neoclassicists make recommendations, suggesting various "human tools" which will facilitate the operation of these processes.

(3) *Structure* provides endless avenues of analysis for the neoclassical theory of organization. The theme is that human behavior disrupts the best laid organizational plans, and thwarts the cleanness of the logical relationships founded in the structure. The neoclassical critique of structure centers on frictions which appear internally among people performing different functions.

Line and staff relations is a problem area, much discussed, in this respect. Many companies seem to have difficulty keeping the line and staff working together harmoniously. Both Dalton[20] and Juran[21] have engaged in research to discover the causes of friction, and to suggest remedies.

Of course, line-staff relations represent only one of the many problems of structural frictions described by the neoclassicists. As often as not, the neoclassicists will offer prescriptions for the elimination of conflict in structure. Among the more important harmony-rendering formulae are participation, junior boards, bottom-up management, joint committees, recognition of human dignity, and "better" communication.

(4) An executive's *span of control* is a function of human determinants, and the reduction of span to a precise, universally applicable ratio is silly, according to the neoclassicists. Some of the determinants of span are individual differences in managerial abilities, the type of people and functions supervised, and the extent of communication effectiveness.

Coupled with the span of control question are the human implications of the type of structure which emerges. That is, is a tall structure with a short span or a flat structure with a wide span more conducive to good human relations and high morale? The answer is situational. Short span results in tight supervision; wide span requires a good deal of delegation with looser controls. Because of individual and organizational differences, sometimes one is better than the other. There is a tendency to favor the looser form of organization, however, for the reason that tall structures

[19] For further discussion of the human relations implications of the scalar and functional processes see: Keith Davis, *op. cit.*, pp. 60–66.

[20] Melville Dalton, "Conflicts between Staff and Line Managerial Officers," *American Sociological Review*, June, 1950, pp. 342–351.

[21] J. M. Juran, "Improving the Relationship between Staff and Line," *Personnel*, May, 1956, pp. 515–524.

breed autocratic leadership, which is often pointed out as a cause of low morale.[22]

The Neoclassical View of the Informal Organization

Nothing more than the barest mention of the informal organization is given even in the most recent classical treatises on organization theory.[23] Systematic discussion of this form of organization has been left to the neoclassicists. The informal organization refers to people in group associations at work, but these associations are not specified in the "blueprint" of the formal organization. The informal organization means natural groupings of people in the work situation.

In a general way, the informal organization appears in response to the social need — the need of people to associate with others. However, for analytical purposes, this explanation is not particularly satisfying. Research has produced the following, more specific determinants underlying the appearance of informal organizations.

(1) The *location* determinant simply states that in order to form into groups of any lasting nature, people have to have frequent face-to-face contact. Thus, the geography of physical location in a plant or office is an important factor in predicting who will be in what group.[24]

(2) *Occupation* is a key factor determining the rise and composition of informal groups. There is a tendency for people performing similar jobs to group together.[25]

(3) *Interests* are another determinant for informal group formation. Even though people might be in the same location, performing similar jobs, differences of interest among them explain why several small, instead of one large, informal organizations emerge.

(4) *Special issues* often result in the formation of informal groups, but this determinant is set apart from the three previously mentioned. In this case, people who do not necessarily have similar interests, occupations, or locations may join together for a common cause. Once the issue is resolved, then the tendency is to revert to the more "natural" group forms.[26] Thus, special issues give rise to a rather impermanent informal association; groups based on the other three determinants tend to be more lasting.

---

[22] Gardner and Moore, *op. cit.*, pp. 237–243.

[23] For example: Brech, *op. cit.*, pp. 27–29; and Allen, *op. cit.*, pp. 61–62.

[24] See: Leon Festinger, Stanley Schachter, and Kurt Back, *Social Pressures in Informal Groups* (New York: Harper and Brothers, 1950), pp. 153–163.

[25] For example see: W. Fred Cottrell, *The Railroader* (Palo Alto: The Stanford University Press, 1940), Chapter 3.

[26] Except in cases where the existence of an organization is necessary for the continued maintenance of employee interest. Under these conditions the previously informal association may emerge as a formal group, such as a union.

When informal organizations come into being they assume certain characteristics. Since understanding these characteristics is important for management practice, they are noted below:

(1) Informal organizations act as agencies of *social control*. They generate a culture based on certain norms of conduct which, in turn, demands conformity from group members. These standards may be at odds with the values set by the formal organization. So an individual may very well find himself in a situation of conflicting demands.

(2) The form of human interrelationships in the informal organization requires *techniques of analysis* different from those used to plot the relationships of people in a formal organization. The method used for determining the structure of the informal group is called sociometric analysis. Sociometry reveals the complex structure of interpersonal relations which is based on premises fundamentally unlike the logic of the formal organization.

(3) Informal organizations have *status and communication* systems peculiar to themselves, not necessarily derived from the formal systems. For example, the grapevine is the subject of much neoclassical study.

(4) Survival of the informal organization requires stable continuing relationships among the people in them. Thus, it has been observed that the informal organization *resists change*.[27] Considerable attention is given by the neoclassicists to overcoming informal resistance to change.

(5) The last aspect of analysis which appears to be central to the neoclassical view of the informal organization is the study of the *informal leader*. Discussion revolves around who the informal leader is, how he assumes this role, what characteristics are peculiar to him, and how he can help the manager accomplish his objectives in the formal organization.[28]

This brief sketch of some of the major facets of informal organization theory has neglected, so far, one important topic treated by the neoclassical school. It is the way in which the formal and informal organizations interact.

A conventional way of looking at the interaction of the two is the "live and let live" point of view. Management should recognize that the informal organization exists, nothing can destroy it, and so the executive might just as well work with it. Working with the informal organization involves not threatening its existence unnecessarily, listening to opinions expressed for the group by the leader, allowing group participation in deci-

[27] Probably the classic study of resistance to change is: Lester Coch and John R. P. French, Jr., "Overcoming Resistance to Change," in Schuyler Dean Hoslett (editor) *Human Factors in Management* (New York: Harper and Brothers, 1951), pp. 242–268.

[28] For example see: Robert Saltonstall, *Human Relations in Administration* (New York: McGraw-Hill Book Company, 1959), pp. 330–331; and Keith Davis, *op. cit.*, pp. 99–101.

sion-making situations, and controlling the grapevine by prompt release of accurate information.[29]

While this approach is management centered, it is not unreasonable to expect that informal group standards and norms could make themselves felt on formal organizational policy. An honestly conceived effort by managers to establish a working relationship with the informal organization could result in an association where both formal and informal views would be reciprocally modified. The danger which at all costs should be avoided is that "working with the informal organization" does not degenerate into a shallow disguise for human manipulation.

Some neoclassical writing in organization theory, especially that coming from the management-oriented segment of this school, gives the impression that the formal and informal organizations are distinct, and at times, quite irreconcilable factors in a company. The interaction which takes place between the two is something akin to the interaction between the company and a labor union, or a government agency, or another company.

The concept of the social system is another approach to the interactional climate. While this concept can be properly classified as neoclassical, it borders on the modern theories of organization. The phrase "social system" means than an organization is a complex of mutually interdepedent, but variable, factors.

These factors include individuals and their attitudes and motives, jobs, the physical work setting, the formal organization, and the informal organizations. These factors, and many others, are woven into an overall pattern of interdependency. From this point of view, the formal and informal organizations lose their distinctiveness, but find real meaning, in terms of human behavior, in the operation of the system as a whole. Thus, the study of organization turns away from descriptions of its component parts, and is refocused on the system of interrelationships among the parts.

One of the major contributions of the Hawthorne studies was the integration of Pareto's idea of the social system into a meaningful method of analysis for the study of behavior in human organizations.[30] This concept is still vitally important. But unfortunately some work in the field of human relations undertaken by the neoclassicists has overlooked, or perhaps discounted, the significance of this consideration.[31]

The fundamental insight regarding the social system, developed and applied to the industrial scene by the Hawthorne researchers, did not find

---

[29] For an example of this approach see: John T. Doutt, "Management Must Manage the Informal Group, Too," *Advanced Management*, May, 1959, pp. 26–28.

[30] See: Roethlisberger and Dickson, *op. cit.*, Chapter 24.

[31] A check of management human relations texts, the organization and human relations chapters of principles of management texts, and texts on conventional organization theory for management courses reveals little or no treatment of the concept of the social system.

much extension in subsequent work in the neoclassical vein. Indeed, the neoclassical school after the Hawthorne studies generally seemed content to engage in descriptive generalizations, or particularized empirical research studies which did not have much meaning outside their own context.

The neoclassical school of organization theory has been called bankrupt. Criticisms range from, "human relations is a tool for cynical puppeteering of people," to "human relations is nothing more than a trifling body of empirical and descriptive information." There is a good deal of truth in both criticisms, but another appraisal of the neoclassical school of organization theory is offered here. The neoclassical approach has provided valuable contributions to lore of organization. But, like the classical theory, the neoclassical doctrine suffers from incompleteness, a shortsighted perspective, and lack of integration among the many facets of human behavior studied by it. Modern organization theory has made a move to cover the shortcomings of the current body of theoretical knowledge.

Modern Organization Theory

The distinctive qualities of modern organization theory are its conceptual-analytical base, its reliance on empirical research data and, above all, its integrating nature. These qualities are framed in a philosophy which accepts the premise that the only meaningful way to study organization is to study it as a system. As Henderson put it, the study of a system must rely on a method of analysis, ". . . involving the simultaneous variations of mutually dependent variables."[32] Human systems, of course, contain a huge number of dependent variables which defy the most complex simultaneous equations to solve.

Nevertheless, system analysis has its own peculiar point of view which aims to study organization in the way Henderson suggests. It treats organization as a system of mutually dependent variables. As a result, modern organization theory, which accepts system analysis, shifts the conceptual level of organization study above the classical and neoclassical theories. Modern organization theory asks a range of interrelated questions which are not seriously considered by the two other theories.

Key among these questions are: (1) What are the strategic parts of the system? (2) What is the nature of their mutual dependency? (3) What are the main processes in the system which link the parts together, and facilitate their adjustment to each other? (4) What are the goals sought by systems?[33]

[32] Lawrence J. Henderson, *Pareto's General Sociology* (Cambridge: Harvard University Press, 1935), p. 13.

[33] There is another question which cannot be treated in the scope of this paper. It asks, what research tools should be used for the study of the system?

Modern organization theory is in no way a unified body of thought. Each writer and researcher has his special emphasis when he considers the system. Perhaps the most evident unifying thread in the study of systems is the effort to look at the organization in its totality. Representative books in this field are March and Simon, *Organizations*,[34] and Haire's anthology, *Modern Organization Theory*.[35]

Instead of attempting a review of different writers' contributions to modern organization theory, it will be more useful to discuss the various ingredients involved in system analysis. They are the parts, the interactions, the processes, and the goals of systems.

The Parts of the System and Their Interdependency

The first basic part of the system is the *individual*, and the personality structure he brings to the organization. Elementary to an individual's personality are motives and attitudes which condition the range of expectancies he hopes to satisfy by participating in the system.

The second part of the system is the formal arrangement of functions, usually called the *formal organization*. The formal organization is the interrelated pattern of jobs which make up the structure of a system. Certain writers, like Argyris, see a fundamental conflict resulting from the demands made by the system, and the structure of the mature, normal personality. In any event, the individual has expectancies regarding the job he is to perform; and, conversely, the job makes demands on, or has expectancies relating to, the performance of the individual. Considerable attention has been given by writers in modern organization theory to incongruencies resulting from the interaction of organizational and individual demands.[36]

The third part in the organization system is the *informal organization*. Enough has been said already about the nature of this organization. But it must be noted that an interactional pattern exists between the individual and the informal group. This interactional arrangement can be conveniently discussed as the mutual modification of expectancies. The informal organization has demands which it makes on members in terms of anticipated forms of behavior, and the individual has expectancies of satisfaction he hopes to derive from association with people on the job. Both these sets of expectancies interact, resulting in the individual modifying his behavior to accord with the demands of the group, and the group, perhaps,

[34] James G. March and Herbert A. Simon, *Organizations* (New York: John Wiley and Sons, 1958).

[35] Mason Haire, (editor) *Modern Organization Theory* (New York: John Wiley and Sons, 1959).

[36] See Chris Argyris, *Personality and Organization* (New York: Harper and Brothers, 1957), esp. Chapters 2, 3, 7.

modifying what it expects from an individual because of the impact of his personality on group norms.[37]

Much of what has been said about the various expectancy systems in an organization can also be treated using status and role concepts. Part of modern organization theory rests on research findings in social psychology relative to reciprocal patterns of behavior stemming from role demands generated by both the formal and informal organizations, and role perceptions peculiar to the individual. Bakke's *fusion process* is largely concerned with the modification of role expectancies. The fusion process is a force, according to Bakke, which acts to weld divergent elements together for the preservation of organizational integrity.[38]

The fifth part of system analysis is the *physical setting* in which the job is performed. Although this element of the system may be implicit in what has been said already about the formal organization and its functions, it is well to separate it. In the physical surroundings of work, interactions are present in complex man-machine systems. The "human engineer" cannot approach the problems posed by such interrelationships in a purely technical, engineering fashion. As Haire says, these problems lie in the domain of the social theorist.[39] Attention must be centered on responses demanded from a logically ordered production function, often with the view of minimizing the error in the system. From this standpoint, work cannot be effectively organized unless the psychological, social, and physiological characteristics of people participating in the work environment are considered. Machines and processes should be designed to fit certain generally observed psychological and physiological properties of men, rather than hiring men to fit machines.

In summary, the parts of the system which appear to be of strategic importance are the individual, the formal structure, the informal organization, status and role patterns, and the physical environment of work. Again, these parts are woven into a configuration called the organizational system. The processes which link the parts are taken up next.

The Linking Processes

One can say, with a good deal of glibness, that all the parts mentioned above are interrelated. Although this observation is quite correct, it does not mean too much in terms of system theory unless some attempt is made

[37] For a larger treatment of this subject see: George C. Homans, *The Human Group* (New York: Harcourt, Brace and Company, 1950), Chapter 5.

[38] E. Wight Bakke, "Concept of the Social Organization," in *Modern Organization Theory, op. cit.,* pp. 60–61.

[39] Mason Haire, "Psychology and the Study of Business: Joint Behavioral Sciences," in *Social Science Research on Business: Product and Potential* (New York: Columbia University Press, 1959), pp. 53–59.

to analyze the processes by which the interaction is achieved. Role theory is devoted to certain types of interactional processes. In addition, modern organization theorists point to three other linking activities which appear to be universal to human systems of organized behavior. These processes are communication, balance, and decision making.

(1) Communication is mentioned often in neoclassical theory, but the emphasis is on description of forms of communication activity, i.e., formal-informal, vertical-horizontal, line-staff. Communication, as a mechanism which links the segments of the system together, is overlooked by way of much considered analysis.

One aspect of modern organization theory is study of the communication network in the system. Communication is viewed as the method by which action is evoked from the parts of the system. Communication acts not only as stimuli resulting in action, but also as a control and coordination mechanism linking the decision centers in the system into a synchronized pattern. Deutsch points out that organizations are composed of parts which communicate with each other, receive messages from the outside world, and store information. Taken together, these communication functions of the parts comprise a configuration representing the total system.[40] More is to be said about communication later in the discussion of the cybernetic model.

(2) The concept of *balance* as a linking process involves a series of some rather complex ideas. Balance refers to an equilibrating mechanism whereby the various parts of the system are maintained in a harmoniously structured relationship to each other.

The necessity for the balance concept logically flows from the nature of systems themselves. It is impossible to conceive of an ordered relationship among the parts of a system without also introducing the idea of a stabilizing or an adapting mechanism.

Balance appears in two varieties — quasi-automatic and innovative. Both forms of balance act to insure system integrity in face of changing conditions, either internal or external to the system. The first form of balance, quasi-automatic, refers to what some think are "homeostatic" properties of systems. That is, systems seem to exhibit built-in propensities to maintain steady states.

If human organizations are open, self-maintaining systems, then control and regulatory processes are necessary. The issue hinges on the degree to which stabilizing processes in systems, when adapting to change, are automatic. March and Simon have an interesting answer to this problem, which in part is based on the type of change and the adjustment necessary to adapt to the change. Systems have programs of action which are put

[40] Karl W. Deutsch "On Communication Models in the Social Sciences," *Public Opinion Quarterly*, 16 (1952), pp. 356–380.

into effect when a change is perceived. If the change is relatively minor, and if the change comes within the purview of established programs of action, then it might be fairly confidently predicted that the adaptation made by the system will be quasi-automatic.[41]

The role of innovative, creative balancing efforts now needs to be examined. The need for innovation arises when adaptation to a change is outside the scope of existing programs designed for the purpose of keeping the system in balance. New programs have to be evolved in order for the system to maintain internal harmony.

New programs are created by trial and error search for feasible action alternatives to cope with a given change. But innovation is subject to the limitations and possibilities inherent in the quantity and variety of information present in a system at a particular time. New combinations of alternatives for innovative purposes depend on:

(a) the possible range of output of the system, or the capacity of the system to supply information.

(b) the range of available information in the memory of the system.

(c) the operating rules (program) governing the analysis and flow of information within the system.

(d) the ability of the system to "forget" previously learned solutions to change problems.[42] A system with too good a memory might narrow its behavioral choices to such an extent as to stifle innovation. In simpler language, old learned programs might be used to adapt to change, when newly innovated programs are necessary.[43]

Much of what has been said about communication and balance brings to mind a cybernetic model in which both these processes have vital roles. Cybernetics has to do with feedback and control in all kinds of systems. Its purpose is to maintain system stability in the face of change. Cybernetics cannot be studied without considering communication networks, information flow, and some kind of balancing process aimed at preserving the integrity of the system.

Cybernetics directs attention to key questions regarding the system. These questions are: How are communication centers connected, and how are they maintained? Corollary to this question: what is the structure of the feedback system? Next, what information is stored in the organization, and at what points? And as a corollary: how accessible is this information to decision-making centers? Third, how conscious is the organization of the operation of its own parts? That is, to what extent do the policy centers receive control information with sufficient frequency and relevancy

---

[41] March and Simon, *op. cit.*, pp. 139–140.

[42] Mervyn L. Cadwallader "The Cybernetic Analysis of Change in Complex Social Organization," *The American Journal of Sociology*, September, 1959, p. 156.

[43] It is conceivable for innovative behavior to be programmed into the system.

to create a real awareness of the operation of the segments of the system? Finally, what are the learning (innovating) capabilities of the system?[44]

Answers to the questions posed by cybernetics are crucial to understanding both the balancing and communication processes in systems.[45] Although cybernetics has been applied largely to technical-engineering problems of automation, the model of feedback, control, and regulation in all systems has a good deal of generality. Cybernetics is a fruitful area which can be used to synthesize the processes of communication and balance.

(3) A wide spectrum of topics dealing with types of decisions in human systems makes up the core of analysis of another important process in organizations. Decision analysis is one of the major contributions of March and Simon in their book *Organizations*. The two major classes of decisions they discuss are decisions to produce and decisions to participate in the system.[46]

Decisions to produce are largely a result of an interaction between individual attitudes and the demands of organization. Motivation analysis becomes central to studying the nature and results of the interaction. Individual decisions to participate in the organization reflect on such issues as the relationship between organizational rewards versus the demands made by the organization. Participation decisions also focus attention on the reasons why individuals remain in or leave organizations.

March and Simon treat decisions as internal variables in an organization which depend on jobs individual expectations and motivations, and organizational structure. Marschak[47] looks on the decision process as an independent variable upon which the survival of the organization is based. In this case, the organization is viewed as having, inherent in its structure, the ability to maximize survival requisites through its established decision processes.

The Goals of Organization

Organization has three goals which may be either intermeshed or independent ends in themselves. They are growth, stability, and interaction. The last goal refers to organizations which exist primarily to provide a medium for association of its members with others. Interestingly enough

---

[44] These are questions adapted from Deutsch, *op. cit.*, 368–370.

[45] Answers to these questions would require a comprehensive volume. One of the best approaches currently available is Stafford Beer, *Cybernetics and Management* (New York: John Wiley and Sons, 1959).

[46] March and Simon, *op. cit.*, Chapters 3 and 4.

[47] Jacob Marschak, "Efficient and Viable Organizational Forms" in *Modern Organization Theory*, Mason Haire, editor, (New York: John Wiley and Sons, 1959), pp. 307–320.

these goals seem to apply to different forms of organization at varying levels of complexity, ranging from simple clockwork mechanisms to social systems.

These similarities in organizational purposes have been observed by a number of people, and a field of thought and research called general system theory has developed, dedicated to the task of discovering organizationed universals. The dream of general system theory is to create a science of organizational universals, or if you will, a universal science using common organizational elements found in all systems as a starting point.

Modern organization theory is on the periphery of general system theory. Both general system theory and modern organization theory study:

(1) the parts (individuals) in aggregates, and the movement of individuals into and out of the system.

(2) the interaction of individuals with the environment found in the system.

(3) the interactions among individuals in the system.

(4) general growth and stability problems of systems.[48]

Modern organization theory and general system theory are similar in that they look at organization as an integrated whole. They differ, however, in terms of their generality. General system theory is concerned with every level of system, whereas modern organizational theory focuses primarily on human organization.

The question might be asked, what can the science of administration gain by the study of system levels other than human? Before attempting an answer, note should be made of what these other levels are. Boulding presents a convenient method of classification:

(1) The static structure — a level of framework, the anatomy of a system; for example, the structure of the universe.

(2) The simple dynamic system — the level of clockworks, predetermined necessary motions.

(3) The cybernetic system — the level of the thermostat, the system moves to maintain a given equilibrium through a process of self-regulation.

(4) The open system — level of self-maintaining systems, moves toward and includes living organisms.

(5) The genetic-societal system — level of cell society, characterized by a division of labor among cells.

(6) Animal systems — level of mobility, evidence of goal-directed behavior.

(7) Human systems — level of symbol interpretation and idea communication.

(8) Social system — level of human organization.

[48] Kenneth E. Boulding, "General System Theory — The Skeleton of a Science," *Management Science*, April, 1956, pp. 200–202.

(9) Transcendental systems — level of ultimates and absolutes which exhibit systematic structure but are unknowable in essence.[49]

This approach to the study of systems by finding universals common at all levels of organization offers intriguing possibilities for administrative organization theory. A good deal of light could be thrown on social systems if structurally analogous elements could be found in the simpler types of systems. For example, cybernetic systems have characteristics which seem to be similar to feedback, regulation, and control phenomena in human organizations. Thus, certain facets of cybernetic models could be generalized to human organization. Considerable danger, however, lies in poorly founded analogies. Superficial similarities between simpler system forms and social systems are apparent everywhere. Instinctually based ant societies, for example, do not yield particularly instructive lessons for understanding rationally conceived human organizations. Thus, care should be taken that analogies used to bridge system levels are not mere devices for literary enrichment. For analogies to have usefulness and validity, they must exhibit inherent structural similarities or implicitly identical operational principles.[50]

Modern organization theory leads, as it has been shown, almost inevitably into a discussion of general system theory. A science of organization universals has some strong advocates, particularly among biologists.[51] Organization theorists in administrative science cannot afford to overlook the contributions of general system theory. Indeed, modern organization concepts could offer a great deal to those working with general system theory. But the ideas dealt with in the general theory are exceedingly elusive.

Speaking of the concept of equilibrium as a unifying element in all systems, Easton says, "It (equilibrium) leaves the impression that we have a useful general theory when in fact, lacking measurability, it is a mere pretense for knowledge."[52] The inability to quantify and measure universal organization elements undermines the success of pragmatic tests to which general system theory might be put.

[49] *Ibid.*, pp. 202–205.

[50] Seidenberg, *op. cit.*, p. 136. The fruitful use of the type of analogies spoken of by Seidenberg is evident in the application of thermodynamic principles, particularly the entropy concept, to communication theory. See: Claude E. Shannon and Warren Weaver, *The Mathematical Theory of Communication*, (Urbana: The University of Illinois Press, 1949). Further, the existence of a complete analogy between the operational behavior of thermodynamic systems, electrical communication systems, and biological systems has been noted by: Y. S. Touloukian, *The Concept of Entropy in Communication, Living Organisms, and Thermodynamics*, Research Bulletin 130, Purdue Engineering Experiment Station.

[51] For example see: Ludwig von Bertalanffy, *Problem of Life* (London: Watts and Company, 1952).

[52] David Easton, "Limits of the Equilibrium Model in Social Research," in *Profits and Problems of Homeostatic Models in the Behavioral Sciences*, Publication 1, Chicago Behavioral Sciences, 1953, p. 39.

Organization Theory: Quo Vadis?

Most sciences have a vision of the universe to which they are applied, and administrative science is not an exception. This universe is composed of parts. One purpose of science is to synthesize the parts into an organized conception of its field of study. As a science matures, its theorems about the configuration of its universe change. The direction of change in three sciences, physics, economics, and sociology, are noted briefly for comparison with the development of an administrative view of human organization.

The first comprehensive and empirically verifiable outlook of the physical universe was presented by Newton in his *Principia*. Classical physics, founded on Newton's work, constitutes a grand scheme in which a wide range of physical phenomena could be organized and predicted. Newtonian physics may rightfully be regarded as "macro" in nature, because its system of organization was concerned largely with gross events of which the movement of celestial bodies, waves, energy forms, and strain are examples. For years classical physics was supreme, being applied continuously to smaller and smaller classes of phenomena in the physical universe. Physicists at one time adopted the view that everything in their realm could be discovered by simply subdividing problems. Physics thus moved into the "micro" order.

But in the nineteenth century a revolution took place motivated largely because events were being noted which could not be explained adequately by the conceptual framework supplied by the classical school. The consequences of this revolution are brilliantly described by Eddington:

> From the point of view of philosophy of science the conception associated with entropy must I think be ranked as the great contribution of the nineteenth century to scientific thought. It marked a reaction from the view that everything to which science need pay attention is discovered by microscopic dissection of objects. It provided an alternative standpoint in which the centre of interest is shifted from the entities reached by the customary analysis (atoms, electric potentials, etc.) to qualities possessed by the system as a whole, which cannot be split up and located — a little bit here, and a little bit there. . . .
>
> We often think that when we have completed our study of *one* we know all about *two*, because "two" is "one and one." We forget that we have still to make a study of "and." Secondary physics is the study of "and" — that is to say, of organization.[53]

Although modern physics often deals in minute quantities and oscillations, the conception of the physicist is on the "macro" scale. He is con-

[53] Sir Arthur Eddington, *The Nature of the Physical World* (Ann Arbor: The University of Michigan Press, 1958), pp. 103–104.

cerned with the "and," or the organization of the world in which the events occur. These developments did not invalidate classical physics as to its usefulness for explaining a certain range of phenomena. But classical physics is no longer the undisputed law of the universe. It is a special case.

Early economic theory, and Adam Smith's *Wealth of Nations* comes to mind, examined economic problems in the macro order. The *Wealth of Nations* is mainly concerned with matters of national income and welfare. Later, the economics of the firm, micro-economics, dominated the theoretical scene in this science. And, finally, with Keynes' *The General Theory of Employment Interest and Money*, a systematic approach to the economic universe was re-introduced on the macro level.

The first era of the developing science of sociology was occupied by the great social "system builders." Comte, the so-called father of sociology, had a macro view of society in that his chief works are devoted to social reorganization. Comte was concerned with the interrelationships among social, political, religious, and educational institutions. As sociology progressed, the science of society compressed. Emphasis shifted from the macro approach of the pioneers to detailed, empirical study of small social units. The compression of sociological analysis was accompanied by study of social pathology or disorganization.

In general, physics, economics, and sociology appear to have two things in common. First, they offered a macro point of view as their initial systematic comprehension of their area of study. Second, as the science developed, attention fragmented into analysis of the parts of the organization, rather than attending to the system as a whole. This is the micro phase.

In physics and economics, discontent was evidenced by some scientists at the continual atomization of the universe. The reaction to the micro approach was a new theory or theories dealing with the total system, on the macro level again. This third phase of scientific development seems to be more evident in physics and economics than in sociology.

The reason for the "macro-micro-macro" order of scientific progress lies, perhaps, in the hypothesis that usually the things which strike man first are of great magnitude. The scientist attempts to discover order in the vastness. But after macro laws or models of systems are postulated, variations appear which demand analysis, not so much in terms of the entire system, but more in terms of the specific parts which make it up. Then, intense study of microcosm may result in new general laws, replacing the old models of organization. Or, the old and the new models may stand together, each explaining a different class of phenomenon. Or, the old and the new concepts of organization may be welded to produce a single creative synthesis.

Now, what does all this have to do with the problem of organization in administrative science? Organization concepts seem to have gone through the same order of development in this field as in the three just mentioned. It is evident that the classical theory of organization, particularly as in the work of Mooney and Reiley, is concerned with principles common to all organizations. It is a macro-organizational view. The classical approach to organization, however, dealt with the gross anatomical parts and processes of the formal organization. Like classical physics, the classical theory of organization is a special case. Neither are especially well equipped to account for variation from their established framework.

Many variations in the classical administrative model result from human behavior. The only way these variations could be understood was by a microscopic examination of particularized, situational aspects of human behavior. The mission of the neoclassical school thus is "micro-analysis."

It was observed earlier, that somewhere along the line the concept of the social system, which is the key to understanding the Hawthorne studies, faded into the background. Maybe the idea is so obvious that it was lost to the view of researchers and writers in human relations. In any event, the press of research in the micro-cosmic universes of the informal organization, morale and productivity, leadership, participation, and the like forced the notion of the social system into limbo. Now, with the advent of modern organization theory, the social system has been resurrected.

Modern organization theory appears to be concerned with Eddington's "and." This school claims that its operational hypothesis is based on a macro point of view; that is, the study of organization as a whole. This nobility of purpose should not obscure, however, certain difficulties faced by this field as it is presently constituted. Modern organization theory raises two questions which should be explored further. First, would it not be more accurate to speak of modern organization theories? Second, just how much of modern organization theory is modern?

The first question can be answered with a quick affirmative. Aside from the notion of the system, there are few, if any, other ideas of a unifying nature. Except for several important exceptions,[54] modern organization theorists tend to pursue their pet points of view,[55] suggesting they are part of system theory, but not troubling to show by what mystical means they arrive at this conclusion.

The irony of it all is that a field dealing with systems has, indeed, little system. Modern organization theory needs a framework, and it needs an integration of issues into a common conception of organization. Admittedly, this is a large order. But it is curious not to find serious analytical treatment of subjects like cybernetics or general system theory in Haire's, *Modern Organizational Theory* which claims to be a representative example of work in this field. Beer has ample evidence in his book *Cyber-*

[54] For example: E. Wight Bakke, *op. cit.*, pp. 18–75.
[55] There is a large selection including decision theory, individual-organization interaction, motivation, vitality, stability, growth, and graph theory, to menton a few.

netics and Management that cybernetics, if imaginatively approached, provides a valuable conceptual base for the study of systems.

The second question suggests an ambiguous answer. Modern organization theory is in part a product of the past; system analysis is not a new idea. Further, modern organization theory relies for supporting data on microcosmic research studies, generally drawn from the journals of the last ten years. The newness of modern organization theory, perhaps, is its effort to synthesize recent research contributions of many fields into a system theory characterized by a reoriented conception of organization.

One might ask, but what is the modern theorist reorienting? A clue is found in the almost snobbish disdain assumed by some authors of the neo-classical human relations school, and particularly, the classical school. Re-evaluation of the classical school of organization is overdue. However, this does not mean that its contributions to organization theory are irrelevant and should be overlooked in the rush to get on the "behavioral science bandwagon."

Haire announces that the papers appearing in *Modern Organization Theory* constitute, "the ragged leading edge of a wave of theoretical development."[56] Ragged, yes; but leading no! The papers appearing in this book do not represent a theoretical breakthrough in the concept of organization. Haire's collection in an interesting potpourri with several contributions of considerable significance. But readers should beware that they will not find vastly new insights into organizational behavior in this book, if they have kept up with the literature of the social sciences, and have dabbled to some extent in the esoteria of biological theories of growth, information theory, and mathematical model building. For those who have not maintained the pace, *Modern Organization Theory* serves the admirable purpose of bringing them up-to-date on a rather diversified number of subjects.

Some work in modern organization theory is pioneering, making its appraisal difficult and future uncertain. While the direction of this endeavor is unclear, one thing is patently true. Human behavior in organizations, and indeed, organization itself, cannot be adequately understood within the ground rules of classical and neo-classical doctrines. Appreciation of human organization requires a *creative* synthesis of massive amounts of empirical data, a high order of deductive reasoning, imaginative research studies, and a taste for individual and social values. Accomplishment of all these objectives, and the inclusion of them into a framework of the concept of the system, appears to be the goal of modern organization theory. The vitality of administrative science rests on the advances modern theorists make along this line.

[56] Mason Haire, "General Issues," in Mason Haire (editor), *Modern Organization Theory, op. cit.,* p. 2.

Modern organization theory, 1960 style, is an amorphous aggregation of synthesizers and restaters, with a few extending leadership on the frontier. For the sake of these few, it is well to admonish that pouring old wine into new bottles may make the spirits cloudy. Unfortunately, modern organization theory has almost succeeded in achieving the status of a fad. Popularization and exploitation contributed to the disrepute into which human relations has fallen. It would be a great waste if modern organization theory yields to the same fate, particularly since both modern organization theory and human relations draw from the same promising source of inspiration — system analysis.

Modern organization theory needs tools of analysis and a conceptual framework uniquely its own, but it must also allow for the incorporation of relevant contributions of many fields. It may be that the framework will come from general system theory. New areas of research such as decision theory, information theory, and cybernetics also offer reasonable expectations of analytical and conceptual tools. Modern organization theory represents a frontier of research which has great significance for management. The potential is great, because it offers the opportunity for uniting what is valuable in classical theory with the social and natural sciences into a systematic and integrated conception of human organization.

13

Recent Breakthroughs in Methods of
Research on Organizations[*]

Albert H. Rubenstein

Northwestern University

Professor Rubenstein reaffirms a point made by Professor Scott in the preceding article, that advances in organization theory depend upon its success in developing new tools and equipment for research. Various tools have been widely used. Some, such as small group laboratories and field study methods, emerged from early human relations research. Mathematical models and computer methods are among the more recent ways of developing and testing theory. The author defines organization research as including any effort to understand the behavior of people in organizations. Many theorists prefer a narrower basis for defining organization, such as structural relationships.

Many of us maintain the image of the basic or pure researcher in science as the lone wolf who operates in the solitude of his one-man laboratory or at his desk. Paper and pencil or chalk are his main weapons against the unknown, in addition to his knowledge and reasoning power.

We have often tended to regard the equipment-filled large laboratory or the team of researchers milling around as characteristic of the more applied or less basic research effort.

While this image has never been completely accurate in the modern scientific era, it is becoming less and less accurate today in most fields of scientific research — physical, life, and behavioral. It is true that most of the important breakthroughs in scientific theory have been the result of the reasoning power or sudden insight of individuals. But it is also

[*] Taken and adapted from *Proceedings of the Annual Meeting,* Academy of Management, December, 1960, pp. 17–25.

true that many of these individuals have worked up to the point of break-through or insight and after that point in environments characterized by groups of people and complexes of equipment.

There is hardly an area of basic research today that has not benefited, and in many cases depended on, the development and availability of new equipment and techniques for observing, measuring, analyzing, or simulating the phenomena under study. Some examples are the cyclotron, the reactor, the high altitude balloon, the arctic airlift, the high speed computer, the ultracentrifuge, the electron microscope, and many more.

All this is a prelude to saying that if the field of organization theory — which is indeed emerging as a field for scientific study — is to progress, it too must utilize new tools and equipment for research.

Some of these techniques and tools are already in use, although on a very limited scale. Most of them are not as dramatic as high altitude balloons, satellites, or nuclear reactors. For the purposes of building organization theories, however, they may be equally powerful.

I should like to discuss four such tools or techniques, some of which have been in use for as long as 30 years, some for only 10. In my opinion, they have not as yet been fully exploited as research tools to develop organizational theories which can help us to explain, predict, and eventually to systematically influence organizational behavior. These four tools are:

1. The small group experimental laboratory
2. Simulation of behavior on computers and in "almost-real-life" situations
3. Mathematical models
4. The field study methods of the anthropologist

Before discussing these, I would like to comment on the level of activity and the boundaries of the field of research in organization theory. As an outside estimate of the approximate level of research in organization theory, we can look at a National Science Foundation figure for total costs for research and development in social sciences in colleges and universities in 1958.[1] This, of course, included a lot of work that could not, by any stretch of the imagination, be called research on organization theory; but this excess probably balances out the work on organization theory in such places as Rand Corporation, the Air University, etc., which are not included in the survey and the proportion of work in psychology that is related to organization theory.

[1] National Science Foundation, "Funds for Research and Development in Colleges and Universities, Fiscal Year 1958: A Preliminary Report." *Reviews of Data on Research & Development*, no. 19, April, 1960.

This total is a little less than $24 million, an amount equal to the annual research and development budget of a number of individual industrial corporations. The situation has improved somewhat, due to increased government and foundation support, but is still at a fairly low level compared to research in the physical and life sciences.

With respect to the boundaries of the field, I find it useful to visualize them as wide open, for the present, as our traditional disciplinary definitions will permit us. The criterion for inclusion that I propose in this early stage of research on organization theory is: any contribution or potential contribution, deliberate or not, from any field, that increases our understanding of the behavior of people in organizations. Thus I would include the work of some psychologists, sociologists, economists, mathematicians, anthropologists, statisticians, biologists, animal sociologists, and various types of engineers, as well as scientifically minded practitioners such as businessmen and administrators of various kinds. Members of all of these professional specialties and more have already made contributions, some unwittingly, to our ability to understand, predict, and influence organizational behavior such as:

Communication
Decision-making
Leadership
Control and evaluation
Power and influence
Work assignment and work flow

In addition to the diversity of disciplinary fields from which contributions to organization theory are coming, it is also interesting to note the diversity of approach or method employed. One reason that the field of "organization theory" appears so un-unified and disorderly to an observer is because it *is* un-unified and disorderly, in terms of common concepts, research methods, and objectives of the researchers.

In attempting to classify current research in this area, the following dimensions might be useful. Each person working in the field can be cross-classified according to several of these dimensions, although I hesitate to make the actual classifications of fellow researchers in this field outside of the classroom. (Sometimes categories are employed as epithets!) The suggested dimensions are:

1. A continuum ranging from *operational or positivistic* toward one end to what might be called *mystical* at the other end. This dimension relates to the source from which the researcher is willing to accept his data. In the first instance, represented best perhaps by the applied anthropologist, he insists that the data he uses be analogous to that employed in the natural sciences. He insists on observability, measurability, communicability, and reproducibility. In doing so, according to adherents to the other end of the continuum, he may be throwing out the baby with

the bath water. He may be getting good measurements, indeed, but he may also be getting trivial measurements, while overlooking the important data that are not so scientifically neat.

The counter-argument, of course, is that data which is generated in the mind of an individual researcher and which is not subject to replication or testing by other researchers is hardly admissible in the game of science. And yet, it is clear even at this early stage, that some of the most brilliant insights in the behavioral sciences have involved this latter type of data. Perhaps refinement and further development of our research methods can reconcile the ends of this particular continuum.

2. Another set of extremes — on a second continuum — is gradually being brought closer together through one of the tools I will discuss. This dimension might be called the *relative degree of abstraction* or the *verbal-quantitative* continuum. Here the extremes are represented by, on the one hand, verbal descriptions of phenomena, variables, relationships, and theories. On the other hand is the extreme use of mathematical models and the language of mathematics to represent these same things.

Unfortunately, some of the reconciliation I referred to is more apparent than real, due to the investment that individual researchers have in their own particular language. One group might argue that mathematics is too wasteful of information and sacrifices the richness of data available on the verbal level for the perhaps dubious advantage of precision.

The mathematically-minded will argue, of course, that ordinary English or disciplinary jargon is too loose and *inexact* for any useful analytical purposes. The reconciliation of the people at the extremes is not easy. The great hope lies in those people who are competent in both languages and who can translate from one into the other.[2] Such people are being trained in small numbers through the efforts of various universities and foundations, but many more are needed.

3. A third dimension, where reconciliation of the extremes may be a forlorn hope, at least in some areas, is represented by a continuum we might call *Prescriptive* . . . to . . .*Descriptive*. This is not the same sense in which descriptive is often used — to connote verbal. Another set of words for this continuum, well known to economists, is *Normative* . . . to . . .*Positive*.

The issue here is whether the researcher is primarily interested in stating "theories" or principles which are *prescriptive*, in the sense that they tell people how they *should* behave, or whether he is primarily interested in stating theories that are *descriptive* — merely describing how people *do*, in fact, behave. In the latter case, he leaves it up to the consumer of his theories to make inferences about how he *ought* to behave.

---

[2] James Coleman, "Rashevsky's Social Behavior Models." Bureau of Applied Social Research, Columbia University, August, 1952.

In physical science, this dimension poses little difficulty, since the criteria for theory are clear: does your theory predict actual behavior and can it be tested in a generally accepted systematic way by any competent researcher. Physicists and chemists do make statements that appear prescriptive or normative, but they are only superficially so. Such a statement, if made properly, will have the form: "You should behave in such-and-such a way because if you do, these will be the consequences, and they can be demonstrated empirically or experimentally."

This is in sharp contrast with the normative and prescriptive statements which are frequently encountered in the behavioral area. Many of them have the form: "You should behave in such-and-such a way because I tell you to and I know because of my superior experience or reasoning power."

4. A fourth dimension, and one that is much less controversial and emotionally charged, might be called a *"taste"* continuum. It describes the variation in tastes of researchers for the specific *level* of phenomena which they choose to study. Quite often this choice stems from deep conviction that the level chosen is the only *proper* one for an understanding of organizational behavior, but there is no good evidence yet to support such a contention by any group of partisans along this continuum. This is the continuum that unites, rather loosely, so many different disciplines in the study of organizational behavior. It ranges from the detailed study of *individual behavior,* or even further, the study of the *individual roles* taken by an individual in an organization, through *small face-to-face groups, larger aggregates* that are major parts of an organization, through *whole organizations* such as business firms or hospitals, into *classes of organizations* such as labor unions, and finally perhaps into studies of *societies as a whole.*

People studying all of these levels have already made and continue to make contributions to organization theory, according to my earlier criterion. The fond hope of many of them is that a full understanding of behavior at their level — the individual or the group or the whole organization — will lead to answers at all other levels.

These, of course, have been arbitrarily chosen categories or dimensions. Alternative methods of slicing the field may be equally useful in helping to prognosticate about the future of research in this field and for purposes of overall research strategy.

The first of the research tools I want to discuss is perhaps the best known of the four. It is also the only one that is truly a piece of equipment of hardware analogous to some used in the natural sciences. This is the Small Group Laboratory. In its pure form it is a complex instrument for establishing experimental conditions and providing observations of the experiment in progress. One of the earliest such laboratories, perhaps the first, was the one at Harvard in the Department of Social Relations, designed and built under the direction of R. F. Bales over ten years ago.[3] Its principal feature was a one way mirror for observing the members of small groups without, in turn, being observed.

Certainly this was not the first time that anyone had observed small groups in action, but with the development and refinement of the laboratory, a degree of control began to be achieved which was a distinct advance in the art of experimentation. Other rooms were designed and built, some based directly on the Harvard one, others incorporating innovations.

At the same time that such experimental rooms — and there are now dozens of them in the U.S. and abroad — helped toward achieving the experimenter's dream of a behavioral experiment not influenced by the presence of the experimenter, it has raised certain ethical and practical questions associated with secret observation. Such questions are not unique to this research method; they also apply to the participant-observer in field studies and the role of the experimenter in simulation studies. They do come closest, however, to our cultural image of white mice or guinea pigs being manipulated in a cage.

Despite such possible drawbacks, the small group experimental room has been the first real experimental tool or piece of equipment for studying organized human behavior. As one might expect, when researchers at M.I.T. became interested in small group research — notably the famous Bavelas experiments — [4] they added technological refinements in the form of electronic controls and analytical tools, i.e., a computer.

The question of what researchers do with these experimental rooms is another matter. One of the major drawbacks that has been recognized in some fields of physical sciences research is the tendency to become equipment-centered and to carry out studies which are adaptable to the tools available, whether they are significant or of prime interest to the researcher or not. This tendency is noticeable in the behavior of many engineers who rush into the laboratory and begin manipulating equipment in favor of sitting and developing adequate theory and hypotheses.

Some of the small group experimenters, with or without the aid of the experimental lab, are primarily interested in small group phenomena as such. They may see possible direct applications of findings to committees, problem-solving groups, or play and work groups; or they may, as one of my colleagues is, be fascinated by the esthetics of the experimental group itself as a phenomenon worth studying, even if the experimental groups consist of the perennial college sophomores.

Other small group experimenters are interested in the kind of extrapolations or interpolations. I mentioned in discussing the fourth dimension — the possibilities of generalizing from the results of small group

---

[3] R. F. Bales, *Interaction Process Analysis.* Addison-Wesley, Cambridge, Mass., 1950.
[4] A. Bavelas, "Communication Patterns in Task-Oriented Groups." *Journal of Acoustical Society of America,* 1950, pp. 725–730.

experiments to the organization or society as a whole, or interpolating observed organizational behavior through the refinements possible by experimentation. This latter procedure — the interaction between empirical observation and laboratory experiments — I believe holds great promise for advancing the field.[5] This has been one of the major research strategies of the Research Center for Group Dynamics at the University of Michigan[6] and is being used increasingly by the organizational behavior group at Carnegie Tech.

The second research tool or method is partly hardware and partly experimental design. It is the simulation of organizational behavior. This simulation is being performed in two ways: on high speed computers and in organizational laboratories.

Simulation by computer is just getting under way, with only a few actual studies in the literature. One of the earliest of these was the simulation of small group decision-making done in the Summer of 1951 at the Rand Corporation. The start of this exercise was to write a series of memoranda setting forth the essential features of the small group interaction process as observed by Bales in his small group laboratory. A. S. Householder rewrote some parts of these interaction models in mathematical form and prepared flow diagrams to guide a Monte Carlo computation of the models.[7] Severe mathematical and computational difficulties were encountered in this work, including the estimation of parameter values from experimental data.

The most recent computer simulation I am aware of is the current work at Carnegie Tech, reported by Cyert and March,[8] on simulating some of the decision-making behavior of a buyer in a department store, namely, ordering and pricing decisions.

With the increased availability of high speed computational facilities all over the country and increased access to them for behavioral research, this method holds tremendous promise for breakthroughs in the field. The major obstacles encountered by the Rand experimenters, however, still persist. The computer can approach reality only in relation to our systematic knowledge of reality. That is, nonsense instructions on human behavior, fed into a simulation, will produce nonsense results. Computer simulation, despite its great promise, cannot stand alone without adequate formal — that is, mathematical — theory and good empirical or experi-

[5] Nicholas J. Demerath and John W. Thibaut, "Small Groups and Administrative Organizations." *Administrative Science Quarterly*, vol. 1, no. 2, September, 1956.

[6] Harold Guetzkow, ed., *Groups, Leadership and Men.* Carnegie Press, Carnegie Institute of Technology, 1951.

[7] R. F. Bales, M. M. Flood, and A. S. Householder, *Some Group Interaction Models.* RM–953, Rand Corporation, October 10, 1952.

[8] Richard M. Cyert and James G. March, "A Specific Price and Output Model." Carnegie Institute of Technology, Behavioral Theory of the Firm Project, Working Paper no. 23, November, 1960.

mental data. The beauty of simulation experimentation, of course, is its economy of time and money (depending on whether you can get computer time free). Organizational parameters such as growth rates, size, status, relationships, decision rules, etc. can readily be changed to see what *would* happen, or what *might* happen. One can start with very simple models and gradually increase their complexity so as to approach real life.

The other major method of simulation involves controlled experiments on organizations in an almost-real-life situation. This is about the closest we can come to real, real life, because in real, real life there are no experimenters, at least none that we are aware of.

Again, one of the earliest and still the largest scale simulation of this type was done at Rand, starting about ten years ago.[9] This work has been carried on by the System Development Corporation, an offshoot of Rand, which specializes in this kind of research. The salient feature of this kind of simulation is that actual people are involved, with all of the richness of perception and behavioral potential that is human. The control is achieved through control over the inputs to the system (i.e. information, assigned tasks, etc.), the reward and penalty system, and the ability to manipulate certain other environmental constraints and inter-personal relations. For example, communication patterns can be systematically varied, alternative decision rules can be tried, and so on.

This method of experimentation, used extensively by the military under the heading of war gaming, is a very powerful tool, but very expensive and much less neat (in an experimental sense) than group laboratory experimenting or computer simulation. Control is difficult to achieve, observation is difficult, and the degree of complexity is very high.

Two other examples of such simulation may be mentioned. One is the ill-fated but extremely interesting work at the Air Force Survival Training School,[10] where the degree of reality achieved aroused the public and led to modification of the program. Another is the work currently being done by Harold Guetzkow at Northwestern in simulating international relations.[11]

The third and perhaps most powerful research method in organizational theory has been in general use less than ten years. It is the use of mathematical models for describing and representing organizational behavior. It is also, perhaps, the most controversial.

[9] Robert L. Chapman and John L. Kennedy, "The Background and Implications of the Rand Corporation Systems Research Laboratory Studies," in A. H. Rubenstein and C. J. Haberstroh, eds., *Some Theories of Organization*, Irwin–Dorsey, 1960, pp. 139–146.

[10] E. Paul Torrance, "Function of Expressed Disagreement in Small Group Processes." *Social Forces*, vol. 35, no. 4, 1957.

[11] Harold Guetzkow, "A Use for Simulation in the Study of Inter-Nation Relations." *Behavioral Science*, vol. 4, no. 3, July, 1959.

This controversy is well exemplified in a paper by Abraham Kaplan, called "Sociology Learns the Language of Mathematics."[12] In it he criticizes the vast amount of pseudo-mathematics and non-applicable mathematics that has entered the literature. There have been attempts prior to the recent upsurge in mathematical modeling to apply directly the mathematical methods and specific mathematical models from various fields of science and engineering to the study of organizational behavior. Most of them have not been very useful so far in advancing the field. Their major effect has been stimulatory and in some cases of help in building an abstraction of real life situations. It is possible that as simulation techniques and other data collection and experimental methods advance, some of these models and analytical tools such as servo-mechanism theory, information theory, game theory, etc., may produce important insights or breakthroughs.

Certainly much has already been gained in making the concepts and data more precise by the introduction of the rigor, and in some cases, specific models or mathematical relationships. One of the most striking examples was the paper by Herbert Simon in which he expressed a number of the basic relationships in George Homan's book, *The Human Group*, in a set of three differential equations.[13]

Among the most exciting possibilities has been the work in stochastic learning theory, decision theory, and other frameworks which can account for the probabilistic and dynamic nature of human behavior. Some of the models in operations research, where it is powerful enough to handle these probabilistic and dynamic aspects, also hold promise for the future.

A milestone in this area was the paper on "Mathematical Models in the Social Sciences," by Kenneth Arrow, over ten years ago.[14] Subsequent work in the field by cross-disciplinary groups is also noteworthy — e.g., the Behavioral Models project at Columbia, the work in the Cowles Commission, the Organization and Psychology group at Rand, and the work at Carnegie Tech.

The fourth tool — the field study methods of the anthropologist — is the one of most direct interest to me in my teaching and research on organization theory. In all the courses in organization theory which I have taught over the past ten years, field studies have been an integral part. At Northwestern, I have just initiated a separate course in organizational field studies as a follow up to the theory course.

With proper interplay between the other research methods and this

[12] Abraham Kaplan, "Sociology Learns the Language of Mathematics." *Commentary*, 1951.

[13] Herbert A. Simon, "A Formal Theory of Interaction in Social Groups." *American Sociological Review*, vol. 17, no. 2, April, 1952.

[14] K. J. Arrow, "Mathematical Models in the Social Sciences," in Daniel Lerner and H. D. Lasswell, eds., *The Policy Sciences*, Stanford University, Stanford University Press, 1951.

one, I believe that field study *experiments* — not mere data collection exercises or case studies of current practice — provide the greatest hope for increasing our understanding of organizational behavior.

Although the Hawthorne studies incorporated some of the techniques used in such studies, the real impetus to this kind of research was provided by the formation of the Society for Applied Anthropology about twenty years ago in Cambridge. Unfortunately, field studies have not been easily worked into the curricula of most of the social sciences as yet — many prefer the laboratory or the library — and so the total amount of such activity is not very high as yet. There is increasing interest in it, however, and I believe we will see some dramatic results from its use in the next few years.

There are two common categories of such field studies, each with its own advantages and procedural difficulties. The traditional method, borrowed directly from social anthropology, uses an observer who is clearly a researcher — an outsider to the group or organization being studied.

The second kind, which is rather hazardous both methodologically and physically at times, is the participant-observer method. Here the researcher is actually part of the organization being studied, either through design or by chance.

Aside from the high potential for contributions to organization theory, I have found the field study experiment — designed and conducted as rigorously as a simulation or laboratory experiment, but adapted to field circumstances — to be a very valuable teaching device.

One indication that the field of organization theory is being recognized as a legitimate area for research and teaching is the recent appearance of several new books. Several are intended primarily as introductory texts, and the rest as research materials. The titles include: *Personality and Organization*,[15] *Organizations*,[16] *Modern Organization Theory*,[17] and *Some Theories of Organization*.[18] The first two are summary and integrative efforts in which the literature has been brought into the conceptual or methodological framework of the writers. The latter two are collections of research articles in the field.

Two other books — *Models of Man*[19] and *Understanding Organizational Behavior*[20] — are reflections of the particular viewpoints on studying

[15] Chris Argyris, *Personality and Organization*. New York, Harper & Bros., 1957.
[16] James G. March and Herbert A. Simon, *Organizations*. New York, John Wiley & Sons, Inc., 1958.
[17] Mason Haire, ed., *Modern Organization Theory*. New York, John Wiley & Sons, Inc., 1959.
[18] A. H. Rubenstein and C. J. Haberstroh, eds., *Some Theories of Organization*. Homewood, Ill., Richard D. Irwin, Inc., and The Dorsey Press, 1960.
[19] Herbert A. Simon, *Models of Man*. New York, John Wiley & Sons, Inc., 1957.
[20] Chris Argyris, *Understanding Organization Behavior*. Homewood, Ill., The Dorsey Press, Inc. 1960.

organizational behavior by two people toward the extremes of the second dimension.

Additional evidence for the emergence of organizational theory as a field of cross-disciplinary study is the development, over the past ten years, of major cooperative teaching and research ventures between previously non-cooperating disciplines on several university campuses. For example, at Northwestern we are in the process of developing a between-schools interest in organization theory through the medium of joint seminars, exchanging graduate students, and co-sponsoring visiting scholars in the field. Thus far we have achieved such cooperation between the schools of Education, Business, Engineering, Speech, and Liberal Arts (which includes our departments of Sociology, Psychology, and Political Science).

With the advent of these new research tools and methods, with the increased interest in organizational behavior by many young people in many disciplines, and with the increased support of these activities by universities and foundations, I look for important developments in organization theory over the next few decades. We will probably not achieve a unified theory of organizations, but will certainly make major advances in our understanding, prediction, and ability to systematically influence organizational behavior.

14

Organizational Constructs: An Approach to Understanding Organizations*

William B. Wolf

University of Southern California

In this article Professor Wolf discusses Barnard's concept of "organizational constructs" as one approach to the study of functioning organizations. After defining an organizational construct as the system of causality which determines an organization's character, he proceeds by analyzing the interacting forces that tend to determine this character.

The purpose of this paper is to outline the essence of an approach for understanding the functioning of formal organizations.[1] Probably the best way to begin describing this approach is to explain how it came to my attention.

* Taken and adapted from the *Journal of the Academy of Management*, April, 1958, vol. 1, no. 1, pp. 7–15.

[1] In this article, we deal primarily with manufacturing organizations, but what is said is equally applicable as an approach to understanding other formal organizations such as churches, clubs, schools, and so forth. For our purpose we may define an organization as: a group of people in a cooperative task in which specific goals are given for the group as a whole. In its broadest sense an organization is any group of persons formally brought together to work toward a common end or ends.

It is easier to describe than to define what we mean by an organization. The following may be considered its principal characteristics:

1. An organization is a formal grouping of people. We are not concerned with spontaneous informal groupings except as they occur within the framework of a formal organization.
2. An organization has fundamental needs or goals under which it unites people in interrelated tasks.
3. An organization involves deliberate and purposeful actions among men in order to maintain the cooperative system.

In 1943 I was working for a relatively large manufacturing firm. My duties brought me into contact with several of its plants. As I moved from one unit to another, it was apparent that each had a different atmosphere. The plants were like people in that each had its own personality or character. This fact was reflected in the manner in which jobs were done, the type of persons who fitted into the organization, the modes of dress, and the manner in which the techniques of management were used.[2] Later, around 1946, I began to write a book on production management. It was to be a "how to do it" manual oriented toward solving specific problems of manufacturing plants. It was based on empirical evidence gained through clinical studies of a variety of plants. However, as I proceeded to study different plants, the "whys" for actions appeared to be of primary importance. It was necessary to deal with fundamentals and to have a sound theory of organization before one could be so bold as to write a "how to do it" manual.

In reviewing the existing literature on organization, I have been unable to find a treatment of the subject that provides a framework for what I am attempting to do. Excellent work has been done in describing specific organizations and in analyzing their common features. Work has also been done in describing specific techniques and comparing special aspects of manufacturing plants. Yet to the best of my knowledge none of these deals with organizations in a manner that focuses attention upon those areas which my research has indicated are of primary importance in understanding the functioning organization.

---

4. An organization is a social system. It has a formal structure that designates the superior and subordinate relationship.
5. Every relatively permanent organization has a body of doctrines and techniques. While these may, in a broad and general way, be common to other similar organizations, they also are to a certain extent unique and they give each organization a synthetic character of its own.
6. Every relatively permanent organization develops its own internal life which tends toward a closed system. The organization develops needs of its own that are separate and distinct from the over-all goals. They deal with providing continuity in policy and leadership and the maintenance of continuous consent of the individuals who make up the organization as a whole.
7. In addition to its internal needs the organization has to adjust to a broader environment. It is subjected to a number of pressures from sources outside its immediate control.

In short, we describe an organization as a living thing: it has a concrete social environment, a formal structure, recognized goals, and a variety of needs. It is continually adjusting and changing to perpetuate itself and to achieve its over-all goals.

[2] A number of writers have attempted to describe this phenomenon. For example: Buchele calls it "Company Character" and Bakke refers to it as a "small society." Robert Buchele, "Company Character and the Effectiveness of Personnel Management," *Personnel*, January, 1955, pp. 289–302. E. Wight Bakke, *Bonds of Organization*, New York, Harper and Brothers, 1950.

Thus, this paper describes an approach to the study of organizations which may, upon further study and research, supply a general theory of organization. It does so by considering the following subjects: (1) the nature of organizational constructs: (2) the problems of studying constructs; (3) a description of the study of an organizational construct; and (4) some of the implications of organizational constructs for research and teaching in the field of business administration.

The Nature of an Organizational Construct

In effect, every organization is an organizational construct, for, by "organizational construct," we are referring to that *system of causality* which determines an organization's character. The term organizational construct is used here to emphasize that we are dealing with the *system of causality*, not its parts in isolation. In short, the term has been selected to focus attention upon the fact that the manner in which a given organization functions is the net result of the complexity of the relationships of its parts to it as a whole and to each other. Each organization is more than a system of parts, components, and relations. It is also the interaction of the forces and parts.

The Problems in Studying Organizational Constructs

It must be realized that an organizational construct is a system involving a complex of mutually related parts that act and interact to create and maintain the organization, which at the same time patterns the activities of its parts and forces. This is to say, the study of organizational constructs involves numerous variables that are mutually dependent and which at the same time have their impacts determined by the over-all construct which they help maintain. This type of relationship can be illustrated by considering one of the variables in an organizational construct. Take, for example, leadership. The effective leader in an organization is effective in part because he has special characteristics which meet the needs of his organization. Yet, at the same time, his effectiveness is in part a function of the impact he makes on that organization. We may think of his effectiveness as being determined by the character of the organization and at the same time determining the nature of that character.

Recognizing the nature of organizational constructs, it becomes apparent that there is only limited value in studying them by applying simple cause and effect reasoning to *ad hoc* problems. Each part and its functioning is an aspect, or dimension, of a complex of many dimensions. The construct as a whole is not a super-entity produced by adding its respective parts. It isn't valid to fractionate or reify observations of the various dimensions of the construct, for each is interrelated to the others and each has a relative magnitude which is a function of the whole of which it is a part.[3]

Furthermore, we should perceive that the use of statistical methods has only limited applicability in providing an understanding of an organizational construct. The measurement of any specific dimension is significant primarily in relation to its other dimensions. Although we may arbitrarily divide a construct into parts, in order to understand the functioning of the parts, we must reconstruct the construct as a whole in order to understand it as a functioning whole.

It is evident that the study of organizations should deal not only with its specific parts but also with functioning wholes. Yet the complexity of constructs poses special problems. We are caught in the "parts versus the whole" conflict. To study the parts in isolation fails to give one a knowledge of the whole. It is like the old parable in which a Rajah placed an elephant in the midst of a number of blind wise men. One blind man felt the tusk of the elephant, another the ear, another a leg, and so forth. When asked to describe the elephant, one said that an elephant was a large stone, another that it was a winnowing fan, another that it was a tree trunk, and so on. Each described the elephant as the part which he felt. None, by himself, could describe the elephant as it really was.

The alternative of studying organizational constructs as wholes appears to be an unmanageable job. The whole is too vast and intricate. We are apt to end up with nothing more than the statement that "everything is related to everything else."

The answer to this dilemma is to study the parts but to do so in a manner which relates them to the construct as a whole and to each other. We are forced to treat the parts in isolation, but we may do so in a manner that will provide us with an understanding of the functioning organization. The procedure is to examine the principal parts one at a time and to make the tentative assumption that the part being examined is the only independent variable. In this way we can note any tendencies that it may have as a determining agent.

In making such an analysis we must recognize the artificiality of our assumption. Furthermore, we should recognize the need for the assumption — by analyzing the parts in this manner we may be able to discern their roles and interactions in a given construct.

[3] This observation has been noted by many. It is even suggested in early religious writings. For example, in summarizing the principles of Buddhism, Christmas Humphreys states, "But there is no such thing as two, for no two things can be conceived without their relationship, and this makes three . . ." *Buddhism*, Harmondsworth, Middlesex, England, Penguin Books, 1951, p. 16. See also: Edward H. Litchfield, "Notes on a General Theory of Administration," *Administrative Science Quarterly*, Vol. 1, No. 1, June, 1956, p. 10.

Thus the manner by which we will proceed is to first analyze the parts. From our analysis we shall draw tentative inferences about the construct. Where such conclusions are reinforced by the inferences drawn from analysis of a number of parts we shall tentatively assume that our deductions represent existing facts. In this manner we may develop a perspective of the organization as a whole.

What I am describing as an approach to the study of organizations is in reality nothing new.[4] Most successful consultants follow this procedure in the first phase of their study of a new client's company. They call it a management survey.

Interviews with successful consultants indicate that frequently what they call their "common sense" or their "intuition" involves thinking in terms of organizational constructs. The consultants, of course, are not fully conscious of this. It appears that they have acquired a considerable amount of knowledge about the surroundings they work in and have learned to make a vast number of adaptations to it. However, they have learned in a pragmatic way and are not completely aware of the learning process or the theory underlying what they do.

A Description of the Study of an Organizational Construct

Probably the best way to illustrate the method for studying an organizational construct is by citing an example. Once this has been done we shall turn to some of its implications. The following is a cursory example. Its purpose is simply to illustrate the method.

Let us suppose that we are about to study the manufacturing plant of a firm that makes specialized machinery for the lumber industry. At the outset we are told that the firm manufactures a quality line of heavy equipment for sawmills, that it is an old and well established firm, that most

[4] Actually this is the method of all science. As Einstein and Infeld point out, scientific enquiry is like a mystery story. Albert Einstein and Leopold Infeld, *The Evolution of Physics*, New York, Simon and Schuster, 1938, Chapter I. In fact, the approach is well illustrated by that greatest of all writers of mystery stories, A. Conan Doyle, in his adventures of Sherlock Holmes. For example, Holmes explains his method to Doctor Watson by telling how he deduced that Watson had recently come from Afghanistan. Watson states: "You were told, no doubt, that I came from Afghanistan." Holmes replies: "Nothing of the sort. I knew you came from Afghanistan. From the long habit the train of thoughts ran so swiftly through my mind that I arrived at the conclusion without being conscious of intermediate steps. There were such steps, however, the train of reasoning ran: Here is a gentleman of a medical type but with the air of a military man — clearly an army doctor, then. He has just come from the tropics, for his face is dark; and that is not the natural tint of his skin, for his wrists are fair. He has undergone hardship and sickness, as his haggard face says clearly. His left arm has been injured. He holds it in a stiff and unnatural manner. Where in the tropics could an English army doctor have seen such hardship and got his arm wounded? Clearly in Afghanistan!" A. Conan Doyle, "A Study in Scarlet," *The Complete Sherlock Holmes*, New York, The Literary Guild, 1936, p. 14.

of its equipment is manufactured to order, that the individual machines sell within a price range of $10,000 to $30,000, that the company was recently purchased by a private party, and so forth. Our job is then to develop an understanding of how this specific plant functions, what its operating problems are, and what methods can be used to mitigate or solve its problems.

What we would do is size up the organization in terms of the principal forces operating in its construct. As we noted these forces we would draw logical inferences as to their roles in the construct. We would analyze each force so as to ascertain its probable role-relationship with the other forces and with the construct as a whole. Thus, if we noted a recent change in the leadership of the firm we would expect to find a communications problem, a morale problem among key supervisors, and the other aspects of the syndrome that is usually associated with a change in the leadership of a manufacturing firm.[5]

The hypotheses underlying such deductions hold that in most organizations there is one individual whose shadow is reflected throughout the entire unit.[6] We call such an individual a "leader." The leader, in this connotation, is to be differentiated from other key or supervisory personnel by the degree to which he influences the activities, beliefs, and interests of the people in the organization.

The leader usually dominates the organization due to his ability to structure the work environment and because of his control over individuals in that environment. He selects supervisors and key personnel and he has the final say in promotions and raises. Thus the persons in the organization are under economic as well as social pressure to adjust to the interests of the leader.

Of course, it should be recognized that the extent to which the leader's shadow influences the organization will vary from one organization to another. It will depend upon the specific constructs. The point to be emphasized is that the tendency for the leader to dominate does exist,

[5] In the management literature there is scarcely anything written on the complications of changes in leadership. Most attention is focused on training executives and selecting executives. Yet my experience indicates that the best techniques of selection and training may be of little use if the actual succession is handled poorly. One excellent discussion of this subject appears in Alvin W. Gouldner's book, *Patterns of Industrial Bureaucracy*, Glencoe, Illinois, The Free Press, 1954, pp. 70–101. It appears that more attention is given to the matter in England. For example, see Rosemary Stewart, "Management Succession." *The Manager*, August 23, 1955, pp. 579–582, and September 23, 1955, pp. 676–679. See also Cyril Sofer, "Reactions to Administrative Change: A Study of Staff Relations in Three British Hospitals," *Human Relations*, 1955, pp. 291–316. Both of these studies were conducted by the Acton Society Trust in England.

[6] This point has been emphasized by Perry Rohrer. See "Planning and Building an Organization," a panel discussion by Rex Reeder, Perry Rohrer, Neele Stearns, and W. N. Mitchell as abstracted by Joseph L. Massie, *The Journal of Business*, Papers and Proceedings of the Management Conference, April, 1954, p. 30.

and consequently we assume that if we can identify and come to know the leader of the organization, we can make a number of deductions about the nature of that organizational construct. Conversely, if we know a number of facts about the construct we may make a number of predictions about its leadership.

In our hypothetical case we would infer that the organization would change to accommodate its new leader, and the leader would also change to accommodate the organization.[7] Furthermore, we would assume that changes in leadership are accompanied by a pattern of reactions among the personnel in the organization. The underlying hypothesis — grossly simplified — runs something like this: The new leader has a "feeling out" period during which he attempts to size up his organization and get on top of his job. One of his first and most difficult hurdles is to establish reliable communications throughout the organization. In this task he is hindered by a lack of knowledge of the social organization of the plant, lack of loyalty toward him by members of the organization, and, in certain cases, definite resistance to his leadership. Faced with these and similar problems, the new leader will tend to rely on formal reports, that is, budgets, cost reports, and so on, to supply him with the necessary data to perform his job. And he will tend to build his own organization by bringing in people from the outside, for example, friends and former colleagues, and by redefining jobs and reassigning personnel.

The above description is by no means a complete analysis of the role of leadership or the significance of changes in leadership. The purpose in describing these matters is simply to illustrate the type of reasoning that is needed in using the organizational construct approach.

Before arriving at some tentative conclusions regarding this case, we must carefully examine our deductions in relation to other significant aspects of the construct. For example, our deductions about the change in leadership indicate that the new leader is faced with a problem of low morale and poor communications. Whether or not we accept these inferences will depend upon other aspects of the construct, such as the nature of the supervisory work force, the tradition of leadership in the organization, and so forth. If we find that the new leader reflects the old, or if the old leadership was ineffective and disliked, our inferences about the problems of the new leader will have to be modified.

Let us suppose that our first deductions are supported by the analysis of the other factors in the complex. We then have a clustering of inferences that supports the assumption that the plant is faced with problems dealing with morale and communications. If this is so, we accept these inferences as existing facts.

---

[7] An area of research that should prove fruitful is that dealing with the changes in attitudes and actions of leaders as they move into a new construct.

In a similar manner, we evaluate the other principal forces in the organizational construct. Moreover, the same type of reasoning is followed in suggesting corrective actions for dealing with operating problems. For example, if we were advising a new leader on the most suitable action to take in improving his organization, we would take into account a wide variety of factors: If we were dealing with a firm in a small rural community, we would hesitate to suggest firing key personnel or bringing in outsiders. We would recognize the close relationship between the life in the plant and that in the community as a whole. In contrast, if we were dealing with a plant in a large urban center, the role of the community would be considered in a different light.

In analyzing the organizational construct of a manufacturing unit, say a plant, a large number of areas must be considered. The following are a few of them: the goals of the organization; the formal structure; the relationship between ownership and control; the financial structure; the size of the operating unit; the size of the company to which this operating unit belongs; the existence of other plants in the company which perform similar functions; the location of the plant; the equipment and machinery used; the layout of equipment; the commonly held moral precepts of the society in which the plant operates; the plant's history and its traditions; the nature of the union, if one exists in the plant; the labor market; the ethnic backgrounds and characteristics of the labor force; the general level of economic activity; the legal framework of the society in which the plant exists; the demand for the product or products; the manner of distribution of the product or products; and the cost structure of the plant.

The above is by no means a complete list. However, it directs attention to the variety of forces that must be considered if one is to understand how decisions are reached and carried out in the typical organization.

The Implications of the Organizational Construct Approach to Research and Teaching in the Field of Business Administration

If we accept the basic premise of the organization construct approach (that is, that to understand a functioning organization one must see it as a whole and see the interactions of its various parts as both determining and determined forces in that whole), a number of deductions follow with respect to the research that needs to be done and the manner in which business administration should be taught.

The implication for research: The research job that needs to be done is of monumental size. It involves bringing together into one or several volumes a systematic analysis of organizational constructs. Such a work would deal with: (1) the concept of organizational constructs; (2) analysis of the principal determinants of constructs; (3) analysis of the interactions of these determinants, and (4) case studies illustrating applications of the organizational construct approach to present day problems.

Such a work will require an interdisciplinary team of writers and researchers. In many areas it will be necessary to carry on basic research to give us a better understanding of the roles of the various determining forces and their interactions. In addition, it will require a considerable amount of rigorous scholarship in order to relate the existing literature to the organizational construct approach.

The implications for teaching business administration: The primary implication of the organizational construct approach to the teaching of business administration is that we must always relate the use of specific business techniques to the construct in which they are used if we are to understand how they function in actual practice. Happily, most curricula in business administration include courses which attempt to "integrate" the subject matter. The differences in course content that do exist appear to relate more to the means for attaining the goal of "integration" than to the goal itself.

One approach for teaching undergraduates that appears reasonable is first to focus the attention of the students upon the nature of going business concerns as functioning wholes.[8] The consideration of the different businesses would be at a fairly superficial level. Probably the method for achieving this goal would be to develop a number of motion pictures and supporting case materials that would give the students a feeling for the characters of a variety of businesses. What I have in mind are films produced primarily for use in the classroom. In them the personnel at various levels in the hierarchy of the organization that is being studied would be interviewed with respect to what they do, what they used to do, what happens in a typical day, what types of problems come up, and so forth. In addition, the market for the firm's products, the histories and traditions of the firm, and so forth would be discussed. During the school term, the beginning student would study several such cases. His attention would be focused on the general nature of things done in each firm and the differences that existed between the cases. In this way, the emphasis in the first course would be on the general nature of organizational constructs. The course would serve to familiarize the students with the concept of constructs and the differences occurring among specific constructs as revealed by comparison of the case materials.

The second level of study would deal with the techniques and tools used by management. In teaching at this level, the emphasis would be on the logic underlying the specific tools and the ways in which they may be used in different constructs. Here the case materials would be taken

[8] Here again many curricula are set up to achieve this result. The major differences are in methods.

from the cases studied in the first course. This would serve to reduce the amount of ephemeral detail the student has to learn in dealing with cases, and to reinforce his understanding of the nature of constructs and their implications to efficient management.

The top level course for the student working for the bachelor's degree would be one which required the student to study specific constructs. The course would be similar to the study of pathology. The students would be given cases to analyze. They would make their own diagnoses and prescribe the means for mitigating or solving problems. In many respects the course would be similar to the case courses now given in most schools of business. The major innovation would be that the student's earlier training would have focused his attention on organizational constructs — he will have been alerted to many of the tendencies (clues) evolving from the various forces in the construct. Furthermore, the cases would be more complete than those generally used. It should be added that a course such as I am describing will require the assembling of a volume dealing with typical functional roles of the various aspects of a construct as both determining and determined forces in an evolving organizational situation.

Conclusion

The above represents an approach to the study of functioning organizations. In final analysis it is neither new nor startling. But the fact of the matter is that much of the work being done in both teaching and in research has neglected the implications of the system of causality that determines an organization's character. Hence, it is hoped that this paper will stimulate discussion and research so that we shall eventually develop a general theory of organization that is inherently sound and at the same time of immense practicability in dealing with real world situations.

15

Decentralization of

Authority in a Bureaucracy[*]

Bernard H. Baum

Continental Casualty Company

[Organization theorists, whether classical, neo-classical, or modern, have been fascinated with the concept of decentralization of authority. Practicing managers, too, have devoted substantial attention to it as an operating device for their companies. This article explores the operational meaning of decentralization of authority, and the crucial question of how and to whom authority should be decentralized.] Then questions were studied in the context of classification decisions in a large government agency.

The purpose of this paper is not to discuss the specific details of decentralization of authority in the Federal Civil Service, but rather some of the more general problems of decentralization of authority in bureaucracy which my research highlights.[1] Students of management have become increasingly interested in the behavioral science approach to organization and administration, and this interest is reflected in the papers presented at past meetings. From my perspective as a sociologist, this is as it should be.

Let me note briefly the basis and limits of my observations. This case study involved the U.S. Civil Service Commission's[2] program of decentralization of authority for personnel management to the independent operating Federal agencies. This study should be applicable to business management, then, to the extent that it is based on:

---

[*] Taken and adapted from *Proceedings of the Annual Meeting*, Academy of Management, 1960.

[1] Bernard H. Baum, *Decentralization of Authority in a Bureaucracy*, (Englewood Cliffs, New Jersey: Prentice-Hall, Inc., 1961).

[2] Hereinafter referred to as the Commission.

1. Governmental activity-decentralization of authority was legislated on a "blanket-wide" basis and bound up in rules and regulations;
2. Specifically and only authority for personnel administration — involving only a segment of management responsibility; and
3. A case of decentralization of authority to outside agencies — although this is not peculiar to the government; (an analogous case in industry for example, is Sears, Roebuck and Company decentralizing authority to manufacturing companies to write up order forms for Sears stores, at the suppliers' discretion, on Sears order forms.

The basic question is generally applicable: What does decentralization of authority mean in operation? As business organizations become larger and more bureaucratic, a crucial question confronting management is how and to whom authority should be decentralized. To help determine the answer I compared actual patterns of human behavior with the norms set forth in official statements.

Analysis of Actions

One of the principal functions of the Commission in implementing the government personnel management system is position classification. Simply stated, position classification is the evaluating and assigning of the multitude of jobs in the civil service within a grade structure to provide equal pay for equal work. Since 1949 the authority to do this has been vested with the operating Federal agencies.

To learn how decentralization of authority actually operates, the research design called for a statistical analysis of classification actions taken by agencies under delegated authority. From my point of view, analysis of classification actions provided an ideal index of agency use of authority for two reasons. First, position classification is precisely the function in which "institutional office" and "person" converge. Second, somewhat less academic but more pragmatic, current research pretty well has to involve objective phenomena and quantitative data and position classification decisions provided these.

But these data don't tell the whole story. To understand differences within the total operation — represented by the statistical data — I made an effort to go below the disposition of cases, the rules, and the regulations, and conducted extended interviews. These were designed to reveal the attitudes and thinking, and to explain the actual behavior of participants in the decentralization of authority program, thus spelling out the statistical material.

The basic data are a summary and analysis of a random sample of 1,353 agency classification actions, post-audited by Commission inspectors. The Commission recommended changes in sixteen per cent of these actions. Whether this figure means that the agencies are not highly competent to do this work, or whether it means that standards are so difficult to apply that there is much room for differences of opinion, or whether it means that this is as good or satisfactory a percentage of correct actions as can be expected by anyone, is difficult to determine. Such a determination is in the last analysis arbitrary.

An analysis of the actions changed by the Commission significantly reveals that there is a definite upward pressure of classification within the agencies. Errors in judgment with regard to classification are not random, since 81.6 per cent of the changes recommended by the Commission were changes downward. This is the result of pressure by both the incumbent of a position and the head of the agency for reasons of prestige and status. Any upward changes recommended by the Commission were almost exclusively in lower-grade jobs. (My discussion of a specific Defense agency gave an example of such pressure).

The pressures such as "empire building," "holding 'good' men," etc., for upward classification, are relatively constant, yet their effect varies between agencies. The grossest violations were found in the Defense Department. There, officials favored a wide area of discretion for themselves and were highly critical of the Commission's claims of decentralization of authority. It may be noted that most of the heads of these agencies were active military officers. Differences in agency functions and the characteristics of agency officials account in part for variations in pressure from agency to agency.

There are two possible ways in which errors can occur in classification: poor judgment (or lack of technical data) and mal-intent. One significant way to remove the errors caused by mal-intent would be removal of available techniques for exerting adverse pressure. One such technique is the working of a classification description so as to make the position appear to require a higher grade than it does. A second technique is the classification of a job so that no suitable Commission list of eligibles exists and thus the agencies can hire whom they choose. In the area of recruiting and placement, agencies often have ways of discouraging prospective applicants who are considered undesirable, so that these applicants never, in fact, apply for a position. Since authority has been essentially decentralized to "offices" and not "persons," the use of such techniques varies, and the nature of agency personnel is a crucial variable.

Interview Findings

A most significant finding of my research was the discovery of a dichotomy, or a continuum, of evaluation of what had been decentralized to the agency, as viewed by agency personnel. Some saw a decentralization of authority; others saw work. The basic distinguishing characteristic was the right to make decisions within the broader framework of policy. In the "excellent" agencies (as rated by the Commission), officials viewed what had been delegated to them as authority. It would seem that these officials have internalized the Commission's basic policies and philosophy. In the "poor" agencies, officials viewed what had been delegated as work. Apparently, in these cases, the Commission had been unable or had failed to place people in the socio-psychological environment that would adapt their decisions to the Commission's objectives. Thus, in "poor" agencies, officials feel that they are doing Commission work with agency money and personnel. In the "average" group, the heads rated what had been delegated as work while the directors of personnel viewed it as authority. We might hypothesize that the basic commitment of the agency head is to the functioning and goal of his agency, whereas the personnel director's basic commitment is to personnel administration. The differences in conception may be a reflection of the conflicts of interests, and the meaning and role of this differential perception in decentralization of authority warrants further research.

On the basis of these observations, it appears that if decentralization of authority is to be effective, from the Commission's viewpoint, the Commission must: (1) do more with education of agency officials in basic Commission philosophy, (2) take a more active part in advising the Executive Branch with regard to appointments, and (3) most significantly, be selective in its decentralization of authority.

The relationship between the Commission's rules and regulations and the merit system, and actual operations is ultimately a quasi-legal question and reflects the disparity between law and actual human behavior. The interviews of Commission personnel reflected a vague feeling of uneasiness regarding their role vis-a-vis the agencies, a conflict between exaggerating deviation to show the need for the Commission and holding down the number of such violations noted to keep personnel work in the agencies. In written reports, the Commission tends to minimize all except the most flagrant violations in order to maintain its vested interest. In audit reports and actions, the personnel director is frequently found to be "caught in the middle."

Another issue in the reliability of such audit reports is the weighting or importance given to specific standards by Commission Inspectors themselves. Public Commission statements concerning the requirement of strict adherence to the law are unrealistic since corrections of violations are made only where errors are discovered. According to Commission officials, a three per cent violation rate is considered satisfactory. Decentralization of authority has never been revoked by the Commission for reasons of undue violation!

Since the Commission is a collection of individuals who, although working in a single organization, do not present a united front, it seems that the personal equation might well receive more consideration in terms of decentralization of authority within the Commission itself.

The extended interviews with persons in the Commission and agencies were conducted with a view to determining how Commission and agency personnel actually view the decentralization of authority program. The first question which we asked of these persons was: What does the Commission's program of decentralization of authority mean to you? How would you define and explain it in terms of human behavior rather than legalistic terms?

In the above question we tried to avoid biasing the answer of the respondents while, at the same time, discouraging their answering the question in purely technical terms which did, in fact, occur. On the whole, Commission officials saw the decentralization-of-authority program as a not altogether successful effort to delegate personnel work but deplored the opening of the door to agency machinations. All officials highlighted the technical considerations of "speed" and "efficiency." The program was also seen as a reflection of a change in the role of the Commission within the total configuration. Only one respondent saw the program as an opportunity for greater individual participation and development, although this point is much stressed in the literature.

The responses of agency heads reflected their orientation toward their operating function. Career-minded agency officials are prone to manipulate Commission authority as part of the process of accommodation. Heads tend to view claims of decentralization of authority as an attempt by the Commission to disguise the fact that agency officials have little real freedom in decision-making.

In answer to a question concerning the advantages and disadvantages of the decentralization of authority program as compared with the old system, the major advantage universally mentioned by the respondents was speed. This highlights the fact that formal and technical considerations of the program predominated in the thinking of officials, and the extent to which other goals are being served by the program might well be questioned.

Despite their reservations regarding the current program, agency officials, en masse, list only advantages to the program as compared to the old system. To the Commission officials, such advantages as speed, flexibility, and knowledge of local conditions tend to lean toward the benefit of the agencies. These latter may imply a disadvantage from the Commission's viewpoint, that is, the extent to which they offer the possibility of circumvention of Commission policy. The Commission's conception of personnel administration can then be placed in whatever position within the agency the head's hierarchy of values dictates. This, from the Commission point of view, limits cooperation and uniformity. The loss of uniformity, while posing no problem to the agencies, is seen by the Commission as foreshadowing the cessation of a single system of personnel administration.

Responses indicate that a crucial variable is not only the system, per se, but the existence of the Commission viewed by the agencies as an opposing force within that system. There are variations in the degree of unity of goals. In an effort to determine how agency officials do, in fact, conceive of their relationship with the Commission, I asked them how they would characterize their relationship with that Office and how this relationship differs, if at all, from the relationship prior to decentralization of authority. All indications are that there has been a minimization of fear in the relationship. Depending on the nature of the agency and its officials, the relationship is more or less on a continuum of friendliness to antagonism.

As the interviews proceeded, it became clear that responses followed a limited pattern revolving around respondents basic orientation and that a limitation in variables existed which we caught in the first few questions.

Related to the lack of a unified goal, and a recurring theme through much of the material collected, was the lack of sufficient training in personnel administration and education for the acceptance of responsibility under a philosophy of decentralization of authority. This represented a problem area in the case at hand.

A limitation in achieving a unified goal, from the viewpoint of Commission officials, is what they perceive as the poor caliber of some personnel officers, in addition to the lack of sufficient financial resources for adequate training. Agency officials, however, see somewhat different problems in the decentralization of authority program, but the underlying problem, as they view it, is the failure of the Commission and its staff to understand and appreciate the problems of the individual agency in operation.

We found that our sample of agency officials vehemently opposed an idea, originally proposed by the Commission in 1932, that agency personnel directors be Commission employees. In various ways, they expressed the general feeling that there exist pressures, loyalties, and human feelings in personnel administration and these should be in the direction of the agencies. The responses of Commission officials were mixed, but both agency and Commission officials indicated that bias and organizational loyalties are a determining factor in the behavior of personnel officials. Thus we find that only to the extent that the system, as fixed by Commission, and the agency heads are in harmony can there be no conflict of interests.

The basic difference in the orientation of Commission and agency officials lies in the existence of a divergent hierarchy of values. The Commission exists, in part at least, to maintain standards and has, as one of its governing principles, the implementation of such standards. Agencies exist for a diversity of purposes and their officials view their function as fulfilling the purpose for which the agency was created. Personnel admin-istration is simply one phase of their activity. In operation, we find that agency officials tend to view the Commission as a negative force, even under decentralization of authority, while they tend to view themselves as a positive force.

Just a few words about the terminology in which the program is formulated. It makes a difference. In this case for example, the Commis-sion representatives who visit the agencies are called "inspectors" — not "advisors" or simply "representatives." On the other hand the Commis-sion uses the term "recommendation" in a rather euphemistic sense, since (and I quote) "compliance with recommendations is required."[3] I would submit, as regards the term "recommendation," that "a rose by any other name" appears to apply. In terms of decentralization of authority, in effect, it could as well read, "corrective action ordered."

Conclusions

This study indicated five basic, interrelated factors crucial to an under-standing of decentralization of authority in a bureacracy. First and fore-most is the observation that decentralization of authority, was conceived and implemented to maintain the existence of the Commission. Thus we conclude that this decentralization program is a strategy designed to save a vested interest. There is evidence that delegatees' viewing of this program as a strategy actually hinders the development of what is classi-cally conceived as the essence of decentralization of authority — individual judgment, initiative, and improved morale.

The second observation is that blanket-wide decentralization of au-thority characterized our case and represents a critical problem area.

Thirdly, the effort of the Commission to change its role, from a 'police' to an advisory body, has not been universally recognized as successful within the Government itself. The problem of reconciling role can be seen in the dilemma of control and decentralization of authority, and the fact that the Commission cannot rid itself of responsibility for accom-plishing its function.

The fourth significant finding of this study is that there exists in the Federal Civil Service a lack of unity of goals. It would appear to us that to decentralize authority without adequate achievement of a reasonable harmony of goals, as was the case here, may well result in the problem situations I observed.

My fifth observation is that decentralization of authority occurred in an organized hierarchy of functional positions lacking adequate reference to the incumbents. Such decentralization of authority leads to the "sci-entific management" approach to decentralization of authority rather than

[3] U.S. Civil Service Commission, *Inspection Procedures*, Civil Service handbook A-901 (Washington: Government Printing Office, 1955), p. 25

the "human relations" approach. To the extent that agencies fulfill Commission expectations, decentralization of authority operates in an optimum manner, but where they do not, the program is hampered and agency officials claim that what they get is work, not authority. Under the Commission's legalistic interpretation, a rule having been issued defines authority. Realistically, a greater degree of authority rests with the agencies.

Basically, I concur with the late Leonard D. White that authority should be decentralized, subject to conformity with basic principles and policies as set down by legislative bodies. This requires the implementation of experts in the field, and the Commission is presumably a basis on which to build such an organization of experts. Its position, however, would not be one of line authority, for it has been shown that conflict can arise from line and staff functions combined in a single organization.

The question is not *whether* authority ought to be decentralized but, when, how and to whom it is decentralized.

Implications

This research allows us to make limited inferences concerning the study of decentralization of authority. One factor to be taken into account in such studies is not the objective existence of an articulated program of decentralization of authority but rather how persons involved in the program and thus affected by it, perceive it. This conception helps to determine and explain actual behavior. We might say that the degree of successful integration that may be achieved by a central authority with its operating units in the performance of functions, is directly proportionate to the degree of successful decentralization of authority. This implies the existence of an adjusted goal, symbolic of an understanding which would tend to spread outward from the point of integration to both parties.

A mutually satisfactory decentralization of authority program appears to require delegation of practically all minutiae of administration to the agencies. This the Commission failed to do. Indeed, the current setting of decentralization of authority in the Federal Civil Service is probably best revealed in the following Commission statement:

> The size of Government requires that personnel work be decentralized — that is, authority to hire, promote, etc., must be given to the man directing operations in the job. At the same time, the Government is regarded as a single employer, and employees in different agencies and different places must have the same general conditions of employment. A fairly complex set of governing regulations is required to reconcile these two needs.[4]

[4] U.S. Civil Service Commission, *The Government Personnel System*, Personnel Management Series No. 4 (Washington: Government Printing Office, September, 1954). My italics.

The realism, in terms of human behavior, of reconciling a dilemma of this nature through the use of a "complex set of governing regulations" is subject to careful study.

Premised on the orientation and competence of agency officials, the rewards for independent judgment should be greater than the penalties for failing to conform to the higher authority's pattern of thought. The additional requirement is the clarification of the role of the central authority in decision-making.

Basically, it is the system and perception of the system, rather than any single control, which produces such frustration and negativism as is found. Fundamentally, mutual confidence, trust, and orientation must precede, to the maximum extent possible, decentralization of authority.

A study of this scope can, at best, afford a starting point for a discussion of characteristics and problems of decentralization of authority and other similar processes in bureaucracy. It should be one of many more specific studies. From these a more rigorous classification of systems of decentralization of authority might be developed and patterns of behavior could be analyzed in terms of this resulting typography.

My research indicates that decentralization of authority in the government was conceived as a technical procedure, imbedded in rules and regulations. It appears to me that effective decentralization of authority must be conceived of in human relations terms; i.e., we must view organization as a flexible and dynamic organism so that decentralization of authority proceeds as a reflection of the philosophy of management and takes into account differences in qualifications and orientations of subunits and incumbents of positions. To put it succinctly, one can't draw a new organization chart and say that authority has been effectively decentralized.

16

Management Science and Group Behavior:
Work-Unit Cohesiveness[*]

Robert T. Golembiewski

University of Georgia

The concern of preceding articles with models and methods of research is also reflected in this article. The author uses small group research methodologies to explore cohesiveness as a strategic organizational concept. He analyzes the complex nature of cohesiveness, and explores the operational problems facing the researcher studying this important concept. Finally, a review of cohesiveness research shows incomplete analytical development mixed with demonstrated theoretical importance of this concept.

Awareness of the multiple bases of human behavior has developed gradually over the past half-century from demonstrations of the influence of groups upon behavior. The burgeoning small-group literature is a recent product of this awareness. In contrast to the descriptive nature of the early group literature,[1] the experimental study of *ad hoc* collectivities characterizes recent work. Sociologists and psychologists have spearheaded this research, the goal of which is to develop concepts and operational methods for the detailed description of group behavior.

The rigorous study of the small group is highly relevant to management science. Primarily, this relevance derives from the traditional emphasis in the literature, as in organizational theory, upon formal organization and the individual.[2] The stress on informal organization is a departure from

* Taken and adapted from *The Journal of the Academy of Management*, vol. 4, no. 2, August, 1961, pp. 87–99.

[1] A large number of these studies are analyzed in Muzafer and Carolyn Sherif, *An Integration of Studies On Intergroup Relations*, New York: Harper and Brothers, 1953.

[2] This is the point of such work as that of Chris Argyris, *Personality and Organization: The Conflict Between System and the Individual*, New York: Harper and Brothers, 1957.

this position, but definitions of the concept have been various and general. Thus small-group analysis, in addition, can help develop a more precise specification of informal organization. The three panels of small-group variables suggest the range of this specificity:

1. *a structural panel,* which includes variables relevant to the description of the relations which exist between group members, e.g., leadership status;
2. *a style panel,* which includes variables relevant to the description of modes of group behavior, e.g., a group with a permissive style of supervision; and
3. *a population panel,* which includes variables relevant to the description of the properties of group members which are significant for group functioning.

Concurrently, small-group analysis provides a model of the research methods necessary in behavioral studies of business.

The purpose of this article is to analyze a conceptual and operational development in small-group behavior to exploit this utility. The focus is upon cohesiveness, a strategic concept in small-group analysis. Its analysis provides a useful illustration-in-depth. But the approach has a dysfunctional narrowness as well.

Cohesiveness: Concepts

Cohesiveness taps a basic property of the small group: its "stick-togetherness," or the member loyalty which defines the group system. However, several overlapping but distinct conceptions of cohesiveness have been employed. Three general classes of such meanings may be noted:

1. the attraction of a group for its members;
2. the coordination of the efforts of members; and
3. the level of motivation of group members to do a task with zeal and efficiency.

The three meanings could not be included in a single concept. Thus the general restriction of the concept to meaning 1 constituted the first major clarification of cohesiveness. Meanings 2 and 3 do not appear to be unidimensional. They have also been interpreted with an "external" bias. The failure to validate hypotheses derived from meanings 2 and 3 substantiates these observations. Such hypotheses proposed that groups characterized by a high internal "togetherness" (for example) will have high output on an experimental task. Mixed experimental results revealed the too-facile association of a group characteristic with a measure of performance that has an extra-group basis, since a small group characterized by high cohesiveness could be a high producer — that is, more able to control member behavior than a group with low cohesiveness. Or, a small group could be a low producer, i.e., more able to resist extra-group demands than low-cohesiveness groups.

Several concepts of cohesiveness have been developed as "attraction." The earliest modern formulation of cohesiveness held that it "is the total field of forces which act on members to remain in the group. . . ."[3] The deficiencies of this conceptualization may be summarized:

1. The concept emphasizes the "total field of forces" rather than the group, with (as will be shown) important consequences for operational definitions of cohesiveness;
2. The concept is not uni-dimensional, since the "total field of forces" might contain a preponderant weight of elements (such as a prison sentence) which would permit this, as well as the converse, formulation: The greater the forces acting upon individuals to stay in a group, the less attractive the group is to those individuals; and
3. It is impossible to measure the "total field of forces" directly and each indirect operational definition is (at best) a partial measure of, or (at the worst) not related to, the "total field of forces."

More recent work has remedied some of these conceptual problems. Thus one progressive conceptualization emphasized cohesiveness as a group property. It provided, in a subtle but significant change, that "cohesiveness is a . . . property of groups, the attraction which it has for its members, or the forces which are exerted on the members to stay in the group . . ."[4] Unlike the earlier version, the emphasis is upon a potentially-measurable phenomenon, member attraction-to-group. But the second difficulty noted above still prevails. As a result, reinforced by experimental findings, cohesiveness was further clarified to be a function of the individual members' resultant attraction-to-group.[5] The "resultant" scores for individuals are a function of two classes of factors: group properties; and the motivational states of the persons involved, which are a function of personal needs and characteristics. As Libo put it, cohesiveness "may be hypothesized as a function of the degree to which there is a correspondence between the need structure of all the individual members and the need-satisfying in the group."[6] Variables in all three small-group research

[3] Festinger, Leon, Stanley Schachter, and Kurt Back, *Social Pressures In Informal Groups: A Study of Human Factors In Housing*, New York: Harper and Brothers, 1950, pp. 164–65.

[4] Festinger, Leon, *et al.*, *Theory and Experiment In Social Communication*, Ann Arbor: Institute for Social Research, 150, p. 21.

[5] Cartwright, Dorwin, and Alvin Zander, editors, *Group Dynamics: Research and Theory*, Evanston: Row, Peterson, 1953, pp. 77–78.

[6] Libo, Lester M., *Measuring Group Cohesiveness*, Ann Arbor: Research Center for Group Dynamics, University of Michigan, 1953.

panels, then, are relevant to cohesiveness. Figure 16.1 schematically out-
lines this final conceptualization.[7]

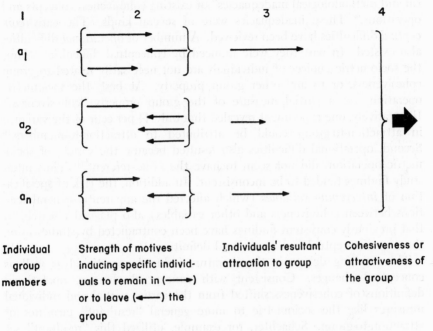

Individual	Strength of motives	Individuals' resultant	Cohesiveness or
group	inducing specific individ-	attraction to group	attractiveness of
members	uals to remain in (———➤)		the group
	or to leave (◄———) the		
	group		

Figure 16.1   Conceptual schema for the determination of group cohesiveness.

Cohesiveness: Operational Problems

The conceptional clarification of cohesiveness, however, did not solve
operational problems. That is, deciding upon *what* is to be measured did
not solve the problem of *how* it is to be measured. But the clarification did
permit a clear indication of what operational developments were necessary.

To develop the point, the early operational definitions of cohesiveness
usually were based on indexes of sociometric choice (e.g., indexes developed
from answers to questions such as: Who are your friends in group x?).
Promising results prompted a series of studies of natural-state groups which
utilized a number of similar (but not identical) sociometric operational
definitions of cohesiveness. The results of such studies may be briefly
noted: some strongly confirmed predicted relations of cohesiveness and

[7] A similar schematization is utilized by Joachim Israel, *Self-Evaluation and Rejection
In Groups: Three Experimental Studies and a Conceptual Outline*, Uppsala: Almkvist
and Wiksells, 1956, p. 26.

other variables; others supplied positive but unexciting support; and others yielded unexpected and contradictory results.[8]

Gross and Martin concluded that such mixed results indicated the "logical and methodological inadequacies" of existing cohesiveness concepts and operations.[9] These inadequacies were of several kinds. The early *conceptual* difficulties have been reviewed. A number of *operational* difficulties also existed. In part they were induced by conceptual difficulties. Thus the sociometric choices of individuals are not necessarily related to group cohesiveness, or to any other group property. At best, the sociometric operation was a partial measure of the group property "cohesiveness." Illustratively, one experiment revealed that only 44 per cent of the variance in attraction-to-group could be attributed to attraction-to-members.[10] Second, operational difficulties also resulted because the variety of sociometric operations did not seem to have the same referent.[11] Thus interstudy findings tended to be inconsistent. In addition, the lack of specification of *intervening variables* (which affected the apparently general relations between cohesiveness and other variables) also plagued research, so that previously consistent findings have been contradicted by studies using the same conceptual and operational definitions.[12]

The resulting debate in the literature induced operational as well as conceptual changes. Consistent with conceptual changes, operational definitions of cohesiveness shifted from the earlier partial and individual measures like the sociometric to more general "resultant" measures of attraction-to-group. Schachter, for example, utilized this "resultant" set of questions to measure cohesiveness:[13]

1. Do you want to remain a member of this group?
2. How often do you think this group should meet?
3. If enough members decide not to stay so that it seems this group may discontinue, would you like the chance to persuade others to stay?

[8] See, for example, John G. Darley, N. Gross, and W. E. Martin, "Studies of Group Behavior: The Stability, Change, and Interrelations of Psychometric and Sociometric Variables," *Journal of Abnormal and Social Psychology*, vol. 46 (1951), pp. 565–76; and J. G. Darley, N. Gross, W. E. Martin, "Studies In Group Behavior: Factors Associated With the Productivity of Groups," *Journal of Applied Psychology*, vol. 36 (1952), pp. 396–403.

[9] Gross, N. and Martin, W. E., "On Group Cohesiveness," *American Journal of Sociology*, vol. 57 (1952), p. 547.

[10] Bovard, Everett W., Jr., "Interaction and Attraction to the Group," *Human Relations*, vol. 9 (1956), p. 482n.

[11] This point was established by Bernice Eisman, "Some Operational Measures of Cohesiveness and Their Interrelations," *Human Relations*, vol. 12 (1959), pp. 183–89.

[12] See John Downing, "Cohesiveness, Perception, and Values," *Human Relations*, vol. 11 (1958), pp. 157–66.

[13] Schachter, S., "Deviation, Rejection, and Communication," *Journal of Abnormal and Social Psychology*, vol. 46 (1951), pp. 190–207. See especially the reprint of the article in Cartwright and Zander, *op. cit.*, p. 228.

The "resultant" approach avoids the particularistic deficiencies of such operations as the sociometric. It also taps member attraction to a specific group, again in contrast to the sociometric operation which isolates relations between pairs of individuals. Finally, such "resultant" measures have proved effective in differentiating subjects exposed to high and low cohesiveness-inducing experimental treatments.[14] The use of such "resultant" operations, however, has been limited.

Despite such developments, important operational problems remain open. First, in terms of Figure 16.1, the translation of the "resultant" attraction-to-group scores of members (step 3) into group cohesiveness (step 4) presents a major difficulty. Thus far, the temporary expedient has been to average the several attraction-to-group scores. The expedient is not satisfactory. For such a mean may disguise within-group differences of a significant nature. Indeed, high intra-set differences may indicate that the entire group is not behaviorally relevant for all members. That is, that the group is categoric rather than psychological. Therefore, cohesiveness operations of substantial predictive utility must measure the "spread" of the data treated in the aggregate.

A second translation difficulty involved steps 3 and 4 in Figure 16.1. The equal weighting of member attraction-to-group scores in existing cohesiveness operations has a serious defect. For group status may be a crucial element in the weighting of these scores in total group cohesiveness. This position is a tenable one. But the unresolved conceptual and operational difficulties with the structural variable "status" inhibit its implementation.

A third problem is that differences in cohesiveness sources seem important at steps 2, 3, and 4 in Figure 16.1. Relevant evidence, however, is thin. This evidence may be reviewed in terms of answers to three questions:

1. *What are the sources of attraction-to-group?* Three have been emphasized: (a) personal attractiveness of group members, (b) the attractiveness of the task with which the group mediates, and (c) the prestige of group membership. These sources of attraction are convenient. For they have been induced in experimental subjects by instructions (1 and 3) and planned assignment (2). But they also cover only a limited range. Ideally, however, cohesiveness should be related to a large number of sources in properties in the structural, style, and population panels.

2. *Do different sources of attraction have similar group consequences?* Research by Back presents mixed evidence.[15] Three batches of experimental collectivities were treated so as to expose each batch to one of these sources of attraction: personal attraction; task attraction; and membership

---

[14] Libo, *op. cit.*, especially pp. 30–31.

[15] Back, K., "Influence Through Social Communication," *Journal of Abnormal and Social Psychology*, vol. 46 (1951), especially pp. 19, 20, 23.

prestige gains. Two-member groups were given the task of the joint preparation of stories about several pictures. Each subject was given slightly different pictures to study alone in order to encourage the exertion of influence in the joint story-preparation. As expected, members of high cohesiveness (HiCo) groups exercised a greater and more equal mutual influence. HiCo members also displayed more equal participation in the group discussion than members of low cohesiveness (LoCo) groups. This consistently reflects greater HiCo involvement in, or greater felt-importance of, the discussion. Back thus concluded that "cohesiveness can be considered as a unitary concept." But there also were quite distinctive inter-source effects on the group process between cohesiveness treatments. To illustrate:

> "The Effect of Task Direction. The relationship created by setting up a goal which can be reached by the group activity tends to have somewhat opposite effects from those of the personal attraction relationship. Group activity is seen as a necessity which is to be completed as quickly and as efficiently as possible."
> ". . . If cohesiveness was based on personal attraction, group members wanted to transform the discussion into a longish, pleasant conversation."

Thus, as expected, intervening variables must be specified if cohesiveness is to have high and consistent predictive utility. This complements common-sense expectations and some experimental work. Consider, for example, cohesiveness which is "leader-centered" (as in traditional organization theory) versus cohesiveness which is "member-centered" (as in much of the small-group literature). A *priori*, these types of cohesiveness would have markedly different group effects over a wide range. To suggest the point, small-group style differences (e.g., directive vs. permissive atmospheres) and population differences (e.g., more members who are high vs. low scorers on "authoritarianism") have been observed in groups with leader-centered cohesiveness vs. groups with a member-centered cohesiveness.[16]

3. *Does attraction-to-group from different sources yield increased total attractiveness?* The crucial experiment has not been performed. But its necessary design seems clear enough. Thus a batch of groups could be treated so as to induce only one of the three sources of cohesiveness in any group; and a batch could be exposed to the three sources simultaneously. The test for between-treatment differences would answer this third ques-

[16] See the suggestive evidence in William Haythorn, Arthur Couch, Peter Langham, and Launor F. Carter, "The Behavior of Authoritarian and Equalitarian Personalities In Groups," *Human Relations*, vol. 9 (1956), pp. 57–74.

tion. Such an experiment might also reveal the sensitivity of existing "resultant" operations for measuring cohesiveness.

Cohesiveness: "Group" Designation

A central problem — the "unit" to which these concepts and operations applied — was not raised directly in re-evaluating cohesiveness. Paradoxically, however, this problem contributed significantly to that re-evaluation. Most early studies of cohesiveness analyzed "formal" groups, such as courts in a housing development, classrooms, and work units. But the problem, as Festinger, Schachter, and Back noted, was that mutual sociometric choices often seemed to reflect "a kind of subgroup development." They went on:

> "It is, of course, impossible in the absence of more empirical data to decide just how much such *excess mutual choices* detract from the cohesiveness of the group as a whole. . . . We should not want to subtract the mutual choices completely since the fact that they are mutual certainly does not nullify their contribution to the cohesiveness of the group. As an approximation, we shall correct the proportion of "in-court" choices by subtracting . . . one half of the mutual choice pairs which occurred."[17]

Festinger, Schachter, and Back were interested in the relation between cohesiveness of the courts of a housing development and opinion of, and activity in, a tenants' association. It was hypothesized that high cohesiveness would be associated with a low percentage of "deviants" from court patterns of opinion and activity. The modification for "excess mutual choices" resulted in appreciably higher negative correlations between cohesiveness and percentage of deviants in one case (Westgate courts). There the percentage of total variance accounted for by the correlation increased from 28 per cent to 55 per cent. In another case (Westgate West courts) the change was in the same direction, but not significantly so. The adjustment was quite delicate, however. For a mutual sociometric choice reflects a very strong friendship bond. Thus the position that "excess" choices decreased the attractiveness of the group was, without considerable clarification, quite peculiar. Such clarification was not offered.

Such results, however, may be explained. Consider the three general types of sociometric choice-patterns given in Figure 16.2. To the degree that formal groups approximate Type I, it seems unnecessary to compensate for "excess mutual choices." For Type I formal groups display a member choice "togetherness" which makes it reasonable to argue that the choice pattern is associated with an underlying opinional agreement. In Type III

[17] Festinger, Schachter, and Back, *op. cit.*, p. 95 (Italics are the author's).

formal groups, by way of sharp contrast, the formal group is categoric only. Thus "groups" of this type are probably not characterized by any marked, group-induced opinional agreement. However, the case for two sets of opinional agreements is presumptively strong. Sociometrically-defined cohesiveness of Type III formal groups would then probably yield results at odds with those predictable from the general group-theory in which

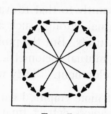

Type I

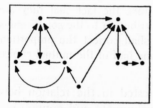

Type II

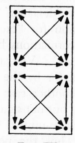

Type III

Figure 16.2 Hypothetical patterns of positive sociometric choices in formal groups.

Legend ⟶ _a_ chooses _b_
⟷ _a_ and _b_ choose each other

cohesiveness is imbedded. For this theory presupposes that a "group" reflects substantial behavioral similarity. Type II formal groups, finally, are intermediate to Types I and III. This type is characterized by a moderately unified choice pattern and thus, reasonably, by a moderate tendency to share opinions.

Some distribution of these general types may be expected in any batch of small, formal units. This permits an explanation of the higher correlation which resulted from the "adjustment" for mutual pairs. Westgate courts (hypothetically) tended toward Types II and especially III. To explain, the "adjustment" reduced the estimates of the cohesiveness of Type III groups significantly more than those of Type II groups. Type III groups (by definition) also would have a greater percentage of deviants. Hence the higher post-adjustment correlation between "per cent deviants" and court cohesiveness in Westgate. A similar argument can be developed to explain the less marked effect of the "adjustment" in Westgate West.

Thus the concentration on a formal unit begged the basic question of "group" designation. The estimates of a group's cohesiveness were "mixed" because the behaviorally-relevant part of a particular formal unit varied from respondent to respondent. These exhortations, of course, do not solve the designational difficulties. The point here is the more limited one of demonstrating how differences in "group" designations affect cohesiveness research. Incidentally, as attempts with matrix algebra and graph theory demonstrate, "group" designation (especially when large data batches are involved) is an effort in which the exact sciences will be indispensable.[18]

Cohesiveness: Management-Relevant Findings

Shortcomings notwithstanding, cohesiveness has been valuable in the study of significant problems of group life relevant to management science and practice. On the broadest level, whether in experimental or natural-state situations, the small group may serve four functions:[19]

1. The group may be an agency through which members obtain and evaluate information about their environment;
2. The group may create some aspects of reality which are relevant for the individual and may control some aspects of the physical and social environment of consequence to individual members;
3. The group may fill a need for affiliation and affect; and
4. The group may function as a defense against the extra-group environment.

These functions imply a basic law of the social physics of groups. The more effective a group is in serving such functions, the greater its cohesiveness (and vice versa). And greater cohesiveness means greater group de-

---

[18] Weiss, Robert S., and Eugene Jacobson, "A Method for the Analysis of the Structure of Complex Organizations," *American Sociological Review*, vol. 20 (1955), pp. 661–68; and Dorwin Cartwright, "The Potential Contribution of Graph Theory to Organization Theory," in Mason Haire, editor, *Modern Organization Theory: A Symposium of the Foundation for Research on Human Behavior*, New York: Wiley, 1959, pp. 254–71.

[19] See Festinger, Back, Schachter Kelley, and Thibault, *op. cit.*, for the development of the underlying theory.

mands which may be placed upon members before their withdrawal is forced. Experimental studies have validated a number of logical derivations from this basic statement of relations. One class of such studies, for example, deals with the change of individual behavior. It has a patent relevance to management. The general hypothesis underlying this research is that the "magnitude of the change which the group can induce (in its internal power) will be equal to or less than the magnitude of . . . its cohesiveness."[20] The main results of experiments confirming this hypothesis may be abstracted:[21]

1. *amount and intensity of communications:* studies have generally shown that participation is more equal and more intense in HiCo than in LoCo groups, consistent with the prediction that participation in HiCo groups is more valued by members;

2. *rejection of deviants:* HiCo groups tend to reject those who deviate from group opinion more than LoCo groups do; and communication directed toward deviants tend to be initially more frequent as well as finally less frequent in HiCo groups than in LoCo, which reflects more marked attempts in HiCo groups to preserve the psychological group first by conversion of the deviant and then by rejecting him convincingly when conversion does not result;

3. *willingness to accept influence:* HiCo members are more susceptible to group influence than LoCo members, a relation most interestingly reflected in experimental demonstrations than HiCo groups are more successful in maintaining high *or* low production levels than LoCo groups; and

4. *reactions toward external threat or deprivation:* HiCo groups are more capable of producing and sustaining a hostile reaction against "external" threat than LoCo groups.

In addition, cohesiveness has been used successfully as an intervening variable to reconcile seemingly conflicting, or to relate previously disparate, findings. This further reinforces the support of the theoretical underpinning of cohesiveness research.

The conclusion is that many group processes with organization counterparts are related to cohesiveness. This connection receives direct support from such well-managed studies within organizations as that by Seashore.[22] Seashore studied 228 relatively small, formal work-units in a plant manufacturing heavy machinery. Two elements limit his analysis of these work

[20] Festinger, Schachter, and Back, *op. cit.*, p. 166.

[21] Consult Schachter, *op. cit.*; and Leonard Berkowitz, "Group Standards, Cohesive-and Productivity," *Human Relations*, vol. 7 (1954), pp. 509–19.

[22] Seashore, Stanley E., *Group Cohesiveness In the Industrial Work Group*, Ann Arbor: Survey Research Center, University of Michigan, 1954, especially pp. 39, 38, 36.

units. First, Seashore used an index of cohesiveness based upon data from answers to five fixed-response questions tapping these areas:

1. Are you really a part of the group?
2. Do you want to stay in the group?
3. How do the men get along?
4. Do the men stick together?
5. Do the men help each other?

There are, however, sharp limits on the use of the combined data derived from answers to these questions. Thus only questions 1 and 2, as Seashore noted "appear to be relatively pure translations from the [resultant] definition of cohesiveness." Moreover, the low intercorrelations of data sets from questions 1 and 2 with each other (.30) and with questions 3–5 (tending toward the low end of the range .15–.38) also advise caution in interpreting the cohesiveness index.

Second, the high intercorrelations of the data sets from questions 3–5 (.62, .64, and .70) also suggest that the choice-base was often narrower than the formal work-unit. Among other possibilities, questions 3–5 may tap responses referring to psychologically-relevant systems within the work units, while questions 1 and 2 may reflect judgments about the entire formal unit. The nature of the questions supports this surmise. In any case, Seashore realized that his research units were not necessarily psychological groups. But the analysis of variance of the cohesiveness scores by work unit proved statistically significant. This provided some justification for treating the work teams as psychological groups.

Seashore's findings underscore the generality and importance of cohesiveness. His findings are consistent with laboratory research or are logically derivable from it. The findings are particularly noteworthy because the two reservations noted above would probably tend to dilute the strength of the relations in the data sample. Seashore's work tapped the co-variation of cohesiveness and three classes of variables: (1) work-related anxiety, (2) productivity, and (3) situational characteristics of formal work-units and their members. His findings are consistent. The findings closely tie the several significant work-site variables to cohesiveness relations. Seashore's findings may be abstracted and commented upon briefly:[23]

1. The hypothesis that the "cohesive work group promotes effective support for the individual in his encounters with anxiety-producing aspects of his work environment" was generally and sometimes significantly supported. Such findings are consistent with the "resultant" conception of cohesiveness discussed above. Moreover, the tension-reduction associated with the cohesiveness helps to explain group influence over member be-

[23] Seashore, *op. cit.*, p. 61 (I); pp. 63, 67, 70 (II); and pp. 88–91 (III).

havior. This finding also has a patent practical importance. For high tension has many dysfunctional consequences in organization.[24]

2. The hypothesis that "the degree of cohesiveness . . . determines the power of the group to induce forces toward uniformity of work standards within the group and toward the formation of differential standards between groups" was demonstrated in two ways: (a) worker productivity was more uniform in HiCo than LoCo work units, and (b) productivity differences between work units were greater in HiCo than LoCo units. These findings are consistent with laboratory research. Cohesiveness, however, often has been associated with "good" (e.g., high productivity) group characteristics. Seashore's findings underscore the importance of the specification of intervening variables such as the style characteristics of groups. The centrality of cohesiveness — whether the style it supports is high or low productivity — is patent for management.

3. Cohesiveness was related to two measures of the "opportunity for interaction": (a) cohesiveness was related to the percentage of work unit members with three or more years on their current job, and (b) cohesiveness was curvilinearly related to work unit size, i.e., both high and low cohesiveness were related to smaller size. Relevant "situational characteristics" should include structural, style, and population properties. Seashore's main emphasis was thus narrow. But his findings were consistent with cohesive theory. Length of service reasonably reflects attraction-to-group, for transfers out of hostile work units would be expected. And small size — when length of service is not controlled — understandably encourages high (or low) cohesiveness because of the greater intimacy (or unfavorable reaction) possible in smaller units. These findings also suggest possible management techniques for manipulating cohesiveness.

Conclusion

This review of cohesiveness research sketches a mixed picture of incomplete analytical development and demonstrated theoretical importance. Despite the unsolved problems, however, four things seem clear. First, cohesiveness is administratively relevant. Existing organization theory (such as the principles of administration) does not provide for such differences. Indeed, this theory implies a mechanics rather than a psychology, as critics have long noted. Wide recognition of this theoretical bias induced the general emphasis on informal organization. But informal organization rephrased the research question. The development of concepts like cohesiveness is necessary to exploit such macroscopic insights. In an applied sense, cohesiveness also has important pay-offs. For organi-

---

[24] Some of the dysfunctional consequences of tension from budgets on first-line supervisors are isolated and analyzed in Chris Argyris, *The Impact of Budgets On People*, Controllership Foundation, Inc., 1952, especially pp. 16–23.

zation is controlled behavior, and cohesiveness is related to the degree of behavioral control which may be exerted by a group. Thus the simple technique of allowing work-unit members to choose each other often results in higher output. This method is more likely to induce high work-unit cohesiveness than assignment by formal authority. For, *ceteris paribus*, the "personal attractiveness" source of cohesiveness is more likely to be induced when self-choice is permitted. In one case, to illustrate, self-selection vs. selection by management of construction teams reveals that self-selected teams were more effective on four criteria: job satisfaction; turnover rate; an index of labor cost; and an index of materials cost.[25]

Second, cohesiveness research provides convenient conceptual and operational tools for natural-state empirical studies. The wide use of these analytical tools is necessary as well as convenient. For small-group analysis depends largely on the study of isolated, *ad hoc* groups in laboratory situations. The study of small groups in formal organizations, then, may validate and/or redirect laboratory research.

Third, such research will have important side effects. Thus the physical sciences have dealt with levels of organization (the atom, the molecule) and with their integration (e.g., "valence"). Analogically, the small group is a level of informal organization important in itself, but not capable of accounting for behavior or other levels.[26] In short, small-group theory must be integrated with the theory derived from other levels of formal and informal organization.[27] The contributions of students from disciplines concerned with management and organization will be valuable in this effort. For such disciplines have developed useful descriptive literatures dealing with macroscopic levels of organization. In any case, the research involvement of large numbers of researchers from a number of disciplines will at lease serve to acquaint them with a style of research that has paid significant dividends.

Fourth, cohesiveness research suggests the outline of the task of the application of the exact sciences to the problems of management. As in the physical sciences, empirical research demands the development of limited and general theoretical statements and of the mathematics such statements require.[28] The degree to which such demands are met and fed back into empirical research will influence substantially the pace of development of management science.

[25] Van Zelst, Raymond H., "Validation of A Sociometric Regrouping Procedure," *Journal of Abnormal and Social Psychology*, vol. 47 (1952), pp. 299–301.

[26] Novikoff, A. B., "The Concept of Integrative Levels In Biology," *Science*, vol. 101 (1945), pp. 209–15.

[27] Simon, Herbert A., "Comments On the Theory of Organizations," *American Political Science Review*, vol. 46 (1952), pp. 1130–39.

[28] Such a treatment of cohesiveness, for example, is provided by Herbert A. Simon and Harold C. Guetzkow, "A Model of Short- and Long-Run Mechanisms Involved in Pressures Toward Uniformity In Groups," *Psychological Review*, vol. 62 (1955), pp. 56–68.

17

The Application of Queuing Theory
to the Span of Control*

Lawrence S. Hill

The RAND Corporation

Little effort has been made to apply mathematical tools of analysis to the study of organization. This article describes the use of queuing theory applied to the span of control problem at the level of first-line supervision. The publication of this article generated much discussion and debate. Some of the opinions elicited in the debate appear at the end of this article.

Modern organizations are so complex that it is appropriate to consider application of some of the more recently advanced (but not new) mathematical techniques to the essence of management itself, the organizational structure.[1] The intent is to evolve a framework for an economic or least-cost decision.[2]

In this article, queuing (or waiting line) theory is applied to the problem of how many subordinates can be efficiently directed by one superior. This worker-to-supervisor ratio is commonly referred to as the "span of control." The primary orientation of this study is toward first line manufacturing supervision, that is, the foreman and shop worker. The economic model

---

* Taken and adapted from *The Journal of the Academy of Management*, vol. 6, no. 1, March, 1963, pp. 58–69.

[1] This article has benefited from helpful suggestions from the following individuals: John J. Coleman and Stanley Hauer, Space Technology Laboratories, Inc., and Lecturers, University of Southern California; David Felber Jr., Bendix Corporation; M. C. Heuston and Milton Kamins, The RAND Corporation.

[2] This is not to imply, however, that cost is the sole determinant in this, or for that matter, any other decision process. For a discussion of the role of cost models in the decision-making procedure refer, for example, to C. E. Bullinger, "The Estimating Function in Decision Making, Its Development, Characteristics and Use," *The Journal of Industrial Engineering*, vol. 13, January–February, 1962, pp. 3–7.

developed here, however, may be adaptable to other levels of supervision and to elements of other organizational structures, such as the military.

The problem of how many machines to assign to a single operator, sometimes referred to as the machine interference problem, was one of the first non-telephone applications of waiting line theory. Ramifications of the machine problem have been explored through the years. However, such studies are of less practical import at this time because management's prerogative in machine assignment is currently somewhat limited. Once production processes are established in union shops, it is often difficult to effect changes.

The principle of span of control, like unity of command, may result in criticism when expressed in a dogmatic manner. Hardly anyone would deny, however, that supervision of an inordinate number of subordinates by one individual can lead to trouble. The supervisor will not have the time to do an adequate job. While mechanical application of the principle is not expounded here, it appears sensible that the organizational planner should consider whether too many or too few subordinates are reporting to a single supervisor.

"Span of control" is usually considered to be a set of abstract rules and generalizations regarding the number of individuals a given manager can supervise and how much time he can devote to each. The principle is applicable in what have been described as four general steps of organizing: setting up the structure, developing the procedure, determining the requirements, and allocating the resources.

The trend in management science today is that traditional "rule-of-thumb" methods and aphorisms are being replaced by more sophisticated approaches. This is no reflection on Frederick W. Taylor's pioneering work in this field at the turn of the century nor V. A. Graicunas' early formulation of organizational relationships. The value of much of this work is rarely questioned today.

Span of Control in Retrospect

A review of some of the literature pertaining to span of control indicates how it has been applied and on what basis quantitative values have been derived. Davis has stated, for example, that although it is impossible to lay down any fixed rule as to the number of executives for whom a superior should be responsible, experience indicates that it should not be fewer than three or more than seven. He further noted that the optimum number seems to be five for the average *executive*. Citing one case where 26 departments and major committees reported directly to the major coordinating executive, he remarked that it was necessary for this manager to work more or less regularly from ten to sixteen hours a day.

In another publication concerned with first-line supervision, the same author has stated:

> Experience indicates that the range of effective size for units of supervision is from 10 to 30 employees. While many reasons for this limitation have been advanced, we have no rational, objective method for determining the optimum size of a unit of supervision in a given case. Its determination is still largely a matter of trial and error.[3]

Yoder has written that some management specialists contend that no one can direct more than six subordinates efficiently. Taking into account the tenuous nature of assigning an exact ratio, he noted that the important thing is that the basic principle be clearly recognized.

In referring to the existence of a belief that there is a span of control which limits the rate at which the pyramid can spread out beneath the top executive, Haire noted that the concept is often traced to the military. He argued, however, that the idea of the squad organization is relatively new in American military history. General officers during the Civil War attempted to control directly the activities of whole armies or corps, which may account for the appalling loss of high-ranking officers on both sides.

Improved weapons technology subsequently forced American armies into a smaller span of control (the advent of the Minie ball and its effectiveness made massed formations lethal). At the same time the beginnings of telegraphic communications made strategic, if not tactical, control of the battlefield possible.

In this regard it is important to note a parallel drawn between the squad leader in the military and the first-line supervisor in business by Petersen and Plowman. These authors state with strong emphasis that these are analogous functions.

In citing some empirical work performed at the Institute of Industrial Relations at the University of California, Berkeley, Haire found that "the simple ratio of one to eight line production workers supervised by a first-line foreman does not stand up." In four companies studied, the ratio of men reporting to a supervisor averaged fourteen to one. The range was from seven to nineteen (to one).

Critics of the span of control principle have shown that a reduction in the number of subordinates reporting to each superior sometimes requires an increase in the number of organizational tiers. This will increase the distance from top management to the bottom of the hierarchy with pos-

---

[3] Subsequent to the completion of this study, an article by Dr. Alan J. Rowe was brought to the author's attention. In this publication, Rowe suggested that since the supervisor is a decision processor, an economic span of control *could* be determined. "If the supervisor is always available," he put it, "there would be a high idle cost; however, if there were too many subordinates, decisions would be held up due to the supervisor being unavailable." See Alan J. Rowe, "Management by Computer . . . How and When?" *Aerospace Management*, vol. 4, no. 10, October, 1961, pp. 66–72.

sible adverse effects on upward and downward communications.[4] Sears, Roebuck, for example, has widened the span in an attempt to reduce this distance.

Waiting Line Analog

Many production problems are attributable in some part to the build-up of waiting line. Implicit to these problems are men, machines, parts or subassemblies requiring service at random time intervals. Other typical examples are delays encountered at toll stations on highways and counters of a supermarket.

The various properties of a waiting line, such as the number in line at a given instant and the waiting time experienced by a particular arrival, are random variables. This is because, in general, arrivals are random events in time and service times are random variables as well.

Operations within service and manufacturing fields can be considered as a "gate." Each person arriving at the gate requires a certain *service* time before the next person can be accepted. The reciprocal of the service time is the rate capacity of the gate. If demand on the gate or the input exceeds capacity for a short time, a queue will form.

Waiting line theory provides a means for forecasting the probable number of units waiting for service and the probable average delay or waiting time, as well as other important data. The theory was developed to provide a model to predict the behavior of systems which attempted to provide services arising from random demands.

Waiting line or queuing theory had its origins in the study of telephone service. The first major study is generally acknowledged to be that undertaken by A. K. Erlang under the auspices of the Copenhagen Telephone Company. For telephone service, the number of customers is so large that the population may be considered infinite. The case to be discussed in this article is a finite queue, since the demand arises from a finite source.

Generalized Model

The basic inputs and expected output of the system considered in this article are presented next. These are shown as an input-output diagram in Figure 17.1 in order to aid in over-all conceptualization of the problem. The inputs are discussed in more detail below.

Classically, the rationale for the span of control concept is that delay, friction, and confusion can be traced to the fact that too many subordinates

---

[4] The span of control is inextricably related to today's interest in mechanized management information systems. The cost function developed in this article with its attendant effects on levels of supervision has a direct bearing on the speed and accuracy of information flows required for automatic data processing. See, for example, L. S. Hill, "A Punched Card Approach to Production Control," *Journal of Machine Accounting*, vol. 13, June, 1962, pp. 45–52.

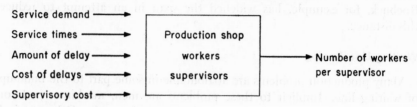

Figure 17.1. The generalized system.

are assigned to a single superior. In its basic form the span of control may be represented as a function of the variables shown as follows:

$$\text{Span of Control} = f(T, C_s, C_w, k) \qquad [1]$$

where:

T = average service time (consultation of worker with supervisor),[5]

C_s = cost per unit of supervisory time,

C_w = cost of worker waiting per time unit,

k = evaluative factor assessing effects of non-productive worker time when supervisor is unavailable while needed.

Mathematical Formulation

Management's objective in queuing systems is to select a "best" of system operating alternatives, that is, one which maintains an economic balance between waiting times and service (supervisory) capacity. The role of waiting line theory in the "span of control" application is to furnish data as to the fraction of time each worker will be waiting for varying worker-to-supervisor ratios. Given these data and the cost of worker and supervisor time, the total nonproductive costs can be derived for each ratio and the minimum found for each specified case.

The following additional symbols are used in development of the model for this system:

N = population (number of workers),

M = service channels (number of supervisors),

[5] The amount of service time (T) is dependent upon a number of considerations which influence the average value. These may be shown as:

$$T = f(I, S, E, M, G, Z)$$

where

  I = type of organization,
  S = training and ability of supervisor,
  E = training and ability of worker,
  M = attitude of management toward delegation and decentralization and availability of staff organizations,
  G = spatial considerations relative to worker-supervisor,
  Z = miscellaneous factors which may include, for example, fatigue considerations.
The above factors are not necessarily mutually exclusive.

W = average waiting time of worker,

U = average productive worker time (time not calling for service),

H = average number of workers waiting for service = $\dfrac{NT}{(U + W + T)}$,

L = average number of workers being serviced = $\dfrac{NW}{(U + W + T)}$,

J = average number of workers doing productive work = $\dfrac{NU}{(U + W + T)}$,

F = system efficiency factor = $\dfrac{J + H}{J + L + H}$,

X = service factor = $\dfrac{T}{T + U}$.

The formula for the average number of units waiting for service (L) may be expressed as:[6]

$$L = N(1 - F) \qquad [2]$$

The variable cost of workers waiting is:

$$VC_w = kC_w N(1 - F) \qquad [3]$$

The variable cost of supervisory time is:

$$VC_s = \frac{M\,C_s}{N} \qquad [4]$$

The total variable cost (TVC) associated with a variation in N is the sum of these last two equations:

$$TVC = kC_w N(1 - F) + \frac{M\,C_s}{N} \qquad [5]$$

The requirement is to determine the value of N, for given values of F (determined by T and U), M, and C_w and C_s, which will minimize this expression.

A summary of the nomenclature used to represent the occurrences in a finite queuing problem is shown in Table 17.1. As indicated in the matrix, a unit (worker) is either engaged in productive work, waiting service from the supervisor, or receiving service from the supervisor. Also, N = J + L + H.

[6] Additional information on the mathematical formulation and probability considerations may be found in L. G. Peck and R. N. Hazelwood, *Finite Queuing Tables*, ORSA Publications in Operations Research, No. 2, New York, John Wiley and Sons, Inc., 1958, pp. xi–xvi.

Table 17.1.   Summary of nomenclature

Units \ Status	Working	Waiting	Conference
Average time	U	W	T
Average number workers	J	L	H

A diagram of the waiting-line system is presented in Figure 17.2. At the instant pictured, there are two units (workers) in the queue requiring service from the foreman and one unit receiving service.

Figure 17.2   A queue with two units waiting.

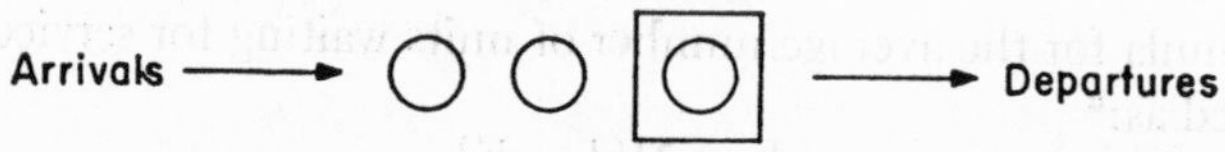

Arrivals ⟶ ○ ○ ▢ ⟶ Departures

Equation [5] assumes the existence of random calls for the foreman's service. Needless to say, the calls result from production problems and may be initiated by either the supervisor or worker. The service times are assumed to be exponential distributions. Empirical data such as time studies or records may be used for determination of specific distributions.

The evaluation factor k must be judged for each application either on a microscopic or a macroscopic basis. For example, if the worker is unable to perform other duties while waiting for the supervisor but other operations are not affected by his idleness, use 1; if the worker can perform other duties but of a lesser or degraded value, use ½; if a "chain reaction" of enforced delays would result, use, say, 3. Implications of the effects of delays on the entire operation are discussed further below in the section on costs.

Judgment factors are commonly used in standard time determination or in job evaluation in industrial engineering. Furthermore, the concept is compatible with other inputs in queuing theory.

Cost Considerations

The question of cost determination in the model is complex. In the calculations for this study, the supervisor's time (C_s) was valued at twice that of a worker. Thus C_w and C_s, as reflected in the computations shown subsequently, represent the *effect* of wages only. Such a generalized approach enables one to determine the economic worker-to-supervisor ratio.

Actually, as in many estimating procedures, the results of the computations may be best expressed as a range. In a given situation there may be relatively little cost significance between the assignment of six, seven, or eight subordinates to a supervisor, and furthermore the difference may not be statistically or otherwise valid. However, there is a definite and unmistakable difference between, say, six and twelve. When this is viewed either in light of the total plant population or as a percentage, a significant number of dollars may be at stake.

There are, of course, other costs which should be considered. These may include the expense of idle machine capacity, costs associated with a delay in performance, and adverse effects of friction and confusion. This type of cost determination is common in many situations, but a categorical answer has never been provided. The difficulty is that the cost is comprised of many elements, some provable and some theoretical. Moreover, the secondary effects may be of more significance than the primary. Such costs may be somewhat accounted for by the "k" factor.

Suffice it to say that idle time is never desirable and the cost theoretic optimum, or adjacent value, are more to be desired than those at the other ends of the spectrum, if allegiance to the span of control concept is sought. Economy of manpower is one of the first considerations of management.

Davis has shown that direct supervisory overhead expense is affected materially by variations in the unit of supervision and the span of control. The greatest effect, according to this author, is on the expense of minor supervision, because this class of supervision has the largest payroll in most concerns. Whether the last statement is unequivocally true or not, it is apparent that the span of control does influence the direct overhead expense accounts.

Fundamental to this particular study is the realization that requirements for *direct* supervision increase greatly at lower hierarchial positions. In addition, a basic amount of supervisory time is necessary to maintain production, even in the absence of immediate problems. Much supervisory time may also be required near the apex of the organization, but for different reasons, namely, policy decisions as contrasted to procedural direction at lower levels. Another distinction is that administrative management is almost entirely mental. First-line supervision may be somewhat physical, for example, shop training. Somewhere else on the continuum is the research organization where there may be relatively little direction exercised by supervision.

Area for Further Research

Equation [5] has been designed to take into account the variables which have been delineated by equation [1]. However, this investigation and the resultant model are concerned *only* with direct single relationships between the supervisor and those who report to him. Consideration of direct group and cross relationships might be incorporated through additional analysis. These, however, would undoubtedly result in an interrupted finite queuing problem, the mathematics of which are extremely complicated. The published literature to date does not contain a solution to an interrupted finite application.

Application of Model

The successive difference with respect to N in the economic model may be expressed as:

$$\frac{\Delta TVC}{\Delta N} = \left[kC_wN + 1(1-F) + \frac{MC_s}{N+1} \right] - \left[kC_wN(1-F) + \frac{MC_s}{N} \right] = 0 \ [6]$$

Calculations were made for a range of workers (N) from 4 to 12, where the service time (T) was considered to be $\frac{1}{2}$ hr, U (the time between service sessions) $= 7.5$ hr, M (the number of supervisors) $= 1$, and $k = 1$. Calculations were also completed for a service time of $\frac{1}{4}$ hr with U $= .75$ hr for the same parameters for a range of N from 4 to 16. As previously noted, the cost per unit of supervisory time (C_s) was simply considered to be twice the cost of worker waiting time (C_w).

Peck and Hazelwood gives tables for the finite queue problem. Based on the parameters given, the results of the computations for a $\frac{1}{2}$-hr service time are shown in Table 17.2. The table reveals the increasing costs of worker waiting time and decreasing costs of supervision as the span of control increases.

Table 17.2. Measure of Non-Productive Costs Per Hour
(M = 1, T = $\frac{1}{2}$, k = 1)

Em-ployees N	Service factor X	Effi-ciency factor F	1 − F	Worker waiting costs kC_wN $(1-F)$	Super-visory costs $\frac{C_s}{N}$	Σ
4	0.0625	0.987	0.013	0.052	0.500	0.552
5	0.0625	0.982	0.018	0.090	0.400	0.490
6	0.0625	0.976	0.024	0.144	0.333	0.477
7	0.0625	0.969	0.031	0.217	0.286	0.503
8	0.0625	0.961	0.039	0.312	0.250	0.562
9	0.0625	0.953	0.047	0.423	0.222	0.645
10	0.0625	0.944	0.056	0.560	0.200	0.760
11	0.0625	0.933	0.067	0.737	0.182	0.919
12	0.0625	0.921	0.079	0.948	0.167	1.115

The economic ratio would be six workers to one supervisor. Contiguous values of N, say, two on either side of the minimum, would be equally suitable from the cost perspective. The economic span of control for this case is shown graphically in Figure 17.3.

For the same conditions, but with a ¼-hr service time, the economic span of control was found to be 9 or 10 workers to one supervisor. The caveat that values adjacent to the optimum would be just as suitable is also true here, of course. While the differences near the minimum point of the curve are less pronounced than in the ½-hr case, it should be remembered that the final costs are a function of the number of employees. The multiplier is greater for the ¼-hr situation, placing more significance on the differences. The computations are presented in Table 17.3 and the economic span of control for this case is shown graphically in Figure 17.4.

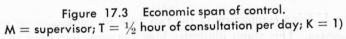

Figure 17.3   Economic span of control.
M = supervisor; T = ½ hour of consultation per day; K = 1)

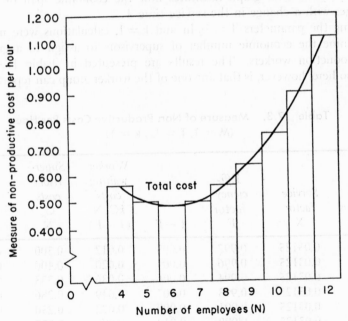

The same calculations were repeated for k = ½. For the first instance, the cost theoretic optimum shifted from six to seven and the second, from nine or ten to ten or eleven. Thus the model is relatively insensitive to values of k. A reduction in k naturally does result in a diminution of the measure of non-productive costs.

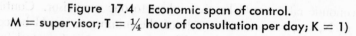

Figure 17.4   Economic span of control.
(M = supervisor; $T = \frac{1}{4}$ hour of consultation per day; $K = 1$)

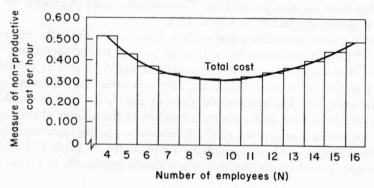

Figure 17.5 is a comparison of the two cases for corresponding numbers of employees. This graph illustrates how the economic span of control changes with a change in the service time T.

Using the parameters $T = \frac{1}{2}$-hr and $k = 1$, calculations were made to determine the economic number of supervisors to assign to a group of 50 production workers. The results are presented in Table 17.4. The proviso here, however, is that any one of the worker group can report to any

Table 17.3.   Measure of Non-Productive Costs Per Hour
($M = 1, T = \frac{1}{4}, k = 1$)

Employees N	Service factor X	Efficiency factor F	$1 - F$	Worker waiting costs kC_wN $(1 - F)$	Supervisory costs $\dfrac{C_s}{N}$	Σ
4	0.03125	0.997	0.003	0.012	0.500	0.512
5	0.03125	0.996	0.004	0.020	0.400	0.420
6	0.03125	0.994	0.006	0.036	0.333	0.369
7	0.03125	0.993	0.007	0.049	0.286	0.335
8	0.03125	0.991	0.009	0.072	0.250	0.322
9	0.03125	0.990	0.010	0.090	0.222	0.312
10	0.03125	0.989	0.011	0.110	0.200	0.310
11	0.03125	0.987	0.013	0.143	0.182	0.325
12	0.03125	0.985	0.015	0.180	0.167	0.347
13	0.03125	0.983	0.017	0.221	0.154	0.375
14	0.03125	0.981	0.019	0.266	0.143	0.409
15	0.03125	0.979	0.021	0.315	0.133	0.448
16	0.03125	0.977	0.023	0.368	0.125	0.493

Table 17.4.   Measure of Non-Productive Costs Per Hour
$(N = 50, T = \frac{1}{2}, k = 1)$

Supervisors M	Service factor X	Efficiency factor F	$1 - F$	Worker waiting costs kC_wN $(1 - F)$	Supervisory costs C_sM	Σ
3	0.0625	0.898	0.102	5.10	6.0	11.1
4	0.0625	0.976	0.024	1.20	8.0	9.2
5	0.0625	0.994	0.006	0.30	10.0	10.3
6	0.0625	0.998	0.002	0.10	12.0	12.1
7	0.0625	0.999+	<0.001	<0.05	14.0	14.0

foreman for consultation. Here the cost theoretic optimum assignment would be four supervisors and the attendant span of control would be about 12 subordinates. Thus the number of required supervisors may be reduced substantially with the condition of interchangeability of reporting. Naturally other trade-offs must be considered for such an arrangement;

Figure 17.5   Comparison of economic span of control for two service times. $(M = 1$ supervisor; $K = 1)$

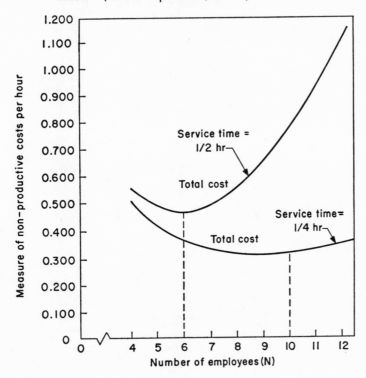

but this appears to be a lesser evil if the only alternative is to increase the span of control beyond a given point.

Some Suggested Uses

The economic model developed here may be used for personnel planning purposes. An *a priori* application would be in the design of new organizations. It may be used *a posteriori* for evaluative purposes. However, much more work would have to be accomplished to demonstrate diverse possible uses and to iron out difficulties in variant applications with attendant ramifications. The use of waiting-line theory does appear to be be a useful method for studying and obtaining answers to many personnel assignment problems. The span of control is an important contribution to good organization structure which in turn is of importance to operating economy and effectiveness.

Discussion: Queuing Theory Revisited*

Joel Zelnick

Lybrand, Ross Brothers, and Montgomery

In his recent article (*Journal of the Academy of Management*, April 1962 issue) Hill suggests queuing theory as an approach to determine the number of employees reporting to a supervisor. The author does not indicate, however, the limitations inherent in the use of this approach.

Yet, it is important to understand and appreciate the limitations of queuing analysis before an attempt is made to implement the approach. In the first place, the solution of queuing problems is tedious and time consuming. Consequently, their calculation is usually computerized, which places a cost on the solution obtained.

In the second place, and perhaps more importantly, there isn't one queuing theory model as implied. On the contrary, there are many queuing models whose underlying assumptions apply to different sets of conditions. In fact, the particular model discussed in the article is the poisson input and exponential holding time model.

In many practical situations, it is difficult to collect the data to substantiate the model that has been assumed to be applicable. Because of this problem, general-purpose queuing simulators have been developed for which no underlying assumptions are necessary. The queuing simulation takes into account the complexity of most real life situations which the basic queuing models assume to be given or ignore completely. For example, in Mr. Hill's article it is difficult to apply the model to a real life situation because the model ignores three basic conditions:

1) The interrelationship of the foreman to his supervisor and to other staff employees.
2) As he indicates the foreman may initiate contacts. This by itself negates the existence of random calls.

* Taken from the *Journal of the Academy of Management*, vol. 6, no. 2, June, 1963, p. 173.

231

3) Additionally, the foreman has many tasks peripheral to his contact with employees on production problems. For instance, he fills out appropriate forms for management reports.

The reliability of input data into the model could be suspected in most cases, because of the uncontrolled manner in which it is usually collected. Thus, in most practical solutions, it must be realized that at best the data will be approximations.

From the above discussion, it can be seen that the implementation of queuing analysis to practical problems can be costly and time consuming. Moreover, the assumptions of the model must be carefully analyzed to insure that it approximates the conditions being studied.

Therefore, these factors must be weighed against the potential benefits derived from the use of this approach.

Discussion: Some Comments
on "Queuing Theory Revisited"*

L. S. Hill

The RAND Corporation

In his discussion, "Queuing Theory Revisited" (*Academy of Management Journal*, June 1963), Mr. Joel Zelnick apparently missed the point that the procedure presented in "The Application of Queuing Theory to the Span of Control" (*Academy of Management Journal*, March 1963), is a *simplified* and *inexpensive* approach to the solution of queuing problems. His suggested alternative is inordinately more expensive with no prospect of an improvement in effectiveness or utility commensurate with such increased cost. Moreover, much time is usually necessary to attain results from simulation.

A complete array of solutions to the queuing formula presented in the original paper can be easily extracted from the Peck and Hazelwood tables.[1] Bell and Kamins have presented an example of the type of analysis which can be accomplished with these tables on a day-to-day basis with a negligible cost impact.[2] Furthermore, these authors examined the assumption of exponentially-distributed service times in the light of relevant prior work on the subject and noted that it gave waiting times which were only slightly too high. They concluded, "In most instances, and particularly for low numbers of units, (that is, service channels) the exponential assumption

* Taken from the *Journal of the Academy of Management*, vol. 6, no. 3, September, 1963, pp. 245–246.

[1] Peck, L. G., and R. N. Hazelwood, *Finite Queuing Tables*, John Wiley and Sons, Inc., New York, 1958.

[2] Bell, C. F., Jr., and Milton Kamins, *Determining Economic Quantities of Maintenance Resources: A Minuteman Application*, The RAND Corporation, RM-3308, June, 1963.

gives an identical answer to more comprehensive, ambitious, exact or exotic solutions."[3]

A complete discussion of the mathematical assumptions underlying the application of queuing theory would be much too lengthy to include here, as was equally true in the original article. Suffice it to say, initiation of calls by the foreman in the case analyzed, like those of the workers, was assumed to be production-oriented. Other assumptions, however, would *not* materially affect the approximate results shown. As noted in the article, inclusion of all possible considerations would result in a problem extremely difficult to solve mathematically. Rather than accede to probable impasses, progress can be made (and in a scientific manner) through the acceptance of certain assumptions — a characteristic of any estimating process.

Mr. Zelnick contends that reliable data cannot be obtained for use as inputs into queuing formulae. On the contrary, professional industrial engineers have effectively taken time studies for decades. They are as well trained in scientific methods as practitioners in other disciplines and possess superior knowledge of *actual* operations.

In summary, the entire tenor of the original article suggests that the span of control problem is not amenable to a finite solution. Furthermore, no universality of application of the formula was claimed. While misinterpretation of the former idea by Mr. Zelnick is puzzling, it is more difficult to perceive how he by-passed the latter consideration when, in the concluding remarks, it was explicitly stated that ". . . much work would have to be accomplished to demonstrate diverse possible uses and to iron out difficulties in variant applications with attendant ramifications."

Queuing theory, as well as any other technique, is not able, and probably never will be able, to give completely *exact* answers to problems in the management field because of the human element involved. Nevertheless, queuing theory, simulation models, and other methodologies can continue to provide a useful and practical basis for making management decisions.

[3] *Ibid.*, pages 30–31. Also pertinent to this topic are the conclusions of D. G. Kendall, in "Some Problems in the Theory of Queues," *Journal of the Royal Statistical Society,* Series B, vol. 13, no. 2, 1951, and M. Kamins, *Two Notes on the Lognormal Distribution,* The RAND Corporation, RM-3781-PR (to be published).

Comment: Queuing Theory Revisited* Once Again

L. S. Hill

The RAND Corporation

The notation was made in "Some Comments on 'Queuing Theory Revisited'," *Academy of Management Journal*, September, 1963, that the suggested analytical procedure for determination of an economically efficient span of control is a simplified approach to the solution of *queuing problems, not* to the span of control problem, as Mr. Zelnick has erroneously reported. The simplification refers to the use of the Peck and Hazlewood tables as contrasted to manual calculations. As even a cursory examination of Peck and Hazlewood and other cited references would reveal, use of these tables *per se* bears no relationship whatever to the accuracy in queuing theory.

In my original article, "The Application of Queuing Theory to the Span of Control," *Academy of Management Journal*, March, 1963, it was stated that the literature dealing with the span of control showed that an acceptable span of control varied somewhere between three and thirty employees per supervisor. Little quantitative effort had apparently been devoted to clarification of underlying reasons for these variations, either on a departmental, company, or industry-wide basis. Analytical methods *can* be developed to determine span of control for a given application, but in the same way that individual time studies are made to determine work standards.

With current rapid advances in industrial technology, it would appear essential that the development of quantitative techniques applicable to problems of industrial engineering and management should not be laid

---

* Taken from the *Journal of the Academy of Management*, vol. 7, no. 4, December, 1964, p. 317.

aside or discouraged in deference, as Mr. Zelnick puts it, to "ouija boards or other methods." A technique which can supply estimates reliable within a certain range — say a span of control from six to eight — is inevitably better than a *purely* intuitive guess.

Ten years ago it was thought by many that mathematical techniques could not be applied to problems of physiology. Today quantitative techniques are being utilized in biomedical research with every promise of giving medical investigators powerful tools with which to make new discoveries and break-throughs in medicine.[1]

The quantitative method, as applied to management problems, must be supplemented by human judgment. The primary purpose of quantitative analysis is *not* to "make" the decisions but to assist the decision-maker.[2]

We do not attempt to design supersonic aircraft and space vehicles by the predominantly intuitive and trial-and-error methods by which ocean-going ships and aircraft were conceived in earlier years. Tomorrow, the dictates of increasingly complex, highly interrelated, and considerably more rapid production processes — combined with the availability of high speed data processing equipment — will make it necessary to provide the decision-maker with increasingly more sophisticated analyses in order to sharpen his intuition and judgment.

---

[1] Richard Bellman, in the mid-1950's, visited the Sloan-Kettering Institute where he talked to John Jacquez, a physician who, in Bellman's words, "understood the power of mathematics." At that time Bellman and Jacquez decided to work on chemotherapy together with two other collaborators. As Bellman has written: "Unfortunately the major control problems of medicine are several orders of magnitude more difficult in every possible way than those which we encounter in engineering and applied mathematics in general." See R. Bellman, *Magic, Mathematics and Mystery*, P-2930, The RAND Corporation, June, 1964.

[2] For a discussion of the suitable role of quantitative analysis in the over-all decision-making process, with emphasis on cost-utility analysis, see G. H. Fisher, *The Role of Cost-Utility Analysis in Program Budgeting*, RM-4279-RC, The RAND Corporation, September, 1964.

18

Decisions and Research in Staff Utilization[*]

Alan C. Filley

University of Wisconsin

The staff concept ranks high in the list of pivotal, strategic management concepts. In recent years this concept has come under heavy attack. Managers and scholars alike manifest doubts about the viability of the staff concept, finding it to be confusing and complex. Professor Filley examines the way companies make use of staff units, and states a theory of staff based on his studies of staff development. His conclusion that the staff concept can be accepted is developed within the framework of decision theory.

Rather startling changes have developed in the field of organization and management during the last ten years. Scientists of many disciplines have turned their attention to the problems of group design and behavior yielding fruitful contributions. Students and scholars of business management have become infused with a zeal for empirical evaluation of traditional concepts that have been all too frequently taken for granted. In many cases traditional theory withstands the hard appraisal with great success. The principles of management, one finds, are not so mythical after all.

There are certain concepts in the body of traditional structural-functional theory that do not fare so well, however. Outstanding in this respect is the staff concept. One finds, upon trying to classify organization personnel or units into a line or staff designation that many jobs defy a tidy accounting. Furthermore, upon discussing line-staff relations with executives one discovers that many managers are unfamiliar with the concepts, though their organizations arrange themselves in suitable patterns anyway.

[*] Taken and adapted from *The Journal of the Academy of Management*, vol. 6, no. 3, September, 1963, pp. 220–231. A paper delivered at the annual meeting of the Midwest Division of the Academy of Management, at Columbus, Ohio, April 26–27, 1963.

After a few of these experiences, and after finding a profusion of contradictory statements in management literature about the proper role and use of staff one finds himself at various times ready to reject the whole idea of staff, prepared to coin new terms, or desirous of developing different classifications. The writer admits to using all of these approaches, and the present article is further admission of a final willingness to accept the staff concept, though on a somewhat different basis.

The following discussion reports theory, observations, and research having to do with staff in business organizations. It first summarizes what appear to be the general characteristics of staff use. Then it evaluates traditional theory in terms of several studies of staff development, and suggests a decision theory of staff growth that is consistent with that research. Finally, a critical hypothesis in the decision theory having to do with personal staff is tested and reported.[1]

Staff Role and Functions

The most satisfactory means of distinguishing staff units in an organization seems to be on the basis of their objectives. A unit, whether an individual, department, or division, can generally be recognized as line if it adds direct salable value to the product or service produced, or staff if it adds value primarily to the organization itself. On this basis a truck driver delivering the product to a customer is line, an engineer preparing working drawings for use in the production process is staff, while another engineer designing installation systems for a customer is line.

The primary mission of a unit must be distinguished from a single line or staff function. Many line units perform staff functions, as when the sales department advises production on customer complaints; or the reverse, as is the case when a purchasing department exercises functional authority by rejecting a purchase order. Staff functions are primarily supportive, while line functions are those of command.

The formal authority of a staff unit ranges from rights of observation and comment at one extreme to the exercise of command functions at the other. Included between these extremes are arrangements in which the staff must be consulted by a line unit, or those in which the staff must concur with the inquiring line unit before a final decision is made. Organizational committees, which are staff units themselves, may be seen to exercise any or several of these forms of formal authority.

---

[1] Research on staff growth reported here is part of a larger study by the writer on the characteristics of internal business growth to be published in full in forthcoming monograph. Research on the use of personal staff is part of a study entitled "Some Organizational Determinants of Managerial Behavior" (with Dr. R. J. House) sponsored by the Graduate School, University of Wisconsin.

Besides formal relationships the staff also exercises power, giving it greater influence in organization matters than formal authority would indicate. Staff units derive their power from such characteristics as expertise, closeness to the top administration, status, superior articulation of ideas, or control of sanctions. Indeed, the effect of a staff suggestion upon a line manager often rests importantly upon a power balance between both parties, particularly where formal authority is poorly defined or inoperative.

The subtle difference in power balances may be determined by investigating practices of appeal. Dr. Robert House and I have investigated power centers in research and development divisions of three large corporations. We asked executives to name those people in a position to initiate action on their part or to veto decisions which they made. Where a power center was in doubt, we asked "What would you do if you disagreed with a request for action (or veto of your decision)?" If the respondent said "I appeal to my boss" then the balance of power was not in the respondent's favor and the other source was counted as a power center or "boss." If on the other hand the answer was "I reject the request and let him take it through channels," then the outside initiator lacked sufficient power to be called a boss or power center. Our research indicates that where the formal authority is well-defined, power centers are less numerous.

One finds two important kinds of staff in organizations. The first is personal staff, of which the most clear-cut example is the assistant–to position. Operating with or without organizational sanction, the assistant–to functions as the arms and legs of his principal: operating within the principal's area of authority, performing a variety of unstandardized activities, and frequently acting in the name of the official for whom he works. More will be said about this type of staff later in this article.

The second type is the organizational staff. These units engage in various planning and control activities, giving service, advice, and coordinative support to other units. The supportive role must be emphasized: the need for staff arises from the complexities of operating large rather than small organizations, and efficient rather than inefficient institutions. The implications of the staff role may be seen in the growth of staff as organizations increase in size.

Staff Growth

Classical theory of organization has described an increasing complexity of functional relationships which develop during growth. The theory prescribes how the organization should deal with this complexity through a balance of vertical and horizontal specialization controlled by scalar levels, departmentation, and spans of control. The concept of increasing functional complexity is expressed in the literature by the Law of Functional Growth:

> The various functions of an organization increase in scope and complexity, as well as the amount of work and the technical requirements for their proper performance, as the volume of business grows. The complexity of functional relationships tends to increase in geometric progression as the volume of work that the organization must handle increases in arithmetic progression.[2]

An important means for dealing with increasing complexity is through the establishment and utilization of staff units. Staff functions are assumed to be withdrawn from line units through functional differentiation, aiding the line in specialized planning and control. Since the theory assumes an increase in functional complexity at a geometric rate, it logically implies a similar increase in the rate of staff growth, stating that "staff functions [and presumably staff units] tend to grow faster than the line organizations they serve."[3]

If one assumes the supportive role of staff, the classical position is also supported logically by the square-cube law.[4] The law states simply that as volume increases by a cubic function the surface inclosing it increases by a square function, increasing as it does only in two dimensions. Thus, when applied to organizational growth, staff should grow at a rate faster than the growth of total organization, lest it collapse from lack of support.

Empirical studies of staff growth do not support the predicted pattern, however. Three earlier studies and one of my own show that, except for early stages of business growth, staff grows at either a linear or mixed pattern.

The first two studies to be noted were cross-sectional, or "point-in-time" analyses, comparing an average of line and staff employment among many firms at an instant of time, arranged by size of employment. Baker and Davis made such a study in 1954.[5]

Using data from 211 companies of less than 25 to 4,000 employees they computed the relationship between all line, represented by direct production labor excluding supervision, and all staff, represented by indirect

[2] Ralph C. Davis, *The Fundamentals of Top Management*, New York: Harper and Brothers, 1951, p. 232.

[3] *Ibid.*, p. 232.

[4] Mason Haire has utilized this law in developing a provocative theory of business growth based upon a biological analogy. He uses the law to posit a relationship between internal and external employees, rather than to continue his logic to the relationship between line and staff. Mason Haire, "Biological Models and Empirical Histories of the Growth of Organizations," *Modern Organization Theory*, New York: John Wiley and Sons, Inc., 1959, p. 292.

[5] Alton W. Baker and Ralph C. Davis, *Ratios of Staff to Line Employees and Stages of Differentiation of Staff Functions*, Bureau of Business Research, The Ohio State University, Research Monograph No. 72, 1954.

labor plus lower levels of supervision. They also showed the relationship between individual kinds of staff and total line employment. The results in each case were expressed as a linear regression line fit to the mean level of staff at each size category of line employment. Using this data staff would be about 42% of total employment at all levels, and 75% of direct production employment.[6]

Contrary to the normative prediction of a geometric increase in staff as size increases, the Baker-Davis analysis indicated that there is a linear relationship between line and staff growth: as shown in Figure 18.1 staff

Figure 18.1 Line—staff relationship in Baker-Davis study.

Total number of indirect employees and direct employees, manufacturing companies, Ohio, 1951.

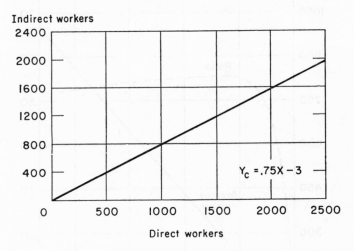

Source: Alton W. Baker and Ralph C. Davis, *Ratios of Staff to Line Employees and Stages of Differentiation of Staff Functions*, Bureau of Business Research, The Ohio State University, Number 72, 1954, p. 15. Used by permission.

employment remained the same percentage of total employment at each increasing size level. However, the researchers found differing rates of growth for individual staff functions. Inspection, cafeteria, maintenance, engineering, tool design, and tool and pattern units each increased at an increasing rate as the number of direct workers increased. Supervisors and executives of direct workers, purchasing, tool handling, personnel, accounting, time and motion study, and production control each increased at a constant rate. Finally top management executives and the staff units of

[6] Regression equation for direct to indirect labor, $y = .75x - 3$; coeff. of corr. .97.

plant protection and shipping and receiving each increased at a decreasing rate.

Another study was made with similar methodology by DeSpelder in 1956.[7] It presented a cross-sectional analysis of 155 companies in the automotive parts manufacturing industry ranging in size from 5 to 2,400 employees, comparing staff employment to different levels of line employ-

Figure 18.2   Line–staff relationship in DeSpelder study.

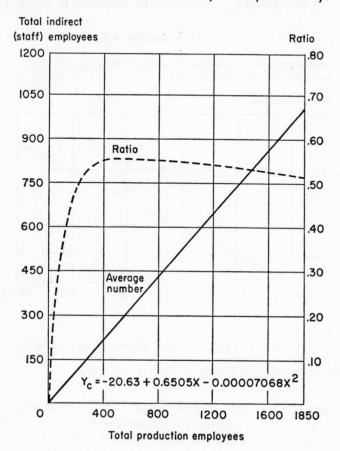

Total indirect (staff) employees

Ratio

$$Y_c = -20.63 + 0.6505X - 0.00007068X^2$$

Total production employees

Source: Bruce E. DeSpelder, *Ratios of Staff to Line Personnel*, Bureau of Business Research, The Ohio State University, Research Monograph No. 106, 1962. Used by permission.

[7] Bruce DeSpelder, *Ratios of Staff to Line Personnel*, Bureau of Business Research, The Ohio State University, Research Monograph No. 106, 1962.

ment, not including sales, top management, or multiple assignment employees. As indicated in Figure 18.2, results showed the percentage of staff employment growing rapidly to a total employment level of about 866 employees, or direct production employment level of about 550, and declining slightly as a percentage of employment after that point.[8] Once the peak was reached, staff declined as a percentage of estimated total employment from 36 per cent to 34 per cent, or as a percentage of direct production employment from 57 per cent to 51 per cent.

As in the previous study, different patterns of growth were noted for different types of staff. Surprisingly, however, the growth of individual types of staff was seldom in agreement with the same staffs cited in the Baker-Davis study. Like the other study, however, top management became a smaller percentage of total employment.

In general, it may be said that DeSpelder confirmed the Baker-Davis results, except for small-sized firms. Staff growth beyond the initial increase in the former, was linear or nearly linear in both cases. One must use care in generalizing about growth from cross-section studies such as this, however, for changing conditions during the growth of a single firm are not shown in firms arranged by size categories. Furthermore, what is measured is actually those individuals or departments which may be recognized as staff rather than all staff functions performed by any line or staff unit. Viewed in this light, it is not surprising that defined or recognized staff should grow rapidly at early stages of business growth.

Contrasted with the cross-section analyses, two longitudinal studies have compared the ratio of line or staff employment to total employment for each year during the growth of firms analyzed. The first was conducted by Mason Haire and reported in 1959.[9] Haire studied the growth in line and staff employment in four firms which had, respectively, about 2,000, 275, 200, and 300 employees. Employment for each year during company growth was classified as line or staff, and each of these classifications was presented as a percentage of total employment, as indicated in Figure 18.3.

The results showed that staff employment grew at an increasing rate during the early period of business growth in all four firms. In later years staff grew at the same rate as total employment, stabilizing in two cases at about 50 per cent of employment and at about 25 per cent in the other two. Thus the time series data for each of the four firms also conflict with the theoretical contention that staff grows at an increasing rate.

Utilizing similar methodology the present writer computed the growth of staff in five firms, shown in Figure 18.4 as firm A through E. These com-

[8] Regression equation for indirect employment to total production employees, $y = -20.63 + 0.6505x - 0.00007068x^2$.

[9] Haire, *op. cit.*, p. 292.

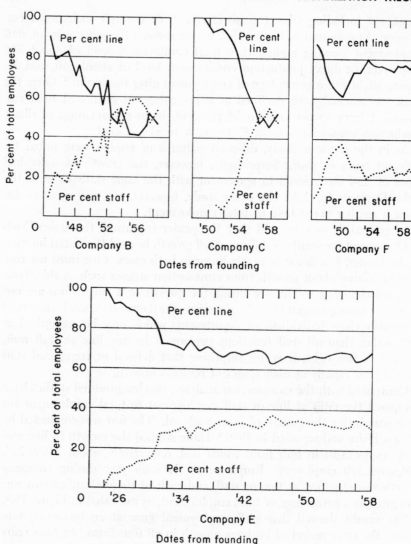

Figure 18.3   Per cent of line and staff personnel during growth of companies in Haire study.

Source: Mason Haire, *Modern Organization Theory* (New York: John Wiley and Sons, 1959) pp. 288–291. Used by permission.

panies had a peak employment of 450, 59, 70, 37, and 378 respectively. Total employment was highest in Companies A, C, and E in final year shown and peaked in Company B in 1950 and D in 1956. Firm A shows an increasing rate of staff growth during the first six years, stabilizing after that point. Firm B shows a slight long-run increase in staff, both before and after employment reached a maximum. Firm C has a clear upward trend in staff during the early period, with what appears to be stabilization at about 20 per cent of employment. Firm D has also had staff employment fluctuating around the 20 per cent level, declining after total employment declined. Finally, Firm E with 378 employees has experienced staff growth at around 10 per cent of employment during its lifetime.

The five firms show little similarity in their patterns of staff growth. Though the earlier cross-section studies might cause one to predict rapid

Figure 18.4   Historical staff growth in five firms.

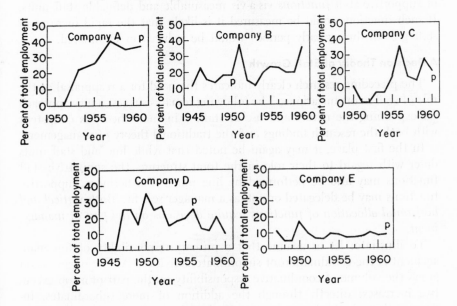

p – Maximum size of total employment

increase in staff among such small firms, they show no uniform rapid increase in staff percentage during growth of employment, nor do they show any clear-cut linear relationship with employment growth. The mixed evidence does show, however, that staff growth is not solely a function of total employment.

A study of the internal conditions of management and organization structure in each of the firms during their growth histories failed to show any correlation of staff growth with the development of a formal, bureaucratic system of organization and management. For example, staff growth was not related to the development of formal administrative management positions.[10] Nor was it to the rationalization of the organization structure.[11]

It should be noted that this and the preceding study do not show what *should be*, but rather *what is*. At least two of the firms experienced clear economies of operation upon the addition of staff, indicating the need for guidelines in staff use and further indicating that an effort to minimize indirect labor may create serious diseconomies of operation. It would seem that further studies of individual types of staff along the lines of the cross-section studies cited earlier is more useful than prediction of total staff utilization, particularly if some measures of efficiency can be determined.

Furthermore, none of the studies cited actually measures the existence of supportive staff *functions* vis-a-vis measurable and definable staff units. If such functions could be measured it is likely that the rapid increase in staff growth during early periods would be reduced or eliminated.

A Decision Theory of Staff Growth

The preceding research clearly indicates the need for a reappraisal of the role of staff in organizations. The following remarks suggest a new approach for explaining the nature and use of staff. This new theory is consistent with both the research findings and the traditional theory of management.

In the first place, it may again be noted that while line and staff units differ with regard to their role in the total structure, the supportive staff functions may also be performed by line units. Furthermore, supportive functions may be delegated or not, as a manager sees fit. *Both vertical and horizontal allocation of functions require decisions on the part of management.*

To illustrate: let us assume that a primary responsibility of top management is the coordination of subordinate activities. As the organization grows the volume of coordinative responsibility on the part of a top executive increases: directly through the addition of more subordinates; indirectly through the increasing complexity of organizational relationships.

Faced with this increased burden a top management executive has two primary courses of action. He may (a) increase his own capacity, or he

[10] Administrative management positions are those which deal with setting long-range objectives and policy for the firm, or of some major division in the firm, and coordinate the activities of diverse functional units. For an excellent historical treatment of the development of administrative management in American business see Alfred D. Chandler and Fritz Redlich, "Recent Developments in American Business Administration and Their Conceptualization," *Business History Review*, Vol. XXXV, no. 1 (Spring 1961), p. 1.

[11] A rational organization structure is one characterized by a legal system of authority; clearly defined objectives, hierarchy, and job relationships; and clearly defined spheres of job competence. See Davis, *op. cit.*, Chaps. VI and XIV, and Max Weber, *Theory of Social and Economic Organization*, translated and edited by A. M. Henderson and T. Parsons, (New York: Oxford University Press, 1947), pp. 335–336.

may (b) delegate coordinative responsibility to others. An increase in his own capacity or ability may be accomplished by increasing his efficiency, by working more intensively, by working more extensively, e.g., longer hours, or by extending his capacity through personal staff, e.g., "assistants-to."

If the executive chooses, on the other hand, to delegate coordinative functions to subordinates, he may delegate functions either to line subordinates or to new or existing staff units. Thus the allocation of functions and the consequent formation of staff units is based on a rational process of decision-making. If he decides to retain centralized responsibility and performance then staff assistants may be created. If he decides to delegate functions to subordinates, staff may also be created. It may be seen that staff can serve to support either centralization or decentralization.

The fact that either line or staff executives may perform necessary supportive functions seems to have been generally overlooked in management literature and research. Research designs which purport to measure a natural-order result of growth are, in fact, measuring only the extent to which circumstances or policy have dictated the creation or restriction of staff units. Nor do such designs consider the conditions militating toward the retention of such functions by top management and against delegation to subordinates.

A Study of the Assistant–To Position

The decision process staff formation explains why actual growth patterns of staff are unpredictable. It also focuses attention on a particular type of staff that is still to be fully understood, the personal staff assistant. If the previous logic is correct, then the assistant should increase the capacity of his principal. Further, the executive who is unable or unwilling to delegate would be more likely to use personal staff.

Considering the assistant's role in terms of the traditional span of control principle, if the executive's capacity to manage is increased with the addition of an assistant, then an executive with an assistant should be able to utilize a broader span than an executive without an assistant. If the assistant does not have such an effect, or if the executive's span is unlimited, then the presence of an assistant would have no significant effect.

Consideration of existing evidence supports the notions of the assistant's role and the rational span of control. Assistant–to positions were found reporting to the top executive in four of the five firms discussed earlier during the period of growth when the organizations were dominated by charismatic entrepreneurs. Broad spans were also present at such times. Later when bureaucratic organizations became established, assistants were generally eliminated and narrower spans established through intermediate levels of management.

A *Business Week* survey of 300 companies also found that assistants were frequently used when top executives were unwilling to delegate more to subordinates.[12] Further, staff members at the Lockheed Missile Division have concluded that the use of personal assistants increase the optimum span for executives.[13]

An opportunity to study the relationship between the use of personal staff and spans of control occurred during a recent interviewing and testing study of a company research division. The division contains over 2,000 scientific, technical, operative, and managerial personnel, serving a firm in the manufacturing equipment industry. Programs of reorganization and executive development have been started recently, but the structure remains somewhat loose and undefined at present.

Based on the decision theory of staff formation it was hypothesized that managers in the division with broad spans should make significantly greater use of assistant–to positions than those which have spans that are optimum or less. Broad spans, it is assumed, indicate that a manager is unable or unwilling to delegate.[14]

The pattern that emerged was most interesting. It became clear once again that what *is* and what *should be* are two quite different situations. Top management in the division had indicated, for example, that there was a formal company policy against the use of assistant–to positions. Yet when 61 department and section heads of research and development units were interviewed, 31 per cent said that they regularly made use of such assistants. Assistants were defined as persons who regularly performed a variety of duties within the area of authority and responsibility of the principal, acting in his name and representing his interests. Not included were seconds–in–command or persons who took over during vacations or other short periods on a non-regular basis.

The determination of span in the interviews also yielded some intriguing results. Respondents were asked to indicate the number of persons supervised directly; that is, the number with whom they had regular contact and about whose activities they had first-hand knowledge. Not included were persons whose work they reviewed for special purposes, as in the case of a salary review of persons reporting to their own seconds in command.

Given this definition of span, there was a noticeable tendency to mention 6 or 7 subordinates or to jump to a much higher number, often 15 to 20. Upon investigation it was discovered that the difference appeared to be

[12] "Handy Men with Growing Power," *Business Week* (Oct. 19, 1957), p. 193.

[13] Harold Stieglitz, "Optimizing Span of Control," *Management Record*, vol. VVIV, no. 9 (Sept. 1962), p. 25.

[14] No judgment of goodness or badness is necessarily implied when the manager is unwilling or unable to delegate, though the effects may often be negative. Under some circumstances, as under periods of stress, it may be essential that direct control of many operations be maintained. Nor is it necessarily true that conditions will not sometimes permit very broad optimum spans in a decentralized organization. For example, the Catholic Church, Sears, Roebuck, and Bank of America utilize broad spans. Each has separate but similar units whose operating problems change slowly over time, and line units which are supported by a variety of organizational staff units.

caused by leadership styles: managers who were more directive in their approach would by-pass the use of subordinate managers. They regularly directed the efforts of persons nominally reporting to their own subordinates as well as the subordinates themselves. Such directive managers typically mentioned broad spans. On the other hand, where respondents delegated to and made use of subordinate managers, they tended to mention those men only when asked about spans.

In analyzing the results, a narrow span was taken to be eight or less persons directed, while a broad span was taken as more than eight persons. The breaking point was chosen because of the noticeable tendency in the interviews to mention, as a small span, a maximum of 6 or 7. The decision was also consistent with the normative statements in management literature which indicate that the ideal span is probably somewhere between 5 to 8 persons.[15]

As indicated in Table 18.1, of those department heads and section heads with more than eight subordinates, 46.9 per cent had assistant–to positions reporting to them, while among those managers with eight or less subordinates only 13.8 per cent had such personal assistants. The difference is significant beyond the one per cent level, and the pattern is sustained in both the section heads and the department heads as separate categories.

One may infer from these results that the notions of a personal assistant to extend capacity and a rational span of control are supported. Furthermore, support of the hypothesis generated by the staff decision theory adds further empirical credence to the theory itself. Decisions about functional allocation may result in staff units which support either centralization or decentralization.

Table 18.1. Use of Assistant–to Positions Under Broad and Narrow Spans

Level	Span	No. With Asst's	%	No. Without Asst's	%	Total With & Without Asst's	%
Dept. No.	0–8	2	8.0	23	92.0	25	100.0
	9–over	7	58.3	5	41.7	12	100.0
Section No.	0–8	2	14.2	12	85.7	14	100.0
	9–over	8	40.0	12	60.0	20	100.0
All	0–8	4	13.8	25	86.2	29	100.0
	9–over	15	46.9	17	53.1	32	100.0

[15] It must not be inferred that the span of eight is ideal for all organizations under all conditions. The rational span for any one organization must be determined empirically with consideration of interrelationship of work, organization level, quality of leadership and subordinates, coordination needed, use of staff, ecological factors, personnel turnover, importance of decisions, degree of formalization, and many other factors.

Concluding Remarks

It is clear that any natural relationship between the growth of staff as the organization increases in size is unlikely. The geometric increase in staff growth predicted by traditional theory is not likely to be found, and any simple linear relationship between line and staff growth at all levels is based upon some questionable assumptions. Instead, the creation of staff units is the product of decision-making by management. It would be useful to focus our attention upon these decisions of functional allocation in order to determine the best alternative arrangement under a given set of conditions.

19

The PERT System: An Appraisal of
Program Evaluation Review Technique[*]

Daniel D. Roman

Florida State University

Program Evaluation Review Technique (PERT) goes beyond tradi-tional Gantt charts to establish a quantitative approach to program planning and control. Sometimes called the Critical Path Method, it emphasizes a network or flow plan in a system of administrative or procedural activities in the pursuit of goals through time. The sys-tem characteristics yield a type of structural analysis that has impli-cations for organization theory.

Program Evaluation Review Technique, better known as P.E.R.T.,[1] represents a significant step forward in the development of managerial science. The system, developed jointly by the Navy Special Projects Office and Booz-Allen-Hamilton, in conjunction with the Fleet Ballistic Missile Program, has had its major impetus and success in association with the Polaris missile.

PERT is essentially a planning and control concept designed to: focus managerial attention on key program developmental parts; point up po-tential problem areas which could disrupt program goals; evaluate progress toward the attainment of program objectives; give management a prompt mechanical reporting device; and, finally, aid and facilitate decision-making. In the accomplishment of these stated objectives, PERT uses TIME as a common denominator to reflect three categories of factors which influence success — time, resource applications, and required performance specifica-

[*] Taken and adapted from *The Journal of the Academy of Management*, vol. 5, no. 1, April, 1962, pp. 57–65.
[1] The Air Force has also adapted a similar system under the designation, Program Evaluation Procedure (P.E.P.).

tions.[2] The explanation of the PERT program, as set forth in this paper, represents a considerable over-simplification of the system. The basic purpose is to examine PERT as a development in management science. The mechanical composition is therefore not covered in detail.[3]

The Mechanics of PERT

Essentially, PERT is an attempt at quantification of program planning and control. An important characteristic of PERT, as distinguished from existing systems, is the attempt to systemize and mechanize the planning and control process. The *innovation of the system* would seem to lie in the addition of mathematical embellishments, the use of computers and variations of known scheduling methods, such as Gantt Charts, "goes-into," and minus day scheduling. The system goes beyond the traditional Gantt Chart scheduling, but still uses the principle of this technique. In the PERT variation, the Gantt-type bars that indicated various phases of activities measured against a time scale have been eliminated.

The Network

The fundamental tool used in the PERT approach is the network or flow plan. The composition of the network is a series of related events and activities. Events, (required sequential accomplishment points), are most frequently represented by circle or square symbols. Activities are the time consuming element of the program and are used to connect the various events. They are shown in the flow plan as arrows. A simplified model of the flow plan is illustrated in Figure 19.1.

The number of events shown on any flow plan should reflect significant program accomplishments, (such as administrative, intellectual or hardware), and should be in some approximation to the complexity of that program, It should also be noted that some events may depend only on one single prior event, while in other situations there may be an interrelationship of several events leading to the accomplishment of an ultimate objective.

Estimating Elapsed-Time Between Events

To determine the elapsed-time between events, the activity time, responsible engineers evaluate the situation and submit their estimates using three possible completion assumptions: optimistic completion time, most likely completion time and pessimistic completion time. Optimistic com-

[2] Willard Fazar, *Advanced Management Systems For Advanced Weapon Systems* (Presentation Abstract: Washington, D.C.: U.S. Navy Special Projects Office, March,
[3] Detailed information on the mechanics of the PERT system is available through the Special Projects Office of the Department of the Navy, Washington 25, D.C.

FLOW PLAN

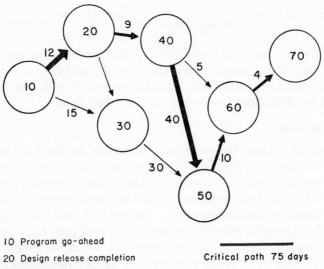

10 Program go-ahead
20 Design release completion
30 Material procurement
40 Model testing
50 Fabrication prototype
60 Full scale testing
70 Production prototype completion

Critical path 75 days

Figure 19.1

pletion time is predicated on minimal difficulties. The most likely completion time represents the most accurate forecast based on normal developments. Pessimistic time is estimated on maximum potential difficulties.

Based on the three-time estimates, a simple formula[4] can be derived which will give the activity time to be used in the system flow plan. The application of the formula gives a time with a 50% chance of realization.

ACTIVITY TIME

O = Optimistic Completion Time
M = Most Likely Completion Time
P = Pessimistic Completion Time

[4] Ben B. Barrett, *Basic Principles of PERT/PEP*, An address before the Controls and Planning Association, Los Angeles, March 22, 1961. For additional calculations in computing activity time see D. G. Malcolm, J. H. Roseboom, C. E. Clark and W. Fazar, *Application of a Technique for Research and Development Program Evaluation*, Operations Research, vol. 7, no. 5, September-October 1959, pp. 651–652.

Assuming $O = 6$ weeks, $M = 8$ weeks and $P = 16$ weeks, the activity time can be computed, using the formula:

$$\frac{0 + 4M + P}{6} = \text{Activity Time} \qquad \frac{6 + 32 + 16}{6} = 9 \text{ weeks}$$

The formula is based on the probability distribution of the time involved in performing the activity.[5] Once the network has been established and all activity times computed, the information on activities and events can be translated into dates based on a program start time.

The Critical Path

The critical path of the program is established by the longest possible time span along the system flow plan. To determine the critical path, data and events are organized in sequence. The starting point for plotting the critical path is the final event in the total network. From the final event, related events are placed sequentially, working backward, until the present is reached. Where the network is simple the critical path can be computed and determined manually. In more complex situations a procedure for sequencing events can be programmed on an electronic computer.[6]

In Figure 19.1, the heavy line indicates the critical path in the network. If the proposed final completion date is to be bettered, indicated by event 70, reappraisal and curtailment of activity time must take place along the critical path.

Inasmuch as the critical path takes the longest time and is the determinant for the project completion, other events may conceivably be completed before the time they are actually needed. The time differential between the scheduled completion of the non-critical events and the time that they are actually required is called the Slack Time. Where excessive Slack Time exists in the program, a re-evaluation should take place. It should be determined which resources, and in what amount, could be transferred to other activities. This, in turn, could shorten the Critical Path or better balance the allocation of resources assigned to the project.

Program Review and Reporting

Once the schedule has been established, frequent review by program participants is required to assess actual progress against planned accomplishment. Inputs are then assembled and programmed into the computer, which prints out the status report of time interval estimates versus actual reported progress.

---

[5] Estimating the time distribution is more fully discussed in, *Pert-Summary Report Phase 1* (Washington, D.C., Special Projects Office, Bureau of Naval Weapons, Department of the Navy, July 1958), p. 6.

[6] Malcolm, *et al., op. cit.*, p. 653.

Reporting can be done bi-weekly, for example, on all items shown in the network or flow plan. The currency and frequency of the reporting promptly alerts management to the events which are deviating from the basic program plan. Where corrective action is not possible and the scheduled date of an objective event has been changed, it will become necessary to recompute the entire program to determine the current anticipated completion dates of all events.[7]

PERT as a Management Tool

There are many dramatic implications of PERT relative to management. Initially and perhaps most important, it focuses management's attention on the importance of planning and control and the coordination of these functions by means of tangible and systematic inputs, audits and reports.

Too often planning and/or control are performed on a segmented basis with inconclusive results and little direction toward a well-defined objective. PERT eliminates uncoordinated segmentation and brings an integrated methodology into program planning. PERT indicates every event critical for program performance and shows the related activity time before the next sequential event(s) can take place. Most control systems also indicate time span and sequence but lack the specificity of PERT in drawing links between the events, the time and the responsibility for functional performance.

While individually none of the ideas employed by PERT represents startling innovation, the total approach takes a major step forward in managerial technique. An appraisal of the system would seem to indicate some significant advantages over existing approaches; these are discussed in the next section.

Participation

The program is planned in detail by the participants. Planning inputs in the PERT system flow upward to be assembled and evaluated as a composite working document. Frequently, in the traditional planning approach basic premises may flow downward and lead to unrealistic assumptions and commitments when program boundaries are predetermined before detailed participation is requested. When the program performers are given limitations such as commencement and completion dates, performance specifications to be met, budget restrictions, and the like, participation may be only partial, even illusory.

---

[7] PERT *Summary Report Phase 1* (Washington, D.C.: Special Projects Office Bureau of Naval Weapons Department of the Navy, July, 1958), p. 13.

In the PERT system, no master plan formulated by management, the project office or a central planning staff is forwarded to the working levels as a compulsory program plan. The people who will ultimately have to meet the program objectives are active contributors from the outset. This can promote teamwork, facilitate communication, encourage a proprietary interest and foster orderly, intelligent planning. After the program ground rules have been established, the people who have participated in the planning are the same people who do the work and report and forecast accomplishment in relation to the original plan.

Perspective, Programming and Interrelationship of Events

PERT departs from normal programming where only key milepost developments are depicted. The PERT network shows the interrelationship between all vital program functions. In short, it attempts to give total program perspective.

The events that are shown on the network or flow plan are broken into meaningful, related segments. The activity time between events may vary from zero to several days or months. As an example, if the activity time is indicated on the network as zero, it alerts the participants to the fact that instantaneous action must take place between certain events before additional sequential development or activity can occur. The flow plan fixes each group's participation time and responsibility and draws attention to each event or chain-event dependency.

Morale and Performance Review

The PERT concept applied to planning and control literally demands the active participation of high level functional personnel. In general practice the detail planning and subsequent control work is usually delegated to secondary staff people. Since the "doers" and the "planners" are different it has often happened that the direction of the plan and the actual direction of the program were only loosely related. By divorcing or estranging planning and performance, the performers felt only a mild sense of obligation to adhere to program boundaries.

PERT has changed this insofar as planning and performance cannot be disassociated. The event and activity time injected in the flow plan represent firm commitments by the person(s) responsible for performing the work. The importance of fulfilling the commitment seems to be a reflection of professional pride and competence. Therefore, an intelligent appraisal and evaluation of the situation is encouraged before events and activities are injected into the entire program. It would be reasonable to assume that if the program segments are well conceived the total program plan should be proportionately better. A good plan well conceived and forcefully executed can be a strong factor in building up organization esprit de corps.

Another consideration is the awareness by technical and scientific personnel that management now has a yardstick of performance evaluation and a means of frequent review. The proximity of planning and performance in one jurisdiction, accountable to an interested management, can stimulate accomplishment and bolster morale.

PERT Schedules Intellectual Activity

A constant source of irritation in program planning is the scheduling of intellectual activities. Scientific and administrative personnel have traditionally been loath to accept time limitations on creative work. As a consequence, scheduling has normally dealt more successfully with tangible accomplishments than with creativity. PERT attempts to show all significant program accomplishment points, including the scheduling of research, administrative activities and decision making. From present indications, it appears that PERT is achieving the scheduling of these points with more than minimal success. The acceptance of this type of scheduling can perhaps be attributed to psychological forces associated with the participative activities, the explanation of total program goals shown in series on interrelated events and increased morale.

PERT and Computers

One of the more important aspects of the PERT system is that its design permits use of the computer. The information is quantified and assembled and programmed into the computer where it can be quickly translated and accurately reported to management for rapid decision making. The quantification and programming of the information into the computers in this new application represents one of the foremost innovations of PERT.

Some of the PERT Problem Areas

In the past several years many new ideas, techniques and tools have been introduced on the business scene. Preliminary successes and elaborate publicity on some of these concepts have led management, in many instances, to embrace them with almost an appalling fanaticism. Quite often acceptance has been on the basis of insufficient study regarding adaptability to the unique problems of a particular business situation. Results have many times been disappointing and costly. Potentially good managerial tools have fallen into disrepute and have become the victims of fadism because of promiscuous application.

While the PERT system holds great promise and obviously can be useful in certain applications, words of caution against uncritical application are appropriate. Many problems pertaining to PERT still have to be solved. Some of the more critical problem areas are the human element, lack of correlation between progress and expenditure and some questions on scheduling practices.

The Human Element

After the total plan has been established, events identified and activity time estimated, the program can be reasonably quantified. However, the basic premises, such as the critical events and the estimated completion times continue to be based on personal evaluation — the human element.

Each contribution to the total program must be carefully analyzed. Incompetent evaluation, general optimism or pessimism can permeate the individual estimates and lead to skewing of the total program. It frequently happens, for example, that representatives of finance and manufacturing are conservative, whereas representatives of engineering and sales may lean toward fairly consistent optimism. Personal variations also exist within functions. Based on functional and personal variations, it would appear that some calibration of individual inputs is necessary to obtain a moderately accurate program forecast.

Another area where the human element cannot be ignored is the review periods when progress is interpreted in relation to schedule. Again, taking into consideration the varying dispositions of the contributing individuals, difficulties can be encountered as a consequence of poor status evaluation. For instance, many times a solution, although elusive, appears imminent and the fact that the problem has not been solved is discounted when giving information to the reviewer. Subsequent scheduled completion dates may not be satisfied because the imminent solution still has not been uncovered. The result may be a slippage of the entire schedule without any prior warning or opportunity to take corrective action. Of course, the converse can be true. While it is not common, completion of a program phase before its schedule time without adequate notification can lead to an uneconomical utilization of resources.

Training of personnel and constant performance evaluation can encourage more accurate forecasting, but it can never completely eliminate the human element. Cursory examination of PERT can obscure the fact that the critical premises are based on personal estimates. As long as this is so, no amount of scientific quantification or methodology can eradicate a foundation built on human error.

Lack of Correlation Between Progress and Expenditure

At least three basic ingredients are in every developmental program: Time, Function and Cost. If these three ingredients are not meaningfully interpreted, it is impossible to determine properly the true program status. A fundamental weakness of the PERT system as it now exists is the failure to correlate progress and expenditures.[8]

---

[8] Research teams are now working on this problem.

If schedule is the sole criteria for status determination, misleading assumptions may develop regarding the progress of the program. Schedules in many instances can be maintained at an accomplishment ratio disproportionate to ultimate function and cost considerations. Without cost inputs it could be possible to maintain schedules, at least initially, by large allocations of expensive resources. Later in the program, when remaining funds were inadequate or exhausted, the cost discrepancy would become apparent and the total status and net accomplishment would have to be reappraised. To date, PERT has not satisfactorily solved this very important problem.

Scheduling Practices

Where program review indicates a slippage of a critical event, rescheduling takes place and new inputs are fed into the computer. Proportional changes are then made in the remainder of the program.

Again the human element in the problem cannot be ignored. The computer cannot think; it can only interpret information at a programmed rate. A computer cannot possibly accurately determine the net effect of the slippage of one critical event on all subsequent events. A critical development may slip schedule-wise, and in many instances proportional slippage does not take place in subsequent events. Related events and activities must be studied and analyzed in relation to new developments. Some events may be affected in direct proportion, other events may slide downstream disproportionately, while in still other instances events may not be adversely affected at all.

Another disturbing element in the PERT process is the method of determining the schedule pattern. The activity time computed by the formula $\frac{O+4M+P}{6}$ represents an estimated average time. Average time assumptions may be adequate under certain conditions. But when they are predicated in an estimate of optimistic, most-likely and pessimistic times they can be skewed in one direction or the other by very high optimism or pessimism.

Quite often on the non-critical paths of the flow plan there is Slack Time. However, there is no Slack Time in the critical path and therefore, there does not appear to be sufficient schedule flexibility in the critical path to allow for unforeseen contingencies. Unless contingency time is initially calculated in the estimated activity times of events along the critical path, serious scheduling difficulties can be encountered.

Finally, it is not clear whether the final event shown on the network represents the committed contractual completion date. Professional schedulers normally build flexibility into the schedule and also provide contingency time between the final scheduled event and the actual requirement time.

Reporting to Management

Under PERT, reporting to management is on a highly systematic basis. The reports are printed out by the E.D.P. equipment on all events programmed into the computer. Most intelligent management is based on the exception principle. Busy managers do not have the time to examine endless information that does not require action and decision. Again, the human element must be injected into PERT. Reports must be condensed and recast for management to point up trouble spots with comprehensive analysis and evaluation of the difficulties. Mechanical reporting to date is neither discriminating nor elucidating enough.

Conclusions

The PERT system has primarily been used in association with program control on military contracts. The Government and defense contractors have been seeking means to correlate program planning and control into some meaningful system which will relate Time, Function and Cost. PERT has thus far not solved the Cost correlation problem, but has had signal success in relating accomplishment to Time and Function. The enthusiastic reception of PERT by the military services in defense contracting is evident in current requirements for PERT or PEP type planning and control systems as a prerequisite for the granting of new military business. If no other justification for the adoption of the system existed, this would exert sufficient pressure for the general adoption of the concept.

As currently conceived, the system is far from perfect. It has not been extensively tried in broad areas of operations planning and control. With some modifications and innovations, it might prove to be a very effective tool. As yet, the system is couched only in general terms as an experimental device in a relatively narrow application. Many of the firms using the system are exploring variations and adopting embellishments peculiar to their specific problems.

Uninhibited acceptance could lead to ultimate disillusionment. For example, small concerns with limited resources may find the system too complex and costly for adaptation. The outstanding criterion of success of the system has been with the Polaris missile. The installation cost of the system and its administration should be projected against potential benefits to be derived.

One of the greatest attributes of the concept is the acceptance of the idea and the participation by scientific, technical and administrative personnel. At this stage it may be too early to go overboard on that account since the idea is unique and has been highly publicized in defense contracting. It is even possible that the initial control groups may have responded to the stimulus of attention, à la the control group in the Hawthorne experiments.

Despite the existing weaknesses in the present system, it is a commendable step. PERT forcefully drives home to management the importance of planning and control. It takes an integrated methodological approach in solving an interrelated problem by encouraging participation and giving perspective; and finally it does attempt to simplify and quantify managerial decision making by elaborating and modifying several of the known managerial tools.

Discussion: A Reporting System for PERT

Joel Zelnick

Lybrand, Ross Brothers and Montgomery

In today's world of paperwork, most managers do not have enough time to read the reports that pass their desk, let alone digest them.

Consequently, any new technique or approach which appreciably increases the number of reports received by them will be looked upon with great reluctance. PERT unfortunately falls into this category because of the voluminous detail reported. In this connection Daniel D. Roman observed in the April 1962 issue of *The Journal of the Academy of Management*:

> ". . . reports are printed out by the E.D.P. equipment on *all events programmed into the computer.* (Emphasis added) Most intelligent management is based on the exception principle. Busy managers do not have the time to examine endless information that does not require action and decision. Again, the human element must be injected into PERT. Reports must be condensed and recast for management to point up trouble spots with comprehensive analysis and evaluation of the difficulties. Mechanical reporting to date is neither discriminating nor elucidating enough."

Exception Reporting

Exception reporting as suggested by Roman is the solution of course, but it requires the development of a formal system to ensure that the right reports are made at the right time. The system must be individually designed to the specific situation, but the principles that must guide such an application, and a generalized system for its use can be suggested.

Step 1

The network should be reviewed at prescribed intervals but the network should be revised only when an activity is completed or when time estimates for an activity have been revised.

Step 2

At the periodic review completed activities should be withdrawn from the networks calculations and added to a sustaining report of the completed activities. If estimates for incomplete activities are revised the network should be recalculated with the revised information. Results of the recalculation should be reported to management only when the change exceeds a prescribed standard. Thus the probability of meeting the schedule dates for the activities on the critical path were let us say 5% or less, then an exception report would be generated for management.

Accompanying this report would be lists of the following:

1. Activities not completed on schedule or whose future time estimates have been revised to cause this condition.
2. Slack-time activities graduated from greatest to least amount of slack.

With this report and supporting lists, management would be equipped with the full information to institute remedial measures, either by overtime scheduling or a re-allocation of facilities from slack-time activities.

Systematic exception reporting could materially reduce the management reporting-reading burden in applications of PERT and yet keep management adequately informed of a project's progress.

20

Toward a Behavioral Science Theory of Wages[*]

David W. Belcher

San Diego State College

One way to test organization theory is to apply it to our "knowledge gaps" in other areas of research. Here the author examines wage theory by substituting behavioral explanations of wage phenomena for economic explanations. The work of leading organization theorists is used to supply behavioral findings. It is the motivational problems in organizational settings which yield the most insight for analyzing wage theory.

Economic wage theory is less than completely satisfactory. In traditional economic theory, the economy is seen as a system of mutually interacting parts in which all transactions are subject to the influence of maximization of personal gain pursued in a stern, impersonal market. Human behavior is held to be rigorously bound by the rules of market behavior. Labor economists point to the inaccuracy of this view when applied to buying and selling labor's services and stress the range of variables — political, psychological, social, and ethical — that impinge on wage determination. Vigorous attempts have been made to build an economic wage theory that accommodates observed wage determination processes and institutions.[1] The attempts have been most successful in explaining the general wage level of a firm, least successful in explaining the internal wage structure, and silent on the effectiveness of wages as motivation.

[*] Taken and adapted from *The Journal of the Academy of Management*, vol. 5, no. 2, August, 1962, pp. 102–116.
[1] George W. Taylor and Frank C. Pierson (eds.), *New Concepts in Wage Determination*, New York: McGraw-Hill Book Company, Inc., 1957, is the most successful.

Meanwhile, behavioral scientists in their study of individuals, groups, and organizations have turned up numerous bits and pieces of evidence that hold promise of filling the gaps left in explanations of wage determination by both general economic theorists and labor economists. This article is an attempt to extract from behavioral science findings and analyses those that appear pertinent to wage theory.

The material has been selected and organized to attempt to fill the largest gaps in economic wage theory. Thus the topics covered are (1) the wage level of the firm, (2) the internal wage structure of the firm, and (3) money as motivation. Because the attention here is to behavioral factors, these factors are employed when an economic explanation would also serve. An explanation is accepted as behavioral (not economic) unless it can be reduced readily to cost-per-unit-of-output terms.[2]

The Wage Level of the Firm

The decision to participate in (join and stay with) an organization has been explained in terms of the inducements-contributions utility balance.[3] In this formulation, the decision to participate in the organization is a function of the balance between the utilities of inducements offered by the organization and contributions made by the participant. The components are (1) the perceived desirability of leaving, which is a function of (a) the individual's satisfaction with his present job, and (b) his perception of alternatives that do not involve his leaving, and (2) the perceived ease of leaving the organization, which is a function of the number of perceived alternatives outside the organization.

Another formulation conceives of labor markets as social institutions. Employers tend to pay what other employers pay in the community and industry. They rely on wage surveys and social pressures discourage paying much above what other employers are paying. Unions reinforce this tendency by insisting that employers who pay below what other employers are paying raise their wages. These institutional forces lead employers to set wages in line with the community or industry.[4]

A third formulation emphasizes the power and influence of firms and unions. Large firms have influence because of their size, money, the in-

---

[2] It is recognized that this definition of economic factors is unduly restrictive for most purposes.

[3] James G. March and Herbert A. Simon, *Organizations*, New York: John Wiley & Sons, Inc., 1958; C. I. Barnard, *The Functions of the Executive*, Cambridge, Mass., 1938, Chapter I.

[4] Robert Dubin, *The World of Work*, Englewood Cliffs, N.J.: Prentice-Hall, Inc., 1958, pp. 229–230.

fluence of the "power elite."[5] "Wage leaders" have influence in labor markets. Unions are political institutions and exert power upon the labor market through their size, money, and the influence of their leaders.[6]

Once participants have joined the organization, it is possible to conceive of non-financial rewards as at least partial substitutes for financial rewards. Representative non-financial rewards are (1) job satisfaction, interest and involvement, (2) power pay (a job of great importance, exclusive jurisdiction over the job), (3) authority pay (promotion, more authority), (4) status pay (giving the individual higher status), (5) privilege pay (giving subordinates opportunities for informal relationships with people of higher authority).[7] The possibility of substitution of non-financial rewards for financial rewards is limited, however, because status tends to equal financial reward in the long run.[8] Non-financial rewards may be more effective than financial rewards in keeping employees on the same job because automatic increases tend to destroy the incentive for stability and merit increases involve difficult administrative decisions.[9]

Internal Wage Structure

Economic theory has perhaps had least success in explaining the internal wage structure of the firm. It is here where a behavioral science wage theory should find its greatest usefulness.

Social Norms

One formulation serving to account for occupational wage differentials emphasizes the force of tradition. The institutions of the community provide customs and traditions which are brought into the organization. The organization and groups within it develop customs and traditions. Some jobs are regarded as more important than others because tradition decrees that these jobs have more prestige. Occupational groups have customs and rituals that affect the position of the occupation in the structure.[10] Wage differentials between jobs in the same plant are correlated with

[5] Robert A. Dahl, in Robert A. Dahl, Mason Haire, and Paul F. Lazarsfeld, *Social Science Research On Business: Product and Potential*, New York: Columbia University Press, 1959, pp. 25–26.

[6] Arthur M. Ross, *Trade Union Wage Policy*, Berkeley: University of California Press, 1948. Ross is a labor economist but his classic work on unions as political organizations is a behavioral analysis.

[7] Dubin, *op. cit.*, pp. 241–246.

[8] Delbert C. Miller and William H. Form, *Industrial Sociology*, New York: Harper & Brothers, 1951, p. 370.

[9] Dubin, *op. cit.*, p. 238.

[10] Miller and Form, *op. cit.*, p. 370.

the degree of skill the jobs once possessed rather than the skill required today.[11]

Simon's social norms theory of executive compensation is similar. He postulates that executive salaries are determined by requirements of "internal consistency" of the salary scale with the formal organization and the norms of proportionality between salaries of executives and their subordinates (norms of span of control and ratio of executive's salary to that of his immediate subordinates). Simon described acceptance of the rate for junior executives paid by other employers as economic determination. In the terms used above even this could be called a social norm.[12]

The Just Price of medieval times, perhaps not unrelated to the "fair wage" to the crafts, provides a wage distribution established from a preestablished status distribution.[13]

Scott reports that there is a close relationship between total rewards and occupational status, but not a close relationship between earnings and occupational status.[14]

Single Factor Explanations

A number of factors have been suggested as explanations of occupational wage differentials. For example, Jeremy Bentham[15] suggested two criteria: (1) that wages of occupations should accord with the social utility of the function performed and (2) that they should accord with the disagreeableness of the occupation. Clark postulated that wages of occupations are correct when people of equal ability receive equal wages in all occupations.[16] Tawney suggested sufficient income to permit a man to perform his work, insisting that what a man is worth is a matter between his own soul and God.[17]

Jaques suggested freedom to act as a factor explaining occupational differentials. He suggested that pay for an occupation (at least at the executive level) be determined by the length of time during which the incum-

11 W. L. Warner and J. O. Low, *The Social System of the Modern Factory: The Strike, a Social Analysis*, New Haven: Yale University Press, 1947.

12 Herbert A. Simon, "The Compensation of Executives," *Sociometry*, March, 1957, pp. 32–35.

13 Theodore Caplow, *The Sociology of Work*, Minneapolis: University of Minnesota Press, 1954; John W. Baldwin, "The Medieval Theories of the Just Price," *Transactions of the American Philosophical Society*, New Series vol. 49, Part 4, July, 1959.

14 W. H. Scott, *et al., Technological Change and Industrial Relations*, Liverpool University Press, 1956.

15 Jeremy Bentham, *A Table of the Springs of Action.*

16 Harold F. Clark, *Economic Theory and Correct Occupational Distribution*, New York: Columbia University, 1931, p. 57.

17 Richard H. Tawney, *The Acquisitive Society*, New York: Harcourt, Brace and Company, 1920.

bent is free to act without checking with his superior.[18] "Behavior control" correlates highly with status according to Caplow.[19]

Sociology of Labor Markets

Sociological analysis of types of labor market indicates the variety of social forces impinging on occupational wages and how different forces govern the different markets. The fact that a given organization may be operating in several types of labor markets accounts for much of the difficulty in maintaining internal wage structures. The following analysis leans heavily on Caplow's *Sociology of Work*.[20]

The Bureaucratic Labor Market. A bureaucracy is an organized hierarchy of social positions complete in itself without reference to the character of individuals who occupy the positions. The key words which identify bureaucracy are rationality and impersonality. Perhaps all large complex organizations are bureaucratic. In a bureaucracy wages are assumed to be proportionate to status rather than vice versa.

The bureaucratic labor market is insulated from economic considerations by three factors. The labor supply problem is solved in large part because recruits enter at the bottom of the hierarchy and are moved up to positions structured in terms of qualifications. The crucial market situations involve promotion and transfer rather than recruiting. The main labor supply problem in a bureaucracy involves the individuals which the bureaucracy cannot train itself, e.g., accountants, engineers, physicians. Labor demand is largely to fill low level positions. In both demand and supply, the closed bureaucracy is largely a self-regulating system. A third insulator is the importance of non-financial incentives, the main one tenure.

In theory, wage determination in a bureaucracy is an administrative decision based upon rational principles. The wage rank order must follow the rank order of training and experience required by positions. Status and wage must be correlated perfectly. Both qualifications and pay for positions with similar work and responsibility must be equal.

In practice, (1) the job classification system is superimposed on a preexisting wage structure, (2) wages for particular occupations should correspond to community rates after allowing for non-financial rewards, (3) most bureaucracies have a pay range for each job.

Conflicts among the stated principles require frequent revision in wage structure. The wage survey creates problems because (1) some of the occupations are not found elsewhere in the community and some only in other bureaucracies (in the latter case, circularity exists), and (2) it brings to the supposedly rational structure inequities attributable to political

[18] Elliott Jaques, *Measurement of Responsibility*, Tavistock Publications, Ltd., 1956.
[19] Caplow, *op. cit.*, p. 55.
[20] Caplow, *ibid.*, pp. 142–176.

pressure, occupational monopoly, or historical accident. The requirement that differences in qualifications be reflected by differences in pay creates conflicts between occupations with only a few subdivisions and those finely divided. Making distinctions between the occupations and keeping the parts in line is difficult.

These problems suggest that a bureaucratic wage structure can only operate with reasonable success in complete isolation or by steady expansion permitting a generous promotion policy. In a stable or declining organization, perhaps the only answer is a steady increase in non-financial rewards. The fact that few bureaucracies are completely closed creates further problems.

The Industrial Labor Market. This is the market for semiskilled labor. Labor supply depends in theory on the local labor force and competition for workers, but in practice is largely irrelevant for wage determination because of collective bargaining. The demand is fluctuating because of freedom of layoff and the type of demand is determined by the employer.[21] The range of wages is the legal minimum (floor) and the "going wage" set by collective bargaining (ceiling). Semiskilled factory labor can be hired at a wide range of prices.

Custom strongly affects these wages. Wage changes are determined with reference to wages previously paid for that kind of work. The higher the proportion of women and minority groups, the lower the average age of working force, the smaller the community, the lower the wage level even with unions. The larger the labor force, the farther north, the smaller the proportion of the population in industrial employment, the higher the wage level. Wage differentials between jobs in the same plant are also influenced by custom and are roughly correlated with the skill assumed necessary for the job. This is closer to skill once required than to skill required today. The occupational hierarchy operates on the assumption that variations in skill required are apparent and easily classified. The assumption is invalid. When a differential exists between two jobs, the holders of the more highly paid job assume it requires more skill and resist any alteration of the differential. Thus both management and union are hesitant to change differentials.

Wage differentials are changed by technological changes, rationalization, and group power struggles. But these changes are almost entirely independent of the market and usually of contract negotiation.

Within the industrial plant there is considerable mobility between departments and jobs, usually in the direction of higher wage rates. A consequence is that in many plants, the high paid jobs are held by high seniority workers, and the wage structure is more closely correlated with seniority

21 Robert L. Raimon, "The Indeterminateness of Wages of Semiskilled Workers," *Industrial and Labor Relations Review*, January, 1953, pp. 180–194.

than skill. In these cases, factory employment is tending toward bureaucracy expressed as high wages paid to those with greatest seniority. In fact, close analysis of the industrial labor market reveals several similarities to the bureaucratic labor market.

The Craft Labor Market. In theory, labor supply of a craft is fixed and the demand variable. Identification is with the craft rather than the employer. Because fluctuating labor demand and fixed labor supply would mean fluctuating wages and cutthroat competition, the craft union operates like a monopolist selling a standardized product. The medieval solution was the "Just Price"; the modern slogan of the "fair wage" carries the same ethical implication.

The wage in prosperity may be the highest price consistent with full employment of the craft. The lowest wage in depression seeks to assure subsistence of all active craftsmen. Adjustment to changed wage rates requires craft control of the distribution of work.

The function of craft control over conditions of sale of craft labor is to preserve the system of selling labor in standardized units by preventing the employer from modifying either the system or the attractiveness of work. Craft markets are essentially local and craft controls operate locally.

These arrangements are inconsistent with both bureaucratic and industrial arrangements. Various compromises are worked out when craftsmen are employed under these systems. One approach is to pay craft wages but withhold all or part of the benefits available to other employees.

The Market for Professional Services. A large proportion of professionals are salaried employees of bureaucracies. Analysis of the market for free professionals not only illustrates the problems of salary determination of professionals in bureaucracies, but provides clues to markets for other types of individualized services.

The supply of professionals is fixed in the short run and tends to decrease with increased demand in that professional controls are tightened. Demand for professional services is highly variable.

The pricing of professional services is subject to a special ideology. Professionals, in theory, are perfectly non-interchangeable. The value of a unit of work is theoretically unmeasurable and not convertible to money.

The fixed supply and varying demand permit the professionals, like the crafts, to fix the price but the professional ethic discourages attempts to standardize prices. Where the professional ethic prevails, the only remaining criterion of payment is what the market will bear, *i.e.*, ability to pay. Basing remuneration on the ability to pay of the client rather than upon the value of the service has been the chief feature of the market for professional services. Recently, however, a trend toward standardized prices in the professions has appeared. The principal concerns of the professional association are to establish minimum prices and to restrict price competition.

The Market for Common Labor. The supply of casual labor is highly variable. Demand is fairly constant in the long run but varies sharply in the short run. Both are highly elastic.

Although the conditions appear to approach the classical market, they do not. Public opinion opposes a continuous price range on ethical grounds and insists that prices be quoted in round figures. Nonmonetary considerations exist and preferences for certain prices. The going wage is a round figure and persists for long periods.

The market for domestic and farm labor is similar to the market for common labor in that the going wage tends to be a round figure and persists for long periods. Usually such workers are isolated and unorganized. Often remuneration is partially in kind. The employer-employee relationship may be close. Personal preferences may result in wages two or three times the going rate or almost zero. The market may go out of balance without reference to general economic conditions, resulting in zero supply or zero demand.

The market for laundry workers in large laundries and for migrant farm workers on large farms has similarities to the common labor market but also to the industrial labor market.

Other Types of Labor Market. The market for unique services (entertainment, sports, journalism, politics, advertising, and certain areas of management) is similar to the market for professionals in that supply is one individual and value of the service is difficult to measure. It is different from the professional market, however, in that the value of unique services is often speculative and is set by individual bargaining or bidding.

The market for commission salesmen and sales managers is another which may offer wages out of any proportion to the individual talent or skill. The strategic element may be the personal relations aspects of the salesman's activity. In most cases, however, salesmen appear to require knowledges and skills quite easily priced in a bureaucratic system.

This sociological analysis of various types of labor markets serves to emphasize the different factors operating in each. The typical large employer must reconcile the various forces operating in all or most of these markets in creating his internal wage structure.

The Employer As a Wage-Setting Institution

Analysis of the various types of labor markets emphasizes the fact that wage determination is a decision-making process that must adapt to numerous, often conflicting influences. To accomplish the purposes of the organization, the employer graduates the pay scale to correspond with the

ranking of the productive contribution of jobs. Jobs that are more important to the purposes of the organization are paid more money. This is
done to see that work gets done and that employees have an incentive to
move to more important jobs.[22]

Job evaluation systems provide a set of norms for classifying jobs. Although they tend to simulate economic reasoning in their quest of objectivity, they remain largely aids to decision-making.

Group Power Theory

Occupational differentials are derived at least in part from group pressures. The strengths and direction of group pressures are functions of (1)
identification of individuals with the group, (2) uniformity of group opinion, (3) group control over the environment, (4) interaction within the
group, (5) cohesiveness of the group, (6) the amount of intergroup competition, (7) the extent to which group pressures support organizational
demands, (8) technology of the plant. Identification of the individual with
the group is a function of (1) prestige of the group, (2) goals shared, (3)
frequency of interaction, (4) number of needs satisfied by the group,
(5) amount of competition among group members, (6) position of the
group. The position of the group is a function of (1) success of the group,
(2) average status level of members, (3) visibility of the group. Visibility
of the group is a function of its (1) distinctiveness, (2) size, (3) rate of
growth.[23]

The organization of the work contributes significantly to the behavior of
work groups. Jobs in the middle range are most susceptible to successful
group action. These are the semiskilled jobs discussed above as character-
izing the industrial labor market. They are not well defined in the labor
market. Uncertainty about the value of the job, ambiguity of status and
skill make for successful group pressure.

These group pressures are an important force operating upon occupational differentials. The worker is occupationally oriented even when a
semiskilled factory worker and behaves as if he belonged to a highly specific occupational group. Certain jobs are ranked as more important or
desirable and are expected to have higher pay. Over a period of time the
action of groups perfects the correlation. The union as well as management is forced by these pressures.[24]

Status has become a group phenomenon and since income tends to be
correlated with status, income tends to be based upon group membership

[22] Dubin, *op. cit.*, p. 233.
[23] March and Simon, *op. cit.*, pp. 59–61, 65–68.
[24] Leonard R. Sayles, *Behavior of Industrial Work Groups*, New York: John Wiley &
Sons, Inc., 1958.

rather than skill inherent in the job. All relations tend to become social relations. Social stratification ensues whenever groups have different social characteristics or functions. All groups tend to regard themselves as separate from and superior to other groups.[25]

Money as Motivation

Economic wage theory assumes maximization of personal gain as a prime mover of the system. Personal gain to labor is measured in wages. Behavioral scientists view this formulation as too narrow a view of motivation. A behavioral science theory of wages should specify the significance of wages as a motivator and the conditions under which wages are effective as motivation.

Definition

An idea of the complexity of motivation may be obtained from Lazarsfeld's definition. He finds it necessary to employ a three-dimensional scheme involving (1) time (present only or including the future), (2) scope (specific or general), and (3) dynamics (passive or driving). Thus motivation is a disposition of general scope with the implication that it drives the bearer toward activities that bridge the present and future. This definition serves to distinguish motivation from preferences, attitudes, wants, expectations, tendencies, and intentions.[26]

Freudian Motivation Theory

Freudian motivation theory postulates the existence in human beings at least in advanced cultures a common hierarchy of needs — (1) physiological, (2) safety, (3) social, (4) esteem, (5) self-actualization. Higher order needs do not appear until the lower level needs are sufficiently satisfied to permit attention to the former. Satisfied needs do not motivate.[27]

Money may be postulated to purchase satisfaction of (1) physiological needs, (2) many safety needs, (3) esteem needs that may be satisfied off the job. By the same reasoning, money (1) only indirectly aids in satisfying social needs, and (2) can only help in satisfying self-actualization needs by removing obstacles. By implication, satisfaction of social, esteem, and self-actualization needs on the job requires satisfactions other than money.[28]

[25] Miller and Form, *op. cit.*, pp. 372, 161.

[26] Lazarsfeld, in *Social Science Research on Business*, pp. 113–114.

[27] A. H. Maslow, *Motivation and Personality*, New York: Harper & Brothers, 1954; Douglas McGregor, *The Human Side of Enterprise*, New York: McGraw-Hill Book Company, Inc., 1960.

[28] Charles D. McDermid, "How Money Motivates Men," *Business Horizons*, Winter, 1960, pp. 93–100.

Self Theory

According to self theory, man lives in a universe of events and objects endowed with meanings by man himself through social definitions couched in language. The individual derives his plans of action from the roles he plays and the statuses he occupies in the groups with which he feels identified — his reference groups. His attitudes toward himself as an object are the best indices to these plans of action, and hence to the action itself, in that they are the anchoring points from which self-evaluations and other evaluations are made. These attitudes serve to guide him even in relatively unfamiliar situations.[29]

Motivation according to self theory is imbedded in the attitudes, values, and roles of individuals in various groups. It becomes a matter of investigation whether the significance of the various motivators (including money) are similar for all groups in our culture[30] or differ between occupational groups.[31]

Social Channelling of Motivation

Motivation, according to this view, is built into the entire social system. It is regarded as highly appropriate to earn a living, "get ahead," provide financial and other security for one's family. By the time a person goes to work, he carries with him these fundamental motivations appropriate to being an employee. Thus every employee comes to a company perceiving the appropriate channels of motivation along which his behavior can be directed. These channels of motivation are the product of society and are given specific form in each business organization. Labor unions operate within the motivational system shared by all citizens and their goals are not concerned with changing the motivation system of society but with influencing management policy in effecting specific rewards for workers in the form of incentives for work. Incentives for work provide the visible rewards for staying within motivational channels — to join an organization, stay with it, and improve performance.[32]

Motivation is intimately tied up with institutional patterns of behavior of society. People behave the way they do in economic organizations because behavior patterns have become institutionalized in such organiza-

---

[29] C. Addison Hickman, and Manford H. Kuhn, *Individuals, Groups, and Economic Behavior*, New York: The Dryden Press, 1956; George H. Meade, *Mind, Self, and Society*, Chicago, 1936.

[30] Dubin, *op. cit.*, p. 228; Miller and Form, *op. cit.*, p. 382.

[31] Scott, *et al.*, *op. cit.*; Talcott Parsons, "Motivation of Economic Activities," *Canadian Journal of Economics and Political Science*, May, 1940, pp. 187–200.

[32] Robert Dubin, *Working Union-Management Relations*, Englewood Cliffs, N.J.: Prentice-Hall, Inc., 1958, p. 16.

tions. It cannot be assumed that self-interest means the same thing in different organizational contexts. The organization molds behavior.[33] The importance of money as a motivator apparently varies also by occupational group[34] and social group.[35]

Work Theory

Many factors outside the work place, some beyond the control of management, shape work conduct and the pattern of social relationships inside the work place — economic variables, social and cultural variables. To get at the meanings people assign to their work, it is necessary to know their group identifications — the groups whose norms and controls they take their cues from. This in turn leads to an analysis of the degree to which different groups embrace different cultural values that define the significance of work.[36]

Apparently most men in our culture will work if they have no need for money — for self-expression, for social relationships, to give meaning to life. There are, however, differences between occupational groups in reasons for working. Professional men cite interest in their field or sense of achievement. Managers and sales people cite keeping occupied and active. At lower levels, the job becomes more important as mere activity.[37]

Studies of non-literate societies report that people work because they must, because everyone else works, and because it is the tradition to work. As among ourselves, labor is performed by non-literate people for reward. But the rewards differ widely in different societies, both in the forms they take and in the degree to which they act as drives. In non-industrial societies, the rewards are direct. Wages, where they exist, are usually paid in kind.

In a vast number of non-literate societies, as in our own, the drive for prestige constitutes a powerful psychological factor in determining behavior. The prestige that accrues to the hard worker, the fast worker, the careful worker, the competent worker, is a significant factor in motivating labor in most societies.[38]

[33] Robert Dubin, *Human Relations in Administration*, New York: Prentice-Hall, Inc., 1951, p. 27.

[34] Scott, *et al., op. cit.*

[35] W. Lloyd Warner, *et al., Social Class in America*, New York: Harper and Brothers, 1949.

[36] Harold L. Wilensky, in *Research in Industrial Human Relations*, New York: Harper and Brothers, 1957, p. 45.

[37] Nancy C. Morse and Robert S. Weiss, "The Function and Meaning of Work and the Job," *American Sociological Review*, April, 1955, pp. 191–198.

[38] Melville J. Herskovitz, *Economic Anthropology*, New York: Alfred A. Knopf, Inc., 1952, pp. 122–123.

Ego-Enhancement

According to Stagner, workers frequently are not conscious of their real motives. No single specific kind of satisfaction can be cited as the key to worker motivation. Workers want more of whatever is needed for satisfaction at any given time: pay, security, praise, recognition, self-expression. In the case of executives, ego-motivation rather than economic motivation is predominant — achievement, prestige, self-expression, power, recognition. Man is concerned about his status. He wants enough food, clothing, other material things to protect him from hardship, but beyond this, he is trying to keep or improve his standing in the community. How he compares with others, with his own ambition, are the crucial questions. Economic motives may in some cases be significant and not in others. Ego-satisfactions frequently have more attraction power for the worker and the executive alike.[39]

Argyris emphasizes self-actualization as the primary motivator. He defines self-actualization as growth toward independence through interaction with others.[40] This may or may not conflict with ego-enhancement.

Variety of Motives

To Brown, there are three motives for working, each related in varying degrees to the work itself: (1) the work may be done as an end in itself, (2) the work may be carried out willingly for other motives directly associated with the work situation (comradeship, status, power), (3) the work may be carried on for genuinely extrinsic motives (money for a variety of purposes).[41]

He takes the position that: (1) There is no one ideal incentive. Incentives vary from one culture to another, one firm to another, one individual to another. (2) The law of diminishing returns applies to all material incentives. (3) Incentives may conflict with other motives. (4) Money is of less significance than had been supposed. (5) But in our culture motives tend to become monetized. People have been taught that money is the key to satisfaction, so when they feel something is wrong with their lives they naturally ask for more money.[42]

Complexity

In motivation theory, the single motive and the monotonic function are objectionable. Two steps must be taken. Factor A must be shown to be

[39] Ross Stagner, "Psychological Aspects of Industrial Conflict, Motivation," *Personnel Psychology*, Spring, 1950, pp. 1–15.

[40] Chris Argyris, *Understanding Organizational Behavior*, Homewood, Illinois: The Dorsey Press, Inc., 1960, pp. 9–10.

[41] J. A. C. Brown, *The Social Psychology of Industry*, Pelican, 1954, p. 206.

[42] Brown, *ibid.*, p. 202.

effective. Then an increase in Factor A must be shown to produce an increment in the dependent variable. If piece-rate incentive plans are to be criticized because (1) they rely on a single motive, and (2) they assume "more reward — more performance," then the same conclusion must be reached about participation, communication, decentralization, and delegation until proven otherwise.[43]

Satisfiers vs. Dissatisfiers

The factors that make for job satisfaction seem to be different from those that make for job dissatisfaction. The factors that make for job satisfaction are those related to the job, to events that indicate success in the performance of work, and to the possibility of growth. The factors that make for job dissatisfaction are conditions that surround the job — supervision, interpersonal relations, physical working conditions, salary, company policy and practice, benefits, and job security. When these latter factors deteriorate, job dissatisfaction ensues and performance suffers — job dissatisfaction actually appears to *interfere* with work. But improving them does not provide job satisfaction, nor increase performance beyond the neutral point.

The job factors are the motivators. Improvement in them can increase performance beyond the neutral position. Money earned as a reward for outstanding performance becomes a reinforcement of recognition and achievement (motivators).[44]

Motivation As a Function of Organization

Much current work on organization theory suggests that organizations can be designed to foster motivation. Likert's modified theory of organization employs a "linking pin function" to tie group communication, influence, decision-making, and thus motivation to the goals of the organization.[45]

McGregor emphasizes arranging work so that people can accomplish their own goals by directing their own efforts toward organizational objectives. His "target approach" stresses the requirement of a commitment before motivation can be expected.[46] Bakke's fusion process appears to have the same basic objective.[47] Drucker's management by objective ap-

[43] Mason Haire, in *Social Science Research in Business*, p. 84.
[44] Frederick Herzberg, *et al.*, *The Motivation to Work*, second edition, New York: John Wiley & Sons, Inc., 1959.
[45] Rensis Likert, "A Motivational Approach to a Modified Theory of Organization and Management," in *Modern Organization Theory*, New York: John Wiley & Sons, Inc., 1958, pp. 184–217.
[46] McGregor, *op. cit.*
[47] E. W. Bakke, *The Fusion Process*, New Haven: Yale University Labor and Management Center, 1953.

proach seeks to achieve motivation by linking personal goals and organizational goals.[48]

Herzberg's study of motivation concludes that: (1) improving conditions surrounding work cannot motivate — they only encourage enjoyment away from work, (2) motivation requires: (a) jobs that demand performance and provide achievement, growth, and responsibility, (b) supervisors who can plan, evaluate, and reward good work, (c) selecting people who fit the work, (d) standards of performance that measure work, (e) rewards geared to performance.[49]

Also applicable here are studies of the geographic ecology of motivation. The structure of the group in the work situation in terms of possibility of interaction has an effect on motivation.[50]

Of equal applicability are the studies showing how individuals are compelled by the group to adopt common ways of behaving. The worker seeks to express his needs by attempting to pull the group in conformity with him. But the group possesses the power to compel the individual to conform. The conflict between individuals and the group under individual incentive plans observed by Whyte, Roy, Dalton, and Sayles is especially pertinent.[51] Methods suggested to resolve this conflict by increased personal involvement of group members do not consistently increase motivation.[52]

The modern tendency to treat organizations as social systems linking individuals to groups and groups to the organization would seem to hold major promise for motivation.

Goal Path Theory

Kahn offers a goal path theory of motivation. Motivation involves goals sought, paths for goal attainment perceived, and barriers which stand between the individual and the goal. Motive consists of two parts: (1) the *need* within the individual and, (2) the *goal* — an object in the environment seen as a source of need satisfaction. The approach the individual

[48] Peter F. Drucker, *The Practice of Management*, New York: Harper and Brothers, 1954.

[49] Herzberg, *et al.*, *op. cit.*

[50] C. R. Walker and R. H. Guest, *The Man On the Assembly Line*, Harvard, 1952; E. Jaques, *The Changing Culture of a Factory*, Dryden Press, 1952.

[51] Melville Dalton, "Economic Incentives and Human Relations," in IRRA, *Industrial Productivity*, 1951; Robert H. Roy, "Do Wage Incentives Reduce Costs," *Industrial and Labor Relations Review*, January, 1952, pp. 195–208; Donald Roy, "Quota Restriction & Goldbricking in a Machine Shop," *American Journal of Sociology*, March, 1952, pp. 427–442; Leonard R. Sayles, "The Impact of Incentives on Inter-Group Work Relations — A Management and Union Problem," *Personnel*, May, 1957, pp. 483–490; William Foote Whyte, *et al.*, *Money and Motivation*, New York: Harper and Brothers, 1955.

[52] Robert Dubin, in Robert Tannenbaum, Irving R. Weschler, and Fred Massarik, *Leadership and Organization*, New York: McGraw-Hill Book Company, Inc., 1961, p. 412.

takes will depend upon what he sees as a *path* toward his goal and the *freedom* (absence of barriers) to take the path.

Thus if a worker sees high productivity as a path leading to attainment of one or more of his personal goals and is free to produce, he will be a high producer. If he sees low productivity as a path to his goals, he will be a low producer. Among workers with a high need for money and freedom to pursue it, 66 per cent of those who saw high productivity as instrumental to the goal of making more money were high producers. Among workers of equally high need for money and equal freedom, but who did not perceive high production as instrumental to their goals, only 22 per cent were high producers.[53]

March-Simon Motivation Thesis

In this formulation, motivation to produce is a function of (1) the character of the evoked set of alternatives, (2) the perceived consequences of evoked alternatives, and (3) the individual goals in terms of which alternatives are evoked. The evoked set of alternatives is a function of (1) the existence of other work alternatives, (2) supervisory practices, (3) the task, (4) the system of rewards, and (5) the work group. The perceived consequences are functions of (1) the perceived alternatives to participation, (2) characteristics of individuals, (3) group pressures, (4) dependence of rewards upon productivity, and (5) operationality of criteria for rewards. Individual goals are a function of (1) the individual's identification with groups, (2) the strength and direction of group pressures, (3) the extent group pressures support organizational demands, and (4) basic values derived from earlier experience.[54]

Non-Motivation

No discussion of motivation can ignore the areas where motivation appears impossible. Herzberg, for example, concludes his study of motivation by insisting that motivation is impossible on machine tending jobs and in bureaucracies and that further rationalization of work prevents motivation on many jobs.[55] It is possible that many clerical, retail sales, custodial, and domestic occupations where promotional possibilities are nonexistent fall into the same category. Wilensky believes we are headed toward an organization of work where only a small group in control will be work-committed and the mass will continue to retreat from work.[56] These conclusions appear to support the wisdom of the March-Simon

---

53 Robert L. Kahn, "Human Relations on the Shop Floor," in E. M. Hugh-Jones (ed.), *Human Relations and Modern Management*, Chicago: Quadrangle Books, 1959, pp. 43–74.

54 March and Simon, *op. cit.*, Chapter 3.

55 Herzberg, *et al.*, *op. cit.*

56 Harold L. Wilensky, "Work, Careers, and Social Integration," *International Social Science Journal*, April, 1960, pp. 543–560.

formulation separating motivation to participate from motivation to produce.[57] If worker motivation becomes impossible on most jobs, motivation to participate in the organization acquires major pertinence.

Conclusion

An attempt has been made to select and organize behavioral science findings and analysis that bear on wage determination. A behavioral science theory of wages should fill gaps left by economic wage theory and institutional analysis. A behavioral science theory of wage level of the firm would include the following elements: (1) the inducements-contributions utility balance, (2) the labor market as a social institution, (3) unions and employers as holders of power and influence,[58] and (4) non-financial rewards as substitutes for financial rewards. A behavioral science theory of internal wage structure would consist of the following elements: (1) the force of social norms and tradition, (2) accommodation of sociologically diverse labor markets, (3) employers as wage-setting institutions, and (4) the force of group power on the internal wage structure. A behavioral science theory of wages as motivation would deal with: (1) basic motivations common to all individuals derived from basic individual needs and the common culture, (2) motives derived from reference groups and varying among the groups, (3) complexity of motivation in operation, *i.e.*, multi-factor, non-linearity in effect, the possibility that some factors are positive motivators and some others negative motivators, (4) perceived alternatives and their consequences, (5) motivation as a function of organization design, (6) non-motivated work.

Although at this stage model-building appears premature, some tentative models may be offered. In behavioral science terms, wage level influences may be postulated. The wage level of the firm will be higher, (1) the lower the level of job satisfaction, (2) the larger the number of alternatives perceived by employees, (3) the more reliance is placed on wage surveys, (4) the more influence exerted by unions, (5) the more the firm desires to be a wage leader, (6) the less the firm substitutes non-financial rewards for financial rewards. Conversely, the wage level of the firm will be lower, (1) the higher the level of job satisfaction, (2) the smaller the number of alternatives perceived by employees, (3) the less reliance placed on wage surveys and the stronger the social pressure exerted by employers on each other, (4) the less influence exerted by unions, (5) the less the firm desires to be a wage leader, (6) the more the firm substitutes non-financial rewards.

Similarly, in behavioral science terms, influences on the internal wage structure of the firm may be postulated. The internal wage structure will

[57] March and Simon, *op. cit.*

[58] This element is not absent in modern economic wage theory.

be more predictable and stable, (1) the more the firm is a closed, isolated bureaucracy, (2) the more semiskilled jobs become bureaucratized, (3) the more professional jobs become bureaucratized, (4) the fewer the craft jobs, (5) the more social norms and tradition correlate with organizational values, (6) the weaker the pressures of groups within the organization. Conversely, the internal wage structure will be less predictable and stable, (1) the more conflict exists between bureaucratic values and social norms and customs in the community, (2) the less semiskilled jobs are bureaucratized, (3) the larger the proportion of professional employees and the more craftlike the professional groups, (4) the more craft jobs, (5) the greater the conflict between organizational values and social norms and tradition in the community, (6) the stronger the group pressures within the organization.

Finally, the effectiveness of money as motivation may be hypothesized in behaviorial science terms. Money will become more effective as motivation as (1) physiological and safety needs are unsatisfied and esteem needs are satisfied off the job, (2) relevant reference groups rate individuals on a monetary scale, (3) society values individuals in monetary terms and equates status with earnings, (4) higher pay provides ego-enhancement for the individual, (5) organizations are designed to assign higher pay as a reinforcement of achievement of organizational goals, (6) pay is perceived as a reward for productivity and productivity is perceived as a path to employee goals. Money will become less effective as motivation as, (1) social and self-actualization needs become important to the individual and attempts are made to satisfy higher order needs on the job, (2) relevant reference groups rate individuals on non-monetary scales, (3) society values individuals in other than monetary terms, (4) men work for reasons other than money, (5) organizations are designed on the assumption that money is the single motivator, positive and continuous in effect, (6) pay is not perceived as a result of productivity.

21

A Behavioral Approach to Wage Administration: Work Flow and Structural Design[*]

Robert T. Golembiewski

University of Georgia

The preceding article stimulated the interest of Professor Golembiewski, who in this article goes more deeply into the problems of work flow and the design of organization structures. He employs the methods of small-group research, concluding that companies will turn increasingly to relatively unorthodox structural designs which ease the problems of measuring performance and encourage the development of informal groups responsible for the total flow of work. These conclusions fit well with emerging themes in recent organization research by sociologists and psychologists.

Belcher recently has drawn compelling attention to the challenge of building behavioral knowledge into a theory of wages.[1] His wide-ranging analysis establishes the general relevance of behavioral research for a wide range of topics within these three areas: (1) the wage level of the firm, (2) the internal wage structure of the firm, and (3) money as motivation. Belcher considers these the three "largest gaps in economic wage theory."[2]

The purpose here is to accept this challenge in a limited area relevant to wage administration. Thus this article has a two-fold focus. It will demonstrate the soundness of Belcher's notice by sketching some significant behavioral factors associated with the flow of work and structural design in organizations, as they affect wage-and-salary administration. Moreover,

---

[*] Taken and adapted from *The Journal of the Academy of Management*, vol. 6, no. 4, December, 1963, pp. 267–277.

[1] David W. Belcher, "Toward a Behavioral Science Theory of Wages," *Journal of the Academy of Management*, vol. 5 (August, 1962), pp. 102–16.

[2] *Ibid.*, p. 102.

this analysis will outline the ways in which an unorthodox structural design will avoid some common and significant difficulties in administering wage-and-salary programs. Notice that the approach here will apply full force only to work situations that have characteristics consistent with those emphasized below. These characteristics, along with being analytically convenient, do commonly occur in operating situations. In cases in which these characteristics exist in less marked degree, or not at all, however, the conclusions of this analysis will apply only to an appropriately diminished degree.

Two Guiding Notions of Wage Administration

Much work in wage and salary administration has been motivated by two underlying hypotheses, that is, two notions of the major properties of an approach that will facilitate cooperative effort. These expectations often are acted upon simultaneously, but need not be. They can be outlined briefly in these terms:

1. *The Symmetry Hypothesis,* which holds that efficiency is increased and administration is facilitated if some structure of jobs is isolated,[3] which structure bears a close correspondence to the idealized or real[4] value of a limited number of classes of jobs to the purposes of the organization, and to which structure are fitted base wage rates; and

2. the *Assymetry Hypothesis,* which holds that employee motivation under a wage and salary program is increased if differences in the performance of individuals on the same or similar jobs are rewarded differently.[5]

These seem reasonable enough guides in general, of course. For they fit closely with ideas of justice widespread in western society, although not in other societies.[6]

It would be an error, however, to argue that these major notions hold under all (or even most) conditions in western society. Development of this point could support a massive analysis. Here, however, we must be content with but a narrow demonstration of the point. In general, attention will be focused on alternate structural designs of an organization as they effect, and are affected by, attempts to act upon the two hypotheses

[3] Four approaches to job evaluation are commonly distinguished. See Robert E. Sibson, "Plan for Management Salary Administration," *Harvard Business Review,* vol. 34 (November–December, 1956), pp. 102–14.

[4] The distinction is a significant one. See Douglas S. Sherwin, "The Job of Job Evaluation," *Harvard Business Review,* vol. 35 (May–June, 1957), pp. 63–71.

[5] Other asymmetries are included in many wage programs, such as those between male vs. female rates, and married vs. single rates. These asymmetries are neglected here.

[6] James Abbeglen, *The Japanese Factory* (Glencoe, Ill.: Free Press, 1958).

above. More specifically, the traditional theory of organization does not induce conditions congenial to the effort to develop policies and procedures based on the Symmetry Hypothesis or the Asymmetry Hypothesis. Fortunately, existing research implies how matters may be improved upon by structural innovation.

The Traditional Theory of Organization: Structure as a Stumbling Block

That the traditional theory of organization poses substantial barriers to acting upon the two hypotheses underlying much work in wage and salary administration requires extensive proof. Figure 21.1 facilitates matters. It depicts the skeletal structure of the lowest three levels of an organization with three "line" processes (A, B, and C) and one "staff" service (D) — each with several operative personnel under a supervisor — that combine their efforts to yield a single product (P_1). All report to a manager (M_{ABCD}).

If patently simplified, Figure 21.1 does not violate common characteristics of organization structures, while it greatly aids analysis. Both points should be clear in the following discussion of four ways in which the traditional theory of organization does not conveniently permit acting upon both the Symmetry Hypothesis and the Asymmetry Hypothesis. This discussion will build upon the elemental facts that:

1. the traditional theory of organization encourages the "vertical fragmentation" of organization units, while the flow of work is in significant respects a horizontal phenomenon;
2. the "line-staff" distinction consistent with the traditional theory of organization reinforces vertical fragmentation and raises significant problems of including "staff" or auxiliary services in wage programs based upon the Asymmetry Hypothesis;
3. the traditional theory of organization encourages, if it does not require, complex wage programs; and
4. the traditional theory of organization implies great tendencies toward inefficiency in sequential operations.

The two hypotheses underlying much work in wage and salary administration, first, do not sit well with the vertical bias of the traditional theory of organization. The terminology may seem curious, but the phenomenon is all too real. Figure 21.2 helps demonstrate the point. Thus the flow of work must be horizontal; it must move across the organization, as in Figure 21.2A. The traditional theory of organization, however, induces strong vertical identifications, and this in social psychological, and practical senses, as in Figure 21.2B. Since the theory emphasizes particular functions and processes, employees can be pardoned for doing the same, whatever the

Figure 21.1   The traditional theory of organization: emphasis upon processes.

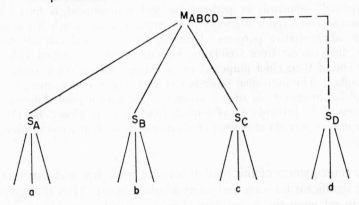

integrative problems caused thereby. The point need not be developed further here, for that task has been accomplished elsewhere with style.[7]

This tension between the flow of work and the vertical orientation induced by the traditional theory of organization can have mischievous consequences. Consider the problems of measuring performance under these conditions: the flow of work is horizontal; and the flow of work depends upon the integration of the contributions of organization units whose orientation is basically vertical. Worthy summarizes the awkwardness of the task in these perceptive terms:[8]

Figure 21.2A   The flow of work.

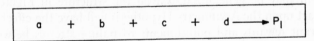

Figure 21.2B   Identifications encouraged by the traditional theory of organization.

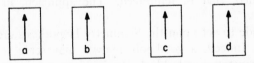

[7] Melville Dalton, *Men Who Manage* (New York: John Wiley & Sons, Inc., 1959), esp. pp. 56–64.

[8] James C. Worthy, "Some Aspects of Organization Structure in Relation to Pressure on Company Decision-Making," pp. 77, in L. Reed Tripp, editor, *Proceedings of the Fifth Annual Meeting of the Industrial Relations Research Association* (IRRA Publication No. 10, 1953).

. . . where the internal structure of the organization is broken down into a series of functional [or processual] divisions, there are no "natural" standards of performance and management is forced to exercise considerable ingenuity in inventing controls which it can use for administrative purposes. Unfortunately, contrived controls such as these, so far from facilitating inter-divisional cooperation (which is one of their chief purposes) often become themselves a source of conflict. The individual supervisor or executive is under strong compulsion to operate in such a manner as to make a good showing in terms of the particular set of controls to which he is subject, and often he does so only at the expense of effective collaboration across divisional lines.

The consequences of this tension between work flow and structural bias can be significant for wage and salary administration. Thus if attempts are made to act upon the Asymmetry Hypothesis, serious problems may arise between the work stations A, B, and C. For operatives at each station are paid only for their partial contributions to P_1, and this lack of responsibility for the total product easily can get the better of them. Consequently, operatives at any work station will tend to choose a pace and tactics that may be suitable for themselves, but may not be suitable for operatives at other work stations. Illustratively, all operatives at all stations will demand rapid service from "staff" unit D, their remuneration being tied to output. The almost-inevitable conflicts about priorities for such service can be sharp.[9] Moreover, the lack of non-arbitrary conventions for parcelling out many charges for integrative slippages does nothing to dampen such "hooray for me" tendencies.

The point may be generalized. Given the structure in Figure 21.1 attempts to act upon the Asymmetry Hypothesis will have the effect of utilizing significant rewards and punishments to induce stresses between work stations that must be integrated. Crudely, the basis of remuneration is individualistic, but the flow of work demands communal effort. And most individuals cannot be expected to perform behaviors that are not consistently rewarded, that is, reinforced. The approach, in short, is self-defeating.

Attempts made to act upon the Symmetry Hypothesis are more neutral in this regard. Indeed, a good job analysis may serve to improve performance by removing such blocks to involvement in work as blatant favoritism to certain job-holders. However, at best, job analysis does not involve a direct and aggressive attack on the vertical fragmentation of a horizontal flow of work encouraged by the traditional theory of organization.

[9] Robert M. Guest, *Organizational Change* (Homewood, Ill.: Irwin-Dorsey, 1962), pp. 65–81.

The "line-staff" relations consistent with the traditional theory of organization, second, also inhibit acting upon the two hypotheses above. The usual distinction, of course, is that the "line" is "on top." "Staff" is "on tap" or "purely advisory," and subordinate to the "line." This according of inferior status to the "staff" can have serious consequences. Patently, for example, it reinforces the vertical fragmentation encouraged by the traditional theory of organization, and this by the very separation of "line" and "staff" into distinct hierarchies. Moreover, the distinction has the effect of separating, on the basis of an arbitrary convention, activities that may in fact contribute simultaneously and significantly to the same flow of work.

The point may be made in more complex, and perhaps more revealing, ways. Consider an automotive plant whose modern technology is based upon the sequential integration of operations, but whose practice is such as to treat each machine virtually as a plant unto itself. That is, large banks of partially-finished goods are located at each station, a stratagem that involves great cost, complicates storage and materials-handling problems, and subverts the plant's technology. This contrast of practice and technology is curious, but not difficult to explain. Thus the production workers ("line") were on an incentive plan (Asymmetry Hypothesis) while, as is commonly the case, maintenance ("staff") was on straight time.

In the rough, the wage program implied a significant tension between the major purposes of the "line" (to maintain or to increase earnings, which implied quick emergency repairs) and the purposes of the maintenance unit (to provide a comprehensive maintenance program, which implied a long-run program of systematic preventive maintenance). Commonly, these purposes were in conflict, many "line" demands for emergency repairs being interpreted as a threat to the overall maintenance program, and thus to maintenance's hope of reducing the need for emergency affairs.

And why should maintenance put itself out merely to increase the wages of the "line?" This was particularly the case since maintenance could argue that the barest attention by the "line" to routine maintenance could have averted most emergencies.

An uneasy adaptation was reached. That is, slow emergency repairs were tolerated, and large banks of semi-finished materials were provided for each operative so that his earnings would not be so affected by leisurely repairs of breakdowns at work stations earlier in the flow of work.[10]

Such awkward situations in large part reflect the compulsive quality of the traditional theory of organization. Thus reserving production bonuses to the "line" is consistent with its superior place in the traditional theory. Moreover, the difficulty of measuring the contributions of "staff" supports

[10] Seymour Melman, *Decision-Making and Productivity* (New York: John Wiley & Sons, Inc., 1958), pp. 6–8.

the "mixed" wage program, and the traditional theory of organization also plays a major role in creating this difficulty in implying the separation of "thinking" from "doing." Later analysis will demonstrate how some unorthodox structural arrangements can avoid significant problems in acting upon the Asymmetry Hypothesis. The traditional theory is no less significant in affecting efforts to act upon the Symmetry Hypothesis. Thus such factors as the number of persons supervised and the size of budget are among the more significant factors that seem to peg a job's value in a job evaluation, thereby giving a great advantage to the contributions of the "line."

Attempts within the context of the traditional theory of organization to act upon the two hypotheses underlying many wage programs, third, induce complex wage programs that can contain significant elements of arbitrariness. Even when only one operation on one item is concerned, one faces the problem of determining the time actually worked under incentive rates and time spent in tooling-up, standing-by and the like. The difficulties of administering a wage program even under these simple conditions can be great. Operators commonly strive to arrange matters, for example, to show a stable level of earnings by claiming greater stand-by time, by "banking" some of their output from a good day, and the like.[11] The administrator of a wage program intrudes blatantly in such matters at this great peril, for even the strongest suspicions are notoriously difficult to prove and the conflict associated with raising embarrassing questions under this head can pollute the wellsprings of cooperative effort for extended periods. The situation reeks of opportunities for arbitrariness and for conflict or inaction.

Matters become worse as reality is approached more closely. That is, commonly, one must deal with one or more operations performed on several items-in-process, each of which presents its own unique problems, in determining an individual's incentive earnings. Some jobs are "stinkers," others permit making a good rate with minimal effort. The problems of allocation are much increased, of course, and some complex behavioral dynamics are induced by the varying requirements and pay-offs of particular tasks. The cost is a complex wage program, resting on an often-arbitrary foundation of "standards" or piece rates and their often-chancy administration. In a coal mining operation, for example, allocations had to be made for the time spent on four to seven major tasks, each with its own rate. Individual organization units were to perform only one task, moreover, but commonly because of technical requirements any unit might spend time on several tasks. A substantial bureaucracy was required to administer the wage program, and foremen were involved in long and

[11] William F. Whyte, *Men At Work* (Homewood, Ill.: Irwin-Dorsey, 1961), pp. 111–13.

heated negotiations about allocating hours to the several tasks. As Herbst noted:[12]

> The method of payment that has grown . . . is of considerable complexity. . . . [In fact] a large proportion of wages is subject to negotiation, if not dispute, with the shift foreman.

And all this comes from the attempt to follow the traditional theory of organization.

The dilemma facing wage and salary administration also has more subtle aspects. Attempts to act on the Asymmetry Hypothesis, for example, often will require close and detailed supervision. And if the Asymmetry Hypothesis is eschewed, close and detailed supervision will, still usually, be required as a motivational goad. Rewards within a class of jobs being largely independent of performance (Symmetry Hypothesis), that is, performance will tend to approach some lower satisfactory level. This is particularly the case because of the difficulty of surmounting the vertical barriers to integrative effort encouraged by the traditional theory of organization. Close and detailed supervision, then, may be equally necessary when acting upon one or both of the hypotheses. The difficulty, of course, is that the research literature is quite definite on the point that close supervision is a poor tactic over the generality of cases, in terms of both its common association with low output and with low employee satisfaction.

When sequential operations are organized as in Figure 21.1 following the traditional theory of organization, fourth, inefficiency is encouraged. Neither the Symmetry Hypothesis nor the Asymmetry Hypothesis help cope with the problem. Consider a simple case suggested by Figure 21.1. S_A, S_B and S_C, for example, will tend to support staffing work station D so as to approach peak levels of demand as closely as conditions (e.g., profits) permit. Obviously, this would serve to limit controversies about priorities, to provide service when needed and in many cases to reduce costs charged against the three "line" stations. S_D often would support this high-side bias. Convenience, of course, is paid for in terms of surplus personnel when demands for service D fall below peak levels. But note that the traditional theory is the culprit. For no one but M_{ABCD} has an institutional interest in resisting convenience continuously, and even he faces rather strict limits in acting over the long haul without the substantial consensus of his subordinates.

A more subtle example goes to the same point. The focus here is on an attempt to act upon the Asymmetry Hypothesis in a coal mine. Separate units performed one of seven tasks in sequence, at different rates of pay.

---

[12] P. G. Herbst, *Autonomous Group Functioning* (London: Tavistock Institute. 1962), p. 33.

But all units often found it necessary to complete or improve upon the work of the previous unit-in-sequence. Or, more bluntly, they found it necessary to do so too often. As Herbst explained:[13]

> Since, in the conventional method, work left over or badly carried out by one task group was paid at a special rate for the succeeding team, a condition arose where the maintenance of some degree of technical inefficiency could become profitable and in some cases was depended on to provide a satisfactory wage level . . .

Variations on this basic theme, of course, are common in industrial and administrative situations. They can make much sport of the most well-intentioned and reasonable wage program.

Neither working hypothesis, underlying much work in wage and salary administration avoids such problems encouraged by the traditional theory of organization. The Symmetry Hypothesis probably implies motivational losses, since considerable social and psychological forces would tend toward an equilibrium biased toward the lower producers in the sequential set of operations. That this often occurs even under incentive programs goes far in supporting the present point. The Asymmetry Hypothesis, moreover, does not meet all of the difficulties implicit in the traditional theory of organization, as was illustrated above.

An Optimistic Approach: Work Flow and Structural Design

This analysis may induce several responses. Thus it might be concluded that one of the two hypotheses underlying much of wage-and-salary administration is inadequate, or that both of them are. Or it might be concluded that the human implies the imperfect, and that one should be content with the mixed blessings of attempts to act upon the two hypotheses.

A more optimistic response will be hazarded here, however, as an alternative to both pessimism and resignation. That is, the administrative advantages of the Symmetry Hypothesis and the motivational advantages of the Asymmetry Hypothesis can be preserved, and this while moderating or eliminating their disadvantages, but if and only if a wage program is tied to an unorthodox structural design that is more sensitive to the flow of work than the traditional theory of organization.

In essence, this unorthodox structure is organized around products, or discrete sub-assemblies. As Figure 21.3 shows each supervisor controls all of the operations required in the total hypothetical flow of work yielding Product P_1. Thus Figure 21.3 organizes work so as to group together in the same unit all of the contributions required for a horizontal flow of work.

---

[13] *Ibid.*, p. 33.

Figure 21.1, in contrast, organizes work so as to isolate in separate units each of the contributions to any horizontal flow of work. Crudely, the latter approach goes against the grain of work and increases integrative problems.

Some substantial experience in organizations indicates that there are two major ways in which the structure in Figure 21.3 may be approached, while wage and salary administration is facilitated. Both approaches serve to permit acting upon the Symmetry Hypothesis and the Asymmetry Hypothesis, although both imply significant changes in conceiving and administering wage programs.

The "Autonomous Group" technique typifies a revolutionary approach to the structure in Figure 21.3.[14] In a British coal mine, for example, the

Figure 21.3 An unorthodox theory of organization: emphasis upon discrete sub-assemblies.

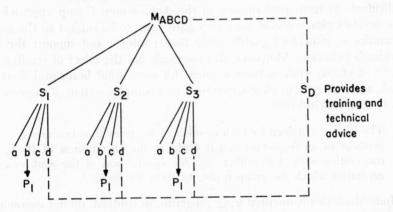

several jobs once performed by separate organizational units were represented on a single team. The several jobs were rotated among team members as they determined, and the team was paid on the basis of an all-in, per-ton price negotiated between the team and management before work started at each coal-face. The team in question decided to share their earnings equally.

The advantages of moving toward the structure in Figure 21.3 via the Autonomous Group proved substantial. Thus the team worked virtually without external supervision, for the team integrated all of the necessary operations. The method of payment, of course, provided the motivation for this integration and was a meaningful measure of performance that permitted general supervision.[15] In addition, the satisfaction of the miners was high, and their work site was admirably maintained. Moreover, the

[14] *Ibid.*
[15] *Ibid.*, p. 4.

men's wages were higher and (at the very least) total labor cost per ton was no higher than that under the earlier pattern of organizing work.[16] And there were great savings deriving from lessened requirements for supervisors and "staff" personnel (see below).

The advantages were no less marked for the wage program. Thus the Autonomous Group approach permitted the scrapping of the cumbersome and troublesome apparatus for administering the complex wage program supporting the orthodox pattern of organization. Removing the complexity and arbitrariness of the original system well suits the Symmetry Hypothesis. Nor were motivational advantages sacrificed (Asymmetry Hypothesis). Of course, rewards were no longer tied to the performance of a single operation by a single individual. And all the better, for such an approach to remuneration would encourage the vertical fragmentation of work stations that have to be integrated in a flow of work. Tying the rewards of individuals to team performance in the Autonomous Group approach is also psychologically sound, for group goals seem to be subject to the same dynamics as individual goals[17] while they reinforce and support the individual's behavior. Moreover, this approach has the effect of tending to unify all of the work stations required for some total horizontal flow of work, and this without close supervision or a complex system of inspection. As Herbst concluded:[18]

> The income obtained by each member of the team thus becomes dependent to an important extent both on the effectiveness of their cooperation with one another, and the effectiveness of the work organization which the group is able to devise for itself.

Individualistically-oriented wage programs, in contrast, do not encourage such cooperation. A complex system of inspection, in addition, would be required so that the induced "hooray for me" attitudes do not get too far out of hand. In Figure 21.1, for example, four separate inspections would be required to eliminate many attempts at "passing the buck," one inspection before and after each of the "line" operations A, B, and C. Such multiplication of "staff" personnel poses significant integrative problems,[19] not to mention cost burdens. In Figure 21.3, in contrast, the art of buck-passing would command less of a premium. For one would be passing the buck to one's teammates, as opposed to those outside one's organizational unit (see Figure 21.1). Moreover, successful buck-passing would not aid team performance. Only constructive solution of any integrative difficulties could

[16] *Ibid.*, pp. 79–81.

[17] Murray Horwitz, "The Recall of Interrupted Group Tasks: An Experimental Study of Individual Motivation in Relation to Social Groups," *Human Relations*, vol. 7 (February, 1954), pp. 3–38.

[18] Herbst, *op. cit.*, p. 4.

accomplish that. In sum, one deals with forces tending toward quite a different direction in Figure 21.3 compared to Figure 21.1.

The Autonomous Group approach may not be applicable to all work situations, although it has been used in this country and abroad.[19] It is possible to approach the structure in Figure 21.3 in a less revolutionary way, however.[20] In an automotive plant in Great Britain, for example, management isolated 15 separate flows of work, to each of which a large number of workers contribute.[21] Conventionally, acting upon the Symmetry Hypothesis, job analysis in this plant yielded a limited number of classes of jobs to which base wage rates were assigned. In addition, acting upon the Asymmetry Hypothesis, production bonuses are awarded, but they are awarded to *all* contributors to any flow of work — whether "line" or "staff" — in proportion to the efficiency of *all* operations within their flow of work.

Such concern with the flow of work can pay significant dividends. The British plant in question, for example, can compete on a cost basis with otherwise comparable firms despite having very significantly higher average wage rates. And in marked contrast to the example of slow maintenance given earlier, emergency repairs are made quickly. In fact, an alarm sounds at the spot that repairs are required, and the necessary personnel rush to the spot. For after all, it is their flow of work that is in trouble! And, of course, their bonus is at stake, as well as that of the production worker.

Organizing structural relations in ways sensitive to the flow of work, in sum, has much to recommend it. Even the brief descriptions above should suffice to demonstrate the ways in which unorthodox structural relations meet the four problems stressed in the previous section. The specific development of the ways in which this is the case can safely be left to the reader, given the transparency of the task and space limitations. Illustratively, however, the structure in Figure 21.3 cuts the ground from beneath the vertical fragmentation of the several work stations by organizing around a total flow of work and by tying rewards to that flow of work.

Conclusion

Behavioral research, then, suggests both the ways in which the traditional theory of organization complicates attempts to act upon the two hypotheses underlying much of wage-and-salary administration, and the ways in which

---

[19] E. L. Trist and H. Murray, "Some Social and Psychological Consequences of the Longwall Method of Coal-Getting," *Human Relations*, vol. 4 (February, 1951), pp. 3–38; and A. K. Rice, "Productivity and Social Organization in an Indian Weaving Shed," *Human Relations*, vol. 6 (November, 1953), pp. 297–329. The technology of modern steel mills, I am told, also has forced similar patterns of organizing in this country and abroad.

[20] See also Eliot D. Chapple and Leonard R. Sayles, *The Measure of Management* (New York: The Macmillan Company, 1962), esp. pp. 27–37.

[21] Melman, *op. cit.*, pp. 12–14.

an unorthodox structure can facilitate such attempts. The relevant research could only be sketched here. Even after the necessarily brief analysis, however, it should be clear that the unorthodox structure provides two important built-in motivators. Thus the unorthodox structure eases the measuring of performance. Moreover, the unorthodox structure encourages the development of informal groups responsible for some total flow of work. This fact, in combination with the possibility of having competing teams producing the same (or similar) discrete sub-assemblies, encourages an upward-orientation in norms of output. And the greater control of the environment by the informal group implicit in the unorthodox structure seems satisfying to most individuals.[22] The benefits, that is to say, can be reciprocal for manager and employee.

[22] Rensis Likert, *New Patterns of Management* (New York: McGraw-Hill Book Company, 1961), pp. 8–10, 20, and many other points.

22

Managerial Authority in the Employment Relationship*

Stanley Young

St. Louis University

Central to organization theory is the concept of authority, as affirmed in the preceding articles by Baum and Filley. Managerial authority has been subject to challenge by employees with the rise of strong labor unions, and by increasing demands in society for the responsible performance of the business enterprise. This article examines the legal and economic bases for the relationship between employer and employee, which is explained as a buyer-seller relationship.

A certain degree of controversy surrounds the issue of managerial authority vis-à-vis the employee.[1] Many of the differences concerning the authority issue seem to emanate from a misunderstanding of the nature of the legal and economic relationship between the manager and non-manager. Although the nature of this relationship is determined by other factors such as psychological, technological, ethical and sociological ones, the scope of this study will be restricted to reviewing briefly the legal and economic aspects of the employment relationship: insofar as they relate to the authority issue. It is hoped that such an analysis will help to resolve some of the incongruities which apparently exist.

* Taken and adapted from *The Journal of the Academy of Management*, vol. 5, no. 3, December, 1962, pp. 207–213. The author is indebted to Henry Manne, LL.D., Associate Professor of Law, George Washington University, Washington, D.C., for his review of the legal aspects of this study.

1 For a brief discussion of the various approaches to managerial authority, see Guest, Robert, *Organizational Change*, Homewood, Ill., The Dorsey Press, Inc., 1962, pp. 118–133; Mandeville, M. J., "Organizational Authority," *Journal of the Academy of Management*, August, 1960, pp. 107–111.

As a working hypothesis, it is here suggested that there exists no authority relationship between manager and employee, only a relationship of exchange between a buyer and a seller.[2] And unless the definition of authority is expanded to include all exchange relationships, the issue of managerial authority is extraneous in a study of the employment relationship.

Legal Characteristics

What are the assumed legal origins of managerial authority and of what validity are they? One assumption found in the formal or classical authority model of the organization has the following elements.[3] Insofar as the employee is concerned, a superior-subordinate relationship exists in which authority is defined as the legal right of the superior (the manager) to command the employee (the subordinate) to behave in a certain manner within the organization. Presumably, the employee has a legal obligation to obey.

It is further assumed that the origin of this authority derives from the property rights of ownership which have been delegated to the manager. Authority is viewed as a downward flow through a chain of command from the stockholders, Board of Directors, to the first line of supervision. This is the familiar pyramidal or hierarchical organization.

The shortcoming of this model is that it assumes a non-existent legal right. There is no property right in which the employee is legally obligated to obey the instructions of the owner. The confusion arises over the definition of property. Property relates to the assets of the firm: materials, equipment, buildings and good will; but it does not include employees. Property rights are concerned with the freedom to use and exchange such assets.[4]

Some managers erroneously assume that they have the same right to determine how the services of employees will be used as they do the machines or materials of the firm. Clearly the stockholders cannot delegate a right to managers which they as stockholders do not have.

---

[2] This study is limited to the employer-employee relationship. The non-employment relationship, as for example found in the family or the military, falls outside the scope of this analysis.

[3] Discussions of the formal authority of management generally include these described characteristics. See: Robert Tannenbaum, Irving R. Weschler, and Fred Massarik, *Leadership and Organization*, New York, McGraw-Hill Book Company, Inc., 1961, pp. 256–276; George Terry, *Principles of Management*, Homewood, Ill., Richard D. Irwin, Inc., 1956, pp. 268–270; Dalton E. McFarland, *Management: Principles and Practices*, New York, The Macmillan Company, 1958, pp. 190–207; Harold Koontz and Cyril O'Donnell, *Principles of Management*, New York, McGraw-Hill Book Company, Inc., 1955, pp. 48–52 and pp. 399–402.

[4] For a discussion concerning the nature of property rights, see: Commons, John, *Legal Foundations of Capitalism*, The Macmillan Company, New York, 1939.

Management's right to command frequently is asserted to originate in the employment contract. It is postulated that when the employee enters into an employment agreement, in exchange for a wage or salary he agrees to accept the authority of the firm. For example, Herbert Simon notes that the entrepreneur gains the right to dispose of the employee's time by entering into an employment contract with him.[5] Koontz and O'Donnell allege that the employment contract provides that the employer will give orders and the employee will obey them.[6]

According to this point of view, the purchase of labor is no different than the purchase of equipment or material. Once a firm pays the vendor for material, the determination of how that material will be used passes from the vendor to the buyer. In similar fashion, it is thought that once the employee agrees to accept a wage, the firm gains the right to determine how his time will be utilized. The assumption that the employment contract is analogous to the exchange of physical goods is not correct.

What are the legal characteristics of the employment agreement? The manager is delegated the legal right or authority to act as a buyer for the firm and use the organization's assets to purchase personal services from the employee, or the seller. The willingness of the employee to render service would in turn be the property which he is exchanging for a consideration from the firm. The employee has the same property rights as respects his person, as the employer does, his assets. Thus an exchange or buyer-seller relationship exists that is comparable to any commercial one.

The employment contract has certain unique characteristics. In the customary verbal, terminal, individual employment contract one finds that initially the parties have only agreed to continue their relationship as long as it remains mutually beneficial.

A manager's orders to an employee can be legally viewed as a buyer's proposal to change the obligations of the seller. The employee has a legal right to reject, accept or make a counter-offer to such demands. He is under no legal obligation to accept the instructions of a manager as is generally assumed. Neither is obligated to accept the proposals of the other; each party must perform only those conditions to which it has mutually agreed.[7] Because the parties do not usually bind themselves to a specific future performance, either one can suggest changes in any aspect of the relationship at will.[8]

---

[5] Simon, Herbert, *Administrative Behavior*, New York, The Macmillan Company, 2nd edition, 1957, p. 7.

[6] Koontz and O'Donnell, *op. cit.*, p. 402.

[7] As to what actually constitutes an agreement, see Eells, Richard and Walton, Clarence, *Conceptual Foundations of Business*, Homewood, Ill., Richard D. Irwin, Inc., 1961, p. 201.

[8] In the terminal agreement, the employer cannot sue for damages concerning violation of contract, because the employee did commit himself to perform services over a

The parties are free to negotiate at any time and in any manner. They can agree to any terms that are mutually acceptable so long as the contract is legally bona fide; that is, the contract must not be fraudulent, mutual consideration should exist, and no law should be violated. The employee can thus propose terms as respects how the property of the firm will be utilized in the same way the manager can suggest how the property of the employee will be used.

Either party can terminate the contract at will, without cause. The employer can discharge the employee; or the employee can quit. Either party can demand the acceptance of certain proposals as a condition for a continued contractual relationship.

John Commons has said, "The contract at the beginning of his (the employee) employment is therefore not a contract. It is a usage, a custom, a habit — it is an understanding between the two, that at each point in the continuous flow of impliedly renewing the contract, the terms of renewal shall conform to what was understood, but without any duty on either side to renew or conform. The laborer is thus continuously on the labor market — even while he is working at his job he is both producing and bargaining and the two are inseparable."[9]

Economic Characteristics

Unfortunately much confusion regarding managerial authority derives from the inability to distinguish the difference between legal rights and economic power.[10] At times it is postulated that the origin of managerial authority derives from the employee's fear of job loss; and rather than face this possibility, the employee accepts the buyer's proposals.

However, this concept of authority is based on the buyer's bargaining capability, rather than his legal rights. If the buyer's bargaining power were of such a nature that the employee followed all instructions, then operationally, it would appear to make little difference whether or not the manager had the right or power to command, because the end result essentially would be the same. But if the concept of managerial authority is restricted to the use of economic sanctions, then the extent to which the employee will conform to managerial instructions would depend upon the relative bargaining power of each party. One cannot assume *a priori* that

---

given period in the future. When a (non)terminal agreement exists, although the employer cannot legally enforce personal performance, he may be able to collect financial damages for lack of performance.

   [9] Commons, *op. cit.*, p. 286.

   [10] Cyril O'Donnell would seem to confuse legal and economic sanctions in his article, "The Source of Managerial Authority," *Political Science Quarterly*, vol. 67, no. 4, December, 1952, pp. 573–588.

acceptance of managerial demands is always preferable to the loss of job; or that the bargaining power of the buyer will under all conditions be superior to that of the seller; or that the buyer's bargaining power will be sufficient to gain acceptance of all his orders. These may be many proposals which the seller will not accept.

The employee can also use economic sanctions in the form of a threat to quit unless his demands are met. At times the bargaining power of the employee will be greater than that of the manager, as in the case of the highly gifted scientist or the productive salesman.

In both instances the parties can threaten not to consummate the contract in order to achieve more favorable terms of exchange. The employment agreement is not unique in this regard, since this is the usual action in any buyer-seller relationship.

The effectiveness of economic coercion depends in large measure on the characteristics of the labor market. As respects what the employer will pay, or what the employee will do, it is generally assumed that given the imperfections of the market place, such conditions will be determined by the familiar supply and demand for labor.[11]

Although it is accepted that the market determines what the employer has to pay for employee services, it is not equally recognized that the market also determines how much or what type of service the manager will receive from his labor expenditure. Most managers know that they must pay the going rate, but they are not equally aware of the fact that they will receive in turn, a "going performance."[12]

If the demand for a particular occupation is increasing and the supply is decreasing, presumably the manager will not only have to pay a higher rate, but he may also receive less service from the seller. The employee may make such demands as shorter hours, longer coffee breaks and greater personal discretion on the job. Hence, the manager's economic power in terms of the extent of cooperation he can purchase, is decreasing. However, if extensive unemployment should exist, then the manager's economic power would increase.

Thus the effectiveness of economic power depends on the availability to each party of alternative economic opportunities. Managerial authority, viewed as though it were resting on an economic base, would be conditioned by the following factors. First, the manager and the employee would each have the authority to exercise this kind of power. Second, it is not unique to the employment exchange but obtains in all exchange relationships.

11 For a real analysis of the extent to which market forces determine the terms of employment, see: Carter, Allen, *Theory of Wages and Employment*, Homewood, Ill., Richard D. Irwin, Inc., 1959.

12 See Rottenberg, Simon, "On Choice in Labor Markets," *Labor and Trade Unionism*, Edited by Galenson, Walter, and Lipset, Seymour, New York, John Wiley & Sons, Inc., 1960, pp. 40–52.

Third, the degree of bargaining power is limited, dynamic and relative to that of the other party; and finally, economic power is circumscribed by market or competitive factors.

Consequently, if by managerial authority it is meant the right to command, then the conclusion must be that no such right exists and that economic ability is affected by those factors noted herein.

Implications of the Analysis

What inferences can be deduced from the foregoing analysis? In reference to the nature of the employment relationship, the question of managerial authority is extraneous to its analysis. An exchange relationship rather than an authority one exists and both relationships can be distinguished in terms of their institution properties.

Authority versus the Exchange Relationship

An authority relationship is usually thought to originate in a higher legal framework (legislation or the common law) which establishes superior-subordinate relationships in which specific legal rights and obligations are fixed and upheld via legal sanctions.

The military may be characterized as having established authority relationships. Legislation (the Articles of War) has stipulated the relationship between officer and soldier; the officer holds the right to command and the soldier has the legal obligation to obey. Violation of orders can lead to use of legal sanctions such as prison or in the case of dire circumstances, the loss of life. Even though there is, perhaps, a limit to the effectiveness of such legal sanctions, nevertheless the military establishment can legally compel a man to perform services against his will; but in the economic organization, this would be unlawful.

On the other hand, in exchange relationships, (which are the existent ones), there are no superior-subordinate relationships, instead there are legal co-equals who voluntarily enter into a contractual relationship which specifies these rights and obligations rather than some external authority. Neither assumes any obligations which are not freely agreed to, nor can one specify an obligation which the other does not accept. The sanctions are economic and contractual terms are dynamic and ever changing.

The characteristics of an authority and exchange relationship are for the most part clear and distinguishable. If all the determinates in an exchange relationship are included in the definition of authority, both the economic and the non-economic ones, then as Professor Mandeville[13] sug-

[13] Mandeville, M. J., "The Nature of Authority:" Comment and reply by Mandeville to an article by Weber, Edward C., in *The Journal of the Academy of Management*, April, 1961, pp. 62–66.

gests, the term authority becomes fairly meaningless. In addition, the term is contrary to accepted usage and provides little in the way of analytical guides.

In buyer-seller relationships (other than employer-employee ones) such as found in the purchase of goods, one does not usually think in terms of an authority relationship. The fact that an individual as a buyer purchases an automobile in no way confers upon him the authority to direct the activities of automobile companies or sellers. Moreover, if one uses the term authority to include the use of economic coercion, then one would have to regard all buyer-seller relationships as authority relationships.

On the other hand, if one initially assumes that the manager-employee relationship is one of exchange rather than one of authority, then the question of managerial authority becomes moot. Although the construction of a theory of organizational negotiations falls outside the scope of this analysis, it is suggested that the exchange construct rather than the authority one provides a more realistic and effective model with which to analyze the determinants of the manager-employee relationship.

For example, insofar as the legal aspects are concerned, the terms of exchange tend to remain relatively stable. These terms represent the parties' mutual obligations and might be viewed as being quasi-legal in nature, or constituting the law of organization.

The conflict between the "classical" and the "human relations" approach can be resolved in terms of the rights and power of the parties' buyer and seller roles. The so-called "zone of acceptance" in the human relations approach can be interpreted as a range of terms of employment that sellers find acceptable. The dynamic quality of such a zone would reflect changing bargaining factors. Leadership characteristics can be subsumed in terms of either personality variables or negotiating style of either the buyer or seller. Agreement concerning terms of exchange would present integration of the parties' objectives. The interaction process is the search for such agreement.

Role Conception

Of what practical significance is it to draw a distinction between an authority relationship and one of exchange? Many managers assume that they do as a matter of fact have authority over the employee. Apart from holding a serious misconception as respects the nature of his role in the relationship, this assumption can prevent him from reaching an effective exchange.

The character of the relationship between the manager and employee is determined largely by legal and economic factors, which neither the manager nor the employee can determine. If the manager desires greater cooperation from the employee, he must negotiate for it. Both our legal and economic systems have already predetermined that this is the manner in which cooperation between the two parties will be established.

The manager has assumed the traditionally entrepreneurial economic functions of both buying and selling. The manager can decide how he will negotiate, but not whether or not he will. In his daily interaction with the employee, he attempts to achieve greater employee cooperation. And whether or not he realizes it implicitly or explicitly, he is continually in a process of negotiating an ever-changing employment contract.

To assume that an authority relationship prevails, tends to over-simplify the problem of gaining employee cooperation. It supposes that there is an existing state of cooperation or obedience on the part of subordinates and that the primary task of the superior is to determine the subordinates' functions. It further implies that there is no necessity to gain the co-operation of subordinates. The manager becomes analogous to the army officer who commands and leads his men.

If the manager clearly recognizes and accepts his role as a buyer of labor, he knows that a mutual working together of the buyer and seller must be sought constantly and negotiated. The manager ever faces the difficult task not only of determining what he wants from the employee, but also of negotiating with the seller in order to obtain his acceptance of the buyer's proposals. Gaining cooperation via negotiations requires considerable skill and is a complex process. It is a process that requires flexibility and com-promise. The principle of quid pro quo is its essence and the skills needed are those of a pioneer trader.

The manager is legally free to adopt any negotiating style he desires; par-ticipating or non-participating, democratic or autocratic, rigid or flexible. Given the many factors, economic and non-economic, that effect the bar-gaining outcome, it is difficult to assess how significant the negotiating style of the buyer is in any given situation, because it would represent only one of the variables.

Another source of confusion concerning the authority issue is that man-agers frequently choose an authoritarian negotiating strategy. Here again there would be little reason to confuse bargaining behavior with the insti-tutional bases of power and authority.

The manager's assumption that he has some form of authority over the employee not only makes the negotiating process difficult, but it may well reduce his effectiveness as a purchaser of labor services. If the objective of the manager is to maximize the return on labor dollar expenditures, then the use of a command strategy is less effective than if alternative strategies were considered by the manager.

PART THREE

Researchers studying the business enterprise face enormous complexity which must be broken into elements in order to reduce problems to manageable dimensions for purposes of research. Some researchers, depending on their disciplinary orientations, prefer to focus on the organization — its processes, its structures, its component units and their interrelationships. Others treat the organization as a context or an environmental system or set of subsystems, examining the behavior of people within this framework. The organization both constrains and causes the behavior of organization members; organization members in turn constrain and cause the behavior of the organization. The articles presented in this section focus on studies emphasizing the behavior of executives in business organizations. The scope of these studies is that of large-scale, complex, bureaucratic types of business enterprises.

A major problem in any business is to create and maintain adequate leadership. Heretofore leadership has been treated as an essentially human characteristic. But the introduction of computer technology raises profound scientific questions about the generation and use of creativity, innovation, and leadership processes. Stanley Stark's article examines

Studies of
Executive Behavior

important gaps in the research literature of psychology, sociology, management, and organization, with respect to our understanding of the capacities and potentials of both human and "metal" brains. He argues that uncertainties about our knowledge of the human brain raises doubts about our knowledge and use of "metal" brains.

Among the more difficult leadership skills is the use of creativity for the planning aspects of leadership and executive behavior. In his article on uncertainty, expectations, and planning theory, Milton H. Spencer argues that until recently researchers have paid insufficient attention to the role of uncertainty in studies of management decision-making and planning. When uncertainty factors are recognized, the executive's most basic functions become those of coordination and supervision. He questions classifications of managerial behavior (which provided for a number of separate managerial functions) from a theoretical and conceptual point of view, although they appear to be useful as expository devices.

Organizations can achieve a partial reduction of uncertainty in dealing with leadership abilities and skills by the nature of their selection systems. Argyris in 1954, and McMurry in 1958, described for bank organizations the selection of the "right type" of manager. William D. Litzinger extends these previous findings in a replication study of branch bank members. He confirms, as found in the two previous studies, the existence of the "right type" concept in centralized banking organizations. However, there may be a new entrepreneurial prototype emerging in branch banking systems. The author suggests that there may be a continuum ranging from the "right type" of executive at one end and the "entrepreneurial" type of executive at the other.

Whereas Spencer focused upon the factors of uncertainty that underlie the executive's planning and decision-making activity, Robert J. House and his colleagues focused upon the measurement of discretionary responsibility as a criterion factor in determining compensation and organizational status for managerial jobs. This article advances and applies concepts put forward by the British consultant and researcher, Elliott Jaques.

By analyzing a large segment of organization and human relations literature, Eugene E. Jennings shows that the concept of the authoritarian culture lag explains a great deal about the reactions against human relations and against company efforts to develop more democracy in the management of the business enterprise. Since the publication of this article, it appears that the lag still exists and that the human relations movement continues to be under severe critical review. The basis of Professor Jennings analysis is rooted in various personality theories, as well as in the general human relations literature. He explains a number of important factors underlying the strong, deep roots of the executive's authoritarian compulsions in business organizations.

There is little doubt about the fact that the efforts for human relations and greater democracy analyzed by Jennings have been geared to workers rather than to managerial levels, as Richard F. Ericson suggests in his paper on rationality and executive motivation. Whereas earlier thinking implied that authoritarian behavior springs from the needs of managers and democracy from the needs of workers, Professor Ericson indicates that the entire range of authority versus democratic behavior patterns should be explored at all levels in the management hierarchy. He traces inter-executive relationships in a number of key studies, concluding that new organization structures and patterns of executive behavior loom on the horizon.

Is a more definitive typology of executives developing in the field of management? Whereas Litzinger studied a typology in banking, and Jennings and Ericson examined the authoritarian and democratic types, Stanley E. Bryan surveys the growing array of types and models being advanced in order to explain executive behavior. He uses as a central integrating and analytical device the concepts of the situation and of the opportunistic elements in executive behavior. Rich in satire and illustration, the article achieves a useful focus on a number of key elements that shape executive behavior, and shows how they are inter-related. It leads the author to state certain modifications of the "law of the situation" advanced by earlier theorists.

Contrasts between the executive's "action" duties and "analytical" duties are described by M. C. Branch, in his discussion of the relations between logical analysis and executive performance. Here the author traces problems of decision-making in large complex organizations. In spite of increased use of scientific methods and the growth of computer and applied mathematical technologies, subjective judgment, appraisal, and intuitive reactions remain important. He argues that executives should not overlook logical analysis as a powerful tool aiding the use of intuitive and subjective judgment.

Among the more interesting concepts in the relationship between man and organization is that of loyalty. What demands for loyalty do organizations make, and what is the result of these demands? Loyalty is frequently asserted to be an important executive qualification and standard of conduct. Yet this complex concept is not well understood. Among the questions of loyalty raised by William R. Gall are: how much loyalty should a company or a supervisor demand? To what or to whom should a person be loyal? What about conflicts of loyalty? What conditions affect the giving of and demand for loyalty? The author suggests certain limits in the balancing of one's loyalties in business organizations. Loyalty for loyalty's sake and "unquestioning" loyalty are suspect. Recognition of loyalty as a fluctuating, continuously tested phenomena, needing to be earned, is suggested. The supreme loyalty demands a sense of integrity and purpose on the part of the executive himself.

The philosophical perspectives inherent in the articles by Jennings, Ericson and Gall are further illuminated by Clarence Walton's article on the concept of the social system. The nature of the American social system is briefly described and analyzed in the framework of techno-logical, social, political, and economic progress and change. Then the implications for management of the business enterprise are carefully traced.

In the final article of this section, Wilmar F. Bernthal studies the values underlying business decision-making by the executive. As in Walton's discussion, this article is concerned with the relationships of the business enterprise to society, and sets forth a number of important implications for executive behavior.

23

Creative Leadership:
Human vs. Metal Brains*

Stanley Stark
Michigan State University

The spectre of man's possible domination by electronic brains has haunted us unrelentingly in recent years. Here the author suggests the divergencies existing within the behavioral literature, and traces similar cleavages in the literature of management and organization. Until these differences are taken into account, we cannot adequately assess the roles of human versus metal brains in creative leadership. Much doubt remains about the creative capacity of the human brain, and hence about the creative capabilities of "metal brains."

Even if Armaggedon never comes, we may still never learn whether metal brains can do everything human brains can do — the reason being that scientists may never agree on what *human* brains can do. Unless we agree about humans, of course, we cannot agree on their being simulated — which makes you think that disagreements about humans would attract a good deal of attention. To my knowledge, (1) there *is* abundant evidence of disagreement about humans, (2) this disagreement extends into the areas of decision and organization theory — especially where creativity and leadership are concerned, and (3) the disagreement — at least in the management and organization literature — has been neither well-publicized nor well-explored.

Hence, I intend in this paper to discuss (1) a few selected materials from the psychological and sociological literature which illustrate what I regard as a fundamental cleavage, and (2) certain other materials which indicate presence of the same cleavage in the management and organiza-

* Taken and adapted from *The Journal of the Academy of Management*, vol. 6, no. 2, June, 1963, pp. 160–169.

tion literature. Unless materials like these are taken into account, I believe it impossible to effectively discuss the role of human vs. metal brains in creative leadership — for they suggest that any debate over human vs. metal brains derives from a prior debate over human vs. *human* brains. In this presentation I shall refer mainly to publications by the following: E. G. Boring, R. H. Waters, G. A. Lundberg, T. R. Sarbin, P. E. Meehl, P. Selznick, and H. A. Simon.

E. G. Boring and R. H. Waters

Let us begin with a day almost 20 years ago when Norbert Wiener "defied" the famous historian and now elder statesman of psychology, E. G. Boring, "to describe a capacity of the human brain which he could not duplicate with electronic devices" (Boring, 1946, p. 178). Professor Boring reports that "I could not at once name him any"; but his inability was not merely a matter of being caught unprepared, for by the time he wrote up this conversation for his colleagues, 18 months had elapsed, and still he could not name him any.

Some might think Professor Boring was suffering some embarrassment over his failure and that he was reporting the conversation to his colleagues by way of seeking their help. A reading of the article does support the notion he was seeking help but not the sort of help you might have guessed; nor does it support at all the notion that he was embarrassed.

Actually, a reading teaches us that Professor Wiener's question had been put to someone completely sympathetic to its viewpoint — "I confess I myself thought it would be salutary to show that all human mental functions have their electronic analogues" (p. 178) — but who lacked a standard inventory of psychological functions with which he might put his sympathy to professional work. In this sense, Professor Boring *was* unprepared: he wanted to be able to agree with Professor Wiener not merely as a layman but as a psychologist whose knowledge of psychological functions was as systematic and exhaustive as the bodily knowledge of a physiologist. And so Professor Boring was calling upon his colleagues for help in inventorying the psychological functions — and to get them started, he submitted a thoughtfully-constructed first approximation of his own.

But a reading teaches us something else, something more central to our interest. Professor Boring saw great value in what he called playing the game of hypothetical robot — not, as some of you might think, because it helps us to discern what in man's mind is essentially mechanical and what is not, but rather because "if you talk about machines, you are more certain to leave out the subjective, anthropomorphic hocus pocus of mentalism" (p. 191). The robot, he says, is "an argument against mentalism, and against vague terms which pass current in psychologists' language while remaining incapable of rigorous definition" (p. 192). In other words, to

engage in what he calls "robotic thinking" is to engage in thought completely free of the metaphysical, teleological and related strains that a
Bertrand Russell sees marring western thought for too long after Leucippus
and Democritus were over-shadowed by Pythagoras, Socrates, Plato, and
Aristotle (1960, pp. 72–73); or, in Professor Boring's framework, to engage
in "robotic thinking" is to immunize oneself against the plague afflicting
"the phenomenologists, the antipositivists, the mystics" and thereby, to
help further the "demonstration of the mechanical nature of man and of
the unity of the sciences" (1946, p. 191).

Some might guess, this time correctly, that Professor Boring's call drew
more than what he meant by "robotic thinking." Rolland H. Waters — a
psychologist who has researched rat maze-learning, analyzed learning
theory, co-edited an animal psychology text, and who therefore, is not too
easily regarded a phenomenologist or mystic — coined a new and pejorative
term to describe the "hypothetical robot" game that Professor Boring had
graciously invited everyone to play. Professor Waters called it *mechano-
morphism,* by which he meant "the ascription of mechanical characteristics to the human individual, and the interpretation of human behavior
in terms of concepts and processes characteristic of machines" (1948,
p. 139). In coining this term, he was, in effect, arming Professor Boring's
opposition with the same kind of weapon Professor Boring used against
them (i.e., anthropomorphism). In doing this, Professor Waters was not
arguing the righteousness of ascribing humanity to infrahumanity but
rather, the sinfulness of ascribing nothing but *infra*-humanity to humanity.

He said that "if one starts with a machine, one ends with a machine"
(p. 141). Precisely, Professor Boring might reply — since we *are* mechanical in our nature, let us from the outset conceptualize mechanistically.
But — Professor Waters might counter — this method cannot possibly
answer Norbert Wiener's question; if all contributions to the inventory of
mental functions must pass a mechanism test, how are we to learn from
such an inventory if any human mental functions are not mechanical?

The answer here for our purpose is that neither Professor Boring nor
Professor Waters has any serious doubt. Professor Boring believes firmly
that man is nothing but machine, Professor Waters believes firmly that he
is something more. Professor Boring wants an inventory not that will help
him to discover truth — he already knows that — but rather that will help
him demonstrate it to those who do not. When, on the other hand, Professor Waters insists *a priori* that any inventory confined to mechanistic
functions is incomplete — an insistence equal to insisting that man is more
than a machine — we know that for him also, the inventory is a demonstration and not an experiment.

But what *would* Professor Waters add if the inventory's metal bars came
down? He does suggest a number of functions, some of which, he notes,

"involve the concept of creative activity"; then he asks rhetorically, "Has this [i.e., creative activity] not been omitted from Boring's inventory" (p. 141)? Certainly, Professor Boring might reply — so has everything else "incapable of rigorous definition."

Could it be, I now rhetorically ask, that what we see here is prototypical of the debate regarding the role of human and metal brains in creative leadership? Could it be, that is, that the kind of creativity that some people attribute to certain leaders is the kind that an E. G. Boring considers "the subjective, anthropomorphic hocus pocus of mentalism"? Our answer should be clear by the time we have finished.

G. A. Lundberg, T. R. Sarbin, and P. E. Meehl

Let us turn now to the subjects of Verstehen and clinical intuition, over which there is long-standing dispute in sociology and psychology. The relevance here for us is that at least since Plato, we have been told that there is a reality higher than the physicochemical, and that only a non-sensory visual capacity can perceive it. In its aristocratic or divine-gift version, it takes the form of Carlyle's seeing eye ("the eye that flashes direct into the heart of things, and sees the truth of them"[101, p. 71]) or (less obviously and less specifically) of Max Weber's charisma;[1] and in its democratic or idle-gift version, it takes the form of Bergson's intuition (1944). As scientists, sociologists and psychologists have focused not on the question of higher reality but on the question of means of knowing it. Is there or is there not a way of knowing which depends primarily upon neither the senses nor the rational-calculative apparatus? (To ask this question is to ask whether there is a way of knowing that has been left out of a real time man/machine system such as SAGE.)

For example, in 1936, George A. Lundberg wrote a critique of what he called "the current attempt to contrast statistical, quantitative, and mathematical methods on the one hand and a method called the method of insight on the other," adding that "sometimes such terms as understanding or intuition are substituted for insight" (p. 40). He argued that insight and understanding are not scientific methods themselves but are the aims or ends of scientific methods. If, in fact, insight and understanding are methods, how are they to be objectively described? "The answer to this demand in some quarters," he scoffs, "is to wear one's collar backwards, to gaze into crystals or tea cups, or go into a trance" (p. 41). He notes in

---

[1] Charisma can take the leadership forms either of personal heroism (through the sword) or of personal revelation (through the word): creative social change is typically associated with either as opposed to patriarchal and bureaucratic leadership. For a hint that Weber's concept of personal revelation was not based entirely on his study of history and current affairs, but that in addition it was something in which he personally believed, see his distinction between education "to awaken charisma" and education "to impart specialized expert training" (Gerth and Mills, 1958, p. 426).

the same mocking vein that "some of the abler magicians, such as Houdini, have acceded to this demand by describing their techniques in verifiable terms" — why not, then, the sociologist-practitioners of *Verstehen?* Indeed, the latter are more obligated than a Houdini, for "verification by other qualified minds is the essence of scientific knowledge" — hence "the progress of science" means "increasingly searching demands that the author of a generalization specify the steps by which he reached it." So, it is not that Professor Lundberg *opposes* the method of *Verstehen:* how *can* he if nobody objectively describes it? "Let us by all means have bigger and better understanding, intuition, and insight," he gibes to the end, but first let its practitioners "let the rest of us in on the technique" (p. 53).

Actually, he believes the technique a myth — a "confusion of language." His introduction makes clear that for him the distinction between *Verstehen* and quantitative methodology is as futile, muddling, and untrue to reality as "other famous specimens of scholastic argument." There is no true dichotomy or even continuum; scientific knowledge is quantitative or or it is not scientific knowledge. What, then, is the source of the misconception? The source is the failure to see that quantitative methodology ranges in formality from the extremely raw — in which state not even numbers may be used, no less algebraic symbols — to the extremely refined. Failing to perceive this formality continuum within quantitative methodology, some people believe they see something essentially different — especially, *Verstehen* — when in fact they are looking at the informal end of the continuum. The truth is, says Professor Lundberg, that "what the critics of the better quantitative methods [i.e., the pro-*Verstehen* wing] seem to prefer is informal, impressionistic, and imaginary statistics supporting their prejudices" (p. 43). In short, there is only one scientific way to the truth, and it is open equally to all: the aristocrats of *Verstehen* are deluded or confused.[2]

In 1941, psychologist Theodore R. Sarbin took up the Lundberg fight in the clinical field. Just as the latter wanted sociology purged of all but its natural science elements, so Professor Sarbin wanted erasure of the artistic image of clinical psychology. An enterprise in which prediction depends entirely on empirical observation and logical inference, and not at all upon artistic, intuitive, magical, or related gift, is a scientific enterprise — and this he argued is the character of the prediction implicit in diagnosis and a choice of therapy. He agreed with Professor Lundberg that "useful diagnoses always proceed from generalizations, whether based on a rigorous statistical method or upon a crude empirical method which has been variously named intuition, insight, *Verstehen*, etc." (1941, p. 394). Diagnoses that strike one's colleagues or oneself as artistic or intuitive can

[2] See his 1941 paper for a more concise statement of the unitary character of all prediction.

usually be revealed, he claimed, to be inferences from previous experience: "that these inferences are informal and not made with the benefit of Hollerith cards and Monroe calculators is beside the point" (p. 395). In the clinic, as Professor Lundberg would say for sociology, there is *no* psychology — Windelband notwithstanding — " 'that cannot be taught and learned, but is the gift of intuitive intelligence' " (p. 397): there is only experience, quantification, and inference. Anything more is "super-empirical," which is to say, non-science.

Thus Professor Sarbin read intuition out of clinical psychology. I am unaware of any response, but when he did it again on an even larger scale in 1944,[3] the following promptly appeared: ". . . while it is correct to attack any attempt to separate psychology from natural science or any attempt to place intuition and 'understanding' above verification, this attack should not be perverted into an attack on intuition itself. Intuition above verification leads to intellectual anarchy. At the same time, those of us who are less intuitively gifted may well afford to adopt some humility in the presence of those who have proven to be more gifted" (Chein, 1945, p. 179). The possible implication is that Professor Sarbin is not very strong in the artistic or intuitive method, and perhaps his perceived lack of strength supplies a motive for his rejecting the method. Whether intended or not, Professor Sarbin's 1944 article alone (see footnote 3) makes it obvious psychologists can generate heat when disagreeing about what human brains can do.

A few years later there appeared in a sociology journal the kind of *Verstehen* description Professor Lundberg had demanded (Abel, 1948). Its author concluded it could not be considered a scientific method (since by itself it neither adds to our knowledge nor serves as a means of verification), and thus seemed to be following the Lundberg-Sarbin line; but he emphasized something else which neither of them had even mentioned — the creative role of *Verstehen*. He said that when we think about human behavior — specifically, when we think about possible antecedents of a given response or possible responses to a given stimulus — we create hypotheses. These hypotheses arise out of "hunches" or "intuitions" — which, he suggested, "originate from the application of the operation of *Verstehen*" (p. 217). In emphasizing the creative role of *Verstehen*, this author in effect aligned himself with the critic who accused Professor Sarbin of perverting an attack on the attempt to place "intuition

[3] And probably more provocatively as well. For example, proponents and/or practioners of the intuitionist method either "fail to recognize the frame of reference into which they have fitted their generalizations or else they engage in non-scientific guesswork . . . they are making statistical predictions in an informal, subjective, and uncontrolled way, or else they are performing purely verbal manipulations which are unverifiable and akin to magic" (1944, p. 214); also "talking about such super-empirical vagaries as the 'gift of intuitive intelligence' is little short of autistic conduct" (p. 219).

and 'understanding' above verification . . . into an attack on intuition itself" (Chein: see above). For both, the operation called Verstehen is involved in creative thought, and as long as its limitations are understood,[4] it is a legitimate part of the scientific enterprise, whether in the laboratory, field, or clinic. For Professors Lundberg and Sarbin, on the other hand, Verstehen is either disguised, unrecognized empirical method or it is nothing that belongs in science.

In 1954, as part of a review monograph on the clinical vs. statistical prediction controversy, the psychologist Paul E. Meehl undertook to defend those clinicians who, like one of his colleagues,[5] resented "that certain statisticians apparently wanted him to substitute a Hollerith machine for his eyes and his brain" (Meehl, 1954, p. 6). He argued along the dualistic Verstehen line that we have already seen, namely, that the experience-quantification-inference pattern considered by the Lundberg-Sarbin line to be *the* scientific pattern is, in fact, only one of two — that there is, in addition, an intuitive pattern of which a Hollerith machine is incapable — a pattern that terminates in creative hypotheses and moreover, which is essentially similar to the mental process involved in the creation of scientific theory. The fact that we cannot specify the logic of this creative pattern (and may never be able to) is grounds for calling it "intuitive" but *not* for concluding that its results cannot be tested or validated: to so conclude is to equate "nondeductive" or "nonformal" with "irrational," an equation Professor Meehl cannot accept.

Time limitation prevents me from bringing this controversy up to date. Suffice it to say that as of August 1962, Professor Sarbin and two associates were protesting that Professor Meehl's review of their new book "has gone beyond the usually accepted bounds of criticism" and were hoping that the journal editor "will consider possible procedural measures . . . to make less likely the promulgation of the more extreme forms of idiosyncrasy."[6]

Formalist vs. Intuitivist Approach

The preceding materials suggest the presence in behavioral science literature of two distinguishable approaches to the human mind, one in which there is exclusive emphasis upon its formal and hence mechanically feasible processes, the other in which these processes share emphasis with another type, virtually unknown except for its products which are often claimed to be creative. The *formalist* approach commonly accompanies loyalty to logical positivism (or logical empiricism) and to the broader movement

[4] For example: "From the point of view of Verstehen alone, any connection that is possible is equally certain" (Abel, 1948, p. 217).

[5] David Rapaport, at the 1947 meeting of the American Psychological Association.

[6] *Contemporary Psychology*, 1962, 7, p. 311. Their book is *Clinical Inference and Cognitive Theory*, which Professor Meehl reviewed in the November 1961 issue.

called scientific empiricism or unity of science, as well as adherence to a view of man as nothing but ordinary physicochemical nature, subject in all respects to the laws of its operation. The *intuitivist* approach commonly accompanies sympathy for humanistic, idealistic philosophy, for a view of life and man as continually being created, and for a view of the human mind as a unique agent in that continuing creation. In other words, those who approach the mind as nothing but mechanism tend to approach man, life, and the universe in a similarly "nothing but" fashion; whereas those who approach the mind as something more than mechanism tend also to find something more in these other domains — though their difficulty in demonstrating their "something more" findings is usually at least as great as it has been in demonstrating *Verstehen.*

How would each of these approaches manifest itself when brought to bear on the domain of large-scale social organizations? Alvin W. Gouldner (1959) has (unintendedly) given us an answer in his distinction between *rational* and *natural system* models of organization — a distinction that builds on the early pages of Philip Selznick's *Leadership in Administration.* It is to this distinction and to this essay that we now turn.

P. Selznick and H. A. Simon

Why did Professor Selznick write this *particular* essay? And why did he title it *Leadership in Administration?* Any reply to the first question should include, I believe, a statement to the following effect: he wrote it as an *intuitivist* supplement, corrective, or antithesis to the *formalist* essay that Herbert A. Simon titled *Administrative Behavior.* And any reply to the second question should include, I believe, a statement to the following effect: leadership in the old-fashioned sense, which stood so high with the *intuitivist* likes of Plato, Carlyle, and Weber, stands very low in the world of scientific empiricism: in *Administrative Behavior* (as in the later March and Simon *Organizations*), the word leadership itself cannot be found in the heading of a single chapter, chapter section, chapter subsection, or *anywhere* in the index.[7]

As for my implication that Professor Selznick's *institutional leadership* is somewhat synonymous with *intuitional* leadership, permit me to document it by putting the following brief speech into his mouth; and, in turn, shall ask you to consider it as best you can from the point of view of Scientific Empiricism, i.e., with the ears of Professors Boring, Lundberg, and Sarbin:

> Certain organizations as a whole and most organizations in their largest
> part are determined in their behavior by precedent, by authority,

[7] I refer to the second edition of *Administrative Behavior* (eighth printing, 1960) and the first edition of *Organizations* (second printing, 1959). In *Administrative Behavior*, "Entrepreneurs" is indexed (p. 256) and is cited three times.

and/or by technical considerations. To say this is to say (1) that they possess a completely or mainly formal-mechanical structure or (2) that their operation is completely or mainly automatic and semi-automatic. The appropriate way to learn about such organizations or operations is the way of the engineer — the student *par excellence* of determinate entities. Human behavior in these determinate entities will be correspondingly determinate, which means that the relevant mental processes are most appropriately studied by psychologists and sociologists closest in spirit and method to the engineer. *Administrative Behavior* (or *Organizations*) is an admirable work in this regard.

My essay, on the other hand, addresses itself mainly to indeterminacy, self-determination, or freedom. This is the meaning of such of my statements as: "leadership is most needed among those organizations, and in those periods of organizational life, where there is most freedom from the determination of decisions by technical goals and methods" (pp. 16–17); "Critical experience calls for leadership. Experience is less critical, and leadership is most dispensable when the range of alternatives is limited by rigid technical criteria. The more limited and refined the task, the more readily can technical criteria prevail in decision-making . . . [when the organization] has the leeway to respond in alternative ways, there is room for character-formation, which enters to give structure to precisely this area of freedom" (pp. 40–41); "leadership declines in importance as the formal structure approaches complete determination of behavior. Management engineering is then fully adequate to the task" (p. 92).

Since I address myself to indeterminacy, self-determination, or freedom, I emphasize not only leadership in administration, but *creativity in leadership* (and even intuition). For example: ". . . policy and administration are interdependent in the special sense that certain areas of organizational activity are peculiarly sensitive to policy matters. Because these areas exist, creative men are needed . . . who know how to transform a neutral body of men into a committed polity. These men are called leaders; their profession is politics. . . . The setting of goals is a creative task. . . . The task of leadership is not only to make policy but to build it into the organization's social structure. This, too, is a creative task. . . . The leadership of any polity fails when it concentrates on sheer survival: institutional survival, properly understood, is a matter of maintaining values and distinctive identity. This is at once one of the most important and least understood functions of leadership. This area (like that of defining institutional mission) is a place where the intuitively knowledgeable leader and the administrative analyst often part company . . ." (pp. 61–63).

Now let us consider whether our simulated sociologist has affronted any simulated (or genuine) scientific empiricist sensibilities. Would the empiricist wonder how he would precisely define certain terms and phrases, e.g., "character-formation, which enters to give structure to precisely this area of freedom," "maintaining values and distinctive identity," "intuitively knowledgeable leader," or in other cases how he would come up with a meaning different from what scientific psychology offers, e.g., "creative men," "setting of goals," "creative task"? My guess is that Professor Simon would wonder much and that Professor Selznick would find it exceedingly difficult to satisfy him. But we *must* satisfy him if we are ever to convince him that at any given time the computer is not doing all the thinking that middle or upper managers do. For example, when he says that "we will have the technical capability, by 1985, to manage corporations by machine" (1960, p. 52), are we entitled to smugly retort, "Sure, but what about *leading, creatively* leading — a la Selznick — by machine?" if we cannot reach agreement on what Professor Selznick means? It is one thing to say to Professor Simon — "You've left creative leadership out of your social psychology and out of your machine" — and another to demonstrate that he has omitted a piece of reality. Just as I believe Professors Boring, Lundberg, and Sarbin would cheerfully agree that they leave *Verstehen* out of their model of man, so I believe Professor Simon would cheerfully receive the news that he omitted "intuitive knowledgeability" — whether Platonic, Carlylean, Weberian, or Selznickean.

Conclusion

From Plato's *Republic* to Selznick's *Leadership in Administration*, western thinkers have associated an ill-defined creative capacity with leadership. To date, the group we have referred to as intuitivist has been shown nothing to persuade it that the digital computer possesses this capacity, but on the other hand, neither has the group we called formalist been shown anything to persuade it that the capacity exists in man. Until the latter group *is* persuaded, we cannot conclude that the metal brain possesses less capacity for creative leadership than the human brain — and it is at least conceivable that the latter group may never be persuaded.

24

Uncertainty, Expectations, and Foundations
of the Theory of Planning[*]

Milton H. Spencer

Wayne State University

Very few people feel that our knowledge of the planning process is adequate. Here the author presents the theoretical concepts he believes important if we are to develop a general theory of planning. He relates planning to a framework of uncertainty, expectations, and coordination, suggesting a reclassification of the managerial functions in such a way as to give coordination a more central role in management theory. Coordination decisions become the key decisions of the executive, and planning becomes an essential activity of coordinative management.

The purpose of this paper is to outline some fundamental theoretical concepts which form an important part of the basis of any general theory of planning. Thus the emphasis here is not on planning methods or on planning techniques, but rather on the underlying elements of pure planning theory. These elements, it will be seen, are rooted in certain aspects of modern decision theory, in the formal theory of uncertainty, and in the development of prediction systems which are the rational bases of all plans.

Modern decision theory is founded on the classic distinction between risk and uncertainty. *Risk*, it will be recalled, may be defined as the quantitative measurement of an outcome, such as a gain or a loss, in a manner such that the probability of the outcome can be predicted. Historical data are usually employed to arrive at a probability measure risk. The use of such data for this purpose assumes that the number of observations is (1) large enough to exhibit stability, (2) repeated in the population or

[*] Taken and adapted from *The Journal of the Academy of Management*, vol. 5, no. 3, December, 1962, pp. 197–206.

universe, and (3) distributed in the manner of a stochastic variable, i.e., at random. A frequency distribution of expected outcomes may then be constructed which the decision maker can use to calculate and subsequently minimize the risks inherent in a prediction problem.

Uncertainty, like risk, is also prediction oriented, but unlike the latter its measurement is not objective and does not assume perfect knowledge. The measurement of uncertainty is a subjective process; no two individuals will view an event and necessarily formulate the same quantitative opinion. This is due to a lack of sufficient historical data on which to base a probability estimate, which in turn is caused by rapid changes in the structural variables that determine each economic environment. In other words, the observations are not repeated often enough to establish a probability figure based on repeated, homogeneous trials, as in the case of risk. Therefore, managers must make decisions in an environment of incomplete knowledge, which they do by forming mental visions of the future that cannot be verified in any quantitative manner.

Under uncertainty, businessmen may be viewed as formulating plans during the present time period, t_0, in anticipation of significant events that they expect will occur at a stated future time period, t_1. These decisions are made under conditions of imperfect knowledge of the future. If the significant event being anticipated is realized, then the plans made in order to fulfill the prediction will turn out to have been correct, and the firm will have made its full (equilibrium) adjustment to uncertainty. But if the significant event is not realized as anticipated, the original plans based on the expectation will be in error, and the plans will have to be revised as t_1 approaches. A significant event is thus an outcome or an occurrence which, if foreseen perfectly, would have influenced a particular plan. Since expectations are often subjective in nature, there will be "degrees of uncertainty" on the part of managers; these degrees may be represented by (subjective) probability distributions of various forms. A basis is thereby formed for calculating the "expected value" for prediction purposes, as has been illustrated and discussed elsewhere.[1]

This is, briefly, the uncertainty framework to which the following paragraphs on planning theory relate. A fuller treatment of uncertainty concepts and of the role of uncertainty in decision theory is available in other sources.[2]

Foundations of Planning Theory

Strictly speaking, when considered in the light of uncertainty theory, it is doubtful whether such terms as "decision making," "planning," and "control" actually denote three mutually exclusive or separate management

[1] See Milton H. Spencer and Louis Siegelman, *Managerial Economics* (Richard D. Irwin, Inc., 1959), Chapter 1.
[2] Cf. *ibid.*, Chapter 1, and the references cited therein.

activities. Indeed, from a conceptual and theoretical standpoint, these activities are sufficiently intertwined to defy true separation. Nevertheless, an element of separation appears useful for expository purposes.

Expectations and Rationality

The existence of uncertainty and the consequent need for planning requires that managers formulate hypotheses about the future. Each manager can then proceed to reduce one or more of his hypotheses to a point of testing in actual operations by integrating facts with expectations in a manner such that his "degree of belief" is greater in one hypothesis than in another. In order to obtain the necessary facts, the manager may survey literature in the form of business magazines and outlook reports, attend conferences, and perform related activities that are pertinent to the gathering of information. In this way he assimilates and integrates facts which he hopes will aid him in formulating hypotheses or mental images of the future with a minimum of error.

How far should managers go in the attempt to gather information? What weights should be placed on various sources and types of information that differ in reliability? The answers to these questions involve problems of choice. Thus, to some extent there is an inverse relationship between the degree of profitable planning and the degree of uncertainty. Management's objective, of course, is to increase (preferably maximize) the former and to decrease (preferably minimize), the latter, which it accomplishes by gathering and synthesizing information about the future that is at best incomplete and unreliable. Expectations or plans could be made more profitable (or uncertainty could be reduced) by expending more funds on improving the completeness and reliability of the information-gathering process. But the likelihood is strong that there is inherent in the process a certain element of diminishing returns, thereby reducing the problem of choice or decision to the basic question:

> To what extent is an increment of expenditure for more or better information worth the resulting improvement in expectations (or reduction in uncertainty)?

Or to put it in different words:

> To what extent should management replace less reliable expectations at lower costs with more reliable expectations at higher costs?

This question, expressed in one form or another, is one of the fundamental decision problems confronting managers in their role as planners. Unfortunately, there is a certain amount of judgment in arriving at an answer. However, an answer is, in effect, arrived at once the decision is made to put the plan into action.

The Planning Horizon

Under uncertainty, the ability to adapt plans to changing expectations or forecasts has a direct bearing on future profits and losses. Unfortunately for decision makers, the real world exercises certain limits on the "time length" of predictions, that is, the distance into the future for which a prediction can be made with a given probability. This leads to the technical notion of the *planning* horizon as a measure of the length of time over which managers plan economic activity.

It was implied above that, ideally, managers formulate a definite set of expectations at one point in time (t_0) for a later point in time (t_4) which they hold at all intermediate points in time (t_1, t_2, t_3). Actually, this description of the planning process does not appear to be in complete accordance with experience. Thus, numerous expectation studies have been made on monthly, quarterly, and annual bases, in which executives were asked to state both their mean and modal estimates of GNP, the level of industrial production, and other economic variables for the coming periods, and their expected range of outcomes of these variables according to given probabilities. The results of these studies have shown that expectations tend to change both within and between periods, and that the range tends to lessen as the end of a period is approached. That is, for many economic variables the range or dispersion of expectations is a function of time, being greatest for dates that extend farthest into the future, and narrowing to eventual convergence as the relevant future date is approached. As often happens, however, a significant change may occur in the structural environment — a major strike, threat of war, or the like — as a result of which the shape of the dispersion or expectations pattern is changed before the relevant date is reached. A new pattern may then emerge which is completely different from the preceding on, and hence a new plan may have to be formulated.

These concepts are illustrated graphically in Figure 24.1. In Figure 24.1A, a plan or course of action is formulated at t_0 to cover the period to t_4. This plan is based on a range of expected outcomes, such as sales, GNP, or some other economic variable which the manager anticipates with a probability of 1.0. The dispersion or range of expectations is relatively wide in the early stages of the plan as shown by the lines *ab*, *cd*, etc., and falls to zero or converges at i at the planning horizon t_4.[3] The result is a single pattern of expectations as distinguished from the kind of multiple

[3] Since the change in range does not yield any further knowledge about such measures as kurtosis, skewness, or variance of the subjective probability distribution, it is at best only a vague and rough measure of the degree of uncertainty that prevails at any given planning date. (Some interesting applications of these ideas to agricultural economics, with relevance to farm prices, appears in E. O. Heady, *Economics of Agricultural Production and Resource Use*, Chapter 16.)

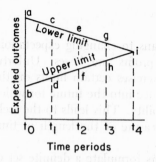

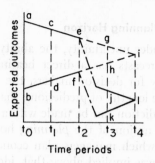

Figure 24.1A. Single Pattern   **Figure 24.1B. Multiple Patterns**

Figure 24.1   Dispersion of Expectations as a Function of Time.

patterns that might emerge in Figure 24.1B. In the latter diagram, a change in one or more of the structural variables that conditions the shape of the dispersion has occurred at time t_2. As a consequence, a period of adjustment takes place during which a new range of expectations (and hence a new plan) is formulated. If no further changes arise to upset this pattern, the convergence of outcomes will occur at l instead of i as previously anticipated. Of course, the planning horizon may now also be extended beyond t_4, although this is not shown on the diagram. Also, the new dispersion or range of outcomes indicated by jk may be less than any dispersion that occurred at t_2 or before as shown in the diagram, but it may also be equal to or greater than any previous dispersion.

How does the length of the planning period, i.e., the planning horizon, differ among individuals? Since expectations are only subjective guesses on the part of each decision maker, it follows that no two managers need view the same facts in the same way; more likely, each will attach different weights or subjective probabilities to the outcomes in question, and will envision different planning horizons in accordance with the financial, marketing, production and institutional framework that characterizes the firm, its markets, and the industry. To be more specific, a discussion of expectation models is needed as a foundation for the theory of planning.

Expectation Models

Businessmen formulate hypotheses or expectations of the future as a basis for establishing plans. These expectation models are largely subjective forecasts based on objective data, the latter usually being of an historical nature. The expectations, of course, vary in degree of refinement. Thus, various studies indicate that some of the more astute and sophisticated businessmen do visualize future outcomes in the form of a probability distribution, with some cognizance at least of a modal or most probable outcome as well as a possible range of outcomes. A larger proportion of businessmen, on the other hand, admittedly do not harbor precise mental visions of probability distributions, but they seem to have at least a cardinal notion of the most likely outcome of an event, as well as some "practical limits" or range within which that outcome will fall. And finally, there is what appears to be the practice of the largest proportion of businessmen, namely, those who tend to think in an ordinal sense by mentally ordering or arranging their expected outcomes from "most likely" to "least likely." In view of these different approaches to the formulation of expectations by businessmen, what can be said about the degree of uncertainty and the accuracy with which such expectations are held?

Degree of Surprise. The British economist G. L. S. Shackle has proposed the "degree of surprise" as an indication of the extent of uncertainty with which managers hold expectations. The degree of surprise, in effect, reflects the disappointment or elation that managers experience over the realization of particular outcomes. Thus a manager who foresees, for example, a relatively narrow range of sales, such as a range of $1.1 to $1.3 million with a probability of 1.0, is not "surprised" if sales of $1.2 million are realized. However, he is very pleasantly surprised if, with the same expected range and probability, sales of $2.0 million are realized, and he is very unpleasantly surprised if sales of $0.5 million are experienced. A competitor, on the other hand, with a substantially wider range of expectations, say $0.8 to $1.6 million, may not be surprised to the same degree if either of the above extreme outcomes is realized.

Other aspects of surprise can be related to the skewness rather than just the range or other measure of dispersion of a distribution. Thus, suppose that the original expectations distribution is such that the most probable level of sales is $1.0 million, with no expectation of sales that are lower but with the possibility of sales that are higher. The surprise at the time of realization may then be low if actual sales are above $1 million, and high if actual sales are below that level. It has been pointed out that while the degree of surprise over outcomes can serve as an indication of both the degree of *ex ante* uncertainty and *ex post* accuracy with which expectations are held, it is possible for an individual to attach high confidence to his expectations and be greatly surprised by the realized outcome.

In some of his research on the economies of expectations done in the late 1930's and early '40's, Albert Hart of Columbia University emphasized the importance of specifying what is meant by fulfillment of anticipations. Thus if we take two (ordered) points in time and designate the first date, t_0, as the original moment of planning, and the second, t_1, as a date slightly later, then the following three conditions are necessary in order to describe the fulfillment of anticipations for any enterprise between these dates:

(1) Events between t_0 and t_1 must follow the expectation-value of the t_0 anticipations.

(2) The expectation-values of t_1 estimates for dates beyond t_1, must be the same as the expectation values of t_0 estimates for the same dates.

(3) The dispersion of t_1 estimates for later dates must be less than of t_0 estimates for the same dates, and the decrease in dispersion must be in accordance with the anticipations of convergence held at t_0.

A failure of any of these conditions results in a *surprise* which may be agreeable or disagreeable. Thus, failure of the first condition results in a primary surprise; failure of the second condition results in a secondary surprise with respect to expectation values; and failure of the third condition results in a secondary surprise with respect to convergence.[4]

It must be emphasized that under uncertainty, the future cannot realistically be viewed as a "series of repeated trials" as is characteristic of the theory of risk. Too many decisions are of a once-and-for-all nature, so that the opportunity for repeating an experiment or correcting a past error does not always exist. It is a relatively rare case when a single anticipated distribution of outcomes can be projected with confidence into the future with the expectation that the outcome of a single time period is but one random value of the probability or frequency distribution that will be repeated in later years.[5] It is an instructive exercise to develop actual illustrations, cases, or conditions under which particular production, investment, marketing, or other types of business decisions can be repeated or corrected in case of error, and under which they cannot.

Classifications of Expectations Models. The ability to predict is evidently essential in the reduction of uncertainty. What methods of prediction have been devised? Actually there are infinitely many, ranging from crude mechanical techniques, rule-of-thumb procedures, and other "naïve" methods to highly elaborate dynamic models of extraordinary elegance and sophistication. Despite their diversity, all methods usually appear to have at least this much in common: (1) they attempt primarily to express subjective expectations on the basis of objective data; (2) they try to predict the probable outcomes of the variables in question; and hence (3) they are not perfect predictors, since uncertainty is ever-present and therefore the possibility of realizing other outcomes always exists. In the following classifications, note the degree of overlap that occurs among alternative proposals.

J. Steindl[6] has proposed that expectation models be placed in one of three broad categories: (1) *The stationary type.* The value of the variable is observed over a certain period, say for a number of years, and the average

---

[4] Cf. A. G. Hart, "Anticipations and Business Planning," *Quarterly Journal of Economics* (Vol. XI).

[5] Cf. G. L. S. Schackle, *Expectations in Economics*, Chapters 1 and 2, *Uncertainty in Economics and Other Reflections*, and Heady, *op. cit.*, Chapter 16.

[6] J. Steindl, "On Risk," *Oxford Economic Papers*, No. 5, 1941, pp. 43 ff.

of these values is then the predicted value for next year and also for future years. The degree of uncertainty depends primarily on fluctuations around the average. (2) *The continuity type*. The last observed variable is the value predicted for the future. This method thus assumes a continuous development of the variable in question. (3) *The quasi-scientific type*. The value of the variable is predicted on the basis of its relationship to other variables, in much the same way as a prediction employing correlation and regression methods.

In somewhat the same vein, G. Stigler[7] has suggested two classes of expectations: (1) *extrapolative*, involving the projection of past trends into the future, and (2) *analytical*, involving the relationship of present and probable future conditions to prices. A. G. Hart[8] has classified anticipations on a three-way basis, according to whether it is assumed that: (1) the recent level of the variable will continue in the future, (2) the recent rate of change of the variable will continue in the future, or (3) the variable will tend toward some "normal" level. And L. Hurwicz,[9] as well as other prominent econometricians, has suggested that expectations can be classified simply as those adapted to (1) least squares regressions, and (2) simultaneous (or systems of) equations.

Evidently, there are sufficient differences in viewpoints so that a synthesis of classifications would appear to be warranted. One such synthesis of prediction or forecasting methods which has been found suitable and meaningful on both "theoretical and practical" grounds is the following:[10]

1. *Naïve methods*. Unsophisticated and unscientific projections based on guesses or on mechanical extrapolations of historical data. As a method of prediction, they may include procedures ranging from simple coin-tossing to determine an upward or downward movement to the projection of trends, auto-correlations, and other more seemingly complex mathematical techniques. Typically, they are distinguished from other forecasting methods listed below in that they are essentially mechanical and are not closely integrated with relevant economic theory and statistical data.

2. *Barometric techniques*. The use of statistical indicators — selected time series of data which, when used in conjunction with one another or when combined in certain ways, provide an indication of the direction in which the economy or particular industries are heading. The series are thus barometers of economic change.

3. *Opinion polling*. The use of sample surveys as a method of prediction. This approach amounts largely to a weighted or unweighted aver-

[7] G. Stigler, *Theory of Competitive Price* (1947).

[8] Hart, *op. cit.*

[9] Leonid Hurwicz, "Theory of the Firm and of Investment," *Econometrica* (Vol. 14).

[10] See Milton H. Spencer, Colin Clark, Peter Hoguet, *Business and Economic Forecasting* (R. D. Irwin, 1961), for numerous applications.

aging of attitudes and expectations. The underlying assumption is that certain attitudes affecting economic decisions can be defined and measured well enough in advance so that predictions can be made of changing business trends. The results are arrived at by asking people who are directly involved, about their expectations as to future economic happenings. Various forms of opinion polls have been employed in economic and in business forecasting.

4. *Econometrics*. An integration of economic theory, mathematics and statistics, in a manner that permits the construction of quantitative models of economic behavior. These models define the most probable inter-relationships among selected variables. Not all econometric models are prediction oriented; some, for example, are descriptive in that they attempt to "explain" the past behavior of the variables in question. Econometric models may be of the single-equation or simultaneous-equation type.

It should be emphasized that these alternative approaches need not be mutually exclusive. Indeed, some of the most sophisticated, durable, and therefore "practical" models have integrated two or more of these methods with considerable success. Admittedly, however, the econometric method is probably the approach which is most logically suited for incorporating the best features of all of the methods, and it is in this integrating direction that econometricians are now moving in their efforts to construct realistic and durable prediction models.

Conclusion: The Concept of Management Under Uncertainty

The purpose of this discussion has been to present some topics and concepts in the formal theory of uncertainty in order to indicate the roles that they play in affecting management decision making and planning. It should be clear that these notions are by no means "theoretical and impractical." Indeed, it is because managers are faced with uncertainty (imperfect knowledge of the future) that they must make decisions the outcomes of which are not known in advance; and it is because they lack perfect knowledge of the future that they must formulate plans which, due to unforeseen (unpredicted) contingencies, may not be realized. Prediction is thus a necessary condition for planning, and it seems probable that a general theory of planning would have to be integrated with the science of prediction if it is to be logically sound and meaningful.

The literature of management is replete with description and statements about the functions of executives. Terms like "decision making," "planning," and "control" have become standard words with fairly standard meanings and implications. Once we recognize the existence of uncertainty, however, these words and the concept of management as a whole take on new meaning and significance in a manner that is not readily appreciated by many writers. How does management function where the future is not known, and plans, which are hardly more than guesses, must be formulated in the face of uncertainty? This is the fundamental question, and some answers have already been indicated in the previous sections. These answers, however, as well as the whole approach to much of modern management thinking, are conditioned by a certain conceptual classification of managerial functions which warrants specific mention at this time.

The Coordinative Function

I submit that the *traditional classifications of managerial functions* (i.e., organizing, planning, directing, etc.) *are both outdated and redundant, in the light of advances in the theory of uncertainty that have taken place in the past several decades!* Some indications of this are apparent from the discussion thus far, whereas a fuller exposition along with a more comprehensive survey of the formal theory of uncertainty are presented in the first chapter of the book cited in footnote 1 above, and in other sources mentioned therein.

When the existence of uncertainty is thus acknowledged as a permanent fact of life, the functions of managers may then be more appropriately classified for purposes of analysis into two distinct levels of activity: one of these is *coordination*; the other is *supervision*. The coordinative function is that of decision making — the process of identifying and selecting alternatives. The need for this function arises in an environment of uncertainty, that is, in situations where the future cannot be predicted with known error, and yet decisions must be made and plans formulated on the basis of expectations. The other phase of management, that of supervision, involves the fulfillment of plans already established, and hence requires little if any coordination of a decision making nature. This classification of management functions, therefore, may be somewhat different from, but it is not in fundamental disagreement with, the analyses underlying the contributions to organization theory by such writers as Chester Barnard, Andreas Papandreou, Herbert Simon, and others. Thus, from a modern standpoint where the *degree of uncertainty* is the crucial consideration, it is management in the coordination sense that occupies virtually all of our attention.

The fundamental role of the coordinating unit — management in its true sense — is that of choosing between alternatives. Problems of choice arise because the material and human resources available to the firm, such as capital, land, labor and managerial ability, are limited and can be employed in alternative uses. The executive function from the coordinative standpoint thus becomes one of making choices or decisions that will provide the optimum means of attaining a desired end, whether the end be the preservation of the existing situation between the firm and its competitors, or the long run attainment of a monopoly in a particular market, or perhaps an intermediate one of profit maximization. But regardless of the goal, the fact is that business managers must make decisions in a realm of uncertainty. If knowledge of the future were perfect, plans could be formulated without error and hence without need for subsequent revision. In the usual case, however, the time involved precludes perfect knowledge of the future. Thus plans are made at one point in time that are based on current knowledge and involve current decisions, in anticipation of a result that will be forthcoming at some future point in time. As more facts become known, plans may have to be revised and a new course of action adopted if the desired objectives are to be attained. Managers are thus engaged in the continuous process of charting a course of action into a hazy horizon.

Recapitulation

The above ideas constitute the essence of the coordinative function, and hence the bare elements of the concept of management under uncertainty. There is a fundamental point in all of this that is worth reiterating: *a firm* (as distinguished from a physical producing plant) *or management in the coordination* (rather than supervisory) *sense, exists because of uncertainty or imperfect knowledge.* If the future were known with certainty, management in the coordination sense would be needed only at the start or initial phase of an investment in order to formulate a plan for the future; thereafter, management in the supervisory sense would be all that is needed for the purpose of administering or carrying out the plan. Apparently, since uncertainty is by far the predominant environment in which businessmen operate, planning, whether done formally or informally, is an essential activity of coordinative management. Much the same can be said for the other managerial functions as well. *Hence the traditional classification of managerial functions results in what is at best a superficial if not illusory description of the managerial process, and at worst an enormous waste of time, unless the separation is made within the framework of uncertainty theory as indicated above.*

In commenting on an earlier version of this paper, a reviewer asked: is decision making an activity coordinate with planning and control, or is it an approach to the analysis of these functions? In the light of the above analysis, my answer is that it is *both* under conditions of uncertainty. I believe that this could probably be most readily verified if not proven by a method of *reductio ad absurdum.*

25

Entrepreneurial Prototype in
Bank Management:
A Comparative Study of Branch Bank Managers[*][1]

William D. Litzinger

Arizona State College

Many researchers believe that more replication studies are needed. This article reports such a study, which tends to confirm the earlier conclusions of Professor Chris Argyris at Yale that a "right type" of individual is found in centralized banking. The author also finds, for a sample of California banks, an emerging entrepreneurial prototype with characteristics similar to those found in other entrepreneurial positions.[1]

Research in banking in the Eastern part of the United States reported by Argyris identified a "right type" individual found predominant among managers and employees in the banking industry.[2] Such individuals were characterized as being quiet, passive, obedient, cautious, and careful. It was further inferred from this research that an employee of the "right type" apparently has (a) a strong desire for security, stability, and predictability in his life; (b) a strong desire to be left alone and to work in relative isolation; and (c) a dislike of aggressiveness and/or hostility in himself or in others.

* Taken and adapted from *The Journal of the Academy of Management*, vol. 6, no. 1, March, 1963, pp. 36–45.

1 This study was conducted in partial fulfillment of the requirements for the doctoral degree in the Graduate School of Business Administration, and was supported in part by a grant from the University of Southern California Research Institute for Business and Economics (USCRIBE), October, 1961.

2 Chris Argyris, "Human Relations in a Bank," *Harvard Business Review*, XXXII (September–October, 1954), 63–72.

Argyris also found that there was a self-selection to the extent that people of the above type gravitated to banking, were hired, remained, and were promoted, so that the bank employee population became purified ("homogenized" so to speak).

McMurry in a later article reaffirms these findings.[3] He posited a functional relationship between the structured, routinized character of banking operations and organization, and the personality configurations of most bank employees. Typically, banking offers security, slow advancement, limited opportunity for initiative and responsibility, and an emphasis upon job stability rather than high economic rewards. Such conditions and attending recruitment policies were noted by McMurry to attract persons with high dependency needs. Such selection criteria proves dysfunctional since such employees do not meet the organizational needs of management succession on a promotion-from-within basis.

However, it is noteworthy to point out that the conclusions regarding the "right type" found in banking resulted from investigations of banks in the Eastern part of the United States. Many such banks are old established institutions having histories in some instances paralleling the industrial development of the areas they serve. As such, most are located under "one roof." Indeed, the laws governing banking in that section of the country prohibit or restrict branch bank operations. Attempts have been made to extend branch banking via mergers in some instances. Also, some attempts have been successful in getting the laws modified to permit branch operations. However, the majority of states today still have limiting legislation in this area.[4]

National Pattern of Banks

During the four decades since 1920, there have been fundamental and far reaching changes in the number of operating banks and branches in the United States (Table 25.1). In 1921, approximately 31,000 banks were in operation, the largest number in the nation's history. From that peak the number of banks has declined to about 14,000. Branches, on the other hand, numbered fewer than 1,500 or less than 5 per cent of all banking offices in 1921; but there are now over 11,000 branches comprising more than 40 per cent of all banking offices.[5]

The fifteen year period since World War II was one of accelerated change. During that time there was a three-fold increase in the number of branch offices while the total number of banks actually declined. Branches comprised 20 per cent of the total banking offices at the beginning of this

[3] Robert N. McMurry, "Recruitment, Dependency, and Morale in the Banking Industry," *Administrative Science Quarterly*, III (June, 1958), 87–106.
[4] *Annual Report of the Federal Deposit Insurance Corporation*, as of June 30, 1960, p. 45.
[5] *Ibid.*, p. 27.

Table 25.1
Number of Banks and Branches in the United States
in Selected Years

Year	Number of banks	Number of branches	Total number of banking offices
1920	31,000	1,500	32,500
1945	14,725	4,168	18,893
1960	13,999	11,106	24,391

Source: *Annual Report of the Federal Deposit Insurance Corporation*, as of June 30, 1960, pp. 27, 45, 126.

period; in 1960, branches had increased in number to where they made up 40 per cent of the total bank offices.

California Banking Picture

The picture of the change in banking in California has been no less spectacular (Table 25.2). There were 717 banks and 179 branches in California in 1920. Branches then comprised approximately 20 per cent of the total banking offices. Today, their numbers have grown to a point where better than 90 per cent of all offices are branch offices.

The fifteen year period since World War II has seen a 188 per cent increase in the number of branch offices. This during a period that shows a 35 per cent reduction in the number of banks. During this time span, an average of nearly 50 new offices a year have been opened in this state.

In the course of the fiscal period June 30, 1960 to June 30, 1961, no less than 131 new banking offices were opened![6]

Table 25.2
Number of Banks and Branches in the State of California
in Selected Years

Year	Number of banks	Number of branches	Total number of banking offices
1920	717	179	896
1945	208	842	1,050
1960	133	1,582	1,715

Source: *Annual Report of the Federal Deposit Insurance Corporation*, as of June 30, 1960, p. 41.
Fifty-First Annual Report of the Superintendent of Banks of the State of California, 1960, p. 9.

[6] *Fifty-Second Annual Report of the Superintendent of Banks of the State of California*, 1961, p. 9.

Decentralization

Branch banking has resulted in decentralization of physical and managerial resources. Though branch banking operations are decentralized in a physical sense, not all banks follow a policy of decentralization of management authority. An important aspect of organizational structure is the level at which decisions are made. Where a great many of the policies, methods, procedures, and programs are decided in the headquarters office, very little decision-making autonomy exists in the branches. A more decentralized picture is presented when operating decisions are pushed well down in the organizational hierarchy.

Although California banks may be physically decentralized, some banks give their branch managers a greater latitude in decision making while others maintain greater centralized managerial control. Such circumstances might lead to the following question: Does the branch bank manager position under a policy of centralized control require individuals of a different "type" than that found necessary in a decentralized environment?

Manager vs. Administrator

A study of the literature on the subject points to the emergence of a dichotomy in managerial roles in terms of organizational needs. To an extent, this divergence reflects changes in the concept of the enterpreneur.

Entrepreneurship has enjoyed a number of definitions that have varied according to time and place. Reviewing the history of this term, Cole has noted:

> . . . At one time, the creative aspects of the entrepreneur was emphasized and he was referred to as a "projector." The modern term came into use in England only in 1878 to signify a "director or manager of a public musical institution" or "one who gets up entertainments." John Stuart Mill mentioned the word as a French term in a footnote to his *Principles* thirty years earlier at which time he expressed regret at the lack of an English equivalent. Recently, the word has been employed to differentiate an active businessman from a slow-moving one. The former "make a market" for new varieties of items whereas the latter carries on a passive trade in traditional goods.[7]

Cole goes on to present a strong argument to show that the entrepreneurial function is both dispersed and concentrated. He noted there is broad participation in the formation of decisions throughout the organization (dispersion), yet there are also seats of major policy decision making which overrule others insofar as there are conflicts and hence represent concentration of entrepreneurial authority. This results from the hierarchical structuring in organization.

[7] Arthur Cole, *Business Enterprise in Its Social Setting* (Cambridge: Harvard University Press, 1959), pp. 6–7.

In a provocative article on the subject, Hartmann explores the various meanings of the term entrepreneur.[8] Initially, the innovative characteristic was given emphasis. Industrialization has been accompanied by the establishment of large permanent organizations wherein it becomes exceedingly difficult for any one individual to greatly affect the course a company is to follow. Under such circumstance, decision making takes on added significance. Hartmann notes that Selznick has differentiated "critical" decision making from the noncritical or "routine" decisions. Decisions involving the setting of goals and shaping the organization are "critical and are made by "managers." Noncritical decisions are handled by "administrators."

After exploring the various approaches, Hartmann suggests that entrepreneurs are those who are the source of all formal authority. The root of such authority is one or more of the following: executive property rights, tradition, or the force of personality (charisma). He then refers to the vernacular of German management today which distinguishes two types of executives, notably those who are leader-initiators (*Führung*) and those who more or less carry out routing administrative procedures (*Leitung*). For Hartmann, managers cannot be the source of all formal authority in in organization, hence not entrepreneurs.

More recently, Odiorne has reaffirmed the German distinction by emphasizing that managers are goal and action oriented whereas administrators merely follow certain procedures mechanically.[9]

Another aspect of distinction among managers was noted in a study of line managers and staff specialists in General Electric.[10] Line managers were found to have higher achievement motives than staff specialists and also preferred intermediate levels of risk whereas staff specialists preferred extreme risks.

In summary, a distinction has been noted between "managers" who set organizational goals versus "administrators" who carry out the routines utilized in achieving the goals. The former represent modern day entrepreneurs. Also, there is evidence to indicate differences among individuals found in line activity as contrasted to staff specialists.

A Comparative Study of Branch Bank Managers
Under Centralization and Decentralization

It would appear that the "right type" identified by Argyris would fit more readily into a highly centralized organization requiring more structuring of functional-support activities since most decisions would flow from

[8] Heinz Hartmann, "Managers and Entrepreneurs: A Useful Distinction?" *Administrative Science Quarterly*, III (March, 1959), pp. 429–451.

[9] George S. Odiorne, *How Managers Make Things Happen* (Englewood Cliffs, N. J.: Prentice-Hall, Inc., 1961).

[10] *Motive Patterns of Managers and Specialists*, Behavioral Research Service, Relations Services, General Electric Company, February, 1960.

headquarters. On the contrary, an organizational environment requiring more decision making at lower levels such as that characterized by a decentralization philosophy, requires more in the way of an "entrepreneurial type." This study was undertaken to ascertain if there are discernible differences between "types" of branch bank managers under divergent managerial policy. To this end, sixty-five (32 decentralized and 33 centralized) incumbent branch bank managers were analyzed in terms of selected personality variables but in different organizational environments, one centralized and the other decentralized.

Selected Personality Variables

In order to begin to differentiate a decentralized branch "manager" from a centralized branch "administrator," some degree of personality assessment is in order, however modest this may be.

Since a manager spends considerable time dealing with people, the values he holds regarding his relationship to other people and their relationship to him are important. As a means of measuring such values, the Gordon Survey of Interpersonal Values was used. It yields scales measuring the following values:

> *Support:* Being treated with understanding, receiving encouragement from others, being treated with kindness and consideration.
> *Conformity:* Doing what is socially correct, following regulations closely doing what is accepted and proper, being a conformist.
> *Recognition:* Being looked up to and admired, being considered important, attracting favorable notice, achieving recognition.
> *Independence:* Having the right to do whatever one wants to do, being free to make one's own decisions, being able to do things in one's own way.
> *Benevolence:* Doing things for other people, sharing with others, helping the unfortunate, being generous.
> *Leadership:* Being in charge of other people, having authority over others, being in a position of leadership or power.[11]

Odiorne, in defining a "manager," noted that such an individual was goal oriented. This factor would appear to be an important element contributing to a distinction between the two general types of individuals with which this study deals. A test which includes a measure of this aspect of an individual's method of influence as a leader is the Fleishman Leadership Opinion Questionnaire. This test was also used and yields scores for two leadership dimensions:

[11] *Manual for the Survey of Interpersonal Values,* Chicago: Science Research Associates, Inc., 1960.

Structure: Reflects the extent to which an individual is likely to define and structure his own role and those of his subordinates toward *goal attainment*. A high score on this dimension characterizes individuals who play a more active role in directing group activities through planning, communicating information, scheduling, criticizing, trying out new ideas, etc.

Consideration: Reflects the extent to which an individual is likely to have job relationships characterized by mutual trust, respect for subordinates' ideas, consideration of their feelings, and a certain warmth between supervisor and subordinate. A high score is indicative of a climate of good rapport and two-way communication. A low score indicates the supervisor is likely to be more impersonal in his relations with group members.[12]

Investment Preference Test

Other studies involving risk preference have attempted to assess it by presenting various gambling type options with known probabilities such as in rolling dice. In an effort to provide a more realistic approach, a test was constructed involving risk decisions with which most branch bank managers are conversant, namely, financial investments. In this test, subjects are asked to make investment decisions among sets (tetrads) of possible investments.

Each set of options in the test is arranged in such a manner as to present a range of risk potential ranging from very safe to rather speculative. While the sequential offering varies, the pattern is repeated in each set of four options. The following pattern is presented in each set: (1) a very safe investment in either a U.S. Treasury Bond or a blue chip company debenture bond; (2) reputable open-end mutual fund stock; (3) blue chip company common stock; (4) a purely speculative venture such as stock in a foreign company, vacant land, etc.

The test uses a constant-sum technique for the quantitative reporting of comparative judgments of investment options. Subjects are directed to distribute $100,000 on a percentage basis over each of the four options. This may itself seem rather artificial. Among the points distilled from the conclusions of many researchers regarding risk, Cerami noted that:

> People are most speculative and devil-may-care when using real money; they are more conservative when dealing with imaginary risks and rewards. . .[13]

Thus such an approach, while appearing somewhat artificial, may in fact mirror reality more closely than actual utilization of personal funds would

[12] *Manual for the Leadership Opinion Questionnaire*, Chicago: Science Research Associates, Inc., 1960.

[13] Charles A. Cerami, "Cut the Risks in Decisions," *Nations Business*, January, 1961, pp. 66–69.

provide. Since managers handle monies for others primarily, a greater approximation of reality is fostered by this technique.

Scoring the Investment Preference Test

Two methods of scoring the Investment Preference Test were developed. A *Total Weighted Score* was arrived at by taking into consideration the relative implicit risks of such securities as comprised the test. Weights were assigned each category of risk for scoring purposes as follows:

Bonds or debentures 1
Mutual fund stock 2
Blue chip common stock 3
Speculative 4

An individual score using this procedure was arrived at by multiplying the percentage the respondent indicated for each option by the corresponding weight and then totaling all the individual products.

While the numerical values of the weights used did not represent any actual percentage yields, they provided a rough relative measure to distinguish the relative risks inherent in the various categories, which are a function of the potential investment risk. A high *Total Weighted Score* indicated a tendency to select predominately higher risk type options (blue chip common stock and/or speculative). Conversely, a low score was indicative of a preference for the safer categories of investments (Government bonds and/or mutual funds common stock). This provided a measure of riskiness *per se*.

A second scoring method yielded an *Extreme Risk Score*. This was obtained by totaling the actual percentages allocated to the safest (bonds) and the riskiest (speculative) investment options. This scoring technique yielded a measure of the propensity for extreme or intermediate risk levels. A high score indicated a preference for taking extremely high and/or extremely low risks, whereas, a low score indicated a tendency toward intermediate risks.

Background Information Questionnaire

A four page questionnaire was used in conjunction with the three tests to elicit two general types of information: (1) objective demographic data such as age, education, children, years as a branch manager, salary; and (2) more subjective job related information such as type of work preferred, amount of risk involved in present position, etc.

Entrepreneurial Prototype

In light of the goal of this study, it was hypothesized that in comparison to administrative "right type" of a centralized bank, the managerial entrepreneur would: place higher values on *independence, leadership,* and *recognition* and lower values on *support, conformity,* and *benevolence;* be significantly higher in "goal attainment orientation" (*structure*) and significantly lower in empathy (*consideration*); and show a significant preference for intermediate risk choices rather than low or high choices.

Results

The centralized branch bank managers were found to be significantly higher in terms of *benevolence* than their decentralized counterparts (Table 25.3). This indicated the centralized managers placed a higher value in doing things for others, sharing, helping the unfortunate, and being generous.

Table 25.3
Chi Square and Frequencies Above and Below
Median of Total Sample on Each Variable

Variable	Central- ized bank +	−	Decentral- ized bank +	−	x^2
Structure	16	17	17	15	.01
Consideration	13	20	18	14	2.12
Support	15	18	14	18	.04
Conformity	18	15	14	18	.75
Recognition	12	21	17	15	1.84
Independence	15	18	15	17	.01
Benevolence	20	13	9	23	6.90*
Leadership	14	19	19	13	2.60
Total weighted risk	15	18	17	15	.02
Extreme risk	25	8	10	22	6.80*
Age	11	22	21	11	6.80*
Years of education	14	19	20	12	2.64
Brothers & sisters	11	22	22	10	8.20*
Number of children	17	16	24	8	3.70*
Years in banking	16	17	17	15	.12
Years as branch manager	11	22	22	10	8.20*
Salary	7	26	28	4	29.10*
Average annual dollar value of loans outstanding	11	22	27	5	17.40*
Number of subordinates	6	27	27	5	28.60*

* Significant at or beyond the .05 level (from Table of Chi Square, 1 *df.*, 3.84).

The two groups did not differ significantly in terms of riskiness *per se.* However, the centralized managers showed a significantly higher preference for extreme risk choices (very safe and/or highly speculative) in comparison with decentralized managers. Thus, in terms of risk preference, the decentralized managers were similar to what had been found to typify individuals acting in a line capacity in the General Electric study of managers and specialists. Centralized branch bank managers, on the other hand, are indicated as being more closely akin to what the G. E. study found regarding staff specialists on this dimension.

Although not statistically significant, the centralized sample tended to place greater emphasis on *consideration* (empathy). The decentralized group tended to place higher values on *leadership*. It has been pointed out that the Median Test used in this study has a power-efficiency approximately equivalent to a t-test using a sample about two-thirds that of this study.[14] This has the effect of increasing the possibility of accepting a null hypothesis (no difference) when it is in fact false. Thus, judgment might well be withheld on these two variables pending additional research.

To test how the two sample groups differed according to the interrelationships of the test variables, intercorrelations among these variables were computed.

A significant difference was found between the two samples in terms of the intercorrelation of *support* and *conformity*. A significant positive relationship between these two values was noted for the decentralized group. Such was not the case among their centralized counterparts. This indicated that managers in the decentralized environment who valued being encouraged, receiving kind treatment, and being understood (*support*) also tended to place a high value in need to conform, that is being socially correct, following regulations, and doing what was accepted and proper.

As a group, the centralized managers tended to be higher and less variable in *conformity*. As a result of this relatively greater homogeneity among this sample, there was less chance to expect any such relationship with *support*.

The two groups differed significantly according to the way *structure* and *support* were intercorrelated. There was a tendency in the centralized sample for those with high *support* needs to have also high need for *structure*. This indicated that those in the centralized environment desirous of being understood and treated with kindness also tended to become more involved with subordinates. That is to say, they felt a greater need to participate actively in the planning, scheduling, and general structuring of the work of their subordinates. The opposite was true of the decentralized sample. Those in the decentralized environment who tended toward more structure perception (need to structure the work for subordinates) showed less concern about being accepted by their subordinates.

Demographically, the decentralized group had significantly larger operating units in terms of average amount of annual loans outstanding and

[14] A. M. Mood, "On the Asymptotic Efficiency of Certain Non-Parametric Two-Sample Tests," *Annals of Mathematical Statistics*, (September, 1954), pp. 514–523.

number of subordinates. They were also older, had more experience as branch managers and were paid higher salaries. Interestingly, the decentralized managers had significantly more brothers and sisters and also had more children of their own.

The centralized branch managers showed a significantly higher preference for the type of work that is self-satisfying rather than that of a prestigious nature. Both groups exhibited a preference for working with people rather than things. In terms of the most significant part of their jobs, both groups indicated responsibilty for the profit or loss of their unit was most important. Each group felt their jobs involved considerable risk rather than an average or little amount of risk.

Conclusions

On balance, this study tended to support Argyris' conclusions that a "right type" individual is to be found in centralized banking. However, a new prototype may be emerging in the decentralized branch bank operations in California with attributes similar to those found in other "entrepreneurial" positions.

It would appear that, rather than a clear-cut delineation of two distinct types on a categorical basis, those found in branch banking may best be classified along a continuum with the "right type" at one end, an "entrepreneurial" type at the other, and gradations along this scale in between.

The failure of this study to note two completely separate types of unit managers may be partly due to self-selection. Also, it may be that a mixture of "types" is required in banking, whether it is a centralized or decentralized operation. Other studies comparing successful branch bank managers with successful bank staff specialists such as loan officers might lead to a more definitive delineation between the administrative "right type" and the managerial entrepreneur.

Suggestions for Further Research

The concept of differing "types" of unit managers associated with centralization or decentralization could be explored in other types of organizations including retailing, manufacturing, etc.

A further refinement of the Investment Preference Test for use with other groups sophisticated in financial matters of an investment nature, such as savings and loan managers or stock brokers, would be a natural extension of research using this tool.

Longitudinal studies of managers using a test of this kind may indicate the pattern of change in these individuals over time in terms of risk preference. The impact of stock market gyrations on risk behavior could be investigated to attempt to determine the degree of influence on investment decisions.

26

Criteria for the Determination
of Compensation and Organizational
Status for Managerial Jobs*

Robert J. House

The McKinsey Foundation for Management Research, Inc.

**Leon E. Peters, Hugh M. Stephenson,
and James E. McElwain**

The National Cash Register Company

The study reported in this article features the joint collaboration of a university researcher with company researchers. The researchers sought to find criteria by which to measure the elements of status and compensation in managerial jobs. Theoretical gaps in the measurement of discretionary responsibility are specified, and three criterion factors are analyzed for the evaluation of managerial positions.

This paper is a report of an analytical attempt to measure and explain the essential factors inherent in the determination of compensation and status for managerial jobs. This study is an outgrowth of a management development program designed and conducted for the Research and Development Division of The National Cash Register Company. As a result of studying compensation and organization theory, the top management of the R & D Division authorized a search for measurements which can be used for assigning compensation and organizational status to managerial jobs, and for rewarding management jobs on the basis of their

* Taken and adapted from the *Proceedings of the Annual Meeting*, Academy of Management, 1962, pp. 67–82.

contribution to organizational objectives. The study was an exploratory effort which will require additional empirical investigation before final consideration is given for implementation. This paper reports the results of the exploratory study.

Purpose

It is our purpose to advance a set of criterion factors which may be used to measure the requisite considerations essential in the determination of status and compensation for management jobs. To date these determinations have been based in large measure on intuitive judgment. The relationships between these criteria variables are specified and a method of measurement is advanced.

There is no intent on the part of the authors to suggest that this evaluating system can be used to replace existing perspectives or explanations of managerial phenomenon. The present model is intended to supplement not supplant existing explanations.

The particular area of existing theory which we found lacking for purposes of organizational design and managerial compensation concerns measurement of discretionary responsibility. True, there are existing job evaluation plans which include discretionary responsibility as a criterion factor. However, we have found only one of these factor definitions to be operational in the sense of being sufficiently precise and discriminating to be useful as a foundation upon which to derive measurement instruments.

Since most existing theories of management consider delegation of responsibility as an essential construct for explaining managerial phenomenon, and since there has been little effort toward measurement of responsibility delegations, we believe this to be an important gap in existing theory, and one worth pursuing at some length. The one study which we found in the literature capable of yielding a useful measurement of responsibility does not explain the factors involved, but merely provides a correlate of delegation assignments. This study is reviewed briefly below.

Background

In 1956 Elliott Jaques, consultant to the Glacier Metal Company, published a work entitled *Measurement of Responsibility*.[1] In this research report Jaques concludes that time-span, the length of time over which one has discretion of how to do a job without being reviewed either directly or indirectly, is an accurate measurement of the responsibility assigned

[1] Elliott Jaques, *Measurement of Responsibility: A Study of Work, Payments and Individual Capacity*. Cambridge, Mass., Harvard University Press, 1961.

to a position. Based on a preliminary study of twenty-five positions, Jaques concluded that all incumbents of these positions "were able to describe their responsibility in terms of maximum time-span and, in a manner *absolutely consistent* with the independent assessment of their (superior) managers;" and, "the distribution of Grade I time-spans was higher than Grade II, which was higher in turn than Grade III,"[2] which was to be expected.

Jaques further concluded that the frequency of work dissatisfactions was highly correlated with inconsistent assignment of pay and status when viewed in the light of the time-span criteria.[3] In 1961 Jaques reports successful application of the time-span measurement in six different firms. In this report he is careful to note that the time-span criteria is not an explanation but more accurately, a measurement of responsibility assignments. In the same way that a thermometer measures, but does not explain temperature, so time-span measures, but does not explain the assignment of responsibility. According to Jaques:

> the criticism has frequently been levelled against the time-span method of measurement that it fails to take aspects of a job other than time into account. Surely, it is argued, such factors as the type of responsibility, or the variety of number of kinds of responsibility, or the importance of the responsibility, or the consequences of bad discretion, or the difficulty of the discretion exercised, ought to be considered. Are they not equally important as the time-span of the discretion? Maybe so. But it is not my endeavor to make these comparisons. The length of a column of mercury in a graduated capillary tube constructed under certain conditions cannot in itself tell very much about the structure or function of the human body. But it is useful in measuring its temperature.[4]

As stated previously, our purpose is to explain, as well as measure, the factors involved in the assignment of responsibility.

Assumptions

It is assumed that delegations have been made rationally and consistently, and defined in writing. As will be shown later, these assumptions are prerequisite to the effective utilization of the proposed criteria. These are the conventional assumptions which are prerequisite to effective utilization of most job evaluation plans.

[2] *Ibid.*, p. 20. Italics are the authors'.
[3] *Ibid.*, pp. 30–31.
[4] Elliott Jaques, *Equitable Payment: A General Theory of Work, Differential Payment, and Individual Progress.* John Wiley and Sons, Inc., New York, 1961, pp. 69–70.

Implications of these assumptions

These assumptions imply that if top management of an organization has not established the organization structure on an explicit and consistent process of delegation, then the criteria advanced here cannot be validly used for purposes of determining compensation and organizational status for positions within structure.

If this criteria were used under conditions where the above assumptions were not valid, the invalidity of the assumptions would be brought to light. The result of this finding would be that top management would either (a) become cognizant of the current situation, or (b) become defensive concerning past practices. Where the former occurs, the proposed evaluation plan can be useful in defining problems of organizational structure and balance. Where the latter occurs, the result is likely to be frustration, disillusionment, and possible impaired morale.

A second assumption is that management has the normal controls over the development and expansion of the organization. The proposed system uses as one of the measurements the number of personnel managed. It is possible therefore that this system of evaluation like any other system can place a premium on over-staffing or empire building. Management must recognize this implication and respond with the normal controls that have always been necessary.

Top Management Must Define Relative Value of Criterion Factors

If the criteria proposed here are to be used successfully, it is necessary that top management assume the responsibilty of defining the relative value of each criterion factor. Measurement of the degree to which each factor exists in a job is meaningless until the factor values have been established by top management in terms of their *relative* contribution to the objectives of the organization. Thus, application of these criteria in actual practice requires active participation of top management in the establishment of values for each variable.

Top management must also define certain constraints. The process of defining constraints is incumbent upon top management because these reflect the managerial philosophy of the organization. Constraints, then, are a question of management philosophy, not measurement technique.

The Basic Factors

The over-all relationships between the criteria factors are diagrammed in Figure 26.1. Reading from right to left, we see that the total job value may be broken down into four classifications of variables. These variables are: a) the ability requirements necessary to carry out the prescribed duties of the job; b) the discretionary decision responsibilities of the job — that is, the degree to which the job incumbent is delegated responsibility to make decisions of a discretionary nature; c) the advisory responsibilities delegated to the job; and, d) factors peculiar to the particular organization.

Further to the left, we have defined two classes of discretionary decisions.

The first class concerns personnel decision responsibility, such as decisions to instruct, coach, reward, censure, and fire. The second concerns responsibility for the commitment of resources. Examples here are commitments of materials, man-hours, or dollars.

Reading further to the left, we see that the personnel decisions can be weighted in terms of the number of people for whom the decision maker has responsibility; the skill level of his people — that is, whether they are skilled, non-skilled, professional or managerial; and the severity of the

Figure 26.1   Relationships Between Factors

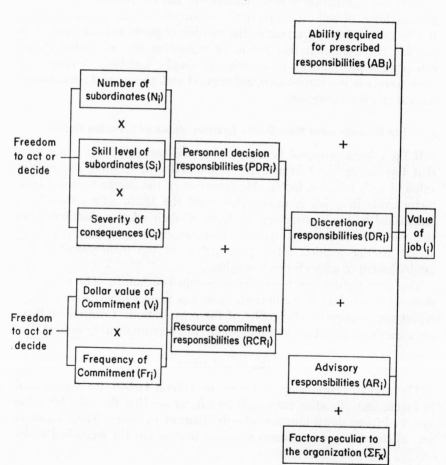

consequences of his personal decisions. For example, decisions to hire and fire are considered more severe than decisions to coach or instruct.

We also see that the resource commitments can be measured in terms of the dollar value of the resources, and the frequency of the commitments. And finally, on the extreme left of this chart, we see that the decision responsibilities are assessed in terms of the degree to which the decision maker has freedom to make a decision. If the decision is made within definite limits as specified by procedures or policies, or if the decision is constrained by the requirement to gain approval from other members of the organization, the decision maker's freedom to act is severely constrained. Thus, the discretionary content of the job is significantly decreased.

The amount of space devoted to the explanation of the discretionary content of a job should not imply that we believe this to be the most important factor. The question as to what is the most important factor for which we assign pay and status must be decided by the top management of the particular organization. Where the organization is engaged in a highly specialized or technical process, and where its life blood is technical innovation, then the managerial pay and status system would most likely emphasize specialized ability. Where the organization is highly decentralized the managerial job would surely be paid more for discretionary responsibility than for specialized ability requirements. If the organization is organized on the basis of checks and balances, then advisory responsibilities and control abilities would receive greater emphasis. The relative weights for the above factors must be determined by top management to answer the question "What do we want to pay for and what do we want to emphasize?" The answer to these questions depends on the essential functions of the organization and the governing management philosophy.

In the following sections we will provide a detailed explanation of the scales which have been developed for measurement of these factors. These scales appear to be operational and useful based on preliminary case experience. Subsequent validation is still necessary at this time.

Discretionary Decision Responsibility

The first factor to be discussed concerns the decisions for which the job incumbent is responsible, and for which he must exercise discretion. In this discussion, attention will be given to two facets of discretionary content; these are first, decisions concerning personnel administration, and second, decisions concerning resource allocation.

Discretionary Responsibility for Personnel Decisions

To evaluate personnel decision responsibility, it is necessary for top management to define the essential nature of the managerial position in the particular organization, consistent with its own management philosophy. If an essential difference between managerial and operative positions is one of leadership, then this difference must be defined explicitly. One dimension of the leadership function is the number of people being led. Thus, for our purposes, a manager may be defined as a person who has leadership responsibility over a specified number of people. Stated another way, we might say that a manager is one who has the responsibility to exercise discretion over no less than X number of people.

Responsibility for X people, according to this definition, constitutes a sufficient condition for the status of first level management. Responsibility for X people also constitutes a necessary *but not* a sufficient condition for higher levels of management. To be assigned organizational status above the first level of management, a position must be delegated the responsibility for X people *plus* either (a) additional people, or (b) some additional responsibility. The actual number of people, or the value of the additional responsibility, must be decided by top management.

As a guide, it is suggested that the number of people be not less than that number which requires formal and systematic supervision. If it is possible under normal conditions for an astute person to lead as many as three people without engaging in deliberate planning and organizing processes, and without establishing formal and systematic means of control, then we would not recommend that three people be used as the minimum number for managerial positions. To use this number as the minimum leadership requirement would be to foster unsystematic rather than a fundamental approach to managing. We recommend that the minimum number of people be that number which, under normal conditions, requires the deliberate performance of the functions of planning, organizing, and controlling in order to provide for effective co-ordination and teamwork of the group. Using this as a general guide for the establishment of a minimum leadership requirement, the job feature recommended here will not only be useful for measuring the relative value of positions, but also for fostering attitude and practices of management consistent with the earlier assumption of planned and rational delegation.

Assuming a manager has some leadership responsibility for the prescribed minimum number of people, the question can be asked, "What amount of discretion does this manager have over these people; and is the leadership of one classification of employees to be more highly valued than another classification? Is the leadership of several people of more or less value than the leadership of the minimum number?" According to our criteria, the value of the positions should reflect the differences in discretionary authority over subordinates, the differences in skill level of subordinates, and the number of subordinates. For example, if a job carries responsibility to instruct, demonstrate, and coach subordinates, it will be awarded a given value for the exercise of this responsibility. However, if it carries the responsibility (and authority) to make higher level and more severe decisions, such as the decision to promote and hire employees, or decisions to dismiss, demote, and to reduce salary, then it would be a proportionately higher value for this additional responsibility. If the job carries responsibility over managers rather than operatives only, this too, should be reflected in the value of the job.

Using the above rationale, the relative value of the personnel decision responsibilities for the particular job can be scaled as illustrated in Figure 26.2. On this chart, classifications of subordinates are scaled down the side. Point values or a numerical index would be established to reflect decision severity as modified by class of employee. Thus, the highest values would be assigned to positions falling within the right hand column at the bottom. A rating determined for each class of people and is then modified by the number of subordinates as indicated at the bottom of the chart. The relative value for the decisions across the top must be decided by top management. Again this decision reflects the managerial philosophy of the organization. Where the management places a high value on human relations and equity considerations, the marginal rate of point increase will be increasingly rapid as one proceeds down the left hand side of the chart. Where the managerial philosophy places a higher value on employee development than on employee selection, the values assigned to the first two columns (instruction and performance appraisal) will be higher than the values assigned to the fourth column (promote and hire).

The personnel decision responsibility as arrived at by this process can be further assessed in terms of the freedom, or discretionary authority, which a decision maker enjoys when making his decisions. Freedom to act also modifies the second classification of discretionary responsibility, namely, the responsibility to commit resources. Therefore, we will advance a set of criteria to measure freedom to act after describing resource commitment responsibility in more detail.

Discretionary Responsibility for Commitment of Resources

A commitment is defined here as any decision or action made on one's own initiative, *not requiring superior line approval*, which results in an *irrevocable*[5] allocation of resources.

To arrive at the value of a commitment, the resource decisions involved in the performance of one's responsibility are specified. These decisions

[5] The location of resources is *not* said to be irrevocable in the sense of being *absolutely* incapable of alteration or reversal so that the ultimate consequence must necessarily be realized. Rather, it is said to be irrevocable in the sense of an irretrievable step having been taken. Thus, a commitment is more than decision, i.e. more than deciding to do something. It implies overt action, the quality of which is assessed at some point after implementation. For that span of time, therefore, the commitment is *de facto* irrevocable.

Figure 26.2 Personnel Decision Responsibilities

	DECISIONS				
	Instruct, Demonstrate, and Coach	Perform Performance Appraisals	Reward Within Established Rate Range	Promote and Hire	Dismiss, Demote and Reduce Salary
NON-SKILLED					
SEMI-SKILLED					
SKILLED					
EXEMPT					
MANAGERIAL					

MODIFIED BY NUMBER OF PEOPLE

No. of People   Modifying Factor
0   X values to be determined
1–3   by top management.)
3–12
12–24
24–50
50–100
Over 100

are measured in terms of two dimensions. The first is the amount of company resources which can be irrevocably committed. To evaluate this dimension, an assessment is made of the direct loss which would result under normal conditions if the intent of the commitment is unsuccessful. Possible losses can be determined by identifying the review techniques used to control the effects of commitments, and by identifying the effects which could possibly occur prior to review. The second dimension for this criterion is the frequency with which such commitments are made.

These dimensions are shown on the left side of Figure 26.3.

For example, if a manager has the responsibility to commit up to $5,000 for direct materials, if this commitment is unreviewed by a superior line manager *before* the commitment is made, and if it could happen that these materials could *not* be used for productive purposes after they are purchased, then the value of these materials, that is, $5,000 constitutes one dimension of the commitment criterion. If it is possible that the purchase of faulty materials would result in idle machine time or lost man-hours, the cost of these lost resources would be added to the $5,000. However, if a safety stock was maintained for such a possibility, then the resources of men and machines would not automatically be committed with the purchase of materials, and the value of the commitment would remain at $5,000. Thus, we see how the value of a commitment is deduced by analysis of the mechanism used to control the effects of the commitments.

Concerning frequency, if the same manager is expected to make such a commitment ten times a year, then the yearly commitment value of this decision is $50,000. Hence, the value of the resource commitment responsibility is a function of the possible loss resulting from the commitment multiplied by the frequency of the commitment.

At this point, we have discussed the two essential discretionary responsibilities, namely personnel and resources, of a managerial job. These responsibilities are modified by the degree to which the manager is free to exercise discretion when carrying out his responsibility.

Discretionary Responsibilities Modified by Freedom to Act

According to our criteria, the discretionary content of a decision is inversely related to the degree to which the decision maker is required to rely upon prescribed courses of action, precedent, advice from others, formula, or supervision of his superior. For example, if the commitment for the purchase of materials is one which is based upon an established and compulsory economic order quantity formula, it may be said to be highly prescribed. Thus, the degree of discretionary content or freedom involved in the commitment is relatively low as compared with decisions

Figure 26.3 Resource Commitment Responsibility

Frequency \ Severity $	Up to 100	100 to 250	250 to 500	500 to 1,000	1,000 to 2,500	2,500 to 12,500	12,500 to 60,000	Over 60,000
Less Often Than Annually								
Annually								
Semi-Annually								
Quarterly								
Monthly								
Weekly								
Daily								

which are made on the basis of choice and which do not lend themselves to policy or formula consideration.

Based on this rationale we advance the proposition that the discretionary content for a given decision is inversely related to the degree to which checks and balances have been established to govern this decision. These checks and balances in organized activities may take the form of (a) direct supervision, (b) influence of other members of the organization, (c) constraints resulting from precedent, policy, rules, or procedure. We have already said that the decision is irrevocable[6] and goes unreviewed by one's superior. Thus, it is not necessary to measure the degree of supervision over these decisions since by definition, there is no such supervision. If the remaining checks and balances can be scaled, and if these scales can be applied to measure the degree to which the factors govern a given decision, then the discretionary content of that decision may be also scaled.

Based on this rationale, a scale for the measurement of discretionary content is illustrated in Figure 26.4.

If (a) the decision is one which is made without advice from other members of the organization, (b) there is no requirement to check with or obtain the approval of other members of the organization and (c) the decision maker is not required to follow established prescriptions, the decision maker is said to be free from external constraints. This is illustrated in degree A of "available guides," Figure 26.4. However, if the decision is constrained by the requirement that the decision maker must get the approval of a staff organization, if he must at least get the advice of other members of the organization, or if his decision is governed by policy, precedent, procedure, or rule, then his decision is relatively constrained, and is considered to be less discretionary. Using Figure 26.4 as criteria for discretionary freedom, we can modify the personnel decision responsibility and resource commitment responsibility to arrive at a final value for the discretionary content of each position throughout the organization structure.

Advisory Responsibility

We have proposed that there are four basic job factors pertinent to the evaluation of managerial positions for purposes of compensation and status. We have discussed discretionary responsibility in some detail. At this point, let us turn to a discussion of the second factor, the advisory responsibility which accompanies a position.

For purposes of this evaluation system, advisory responsibility consists of the obligation to render recommendations *directly* to persons who

---

[6] See discussion of "irrevocable" in footnote 5.

Figure 26.4 Degree of Freedom to Act or Decide

	DEGREES OF CONSTRAINT					
AVAILABLE GUIDES	Only Operational Objectives — No Guides or Precedent	Prior Experience — No Policy or Rules	Established Management Practices Requiring Judgment — No Specific Rules or Procedures	Principles, Procedures, and Rules Requiring Objective Evidence for Exceptions	Principles, Procedures, and Rules Requiring Staff Approval Prior to Exceptions	Highly Specialized Training in Recognized Discipline
STAFF INFLUENCE	No Advice	Voluntary Advice	Compulsory Staff Advice	Compulsory Staff Advice — Staff Can Appeal	Compulsory Staff Advice — Line Can Appeal	Staff Functional Authority
PER CENT OF POINTS FOR EACH DIVISION	100					0

make either personnel decisions or resource commitments. We advance the proposition that the value of the advisory responsibility, when based on a rational process of delegation, is a function of (a) the influence which the advisor is intended to exercise, and (b) the value of the decision to be made by the advisees. Figure 26.5 illustrates this relationship. From Figure 26.5 it can be seen that advisory responsibility constitutes a portion of the total responsibility for a given kind of decision. Thus, the advisory responsibilities are valued at some percentage of the value of the discretion exercised by the advisee. The relative amount of value to be assigned to an advisory responsibility is to be determined by top management since this reflects the degree to which the management philosophy values checks and balances, specialization and control.

To evaluate the advisory responsibilities of a position it is first necessary to evaluate the value of the decisions on which the advice is being rendered. The decisions would either be personnel decisions or resource commitments as described in the preceding section. Once the value of the decisions has been determined a portion of the value would be allotted to the advisor depending upon the influence that he was intended to exert on the decision maker.

Ability Requirements

According to our criteria, all information which is not submitted directly to the decision maker is not considered as advice. The responsibility to render information which is not directly used by the recipient for decision purposes is evaluated by measuring the ability required to perform these responsibilities as illustrated in Figure 25.6.

In analyzing the constituent parts of the ability factor, four sub-factors appear important. They are:

1. Complexity of work flow.
2. Knowledge.
   a. Depth.
   b. Rate of change.
3. Similarity or dissimilarity of functions and/or objectives.
4. Experience.

It is our belief that some overlap exists between complexity of work flow and similarity or dissimilarity of functions and objectives. However, there are definitely mutually exclusive areas within both dimensions. Therefore, they are both included in the matrix.

There is no intent that each of the sub-factors be co-equal. The relative value of these sub-factors must be decided by top management.

Figure 26.5 Degree of Freedom to Act or Decide

AVAILABLE	DEGREES OF CONSTRAINT						
	Only Operational Objectives — No Guides or Precedent	Prior Experience — No Policy or Rules	Established Management Practices Requiring Judgment — No Specific Rules or Procedures	Principles, Procedures, and Rules Requiring Objective Evidence for Exceptions	Principles, Procedures, and Rules Staff Approval Prior to Exceptions	Highly Specialized Training in Recognized Discipline	
STAFF INFLUENCE	No Advice	Voluntary Advice	Compulsory Staff Advice	Compulsory Staff Advice — Staff Can Appeal	Compulsory Staff Advice — Line Can Appeal	Staff Functional Authority	
PER CENT OF POINTS FOR EACH DECISION FOR DECISION MAKER	100					0	100%
PER CENT OF POINTS FOR EACH DECISION FOR THE ADVISOR	0					100	100%
TOTAL	100%	100%	100%	100%	100%	100%	100%

354

Figure 26.6 Ability

	1	2	3	4	5	6
COMPLEXITY OF WORK FLOW	Simple Work Flow Within Group — Little or No Work Relation Between Groups		Complex Internal Relations		Complex Internal & Complex External	
SIMILARITY OR DISSIMILARITY OF FUNCTIONS AND/OR OBJECTIVES	Highly Similar Functions Highly Similar Objectives	Similar Functions & Some Dissimilar Objectives or Similar Objectives & Some Dissimilar Functions	Similar Functions & Dissimilar Objectives or Similar Objectives & Dissimilar Functions	Highly Dissimilar Functions & Similar Objectives or Highly Dissimilar Objectives & Similar Functions	Highly Dissimilar Functions & Highly Dissimilar Objectives	
KNOWLEDGE						
DEPTH	Unskilled	Semi-Skilled	Skilled	One B.S.	M.A. or M.S.	Ph.D
RATE OF CHANGE	Slowly Changing Single Discipline		Multiple Discipline Changing at Moderate Rate or Single Rapidly Changing Discipline		Multiple, Rapidly Changing Discipline	
EXPERIENCE	None Required					8 Yrs. or More

355

As previously stated, the ability factor, although applicable to all jobs, is of principal importance to incumbents having low discretionary job content but providing specialized information to individuals who in turn provide advice directly to a decision maker.

Factors Peculiar to the Organization

A fourth factor entitled "Factors Peculiar to the Organization" is advanced as a consideration. Examples of such sub-factors which might be included are travel, job hazards, pressure of work, and frequency of transfer.

We have discussed the three basic criterion factors which are recommended for the evaluation of managerial positions. For summary purposes, we will briefly describe the steps involved in applying these criteria.

Steps in Measuring Managerial Responsibility

The method of assessment for the jobs of managers can be summarized as follows:

1) To use Jaques' words, it is necessary to "tease out" the decisions, delegated to a particular job.

2) Discover the mechanisms employed to review the use of discretion. By this means, one can discover the controls and constraints imposed upon the job incumbent.

3) Discover the expected results if the discretion were ill-used, that is, if the intent of the discretion were unsuccessful. These expected results can be described in terms of the dollar value of the resources which could be committed but not used and therefore, lost to the organization.

4) Discover the frequency with which the manager is expected to exercise such discretion.

5) Multiply the frequency times the severity (potential value of resource loss) or scaled level (of personal decision) for each area of discretionary content of the job.

6) Combine the result of the above analysis with the result of the measurement of ability required for prescribed action and the measurement of advisory responsibility to arrive at a total value of the position.[7]

---

[7] This method of assessment closely follows that outlined by Jaques on page 32 of the book entitled *Measurement of Responsibility*, but this method considers factors different from those advocated by Jaques.

27

The Authoritarian Cultural Lag in Business*

Eugene Emerson Jennings

Michigan State University

This interpretive analysis develops the concept of the "authoritarian culture lag" as a partial explanation of the growing reactions against the human relations approach. Professor Jennings discusses the research basis of human relations thinking, and traces the ambiguities, tensions and conflicts that abound in attempts to improve essentially authoritarian systems through concepts of democracy. A considerable range of major research work is brought together to show that reactions against human relations are directed toward a renouncement of democracy in the business enterprise.

After enjoying for some thirty years a gradual and somewhat unexpected increase in acceptance, especially verbal, the popularity of the human relations approach seems now to have reached its apex. To some people its future is subject to much doubt. What these critics refer to as its veneer has been cracking for at least five years.

In 1953 Douglas McGregor, then President of Antioch College, warned that business was confused about human relations. He described as a major error of management the assumption that personnel administration consisted largely in dealing with human relations problems. He said that this approach to personnel administration viewed the subject as a repair job instead of as a way to prevent the need for repairs.[1] At the same time, Eugene Lyons, Personnel Vice-President of Merck and Company, accused his own profession of conducting human relations on a day-to-day expediency basis.

---

* Taken and adapted from *The Journal of the Academy of Management,* vol. 2, no. 2, August, 1959, pp. 111–126.
[1] *Business Week,* November 14, 1953, p. 125.

The purpose of this paper is to discuss the problem highlighted by this growing criticism of both the human relations approach and the popular but elusive term "democracy in business." The specific thesis is that the concept "authoritarian cultural lag" offers a partial explanation for this reaction formation that appears to be gathering formidable support.

The attempt to introduce "democracy" into business theory and practice has been urged for a quarter of a century by two principal schools of thought whose intellectual mentors were Elton Mayo and Kurt Lewin. Of course, there are differences between them, but from an over-all standpoint the similarities predominate. For example, both believed that there was too much authoritarianism in business (and society for that matter). Both believed that the small, face-to-face (primary) work group was potentially real to the individual and powerful over him. And both believed that through participation the group could motivate the individual to be more productive and happy.

Mayo and Lewin believed that the individual had lost his sense of worth and was resisting change (increased productivity and efficiency) because he no longer had a way of meaningfully identifying with his organization, society, and, for that matter, his fellow man. Both believed, therefore, that an administrative elite should be trained that would promote the spirit of co-operation and participation. Being academics, they attempted to support their formulations by research, and they believed in education as the basis whereby this administrative elite was to be developed. The approach of Kurt Lewin became known as group dynamics and that of Mayo as human relations.

Just as this brief interpretation hazards the possibility of misinterpretation and faulty generalization, so interpretations made of these two schools of thought by the many subsequent students and practitioners of business administration may have fallen short of the mentors' initial formulations. No doubt some have interpreted "human relations" to mean simply that by increasing management's interest in workers their production would increase. In addition some businessmen may have interpreted human relations to mean increased productivity through increased morale, or increased loyalty through increased participation, or increased acceptance of change through better communications. Or perhaps group dynamics was misinterpreted by the attempt to establish committees, not just for getting better decisions and insuring their acceptance, but for bringing about better conformity and achieving a greater degree of loyalty.

When Erich Fromm and David Riesman accused the business system of being a hotbed for spawning conformity-ridden individuals,[2] or when Malcolm McNair criticized the "human relations" fad for its repeated

---

[2] Erich Fromm, *The Saturday Review*, March 16, 1957, p. 9; David Riesman, *et al.*, *The Lonely Crowd*, Doubleday, 1955.

violation of the dignity of the individual by employing techniques for manipulating people,[3] ample evidence to support their charges probably existed. The reaction formation gathered considerable strength when Clark Kerr, Chancellor of the University of California at Los Angeles, accused the "factory sociologists" of plotting against the privacy and independency of the individual.[4] By the time *Fortune's* William H. Whyte exhibited *The Organization Man*, many had been warmed up to the possibility that George Orwell's authoritarian "Big Brother" was just around the corner.

If the organization is today enslaving the individual, it is of course important to know how much the theories and practices of human relations and group dynamics have contributed. The reaction formation is most biting in its disbelief in the validity of the human relations and group dynamics research data. There is considered opinion that initial formulations by their intellectual mentors were not based on adequate research. Landsberger suggests several shortcomings, among which is the fact that Mayo did not seem to have considered that he was dealing with a situation that was not necessarily a permanent and representative characteristic of America as a whole.[5] Lewin's original idea that "democratic" groups are more productive and satisfied may turn out to be a classic faulty generalization. His conclusion was that "more creative and constructive work products emerged from the high unity of democratic life, with its greater amount of objectivity and co-operativeness of interpersonal relationships."[6] This generalization of higher productivity and morale was premature in terms of the evidence provided at that time. Subsequent studies tried to affirm this generalization,[7] but lately there have appeared several studies that have counteracted this affirmation.[8]

Recently, on behalf of the American Management Association, the author brought together available group dynamics studies dealing with

[3] Malcolm McNair, "Thinking Ahead: What Price Human Relations?" *Harvard Business Review*, March–April, 1957, p. 15.

[4] Clark Kerr, "What Became of the Independent Spirit?" *Fortune*, July, 1953, p. 110.

[5] Henry Landsberger, *Hawthorne Revisited*, Cornell, 1958, p. 71.

[6] R. Lippitt, and R. White, "An Experimental Study of Leadership and Group Life," in T. M. Newcomb and E. L. Hartley, (Eds.), *Readings in Social Psychology* (New York, Henry Holt and Company, 1957), pp. 315–330.

[7] R. L. Kahn, and Daniel Katz, "Leadership Practices in Relation to Productivity and Morale," in *Group Dynamics*, Cartwright and Zander (Eds.) (Evanston, Illinois, Row, Peterson Co., 1953).

M. G. Preston, and R. K. Heintz, "Effects of Participatory and Supervisory Leadership as Group Judgment," *Journal of Abnormal Social Psychology*, 1949, 44, pp. 345–355.

M. A. Deutsch, "A Theory of Co-operation and Competition," *Human Relations*, 1949, 2, pp. 25–52.

G. Lindsey, *Handbook of Social Psychology* (Cambridge, Addison-Wesley Publishing Co., 1954), p. 757.

[8] H. G. McCurdy, and H. W. Eberg, "Democratic or Authoritarian: A Further Investigation of Group Problem Solving," *Journal of Personality*, 1953, 22, pp. 258–269.

democratic and authoritarian leadership and found that he could not be dogmatic in regard to which was superior or in regard to what role either played in morale and productivity.[9] As this group dynamics literature was correlated, Rensis Likert, of the University of Michigan, brought together literature, some of which was duplicate but most of which was provided more directly by "human relations" studies. He concluded that research findings did not support the assumption that there are leadership and supervisory practices which, if followed, will consistently yield appreciably better performance and morale than is obtained from other practices.[10] The situation is apparently much more complex than the initial theorists and their subsequent practical interpreters presumed.

This means that from a research standpoint there is not sufficient empirical data to suggest that the intended effects would have occurred even if management had followed faithfully the initial formulations of the two mentors, Mayo and Lewin. Since there are too few cases where they were applied faithfully, we cannot honestly say to what extent Chancellor Kerr's criticism to the effect that "factory sociologists" are plotting against the privacy and independency of the individual is due to "human relations" or "group dynamics." But if these original formulations were *impotent* in the first place, it does not follow necessarily that either the theory or application of human relations and group dynamics is invalid. These programs nevertheless bear critical watching. Such facts constitute one reason for the academic's reaction formation.

Apparently some businessmen, too, are becoming wary of this "democratic" movement. Inland Steel in 1956 created for William Caples the title of Vice-President of Human Relations. It is not known to what extent the title was at the time based on taking advantage of a popular name; but by the spring of 1958 the title was quietly withdrawn. Mr. Caples not only reported that the acquiring of this title suggested to some that they had either no human relations or "poor" human relations before its adoption, but also that the "Mayoan" school had really never been appreciably adopted by business and industry in the first place.[11] One company had made it clear to the author in the form of written communication that the individual "exchanges his full freedom of action for his place on the payroll." This executive goes on to explain that the individual "must realize that his purpose of being there is to carry out,

[9] E. E. Jennings, "The Democratic and Authoritarian Approaches: A Comparative Survey of Research Findings," *American Management Association Personnel Report* #16, 1958, pp. 42–56.

[10] Rensis Likert, "Effective Supervision: A Culturally Relative Process," Mimeograph, 1947.

[11] William Caples, "Comments on Human Relations," Speech before the Michigan State University Business College Faculty and Graduate Student Seminar, November, 1958.

within his area of responsibility, the objectives of the organization." He concluded, "This is a reality, not just a theory."[12]

If it is not yet altogether fair to say that many companies have recently recaptured the authoritarian spirit, it is clear that many companies have not given it up to an appreciable extent and that some have become ambivalent about the whole affair. The General Electric Company has become one of the foremost training grounds for Mayo's administrative elite.[13] Each year a junior elite is trained in the school of human relations, with heavy emphasis on communications, sensitivity, and other social skills. Yet, at the top level, "Boulwareism" teaches them to believe that intelligent, enlightened leadership should be able to discern what are the needs of the workers and, once having determined these, it is best to hold to them once and for all, regardless of pressure (union) to the contrary.

If apparent rejection (as in the case of Caples) and ambivalence (as in the case of General Electric) may be looked upon as defenses (reaction formation) against the implications of human relations in business, *clarification* may likewise be a form of defense or reaction formation. Donald R. Schoen, Executive Vice-President of the Hays Corporation of Michigan City, Indiana, believing that many advocates of human relations have failed to make clear just what they are talking about, tried to help relieve the misunderstanding and confusion by suggesting that the underlying theme of the human relations approach is an attempt to understand people as they really are and to accept them on this basis.[14]

This of course raises the question as to what people are really like. It is possible, as we shall note in this paper, that executives are *basically* authoritarian and that they are under certain conditions *predisposed* to rely upon an authoritarian structure for their feelings of effectiveness and security.

It should be mentioned that it is not the purpose of this paper to disparage the human relations approach, but rather to show the limitations that are inherent in the optimistic enthusiasm of the human relations people who believe that the unique strength of the democratic work group can be a positive force for accomplishing the objective aims of the larger organization — increased productivity and morale. We have already noted that the empirical evidence is too ambiguous to justify such an optimistic statement at this time. However, there has not been too much elaboration on the reason certain students and practitioners of business administration are today tending to reject the "democratic" thesis.

[12] Personal letter from A. F. Koepcke, Director of Management Development and Educational Services, Borg-Warner Corporation, February 25, 1958.

[13] See *Fortune*, "The Crown Princes of Business," October, 1953, p. 150.

[14] D. R. Schoen, "Human Relations: Boon or Bogle?" *Harvard Business Review*, November–December, 1957, p. 41.

Perhaps the problem involves an insurmountable contradiction. It is a problem of an *authoritarian* system trying to include to an appreciable degree the democratic urges of a society at large as well as those of the subordinate members of the business system per se. Is there a contradiction here in terms of opposing drives that go far deeper than what is normally implied in the "democratic" approach? The "democratic" approach carries the questionable implication that management is psychologically able to incorporate into the administrative structure the democratic process with its emphasis on participation and representation.

The explicit thesis of this paper is that by and large the typical executive does not have this psychological capacity to integrate appreciably with the democratic urges of the primary work group process. Even the practice of coming to the point of appearing to give lip service and some degree of credence to the democratic approach in such things as decision making and policy formation represents for the executive a stretching beyond his psychological capacity. Believing that management can resolve these two conflicting urges, authoritarian and democratic, without performing a major revision of either viewpoint may well be overly optimistic.

Much of the theory that has gone into the study of the authoritarian personality has come from the views of Erich Fromm on the subject of freedom.[15] In line with psychoanalytic theory, the adult relationships are merely blown-up child relationships, with the latter having centered around the parents. The child, being closely attached to his mother for nutriment, love, support, and security comes to require not only physical weaning but emotional separation from his mother as well. Under ideal circumstances, this dependency breaks off by the child's development of emotional strength and self-confidence and the capacity to cope successfully with his environment. Unfortunately, in our interpretation of Fromm, the child's development is less than ideal in the majority of cases and the break-off comes at such a time when the child is not ready to cope with this new freedom. As a result, he rejects the opportunities offered him to stand alone and make his own decisions and he endeavors to find persons who have strength, power, and authority to whom he may attach himself, on whom he may be dependent, and to whom he may become submissive. But this flight into dependence defeats its own ends because it is prone to increase rather than decrease the individual's insecurities. Insecurity and submissiveness compound each other to a point at which they affront and offend his self-ideal as a dynamic, fearless, independent individual. This conflict is displaced onto the very persons to whom he has formed his dependent, submissive attachment. He hates them, and yet he needs their support. In adult life his dependence and submissiveness tend

[15] Erich Fromm, *Escape From Freedom* (New York, Rinehart, 1941).

to make him hard working, and the fact that he is hostile toward authority makes him difficult to supervise. He tends to make his way into large organizations because of this unusual need for security. Most often he is the one who learns how to adapt quickly to demands placed upon him by superior authority and, in turn, to displace such hostility that is normally a result of this submissiveness onto subordinates in such a manner that he becomes viewed as management material.

Norman Martin provided a picture of the executive in an article spelling out Machiavellian tactics and power orientation. He says that beneath the general principles, attitudes, and ideals of "human relations" lie the actual tactics and day-to-day techniques by which executives achieve, maintain, and exercise power. In the current enthusiasm for "democratizing" business procedures, these hard, practical devices tend to be overlooked. Martin says that they nevertheless exist and in many ways do not depart substantially from the scorned advice of Niccolo Machiavelli.[16]

In an article confirming Martin's view of the executive's character formation, Robert McMurry, an Austrian-trained clinical psychologist and senior partner of a Chicago management consulting firm, says that most executives do not want a system of democratic management because they are more likely to be hard-driving, egocentric entrepreneurs who come up outside the business in careers where they have had to keep the power in their hands; or, they may be veteran victors in "no quarter given" fighting for positions of increasing power within the business.[17]

Instead of participative management McMurry describes business as a "benevolent autocracy" wherein the top man stresses the desirability of "humanistic" management but remains undeniably its strong man, while all jobs and relationships are clearly defined and rigidly structured. Henry's view of the executive as being high in drive and achievement, strong in his aspiration to upward mobility, acutely decisive, and possessing a strong sense of self-identity, does not show a tendency in the direction that the "democrats" Mayo and Lewin would greatly appreciate. The capstone of this view of the executive as an authoritarian was provided in a major study by Warner and Abegglen.[18] These authors' description of the mobile executive is strikingly similar to the authoritarian personality described in the final passages of this paper.

The view presented by these several studies enables us to diagnose the "inroad" of "democracy" as basically the result of some kind of external

[16] Norman Martin, "Thinking Ahead," *Harvard Business Review*, November–December, 1956.

[17] See *Harvard Business Review*, January–February, 1958.

[18] W. Lloyd Warner and James C. Abegglen, *Big Business Leaders in America* (New York, Harper and Brothers, 1955).

STUDIES OF EXECUTIVE BEHAVIOR

pressure and not necessarily the manifestation of *inner* conviction on the part of the executive. This accounts for the fact that at the verbal level the "democratic" approach has its greatest manifest acceptance.

If this diagnosis is true, the possibility exists that "democracy" will never become more generally adopted than it now is. But even this prediction is less pessimistic than the more likely development that it will henceforth be attacked more openly or even repudiated by a reversion to a more overt or more rigid authoritarian approach. When this occurs, we shall be in the middle of a situation known as "the authoritarian cultural lag." We are presently entering it. The foregoing evidence of this reaction formation against the "democratic" thesis has been briefly provided not only to highlight the central problem of this paper but to show what authoritarian cultural lag is like in its early stages.

In 1829 Robert Southey made some observations on inventions and technology and their influence on social life. More than a quarter of a century ago, Herbert Hoover, then Secretary of Commerce, wrote an article in one of our journals in which he pointed out the rapid spread of radio and indicated some of the problems which the radio would create. About the same time he wrote the introduction to a book dealing with economic and industrial changes and used the concept as well as the term "lag."[19] However, it was Ogburn who dealt most freely with the term lag and introduced it formally into the literature.[20] He said that where one part of culture changes first, through some discovery or invention, and it occasions changes in some part of culture, this delay is a cultural lag, during which time there may be said to be maladjustment. Furthermore, he saw that changes in the material culture are apt to be more numerous and rapid than changes in non-material culture. Within non-material culture, such as managerial theory and practice, this lag may also occur in the sense of one part being more firmly entrenched than the other in the attitudes and expectations of the members of that culture. In this sense the culture of a society (such as business) is a functionally interrelated whole in which changes in one part may eventually bring about repercussions in the most distant parts of that culture. These repercussions are usually highlighted by reaction formation such as we have described in this present discussion.

The concept of lag is also useful for explaining a reversion to authoritarian leadership after a too drastic attempt to impose democracy on an authoritarian culture. Gilbert used this concept to explain the German demise and also the French disaster. He viewed the assumption by

[19] W. D. Wallis, "The Concept of the Lag," *The Journal of Sociological and Social Research*, 1934–35, 19, p. 399.

[20] William F. Ogburn, *Social Change With Respect to Culture and Original Nature* (New York, The Viking Press, Inc., 1938).

Napoleon of the role of dictator, and then emperor, after getting the whole-hearted support of significant segments of post-revolutionary French society, as illustrative of a fact that has been true of virtually every dictatorship since that time. It is the inability of an authoritarian culture to absorb too much self-government too suddenly without a "regression" to some form of paternalistic-authoritarian rule. From the First French Republic to the German Weimar Republic there has occurred evidence that while the outward forms of democracy may be achieved overnight by revolution, the psychological change necessary to sustain it cannot.[21] This is illustrated by the numerous attempts at restoration in England well after the monarchy had been overthrown.

The failure of the Russian revolution of 1905 may be partially explained by the inability of both theorists and activists to put into practice the very program that represented their ideological beliefs.[22] It is interesting to note that when the lag became manifest to Lenin and the central committee, almost the same kind of reaction formation set in as we found in our discussion: Questioning occurred over what were Marx's and Engel's original formulations, who had deviated, was it merely misinterpretation or willful distortion, and what clarification was necessary to restore the "democratic" movement to parity (reduce the lag) with the authoritarian system (Tsarism). Some recent examples of this authoritarian cultural lag may be found in South America and in Africa, notably, of course, in Egypt.

In America, too, we have had many examples. A society will have a lag which values authority and power and which has democratic urges that constantly threaten or serve to checkmate these authoritarian values. The demand by workers in the 1930's for recognition and representation in management decisions was too sudden and too foreign a demand for the business executive to absorb into his traditionally authoritarian manner of thinking and behaving. As is the case of the French, English, and Russian revolutions, the attempt to dilute the American businessman's authority was, among other things, countered by a surge of paternalistic management largely based on the exertion of personal dominance. We may also note that union members were caught in a lag too, since their freedom from authoritarian management came too suddenly in terms of their limited understanding and skills to make use of it through democratic participation in union affairs.[23] This lag partially contributed to the emergence of authoritarian rule in unions.

Of course, in all of the cases cited, the concept of the authoritarian cultural lag can be used only partially to explain what happened. This is

[21] G. M. Gilbert, *The Psychology of Dictatorship* (New York, The Ronald Press, 1950).

[22] See B. D. Wolfe, *Three Who Made a Revolution* (Beacon Press, Inc., 1948).

[23] See Neil W. Chamberlain, *et al.*, *A Decade of Industrial Relations Research* (Harper and Brothers, 1958).

because major innovations in a culture are produced by a complex set of factors. So far not all the factors have been adequately discerned.

Within the business system one example of an authoritarian cultural lag is particularly interesting. When Ralph Cordiner set up the services division, composed of ten vice-presidents — such as manufacturing, engineering, employee and plant community relations, and public relations — whose only authority, according to *Fortune*, was to go into a division or department and observe for purposes primarily of planning and forecasting, the operating managers tended to reject the informal roles of these vice-presidents as staff men and tended instead to view them as possessing undue authority. Harris, in describing this overhaul of General Electric, stated, "It may well take a new generation of operating managers to accept services for what they are — a service group for operators, not a staff group of bosses."[24] The attempt of Montgomery Ward to move into a less authoritarian tempo upon the release of Sewell Avery is an excellent study of inertia of long established habits and attitudes. Unfortunately this research is just getting underway.

Although he did not explicitly use the term authoritarian cultural lag, it was very much a key to Mayo's initial theoretical formulation. He saw the changes of the last two centuries as having a disturbing influence on traditional social balances. Material and technical achievements had outpaced free and effective communication between groups and the capacity for spontaneous co-operation. As late as 1947 he saw the study of social facts as only beginning to open up knowledge in regard to the magnitude and fundamental character of the disparity between the individual and the organization. Owing to this general ignorance, Mayo saw leaders in many countries relapsing to the ancient practice of compulsion by central authority (authoritarian leadership) in order to achieve their ends. He saw that this affected even those countries that nominally retained the forms of democratic government. Compulsion never succeeded in arousing eager and spontaneous co-operation.[25] Mayo's research led him to the now famous trilogy which, in simple terms, might be stated as follows: spontaneous co-operation is a function of the degree of work satisfaction, and work satisfaction, in turn, depends upon the informal social pattern of the work group.[26]

This trilogy must of course be properly expanded if used for practical purposes, but for our theoretical discussion its brevity will suffice to point

[24] See *Fortune*, December, 1955.

[25] Elton Mayo, *Political Problems of an Industrial Civilization* (Harvard University Press, 1947), p. 24.

[26] Reinhard Bendix and Lloyd H. Fisher, "The Perspectives of Elton Mayo," Berkeley, University of California Report No. 17, 1950.

out that Mayo did not foresee what the future would provide in the way of ameliorative conditions to offset the lack of work satisfaction, civic leadership, and social, political, and charitable activities of a type that would give workers opportunity for social status and expression. Higher wages, more leisure time, greater security, and increasing protection from technological unemployment are but a few of these ameliorative factors and conditions that we might cite in addition to those that were installed in varying degrees by the human relations and group dynamics programs. Furthermore, Mayo did not fully anticipate that the major portion of labor's increased productivity would not come from its own efforts but from technological innovation: The foremost requirement of labor in a highly automated system is to be "reliable" rather than "productive."

It is not unfair to suggest that the development of co-operation and participation to the degree proposed by Mayo and Lewin is not only something that American management lacks the skill to promote, but is also something management fears, since such a degree of co-operation and participation might bring on problems for both workers and executives that require more in terms of time and energy than they are prepared to devote to them. Sufficient evidence however is lacking to prove that the American executive is resisting further invasion of democracy into his business system because of the additional problems and responsibility that are likely to result.

The possibility exists that both Mayo's and Lewin's major misjudgment was the extent to which the authoritarian character trait is imbedded in our society, especially in our business culture. If this is true, these mentors could not have anticipated the resistance to the personality change their formulations required of the members of the administrative elite.

This same mistake in judging the character of the members of the system that one is attempting to revolutionize was made by the Mensheviks during the 1905 rebellion. The Mensheviks believed that rulership from below by a kind of social democracy represented the logical extension of their appraisal of the peasant's character. Lenin, however, appraised the situation differently. He saw that Russian patriarchism was rooted deeply in the undivided family dominated by the father patriarch. The village in turn was dominated by its council of elders, who in turn were led by a village patriarch. At the apex of Russian society the Tsar was the "father of the people." Thus Lenin saw that power in the hands of the peasants would fail to be effective, for they had not the skills, attitudes, or habits necessary for its effective use. He formulated the concept of "democratic dictatorship," which Stalin developed further to a point wherein he took the place of the Tsar as "father of the people." Although, of course, the social theory is different, this concept of "democratic dictatorship" is somewhat akin to McMurry's "benevolent autocrat" or the author's "mature autocrat," which he has employed frequently to show in what manner the reversion to more authoritarian practices will possibly take place in American business.[27]

In short, Mayo and Lewin may have misjudged the extent to which democratic urges represent basic prompting in our national character structure, especially that of the various elites.

Then, too, the authoritarian cultural lag is greatly dependent upon the character formation of the elite which is in power. This, our next point of analysis, requires a description of studies that have recently shed light on the character formation of authoritarian personality.[28]

In determining specifically the characteristics of the authoritarian character structure, a group of California researchers found that the traits included extreme conformity to in-group norms, over-idealization of power figures, unconscious feeling of hostility toward such power figures, and a strong tendency to displace aggression onto weaker and non-retaliative persons.[29] For the purpose at hand, it is desirable to select several aspects of the authoritarian personality syndrome that will cast light on the reaction formation to the "democratic approach" in business theory and practice. In this regard, the most promising aspects are the power, antiambiguity, and conformity sets described below.

In terms of the power set, authoritarians strongly prefer to work in organization climates that are heavily status-laden, to accept strongly directive supervision, and to talk in terms of "power" words when describing "good" superiors.[30] Because they tend to identify with a power structure, they identify with individuals who have displayed this same power orientation and to be repulsed by subordinates or peers who do not show similar respect for "power" figures.

The authoritarian's inner need for power is satisfied in part by identifying with superiors and alienating himself from subordinates. He finds security in a hierarchical organization of superior-subordinate relationships, because this is a means of identifying with power which he so anxiously wants. Thus he is predisposed to accepting the traditional management practices of individual decision-making, unilateral communication flow, and delegation of routine work to subordinate persons and to maintaining a tight control on jobs that require his superior skill and wisdom.

[27] See E. E. Jennings, "The Mature Autocrat," *Nations Business*, September, 1958.

[28] It should be noted that these studies are Freudian-based and the ensuing word choices may be difficult for the reader. He would be greatly aided were he to read the very readable essay by Fromm on the authoritarian personality. See Erich Fromm, *Escape From Freedom* (New York, Rinehart), 1941.

[29] T. W. Adorno, *et al.*, *The Authoritarian Personality* (New York, Harper and Brothers, 1950).

[30] F. H. Sanford, "Leadership Identification and Acceptance," in H. Guetzkow, (ed.), *Groups, Leadership and Men* (New Brunswick, Rutgers University Press, 1950), pp. 158–176.

Very closely related to this power set is the authoritarian personality's anti-ambiguity set, which is manifested by a strong demand for unqualified certainty, definiteness, and concreteness.[31] To the authoritarian personality the uncertain and unpredictable are highly annoying and emotionally upsetting.[32] To accommodate this fear of the ambiguous, there is a marked tendency to unqualified thinking in terms of black and white and either-or solutions and diagnoses. A further tendency is that of a compartmentalized, piece-meal approach to problems accompanied by an absolutizing of specific aspects that are familiar.[33] The quest for certainty creates a dislike for undertaking any project unless there is a pretty good idea as to how it will turn out. Straightforward reasoning appeals to the authoritarian personality, but metaphors and analogies are very distracting.

This anti-ambiguity set combines with the power set to recognize the *individual* rather than the group as the basic unit of the organization structure. The kind of sociological thinking that gives credit to collective units, such as primary groups, is alien to "good" organization and viewed by the authoritarian personality as a sign of weakness.

In addition, the authoritarian tends to be somewhat insensitive to the psychological or personality characteristics of others in their perceptions and judgments.[34] He is more sensitive to such external variables as social status, organization position, and other "power" related factors.[35] In spite of this reduced sensitivity to people as social and psychological subjects, he shows a greater tendency than non-authoritarians to differentiate the social environment in terms of power symbols. Here we see these power and anti-ambiguity sets operate to focus attention on the environment about him in sharp, black-and-white distinctions in which a man is either "great" or "weak" or helpful or not helpful, and the criteria that the authoritarian uses for making these judgments are concrete rather than abstract, impersonal rather than personal, institutional rather than social. The two sets, power and anti-ambiguity, then, reveal that the authoritarian executive views individuals rather than abstract groups as the basic units of organization, and perceives them, and makes judgments about them, based upon power, institutional, and status-laden concepts.

The third set is the conformity set, which is broadly defined here to mean being overly submissive to the demands placed upon the executive

---

[31] H. Webster, N. Sanford, and Mervin Freedman, "A New Instrument for Studying Authoritarianism in Personality," *Journal of Psychology*, 1955, 40, pp. 73–84.

[32] Else Frenkel-Brunswick, "Intolerance of Ambiguity as an Emotional and Perceptual Variable," *Journal of Personality*, 1949, 18, pp. 108–143.

[33] Else Frenkel-Brunswick, "Social Tensions and the Inhibition of Thought," *Social Problems*, 1954–55, 2, pp. 75–83.

[34] Howard E. Jones, "Authoritarianism as a Determinant of First-Impression Formation," *Journal of Personality*, 1957.

[35] M. Wagman, "Attitude Change and Authoritarian Personality," *Journal of Social Psychology*, 1955, 49, pp. 3–24.

by his "power" figures.[36] He tends to inhibit his hostility to them, but in turn to demand conformity from those he considers subordinate.[37] However, is this conformity a result of inner conviction? When a person yields to group opinion in expressing a judgment he may be responding to certain aspects of the situation such as pressure from the group to conform, lack of any objective standard of judgment, or the need to get a job done because of too little harmony. But the authoritarian executive is seen to conform for another reason. He has an *inner need* to conform, especially to power figures and to group pressures. In the latter case, he conforms to group pressure because the act of conforming helps keep hostile impulses against groups suppressed, and thereby functions as a mechanism of defense.[38] Such an executive may agree with group norms and decisions because by so doing he can keep from being *genuinely* influenced by them. The same can be said of conforming to power figures, only in this case the art of conforming will be followed by behavior that agrees with the act of conforming, because of his respect for obeying the demands of a superior-subordinate relationship. But when placed in a permissive setting — such as what Mayo and Lewin would develop — will oftentimes *overtly* conform to the majority view, or he will *overtly* conform to the superior view of a formal power figure. By this means he acts to keep himself from being *genuinely* influenced by others. This inner *need* to conform finally gives us a reason why "democracy" appears to be in business more than it actually may be.

When we now consider all these three sets of the authoritarian executive, we see that he is strongly apt to maintain an authoritarian approach to people because of deep-seated power, anti-ambiguity, and conformity needs and that these needs-satisfactions are integral to his psychological well-being. When faced with the requirement to make use of individuals in the manner suggested by human relations and group dynamics, we see that he is not psychologically capable of doing so with any high degree of conviction and, as a result, may level, compromise, or yield. In this way, he will *use* groups as well as participation procedures, but he will maintain subtle but effective ways of maintaining his personal autonomy.

The authoritarian's personality conflicts headlong with the kind of leader he must become if he is to follow faithfully Mayoan and Lewinian formulations. He is hostile to the very concept of shared leadership and, second, he finds the democratic leadership concept to be very abstract, and there-

[36] Leonard Berkowitz and R. M. Lundy, "Personality Characteristics Related to Susceptibility to Influence by Peers or Authority Figures," *Journal of Personality*, 1957, 25, pp. 306–316.

[37] J. W. Thibaut and H. W. Ricken, "Authoritarianism, Status, and the Communication of Aggression," *Human Relations*, 1955, 8.

[38] Martin L. Hoffman, "Conformity as a Defense Mechanism and a Form of Resistance to Genuine Group Influence," *Journal of Personality*, 1957, 25, pp. 412–424.

fore fear-arousing. The concept of a democratic leader itself suggests that it cannot be rigorously defined. Even to some of the less authoritarian executives, the idea that leadership is largely determined by the demands of the situation and that these demands vary from group to group and situation to situation, is a vague, ambiguous, and terribly frustrating concept to entertain, especially in terms of the requirements found normally in business enterprise. This possibly accounts for the reason why Bendix found in his exhaustive study that the "Mayoan school" contributed more to managerial ideology than to managerial practice.[39]

We may theorize, then, that the current criticism of the human relations approach expresses the beginning of the renouncement of "democracy" in business. The incipient authoritarian cultural lag as we have described it is an expression of the executive's inability to become motivated by the diffused image invoked by the new prototype of leadership found in the human relations and other "democratic" approaches. If it is not motivating to them, it may be taken to mean that the authoritarian prototype has not been displaced as a manifestation of an inner-motivating force.

If the proponents of the democracy, the Mayoans and the Lewinians, address themselves effectively to this growing storm of reaction and in the long run appreciably "democratize" management, they will most likely have done so through a better understanding of the inner-needs of the executives, who are largely products of an authoritarian culture. This struggle represents a long-time affair lasting over several generations. At the present time these proponents' continued use of words of hope and optimism, that completely overlook the psychological inability of authoritarian executives to effectively follow through, is tending to forestall progress toward their desired objective.

[39] Reinhard Bendix, *Work and Authority in Industry* (New York, John Wiley Sons, Inc., 1956), pp. 308–340.

28

Rationality and Executive Motivation*

Richard F. Ericson

The George Washington University

Given a rather stable socio-psychic framework which continually urges the individual to evaluate the worthwhileness of his conduct in terms of whether he is "getting ahead"; and, given the impersonal organization monoliths into which the individual typically is thrust: how are behavior patterns among individual executives most likely to be shaped?

It has become commonplace in modern management literature to recognize that the traditional mechanistically-inclined theory has in recent decades been substantially corrected and supplemented by human relations insights. But the imperative of structuring effective and satisfying moral relations among managers appears yet to receive the kind of study it so richly deserves. E. F. L. Brech has recently called attention to just this deficiency:

> We have, in the past twenty years, heard so much about management-worker cooperation and equally little about inter-management cooperation. Here there is offered a field for research the results of which might well determine the whole future pattern of management in industry and government in national affairs.[1]

To be sure, there has in recent years been a noticeable concentration upon such topics as executive appraisal and the social responsibilities of the executive. But illumination of the dynamics of the day-to-day interaction of managers is in rather short supply. Thus after assaying *The Social Ethic in Management Literature* William G. Scott concludes:

---

* Taken and adapted from *The Journal of the Academy of Management*, vol. 5, no. 1, April, 1962, pp. 7–23.
[1] In Kruisinga, H. J. *The Balance Between Centralization and Decentralization in Managerial Control* (Leiden, Netherlands: H. E. Stenfert Kroese. N. V., 1954), p. 21.

Unfortunately, writers in the area of human relations have tended to concentrate their attention on human motivational problems at the worker level of the organization. . . . Little effort has been expended in research of managerial motivational patterns as they are reflected in cooperative or non-cooperative behavior.[2]

To the extent that the organizational implications and social ramifications of contemporary managerial motivation have been examined, it has largely been in the hands of the novelists. It may be questioned whether management theorists are wise to allow such a division of labor as this to persist.

There are, of course, noteworthy exceptions to the above generalizations. One example is the research of Chris Argyris, as he has explored the significance of Bakke's "fusion process" in industrial and commercial settings. From his investigations Argyris has derived "foundations for effective leadership and human development."[3] His rather pessimistic conclusions concerning the emotional welfare of organization participants are widely known. Even more widely known is W. H. Whyte's delineation of the major sources of the "organization man's" personality aberrations.[4]

Then there are a few investigative efforts such as those of W. E. Henry which bear upon our interest here.[5] Similarly field-researched is A. W. Gouldner's categorization of "cosmopolitans and locals" as the major constellations of organization-personality ideal-types.[6] Melville Dalton's frequently-cited article "Managing the Managers" also deserves note as an illustrative contribution.[7]

Finally, the work of N. H. Martin and J. H. Sims may be singled out as being particularly germane to this present analysis.[8] Martin and Sims have endeavored to analyze the tactics actually observed to be employed by executives as they (the executives) strive to manipulate one another's behavior behind a "human relations" facade.[9]

[2] Studies in Business and Economics, Bulletin No. 4, Bureau of Business and Economic Research, School of Business Administration, Georgia State College of Business Administration, pp. 93–94.

[3] *Personality and Organization* (N.Y.: Harper and Brothers, 1957) p. 211 ff.

[4] *The Organization Man* (N.Y.: Simon and Schuster, 1956).

[5] *Executive Personality and Job Success* (N.Y.: American Management Association, Personnel Series, No. 120, 1948). See also B. B. Gardner "What Makes Successful and Unsuccessful Executives?" *Advanced Management*, September, 1948, pp. 116–124.

[6] "Cosmopolitans and Locals: Toward an Analysis of Latent Social Roles — I" *Administrative Science Quarterly*, December, 1957, p. 281 ff, and — II, March, 1958, p. 444 ff.

[7] *Human Organization*, vol. 14, no. 3, p. 4 ff.

[8] "Thinking Ahead — Power Tactics," *Harvard Business Review*, November-December, 1956, p. 25.

[9] In this connection, a delightful diversion is provided by Bill Conklin in "How to Win a Conference" (reprinted in *The Management Review*, January, 1958, p. 27 ff.) It is bound to strike a responsive chord in those who have themselves fought the battle of the Seige Perilous in business or academic conferences.

The Problem of Executive Rationality

Herbert Simon has argued that "administrative theory is concerned with the control of the nonrational,"[10] and that "it is precisely in the realm where human behavior is *intendedly* rational, but only *limitedly* so, that there is room for a genuine theory of organization and administration."[11] Similarly, Dauten *et al*, take the view that:[12]

> . . . the activities of all managers are guided and controlled broadly by such things as personal goals, aspirations, and values (including culturally determined moral codes), the value system of the organization, the major objectives selected by the firm, and the policies and systems that have been formulated by the policy-making group. Although such human values seem to defy complete anaysis, it is sometimes overlooked that they serve as the master control of all organizational activity.

Such approaches to the study of the realities of managers' behavior are consonant with the focal point of the present analysis. It has sagely been said "Seeing's believing but feeling's the thing."

Applied to inter-executive behavior, particularly that between the subordinate and his superior, it is here contended that the great preponderance of social and cultural forces that impinge upon the individual as he seeks successfully to play his managerial role impress upon him the fundamental necessity of pleasing his boss. Inevitably, in our presently typical organizational arrangements, it is the immediate superior who largely determines the aspiring executive's business-life destiny.

True, "objective" executive appraisals commonly will be made, but even the least sophisticated manager is aware that the degree of reliability of such instruments acknowledgedly diminishes rapidly as one ascends the management hierarchy. In the final analysis, pure subjective judgment combines with a subjective interpretation of "analytical findings" to reveal to superiors which of their subordinates are the best candidates for advancement.

While a certain level of satisfactory job performance is, for the most part, an essential prerequisite to advancement, the subordinate early in his business career quickly becomes intuitively aware that technical competence is perhaps not even half the success story. The *feelings* about him that he and circumstances have generated in the minds and hearts of those who matter in the organization hierarchy: these are the really important differentiators of the "promotables" and the "also rans."[13]

---

[10] *Administrative Behavior* (N.Y.: The Macmillan Company, 1957) p. 244.

[11] *Ibid.*, p. xxiv.

[12] Dauten, P. M. Jr., Gammill, H. L. and Robinson, S. C., "Our Concepts of Controlling Need Re-Thinking," *Journal of the Academy of Management*, December, 1958, p. 41.

[13] In discussing the interaction of individuals engaged in the pursuit of a common goal, Cecil A. Gibb points out that a group member's standing is "dependent not upon the

An individual's definition of success generally stems from cultural — or, more particularly, reference group — norms. In the case of the business executive in our society, these norms place heavy emphasis upon progress up the hierarchial ladder, with all of the tangible and intangible emoluments that appertain. As R. J. Pellegrin and C. H. Coates concluded:

> The executive considers mobility to upper levels essential for success, since his need for esteem and feelings of personal accomplishment can be satisfied *only* by securing a high position. . . . The executive . . . maintains a high level of aspiration and sets continually higher goals for himself as he moves upward in the occupational hierarchy.[14]

Our analysis consequently deals with what Robert V. Presthus has identified as the "upward-mobiles."[15] It is an area of interpersonal behavior in organizations which has received surprisingly disproportionate treatment in the literature.[16] We are concerned with these questions: To what extent is organizational identification a rational process? What is the nature of the psychological forces which influence the behavior of the upward-mobiles? What is the loyalty orientation of executives and how is it manifested? And finally, what are the moral and social implications of the evoked behavior?

Rationality and Organizational Identification

Stemming perhaps mainly from the seminal writing of Chester Barnard some twenty years ago,[17] current management literature often is concerned with the problem of how and to what extent the individual can be made to "internalize" (accept as his own) the organization's goals. The "inducements-contributions" balance has been suggested to conceptualize this phenomenon.[18]

---

possession of . . . special qualities as such, but upon the extent to which his fellows *perceive* him as having these qualities." (In Gardner Lindzey, *Handbook of Social Psychology* (Cambridge, Mass.: Addison-Wesley Publishing Company, Inc., 1954, p. 914).

[14] "Executives and Supervisors: Contrasting Definitions of Career Success," *Administrative Science Quarterly*, March, 1957, p. 517.

[15] Presthus has identified "three general patterns of accommodation to the bureaucratic situation: the upward-mobiles, the indifferents, and the ambivalents." ("Toward a Theory of Organizational Behavior," *Administrative Science Quarterly*, June, 1958, p. 70.)

[16] After surveying the literature in this connection, Chris Argyris concludes: "There do not seem to be any studies that focus on executive upward mobility as an adaptive mechanism. The meager evidence that does exist is obtained indirectly from the studies on executive motivation and behavior observed in various organizations." *Personality and Organization, op. cit.*, p. 81.

[17] *The Functions of the Executive* (Cambridge, Mass.: Harvard University Press, 1938).

[18] See Jones, Manley Howe, *Executive Decision-Making* (Homewood, Illinois: Richard D. Irwin, Inc., 1957) pp. 102–114. This idea has been often and variously expressed in the literature.

A participant is said to have "internalized" the organization's goals when they assume the character of personal goals. He "identifies with" the organization to the extent that he perceives it as being able to aid him in their realization. The inducements-contributions concept thus recognizes the need for management to create an environment in which personal goals (inducements) are at least as fully met in the eyes of the subordinate as are organization goals (contributions).

But this internalization and identification is surely never completely achieved. Residual areas of conflict always remain, at least potentially. The fact that the management employee will rarely acknowledge the existence of incomplete internalization greatly complicates the behavioral environment within which executive roles must be played. In this vein, Manley Howe Jones has written:

> Whether we like it or not, people's personal goals play a dominant role in company decision-making. When a man is making company decisions or deciding to accept and carry out company decisions proposed to him, he examines them in part with a view to whether they will further his own goals . . . in my opinion, it is neither improper nor unethical for a man to work in behalf of his personal goals, *so long as he furthers the company goals and does not injure his fellow men.*[19] (Italics supplied.)

The italicized portion of Jones' thought is, of course, the crux of the matter. It is easily agreed with in the abstract. But, in all but the baldest cases of infidelity and chicanery, how to determine the existence and the degree of such a conflict is the trick. It is the *perceptive* and the *interpretative* aspects of the organization's stated goals which permit men, "in good conscience," to act in ways which may be questioned by others viewing the same set of circumstances.

Let us approach this matter from another direction. The so-called "acceptance" theory posits that, in the final analysis, the source of managerial authority ultimately rests in the behavior of the order-receiver, not in the order-giver. Barnard's "zone of indifference" and Simon's "zone of acceptance" have been offered to explain the fact that most subordinate behavior appears to be almost decisional and unquestioning. Robert Tannenbaum has endeavored to formulate a decisional inequation in terms of which a subordinate will act or will not act in accordance with received instructions: An order will be accepted if $A_a + D_d > A_d + D_a$, that is, if the advantage of accepting plus the disadvantage of declining are greater than the advantages of declining plus the disadvantages of accepting.[20] Notice that the emphasis is upon the *subordinate's* evaluation of these

[19] Ibid., pp. 89–90.
[20] "Managerial Decision-Making," *Journal of Business,* January, 1950, p. 200.

relative advantages and disadvantages as *he* perceives them in terms of *his* goals and objectives.

Thus there may be a strong element of rationality in actions which appear from some points of view totally non-rational, if not irrational. The "rational-nonrational-irrational" trichotomy is consequently sensibly employed only if careful attention is given to the specific complex of goals toward which behavior is directed. Behavior which is "neurotic" from the standpoint of the organization may well be completely "normal" viewed from the individual's preception of organizationally achievable objectives. So unless "irrational" is interpreted to mean "psychotic" behavior — that where the individual is hopelessly incapable of effectively pursuing a means-ends chain, and this kind of behavior is hardly of great interest to administrative theory — this analytical framework is likely to lead to greater confusion than enlightenment.

Motivation Vectors

Thorstein Veblen long ago called attention to what is essentially the "other-directedness" that David Reisman finds in contemporary Western man:

> . . . but for the purpose of a commonplace decent standing in the community these means of repute have been replaced by the acquisition and accumulation of goods. In order to stand well in the eyes of the community, it is necessary to come up to a certain, somewhat indefinite, conventional standard of wealth. . . . Those members of the community who fall short of this, somewhat indefinite, normal degree of prowess or of property suffer in the esteem of their fellow men; and consequently they suffer also in their own esteem, since the usual basis of self-respect is the respect accorded by one's neighbors. Only individuals with an aberrant temperament can in the long run retain their own self-esteem in the face of the dis-esteem of their fellows.[21]

And in his analysis of the "Motivation of Organizational Activities" Talcott Parsons concludes that such attitudes are socially structured:

> It is thus suggested that the much talked of "acquisitiveness" of a capitalistic economic system is not primarily, or even to any very large extent a matter of the peculiar incidence of self-interested elements in the motivation of the typical individual, but of a peculiar institutional structure which has grown up in the Western world. There is reason to believe that the situation with respect to motivation is a great deal more similar in this area to that in other parts of our occupational structure which are not marked by this kind of acquisitiveness than is

[21] *The Theory of the Leisure Class* [N.Y.: The New American Library (Mentor Edition), p. 38.]

generally supposed. . . . One may, then, perhaps say that the whole occupational sphere is dominated by a single fundamental goal, that of "success."[22]

Thus, in our society, conceptions of the "good life" are closely tied to prospects of "getting ahead" materially. This is *par excellence* the way we win the approbation of those about whose opinions we care, for the majority of us.

But it is not only the norms established by typical reference groups that urge the office worker "upward and onward." Indeed, one is occasionally drawn up short by the realization of the institutional depths to which this success imperative has penetrated the social fabric.

For example, recently there appeared in a prominent commercial publication an advertisement seeking to sell the night school services of one of our largest metropolitan universities. The ad showed a shirt-sleeve-and-calculator type office worker carefully peering out of the corner of his eye at two men standing in front of a partially opened door on which the title "Manager" was inscribed. Both men were in suit coats and in every particular suggested confidence and success. One man (obviously the "big boss") was showing the other (obviously the newly-appointed manager) into his office. The caption on the advertisement goaded the reader: "Management keeps its eyes on men who seek to improve themselves through additional education."

Clearly, the implied requirement is impossible of complete fulfillment. *All* cannot "succeed" in terms of socially sanctioned definitions such as these. Not only are organizations hierarchical, they are also notoriously pyramidal. And if the "information technologists" have their way, even greater impediments than now are found may soon block the way of the upward-gazing men in the middle management strata.[23]

If this is the vexing psychological ethos in which the upward mobile must live and work, how is any degree of emotional stability preserved? The fact is, that while evidently a great many powerful forces impinge upon an executive's psyche constraining him to drive ever harder to succeed, there are others in the environments of most of us which serve somewhat to offset or to counterbalance these. Vector psychology will serve to illustrate these relationships.

J. B. Rotter lists six basic categories of human needs: recognition-status; protection-dependency; dominance; independence; love and affection; and physical comfort.[24] The accompanying table (Figure 28.1) suggests the

---

[22] *Canadian Journal of Economics and Political Science*, May, 1940, p. 200.

[23] Leavitt, H. J. and Whisler, T. L., "Management in the 1980's," *Harvard Business Review*, November-December, 1958, p. 41.

[24] *Social Learning and Clinical Psychology* (N.Y.: Prentice-Hall, Inc., 1954).

relationship between these basic needs and his desire to succeed, on the one hand, and his desire to "take it easy," on the other, in terms of the major social groups whose approbation the individual most likely will seek.

Figure 28.1   Vectors in Executive Motivation

Direction of Force Origin of Force	Desire to "Succeed," i.e. Need fulfillment prompted by a desire to "get ahead" VERTICAL VECTORS	Desire to "Get Along," i.e. Need fulfillment prompted by a desire to "live and let live." HORIZONTAL VECTORS
1. Work Associates a. Peer Group	Recognition-Status Dominance Independence	Love and Affection
b. Superiors	Recognition-Status	Protection-Dependency
2. Wife and Children	Physical Comfort Love and Affection	Love and Affection Protection-Dependency
3. Parents and close relatives	Recognition-Status Love and Affection	Physical Comfort
4. Social friends	Love and Affection	Love and Affection

NOTE: The following definitions are given by Rotter:
1. Recognition-Status: Need to be considered competent or good in a professional, social, occupational, or play activity. Need to gain social or vocational position — that is, to be more skilled or better than others.
2. Protection-Dependency: The need to have another person or group of people prevent frustration or punishment and to provide for the satisfaction of other needs.
3. Dominance: Need to direct or control the actions of other people, including members of family and friends. To have any action taken be that which he suggests.
4. Independence: Need to make own decisions, to rely on oneself, together with the need to develop skills for obtaining satisfactions directly without the mediation of other people.
5. Love and Affection: Need for acceptance and indication of liking by other individuals. In contrast to recognition-status, not concerned with social or professional positions of friends, but seeks their warm regard.
6. Physical Comfort: Learned need for physical satisfaction that has become associated with the gaining of security.

It is indicated that while the preponderance of forces, both endogenous and exogenous, seem to be pushing the executive to strive for success, some not insignificant pressures tend to promote the equilibration of his psychological force-field. For example, one might hypothesize that the need for love and affection from his peer group, to the extent the need exists, is more likely to be achieved by not "pushing" too hard, by not employing power tactics which are too overt, by being "one of the boys."[25] Rensis Likert's interpretation of the findings of the Institute for Social Research substantiates such an analysis:

> An examination of the results presented here and of the results from other research shows that every human being earnestly seeks a secure, friendly, and supportive relationship and one that gives him a sense of personal worth in the face-to-face groups most important to him. . . . Either we successfully establish these friendly and supportive relationships or we crack up.[26]

Adam Curle is among those who have pointed out that often the various groups to which an individual is attached make demands upon his behavior which are mutually incompatible.[27] The precise manner in which the individual's need-structure balances the various forces that are playing upon him will relate both to: (1) the relative importance of each of the various categories of needs extant at the moment in the person's psychological makeup; and, (2) the nature and characteristics of the need-determining and need-fulfilling groups to which the individual belongs. Consequently the validity of March and Simon's prediction that "an organizational participant (will) try to select his group memberships so as to keep at a low level the conflict imposed by differences in the demands made upon him"[28] seems apparent. And what if the conflicts and tensions become too great? Tom Burns' analysis of the ego-defense provided by "cliques and cabals in occupational milieux" identifies a kind of comforting behavior to which frustrated organizational co-operators may resort.[29]

Considerations Influencing the Supply of and the Demand for Superior-Oriented Loyalty

The chain of needs linking superior and subordinate is forged in the first instance by the very essence of the process by which men are selected to be

---

[25] The reader is invited to test his agreement with the classifications made in the table. Note that nothing has been speculated even as to the ordinal strength of the forces. All that is attempted to be shown is that an executive's behavior is the resultant of a psychological vector parallelogram which for the most part appears to insist rather overwhelmingly, in the typical case, that the executive "succeed" in the socially approved sense.

[26] *Motivation: The Core of Management* (American Management Association, Personnel Series, No. 155, 1953), p. 16.

[27] Incentives to Work: An Anthropological Appraisal," *Human Relations*, Vol. II, No. 1, p. 41.

[28] March, J. G. and Simon, H. A. *Organizations* (N.Y.: John Wiley & Sons, Inc., 1958), p. 95.

[29] "The Reference of Conduct in Small Groups," *Human Relations*, Vol. VII, No. 4, 1955, p. 467.

position-incumbents. An immediate "fealty nexus" is created. In the words of Cecil Gibb:[30]

> The power of incumbent leaders to determine their own succession and to influence future leadership cannot be overlooked. . . . At the very least it must certainly be true that where succession to leadership is determined by appointment from above the persons so chosen are perceived to meet the needs of the superior sponsoring group and to owe their primary obligations to higher echelons of control. They may or may not be able to function as instruments of satisfaction for their subordinates.

Thus, as an executive's success is attested to by his rise in the power structure of an organization, he often experiences increasing feelings of isolation. Concurrently there may tend to assail him doubts and fears of inadequacy which he hasn't felt lower in the hierarchy. High office brings new stature, prestige, power, authority. It also seems to bring a new need for reinforcement and reassurance.

Indeed, our complex and multi-facted organizations tend to create a psychological environment in which the "boss" often demands of the men around and immediately below him a fidelity toward him, even as opposed to the organization and to the goals it avowedly seeks, should a crisis situation arise. His subordinates are usually only too ready to meet these demands. As Robert Presthus has noted, subordinates may even be over-ready:

> An interesting latent consequence of status-directed behavior is an exaggerated picture of conformity demands, which is often dysfunctional because it aggravates the fear of action and responsibility often seen in big organizations . . . distorted perception reflects the anxiety of the individual to please his superiors . . . such expectations may seem more compelling than they really are. The individual is not inclined to underestimate them for fear of alienating those upon whom his career chances rest. . . .[31]

Another source of demand for superior-oriented loyalties is found in the internecine warfare that often rages between various executive groups in the organization. It is not to the inter-departmental hasseling that reference is made, but rather to the engagements that take place between competing executives intradepartmentally. As aspiring managers come to recognize

[30] In Gardner Lindzey, *op. cit.*, p. 913.

[31] "Toward a Theory of Organizational Behavior," *op. cit.*, p. 65. The general semanticists have stressed that the behavioral manifestations of these commonly-found over-anxieties are reflected in our verbalizations. For example, see Wendell Johnson's discussion of the principles of "delayed reaction" and "optimal tonicity" in Chapter IX of his *People in Quandaries* (N Y.: Harper and Brothers, 1946).

who are their primary rivals for occupancy of the offices higher in the hierarchy, each inclines to build a coterie of loyal followers. All recognize that
if their chief succeeds, the favored subordinate's chances of success are
markedly improved.[32]

So the bond is reciprocally useful: the chief can count upon a loyal
following to help him outmaneuver his rivals, while the subordinates can
count upon the chief to "remember" them if he wins the game. As Ordway
Tead has so succinctly expressed it: "Tell me whose commendation the
executive seeks, and I will tell you in which way his purposes and policies
will be slanted."[33]

It is important to recognize the existence of the superior-subordinates
loyalty bond as one found at all levels of the authority structure. Therefore
as a man is the superior of certain subordinates, he is, even at the presidential level, a subordinate of other superiors. The simultaneous cultiva-
tion of leadership-followership traits is consequently requisite to the successful performance of all organization men. E. P. Hollander and W. B.
Webb have remarked in this connection:

> It appears evident that the popular dichotomy between leadership
> and followership is in need of reappraisal. Rather understandably, the
> nature of our complex, hierarchical institutions demands that the ef-
> fective leader be equally effective as a follower. It may be considerably
> more realistic, therefore, to consider characteristics of followership as
> one functional component of good leadership.[34]

One may consequently visualize among aspiring executives an organizational network of interpersonal loyalties, structured essentially in terms of
a "people who can do the most good" philosophy. This conceptualization
is more than just speculative, as the research of D. C. Pelz has shown.[35]
In a sense, sociometric choices may be said to be made not just in terms of
affective "likes" and "dislikes." Pelz's study concludes that subordinates
are attracted to leaders who are in a position to do them (the subordinates)

---

[32] Robert Presthus similarly views these matters: "An appraisal of authority must also
include the fact that big organizations are composed of many sub-hierarchies, each bound
together by authority, interest, and values in a way similar to that in the total organization. . . . As a result, an upward-looking posture characterizes the whole organization. . . .
Here the ambiguity of personal and organizational goals may be seen. To retain his
position and preserve the hope of future rewards, each subleader must simultaneously
promote organization-wide values and yet retain the loyalty of his immediate associates
by defending their interests against both competing sub-hierarchies and neglect by the
elite." "Toward a Theory of Organizational Behavior," *op. cit.*, p. 58–59.

[33] *The Art of Administration* (N.Y.: McGraw-Hill Book Co., Inc., 1951) p. 18.

[34] "Leadership, Followership, and Friendship: An Analysis of Peer Nominations,"
Journal of Abnormal and Social Psychology, reprinted in E. E. Maccoby *et al.* (eds.)
Readings in Social Psychology (N.Y.: Henry Holt and Company, 1958), pp. 495–496.

[35] "Leadership Within a Hierarchical Organization," *Journal of Social Issues*, 1951,
7, pp. 49–55.

the most good as they seek to achieve their organization goals. Subordinates realize that such superiors must in turn be in the favor of their superiors, and consequently, in the nomenclature of the Ohio State Leadership Studies group, are willing to tolerate a good deal of "initiating structure" at the expense of "consideration."

Finally, we must recognize an often nefariously-employed power which the superior possesses with respect to his subordinates tending to evoke their loyalty to him personally. The influence of the superior on the fortunes of the subordinate extend beyond the immediate milieu both geographically and temporally. In mind is the matter of good references. These are typically of no small moment as men move from one impersonally-structured organization to another. Woe be unto the man who has dared to raise doubts, well-founded or not, in the mind of his erstwhile superior in matters of "loyalty," often miscalled "integrity."

The point is that while such condemnations deserve seriously to be regarded if they arise from intellectual or other dishonesty, infidelity to patent organization goals, and the like, they may often have originated from the subordinate's attempts to "do the right thing" even though this proved somehow to have worked to the personal detriment of the superior. Be this as it may, the fear of a "bad report" is probably more often than not a powerful element tending to skew the subordinate's structure of loyalties heavily in favor of the person of the superior.

But it is not to be thought that an executive in his role as a subordinate is caught up in organizational and inter-personal currents over which he has no control. Quite to the contrary.

How Executives May Influence Superiors', Peers', and Subordinates' Perceptions of "Reality"

"The best way to get ahead in the Air Force is to keep both feet firmly on the ground. The boys that fly don't have time to play politics."[36] This comment was recently reported to have been made by a field grade officer. It represents a feeling and an attitude which is rather commonly to be found in large-scale bureaucracies of all sorts. While it is enlightening and fruitful to observe the various subtle forms such behavior takes, we are not here mainly concerned with what might be called the affective (the "office-politicking") aspects of executive deportment.

We are rather primarily interested in investigating by what general types of means the executive is capable of shaping the *cognitive* ethos of his co-workers, to the end that his fortunes are most favorably developed. We ask: what are the ways in which a subordinate can, most often quite legiti-

[36] Hamil, Fred, "How Officers Get Promoted," *Armed Forces Management*, December, 1958, p. 15.

mately, utilize the power attributes of his office to enhance his tenure in that office and to mold his superior's attitudes towards him so that his chances for favorable consideration for higher offices are increased?

An organization office may be conceived as one of the relays or links in a communications net. Thus conceptualized, the incumbent is an energizer, a transmitter. But human incumbents are much more than this, for what flows out of such a communication link is frequently hardly relatable to what flowed in. Indeed some kind of purposeful change in the input is generally the reason for a reflective, deliberative human link, otherwise an electronic or mechanical relay would probably better serve. It is generally assumed that whatever transformation has occurred between input and output will, at least in the best understanding of the human transformer, lead to an expeditious fulfillment of the organization objectives involved. But a moment's reflection raises doubts that this is necessarily or perhaps even usually the entire fact.

In analyzing the possibilities involved, let us refer to the flow down the hierarchical communication net as "orders" and to the upward flow as "information." Considering the downward flow first, it appears that orders may be classified into three groups (not mutually exclusive) on the basis of their susceptibility to co-worker reality and manipulation. First, there are those routine orders in which the subordinate perceives no worthwhile possibility of personal exploitation. Second, there are those which are susceptible to varying interpretation. (Indeed, such an invitation to interpretation may be implicit in the received order, if not explicit.) And third, there are those orders whose implementation is to some extent left to the discretion of the order-receiver. Clearly, the last two categories are those which may be useful to the upward-mobile executive. (Refer to Figure 28.2a, "Order Transformation Schema.")[37]

What are the possibilities for self-promotion which inhere in order interpretation? An executive may, for example, be selective in his judgment of which elements of the communication are meant to be emphasized. That is, he may have appreciable latitude as to the relative weights that are to be assigned to the several decisional subparts encompassed in the order. Thus, he may be expected to tend more heavily to weigh those which magnify his importance in their execution than those which do not. Or the order-receiver may find it feasible to interpret the order in the broadest possible context, or in the narrowest possible context, as the specifics of the situation dictate will most likely accrue to his best advantage.

Similarly, the executive may recognize that there exist possibilities for self-aggrandizement in order implementation. For example, the exact

[37] Cf. the conceptualization in Figure 28.2 with Stanford Goldman's "Block Diagram of the Real World as a Transducer Between Cause and Effect" in his *Information Theory* (N.Y.: Prentice-Hall, Inc., 1953), p. 308.

mode of execution may be left to the discretion of the order-receiver. In this instance there may be choice as to which of the subordinate staff will be burdened with, or privileged to fulfill, the action requirement. The sequence in which actions are to be taken and the timing of action may also provide the executive with opportunities for exploitation. Or the order may suggest the possibility of justifying a conference, which almost inevitably will provide the shrewd executive with an opportunity to impress upon those around him that he has been entrusted with extremely important responsibilities, and that he is the "man to watch."

The upward flow of communication, "information," provides perhaps even more potential for molding the perceptions of those who matter than does the downward flow. (See Figure 28.2b, "Information Transformation

Figure 28.2 Modes of Communication Transformation

a. Order transformation schema

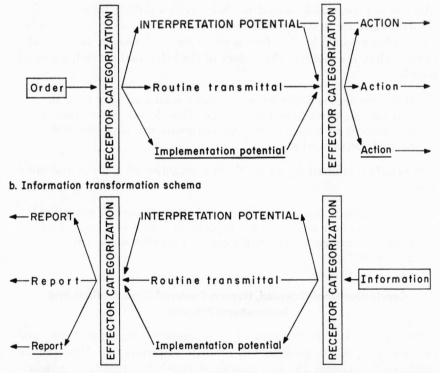

b. Information transformation schema

NOTE: The capitalized and the underscored channels are meant to convey the idea of transformation which leads to enhancement of the executive's status resulting in actions (in the case of the downward flow of orders) and reports (in the case of an upward flow of information) which are different from what they might have been without such interpretation.

Schema.") Appropriate selection, interpretation, and manipulation of the information reaching one's superiors obviously abounds in opportunities for self-promotion.

The really callous executive, bent upon fully exploiting the strategic gains thought to inhere in tactics such as these, realizes of course that an increase in the degree of one's outstandingness is achievable not only by putting one's self in the most favorable light. The manipulator is also made to stand out from his peer-competitors in such proportion as he can detract from their stature, as he can "cut them down to size." One's executive height, then, is capable of increase both by positive measures (self-aggrandizement) and by negative measures (peer degradation). To be sure, the detraction from peers' stature is a dangerous game, because of the irascibility and the implacable hostility likely to be engendered in co-workers should one be found out. But still, such games are played.

Given the major characteristics of the socioculture in which today's executives live and work, it would indeed be surprising were we to find many who did not consciously attend to their decision-making behavior with a constant vigilance to its personal ramifications. The validity of the above analysis is supported by the studied observations of men in various walks of life. Thus, the cautious phraseology of the behavioral researcher Carroll Shartle:

> It is sometimes said that an administrator is on a one-way track and that the only direction he can go is up. Thus, he may make many of his decisions in terms of how their outcomes will affect the status which he hopes to achieve. . . .[38]

is positively reinforced by an on-the-line executive of a major industrial firm:

> I am convinced that a majority of employees still work to please the man who is their superior — not to accomplish what they understand to be their particular piece of the common objective of the entire organization.[39]

Conclusion: Goal-Oriented, Human-Centered Organizations and Sociocultural Progress

Over and over in the literature of contemporary organization theory and practice one is led to consider this ultimate of perplexities: How can we satisfactorily reconcile the ever-growing demands for increased specializa-

[38] *Executive Performance and Leadership* (Englewood Cliffs, N.J.: Prentice-Hall, Inc., 1956), p. 15.
[39] Ben D. Mills (Vice President, Ford Motor Company) "Management Without Meddling," *Think*, October, 1958, p. 9.

tion and high-level knowledge and skill with the apparently contradictory needs of the "mature personality?"

March and Simon, discussing the Selznick model in bureaucratic theory, indicate how dysfunctional consequences, from both the standpoint of the organization and that of the individual, are auto-reinforcing.[40] The reasoning is: desire to control by top echelons of management leads to increased delegation; increased delegation leads to greater departmentation; greater departmentation leads to more minute specialization; this leads to a bifurcation of interests between the subunits of the organization; it follows that subunit decisions will be made increasingly in terms of internal strategies; consequently there is a decrease in the extent to which the organization's goals are achieved. But this only results, according to the model, in increased delegation. The cycle is complete.

Another such endless and mutually detrimental interactional reciprocity is Chris Argyris' model of superior domination, subordinate defensive adaptation, increased superior domination, and so on. Is there no way out of these organizationally-inspired labyrinths?[41]

To pose this question is to have implicitly raised another, more fundamental one. In the circumstances of modern industrial democracy, what *is* the function of executive leadership? Is it to command (the bureaucratic approach), is it to create a "permissive environment," is it to "manage by objectives," or what? Warren G. Bennis' recent useful study of "Leadership Theory and Administrative Behavior" provides some guidance.[42]

Bennis, after a synoptic survey of the state of the theory and the evident alternatives, appears to favor Douglas McGregor's "double reference" approach, which is recognized to be grounded in Peter Drucker's preference for "management by objective." This attempt to mediate the conceptually polar extremes of the bureaucratic and the human relations models hinges upon the doctrine of mutual interdependence of the superior and his subordinates, and their recognition of this fact. Bennis argues that the disparity of power that exists between the superior and his subordinates in typical hierarchical relationships raises the question of the exact nature of this "interdependence." In his view "the nature of negotiation and trading has to be analyzed more fully in order to clarify what each is giving up and what each is gaining from the collaborative relationship."[43] It is hoped that the present paper sheds some light on this point. Bennis himself concludes:

> The decision maker, then, faced with no operable means for evaluating a decision — as is often the case — and with limited data, has no

[40] *Organizations, op. cit.*, pp. 40–42.
[41] *Personality and Organization, op. cit.*, pp. 232–237.
[42] *Administrative Science Quarterly*, December, 1959, p. 259 ff.
[43] *Ibid.*, p. 286.

other recourse than to utilize a group, both as a security operation as well as a validity-tester . . . in today's organizations — scientific, military, government, and education — the consequences of decisions may have such far reaching effects, that no one individual — even if all the knowledge were available on which to make a decision — would feel sufficiently courageous to make it.[44]

Thus, the decision-making superior, in our present-day organization complexes, is almost universally sensitized to the fact that he "needs" his subordinates in a way that was not true perhaps as little as two or three decades ago. And if the potentialities of electronic data processing for routine decision-making are as revolutionary as they now portend, the dependence of the manager upon his "subordinate" corps of experts may well assume new and significantly increased dimensions.

In the light of current events such as these, it seems justifiable to speculate that the subordinate will increase his "reality-shaping potential" *vis a vis* his superior at an accelerated pace in coming years. It appears likely that the manager will increasingly be called upon to adjudicate and to coordinate the activities of his specialized expert staff. Another way of saying this is that the "research administrator problem" of today will lose the relative narrowness it now has among the manifold organization-personality problems with which we struggle. The research administrator is now being referred to as a new "man in the middle" who must, as has long been said of the foreman, be Janus-faced. The research administrator is said to be "frequently caught between the conflicting demands of the scientists and those of higher authority within the organization."[45]

It is predicted that, to an ever-growing extent, all managers of large-scale undertakings will become "men in the middle" in this sense. Peter Drucker has recently put the matter with his usual cogency:

> For the new organization of highly educated people, authority and responsibility may well be the wrong principles of organization. It may well be that we will have to learn to organize not a system of authority and responsibility — a system of command — but an information and decision system — a system of judgment, knowledge, and expectations. . . . We may have to learn to consider authority, responsibility, rank and reward as four separate and distinct variables to be marked in a configuration, rather than as synonyms for the same thing. We may even have to learn to consider authority, responsibility, rank, and reward as four separate and distinct variables to be merged in a configuration, rather than as synonyms for the same thing. We may even have to learn to look at an organization as a process . . . rather than as merely

[44] *Ibid.*, p. 294.
[45] Norman Kaplan, "The Role of the Research Administrator," *Administrative Science Quarterly*, June, 1959, p. 41.

a mechanism; in other words, as something in which there is no "higher" or "lower" but only a "different."[46]

The consequence of all this may well be that perceived superior-subordinate interdependence is not only heightened, but is substantively transmuted. But we are speculating about future trends.

Meanwhile, what of the inter-executive relationships with which we are concerned here? A correction of the inordinate excesses to which some managements imbibed of the pablum that was often mislabeled the "human relations approach" doubtless needed to be made. But is the other extreme of, for example, "benevolent autocracy" *a la* Robert McMurry the alternative?[47] Surely not.

Behavioral scientists such as Morton Deutsch question the validity of the assumptions on which rivalry-structured organizations are built.[48] It is commonly thought that the increasing intensity of competition between aspiring executives as the top of the pyramid comes into view will assure the organization of the most able leadership, according to the "survival of the fittest" principle. Now research raises serious doubts that this is generally the case. It is even suggested that quite the opposite result may often occur. The analysis in this paper is meant to support the conclusion. The "fittest" may more often than not turn out to be the shrewdest, the most adulatory, the most underhanded.

Let us consider the argument on another plane. Our discussion seems inevitably to suggest that essentially, if our enterprise and other institutions are to serve their constituents — employees, stockholders, customers, suppliers, and the general public — at a value approaching their maximum potential, then managers must seek to construct organizational environments in which the intendedly rational behavior of the participants is enabled more closely to meet their basic psychic and emotional requirements. The deeper moral aspirations of the community at large will also be better met than has so often been the case to date.

In addition to the reconceptualizations of industrial organizational structure that may be necessary to meet tomorrow's challenges in the vein suggested by Peter Drucker, it may well be that our sociocultural progress will be closely and functionally related to our ability to conceive newly appropriate *forms* within which organized behavior occurs. The necessity here springs mainly from what G. C. Homans has included as one of the five

---

[46] Fenn, D. H., Jr., *Management's Mission in a New Society* (N.Y.: McGraw-Hill Book Co., Inc., 1959), pp. 174–175.

[47] "The Case for the Benevolent Autocrat," *Harvard Business Review*, January-February, 1958, p. 82 ff.

[48] See his "A Theory of Co-operation and Competition," *Human Relations*, vol. II, no. 1, 1949, p. 129; and his "An Experimental Study of the Effects of Co-operation and Competition upon Group Processes," *Human Relations*, vol. II, no. 3, p. 199.

basic problems of advancing civilization: "circulation."[48a] By circulation Homans means the channels by which the leadership cream of a society is allowed to rise to the top and fill its rightful role. (This is not unrelated, of course, to Pareto's notion of the "circulation of the elite."[49] And it may be noted in passing that Elton Mayo was much concerned with this problem, considering that the elite of his time were in most significant senses an elite best able to cope with the social-organizational problems of a bygone era, not with the problems they faced in their time.[50]

But what of the new forms to which we have alluded? In a penetrating article, Paul H. Appleby has suggested that that level of organizational structure which lies between the social microcosm (single, specialized groups, enterprises, function, and activities) and the social macrocosm (governmental organization of society) is "the intermediate organizational area (which) has been largely ignored in the world of serious study." Moreover, he avers:

> The fact is that the gap between separate organizational policies of all kinds and public policies appropriate for governmental treatment is everywhere much too wide to permit ready translation of the small, special, and private into terms appropriate to general public consideration. . . . The function of intermediate structures may be identified as sifting out issues, translating issues into terms of broader meaning, reducing the range of presumed choice to really feasible alternative courses of action, and identifying or dramatizing those alternatives.[51]

One of the major functions of these "intermediate organizations" would be to contribute to circulation, to assuring that leaders attuned to the times readily found their way into appropriate positions in the organizational structure of society. Appleby's is an urgent call:

> We need rather desperately, I think, to turn more of our attention to organization, to structure, to administration, to decision-making, and to the skills of membership essential to a popularly oriented society and to popular government. We need much more consciously to develop a larger pool of leadership capacities, a larger proportion of persons especially equipped to deal, intellectually and in operational decision-making, with the relationships between innumerable facts, function, and forces which superficially appear highly unlike.[52]

With this point of view the analysis in this paper completely concurs.

It is heartening to note that discussions of business morality and ethical conduct in industry are commencing to confront questions such as these.

[48a] *The Human Group* (N.Y.: Harcourt, Brace and Co., 1950).
[49] Vilfredo Pareto, *The Mind and Society* (N.Y.: Harcourt, Brace and Co., 1935).
[50] *The Human Problems of Industrial Civilization* (Boston, Mass.: Graduate School of Business Administration, Harvard University, 1933).
[51] "Managing Complexity," *Ethics*, January, 1954, pp. 93–94.
[52] *Ibid.*, p. 99.

But it is apparent that even yet only dimly is the critical import of these matters sensed. As Chester Barnard has pointed out:

> . . . it is the moral problem that leads to much frustration and even to pathological behavior. . . . It simply is not known to any wide degree what are the number and the character of the moral problems that are faced by those who do the world's work.[53]

And it is unlikely that we can do better in concluding this exploration of the rationale of executive motivation than with the remedial emphasis Barnard suggests:

> Indeed, it seems to me that the most important of our problems is to convey an understanding of the moral issues that are involved, rather than the technical and scientific questions to which so much of our educational and training processes are directed. . . . It is here, I think, that the universities in the future will have a great opportunity, for I doubt if those within our organizations can be sufficiently adept and objective to give appropriate study to the nature of the moral problems which they face.[54]

---

[53] *Elementary Conditions of Business Morals* (The Barbara Weinstock Lecture on the Morals of Trade, University of California, Berkeley, 1958), pp. 38–39.

[54] *Ibid.*, p. 37 and p. 39.

29

The Situation and the Opportunistic

Executive*

Stanley E. Bryan

Michigan State University

The executive is both the creature of and the creator of his environment. This article discusses the heuristic, opportunistic, situational elements that shape executive behavior and influence the evaluation of the executive and his work. Rich in illustrations and examples, this paper traces the relations between situational forces and executive decision-making, fitting a large body of research literature into related framework.

How much do executives really shape the environments in which they operate? How much do they behave opportunistically in foretelling changing forces in situations not of their own making and responding accordingly? To what degree does the executive discover, create and exploit opportunities in a continuing process of incremental and rational decisions? To what degree does he feel his way through terrain that requires the use of intuition, hunch, judgment and serendipity, yet over which he has relatively little control? To what extent are decisions made on the basis of utilities, payoffs, probabilities, risks and uncertainties, properly quantified and after a full weighing of evidence? To what extent is the whole process heuristic, played part by plan and part by ear, depending on what breaks occur and how those breaks are interpreted? How important is the element of surprise, one relatively little treated in the literature, yet apparently a critical factor in real life? What are the forces to which executives in fact respond? And, where does the "law of the situation" fit into the picture?

* Taken and adapted from *The Journal of the Academy of Management*, vol. 5, no. 1, April, 1962, pp. 36–56.

These and similar questions have led to a search of management literature on executive types and on forces to which executives respond. This
article represents a log of the search.

A Model of a Heuristic Executive

The search starts in the "old country" looking at a venerable old management principle, and pursues its way to "newer territory," moving up
and down numerous trails, all somehow related to the situations which surround the executive. A heuristic executive is considered as he faces uncertainty and non-measurable surprise in the situations that confront him.
The term "heuristic" applies to methods which are persuasive rather than
logically compelling, and which may lead to a solution of a problem, but
offer no guarantee that they will do so. This executive has a more common
name and he will be called by it in this log. It is "opportunistic."

To find a heuristic, opportunistic executive should not suggest discount-
ing the need for skill and ability in the executive process. Actual examples
cited below should not be considered as discrediting the executive abilities
of the men in the cases noted. Although fate, status, power, and surprise
play their part in this presentation the theme is not simply that some men
are "lucky" and others are not. The heuristic and opportunistic concept
is more realistically complex, finding executives in decision-making situations where they are often carried along by the tide of events, sometimes
predictable and sometimes not, and sometimes they are buffeted by non-
ordered, non-measurable, potential surprise.

The Pattern of Search and the Ground Traversed

The pattern of search resulting in this log, though circuitous, is not as
completely random as a Heisenberg particle. It starts with some "older"
management precepts and moves to some "newer" ones. At the same time
it moves from some generalizations to specific cases; no originality is professed. References cited will aid the reader by showing the many divergent
ideas about how executives do, or should, face situations. The aim is to
describe the ground briefly rather than merely record a benchmark referring
to the particular reference. The resulting log is thus a compromise between
(1) recording only benchmarks, and (2) fully describing the territory —
too long for some readers, too short to completely cover the ground.

One theme carries through this search: the situation and the executive
relating himself to it. The ground traversed includes the constant change
in the situation, the forces within the manager himself, executive leaders
and subordinates, the power situation, the models of men and situations,
and the opportunistic executive. Because the search is motivated by an at-

tempt to identify "other forces" which bear upon the executive and the situation, special attention is given to exploring the area of opportunity and opportunism (and the heuristic) in the situation.

The return is to a point of high ground overlooking the "law of the situation," seeing it in different perspective as bordered by uncertainty, status, power, happenstance, non-expectation, fate — and the heuristic.

The "Law of the Situation"

The following generalization has been called the "law of the situation": effective executive leadership depends on the executive's ability and courage to face the facts in the situation, interpret the facts properly in light of the situation's requirements, and follow the course of action they dictate.[1] The mathematical model-maker might prefer to express this group of relationships somewhat as follows, in which the capital letters can be identified as the first letters in items listed above (with preciseness implied):

$$f(D) = f(A) + f(C) + f(F) + f(I)$$

The "law of the situation" is presumably a guide to action for the practicing executive, emphasizing his need for ability and courage to assemble and interpret facts — including the philosophies and viewpoints of the people involved with the decision — and to take action based on the situation.[2] Yet decision-making is almost always performed in an environment of imperfect, fragmentary, and often erroneous information.[3] Anshen, emphasizing the quantification of the factors in a problem, argues that most — possibly all — of management's qualitative judgments can be quantified under compulsion and such quantification need not be accurate to be valuable.[4] He implies that sizeable errors in cost estimates, for example, result in relatively small differences in results.[5] Holt reiterates this concept of quantification error by saying that (in a factory situation under analysis) even if substantial errors are made in estimating the parameters of the cost function, the factory performance measured in cost terms will not suffer seriously.[6] Such arguments pushed too far, however, lead to the

[1] R. C. Davis, *The Fundamentals of Top Management*, New York: Harper & Brothers Publishers, 1951, p. 152.

[2] Keith Davis, *Human Relations in Business*, New York: McGraw-Hill Book Co., Inc., 1957, p. 274.

[3] B. V. Dean, "Application of Operations Research to Managerial Decision-Making," *Administrative Science Quarterly*, December, 1958, p. 412.

[4] Melvin Anshen, "Price Tags for Business Policy," *Harvard Business Review*, January-February, 1960, p. 74.

[5] Melvin Anshen, C. C. Holt, Franco Modigliani, J. F. Muth, and H. A. Simon, "Mathematics for Production Scheduling," *Harvard Business Review*, March-April, 1958, p. 54.

[6] C. C. Holt, Franco Modigliani, J. F. Muth, and H. A. Simon, *Planning Production, Inventories, and Work Force*, Englewood Cliffs: Prentice-Hall, Inc., 1960, p. 59.

generalization that "facts" in the situation are not as important as "quantification." No decision really rests upon the facts alone; but there probably isn't any better starting point than trying to get them.[7] They should be obtained whether they are subject to quantification or not.

In presenting a "law" (or "principle") the writer is aware of views such as Simon's that it is a "fatal defect" of the current principles of management that they are like proverbs, almost always appearing in contradictory pairs.[8] There are predilections in some quarters against attempts to state "laws" or "principles" for business administration.[9] An executive seeking aid in how to approach a situation can readily find in management practices or literature concepts that seem diametrically opposed to one another — yet each with its promulgator and adherents and each apparently effective in sufficient cases to support in practicability.[10] Little wonder then that such an executive is guided by the heuristic process without consciously knowing he is.

Is a generalization such as the "law of the situation" useful, then? Yes. It sets up a criterion for action even though in general terms, and it establishes a point of departure — a proposition for discussion. If the "law of the situation" were only a straw man set up to knock down through discussion it would be useful. As a proverb it is in illustrious biblical company, for generations of men have quoted proverbs to prove their points.

Constant Change in Situations and Ideas

Hegel's dialectic comes to mind.[11] Every idea has an opposite idea, every action results in reaction. The result is a synthesis which starts the process over again. The only constant thing in a dynamic situation is change, often surprising change. Ideas, decisions and forces create new situations and the phenomenon is a spiraling of sequential ideas, decisions and situations. Galbraith's concept of "countervailing power" for American Capitalism is a nicely-phrased generalization that could be applied to management ideas and situations. Men assess situations, and the future effects of alternate ideas or courses of action, differently. Some stress infinite benefit for one

---

[7] R. F. Bales, "In Conference," *Harvard Business Review*, March-April, 1954, p. 44.

[8] H. A. Simon, *Administrative Behavior*, New York: The Macmillan Company, 1958, p. 20.

[9] For example, see A. H. Dunn, III, "Basic Characteristics of the Case Method," in M. P. McNair (Ed.), *The Case Method at the Harvard Business School*, New York: McGraw-Hill Book Co., Inc., 1954, p. 97.

[10] I have added footnotes to this presentation to prove this assertion. One of the fascinating aspects of management for the student is that there are so many differing opinions. The footnotes also serve as direction signs for the numerous trails I have crossed in the preparation of this presentation.

[11] Hegel's dalectic (and his influence upon Karl Marx) appear in more detail in W. N. Loucks and J. W. Hoot, *Comparative Economic Systems*, New York: Harper & Brothers, Publishers, 1948 (3rd Edition), p. 158.

course, utter disaster for another, with the dialectic of exaggeration also brought into the situation and used in the disputation. One might be moved to note that most decisions once taken don't seem as important in restrospect as they did at the time they were being made. One should also note the influence of potential unmeasurable, unexpected surprise in the turn of events even with the best made decisions.

The philosopher could well take a position analogous to a proposition of Galbraith's (in his statement relating to decisions of Government executives) that in situations where organization slack and considerable affluence abounds most decisions are of relatively little importance within and of themselves.[12]

Emboldened by courage to question the sagacity of many decisions, one might even note that the outcomes of many decisions are the result of luck, fate, fortune, nature, or possibly even Omnipotent Power, rather than the working out of plans formulated by the force of man's own feeble mental powers. The capacity of the human mind for formalizing and solving complex problems is very small compared with the size of the problems which in reality face him in the real world.[13] His decisions are likely to come to naught, or result in unanticipated circumstances, as the many strong forces which surround the situation come into play.

Men of affairs know how to "rationalize" decisions after the situation has developed. The seats of honor at the feasts of the successful (in the world of affairs) are reserved for those who can acquire a name for having *prescience*. There is a natural tendency for such men to play down or soft pedal decisions which did not turn out as successfully as they had hoped. The decision-maker is more the artist than the scientists in working with situations which develop. Despite the ever-changing managerial situations, however, the "law of the situation," can help the executive to face these changing elements and make more rational decisions.

The Forces Within the Manager Facing a Situation

Forces of various sorts abound. But three definite *types* of forces seem to be present — in the manager, in the subordinate, and in the situation.[14] Men and events have been mated throughout history. For those who argue that events, not executives, shape the big decisions, history might well be adrift with no master, a pawn in the hands of fortune, chance, or fate. For them, history is the result of innumerable decisions, each one of small

[12] J. K. Galbraith, *American Capitalism: Concept of Countervailing Power*, Boston: Houghton Mifflin Company, 1952, p. 118.

[13] H. A. Simon, *Models of Man*, New York: John Wiley & Sons, Inc., 1957, p. 198.

[14] Robert Tannenbaum and W. H. Schmidt, "How to Choose a Leadership Pattern," *Harvard Business Review*, March-April, 1958, p. 98.

consequence, but in total adding up in a way no man intends, and resulting in history. But another will ask: "What of the pivotal decisions of history (declaring war, dropping the A-bomb, etc.)? They would reply that the "pivotal decisions" might never have been necessary if history had been the creation of another set of innumerable small decisions, so that history, as fate, has decreed there would be no great decision regarding the declaration of war or the dropping of the A-bomb, etc.

A pervasive argument exists for the fact that crises create leaders.[15] Examples range all the way from Moses in biblical times, Florence Nightingale in the past century, to a modern company sales manager faced with the crisis created by a sudden change in demand. Speaking of early history, M. René Sedillot, in *The History of the World* observed that each chapter of history ends in a flood of barbarians — dynasties and empires disappeared.[16] How would Julius Caesar, Charlemagne or Genghis Khan have fared in another time and another place? Or how would the great autocrats of industry fare if they started their careers today? Allen, in his book *The Big Change* points out that great autocrats, such as the late table-pounding George Washington Hill of American Tobacco and the rambunctious Sewell Avery of Montgomery Ward, are in increasingly short supply in today's industry.[17] Gordon sees today's executive more the co-ordinator doing a "management job" approving decisions that flow up to him — doing less and less initiation.[18] Does not the time and the situation mold the leader?

A current case illustrates the interaction between the situation and the personal force of the leader. The case developed at the Underwood Typewriter Company and resulted in the first major U.S. firm to fall into foreign hands.[19] After the prosperous World War II years when Underwood did not produce typewriters but built war materials the company found its traditional market threatened by newcomers. Philip D. Wagoner, chief executive officer in 1952, was faced with a situation in which the company was in poor, but not desperate condition. He "foolishly agreed" (he has since admitted) to the hiring of a well known firm of consultants.[20] Underwood subsequently suffered from the changes initiated largely by the consultants in which the top management was changed three times in three years. Under leadership largely selected by the consultants, old-

[15] G. E. Willis, "The Crisis Technique," in E. C. Bursk (Ed.), *The Management Team*, Cambridge: Harvard University Press, 1955, p. 215.

[16] Rene Sedillot, *The History of the World*, (A Mentor Book), New York: Harcourt, Brace & Company, 1951, p. 86.

[17] F. L. Allen, *The Big Change*, New York: Harper & Brothers Publishers, 1952, p. 250.

[18] R. A. Gordon, *Business Leadership in the Large Corporation*, Washington: Brookings Institution, 1945, p .11.

[19] "What Went Wrong at Underwood," *Fortune*, September, 1960, p. 141.

[20] *Ibid.*

school conservatism first appeared, it is said, followed by experimentation with modern technology. These changes played their parts in Underwood's decline. It was as though Fate decreed that no action decided upon would meet with success. In the desperation which resulted it was considered a good decision and a relief to sell the controlling interest to the Olivetti Company of Italy. Strong "other-forces" prevailed in this case.

Max Weber put great emphasis on the rise of "charismic" leaders as truly revolutionary forces in history — "charismic" meaning possession of the "gift of grace" which caused followers looking for leadership to follow. But he also noted the "routinization of charisma" in which the followers took over the "leadership" of providing for the material interests of the followers as they adapted to the situation.[21] The leader, the led, and the situation are inextricably woven together with the sequential decisions of leaders modifying the situation but sometimes not modifying it in the way they would wish. Sending in the team heroes in the closing minutes of a losing game can't be counted on with any great probability to change defeat into victory. Fate seems to decree defeat in some situations, leave potential leaders dead before the preliminary campaigns are finished, and in other situations allow only Pyrrhic victories.

The Business Executive or Business Leader and the Situation

Gardner, in answering the question, "What makes successful and unsuccessful executives?" says that it is clear that successful business executives have many personality "traits" in common.[22] He suggests eleven "traits" all of which can be spotted in advance by tests and all of which are in the common personality structure of the successful executive, including (for example) "a pervasive fear of failure — the need to overcome a sense of frustration."[23] Schell lists other such traits (e.g., "moral stamina," "scientific trend of mind," etc.).[24] Tead emphasizes "decisiveness" (one of the "traits" listed by Gardner) because, he says, there is danger that studious "scientific minded" individuals in posts of leadership will never stop taking evidence and accumulating and weighing facts.[25]

Gouldner, after reviewing certain traits ("intelligence," etc.), concludes that there is no reliable evidence of the existence of universal leadership

[21] H. H. Gerth and C. W. Mills, (Translators and Editors), *Max Weber — Essays in Sociology*, London: Routledge and Kegan Paul, Ltd., 1948, p. 54.

[22] B. B. Gardner, "What Makes Successful and Unsuccessful Executives?" *Advanced Management*, September, 1948, p. 116, reprinted in F. A. Shull, Jr., (Ed.), *Selected Readings in Management*, Homewood, Ill.: Richard D. Irwin, Inc., 1958, p. 308.

[23] *Ibid.*, p. 311.

[24] E. H. Schell, *Techniques of Executive Control*, New York: McGraw-Hill Book Company, Inc., 1957 (8th Edit.), p. 18.

[25] Ordway Tead, *The Art of Leadership*, New York: McGraw-Hill Book Company, Inc., 1935, p. 121.

traits.[26] Pfiffner and Sherwood say that no consistent pattern of traits has emerged: "We still cannot say there is an elite group of men destined for leadership regardless of the organizational circumstances in which they find themselves."[27] Stogdill in a summary of 124 studies of leadership summarized their findings in broad general categories of traits: "capacity" ("intelligence," etc.), "achievement" (knowledge, etc.), "responsibility," and "status"; then he added "the situation."[28] If the situation is as important as Stogdill and others believe, it represents, as Bellows suggests, "devastating evidence against measurable traits."[29]

The assumption of a leadership syndrome or leader type is "futile."[30] Who becomes the leader of a given group engaging in a particular activity, and what the leadership characteristics are in the given case, are functions of the specific situation including the measuring instruments employed.[31] The degree to which any individual exhibits leadership depends not only on his *characteristics*, but also on the *characteristics of the situation* in which he finds himself.[32]

The situation of the executive includes a definitely structured organizational hierarchy, presumably performing some useful social and economic service and fulfilling its profit objectives. The bonds of his situation include the functional specifications of his work, the status system in operation, and the communication network of the particular organization.[33] Within this general framework many (probably most) of the acts of executives may be regarded as responses to conditions of the environment involving no process of decision requiring deliberation, calculation or thought.[34] The environmental situation in such cases depends largely upon learning to adapt to the organization, experience gained from similar situations, and the occupation of an organizational position to which information, "facts," delegations, and appeals flow for "processing." Interpersonal relationships exist side by side with technical relationships. To be effective the executive

26 W. W. Gouldner (Ed.), *Studies in Leadership*, New York: Harper & Brothers, Publishers, 1950, p. 34.

27 J. M. Pfiffner and F. P. Sherwood, *Administrative Organization*, Englewood Cliffs, N.J.: Prentice-Hall, Inc., 1960, p. 354.

28 R. M. Stogdill, "Personal Factors Associated With Leadership: A Survey of the Field," *The Journal of Psychology*, January, 1948, p. 35.

29 Roger Bellows, *Creative Leadership*, Englewood Cliffs, N.J.: Prentice-Hall, Inc., 1959, p. 293.

30 J. P. Guilford, *Personality*, New York: McGraw-Hill Book Company, Inc., 1959, p. 470.

31 J. A. C. Brown, *The Social Psychology of Industry*, Middlesex, England: Penguin Books, Ltd., 1956, p. 220.

32 Alex Bavelas, "Leadership: Man and Function," *Administrative Science Quarterly*, March, 1960, p. 493.

33 E. W. Bakke, *Bonds of Organization*, New York: Harper & Brothers, Publishers, 1950, p. 186.

34 Chester I. Barnard, *The Functions of the Executive*, Cambridge: Harvard University Press, 1938, p. 200.

must adapt his behavior to fit the expectations, values and interpersonal skills (i.e., the cultural background) of those with whom he is interacting — in all relationships with superiors, peers, and subordinates.[35] Barnard has noted that in any kind of organization good executives know how to get action for which they cannot be given authority of command, but for which they are held accountable and responsible.[36] On the other hand organization structure and experience routinize the handling of many situations which require the "processing" of the *position* and not necessarily the *man* holding the position.

The Subordinates and the Situation

There is an interdependence between executives and their subordinates. Barnard speaks of a "zone of indifference" within which orders issued to subordinates are acceptable and beyond which they are not acceptable.[37] Furthermore a subordinate must understand an order and be able mentally and physically to carry it out before an executive's complete "authority" is consummated. Complete "authority" fails just as much from lip service, lax adherence to the letter of command, or doing the wrong things as from refusal to obey orders. At no time are subordinates completely dependent upon executives. In military situations commanders long ago understood the need for exhortations before battles to work followers up to following their lead in battle. They knew how quickly their army could turn into an uncontrollable retreating mob if fortune turned against them and men sought their own self-interest in flight. In business situations, if the subordinate believes he must contribute too much for the rewards the organization is able to give, he will quit and seek his opportunity elsewhere. March and Simon state this proposition in the technical terms of economics as follows: increases in the balance of inducement utilities over contribution utilities decrease the propensity of the individual participant to leave the organization whereas decreases in the balance have an opposite effect.[38]

The Power Elite vs. the Other Directed — Status Power and the Situation

The power structure related to organization situations has been commented on in management literature in various ways. The structure could

[35] Rensis Likert, "Effective Supervision: A Culturally Relative Process," University of Michigan (Mimeograph), cited in E. E. Jennings, *An Anatomy of Leadership*, New York: Harper & Brothers, Publishers, 1960, p. 176.

[36] Chester I. Barnard, cited in W. H. Newman, *Administrative Action*, Englewood Cliffs, N.J.: Prentice-Hall, Inc., 1951, p. 176.

[37] Chester I. Barnard, *The Functons of the Executive*, p. 169.

[38] J. G. March and H. A. Simon, *Organizations*, New York: John Wiley & Sons, Inc., 1958, p. 93.

be Weber's bureaucracy, or Galbraith's countervailing power, or the concept of private property rights, or the idea of the power elite. Dayton Stoddard, in the novel *Prelude to Night*, presents a "polite circle" of persons who have considerable reciprocal personal influence.[39] He points to a "natural law" to the effect that once one is in the circle that is sufficient and nobody cares how one got there. During one of the political campaigns in the State of Michigan a judge is quoted as saying that "the Party admits no one to the charmed circle unless approved by the high command."[40] Mills makes *The Power Elite* the subject of his book by that name.[41] Mills' elite is not confined to any one particular circle or section of the country, but is a generalization as to how an elite is formed, composed of men whose positions enable them to transcend the ordinary environments of ordinary men and women. The members of the elite occupy positions of positive or potential power, and are members of overlapping and intricately connected circles who "sit on the same terrace," although this might become clear to them only when in mutual defense they come to understand what they have in common and so close their ranks against outsiders.[42]

Hunter, who explored interrelationships among people designated as "top leaders" in the United States found they had relatively close associations with various other members of the group.[43] Hunter speaks of "entry into the circuit — not a tight circle" and of "comers" who others know are being "groomed" and thus will help along even though they personally don't hold them in high esteem.[44] Heuristic executives develop under such circumstances.

At the other extreme is Riesman's "other directed," amorphous leadership, which is no leadership at all and which evokes the rhetorical question, "Is there a ruling class left?"[45] Power in America he says, seems situational and mercurial, resisting attempts to locate it.[46] While Riesman is finding little or no leadership in such organizations as corporations. Hunter is commenting upon the corporate enterprise as the most potent single force on the American scene collectively to control political machinery.[47] But

[39] Dayton Stoddard, *Prelude to Night*, New York: Coward McCann, 1945, p. 287.
[40] *Time* (Latin American Edition), October 24, 1960, p. 15. Detroit Judge W. McKay Skillman is quoted as saying about the Michigan G.O.P. organization in 1951: "The Republican Party admits no one to the charmed circle unless approved by the high command. . . . No little part of Professor (Paul) Bagwell's triumph was that he was able to crash the charmed circle."
[41] C. W. Mills, *The Power Elite*, New York: Oxford University Press, 1957.
[42] *Ibid.*, pp. 3–11, *passim.*
[43] Floyd Hunter, *Top Leadership, U.S.A.*, Chapel Hill: University of North Carolina Press, 1959, p. 259.
[44] *Ibid.*, p. 164.
[45] David Riesman, Reuel Denney and N. Glazer, *The Lonely Crowd*, New Haven, Conn.: Yale University Press, 1950, p. 248.
[46] *Ibid.*, p. 252.
[47] Hunter, *op. cit.*, p. 252.

Hunter also admits that some of his social science colleagues studying top corporate leadership in one city think of it as "gutless" in public policy leadership.[48] Others, of course, have also commented on the seeming lack of identifiable leadership in corporations.[49] Corporate leadership has been described as being like a boy riding his bicycle and shouting with pride, "Look Ma, no hands!" Even Mills, in spite of his concept of the power elite, observes that the men selected for the top positions have many spokesmen, advisers, ghosts, and make-up men who modify their self-conceptions and create their public images as well as shape many of their decisions.[50] "Other-forces" are found here.

The emphasis in depicting executive leadership seems to have swung away from a consideration of the leader as an entity, to a search for significant leader characteristics in situations containing common elements.[51] Where specific personalities are masked by public images, submerged within group elites, and difficult to identify it is understandable that objective "scientists" would prefer to depict their own "model" of an executive leader as he faces a situation. The model might be oversimplified but it allows predictions of decision behavior.

The Model Builders' Men and the Situation

The search for "other-forces" bearing upon the management situation now moves into model builders' territory. This is a populated land, inhabited by beings who have been identified as executives — indeed each has been identified as the essence of *the* executive. This might be called the dream sequence in the search, for these "men" seem "other worldly," peculiarly appropriate in a search for "other forces." The characters are more images than men, abstract, ethereal, individualistic, and not really men at all. They might be thought of as little Frankensteins created by imaginative behavioral and quantitative scientists. But *some* claim that one can understand the American Executive by studying the Zuni Indian, and in the same vein one should not ignore these young fellows as they might grow up to be big Frankensteins who *are* American executives. With the confidence of youth some of these ageless youngsters claim knowledge of the facts in the situations they assume and also are aware of the payoffs. These models have been midwifed by others and described by others, but here it seems appropriate to briefly identify them by characteristics as well as by name.

[48] *Ibid.*

[49] See for example, E. S. Mason, "Have Corporations a Higher Duty Than Profits?" *Fortune*, August, 1960, p. 108.

[50] Mills, *op. cit.*, p. 15.

[51] Robert Tannenbaum and Fred Massarik, "Leadership: A Frame of Reference," *Management Science*, October, 1957, p. 2.

These model men (facing situations) suggest characteristics in the executive without specifically mentioning traits. Emphasis is on motivation rather than traits. They are activists who assume to have certain facts at their disposal and their reactions are sufficiently standardized to form a definite pattern of approach to the situation. Some of theses models have heuristic or opportunistic characteristics implied, depending upon the situation which is assumed to be facing them. Individually they make assumptions as to whether they are facing situations under conditions of certainty, risk, or uncertainty. Most of them know the payoffs and penalties of alternative strategies in advance.

Economic man is a model who has been known by travelers in economics for a long time. He is completely rational. His actions are predictable. If the situation exists on a modern Christmas Eve such that faithful Bob Cratchit's marginal cost has risen above the value of Bob's marginal product, economic man puts Bob out on the street to go home and tell his hungry family he has lost his job. Economic man is an omniscient, rational, ruthless fellow who chooses among well-defined alternatives in such a way as to maximize his profit or utility.

Boulding presents a heroic man who often dominates economic man (and who bears considerable relationship to Weber's charismic leader) who like Alfred Tennyson's six hundred in "The Charge of the Light Brigade" will probably rush in ignoring the costs, penalties or payoffs.[52] He is a counterfoil for the rational models of man such as economic man. It can be argued that the heroic ethic arises and attains power because of the profound uncertainties of life and lack of knowledge of the payoffs. Thus heroic man acts according to his nature and not according to his objective calculations. Without the heroic, man has no meaning; without the economic, he has no sense. On any contest between the heroic and economic the probability in the long run is that economic man would win.[53] Shubik suggests that it is heroic man rather than economic man who starts price wars.[54] He has heuristic characteristics.

March and Simon present a satisficing man who is interested in feasibility and not optimality.[55] The difference between optimizing economic man and satisficing man they say is somewhat like the difference between searching the haystack for the sharpest needle and searching for one to sew with. Satisficing man is sufficiently the realist to realize that the cost of

[52] K. E. Boulding, *The Skills of the Economist*, Cleveland: Howard Allen, Inc., 1958, p. 180. This book was based on lectures given in Rio de Janeiro, Brazil, in August and September, 1953.

[53] *Ibid.*, p. 181.

[54] Martin Shubik, "Studies and Theories of Decision-Making," *Administrative Science Quarterly*, December, 1958, p. 289. Credit for naming some of these model men should probably go to Shubik. See *Business Week*, February 7, 1959, p. 44.

[55] March and Simon, *op. cit.*, p. 141.

search is a factor in determining the optimal alternative. He seeks to improve his profit or payoff not necessarily to maximize it. He has heuristic characteristics.

Von Neumann and Morgenstern present minimax man.[56] Minimax man is a pessimistic individual, usually thinking of himself as the underdog who faces the uncertainty of what strategy a ruthless, aggressive competitor will use against him. Although he is uncertain of his competitor's strategy he knows the payoffs and penalties of each of the strategies which his opponent *can* use. His guide for decision in the situation is based upon opponent capabilities, not opponent intentions. Minimax man plans his own strategy so that no matter which strategy his opponent selects minimax man will minimize his own losses to the extent possible. He evaluates the maximum losses to him of each strategy and selects the strategy which offers the "minimum maximum" loss or minimax loss.[57]

Savage suggests a "minimax regret" man.[58] Minimax regret man is a fifth-cousin to minimax man but he is a Robinson Crusoe-type man who sees his opponent as Nature and not another person. He is a man who, like the woofle-bird, is more concerned with where he has been than where he is going (woofle-birds fly backwards) and knows that in the future he must look backwards with regret if conditions of Nature turn out differently than he predicts. His decision-pattern is to think in terms of payoffs and penalties in *regrets* (which he has the ability to quantify), and select from the strategies available to him in such a way as to minimize the maximum regrets among them. He probably has some heuristic characteristics.

Wald suggests a maximin man.[59] Maximin man is also a Robinson Crusoe-type who sees his opponent as Nature and not another person. If he thought of his opponent as a person rather than nature his opponent might well be minimax man. Maximin man is a pessimist who acts as if Nature (or minimax man) will be malevolent once he himself has selected his strategy. He is the aggressor but he assumes that Nature (or minimax man) will perversely work in such a way as to minimize his payoff. Naturally he evaluates the minimum gains available to him among his various available strategies and selects the strategy with the highest minimum, that is the maximum minimum or maximin.

[56] John von Neumann and Oskar Morgenstern, *Theory of Games and Economic Behavior*, Princeton: 1944.

[57] Unfortunately minimax man finds his choice of strategies becomes more complicated if there doesn't exist an equilibrium pair, that is a combination payoff-penalty to which minimax and maximin equate so the game is a two-person zero-sum game. See for example R. D. Luce and Howard Raiffa, *Games and Decisions*, New York: John Wiley & Sons, Inc., 1957, p. 66ff.

[58] L. G. Savage, *The Foundations of Statistics*, New York: John Wiley & Sons, Inc., 1954, p. 30.

[59] Abraham Wald, *Statistical Decision Functions*, New York: John Wiley & Sons, Inc., 1950.

Hurwicz suggests a more optimistic man.[60] Optimistic man sees his opponent as Nature, but asks, "Why must Nature always be considered perverse?" Optimistic man is a gambler who asks, "Why not look at the best state of Nature, or at a weighted combination of best and worst?" Optimistic man uses a coefficient of optimism to weight his various payoffs and penalties depending upon how probable he thinks the state of Nature associated with each of them will be.[61] If optimistic man is the complete optimist (giving his largest payoff a coefficient of optimism of 1.00) he is maximax man. His decision-pattern is to evaluate the maximum gain associated with each of his possible strategies and to choose the maximum among them, that is the maximum maximum or maximax. He, too, seems to have heuristic characteristics.

The Laplace probability man (equal probability man), like the economic man, is an older fellow who has been around for a long time. He argues that since he doesn't know the probabilities associated with the various ways in which nature will work against his various strategies he will equate the probabilities. For example, probability of "success" and "failure" as the two states of nature (say) are equated. He argues that if there is insufficient reason for a thing to happen it won't happen.[62] He uses the number of states of nature as the denominator to divide the total of the payoffs associated with each strategy. If "success" is $(+)$ and "failure" $(-)$, and if Strategy #1 offers $(+10 -6)$ while Strategy #2 offers $(+5 -3)$, or totals of $(+4)$ and $(+2)$ respectively, he would divide each by two to get $(+2)$ and $(+1)$ respectively, and choose Strategy #1. His decision-pattern is to evaluate the greatest final figure among the totals of the various strategies and pick the strategy with the greatest total, for in the long run this strategy would give him the greatest cumulative payoff. He probably uses the heuristic process in convincing himself that probabilities are equal.

The probabilistic man is a cousin to the LaPlace man. He is a more knowledgeable man than his cousin, however, for he knows the probabilities of the various ways in which Nature will work against his various

[60] Leonid Hurwicz, "Optimality Criteria for Decision Making Under Ignorance," Cowles Commission Discussion Papers, Statistics, No. 370, 1951 (mimeographed), cited in Luce and Raiffa, op. cit. (Note 57), p. 282.

[61] D. W. Miller and M. K. Starr, Executive Decisions and Operations Research, Englewood Cliffs, N.J.: Prentice-Hall, Inc., 1960, p. 69. He would use a coefficient of optimism ranging from 1.00 (completely optimistic) to 0 (completely pessimistic) to weight the respective outcomes or payoffs, using the von Neumann-Morgenstern standard gamble technique.

[62] This proposition is just the reverse of "Murphy's Law: What can happen will happen." (See for example, "The Astronauts, How Long on Earth?" Newsweek, No. 7, 1960, p. 84). Miller and Starr (op. cit., p. 91) tell of one of the best-known arguments of the Middle Ages based upon the principle of equal probability or insufficient reason: Jean Buriden in the first half of the 14th Century invented an ass — Buriden's Ass — which when placed exactly between two identical piles of hay starved to death, having insufficient reason to choose one pile over the other.

strategies. He faces a situation of known risks rather than uncertainties. Whereas the economic man faces a situation of certainty and the other men face a situation of uncertainty, probabilistic man claims knowledge of statistical probabilities associated with the various payoffs and penalties. His criterion for decision is to weight the individual payoffs or penalties of each strategy with the probability that the particular state of Nature will prevail and to select the highest total payoff for the various strategies.

The reader may note that the population of the world is increasing. To the many types of executive leaders described through the use of traits, each varying from the other, add the executive leaders created by innumerable types of situations. To the groups of leaders who make up the charmed circle or circuit — the "power elite" — are added the innumerable "other directed," "position holding" and "executive image" leaders. And to economic man and equal probability man are added a host of other fellows like minimax man and maximin man. A thorough census would uncover many others such as commonsense man and case-study man in the backlands, special types like *homo telephonicus* in the telephone companies, "Murphy's man" (what *can* happen *will* happen) in the engineering laboratories and so on. They each face situations and each make decisions, rationalizing them in various ways. In Appendix A the writer analyzes briefly how each of the more "rational" men would decide in a specific instance. But there is one more type managerial man to add to this gallery of characters.

Opportunistic Man (or Heuristic Man) and the Situation

Malthusian malnutrition has not cut down the population of model men. Another man is discovered on the border of the model builders' territory. He is opportunistic or heuristic man. Opportunistic man is a mixture of inconsistencies, a child of fortune, but with considerable ability to guide his own destiny. He has in him some of the non-rational elements of heroic man as he faces uncertainty and makes decisions largely by the heuristic process. He demonstrates some of economic man's sense and satisficing man's willingness to accept feasibility as a criterion for action. By chance (or persuasion of an occult sort) he picks the right family to be born into, or possibly marry into. By the heuristic process he possibly picks the right company or the right division of the company and the right time to be there (he can guide his own destiny to a large extent). When the tides are running against him he might end up as the poor cousin or unfortunate one. In fact, opportunistic man might be thought of as subject to Dr. Jekyll-Mr. Hyde changes in fate due to chameleonic changes in the situation. But he is not just a "lucky" or "unlucky" fellow. He is a heuristic fellow.

Opportunistic man might be found as the son who shows particular genius in using the heuristic process to improve the profit picture of his company by closing the division in which his father showed so much wisdom earlier in opening. As a poor cousin he might be one of the division executives who is being pruned as "deadwood" because of his loyalty to his father's earlier insistence that this division follow conservatism on plant and product improvement to insure the company's profit picture under the earlier wise conservative management. He was heuristic in accepting the leadership of the father even when he might have gone with a more progressive company at one time at a higher salary because he was so successful in following the conservative policy in earlier days. Opportunistic man finds the heuristic process sometimes fails after he has been persuaded that decisions were successful. One wonders how many situations occur in business where men who by chance are in top management, after a situation deteriorates, use the heuristic process to conclude that lower management was at fault. As top management, they might get credit for wise decisions.[63] The heuristic process is often successful.

Opportunistic man through heuristic decisions can end up in awkward situations. For example, having proved his executive ability and become vice-president of the country's largest electric equipment manufacturing company he might participate in an industry-wide price-fixing conspiracy involving twenty-nine of the largest electrical equipment companies just at the time the Government "cracks down" — and so gets sentenced to be put "behind bars with common criminals who have been convicted of embezzlement and other serious crimes."[64] Here is heuristic man at work under the pressure of great "other forces" from within and outside his company. This man at another time and another place and with different people might be honored for working to achieve price stability in his industry and protecting the welfare of his company. But heuristic man is also "naïve top management" (higher than the vice-presidential level) who deliberately broke "Directive Policy 20.5" (insisting upon strict obedience to the anti-trust laws), and further declares that sympathy for the arrest is misplaced.[65] He also is employing a heuristic process in the face of a rapidly changing situation caused by great "other-forces" that have their effect on him and on the situation. At the same time one of the

---

[63] A somewhat different situation, but involving "new management" is recorded in the following quotation from "U.S. Rubber Moves Ahead," *Business Week*, October 23, 1960, p. 104: "The most dramatic change is the speed with which decisions are made. In an important test of quick action the new management decided at the beginning of the '57–'58 recession to close down the company's old Ft. Wayne plant . . . under the old committee its demise could only have come through rather long wrangling and perhaps needless compromise."

[64] "The Big Conspiracy," *Time* (Latin American Edition), February 17, 1961, p. 62.

[65] *Ibid.*, p. 63.

"nonconformist" executives has his personal lawyers plead that he is an "organization man" who broke the law to keep his job — he would have been fired otherwise.[66] His allusion is to W. H. Whyte's *The Organization Man* and its thesis that men in organizations must be conformists. His plea itself is a heuristic process.

Opportunistic Man Creates Situations — Cases

With ability to guide his own destiny within broad limits and subject to happenstance and non-measurable surprise, opportunistic man creates situations by heuristic processes. Perhaps he is the president of the third largest auto manufacturer in the U.S., who after 27 years with the company is appointed to the presidency of the company only to be summarily fired one month after his appointment due to a conflict of interest (being major owner in one of the company's suppliers).[67] Or perhaps he is the president of the second largest insurance company in the U.S. who is criticized by his company's directors for a personal deal with a client company which involved large tax savings for him and might well be construed to be a conflict of interest, so he faces a situation in which he prefers to resign.[68] These men are good executives. They are heuristic men also. And they are subject to many strong "other-forces" which change the situations they create.

Opportunistic man might protect his own interest by securing a change in stock-option prices to lower prices when the market price of the company's stock *declines* under his stewardship.[69] Or he might be the president of a large company who arranges personal deals involving company funds just before the directors arrange to sell the company to an outside interest which subsequently liquidates the company.[70] These cases illustrate situations created by opportunistic men employing the heuristic process.

[66] "Anti-trust Defendants Quit," *Business Week*, December 3, 1960, p. 34.

[67] See "Behind the Conflict at Chrysler," *Fortune*, November, 1960, p. 132. For additional information: "Waiting for Chrysler to Drop the Other Shoe," *Business Week*, August 6, 1960, p. 22; "Chrysler Searches for a Clean Bill," *Business Week*, August 27, 1960, p. 30; "Chrysler Is Found Not Guilty," *Business Week*, October 8, 1960, p. 32; "Newberg Attacks Chrysler," *Time* (Latin American Edition), January 28, 1961, p. 51; "Chrysler's Troubles Cont'd, *Time* (Latin American Edition), February 3, 1961, p. 51.

[68] See "Man in a Glass House," *Time* (Latin American Edition), August 29, 1960, p. 50; "Toward Freer Circles," *Time* (Latin American Edition), January 2, 1961, p. 47; "Prudential's Choice," *Time* (Latin American Edition), January 20, 1961, p. 51.

[69] *State Journal* (Lansing, Michigan), April 6, 1960, p. 19. Directors who would benefit from change cancelled old officer's options to buy stock at prices currently above the declining market price and re-issue options at a much lower price, below current market price.

[70] See Solomon Barkin, "The Functions of Management," *Business Topics*, Winter, 1960, p. 33.

Failure and Success Amidst Opportunities

Opportunities might lead to success but offer no guarantee that they will. Barnet says that the average length of life of a corporation is short, only seven years.[71] Hutchinson and Newcomer say that the few empirical studies of business failures show a large death rate among firms requiring low capitalization.[72] The *Survey of Current Business* monthly report of business failures continues to average about 1,000 per month in very round figures.[73] Risk of failure is definitely present in the business situation, particularly for small enterprises trying to launch a new product or service. Poor product acceptance is one risk which new business must always face.

The large corporation helps to provide insurance against poor product acceptance. Galbraith points out that no large U.S. corporation which is also large in its industry has failed or been seriously in danger of insolvency in many years and that the large corporation has provided a retreat from risk.[74] He also says that nothing would be more damaging to the executive reputation in companies like General Motors or General Electric than to launch a product without testing the market.[75] The situation is not always that simple. Non-measurable potential surprise caused by "other-forces" often enter the situation to confound the expectations.

The situation at Ford relating to the launching and subsequent elimination of the Edsel car might be thought of as a case of insufficient market research (by hindsight) or it might be a failure registered through the heuristic process. Fortunately it didn't seem to damage the reputation of Ford top managers; although there was the usual turn-over in the lower echelons. This case does illustrate an opportunistic company which was in a position to launch an Edsel and discontinue it shortly afterwards without jeopardizing the whole life of the company. Henry Ford II was in a position decisively to influence the expenditure of a quarter of a billion dollars to develop the Edsel car.[76] He was opportunistic and his decision was heuristic. He was in the position to influence its discontinuance two or three years later.[77]

---

[71] E. M. Barnet, "Management in Perspective: The Problem of Executive Manpower Insolvency," *The Journal of the Academy of Management*, December, 1960, p. 197.

[72] A. R. Hutchinson and Mabel Newcomer, "A Study of Business Mortality," *American Economic Review*, June, 1958, p. 497.

[73] For example, *Survey of Current Business*, December, 1960, Table S-5 shows business failures per month in 1960, January through October ranged from 1,181 to 1,370 (mostly in retail trade). In other years business failures have ranged below and above 1,000 per month. These figures represent only business failures which have been formally recorded in some official way.

[74] J. K. Galbraith, *The Affluent Society*, Boston: Houghton Mifflin Co., 1958, p. 103.

[75] *Ibid.*

[76] "How Edsel Lured Those Dealers," *Fortune*, September, 1957, p. 145.

[77] "Detroit is Flying by the Seat of Its Pants," *Fortune*, January, 1961, p. 145.

One would think that Ford Motor Company executives with know-how, experience, preparation and status power in the industry could successfully establish a new product which they were persuaded was needed in their line. But powerful "other-forces" can buffet even a Ford Company. Henry Ford II applied the "law of the situation" and Edsel is gone. "Joe Smith" in the Edsel Division facing the same general situation of the failure of the Edsel car that faced Henry Ford II, might have to find another job. Both were heuristic men in entering the Edsel venture. Both were buffeted by "other-forces." But the situation is not always so grim. Perhaps good "other-forces" also were at work so that Joe Smith got a better job. Henry Ford II was in a status position of some security and was able to turn his attention to other matters such as the authorization of an expenditure of $363 million for the stock in private hands (to the dismay of some Britons) in order completely to own Ford's British subsidiary.[78] If it hadn't been the Ford Motor Company there might not have been $363 millions left after the Edsel venture. Financial strength and status power are "other-forces" in situations which continue to change. These are the kind of "other-forces" which provide the "retreat from risk" mentioned by Galbraith and which are found in large corporations.

Birth and Death, Opportunity and the Situation

The march of history is proof that opportunistic man can benefit from birth. Studies of social mobility show that persons with less propitious starts in life have more chance in modern American corporate life to rise to the top in recent years than they had in past years. Taussig and Joslyn's study in 1932 led them to state that there was evidence that the representation of the "big business class" among business leaders was tending to increase as time goes by.[79] Newcomer concluded that her study (1955) doesn't seem to substantiate this thesis, as there was a slight decline in the 1950 group of leaders whose fathers were head of the same corporation (from 13.4% in 1925 to 11.6% in 1950).[80] Warner and Abegglen's study

[78] See "Ford Offer Stirs British Ire," *Business Week*, November 19, 1960, p. 50. "Ford Furor," *Time* (Latin American Edition), November 20, 1960, p. 50. The announcement was timed badly for the public relations of the Ford Company as it came just at the time that President Eisenhower had issued orders to conserve $500 million dollars to help stop the gold flow from the country by ordering servicemen's families home from Europe (See "Is the U.S. Dollar in Danger?", *Newsweek*, December 6, 1960, p. 49, and Servicemen — The Big Pullback," *Newsweek*, November 26, 1960, p. 17).

[79] F. W. Taussig and C. S. Joslyn, *American Business Leaders*, New York: Macmillan Company, 1932, p. 97.

[80] Mabel Newcomer, *The Big Business Executive, 1900–1950*, New York: Columbia University Press, 1955, p. 56. Newcomer's mode of question might not follow influence through corporate reorganizations and changes in corporate names. An interesting illustration of how a person might become chief executive of a company through influence

of social mobility in top management showed that top management had a greater percentage of leadership coming from lower level occupations and social classes than it did in the earlier (Taussig and Joslyn) study.[81] These studies are encouraging for those starting recently from less propitious circumstances of birth, but nothing in them indicates that it *hurts* a man's chances of becoming a business leader just because his father was head of the corporation or held controlling interests in other corporations.

An executive can have opportunity thrust upon him due to death. The death of a superior might be the key to advancement of a subordinate. On the other hand it can result in the promising subordinate leaving the company. An interesting example is the case of the company which lost its top executive through death, brought in a man from the outside, and lost the promising subordinate to a competitor. A short time after his appointment as president the new man was killed in a plane crash and the company was left with a distressing vacuum at the top. The decision that the company had made resulted in its losing a good man who might have made a good president, for the short tenure in office of a man with an excellent reputation, followed by chaos. The death of one executive led to one man seeking his opportunity in another company. The death of a second executive led to opportunity for yet another executive not mentioned above. Death of executives might well be one of the elements that Sir Noel F. Hall was commenting on when he said: "What is missing in the general theory of (objective quantitative) inquiry is a theory whose domain is the no-man's land between numerical probability and non-ordered, non-measurable, potential surprise — "[82]

How many times has thrombosis changed the situation and changed the leadership, giving another man the reins of leadership to face an uncertain situation while his colleagues, later known as lesser colleagues, continue to walk in lock-step behind other men whose longevity seems limitless. This is an example of a nebulous "other force" which enters the situation to help or to hinder the heuristic executive in his career.

---

which might not show in a formal questionnaire is that of William Wood Prince, born William Wood and adopted by friend and distant cousin Frederick Henry Prince who promised to give him eventual controlling voice in the Prince trust, now worth $150 million and stewardship over 5% of Armour & Company Stock, the biggest block. When he came into control he authorized the expenditure of millions of dollars to modernize Armour, shut down five huge unprofitable plants and chopped capacity by 20% (See for example, "Armour's Star, William Wood Prince," *Time* (Latin American Edition), March 3, 1961, p. 50.

[81] W. L. Warner and J. C. Abegglen, "Executive Careers Today: Who Gets to the Top," *The Management Review*, February, 1956, p. 83. See also W. L. Warner and J. C. Abegglen, *Occupational Mobility in American Business and Industry*, Minneapolis: University of Minnesota Press, 1955; or Warner and Abegglen, *Big Business Leaders in America*, New York: Harper & Brothers, Publishers, 1955.

[82] N. F. Hall, *The Making of Higher Executives: The Modern Challenges*, New York: New York University, 1958, p. 10.

Back to the Law of the Situation

The route of search returns to the "law of the situation." From a different vantage point and due to changes in perspective along the way the old principle is seen in a modified form. The nebulous "other-forces" are not precisely identified but they can be recognized in a general way as surrounding the principle, some of them being: happenstance, non-measurable surprise, status power, fate, uncertainty, death, and the like. Their existence makes it difficult to bring in collected and quantified facts.

The "other-forces" also made it difficult to create a simple model of an executive. Even if an executive were to know the "traits" that he should possess, furthermore, the chances would be considerable that he would not possess them and possibly could not acquire them. Or given the "objective facts" of the situation and the various strategies available to him, the various conditions of nature or competitor's strategies which might be used against him, it is possible that he could not evaluate payoffs and penalties associated with each or arrange them in an orderly matrix which would help him to objectively maximize or satisfice his gains. And non-ordered, non-measurable, potential surprise can envelope the situation and change it greatly.

But perhaps it is the subjective element that is made clearer by this search. The practicing executive finds much of his environment and many of the situations created by heuristic executives as well as "other-forces." The *observer effect* known as the *Heisenberg uncertainty principle* (coming from quantum physics) might sum up briefly this subjective element. This is the idea that observer and subject are bound together in a mutual relationship so that the model tends to be in the observer's mind and he cannot observe without changing the phenomenon. The executive is bound to the situation in much the same way.[83]

The conclusion is that most men are more heuristic, or opportunistic, in their make-up than has been suggested in management literature, and that "the situation" is modified by the "other forces" outside the executive and the heuristic process within the executive. These are additional "facts" which should be recognized — and faced — in applying the principle known as the "law of the situation."

Appendix A

The rational men identified have different viewpoints on strategy based upon the criteria they use. What should the criterion be by which to judge

[83] The idea is not unlike but not the same as *perception* and *projection* as these terms are used in psychology.

success or failure of a strategy? How should payoff be measured? A perennial difficulty in modelmaking of the analytical type is the illness which might well be known as "criterion trouble."[84] The struggle to evaluate utility is not a new phenomenon — Jeremy Bentham, for example, attempted to develop a "calculus of pleasure and pain" and to apply scientific measurements to the concept.[85] Bernoulli assumed money might be used in an approximation of utility by using the logarithm of the number of money units as a measure of utility.[86] Utility is an important concept in rational decision-making in game theory because preferences must be quantified to make game theory operative, particularly under conditions of risk.[87]

Table 29.1

Battle of Bismark Sea: Matrix of Conditions, Strategies and Payoffs

	Condition 1[a]	Condition 2[b]	Minimum	Maximum	Total	.50–.50 Average
Kenney's strategies:						
Northern Route	2	2	2[c]	2	4	2
Southern Route	1	3	1	3[d]	4	2
Japanese strategies:						
Minimum	−1	−2				
Maximum	−2[e]	−3				
Total	−3	−5				
.50–.50	−1.5[f]	−2.5				

[a] Japanese take Northern Route.
[b] Japanese take Southern Route.
[c] Kenney's *Maximin* (Maximum-Minimum).
[d] Kenney's *Maximax* (Maximum-Maximum).
[e] Japanese *Minimax* (Minimum-Maximum).
[f] Japanese *Equal* Probability Minimum Penalty.

[84] J. D. Williams, *The Compleat Strategyst*, New York: McGraw-Hill Book Co., Inc., 1954, p. 23. Williams points out that rough criteria are sometimes sufficient . . . . It is well known in the Military Establishment, for instance, that a lot of ground can be covered in shoes that do not fit perfectly (cf., Anshen, notes 4 & 5).

[85] See P. C. Newman, *The Development of Economic Thought*, Englewood Cliffs, N.J.: Prentice-Hall, Inc., 1952, p. 59.

[86] Miller and Starr, *op. cit.*, p. 57.

[87] Luce and Raiffa, *op. cit.*, Chapter 2, "Utility Theory."

The situation used here to contrast the strategies which would be selected by the various rational men is one which occurred during the battle of the Bismark Sea.[88] During the struggle for New Guinea the intelligence reports stated that the Japanese planned to move a troop and

Table 29.2

Battle of Bismark Sea: Choice of Strategies of Various Men

Man — Model	Side	Decision	Payoff or Penalty	Note
Minimax	Japanese	Northern Route	−2	Minimizes the maximum penalty to be paid for each of the conditions
Maximin	Kenney's	Northern Route	+2	Maximizes the minimum payoff to be secured for each of the strategies
Maximax	Kenney's	Southern Route	+3	Completely optimistic about the conditions which will result
Equal Probability	Japanese	Northern Route	−1.5	In long run if "game" were repeated time and time again average penalty would be less
Equal Probability	Kenney's	Either	+2	In long run average payoffs would be equal. See Footnote #62 (Buriden's Ass)
Minimax Regret	Japanese	Northern Route	(2)	In *days*. If Kenney went North, Japanese could not reduce penalty. *If* Kenney went South and Japanese went South, Japanese would regret they hadn't chosen North and saved 2 days of bombing

Note: Those who are acquainted with two-person zero-sum games with equilibrium point will note there is one equilibrium point, Northern route-Northern route with penalty-payoff of 2 days of bombing. These were the choices that were made in the actual battle and the Japanese suffered a disastrous defeat. According to game theory both commanders made the correct decision. The reader might conjecture about the decisions the other men might make: Satisficing man (Southern Route with one day payoff)? Opportunistic man (Southern Route, perhaps luck would give him a three day payoff)? Heroic man (might rush right into New Britain)? Etc.?

[88] Described in more detail in O. G. Haywood, Jr., "Military Decision and Game Theory" *Journal of the Operations Research Society of America*, Spring, 1954, p. 365; cited in Luce and Raiffa, *op. cit.*, p. 64. I have added modifications such as substituting "condition" for "Japanese Strategy" so that I could add the decisions of other "men" than Maximin and Minimax, for the other "men" presumably face Nature, not a strategy-selecting opponent. For those interested in policy pronouncements Haywood states that the doctrine of decision of the armed forces of the U.S. is a doctrine based on enemy capabilities (not intentions) (p. 366).

supply convoy from New Britain to New Guinea. The Japanese had a choice of taking a northern route or a southern route. General Kenney and his staff had to make a choice as to whether he should concentrate his reconnaissance aircraft on one route or the other. Once the convoy was sighted the convoy could be bombed until it arrived at New Guinea. The utility or payoff for Kenney and his staff was stated in days of bombing time. For the Japanese the disutility or penalty would be days of bombing time identified with a minus sign.

The matrix of strategies, conditions, and payoffs is shown in Table 29.1. The author's idea of how the various men would choose their respective strategies is shown in Table 29.2.

30

Logical Analysis and Executive Performance*

M. C. Branch

Thompson Ramo Wooldridge Inc., Canoga Park, California

Increasingly complex demands upon the business executive force upon him increasingly complex problems of analysis and decision. Evaluations employing computers, quantitative methods, statistics and other scientific methodologies are also increasing, but are limited in their application by the executive's ability to understand the reasoning, methodology, and subjective judgments under the highly analyzed information reaching him when he needs to make a decision. The author argues that logical analysis is a powerful tool of subjective judgment, capable of making it possible to employ fully the intelligence capabilities of the human mind.

The functions of the executive can be grouped into two general categories. One involves action duties performed through personal contact or communication: leadership, initiation, decision, direction, control, motivation, guidance, inspection, or representation. This operational activity may relate to production, sales, corporate-legal affairs, personnel, public relations, facilities, or any one of a dozen areas of executive concern. The other encompasses responsibilities of an analytical nature requiring careful study: for example, determination of long-range objectives, corporate organization, financial structure and tactics, new product research, or competitive strategies.

Of course, these two categories of activity are by no means mutually exclusive and may be directed toward the same general purposes, but the

* Taken and adapted from *The Journal of the Academy of Management*, vol. 4, no. 1, April, 1961, pp. 27–31.

first emphasizes action, the second analytical thought. One requires the executive to "get up and go" or otherwise act quickly; the other calls for him to "sit down and think" constructively, so he can formulate or approve a solution to a difficult problem, a fundamental policy or strategy, or a longer-range plan for the business. One is extrovertive and more immediate in its emphasis, the other introvertive and longer-range.[1]

Analysis and Executive Performance

The analytical responsibilities of management become more crucial as business and the socio-economic contexts within which it operates becomes organizationally and technically more complex. Many matters which in times past were appraised quite easily, now require extensive analysis. Witness the enormous increase in tax and other data for various governmental purposes incorporated by business in its operational reporting and influencing most corporate decisions. And as the different aspects of business become more interdependent, maintaining an integrated picture of the company as a whole becomes more difficult, and subject to interpretation, judgment, intent, and statistical subtlety.

New analytical mechanisms are being applied and developed in business. Even today, some executives are called upon to decide between strategies of acquisition expressed in matrix form, choose among different inventory policies derived by linear programming, adopt sales projections developed from multiple-probability assumptions, determine the practical significance of the results of the psychological interview of several executive candidates, or approve research expenditures toward a new product recommended because of estimates of the state of a technical art and scientific sampling of opinion. This type of evaluation employing quantification, mathematics, statistics, and scientific method will be more prevalent in the future.[2]

It is possible to present only the final factual results or conclusions of analysis to the executive for review and decision. But if he does not under-

[1] Improvements in analytical method and its increasing application to business affairs are clearly evident in the recent literature. E.g., among the publications of the American Management Association are Felix E. Larkin, "Long-Range Planning at W. R. Grace and Co.," *Management Report No. 3*, 1958, pp. 54–60; Paul V. Manning, "Long Range Planning for Product Research," *Research and Development Series No. 4*, 1957, pp. 54–57; and "Return on Investment — Tool of Modern Management," *Improved Tools of Financial Management*, 1956. See also H. I. Ansoff, "Strategies for Diversification," *Harvard Business Review*, Vol. 35, No. 5, September–October 1957, pp. 113–124.

[2] Cf. Franklin A. Lindsay, *New Techniques for Management Decision Making*, New York (McGraw-Hill Consultant Reports on Current Business Problems), 1958; A. Charnes and W. W. Cooper, "Management Models and Industrial Applications of Linear Programming." *Management Science*, vol. 4, no. 1, October, 1957, p. 38–91.

stand in general the reasoning, methodology, and judgments underlying these results which reach his desk in highly distilled form, he cannot make an intelligent decision. Unless he has sufficient background knowledge to appraise the material critically by asking appropriate questions, he cannot test its accuracy or inclusiveness, request corrections, or suggest constructive improvement. Without this minimum comprehension, he is in effect making decisions half blindly. For him to delegate all analytical decisions to others would, of course, constitute a serious abrogation of his basic responsibility.

At the present time, scientific method can only be applied piecemeal in corporate planning. There are many elements of the business at this level which cannot be quantified reliably, such as employee morale, the success of public relations, most legal situations, or the value of research and development. Even in financial accounting and analysis, with its relatively high degree of quantification attained over the years, there are many aspects as subject to interpretation and subjective judgment as they are to precise calculation. For example, the return on investment of money spent for staff and other indirectly supportive activities cannot be determined with anything approaching the accuracy possible for the direct inputs-outputs of manufacturing.

Although conducted differently by different professional personnel, the diverse elements of a business comprise a single corporate entity or system. A method of comparative measurement which would overcome some of the well-known limitations of the monetary unit (the dollar) would permit a level of analysis now impossible. Since a business organism is constantly changing, a primary value of all analysis is as a basis for projection; even the closing of last year's books is as useful for what it suggests for the future as the legal-operating record it provides. But our methods of applying scientific method to business projections are quite limited. Techniques are needed for coping with constant and unequal change, for determining over-all or composite probabilities.

Because of such limitations, many of the most vital corporate concerns are decided mainly on the basis of subjective judgment and analysis. For some time to come, it will not be possible or practical to calculate numerically the optimum course of action for such important matters as choice among investment alternatives, long-range strategy of diversification, program of research expenditures, improved personnel policies, or the initiation of foreign operations.[3]

---

[3] Cf. Ernest H. Weinwurm, "Limitations of the Scientific Method in Management Science," *Management Science*, vol. 3, no. 3, April 1957, pp. 225–233; Peter F. Drucker, "Management Science and the Manager," *ibid.*, vol. 1, no. 2, January, 1955, pp. 115–126; and *Operations Research Reconsidered — Some Frontiers and Boundaries of Industrial OR*, American Management Association Report No. 10, 1958, 143 pp.

Intuition and Subjective Appraisal

The time-honored methods of subjective appraisal rely on personal experience. To an extent varying widely with the individual and business situation, the executive may perform his own analytical examination and calculation in reaching his conclusions. More often, he depends on intuitive reaction and discernment. If presented with several alternatives, he is more likely to choose one of these specific recommendations than perceive or develop a synthesis solution perhaps preferable from his vantage point to any of the choices submitted. He may consider he does not have the time to resolve the problem himself, believe this can and will be done by others, or is disinclined to spend the time and effort required if he is constitutionally more oriented toward action than analysis. In any event, unless he accepts without question facts, figures, and conclusions as presented to him, he must make some form of quick analytical check for approximate accuracy and content.

Some executives prefer to manufacture logical reasons in an attempt to underpin the intuitive judgment which alone can produce a decision when there is nothing sufficiently definite to analyze meaningfully, or when there is not enough time for conclusive study. And yet, because the greater portion of the mind exists below the surface of immediate consciousness, intuition is far from chance. What is actually occurring is an unconscious or semiconscious utilization of a large mental reservoir which cannot be directly or deliberately tapped; but this accumulation of "forgotten" experiences, conclusions, facts, figures, and impressions absorbed throughout the years is applied nevertheless through intuition. Furthermore, the unconscious mind performs a high degree of effective synthesis between different or conflicting experiences.

The practical value of this intuitive judgment depends on the condition of what might be called the circuitry of the unconscious mind. Significantly crossed emotional wires can short-circuit the mental "computer" in its process of intuitive resolution, and produce a false or uniformly biased answer — not necessarily from the personal point of view of the individual who thinks and acts as he does for some compelling reason, but because judgments in the best interest of an institution require as much objectivity as possible. For most businessmen, the condition of his intuitive circuitry is best evaluated by the *post facto* batting average of the sound conclusions it produces and by comparison with other intuitive minds of proven capability. Unfortunately, it is difficult for most of us to admit or even recognize a low batting average in this respect and limit or check our intuitive judgments accordingly.[4]

4 See Melville C. Branch, Jr., "Psychological Factors in Business Planning," *Journal of the American Institute of Planners,* vol. XXII, no. 3, Summer 1956, pp. 174;

Analytical Limitations of the Human Mind

Although the human mind is a remarkable organism with impressive capabilities, it performs some mental functions less well than others. These relate to what may be described briefly as: scan, correlation, and abstraction.

Most persons do not consciously scan a situation in all important aspects to identify its many different elements and considerations. The frequent assumption that this awareness is widespread ignores our innate tendency to focus on those aspects with which we are most familiar through experience and professional concentration, or toward which we are oriented by our mental-emotional personalities.[5] For most people, the comprehensive view requires deliberate effort or special stimulation. We are also limited in the number of successive correlations we can follow without becoming lost. For example, deriving the outcome of a succession of many different conditional interrelationships is impossible without mathematical knowledge. Confronted with a relatively simple sequence, such as, if $A \leqq B$, $C \geq A$, $D > B$, and $C < D$, most of us cannot readily derive the relation between A and D. In general, we can retain only a very few elements simultaneously in our minds, resolve their respective interrelationships, and determine their combined effect.[6] The average person is also limited in his capability to comprehend and manipulate abstractions. Our inherent preference is for real-life, concrete images rooted in the vast unconscious storage of experiences we have observed directly. In contrast, a characteristic of analytical method is its dependence on abstraction. Unfortunately, the analytical appraisal increasingly essential in executive business decisions involves these very mental activities we perform less effectively.

In time, our capacity to scan, correlate, and deal with abstractions may improve with educational advances, the effects of our ever-changing environment, and continued evolutionary development of the human mind itself. We know how readily children absorb new concepts with which their parents have great difficulty. It is possible that entirely new methods of conceptualization and analysis may be found which will extend those

---

Eugene Raudsepp, "Can You Trust Your Hunches — The Role of Intuition in Executive Decision-Making," *Management Review*, vol. XLIX, no. 4, American Management Association, April 1960, pp. 4–9, 73–76.

[5] Insights into the relationship between individual psychology, career selection, and professional performance are provided by Lawrence S. Kubie, M.D., in "Some Unsolved Problems of the Scientific Career," *American Scientist*, vol. 41, no. 4, October, 1953, pp. 596–613.

[6] E.g. George A. Miller, "The Magical Number Seven, Plus or Minus Two: Some Limits on Our Capacity for Processing Information," *The Psychological Review*, vol. 63, no. 2, March 1956, pp. 81–97.

areas in which we are now cogitatively relatively weak. But since we can hardly wait for evolution or an uncertain intellectual breakthrough, we must rely at least for some time to come on those aids to our mental functioning now available; and perhaps it is the more efficient utilization of these which will likely trigger some significant methodological advance.

In our current fascination with the electronic computer, we may be neglecting to employ fully the capabilities of the most impressive cognitive device of all — the intelligent human mental-nervous system. Coupled with intuition, logical analysis is a powerful tool of subjective judgment.[7]

---

[7] In an invited presentation before the Institute of Management Science's College of Planning, at Los Angeles, California on September 12, 1960, the author elaborated upon the prerequisites to logical analysis and discussed some means and methods that might be employed as an aid to logical reasoning. The article above is an excerpt from this presentation.

31

Not By Loyalty Alone*

William R. Gall

Mead Johnson Institute

Taking a rigorous look at loyalty in its various forms and settings, this article examines a number of implications and problems of the demand for loyalty in a business organization. The author finds the best expression of loyalty to be that of integrity of purpose exhibited by the organization's members. Loyalty alone cannot assure success.

During the early stages of his career as a promising industrial executive, Willis Wayde grappled with the temptation to advance his personal interests at the expense of being loyal to his employer. This fictional character of John P. Marquand's novel was frustrated (momentarily) by the perplexity of it all: "Loyalty was the damndest thing. It was something that kept cropping up in business at eccentric intervals, and it kept requiring a definite definition."[1]

This same thought must plague every executive in industry today. Quite often the decisions which must be made to achieve the objectives of the corporation do not necessarily advance the immediate interests of all the people affected; in such instances, conflicts of loyalty are inevitable and the facts of the matter are often forgotten in favor of "expediency" — in satisfying immediate needs rather than taking the long range viewpoint.

Traditional Loyalty

Loyalty is considered so important in the corporate world that it is one of the most frequently mentioned characteristics essential to the success of an organization. When executives list the qualities they look for in evaluating

---

* Taken and adapted from *The Journal of the Academy of Management*, vol. 5, no. 2, August, 1962, pp. 117–123.
[1] John P. Marquand, *Sincerely, Willis Wayde*, p. 193.

managerial candidates, loyalty is usually included as a requirement. Republic Steel Corporation, for example, lists "a spirit of loyalty" as one of the nine qualifications they seek in young men they hire.[2] Loyalty is one of six standards of conduct considered as important, by one prominent executive, to the success of a company as its clearly defined standards of manufacturing, sales operations, or inventory control.[3] The need for loyalty is, in fact, usually implied in the conditions set forth as prerequisites to achieve the objectives of an organization. Yet, recent evidence indicates that loyalty in business suffers some specific shortcomings.

Josiah Royce, famous professor of philosophy at Harvard University, said that there are two kinds of loyalty.

> One is a devotion to great causes. The patriot who bravely dies for his country exemplifies this kind of loyalty. The other kind isn't so exciting, yet takes a lot of character to see it through. In a way it is more important. The hundreds of faithful duties we must do every day are eloquent examples of — shall we call it pedestrian? — loyalty. It makes the world go around. It's the lifeblood of teamwork. Such loyalty includes duty, promptness, keeping one's promises, steadfastness in adversity, humbleness of spirit.[4]

The history of mankind is interwoven with innumerable examples of the former kind of loyalty — the devotion to great causes. Judas, Arnold, and Rosenberg are names which are synonymous with the term "traitor" and are historically significant because of their acts of disloyalty during critical eras of our history. This type of loyalty — devotion to great causes — is vividly portrayed in Theodore Plievier's book, *Stalingrad*, which depicts the "loyalty" of the Nazi military system. German soldiers, throughout the ranks, had become so accustomed to loyal obedience to orders that Hitler's decision to let his armies die on the field of Stalingrad, rather than surrender, caused no one to question their true fate. The strength of the Communist Party would be negligible were it not for the demanding loyalty to "The Party." Their very solidarity results from an unyielding obedience to an objective which usually requires a subservience of personal motives. The number of purges and defections in Communist controlled states, however, indicates that loyalty to the Party is not as complete as its leaders would have us believe.

The type of loyalty with which businessmen are concerned must obviously fall into the latter category which Royce termed "pedestrian." Al-

[2] W. B. Boyer," What Industry Wants In Business School Graduates," *The Personnel Administrator*, May-June, 1961, p. 5.

[3] Philip B. Niles, "Six Standards for Executive Conduct," *Dun's Review and Modern Industry*, April, 1956, pp. 41–44.

[4] James F. Bender, *The Techniques of Executive Leadership*, pp. 103–105.

though it isn't as exciting, the importance it assumes during the lifetime of a businessman can be just as demanding as a devotion to great causes. The late Chester Barnard stressed its importance in the following manner:

> The most important single contribution required of the executive, certainly the most universal qualification, is loyalty, domination by the organization personality. This is the first necessity because the lines of communication cannot function at all unless the personal contributions of executives will be present at the required position, at the times necessary, without default for ordinary personal reasons. . . . The contribution of personal loyalty and submission is least susceptible to tangible inducements. It cannot be bought either by material inducements or by other positive incentives, except all other things be equal.[5]

Although the recognition of loyalty and its importance to an organization is evident from many sources, does industry understand and appreciate the implications it carries in the business world? As worthy as the quality has proven to be, is loyalty in the business organization properly evaluated in terms of achieving corporate objectives? In an industrial world where corporate and individual competition are ever increasing, loyalty to a "common cause" is often negligible. The morality and integrity of a business organization, as well as the individuals who manage it, are so involved that the question of loyalty in industry deserves careful scrutiny.

Today's Loyalties

Harrison Johnson, editor of *Modern Office Procedures* magazine, recently conducted a survey of 103 business executives which resulted in some alarming comments.[6] Asked whether a man can move up through the ranks of management solely by honest, decent methods, an overwhelming majority of those questioned answered: "No!" Stealing ideas, planting pious doubts, withholding facts, and knifing the absentee were some of the techniques most frequently mentioned as ways for eliminating competition in the quest for personal advancement. Such comments are indicative of the personal motives which often take precedence over corporate goals and objectives.

In another study conducted by three Carnegie Institute of Technology professors, the early management careers of thirty executives, with similar backgrounds and qualifications, were studied to determine why some advanced faster than others.[7] One difference was found to be in the personal goals of the men. The men who were most successful in their advance-

---

[5] Chester I. Barnard, *The Functions of the Executive*, p. 220.
[6] "How To Get The Boss's Job," *Modern Office Procedures*, May, 1961, pp. 15–18.
[7] *Business Week*, August 27, 1960, p. 82.

ment expressed more desire for power, autonomy, income, and status than their less successful colleagues. Their attitude toward the organization was somewhat detached. They seemed to have a definite distrust of the organization as a protector of their own long-run interests.[8]

This opportunity to advance a personal career by shifting from one company to another has become common-place in industry. The technological revolution, coupled with the increased mobility of American businesses and businessmen, has created tremendous opportunities for qualified management personnel. As a result, a competent executive is able to sell his much needed talents to the highest bidder, and it is not uncommon to find top executives who have served in the top management ranks of two or more organizations. It is difficult to say whether American business encourages "pirating" of management personnel or merely tolerates it; whatever the case, the attitude in Europe is one which considers it an act of disloyalty to quit a company.[9] The increasing tendency for qualified management personnel to change jobs, in order to advance their personal careers, must cause some concern in the minds of those who advocate complete "loyalty to the firm." It must be recognized, however, that many successful executives have faithfully served more than one employer during their careers.[10]

The conflict of loyalties which are prevalent in modern industry creates additional barriers to the achievement of maximum loyalty among the organizational group. The conflict of objectives between management and labor has long divided the loyalties of individual employees. The conflicting allegiances between individual subordinates, the group, and the organization are equally serious and have been the basis of numerous sociological and psychological studies on group behavior.

An equally important conflict of objectives is now apparent between the "management mind" and the "scientific mind." With an increasing emphasis on research and development, more and more scientists are actively engaged in the corporate decision making process. Corporate loyalty, however, sometimes has a secondary emphasis to the dedicated scientist. The

[8] It is important to mention, however, that while these men maintained a wide range of outside contacts and were constantly on the lookout for other opportunities, they actually changed companies less often than their less successful classmates.

[9] *Business Week*, August 13, 1960, p. 48.

[10] Of the 58 male executives contributing chapters to H. B. Maynard's *Top Management Handbook*, their personal histories indicate that 26 were employed by more than one company during their career; 12 either founded or inherited their own companies; the remaining 20 were associated with the same organization (or a subsidiary) where they started their industry careers. These men were selected as participating authors because of their outstanding achievements and contributions to the management profession. There might be some doubt that the 26 men with multi-company backgrounds could have realized their true potential had they remained with one company throughout their careers.

conclusion of a study made by Princeton University was that scientists are hard for industry to handle because their system of "colleague authority" clashes with the corporation's system of "executive authority."[11] It was determined that opinions of others in the same scientific field (hence, "colleague authority") are often more important to the scientist than are his boss's opinions. A similar, but more detailed, analysis resulted from a research study made by the Opinion Research Corporation in 1959.[12] Among other findings, it was concluded that the management mind conflicts with the scientific mind in approaching risk-taking and decision making — the management mind is integrative while the scientific mind is analytical. With this basic difference involved, it is not difficult to imagine the conflict which arises in attempting to set common aims and objectives, not to mention the problem of establishing policies and procedures to attain them.

Many people are loyal to an organization primarily because of their loyalty to their immediate superior. If an executive makes a decision which is judged as inferior by top management — and does any executive always make the right decision? — do the subordinates of that executive support his decision, and in effect, turn against the company? Or does the subordinate remain loyal to the company and prove to be a "fair weather" loyal subordinate to the executive? Such situations arise daily, and the man who is sincerely loyal to both his boss and the company is bound to have his loyalties placed under severe pressures. Does all of this mean that the importance of loyalty is waning? Do the desires for personal gain and recognition, the pride of scientists in their professional attainments, the opportunity to change jobs without disrespect and all the other conflicting factors lessen the impact that loyalty can have on a corporation's ultimate success? On the contrary, loyalty is of great significance in the over-all performance of an industrial organization.

The Balance

The preceding discussion merely illustrates some of the loyalty problems which the present-day manager must face, and should recognize, in meeting his leadership responsibilities. If he is to fulfill these responsibilities, then he must acknowledge certain factors which affect the loyalty relationships in American business organizations, and subsequently, limit its importance.

First of all, it must be conceded that some senior, and seemingly truly loyal, employees may exhibit loyalty "for loyalty's sake" alone. There are always to be found those individuals who are primarily interested in tenure

[11] *Business Week*, October 22, 1960, p. 113.

[12] "The Conflict Between the Scientific Mind and the Management Mind," Opinion Research Corporation, September, 1959.

or security, rather than growth and development. These individuals, who are so satiated with their current position and achievements that they refrain from personally initiating any action which might place their status in jeopardy, rarely make significant contributions to the success of the organization. Such situations can be found where seniority is a prerequisite to promotion. This factor was recognized by M. A. Sullivan in the following statement:

> There is also the perpetual conflict between seniority and ability. Designed as a recognition of loyalty, the seniority rule is often a detriment to progress in management. Many utilities, banks, and old-line companies lose able men who refuse to be mere time servers. Any decisions affecting seniority are certain to have significant ethical echoes, with the moral margin favoring the right of a young man to move ahead.[13]

A second factor, which is seldom recognized, is that an organization should not expect, or even desire, "unquestioning" loyalty; (frankly, it seems that this is the trait actually desired by many executives, and probably accounts for much of the job shifting at middle management levels). The day of the one-man rule concept of organization has passed; the competition of modern industry demands that all the skill and judgment possessed by a company be used to its fullest extent. Seldom does one man possess this skill and judgment to such a degree that he can, by himself, make the necessary decisions to assure continued growth and success. As Louis William Norris emphasized in his article on the moral aspects of management: "Leadership rests on an amalgamation of opinion, a fusion of standards. A healthy administrative organization encourages differences and originality of judgment. All this is to the good, but it makes for everyday aches and pains."[14]

A third factor, which combines many of the elements of the first two, involves recognition of the "fusion process."[15] With this recognition comes the realization that loyalty is not a constant factor of organizational behavior. It flows and ebbs with every problem the organization must face; loyalty is tested with each decision, and the ability of the affected individ-

---

[13] "Business Ethics: Policy or Principle?" *Dun's Review and Modern Industry*, November, 1959, p. 69.

[14] Louis William Norris, "Moral Hazards of an Executive," *Harvard Business Review*, September-October, 1960, p. 73.

[15] "The fusion process is defined as the *simultaneous* operation of the *socializing process* by which the organization seeks to make an agent of the individual for the achievement of organizational objectives, and of the *personalizing process* by which the individual seeks to make an agency of the organization for the achievement of his personal objectives." The total analysis of this process is explained in the interim report by E. Wight Bakke, "The Fusion Process," published by the Labor and Management Center, Yale University.

uals to place long term objectives ahead of short term satisfactions determines the degree to which loyalty is achieved. Obviously loyalty has to be earned, and it is the responsibility of the leader to direct and channel the efforts of his subordinates toward those long range objectives. The fact that divided loyalties do exist, and that organizational loyalty is ever on trial, should not deter the company's pursuit toward its objectives. It does emphasize, however, that these objectives should insure the well-being and the growth and development opportunities of each individual employee.

A fourth and final factor must also be mentioned: "Humanism demands that the world's work be done, but not at the expense of a man's loyalty to his code of personal ethics or his freedom of decision within legal bounds."[16] Although most business men endeavor to adhere to ethical and legal principles, the recent probe into the price-fixing activities of several large corporations indicates internal problems inherent to competitive enterprise. While it may never be known to what extent, if any, that top management was involved in the price fixing of electrical equipment, two conclusions can be drawn: first, the men who were found guilty became involved in the price-fixing scheme because their personal ethics and interpretation of existing law did not oppose such activities; or second, the guilty individuals aided in the manipulation of prices with competing companies, in spite of their personal ethics, because the resultant profits would increase their promotional opportunities in the company. (Various newspaper accounts of the trial testimony revealed that most of the accused fell in one of these categories.) The legal implications of company loyalty assumed even more explicit terms in the recent management conflict at Chrysler Corporation. The corporation filed a lawsuit against Ben Stone, the Detroit business partner of William C. Newberg, former Chrysler president. The suit charged that Newberg had violated his trust to Chrysler and defined this trust in these terms:

> In his capacity as an officer and director of the plaintiff . . . William C. Newberg occupied the position of a fiduciary with respect to the plaintiff corporation and its shareholders and at all times owed the plaintiff the fiduciary obligations and responsibilities attendant upon his various positions, including, among others, the duty of undivided loyalty to the plaintiff.[17]

The fact that two such newsworthy cases occurred within a year's time should be sufficient warning to all industrial organizations that *loyalty to the firm can be rationalized to condone even illegal actions.*

In the final analysis, it would be a mistake to stress the need for loyalty without also advocating the necessity for integrity. The dictionary defines

[16] "Men, Morality, and Management," *Dun's Review and Modern Industry*, October, 1959, pp. 58–72.

[17] "Behind the Conflict at Chrysler," *Fortune*, November, 1960, p. 137.

integrity as moral soundness; honesty; uprightness. It is this characteristic that gives an organization stability that will prove of value when loyalties are divided. Philip Selznick has written what is probably the most realistic and forceful interpretation of this characteristics. In his discussion, "Beyond Organization," he stresses that certain firms can be identified by their distinctive ways of making decisions or by peculiar commitments to aims, methods, or clienteles.[18] In this manner the organization takes on values and as a vehicle of group integrity it becomes, to some degree, an end in itself. This process of becoming infused with value is what is meant as institutionalization, and as this occurs, *organization management* becomes *institutional leadership*. The integrity of an enterprise goes beyond organization forms and procedures, efficiency, and even beyond group cohesion — integrity combines organization and policy. It is the unity that emerges when a particular orientation becomes so firmly a part of group life that it influences and directs a divergence of attitudes, decisions, and forms of the organization, and does so at many levels of experience. The building of integrity is part of what Mr. Selznick calls the "institutional embodiment of purpose," and its protection is a major function of leadership. The responsible leader must also have a concern for change and reconstruction, and what can be done to establish policy internally depends upon the changing relation between the organization and its environment. The inbuilding of purpose is a challenge to creativity because it involves the transformation of men and groups from neutral, technical units into participants who have a peculiar stamp, sensitivity, and commitment. This entire concept is summarized as follows:

> The main practical import of this effect is that policy will gain spontaneous and reasoned support. Desired ends and means are sustained and furthered, not through continuous command, but as a free expression of truly accepted principles. This presumes that at least the core participants combine loyalty to the enterprise with a sensitive awareness of the principles by which it is guided. Loyalty by itself is not enough, just as blind patriotism is insufficient. There must also be an ability to sense when a course of action threatens institutional integrity.[19]

Any company that has this institutional embodiment of purpose is to be envied, but the fact that such companies do exist indicates that loyalty problems can be overcome. A careful observation of these companies will reveal a management team of dedicated and loyal executives who exercise integrity with their decision making powers.

Yes, as Willis Wayde observed, "Loyalty is the damndest thing." It does keep cropping up at eccentric intervals, and we keep searching for a definite

[18] Philip Selznick, *Leadership in Administration*, pp. 138–140.
[19] *Ibid.*, p. 150.

definition. *Loyalty in industry is best expressed by the integrity of purpose exhibited by the members of an organization while striving to achieve corporate objectives.* It is a real and frustrating challenge, and one that will not diminish as competition for profits and service become more severe. The fact that it will always prove a frustration should alert all management leaders to the realization that loyalty in itself does not assure success. Loyalty must be tempered with integrity, and the successful leaders of American business will continue to be those individuals who don't always look out for themselves.

32

Business and the Social System:
End of the Brumaire*

Clarence C. Walton

Columbia University

The concept of a social system has been a pervasive concept for many years in behavioral science, and in recent years has been widely applied in the analysis of numerous problems of the business enterprise. Professor Walton explains the concept of a social system, which he then relates to the American system. With this as background, the article discusses two major trends faced by professional managers: (1) increasing rigor of decision-making through the use of computers, and (2) the emerging international and multi-national character of corporations. Such developments intensify problems of human relations, and the corporate environment thus becomes highly relevant.

The Essayable Teleology

There was a time in our recent past when vocal groups of perceptive men were repelled by excessive concentrations of industrial and economic power, and angered by what was felt to be the moral bankruptcy of those interlocking directorates which controlled such combinations. The time and the reaction were not unlike that murky twilight of the French Directorate when Abbe Sieyes successfully upset the old oligarchy and created a new one called the Consulate. That interim period, the brumaire, was a time when Frenchmen knew what they disliked but were unsure to what institutional forms should be entrusted the nation's future.

Some of the same uncertainties mark the present. What Charles and Mary Beard felicitously called America in Midpassage marks a stage in a

* Taken and adapted from *Proceedings of The Annual Meeting*, 1961, Academy of Management.

431

journey that is tumultuous enough to generate perplexity on the real goals of our society and the part business should play towards their achievement.[1]

Even within the limited perspective of the last twenty years it is evident that the peaceful revolution has swept many old practices into oblivion. Defense spending has dramatically eroded the notion of competition for several major industries, notably in electronics and in aircraft, and has replaced the old market mores with a concept of negotiated arrangements. Urbanization has reached such an intensive stage of development that "megalopolis" is the latest semantic innovation embossed on the coinage of our intellectual exchange system to describe the phenomenon. Affluence has so replaced scarcity as a major concept in economic theory as to encourage Galbraith to essay a reformulation of the historic law of supply and demand; and automation has become a business opportunity and a national challenge. And so it goes.

If the major changes in society and in business institutions are fairly obvious, the implications are not. The traditional national penchant for hasty and ingenious improvisation in the face of new demands must be complemented with a more rationally developed kind of social innovation lest, like Telegonous, we unwittingly kill the father of so much in our national progress. These observations lead inexorably, if leisurely, to a confession of need for re-examination of the relationship between a democratic society and a dynamic economy. While a kind of enlightened eclecticism is required to sort out the major characteristics of modern society and modern business, the teleology which governs this inquiry is concerned less with this aspect and far more with probing into the implications these new facets have for the future. A "fact-oriented" approach can itself be misleading unless facts are placed within a certain context.[2] Worse still is the ever-present danger of asserting as fact that which is assumption, and then going on to develop with enormous ingenuity the relationship among them. History abounds with intriguing examples of first-rate minds explaining facts that never were.

> Consider only . . . Hegel solemnly explaining why there could be only seven planets and none between Mars and Jupiter just as Piazzi was discovering Ceres in that very region; the talented physiologist Johannes Müller explaining why the rate of transmission of the nerve impulse could never be measured just a few years before Helmholtz

[1] See Henry Wriston, ed., *Goals for Americans*, (Englewood Cliffs, Prentice-Hall, Inc., 1960), and *Strategy for the Sixties*, (Washington, D.C., Foreign Policy Clearing House, 1960).

[2] Carl Becker, "What are Historical Facts," *The Western Political Quarterly*, VIII (September, 1935). "We know where we are when we say 'we get down to facts' but even the established facts of history are illusive unless placed in a certain context," p. 327.

proceeded to measure it; J. S. Mill explaining the impossibility of sound statistical studies of human behavior long after Quetelet and others had conducted such studies.[3]

When micro-analytical studies reveal such tendencies, the dangers inherent in a macro approach such as this become doubly hazardous. Yet, in its rich and variegated detail, American society is more a Bayeux tapestry where the whole must be distinguished from the detailed components. To begin the search for perspective it is proposed to raise four major questions:

1. What is meant analytically by the generic term "social system"?
2. What are the specific attributes of the American social system?
3. What are some of the primary questions which have special relevance for the business community in its relationship with the larger society?
4. What are the implications of the foregoing issues for professional education in business?

If it is clearly understood that the questions are put in a general way to excite further discussions and not elicit definitive answers, this treatment may be modestly productive.

The Meaning of a "Social System"

A preference for the term "social system" over the term "society" has been deliberately indicated. "Society" generates paradoxes since it is used at times in too restrictive a sense and, on other occasions, in too embracive a context. In a restricted way, it can be legitimately applied to as few as two human beings — such as husband and wife — and in a universalistic sense it can be applied to the nation-state or, indeed, the world community. Society embraces all facets of human living whereas social systems relate to the observable structure and organization through which basic human needs (religious, sexual, political, economic, and cultural) are satisfied. Since systems have structure and organization they imply permanence, are more subject to scientific scrutiny, and operate according to defined principles.

Economic life is thus a social system. As such, it has within its own sphere an autonomy and a body of governing principles by which it can be explained. Since the system exists to meet a basic need for goods and services, it cannot be decreed out of existence by other social systems even when these others are essentially hostile to it. Thus, for example, the hostility of the early Greeks and Romans toward the business system may

[3] Robert K. Merton, Leonard Broom, L. S. Cottrell, Jr., *Sociology Today* (New York, Basic Books, Inc., 1959), p. xiii.

have hobbled the effectiveness of business but surely could not destroy it. Similarly, the Church Fathers were ill disposed toward the merchant class but recognized that the exchange function had to operate within a certain context. Slowly even the "laws" of the market were grudgingly given a rightful recognition.

If there is autonomy within its sphere, it does not follow that there is isolation between the social systems. All are contrived to serve man. All have, therefore, a common focus emerging from a common object. Since man has different priorities for needs which flow from his essential nature and from the changing circumstances in which he finds himself, it is evident that a constant interplay occurs among the various social systems.

Perhaps the logic of this section can be shunted to one major proposition which asserts that there can be no real dichotomy between business and other major institutions which comprise the total society. This apparently tautological view has important implications. It repudiates, for example, the major assumptions of classical economics which held that the economic order not only operated under the sovereign and impersonal rules of the market place but that individualistic self-seeking — subsumed under the profit motive — automatically assured the social good.[4] It furthermore is hesitant to accept the major thesis of a recent study which held that industrialism ("social organization where industries, including many large-scale industries, are the dominant method of production") must inexorably forge "new and fewer distinctive cultural patterns." "Authority must be concentrated," according to this study; further, consent becomes more crucial than coercion, and the State will survive and prosper.[5]

When it is remembered that the nineteenth century apotheosis of the economic system had enormous significance for political theory (witness the Spencerian version of the State as being a necessary evil whose raison d' etre is found only in the requirements for protecting property rights and assuring national security), it is not illogical to assume that any similar attempt to place primacy for society's purposes and systems on industrialism must likewise have similar implications. It is our own view that the interplay is constant, and that no single system can be assumed to possess an eternal primacy. At one time political needs may dominate and, at quite another, cultural considerations.

In terms of a general and analytical framework we can conclude, therefore, that while each social system must be studied within the framework of that system's purposes and principles it is inaccurate to conclude that (1) a splendid isolation — even when maintained in theory — can be sustained in fact, and (2) that any single social system provides the primary

---

[4] Edward Mason, "Apologetics of Managerialism," *Journal of Business*, XXXI, (January, 1958), pp. 1–11.

[5] Clark Kerr, John Dunlop, Frederick Harbison, and Charles Myers, *Industrialism and Industrial Man* (Cambridge: Harvard University Press, 1960), pp. 97 and 288–90.

determinant for a given society. Consequently, rich cultural diversities can exist even when other systems — like the industrial one — may become quite uniform. The actual interplay can be worked out historically by disparate systems in quite different ways. If comparative studies can start from certain common bases, they must also move fruitfully to identify specific differences.

The Specific Attributes of the American System

To a general understanding of social systems must be added those features of American society which have burgeoned from that unique amalgam of new people exploiting virgin land under demonstrably different historical conditions. Eminent scholars like Hacker are quite prepared to establish those differences which have provided the color and romance for the American epic.[6] But tradition, too, is subject to refinement and adaptation, and we must address ourselves to the significant changes in our American system. The past century provides a ready-made model for analysis.

The watershed is 1890 and the census of that year is possibly the most significant decennial report in the country's history. Prior to 1890 the characteristics of our society could be lumped under four headings: agrarianism, individualism, parochialism, and optimism. Against these may be posited the lineaments of the new America: industrialism, organizationalism, internationalism, and a grim kind of realism. A cursory review of the respective halves of the century is illuminating.

During the last half of the nineteenth century most Americans earned their livelihood by tilling the soil. Homespun virtues of rural life were evidenced in a passionate belief in God and Divine Providence, in personal frugality and industriousness, in affection for such simple fictional heroes as Mark Twain and Huckleberry Finn. Within the business sector the dimensions easily perceived by observers were the same ones which impressed themselves on the far-ranging vision of Adam Smith. Individual enterprise meant precisely that and skepticism of combinations was still strong despite stirrings by the Rockefellers and Carnegies. The market was still the arbiter of business operations; supply and demand made themselves felt under a brand of competition that created quick bankruptcies as well as quick profits. And the entrepreneur put his own money and energies on the line. His enterprise's success was his personal success and societal expectations, slowly changing, nevertheless recognized that the fruits were his to dispose as he willed.[7] For all practical purposes, the

[6] Louis Hacker, *Triumph of American Capitalism* (New York: Simon and Schuster, 1940). "The tradition of the Enlightenment, the American Revolution, Jeffersonianism, Old Radical Republicanism, Populism — this is the American tradition," p. 435.

[7] Sigmund Diamond, *The Regulation of the American Businessman* (Cambridge: Harvard University Press, 1955).

Revolutionary ideal of small businesses run by small businessmen remained the ideal for the American economy.

Parochialism, the third aspect of the post-Civil War period, is a form of shorthand to describe the country's intense preoccupation with internal growth and development. The vast sweep of land from ocean to ocean provided a common market of truly heroic proportions. Americans still bought more from abroad than they sold and only a few venturesome souls dared suggest that the pattern was soon to be reversed. The 1890 census revealed as a fact what a few suggested, namely, that for the first time in its development America recorded a favorable trade balance. The sequence of events was easy to discern. Overseas markets meant need for merchant shipping; merchant ships required naval protection; combat vessels required refuelling and repair stations. Within a decade the flag flew over Hawaii, Guam and the Philippines in the Pacific and the Virgin Islands and Puerto Rico in the Atlantic. The myth of isolation defied the fact!

Events outpace the narrative. Returning to the pre-1890 period we note that the country was literally saturated in a doctrine of progress quite translatable in terms of Condorcet's easy formula: every day in every way things are getting better and better. If there is an inclination to decry such buoyant optimism it must be restated that there was ample ground for the conviction and ample support from theoreticians who sought to rationalize it. The American character was thought to be something special over and above that of the ordinary men populating other nations.[8]

But behind the facade profound changes were taking place. The prevailing value system rested on an individualistic ethic — defined crudely as reliance on the enlightened self-interest of the single human person for the achievement of his own destiny. The social good was presumed to result from the sum of individual goods. This individualistic ethic had long historical underpinnings. Renaissance secularism, Protestant subjectivism, and economic liberalism were European imports engrafted on native soil. According to Frederick Jackson Turner the frontier became the catalyst for transmuting secularism, Protestantism and liberalism into meaningful terms for Americans.[9]

Yet, like the political isolation rooted in American parochialism, the individualism rooted in the European and American amalgam was under assault. The religious content of the individual ethic was being eroded in western Europe by men like Giosue Carducci in Italy, Ernest Roman in France, and Friedrich Wilhelm Nietzsche in Germany. A partially acknowledged anti-Judaism intermingled with a fully acknowledged anti-

---

[8] See for example, J. K. Mehta, *Lectures on Modern Economic Theory* (Allahabad: Chaitanga Publishing House, 1959), especially Ch. XI wherein the Indian scholar talks of "character" as the prime ingredient in growth.

[9] *The Frontier in American History* (New York: Henry Holt, 1920).

Christianity to provide mortar for the intellectual bombardment against western religions on grounds that they were oriental and, therefore, repulsive to the European tradition. Renan's *Origins of Christianity* particularly stressed the fact that Jesus and his followers were Jews and part of a barbarous Asiatic tradition. Carducci glorified paganism in his hymn, *To Satan*, as the source of liberty even as religion was its antithesis. Riding a chariot of fire, Satan is the emblem of revolt against Jehovah and the symbol of modern scientific progress. Note that progress was retained but emasculated of its theological base. Nietzsche castigated Christianity as a Jewish trick for revenge against the Romans and the whole world which treated them so shabbily.[10]

The drama was waged far less spectacularly in this country, but it is undeniable that Church influences moved from a confident and assertive posture typical of the Jonathan Edwards tradition to an unsure and defensive status typified by the Reverend President of Yale, Noah Porter, whose own course in "First Principles" lost many of those bright students to the new secularism that Porter had set out to demolish. The powerful puritan bellowing of Edwards still found some echo. An extreme case is found in a young Vermont mystic, John Humphrey Noyes, who wrote Henry Lloyd Garrison that the Holy Spirit had moved Noyes to "nominate Jesus Christ for the Presidency, not only of the United States but of the world."[11] Successive generations of ministers were to entertain far less sweeping ambitions. This decline in religion's importance to the individualistic ethic becomes even more pronounced when juxtaposed against the rising popularity of Social Darwinism.[12] With its emphasis on ruthless competition, struggle for survival, and belief that social improvement was sustained as a necessary consequence of those two operations, it was apparent that individualistic businessmen had a new ethic delicately attuned to justify the ruthlessness of the most extreme of the so-called robber barons.[13]

Now the foregoing had this one important lesson for business leaders: namely, that business was not totally responsible for the excesses it admittedly committed during the infancy of the industrial movement. This seems to embody an internal contradiction. Surely long hours of work in unsanitary conditions, surely assumption by owners of dictatorial powers over the lives of workers, and surely the single-minded dedication to profits regardless of social costs, conspire to make business the villain. Yet is

[10] *Ibid.*
[11] Quoted by V. L. Parrington, *Main Currents in American Thought* (New York: Harcourt Brace, 1930), 11, p. 344.
[12] Richard Hofstadter, *Social Darwinism in American Thought* (Boston: Beacon Press, 1955), esp. pp. 20–23.
[13] *Ibid.*, Chapter Three on William Graham Sumner.

not the real question not related to business practices and practitioners and more to an ethos that generally condoned and often approved? As Brooks Adams wryly remarked, the American male thought first of his dinner and next of his girl. Within this variant of the individualistic ethic business had not been less a force for change in values, as it had been an instinctive and effective adaptor to changes in values that had already been established.

These changes in the value constructs can be schematically related within the following diagram.

Pre 1890	Post
Calvinist work — production — success ethic	Leisure and consumption orientation
Strict interpretation of the Decalogue	Ethical relativism
Individualism — independence	Socialization — interdependence
Crusade for progress: optimistic future	Containment: uncertain or pessimistic future
Belief in nationalism	Regionalism — internationalism

After 1890 we moved to the period characterized in 1930 by John Dewey[14] as "United States Incorporated" and by Kenneth Boulding some twenty years later as the era of the "Organizational Revolution."[15] The story is almost a cliche by now. Owner-managers were replaced by non-owning professionals; small businesses were dwarfed by corporate giants;[16] individualism yielded to a spirit of conformity; parochialism was replaced by an internationalism that left no room for isolation as a policy of national illusion. For business mores, the significant shift was to a management ideology[17] with a recognizable affinity toward a new social ethic. The social ethic emphasized human interdependence and not man's independence; it stressed cooperation and participative teamwork and tended to sub-

[14] John Dewey, *Individualism, Old and New* (New York: G. P. Putnam, 1930).

[15] Kenneth Boulding, *The Organizational Revolution* (New York: Harper and Brothers, 1953).

[16] See Ralph Nelson, *Merger Movements in American Industry, 1895–1956* (Princeton: Princeton University Press, 1959).

[17] Ideology is a difficult word to describe satisfactorily. Karl Mannheim uses the term to include an accepted body of beliefs and ethical codes, in *Ideology and Utopia* (London: Routledge and Kegan Paul, 1936), pp. 17–21; whereas Carl Friedrich and Zbigniew Brzezinski equate ideology with a "reasonably coherent body of ideas concerning the practical means of how to change and reform society . . . ," *Totalitarian Dictatorship and Autocracy* (Cambridge: Harvard University Press, 1956), p. 74. It can be argued that in contemporary terms ideology is less concerned with ideas for reform and more concerned with pragmatic rationales developed by their protagonists to defend them. In the newer testaments speculation of the kind exemplified by Aristotle or Burke or by the writers of *The Federalist* — despite their concern for pragmatic change — is no longer the hallmark of an ideology. See, for example, J. J. Roucek, *Contemporary Political Ideologies* (New York: Philosophical Library, 1960).

ordinate the role of the business hero; it placed a premium on human solidarity and social harmony and eschewed the rigors of rough competition and open conflict. By and large, it reflected a concern with security and status with group responsibility and personal dignity that is suggestive of a new kind of feudalism.[18]

Some Primary Questions for American Business

If professional management is called upon to handle problems emerging from an urbanized, industrialized and internationalized world, and if management is committed more and more to practice a social ethic,[19] what developments are in the offing which suggest further dramatic change in the main contours for decision-making and for organizational arrangements? A number of trends can be discerned but the following two have been selected for identification because they are felt to be among the most significant.

Two propositions are advanced to indicate the line of reasoning that will be pursued. (1) Decision-making is likely to become more rigorously analytical and rational in the future mainly because of widespread utilization of the computer, and (2) the corporation will become international of multinational in nature. Both have interesting applications.

The most eloquent spokesman for the first proposition is Herbert Simon who argues that the machine will influence business management importantly at three levels. At the lowest level of clerical and repetitive work, the machine will literally take over completely; at the mid-management level many of the functions now performed by human beings because of their experiences and intuitions — such as production scheduling and inventory controls — will be transferred to the machine. More startling is Simon's conclusion that many top-level management assignments which involve judgment and insight will increasingly pass to the computer — especially as the machines are improved to do heuristic programming (nonnumerical tasks, use of humanoid problem-solving techniques, and even ability to employ a learning process).[20]

Allowing for a substantial margin of error it is still true that management functions are in for heavy seige. What, then, are to be the primary

[18] R. A. Nisbet, *Quest for Community* (New York: Oxford University Press, 1953).

[19] Marshall Dimock has argued, for example, that the advocates of a "science of administration come nearer to making philosophical assumptions than they do to proving universal laws" and that instead of assumptions there is need "to think more clearly . . . about the ethical or moral content of our aims, our plans, our administrative methods." *A Philosophy of Administration* (New York: Harper and Brothers, 1959), p. 55.

[20] See Simon's fascinating essay, "The Corporation: Will It Be Managed by Machines?" in Melvin Anshen and G. L. Bach, eds., *Management and Corporations 1985* (New York: McGraw-Hill Book Company, 1960), pp. 17–55.

functions that will remain with management? It would seem likely that, above all other considerations, the future manager will be absorbed with problems of "human relationships." There can be no such relationships without value relationships. Unlike the machine or the ledger or the computer, the human being carries within him a complex of drives and ambitions which he regulates and utilizes in a certain framework of values established by his own will and by society. Insights from the social scientists,[21] and from the philosophers,[22] and theologians will become increasingly necessary in the conceptual apparatus of the manager. Now these have never been the particular forte of business leadership. The executive must now speak and act from a new and higher level of discourse and frame of reference.

If human relationships will generate the primary problems for the future business executive, the question of the "environment" in which these problems will be spawned and, hopefully, settled become relevant. It has been pointed out that parochialism yielded to internationalism for the American society. It is now apparent that the corporation is undergoing the same metamorphosis that the nation has already passed through. Increasingly large American corporations have their homes in the United States, yet have subsidiaries which operate and live under the laws and customs of other countries as well. David Lilienthal calls these organizations the "multinational corporations";[23] Wolfgang Friedmann speaks of "joint ventures";[24] Emile Benoit simply calls them "international corporations."[25]

More important than nomenclature is the substance. What does this extra-national movement mean to management? An easy catalog is hard to come by. Clearly knowledge of foreign cultures and foreign tongues becomes more important. The graduate of the Ecole Polytechnique will increasingly compete with the graduate of top American universities for key positions in major corporations. There will likely be an outflow of accountants and tax experts to underdeveloped parts of the world. Stock ownership may become universal and new forms of competition may challenge our anti-trust laws. The use of national currencies like the dollar as international reserves will possibly become an anachronism, and in foreign investments, American managements may be forced to deal more with the

---

[21] George B. Strother, ed., *Social Science Approaches to Business Behavior* (Homewood, Ill., The Dorsey Press and Richard D. Irwin, Inc., 1962).

[22] An effort worth noting is that of C. West Churchman, *Prediction and Optimal Decision* (Englewood Cliffs, N.J., Prentice-Hall, Inc., 1961). See especially Chapter 9 on "additivity of values."

[23] Lilienthal in Anshen and Bach, *op. cit.*, pp. 119–158.

[24] Wolfgang Friedmann and George Kalmanoff, eds., *Joint International Business Ventures* (New York: Columbia University Press, 1961).

[25] Emile Benoit, *Europe at Sixes and Sevens* (New York: Columbia University Press, 1961), esp. Ch. 5.

International Monetary Fund or U.N. banking instrumentalities and less with their own.[26] To place the problem of adjusting human relationships in a world-wide setting and a global environment is to adjust some measure of the challenges for management in the immediate years ahead.

There are those, like Robert Heilbroner, who argue brilliantly that the American business leadership is destined for a more subordinate role than ever before.[27] Yet, like Edward Carr, the British historian, we tend toward his persuasion — if not to his conclusions — that "progress in human affairs, whether in science or in history or in society, has come mainly through the bold readiness of human beings not to confine themselves to seeking piecemeal improvements in the way things are done, but to present fundamental challenges in the name of reason to the current way of doing things and to the avowed or hidden assumptions on which it rests."[28]

How can some of these fundamental challenges be viewed? Perhaps the most effective way comes from statements which — combining fact and assumption — lead to a sharp question.

1. Fact: Engineering skills are obsolescent within a decade.
   Assumption: Management skills are likely to follow the same general pattern and corporation will move to provide for re-educating managers.
   Query: Should corporations also undertake a primary responsibility toward re-educating workers whose manual skills are outstripped by technology?

2. Fact: Corporate centralization in headquarters remote from satellite offices and branch factories is the prevailing way of conducting manufacturing operations.
   Assumption: The pattern will become increasingly marked in the future where manufacturing units abroad may even compete with an already established American unit.
   Query: What is the obligation of absentee landlordism to local communities under these new conditions?

3. Fact: Stock options and incentive plans are fairly common for top and middle management.
   Assumption: The worker is an equally essential partner with management on the productivity team.
   Query: Should workers share automatically (through profit sharing plans) in any increase in annual profits?

[26] Robert Triffin, *Gold and the Dollar Crisis* (New Haven: Yale University Press, 1961), pp. 10–14, and Chs. 6 and 7.
[27] *The Future as History* (New York: Grove Press, 1960), Ch. IV.
[28] Edward Hallet Carr, *What is History* (New York: Alfred Knopf, 1961), p. 207.

4. Fact: The Department of Labor is slowly changing its role from mediator to champion of the "national interests" in labor-management disputes which threaten the economy.

   Assumption: Organized labor, which is resisting this tendency, will move to enlist the support of organized industry in a resistance movement.

   Query: What should be the question of corporate leadership on this matter?

5. Fact: History has demonstrated that when an enterprise becomes both profitable and powerful the community makes demands on it (as did the Italian communities against the medieval Casas) for support of schools, hospitals and the like.

   Assumption: The pattern in America will follow this historic route.

   Query: What is the corporation's primary relationship to philanthropy?

Implications for Education in Business

The new styles in business obviously carry implications for the kinds of appropriate educational preparation required by that vocation. Unlike so many past developments, however, the current efforts to revitalize the curricula have a forward look.[29] There are stirrings on many campuses and in many executive programs which reflect a desire to achieve constructive reformulations.

Looking at the problem in terms of curriculum, student-preparation, and teacher recruitment, the following observations can be hazarded. Curricula everywhere are under intensive scrutiny, but there is no clear consensus on how to provide an educational experience which seeks to explain American business and society in terms of analytical, historical, and comparative data. In some cases there is a growing re-emphasis on business history and an assertion by scholars like Professor A. K. Steigerwalt of Michigan that this discipline must assume a central — as opposed to a peripheral — role in the curriculum if society-business relationships are to be rigorously analyzed.

At Harvard the well-known BRAS course, "Business Responsibilities in the American Society," is undergoing intensive analysis and refinement. In still other cases, business law courses have either gone on the defensive

[29] Saarsalmi, Meeri Marjatta: *Some Aspects of the Thought Underlying Higher Education for Business in the United States* (Bloomington: Bureau of Business Research, Indiana University, 1955).

or else are being readjusted substantially to include the larger legal-social environment in which business institutions have originated and developed. At Northwestern University interesting experiments have been done with the course called, "Competition of Ideas," which utilizes almost exclusively a case-method approach to the problem of competing values within the business system.

At Columbia a somewhat revolutionary tack has been taken with the new course called, "Conceptual Foundations of Business." Combining readings from a wide range of sources in history, philosophy, and the social sciences, it seeks to focus on current developments with a "rear-view" mirror on the relevant past, and to compare these with developments in other countries.[30]

In terms of student preparation, there is a real question on the part of the graduate schools, particularly, whether to insist on undergraduate preparation in the humanities as a prerequisite for admission to those professional courses which seek to probe into the problems of the economic system in a larger society. Even as there is growing insistence on intensive undergraduate preparation in mathematics, there are beginning efforts to require equally rigorous preparation in the humanities. The need for effective working partnerships with college liberal arts divisions is obvious, but an unfortunate legacy of mutual suspicion makes such arrangement difficult. There is the further question whether to recruit, for example, philosophers who show an interest in business problems or utilize professors of business who show an interest in philosophical problems.

The range for diversity of approach and for imaginative experimentation is enormous, and this opportunity will properly provide grist for exciting and animated discussion at many professional meetings over the next few years.

[30] Robert J. Senkier, *Revising a Business Curriculum — The Columbia Experience* (New York: Graduate School of Business, Columbia University, 1961).

33

Value Perspectives in Management Decisions*

Wilmar F. Bernthal

University of Colorado

Relationships between business and society present issues of vital concern to businessmen, students, and scholars. This exploration of the values that underlie management decisions and the character of corporate business enterprises usefully extends the analysis presented in the preceding selection. The article calls for the manager's awareness of the values he holds and of the assumptions he makes. A hierarchy of values is suggested as a guide to decision-making.

What are the values that guide managers in making business decisions? Do, can, and should these values encompass more than the immediate profit-making of the business firm? Is there such a thing as "enlightened" business management? If so, what is its nature, and what are its economic and social consequences?

These are questions raised by both the critic and the student of business administration. They are questions that need to be faced more boldly by the management profession, and need to be reckoned with more openly and forthrightly by schools of business administration.

In this paper I will attempt to bring these issues into focus, and then propose a model of a hierarchy of values for management decision from which a manager, or a student of management, can better deduce his own values and make some tentative judgments on criteria which will guide him in his management decisions.

* Taken and adapted from *The Journal of the Academy of Management*, vol. 5, no. 3, December, 1962, pp. 190–196.

The Management Dilemma: Business and Society

Much as the business community is frequently subjected to criticism, perhaps uninformed but nevertheless real, that its activities are contrary to the public interest, so also business schools are often suspected of advancing the cause of a vested interest group which somehow operates to its own benefit at the expense of society in general.

The goals of management education frequently are perceived differently by the social scientist and the teacher of business administration. The social scientist generally assumes he represents the broad interests of humanity, and that the goals of business administration are in conflict with such broad interests. Furthermore, he assumes that this conflict between the micro-outlook of business and the macro-outlook of economics and the other social sciences is inherent and cannot be reconciled. This can lead him to the conclusions that business administration as such should neither be taught nor supported with behavioral science research.[1]

The student, as the degree-carrying product of the business school, becomes involved in this apparent conflict between business and society as soon as he decides to enter a business school for his higher education. Many a student seeks a business school education with the avowed purpose of learning how to better exploit business opportunities for his personal benefit, with little concern for the ultimate consequences of his actions upon the economic system and upon society in general. If he leaves the business school with the same notion more firmly entrenched, he becomes a living testimonial that the critics may not be altogether wrong. And yet, what he seeks from the business school is a "practical" education to equip him for a very "practical" business career.

The business community itself is caught up in this dilemma of the function of business schools. As a practical matter, business looks to these schools for a manpower reservoir, reasonably equipped to perform on an entry job and to "learn the business." But despite some lofty statements about the need for the liberally educated student as the key to business survival and growth, it is likely that the great majority of businessmen are recruiting not the well-educated student as much as they are seeking a well-trained, loyal, and hardworking subordinate who will not question too much the assumption and values of the firm as perpetuated by the existing hierachy of managers.

What does all this imply for the teaching of management? It means at least the following:

1. Many misunderstandings arise out of differing goals and values.

2. These goals and values, unless spelled out precisely, do not communicate automatically.

[1] For an illustration of this position, see Loren Baritz, *The Servants of Power* (Middletown, Conn.: Wesleyan University Press, 1960).

3. Individual goals and values are subjectively arrived at, and differ markedly between individuals.

4. There is a tendency for individuals to assume that their goals are "normal" and that the other people should accept and/or adopt these goals.

5. Most people (businessmen, students, even college professors) are largely unaware of their own assumptions and value judgments, particularly as they relate to their own specialty.

6. An educated person is one who can see himself and his subject in a broader perspective, who is aware of differing and often conflicting values and goals, who is cognizant of his own hierarchy of values by which his decisions are guided, and who then makes decisions with full awareness of their consequences.

This poses some complex problems for the teaching of management. Since decision-making is the essence of management, the question of values cannot be ignored. Management cannot be taught in a vacuum, for it must be practiced in a social context rather than in isolation. On the other hand, to impose one particular set of values upon the student amounts to indoctrination, and violates his individuality and human dignity. The contribution that the teacher of management can make, however, lies in making the student fully aware of the value context of management, in clearly labelling his own values when he discusses management issues, and in encouraging — even compelling — the student to think through his own hierarchy of values which guide and motivate him. The student thus becomes educated to consider the whole range of consequences, immediate and long run, of acting upon his set of values.

The Firm as the Focal Point of Management Decisions

Management is conceived as the process of achieving objectives through the efficient use of physical and human resources. The "objectives" are usually assumed as "given," and are implied or expressed as those of the "organization" — in a business context, those of the business firm.

Ask any businessman, and almost any business student, what the objectives of the firm are, and the answer is a loud and clear: "Profits." A second thought might add such related goals as "survival" and "growth," and a more thoughtful answer might even qualify this with the addition of "through the production and distribution of goods and services," or "through the creation of economic utility."

It is not to be denied that this focus is a proper one for the study of business administration. The question, however, is whether it is broad enough to place the business firm into perspective. Does it recognize the assumptions implied in holding out "pursuit of profit" as management's objective?

For one thing, the "profit" objective would be considerably modified under an economic system in which private competitive enterprise is not the accepted mode of production and distribution. The profit objective assumes free enterprise and competition.

Furthermore, the profit objective often assumes the Adam Smith model of perfect competition in which each businessman in seeking to maximize his own gain is led "as if by an invisible hand" to also provide for the social good. Granted this assumption, the "blind" pursuit of profit can become a comfortable and satisfying level of aspiration for the business manager. The fact that competition is not, and seldom has been, a very precise internal regulator of business actions is well recognized by thoughtful observers of the American business scene.[2] It is somewhat alarming, however, to note the frequency with which free enterprise (perhaps *laissez faire*) is promoted on the assumption that all profit-getting will redound to the greatest social good.

When competition does not regulate effectively, what shall be substituted? The Utopian ideal of free enterprise would assume individual responsibility of the businessman not to violate his freedom — that is, it would assume "enlightened" free enterprise. But to the extent that such enlightenment is not a part of the vision of the businessman, the other regulators, such as government regulation and the countervailing power of other large groups, such as labor and consumer groups, are bound to limit the "freedom" of free enterprise.

Even though the greatest emphasis in teaching management must remain on how to maximize efficiency in the performance of the firm, it is not enough to assume as "given" and "virtuous" the objective of "profits." The perspective of the manager must be broad enough to consider the goals of the economic system in the service of which the existence of the firm can be justified.

The Perspective of the Firm within the Economic System

In viewing the business firm in the context of an economic system, the student of management is confronted with a hierarchy of values. Free enterprise (and profit making) can be justified only as long as it serves the higher goals of the economic system — those of allocation of scarce resources through production and distribution. To the extent that the firm is unable, or unwilling, to further these higher goals, its own existence will be short-lived. It may lose the support of a customer who has free choice to buy

[2] See, for example, Edward S. Mason, "The Apologetics of 'Managerialism,'" *The Journal of Business*, January, 1958; Gerhard R. Andlinger, "The Crucible of our Business Creeds," *Business Horizons*, Fall, 1959; and Adolf A. Berle, *Power Without Property*, (Harcourt, Brace, 1959).

elsewhere. Or, if the customer does not have free choice, the firm's profit-making will be regulated by society (government). If the customer is exploited by pricing conspiracies or if labor is abused through discriminatory or exploitive personnel practices, society, through labor or consumer organizations, or through government intervention, very effectively curtails the freedom of "free" enterprise.

The rationalization, based on the Adam Smith economic model, of the nonresponsibility of the businessman for the broader economic consequences of his action, may, in fact, be an excuse for irresponsibility in his actions. If the business decision-maker limits himself to a micro-view of the firm in a vacuum, and assumes that the system will survive automatically, his actions may contribute to the erosion of free enterprise upon which he depends for long-term survival and growth.

A healthy dose of macro-economics, together with a reasonable sprinkling of work in history, political science, and philosophy, will help build a foundation for viewing the firm in context of an economic system. But unless this context is kept alive in the study of business administration, the relevance may be lost. A management perspective that ignores the economic context within which the firm operates is shortsighted and inadequate if private enterprise is to prevail.

The Broader Context of Society Itself

The model of a hierarchy of economic values, based upon the pursuit of profit within an economic system that assures consumer values, can be justified in terms of enlightened economic self-interest. However, a broad perspective for the teaching of management admits other values besides the economic. Surely, life is more than making a living, the purpose of human society is greater than its economic survival and prosperity. But economic survival and comfort are a necessary prerequisite to broader social progress. Throughout history, peaks of economic well-being have accompanied or preceded those periods which are regarded as peaks of civilization in various cultures.[3] It is the great American dream that for the first time in human history we can build a culture and civilization in which high economic welfare is widely distributed among all members of society, and the opportunities for personal growth and development are available equally to all.

To put the economic aspect of life into a broader perspective, it is necessary to see the importance to a culture and civilization of developing not only vigor in economic activity, but also of devoting man's energies to the

---

[3] This thesis is demonstrated by Shepard B. Clough in *The Rise and Fall of Civilization* (New York: McGraw-Hill Book Company, Inc., 1951) and *The American Way: The Economic Basis of our Civilization* (New York: Thomas Y. Crowell Company, 1953).

civilizing process, once economic survival is assured. A surplus of goods beyond that necessary for maintaining life makes it possible for man to devote more energy and attention to the creation of works of literature, architecture, sculpture, music; to the establishment of orderly societies where the conduct of people conforms to known and just rules with a maximum of freedom of opportunity for self-expression. The economic factor is of great importance in attaining and protecting great heights of freedom, self-expression, and culture. Yet an undue preoccupation with the economic process as an end in itself may unwittingly interfere with the creation of these "finer things in life" which it initially makes possible.

In a hierarchy of values, the goals of society become much more subjective than the goals of an economic system. Individuals will vary greatly in the value they place upon creative achievement, justice, order, esthetic values, happiness, and beauty as the real stuff of civilization. Yet, as economic wellbeing becomes more widespread and taken for granted, it is these questions of "higher" values which will impinge on many business decisions. As a minimum, a value system must give some guidance as to the limits within which business must operate so as not to interfere with the development of a higher culture. This raises many immediate questions about "social responsibility" in such decision matters as community welfare, air and stream pollution, resource conservation, Madison Avenue techniques for sales promotion, and so forth. On the positive side, it opens up the whole area of business opportunity and responsibility, not only for interfering, but particularly for helping to promote and develop the broader culture and greater civilization that is within our grasp.

The Search for Ultimate Values

Man's search for ultimate values is the story of life itself. Implied in every decision he makes is a judgment in terms of a priority of values, when goals come into conflict, and in terms of the ultimate decision criterion. In every business decision, the manager acts upon his own response to the basic philosophical question, "What is the nature of man?" Whether expressed or implied, the decision-maker reveals his own philosophy of life in making these critical decisions.

As is true with social values, ultimate values also are subjective with the individual. There is, however, rather widespread general agreement within a given cultural context on the nature of these values. In the American tradition, rooted in the Judaeo-Christian ethic and democratic political philosophy, the *individual* is presumed to be the basic unit of satisfaction, and all social, political, and economic arrangements are designed to help him achieve self-fulfillment. This view contrasts sharply with opposing philosophies which consider the state the ultimate value, with the individual an instrument in helping the state achieve its historic destiny.

In the American cultural context, the ultimate goals or objectives of the individual are generalized as freedom, opportunity, self-realization, human dignity. These values assume a respect for the rights of others, a concern over justice and order under law, a responsibility for maintaining and perpetuating systems that make this freedom possible.

In a cultural context in which individual freedom and human dignity are of ultimate concern, the decision-maker in business is forced to assess his economic decisions in terms of their social and human consequences. The limits of his freedom in economic decision-making become readily apparent in terms of a value hierarchy that places economic values into perspective with other human values.

The Value Hierarchy as a Guide to Decision-making

The model of a hierarchy of values for management decisions discussed above is portrayed in Figure 33.1. It shows how limits of freedom in pur-

Figure 33.1   The Value Hierarchy — A Model for Management Decision

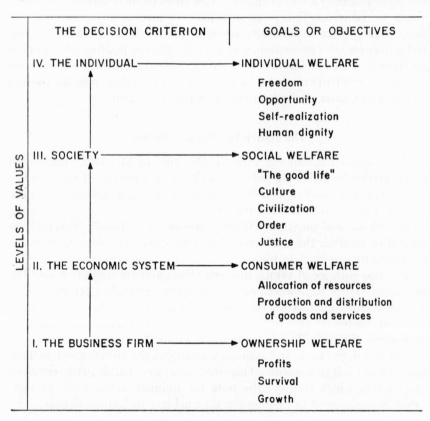

	THE DECISION CRITERION	GOALS OR OBJECTIVES
	IV. THE INDIVIDUAL────────────→	INDIVIDUAL WELFARE
		Freedom
		Opportunity
		Self-realization
		Human dignity
III. SOCIETY────────────────→		SOCIAL WELFARE
		"The good life"
		Culture
		Civilization
		Order
		Justice
II. THE ECONOMIC SYSTEM────────→		CONSUMER WELFARE
		Allocation of resources
		Production and distribution of goods and services
I. THE BUSINESS FIRM ──────────→		OWNERSHIP WELFARE
		Profits
		Survival
		Growth

LEVELS OF VALUES

suing objectives at a given level are set by the goals or values at a higher level. It suggests that responsible business management requires decisions and actions that contribute to the goals of the firm without violating higher values or goals.

This model places human values above economic values. It assumes that economic objectives can be achieved without denying the individual his basic rights as a human being. The value judgments the business manager faces, then, are largely those in which his decisions affect other human beings in their roles either as consumers or as employees.

The human being plays many roles in society. He creates human organizations through which he pursues his own goals in life. He (more or less) voluntarily associates himself with a variety of organizations — social, religious, political, business — and subordinates himself to the norms, rules, laws, policies, and traditions of those organizations. In his role as consumer he exercises considerable freedom of choice in supporting those economic organizations that serve his needs best. In his role as employee, he also has some freedom of opportunity in seeking employment, and, theoretically, freedom to leave an employer who violates his human dignity.

To the extent, however, that the job is the individual's medium for economic self-preservation, he is dependent on the employer for conditions of work which, hopefully, provide a broader range of satisfactions than economic survival. The manager creates or determines the work environment in which the employment relationship is carried out. In this context he faces an array of critical decisions involving human values of the individual and economic goals of the firm. Fortunately, in the great majority of cases, the human values and economic values reinforce each other, and are not in conflict. Nevertheless, when they do come into conflict, the manager's value system is put to the test, and his decisions may have consequences that determine not only the immediate effectiveness of the firm, but ultimately the type of economic, social, and political environment in which he will operate.

Conclusion

I believe that an awareness by the manager of the assumptions he makes and the values he holds is critical to effective management decision-making. The model of a hierarchy of values here proposed suggests that a manager should be aware of not only the immediate economic consequences of his decisions, but also of their ultimate consequences in terms of different levels of values. Training for management that keeps the question of values in view achieves not only better business decisions in the long run, but also develops a sense of social or citizenship responsibility which is the mark of an educated person. Schools of business have a great opportunity and responsibility here to measure up to their potential as educational institutions.

PART FOUR

Developments on the political, social, and economic scene throughout the world have focused increasing attention on management philosophies, on the behavior of executives, and on management theory and practice, in varying cultural settings. Less developed nations throughout the world are setting their courses for greater industrialization, with increasing demands for the export of management knowledge and skills. The extent of this knowledge exchange is at least in part indicated by the interchange of scholars between the United States and other nations. In the academic year 1963–1964, a total of 3,366 American scholars served abroad for periods of greater than thirty days. During this same period, 8,377 foreign scholars worked in the United States for periods greater than thirty days.[1]

The articles in this section provide examples of work by United States researchers in foreign countries. As would be expected, the researchers had to take account of cultural differences between countries where concepts originate and countries in which they are being applied. While the authors of these articles take a cautious view of the applicability of concepts developed out of American experience, they remain gen-

[1] *Open Doors: Report on International Exchange*, New York, Institute of International Education, Inc., July, 1964.

Problems of International Management

erally optimistic about the fruitfulness of attempts to export a large part of this knowledge and experience, and about the gains to be achieved by learning about management in other cultures.

The contrasts between the United States and management in other countries is perhaps most dramatic in cultures of the Orient. In his article on Japanese organization and management, Joseph N. Froomkin, notes great productivity increases under a system of little formality, little delegation, and practically no staff work. Organization and management methods are transmitted by tradition, rather than through a recorded, formally established body of systematic knowledge. Strong centralization, coupled with a strong sense of leadership and duty toward one's followers, are the keynotes. These precepts lead to difficulties of inter-departmental or inter-divisional communication, and in getting new functions started. But the author sees a number of ideas which he believes United States managers would find it worth while to consider.

Not only has scholarly knowledge been transmitted between cultures, but the skills, techniques, and practices of management have been exported by American companies operating overseas. Richard F. Gonzalez and Claude McMillan, Jr., show how United States executives face marked contrasts between their own business environment and that of a foreign country. Based on their two-year studies in Brazil, these authors believe that there is a uniquely American management philosophy and approach to business management, and moreover, that this unique philosophy is a special case, limited in applicability to economies and cultures comparable to that of the United States. They describe and illustrate several points at which the cultural bases of American managerial action clash with those of Brazil.

The fact that management philosophies are highly culture-bound has also interested Winston Oberg. While on a two-year assignment in Brazil, he made a study of the typical problems facing Brazilian managers in a cross-section of industries. In this article, he compares these problems with the typical problems faced by a sample of Michigan business managers. He, too, concludes that there are enough cultural variations to throw substantial doubt on the concept of universality of management principles. If there are such principles, he believes they should be subjected to more rigorous and more sophisticated testing.[2]

In the final article of this section, Barry M. Richman reports an incisive and extensive study of managerial motivation in Soviet and Czechoslovak industries. As Oberg does, he investigates the "rules of the game" by which managers in the two cultures act. His studies show that change occurs in communist states, as elsewhere. He compares how these two industrial states reached subtantially different conclusions concerning the same types of problems. Not only have major structural changes occurred in the environments in which managers in these two countries operate, but further major changes can be expected in the future. Richman concludes that Czech reforms have improved their system and that it currently has advantages over the Soviet system. He finds the potential for further change somewhat greater for the Soviets, who are still struggling to attain improved motivation and productivity of their system, than for the Czechs.[3]

It is clear, as indicated by the articles in this section, that the international dimension of management is a two-way system. Representatives of Culture A, when they operate in Culture B, not only transmit their own techniques and philosophies, but also modify their own as Culture B makes its advantages more apparent. Scholars and managers working abroad can do much to aid each other, and to aid industrializing notions, in the evolution of the science of management.

---

[2] In the United States, Ernest Dale has remained critical of the concept of universal managership. See Ernest Dale, "The Functional Approach to Management," in Harold Koontz, (Ed.), *Toward a Unified Theory of Management*, New York, The McGraw-Hill Book Company, Inc., 1964, pp. 20–40.

[3] For a further analysis of Soviet management and a comparison with American environment, see Barry M. Richman, *Soviet Management*, Englewood Cliffs, N.J., Prentice-Hall, Inc., 1965.

34

Management and Organization
In Japanese Industry*

Joseph N. Froomkin

International Business Machines Corporation

Cultural differences between Japanese and American businesses are examined and compared. The results of such a comparison do not always favor American management. However, little is really known about Japanese management practices, since secrecy and privacy are features of the Japanese business environment. The author presents a generally favorable analysis of Japanese management practice, with allowance for cultural values and problems of rapid growth and change.

Americans who look at the organization and practice of Japanese management always have the same initial reaction: Can this really work?

There is little formal organization, less delegation of authority and little reliance on staff work even in the largest firms. Nevertheless, Japanese industry has supported a rise in Gross National Product of 6.5% a year and industrial production has increased by 12% per annum. Management practices which make such growth possible deserve attention from all businessmen.

The practices underlying Japanese business organization are not extensively documented. There is very little literature on the subject. The dearth of information is no accident, but is due to the unwillingness of most Japanese businessmen to discuss their practices with outsiders. A Japanese corporation is a private preserve, and the internal method of operation, in the opinion of Japanese executives, is of no concern to any-

* Taken and adapted from *The Journal of the Academy of Management*, vol. 7, no. 1, March, 1964, pp. 71–76.

body outside the establishment. A definitive or detailed study of Japanese business will be done only when some top Japanese executive analyzes his organization after his retirement. In the meanwhile, the following notes gathered during a consulting trip in Japan might highlight some of the features of interest to U.S. managers.

Organization Follows Tradition

Despite the absence of an accepted or recorded theory of organization, most Japanese firms follow a single pattern in their organization and employment practices. This similarity reflects the impact of specific social values. Japanese society stresses the duties of leadership and assures rewards to followers. Most large Japanese firms translate these principles into the centralization of decision-making power and the no-firing rule — the so-called permanent employment policy. This common ground has made it possible to evolve strikingly similar practices in management.

The degree of centralization of decision-making power, however, varies from company to company. In some smaller companies it is so extreme that all decisions originate with the president of the company. This strong individual generally represents the ownership interest or is a major stockholder of the corporation. Though companies ruled by such a dictator still exist today, they are the exception rather than the rule.

In most of the large companies that I dealt with, strong leadership is equally evident but it is parceled out along functional lines. The absolute power to make decisions and to give instructions is clearly vested in a single person in each different area of the business, such as the plant manager, etc. Each one of these leaders possesses specific spheres of authority to the exclusion of all others. In contrast to some American business practices, the committee form of organization and "touching bases" before making a decision are almost unknown.

The leaders in the various management fields are accustomed to making independent decisions, but not to working together. As numerous American businessmen who have tried to reach agreements with Japanese firms have found out, it is difficult to get the leaders from different areas of the same business to agree. Japanese managers are not accustomed to interdepartmental give-and-take, and hence take an unconscionably long time to make up their minds on matters which involve more than one department.

As an American businessman who distributes the consumer electronic line for a large Japanese concern learned, for instance, it is extremely time consuming to have the managers of the portable and the standard radio divisions agree to a joint design for the line. It is much simpler to formalize the designs and then negotiate with the managers of the two lines separately.

Communicating Centralized Decisions

Although decisions are generally reached rapidly in Japanese business, the communication process requires that they be transmitted and discussed slowly.

In order to preserve the dignity of fellow employees, the communication of policy decisions takes the form of long and over-polite meetings, during which the pros and cons are discussed at great length, and the consensus demanded by the top manager is reached unanimously. This is achieved by carefully watching the important persons involved. On balance, this takes less time than most "brainstorming" or committee meetings in the U.S. — except for the rare decisions which cross departmental lines.

Many top managers of medium and large companies told me that the decision-making process had been democratized since the end of World War II. Nowadays, these managers permit their decisions to be discussed by their immediate subordinates in their own departments before such decisions are implemented. Sometimes, but not often, the subordinates' arguments are considered and the decisions reversed. This free discussion occurs most often in the marketing area, where Japanese managers have the least experience. Nevertheless, in all cases the final decision rests with the top manager.

New Functions Often Difficult to Start

A weakness of such centralized decision-making is the difficulty which Japanese firms have in adding new functions to their present organization. A box in the organization chart is not sufficient to get the operation going; it must have the backing of an important leader to be effective. Often this leader will hesitate to push the new function lest he upset the status quo and the working relationship with other important leaders. Thus centralized product design departments or audits of market share are seldom established in Japanese multiple-division companies, for fear they would impose an unbearable outside control over the heads of the division.

More than in the United States, adaptation to strong leadership takes precedence over the organization chart. When a new firm was formed by the merger of two companies a few years ago, for instance, an outside consultant was called in to set up the new organization. His organization chart still remains in force, but it does not describe the true power-centers of the company. In one part of the business, most important decisions are made by the head of the administrative department, and in the other, by the sales manager. All other departmental managers consult (really report to) these two men. The organizational chart is used to save the prestige of a large number of employees in the merged companies. The titles on the chart do not correspond to the functions.

Many employees of Japanese firms have titles such as chief of department, head of section, etc., and even more employees are assistants to these chiefs. These titles are usually devoid of any real decision-making power; they were created to accommodate the psychological needs of employees with many years of seniority.

Since the Japanese seem unable to cut up the operations of a business into relatively small and easy-to-manage functions, a strong and independent leader must be found for each important facet of the firm. On the whole, Japanese firms have succeeded in developing this type of leadership, even though the process may take considerable time. Yet, some functions are more difficult to start than others.

The Tough Road of Marketing — A New Function

Traditionally, the output of large Japanese companies is sold or consigned to an agent who distributes it to wholesalers. These wholesalers, in turn, sell to retailers. Dealing directly with retailers or establishing retail locations is considered a low-status occupation — one to which, therefore, it was difficult to draw top management attention.

In several instances, in the postwar period, marketing was neglected by large Japanese companies (it is still neglected by one of the biggest trading groups) because strong leaders could not be found within the company to head this function. The appointment of a marketing manager was not sufficient to overcome existing prejudices.

This lack of attention from top management precluded the appointment of men with leadership talent to handle these problems. Right after the war, a number of small, aggressive merchandisers started to eat into the traditional markets of large companies. The giants' reaction was not to make drastic changes in their organization, introduce tighter controls in marketing, or shorten the gap between the producer and the retailer. Instead, they tried to regain their share of the market by cutting prices. These price cuts generally were met by the competition. The market expanded, but the large companies did not recover their share of it. Only then did top management's attitude to marketing change. The difficult job of convincing likely candidates to accept positions in a low-status field was accomplished.

By now the majority of large companies have established their own distribution outlets and have set quotas to distributors based on share of market. They are slowly introducing training schools for retailers. The traditional annual banquet or outing for agents and retailers is no longer a purely social occasion, but is increasingly taking on the aspect of an industry training school.

The past ten years' progress in this field is very impressive. This was made clear to me by a sales call demonstration during the sales meeting of one of the largest consumer goods companies in Japan. Apart from the somewhat slower pace necessitated by the courtesy of Japanese life, the sales call could have been made in the U.S. It even suffered from the most general shortcoming of American sales calls — the absence of stress on the reason why the retailer should push the salesman's brand over that of competitors. I suggested that the script be amended to include references to the high quality of the company's product, which had won a prize at a trade fair, as well as reports of other retailers' success with the product. The eagerness with which these suggestions were accepted by salesmen — and later followed up at the regional sales meeting — indicated new flexibility in marketing techniques.

Keeping Up Morale in a Period of Change

How do Japanese companies carry off drastic changes in their organization and orientation without hiring outside personnel or destroying the firm's morale? The answer probably lies in their method of selecting and training managers. The characteristic attitude of management in Japanese firms is one of patient dedication. Most Japanese companies recruit young men immediately upon their graduation from a university. The best-known firms hire graduates from the equivalent of Ivy League schools, while smaller and foreign companies must content themselves with graduates of lower-ranking universities. In most cases, the first job is the only job these college graduates will ever have.

After joining the company, all college graduates go through a period of apprenticeship which lasts from 10 to 15 years. During this period they are all treated and remunerated on an equal basis. In the larger companies it is quite easy to guess a younger employee's salary by determining the number of years he has been employed. Only after this initial period are some apprentice managers advanced more speedily than others. The less able will remain in the firm until retirement and still receive minimal seniority increases.

This preservation of harmony within a firm by giving the illusion that nobody loses and everybody wins is difficult for outsiders to understand. An American sales executive complained that although the Japanese subsidiary management seemed to pay lip service to his efforts to introduce the merit system of promotion, they did nothing to bring it to life. After a particularly long lecture, which seemed to elicit agreement, he asked the local sales manager whether he would now promote an outstanding young man rather than a seasoned and mediocre older man. The Japanese sales manager replied that he was still convinced that he was obliged to promote the older man.

No Japanese manager would dare make a promotion that is blatantly out of turn — not only because it would rock the morale of the firm, but also because the apprenticeship period is valued for its "character build-ing" qualities. The period is spent in cementing relationships with one's contemporaries, and being observed by an important manager. A young man at this stage can have no greater joy than to perform a favor for a manager. On the other hand, the senior manager is always on the de-fensive against accepting such favors, lest he be morally obliged to further the young man's career. And an understanding of this facet of Japanese life sheds light on the willingness of young college graduates to work as house servants or errand boys for the heads of large enterprises. The young men are investing in a personal relationship, and their behavior closely resembles that of American business school graduates who buck for the job of administrative assistant to the president of the company.

The long apprenticeship period and the systematic method of advance-ment have both good and bad results. While they encourage extreme devotion and loyalty to the firm, they may also lead to an atmosphere of Balkan politics within the company. Loyalty to the organization is bal-anced by the expectation of rewards stemming from the firm. However, loyalty to the firm may be perverted into devotion to an individual senior manager in the expectation that this devotion will be rewarded. In the final round of promotions, when leaders are chosen to head the decision centers, Japanese firms pay a great deal of attention to "noble character" — a euphemism for the broader loyalty.

The most intriguing feature of the system is the fact that accepting decisions — as well as detailed instructions for their implementation — over such a long period of time seems to further, rather than hinder, the growth of leadership. It appears to develop the ability both to make decisions and to provide guidance after promotion to a manager's job. The close contact between leaders and followers also appears to favor the promotion of the ablest of the top-level jobs, possibly more so than under our own system. By contrast, promotions to intermediate positions in Japanese business are done on a routine basis, purely according to seniority.

What Is Good About Japanese Practices

The Japanese system of management development is responsible, to a large extent, for enabling Japanese industry to grow fast. The emphasis on broader loyalties and ability in choosing high level executives gives a solid topping to the management pyramid. At the same time, clear-cut responsi-bilities and loyalty to the firm make Japanese top managers eager to im-prove operations. The important manager does not end his development as a manager when he is promoted to a decision center. On the contrary, he begins it then. Courses in executive development seldom arouse much interest among younger employees; however, older employees request them. These courses are extremely difficult to plan. Having come up the hard way, most managers are not satisfied with generalities, but are interested in specific applications of principles of their own areas. They know their operations intimately, and are exceedingly critical of superficial recommendations.

The rapid growth of the Japanese economy has required only minor modifications in the organization of the management hierarchy. Many firms that grew relatively fast in the postwar period have had to promote younger managers somewhat faster than was customary. Other firms that rose from humbler beginnings and became important have adopted the traditional practices, taking care of older staff members who usually remained in key positions despite the firms' high rate of growth.

It is true that impatient young men with a modern outlook now have a few avenues open to chance-taking and rebellion. A few firms, especially in the electronics industry, hire, fire, and promote employees on the American pattern. But these firms remain very much in the minority, and there are signs that with increasing maturity they, too, will conform to the modes of the Japanese business pattern.

In the meantime, to stave off raids for personnel from unconventional firms, some large companies have attempted a light modification in their remuneration policies. Without disrupting the hierarchical ranking of employees by age, an additional dimension, that of merit, has been added to the salary structure. Raises of this type have usually occurred in new areas, such as marketing or data-processing, where problems with by-passed senior personnel have been minimized.

What lessons can American enterprise learn from the Japanese experience? Probably by far the most important is that management development can occur very satisfactorily in an atmosphere where security predominates. Secondly, that good management can be developed well, if not better, under conditions where guidance is given, rather than by the trial-and-error method practiced by many U.S. firms. Thirdly, that an important ingredient for fast and profitable growth is the existence of strong decision centers.

The security, the close supervision, and the close contact with strong decision makers must be contrasted with the competitive environment, the much looser supervision, and the emphasis on committee responsibility in American business. The results of the comparison will not always favor conditions here. If risk-taking is inhibited by lack of security, and the unsuccessful innovator is heavily penalized, then the Japanese pattern is to be preferred. Also, if young managers sink or swim because of fortuitous circumstances, as authority is delegated to them without any guidelines for the implementation of their tasks, it may be better to adopt some features of Japanese management practices. Finally, U.S. businessmen should keep in mind that a strong decision-maker and manager may also make a good coordinator, and that it may be possible to have the best of both worlds.

35

The Universality of American
Management Philosophy*

Richard F. Gonzalez

Claude McMillan, Jr.

Michigan State University

The authors of this paper share with Professor Oberg a certain skepticism about the universality of management precepts and philosophies in all cultures regardless of their stage of development. Some of the contrasting cultural factors between Brazilian and United States managerial philosophies are traced and illustrated. Their conclusions suggest the care with which American management know-how should be applied in other cultures.

There is a growing interest among scholars and executives in international business management. With increasing frequency books and articles dealing with international management are appearing on the market. Titles like these indicate the scope and direction of these publications: *Management Guide to Overseas Operations, The Executive Overseas, Management of International Operations, Management in the Industrial World.* Recently two new periodicals have appeared: *The International Executive,* and *Management International.*

Initially the viewpoint of writers in this field was the viewpoint of the stateside manager who had supervisory responsibility over the overseas operation. Harbison and Myers have portrayed the characteristics of national managers abroad, functioning in their own cultures.[1] More recently, writers have turned to the problems of the American manager serving over-

* Taken and adapted from *The Journal of the Academy of Management,* vol. 3, no. 1, April, 1961, pp. 33–41.
[1] Frederick Harbison and Charles A. Myers, *Management in the Industrial World,* New York, McGraw-Hill Book Company, Inc., 1959.

seas with his company's foreign branch or subsidiary. This change of emphasis is appropriate. Since the end of World War II the involvement of U.S. professional management in the economies of the world has increased enormously. U.S. international business operations no longer involve predominantly the stateside export manager, but rather involve the U.S. executive as entrepreneur, as politician, as professional administrator in a a culture and economy foreign to his own.

These U.S. expatriate executives find themselves in contrasting decision-making environments, dealing with problems foreign to their stateside experience. Aspects of these contrasting environments call into question the applicability of the U.S. managerial approach to certain business problems. The thesis of this article, based on the author's two-year study of American management in South America, is that (1) there is a uniquely American management philosophy, an American approach to business management, and (2) this unique American philosophy is a special case, limited in applicability to economies and cultures comparable to that of the United States.

The American Philosophy of Management

Within the structure of American management there are elements of numerous philosophies. However, the public avowals of business leaders, the policy statements of American firms, and the writings of those who concern themselves with management science provide a common thread of ideas which embody contemporary American management philosophy. This philosophy is comprised of a system of attitudes, approaches, precepts, broad guide lines, principles and values by reference to which the American businessman deals with business problems.

American managers have this philosophy in common. It is deeply ingrained in their thinking and apparent in their actions. They hold this philosophy in common because they are, to a greater or lesser extent, products of a common American ethic and a common social and economic structure.

The uniqueness of this philosophy is apparent to anthropologists and sociologists who study contrasting cultures. It is increasingly apparent to American management personnel who serve their parent company overseas and find themselves in a contrasting environment. The great bulk of U.S. investment abroad is in the underdeveloped nations of the world, where economies and cultures are least like that of the U.S. The bulk of this investment involves firms which had little if any overseas investment 30 years ago.

The U.S. today occupies the place of eminence in the world of international enterprise which Britain occupied in 1913. But whereas the British export was largely financial, the American export is also technological, entrepreneurial, and particularly managerial. Whereas the British investor was the wealthy English individual, the U.S. investor abroad today is the large American business enterprise. The export is a package including equipment, funds, international market connections, and technological and managerial know-how — a small replica of the stateside enterprise. The managers who accompany this package abroad are professional American managers, products of the U.S. culture, imbued with the American managerial philosophy, and dedicated to their parent firm's particular set of policies and standards.

Management principles have relevance in a total social framework. When a new American professional manager arrives at his post abroad he soon learns that the propriety of his approach to many management problems is questioned alike by his more experienced American manager predecessors, by his subordinates, and by his counterpart national businessmen.

That there are contrasts in the American manager's decision-making environment abroad cannot be denied. Let us examine these contrasts briefly.

The contrasts in the American manager's decision-making environment abroad readily fall into two categories: (1) those which arise out of the contrasting state of economic development — chiefly the state of industrialization of the country, and (2) those which can be attributed to the culture of the country. By definition, the underdeveloped and developing nations present a contrasting physical-facilitative environment within which the overseas manager must operate. There results what may be termed mechanical problems for the overseas operation. These contrasts are examined below approximately in the order in which the manager might encounter them when setting up the overseas enterprise.

The Decision Environment and the State of Development

There is initially the task of deciding the nature and scope of the operations, a task made difficult because of a general lack of basic economic information which is both timely and reliable. Market research services are lacking. Where the product is new or different in some respect there is little basis for estimating product acceptance or the limits of the market. Often the smallest unit of production capacity far exceeds demands of the local market. A seamless tube mill, for example, was set up in a Latin American country to supply the newly expanded automotive industry. Mill capacity of a few hours a day could provide that industry's requirement. The firm had to expand the scope of operations to include forming and preparation of tube assemblies, a phase of operations not originally planned.

Anticipating the promotion and distribution of the product, the American manager will learn that conventional appeals, channels of communication and distribution, are different. An anticipated nation-wide market may be restricted to a single city because of the absolute absence of transportation facilities. The sales effort required to enlarge the market may depend on the efforts of a widely scattered sales force only slightly controllable by the home office.

Once the decision to operate abroad at a given scale is made, the next question is one of providing the product. It can be imported, in which case the manager may face staggering red tape, documentation, petty bribery, and most frequently, the disinclination of the host government to allow or encourage importation of finished products into the country. The subsidiary must go into the local money market to pay for the imported goods and is met with restrictions designed to regulate the manner in which typically short dollar supplies may be allocated. An additional problem may stem from the inflation which plagues many underdeveloped nations. Manipulated, multiple and special-category exchange rate structures make it extremely difficult for the American to plan an orderly flow of importations and to control his inventories as he can in the United States. Any disparity between price and exchange rate levels renders inventory management a speculative, if not a gambling, process.

If, on the other hand, the decision is made to set up physical plant facilities, other contrasts are faced. Building materials, methods, and specifications will differ. Equipment must generally be imported with the problem of securing permission and arranging conditions under which the equipment will be valued, taxed, and later replaced. To an increasing degree, Americans are using equipment which is not of U.S. design and manufacture because of unfavorable cost and tariff structures which exist between the U.S. and the host country.

The maintenance of the plant and equipment presents a major problem to operating managers. Workers are not maintenance minded and typically lack an awareness of the value of equipment. Facilities for repair parts and specialized maintenance service are not available. Climatic conditions often result in accelerated wear of equipment.

Staffing the manufacturing operation is a further study in contrasts. The labor market cannot supply the variety of specialized skills needed for operations and administration. The labor force is relatively unskilled, immobile, and not always susceptible to motivations which American managers employ. The relationships between worker and manager may be carried on within a labor organization which is in reality an agency of the federal government. Not only might wages and working conditions be prescribed by law, but measures to insure the security of workers go far beyond those known to Americans.[2] The writers learned that nationals

[2] The indemnification laws, common in most Latin American countries, virtually prevent discharge of an employee after 10 years continuous service. The result is an almost

employed by U.S. firms privately consider their working conditions and treatment to be superior to conditions in national firms. These workers, however, are not prone to make these feelings known publicly in the face of an official union position to the contrary.

For many middle and upper managerial positions the American subsidiary will have to recruit from the ranks of the parent company with all the attendant problems of selecting and transferring personnel. The nature of a mixed and stratified staff will in many cases lead to misunderstanding on the part of the nationals employed by the subsidiary. Few companies thus engaged seem to plan for the orderly staffing of the subsidiary and few are aware of the personal problems faced by the newly assigned managers.

As frequently happens, the subsidiary is part of the parent firm's international division. However, the manufacturing operations are typically staffed directly from the stateside manufacturing organization. Less autonomy for the local management results. The production executives find it necessary to communicate with the home plant for numerous engineering changes and approval to substitute or modify components. In some cases final inspection approval must be forthcoming from the home office for each production run.[3] The division of final authority between the international and the domestic divisions of the home firm, plus the difficulty of communicating at great distances complicates the subsidiary manager's role.

Of all contrasts, perhaps the legal-financial setting is the sharpest. Here the American is most aware that he is operating in a foreign country. He will tend to find the money market poorly developed as a regular source of funds. This becomes important wherever the local government imposes limits on the amount of outside capital which may be brought in, or where there are provisions that a given percentage of the total capitalization shall be held by nationals in the host country. Assuming the prevalent condition of inflation, there is little incentive to defer consumption and save in order to make funds available for long term investment. There is a propensity to view with favor non-industrial investments, as for example, land and construction.

Most capital markets in the developing economies sharply limit their operations geographically and do not provide the information or services

---

automatic discharge before an employee attains this favored position. Turnover is relatively greater and the American concepts of seniority and longevity are unknown. U.S. executives for the most part maintain that they are not influenced by these indemnification laws. In many cases the subsidiaries have yet to face up to the problem because of the relative newness of operations.

[3] Eli Lilly and Company of Brazil is a typical case. Samples of all new products must be submitted to the parent firm for assay and authorization to manufacture — a time-consuming procedure.

to which the American business man is accustomed. Consequently the American will either attempt to bring in funds from the parent company which will be subject to local government regulation, or he will solicit funds from individuals or the government of the host country. The latter source may be significant. It is not uncommon to be in partnership with the government which may have extended an initial invitation or which may have solicited foreign investment under one of a myriad of developmental agencies which exist in most of these countries.

The legal framework of the host country poses further contrast. Included are widely differing laws of incorporation and liability, employer-employee relations, workers' compensation and indemnification, income tax and accounting procedures as well as the multiple rulings of the quasi-legislative-executive agencies of the federal and local governments. These commonly treat such matters as foreign exchange, export-import licensing, economic planning, and the numerous specialized efforts to encourage specific types of economic development, monetary and fiscal control and the tariff. Interestingly it is in the legal area where the Americans must learn rapidly to work with local counsel. The subsidiary in many cases cannot be represented by stateside counsel who have no standing before the Latin American bar.

All of the above are superimposed upon a framework of differing political-governmental institutions. To the degree that these reflect cultural contrasts they are treated later on. However the economic goals of host governments lead them to play an ever increasing role in the business area. The American will find his traditional role as a decision-maker curtailed. In many cases the growth of the subsidiary will be dictated, encouraged or discouraged by direct government action.

Finally there are those contrasts still reflecting the differences due to the state of economic development, which are seen in the under-developed state of many of the supporting economic institutions which the American assumes to be part of the business environment. These include banking services and the banking system itself, commercial credit facilities, a sophisticated communications and distribution system, and perhaps the lack of an attitude of professionalism among those who engage in business activity. The list is scarcely exhaustive.

The Decision Environment and Contrasting Cultures

The under-developed nations of the world have in common many economic, cultural and political characteristics which stand in contrast to U.S. society. Most of these nations have little tradition of personal freedom as do Americans and they strive for it today far less than they strive for desirable national attributes such as economic well-being, social order, prestige, and power. Perhaps today more than any time in recent decades they are willing to forego many of their present freedoms with the hope that by so doing they can achieve more desirable material advances.

It is frequently suggested that the economies of these nations are comparable to that of the U.S. seventy-five years ago. Their productive wealth is in the hands of the aristocratic few, who feel little obligation in the way of public service. These same aristocratic owners tend to be the political leaders of their countries, to own the newspapers and radio broadcasting systems, and to be molders if not makers of public opinion. They view a truly free market with suspicion. In a way they are in the "public be damned" stage of business leadership.

As already indicated, these economies are characterized by a great want of personal devotion to saving. This is due in part to the lack of an ethical tradition which placed great premium on hard work and frugality as virtues. But it is due in larger part today to inflation whose toll in decreased purchasing power makes saving illogical.

These nations tend to be afflicted with a reluctance to cooperate; there is wanting a network of compatible, cooperating institutions which serve to unify social activities and to provide the economic framework within which the talents and energies of the entrepreneur can be challenged and utilized for the benefit of all. There is a lesser disposition to respect the law, to conform to the rules in the interests of order, progress, and efficiency. The great majority of American executives with whom the authors came in contact in South America viewed this as a difficult and serious problem in everyday business affairs. The American manufacturer who endeavors to comply with laws, to pay taxes and conform to prescribed employment rules is at a decided disadvantage among competitors whose culture attaches little importance to ethical business conduct.

There is a difference in temperament. Distrust, relatively, seems to be a national heritage. Americans tend to organize and conduct their lives in society on the assumption that most people can be trusted. Abroad, distrust is particularly manifest towards strangers and those who are not of the social elite. This helps explain the foreign national's preference for doing business with those whom he knows as intimate friends. Factors such as terms, quality, service, and price tend to be cast aside in favor of personal contacts when important dealings are made. This same preference for intricate, individual, and personal relationships accounts for the fact that political parties are thought of and dealt with not as institutions but in terms of the identity of their strong authoritarian leaders. It is not the party, the business organization, the educational institution, the foundation or the government to which one owes allegiance, but rather the leader's personality.

Failure to recognize this has resulted in costly blunders for some American firms abroad. In 1958 the American Can Company's entry into the

Brazilian market was set back several years by well organized public manifestations of hostility. The company had cleared its proposed program of container manufacture with the appropriate Brazilian government agency. But in advertising its proposed program as a boon to the economy of Brazil it failed to reckon with the susceptibility of the Brazilian people to allegiance with a favored Brazilian family: The Matarazzos. The mass of public opinion was much less responsive to American Can's offer of additional production capacity, greater competition, more and better customer service than they were to organized sympathy for the Matarazzo interests. Economic abstractions meant much less than did damage to the personal interests of the empire which bore a well-known name.

Thus the Matarazzo container monopoly which bore partial responsibility for Brazil's inability to feed itself was able to continue without competition for another few years.

In summary, the American tends to assume a free economy in which business is aware of its service obligation. Competition is advocated and it is assumed that people can generally be trusted to so govern themselves as to promote a larger social purpose. In contrast, people in the underdeveloped areas of the world assume that a free economy is not entirely trustworthy, that government by strong individuals who can be expected to grow rich in office is the norm, and that manifestation of concern for the masses is to be viewed with suspicion.

The Appropriateness of American Management Philosophy Abroad

Management is both science and art. That portion of the managerial function which is susceptible to the application of scientific principles is ever increasing. The science of management has reached its highest state of development in the U.S., and it is for this knowledge, this know-how, that American management is most highly respected abroad. Transferred abroad, this know-how is first viewed with skepticism. Foreign national employees and partners are slow to respond and understand the American scientific approach to management problems. However, once fully indoctrinated they accept and support this way of doing things. The superiority of this more objective, systematic, orderly and controlled approach to problems is seen and accepted. For the host country, for American international relations, and for the American parent firm itself the export of American managerial know-how as well as technological know-how has yielded great dividends.

Our claim that management can be scientific is thus supported by the evident universality of this aspect of managerial know-how. But all aspects of the American approach to management are not universally respected abroad and in the adaptations which successful American managers make to a foreign environment there is evidence of a lack of universality in contemporary American management philosophy. That aspect of management which lacks universality has to do with interpersonal relationships, including those between management and workers, management and suppliers, management and the customer, the community, competition and government.

Those writers who deal most extensively with managerial philosophy have dealt most intensively with management-employee relations. In the field of international management this pattern has been maintained. Thus Fayerweather and Harbison and Myers, in discussing management abroad, emphasize management-employee relations.[4] Fayerweather deals chiefly with American management and employee relations in foreign countries while Harbison and Myers deal with contrasting relations between management and employees in their own countries throughout the world. But management philosophy involves more than a philosophy of management and labor relations. As Professor R. C. Davis has suggested, a management philosophy can and should supply the basis for a broader range of management problems.[5]

A complete philosophy of management involves all managerial relationships and is based on broad and fundamental tenets. The American philosophy is closely associated with the American ideal which places great emphasis on personal freedom, the rights of private property, the sanctity of contract and the stewardship or service responsibility of those in positions of leadership. It tolerates a limited degree of government regulation but relies primarily on competitive market forces in a free economy to exercise control. It assumes that individual initiative, given the opportunity to seek self-aggrandizement, will manifest itself for the common good. It professes belief in the Protestant ethic, subscribing to the virtues of hard work and thrift.

Yet these are abstract concepts, and the complete managerial philosophy also depends for its identity on the way in which these concepts are applied to the solution of business problems. The successful manager is something of a politician. He must adapt to his environment. As Harbison and Myers state: "His (the manager's) policies are thus the result of accommodations, and his philosophy at any one period is likely to be a rationalization of the cumulative impact of the pressures which have been brought to bear upon him. In other words, management must adjust to its environment."[6]

---

[4] John Fayerweather, *The Executive Overseas*, and *Management of International Operations*; Frederick Harbison and Charles A. Myers, *op. cit.*

[5] Ralph C. Davis, "A Philosophy of Management," *The Journal of the Academy of Management*, December, 1958.

[6] Harbison and Myers, *op. cit.*, p. 61.

In a study of American executives in South America from 1958 to 1960 the authors found that the American businessman recognizes this need to adapt. Few of these businessmen could identify in what precise way the new American assignee's approach and understanding were inadequate. But all manifested an awareness that several years on the job abroad yields an alteration in the man as a manager — that perhaps intuitively he adopts a new attitude, a new approach or philosophy which is more conducive to managerial effectiveness.

The validity of this thesis is further supported by the change in American management philosophy through time. Our own management philosophy today is a product of the past. It has appropriately changed through time as public opinion, unionization, and government policy have altered the businessman's decision-making environment.

Today's concept of what constitutes appropriate and effective conduct among business leaders stands in vivid contrast to that which prevailed seventy-five years ago in the U.S. American management philosophy of 1875 would hardly be appropriate for the U.S. in 1960. Similarly a management philosophy which is appropriate for Chicago today is not necessarily appropriate for Calcutta or Buenos Aires.

We tend to strive for a unified, universally valid philosophy by reference to which management action is appropriate and meaningful. Professor R. C. Davis, in discussing a management philosophy, suggests that a philosophy can and should be scientific in that it is based upon and derived from valid tenets and is applicable to the solution of managerial problems anywhere.[7] But if the resultant philosophy is appropriate and valid only for a given economic-cultural framework, it cannot be universal.

American management experience abroad provides evidence that our uniquely American philosophy of management is not universally applicable but rather is a special case. For American enterprise and American management, recognizing this fact is important.

[7] R. C. Davis, *op. cit.*

36

Cross-Cultural Perspectives on
Management Principles*
Winston Oberg

Michigan State University

This article reports a study which compared data from a sample of top Brazilian managers with a sample of top managers in the State of Michigan. The purpose was to determine whether the ground rules for the game of management are closely similar or widely divergent in the two cultures, as a test of the validity of the universality of management principles. The author believes that cultural differences are more significant than is commonly recognized. Ten specific problems of concern to top management, in both places, are examined and compared.

The perennial argument between those who hold that management is a science governed by universal principles which can be discovered by research and those who say it is an art whose successful practice is dependent on a lengthy apprenticeship in a specific highly culture-bound situation will probably be intensified as the results of current cross-cultural studies of management become more widely known. Harbison and Myers,[1] for example, in their study of management development practices in twenty-three countries, made a number of generalizations about management and management development which suggested that these did not differ fundamentally from country to country. Bendix[2] compared the management situation in the U.S. today with that of British and Russian management

* Taken and adapted from *The Journal of the Academy of Management*, vol. 6, no. 2, June, 1963, pp. 129–143.

[1] Frederick Harbison and Charles A. Myers, *Management in the Industrial World*, (McGraw-Hill Book Company, Inc., New York, 1959).

[2] Reinhard Bendix, *Work and Authority in Industry*, (John Wiley & Sons, Inc., New York, 1956).

at the turn of the century and management in East Germany today and found many common elements. On the other hand, Gonzalez and McMillan,[3] after serving as consultants on business administration training in Brazil, concluded that management philosophies are highly culture-bound.

An important issue is whether or not the requirements for managerial success and the ground rules under which managers operate are quite similar from country to country or whether they differ so significantly as to make any attempt to generalize meaningless and futile. The study of the ground rules under which managers operate appears to be particularly significant in this analysis. Should the ground rules be the same or similar there would be a presumption that the qualities required and the strategy or "science" involved do not differ too much from country to country. If on the other hand the ground rules are markedly different — or, using an analogy from sports, if the "game" of management is played according to one set of rules in the United States and quite different rules in France and still other rules in Brazil, it would be as fruitful to study the strategy of baseball in one country the strategy of soccer in another, and the strategy of cricket in still a third country to derive a set of common principles or generalizations as it would to try to generalize about management when practiced under so many different national conditions.

My own experience in international management leads me to believe that cultural differences from one country to another are more significant than many writers now appear to recognize. For example, the skills that lead to managerial success in the U.S. may not be the skills that lead to managerial success in Brazil, to take the two countries with whose managers I am most familiar. Certainly the problems which managers face in these two cultures differ and the ground rules under which managers operate are almost as unlike in these two countries as the ground rules under which the two countries' national games are played. If, as it appears, the Brazilian manager is playing a form of "soccer" while the U.S. manager is playing "baseball," it is difficult to see how basic generalizations will apply with anywhere equal force to the two situations.

An illustration may clarify this point for the reader. Between August, 1959, and July, 1960, I served as a technical assistant to the University of Rio Grande do Sul (Brazil) under an I.C.A. agreement between my university and the Brazilian government. My role was to help the University of Rio Grande do Sul develop a business administration curriculum and train business administration professors. Part of my responsibility was to initiate a series of management seminars to demonstrate to the local

[3] Richard F. Gonzalez and Claude McMillan Jr., "The Universality of American Management Philosophy" *Journal of the Academy of Management*, vol. 4, no. 1, (April 1961) pp. 33–41. (See Selection Number 35 of this book).

community the value of the kind of curriculum we were hoping to develop. In preparation for these seminars, I visited a cross-section of businessmen in the state of Rio Grande do Sul (southernmost state in Brazil and the state that holds the dubious distinction of having expropriated more United States-owned businesses than any other in Brazil).[4] In these visits, I attempted to gain an understanding of the main problems or worries that these men were concerning themselves with. Altogether, I visited 34 companies and talked to 51 presidents, vice presidents, or managing directors. Organizations ranged from manufacturing firms to insurance companies and included banks, newspapers, importing and exporting firms, wholesaling and retailing establishments and even one airline. Their size ranged from around 30 to 1,900 employees. (This last company was the largest in that part of Brazil.)

As a cross-section, this was as representative a selection as local businessmen, serving as my advisers, were able to select. The problems which came out of the study can, therefore, be regarded as the typical problems facing top managers in that state in late 1959 and early 1960. These problems will be compared with a subsequent U.S. study designed to get a parallel list of problems from top businessmen in the state of Michigan whose firms compared in size and activity with the Brazilian firms. In early 1962 we sent to some 1,700 small- and medium-sized firms in the state a questionnaire which, among other things, asked for the two or three most difficult problems the small businessman in Michigan was facing. Although the survey was carried out by mail and the approach was in other respects not identical with that used in Brazil, the focus on management problems was quite similar. The size of the companies surveyed was also parallel to that of Brazil. The range was from a low of three employees to a high of 2,000.

Although response to the questionnaire survey was disappointingly low, (less than 10% of the companies responded), there is no apparent reason to feel that the problems which were reported were unrepresentative of the population covered. One hundred and six usable responses to the question about the Michigan small businessman's problems were received. These will be presented immediately following the list of Brazilian managers' problems. Both samples covered predominantly top management. In the Michigan survey, roughly four out of five respondents were at the vice presidential level or higher. In the Rio Grande do Sul survey, three out of four were at that level. A comparison of the problems of these two sets of managers suggests that although some problems are similar a strikingly different total situation exists in Brazil from that in the U.S. The "game" the two sets of managers are playing may conceivably be the same, in some

---

[4] Between 1959 and 1962, two U.S. owned utilities were expropriated by Leonel Brizolo, governor of the state.

of its fundamentals, but the local ground rules are so different that the reader may well ask how any kind of general strategy, or any set of generalizations or principles can possibly apply to both situations.

The "Game" of Management — Played by Rio Grande do Sul (Brazil) Ground Rules

Brazilian managers mentioned more than 80 different problems.[5] Since many of them were similar, it was possible to group the problems into some 15 categories. The ten most frequently mentioned categories are reported here in detail. (See Table 36.1.)

Table 36.1
The Ten Most Common Problems Mentioned by 51 Rio Grande do Sul (Brazil) Top Managers in 1960

Rank	Problem	% Mentioning
1	Shortage of capital	32
2	Competition with other states	29
3 (tie)	Finding and training high-level executives	26
3 (tie)	Getting good skilled or technical workers	26
5	Inflation	24
6	The farm problems and its effect on business	21
7	Getting good foremen	18
8 (tie)	Tenure	15
8 (tie)	Illiterate or barely literate workers	15
10	The transportation problem	12

1) *The Problem of Raising Money — the Shortage of Capital*

Of the fifteen problems mentioned, this one came up most frequently. 32% (11 of the 34 companies) mentioned it in one way or another. Managers complained about the shortage of money, the difficulty of raising capital, the difficulty in financing credit sales. Here are some typical comments:

> We buy on 90-day terms and sell on 120- to 300-day terms. It is difficult to finance these long-term sales, but we have to because our competitors do.

> Many of our sales are to the government and they take up to three years to pay. This puts a great strain on our capital. It is even worse when a new government takes over. They don't like to pay the bills of the former government.

[5] Survey results were presented at a conference of Rio Grande do Sul managers held in Porto Alegre, Brazil, and were subsequently published: Winston Oberg, "Como a Universidade Pode Ajudar o Homem de Negocios" *Correio do Povo*, Porto Alegre, Brazil, July 3, 1960, p. 26.

Seventy-five per cent of the money printed in Brazil is in Rio, São Paulo, and Belo Horizonte. There is a real shortage of money down here.

Money is shifted to other states for political reasons. Eight banks in Porto Alegre (capital of Rio Grande do Sul) have only half the assets of one bank in Minas. The president of the country is from Minas and has been favoring that state.

As will be seen, this problem is closely related to several of the subsequent problems. In part, the difficulties are due to the country's galloping inflation and to the consequent flight of money out of the country (the "investment in dollars") or the flight into such inflation hedges as real estate projects.

2) *The Problem of Competition with Other States, Particularly São Paulo, Minas Gerais, and Rio de Janeiro*

29% of the companies mentioned this problem in different ways. Some sample comments:

Our main markets are in the triangle: São Paulo, Minas, Rio. We are at a disadvantage being located down here. Transportation costs to the main market put us at a disadvantage.

We are thinking of moving our headquarters out of Rio Grande do Sul to central Brazil. The future looks better there.

The money that is taken out of Rio Grande do Sul by taxes and spent elsewhere in Brazil makes it difficult for local businesses. Our business down here is discriminated against in favor of some other states.

At the time of these interviews, this problem was probably in its most acute stage. Brazil's new capital, Brasilia, was just being completed. Industrial states nearest to Brasilia — São Paulo, Minas Gerais, Rio — had benefited most from the flow of printing press money which had paid for the construction of the new Brazilian capital. Rio Grande do Sul, more than 1,000 miles to the south, had not participated to any great extent in the Brasilia-generated demand for products. Bank deposits and tax money had in large quantities gone north to the states around Brasilia.

3) *The Problem of Finding and Training Executives or High-Level Managers*

26% of the companies mentioned this problem in one way or another. Here are some of the comments:

Our businessmen have had no training. In many cases, a man gets to be director because he's the only man available, not because he's well qualified or the best man for the job. Rio Grande do Sul managements are getting old. They're not keeping up with the progress of the country.

> We can't get good management trainees. The universities don't produce them. We tried to get men from the university. They haven't worked out. The people here who are managers have all started as clerks.

> We can't replace the directors if they leave. We don't have anybody who can take their places.

> We've grown, but our people have not. We've grown too fast for our management.

> We need to decentralize but we can't. We don't have any people to give the responsibility to. You can't delegate responsibility. People won't accept it.

Finally, here is a remarkably candid and revealing comment:

> The family idea here is strong. You get a young fellow with ability and he works hard expecting to get ahead and then along comes the 20-year old son of the owner and he's boss. It discourages people who aren't relatives. Of course, it's pretty important to have close family control at the top because you need absolute loyalty. No one in Brazil considers it dishonest to cheat the government. But to cheat, you need close family-type management and control. You can't afford to let outsiders in. You have to keep the management in the family. It's possible that this will change now that the government is getting more successful in its tax collection. It's getting quite a bit tougher to cheat.

Tied for 3) *The Problem of Getting Good Skilled or Technical Workers*

This problem was also mentioned by 26% of the companies. Here are some of the comments:

> We can buy machinery easier than we can get good men to run the machinery. It takes up to two years to train a good lathe man.

> There is a real shortage of good technical people in the shop and office.

> We have to train our mechanics. We can't hire any. Then we have the problem that when you train a man you often lose him. Other companies hire him away from you after you've spent the time and money to train him.

5) *The Problem of Inflation*

In an article published in 1955 on Brazilian economic progress, Spiegel wrote:

> Inflation, Keynes quotes Lenin, is the best way to destroy the capitalist system. . . . Inflation tends to confound all values, and its persistence in Brazil may at least in part be held responsible for what Lord Bryce once called 'the habit of mistaking words for facts and aspirations for achievements.' . . . To raise the question whether governmental ideology favors inflation as a means of forcing saving is to inquire whether

the government openly favors sin. There are few Brazilian statesmen in responsible positions who have not, time and again, and in the strongest terms, professed profound aversion to inflation and promised prevention or relief. Inflation has progressed notwithstanding. . . .[6]

Spiegel was writing before the 1955 election of President Kubitschek and hence before Brasilia. Even then, inflation was a far more serious problem than anything we in the U.S. have ever faced. By way of illustration, the consumer price index for the city of Porto Alegre computed by the University of Rio Grande do Sul rose nearly 50% in 1954 and another 20% in 1955. Following the election of Kubitschek in 1955, inflation maintained a fairly steady pace, ranging between 10% and 20% per year until 1959. Then the consumer price index began to rise more rapidly, reaching a rate of nearly 40% per year. In the first eight months of 1959, alone, the index rose more than 25%. The index stood at 472 in December, 1958, and by August, 1959, it had reached 588 (1948 prices equal 100).[7] Considering the nature of the inflationary problem, it is somewhat surprising that only 24% of the companies mentioned the problem during the interviews. Possibly there was some censorship of problems during the interview—some limitation of problems to those about which I or the university might be of some assistance; or possibly, inflation generated an appearance of prosperity and high demand which gave it a beneficial appearance to some managers. In any case, the comments of those who realized the problem left no doubts as to its seriousness:

> The big problem is how to maintain your capital in the face of inflation. Paper profits aren't real profits. Some of our competitors don't realize what their real costs and profits are. So they charge unrealistically low prices. They think they're making a profit, but actually they're eating into their capital.

> Big farmers and businessmen in general are not putting their money back into the farm or business to produce more but are putting it into city real estate. This cuts down on the amount of things produced and just makes inflation worse.

6) *The Farm Problem and Its Effect on Business*

Rio Grande do Sul historically had been one of the most important agricultural states in Brazil. In 1959, it still accounted for more than two-thirds of Brazil's production of beans, alfalfa, barley, wool, and grapes to mention only a few of the state's agricultural products. However in the

---

[6] Henry William Spiegel, "Brazil: The State and Economic Growth" in Simon Kuznets, ed. "Economic Growth: Brazil, India, Japan" (Duke University Press, Durham, N. C. 1955) pp. 415–416.

[7] Statistics reported in "Boletim Informativo" of the Faculdade de Ciencias Economicas, Universidade de Rio Grande do Sul, Ano V, 1958 and Ano VI, 1959.

years immediately preceding 1959 the government's de-emphasis of agriculture and intensive encouragement of industrialization had sharply decreased some kinds of agricultural production in the state, with resulting dislocations in the economy of Rio Grande do Sul. Several of the businessmen interviewed had been adversely affected by this de-emphasis of agriculture. 21% of them mentioned this problem in one way or another. Here are some of their comments:

> Agriculture will always be the main source of income here. We're giving too much attention to industry. We used to feed all of Brazil but now Rio Grande do Sul is even having to import black beans.

> Our state is mainly agricultural. Industry should be based on agriculture. Our companies should either be using what the farms produce or making things for the farms to use.

> We are trying to do too much and not being realistic. This state should try to improve the quality of its farming first before worrying about industry.

> This is an agricultural state. Our money comes from agriculture but we are trying to impose on this an industrial economy. Rio Grande do Sul should concentrate on agriculture. That's where the money is.

7) *The Problem of Getting Good Foremen*

Closely related to the first personnel problem, that of getting good executives, is the problem of finding capable foremen. 18% of the companies mentioned this as a problem:

> People don't know how to handle the people working for them, how to get the most out of people. Sometimes they get too friendly with subordinates hoping this will get more cooperation, but just the reverse happens.

> There just aren't enough good foremen.

> Some good men don't want to be foremen. They don't want to be the boss of their colleagues, don't want responsibility.

> This is a family company so we can't have much trouble at the top, but the people below this level — the foremen and sub-foremen — give trouble.

8) *The Problem of Tenure*

This very interesting problem has no exact U.S. counterpart. Under Brazilian social legislation, companies must give severance pay to anyone who has been employed by them for more than a year. Until a man has ten years of service, a company can discharge him relatively simply by paying him one month's salary for every year of continuous service. After a man has been employed for more than ten consecutive years, he receives permanent tenure and may not be dismissed except for serious misdemeanor. If the company is successful in getting a labor court to allow it to discharge a man with tenure, the company still must pay the man two months' pay for every year of continuous company service. (This law applies to rank and file workers only. Persons occupying positions of trust and confidence are guaranteed only severance pay in the amount of one month's pay for every year of continuous company service.) The tenure law is a constant source of irritation to many employers. 15% of the companies mentioned it during the interviews:

> If you keep a man more than ten years, it's very hard to fire him. Even if he is a very good worker before then, he sometimes starts to loaf once he gets tenure. He knows you won't fire him. So, you generally get rid of your men before they've been with you ten years. This means you lose some good people.

> More than 20% of the men we fire are good men who just want to collect severance pay.

> The permanent tenure law leads to high turnover. We have to let people go before they get tenure. This is an especially bad thing as far as our mechanics and our salesmen are concerned. You have a real investment in these people and it's expensive to replace them. But you have to.

> One of our big problems is what to do about some of our older employees who have got tenure. What can you do to get them to do a good job? Many of them are just trying to get fired to collect severance pay.

Tied for 8) *The Problem of Illiterate or Barely Literate Workers*

Rio Grande do Sul boasts the highest literacy rate in Brazil. Yet a third of its adult citizens cannot read or write. Only some 18% of its inhabitants have finished primary school (the first four grades), 21% have finished secondary school (high school), and about one half of 1% have finished the university. The following comments indicate that the lack of good, universal, compulsory, primary education presents serious problems to industrial and commercial managers. 15% of the companies mentioned this problem:

> The basic problem in Brazil is the weakness of primary education. It is difficult to get good help. Workers are willing and intelligent but they have had only four years of schooling and they can't do simple arithmetic problems.

> Our big problem is the low quality of primary schools in Brazil. Workers can't understand technical orders.

> The level of our people is very low. They lack ability to understand mathematics, designs, or drawings. . . .

Our big problem is to reach the rural people who are leaving the farms for industry. They need to be taught to read and do simple mathematics.

10) *The Transportation Problem*

Another victim of recent government policy, according to businessmen, was the state's transportation system. Although the state has hundreds of miles of navigable rivers, transportation on the rivers has declined in recent years. Highways, many times built along the rivers themselves, were accounting for more and more freight traffic. Even airplanes were taking freight away from river and coastwise shipping. 12% of the businessmen pointed this out and attempted to fix the responsibility for the decline in river and coastwise traffic.

We ship refrigerators to the São Paulo market. You will find this hard to believe, but its true: it costs more to ship them by boat than it does to ship them by air.

The big problem in this state is transportation. We're neglecting our river and coastal shipping, which is the cheapest possible kind of transportation, and building expensive roads that run right alongside the rivers. Social laws have ruined river traffic by requiring so many employees.

We can ship iron by truck to Rio cheaper than by boat. This is completely foolish. The main reason is that when you ship by boat you have to go through customs twice.

The reform that is most urgently needed by this state is a reform in the labor legislation having to do with river and coastal shipping. Without injuring the just rights of the workers, we need to apply common sense to the problem of providing low cost ship transportation.

The ideal solution would be to transfer all shipping from the control of the government to private companies, giving them special financial help or concessions to encourage them to replace obsolete boats with more modern ones.

This concludes the list of the ten most frequently mentioned problems which came out of my interviews with 51 Brazilian top executives. It should already be obvious that a number of major differences exist between the U.S. situation and that of Brazil. Inflation, inadequate transportation, apparent government favoritism to certain regions of the country, scarcity of managers, scarcity of technicians, a tenure law, featherbedding social legislation, and wholesale evasion of tax laws are virtually unique aspects of the Brazilian businessman's situation. While one or two of these conditions have their counterparts in the U.S., for the most part they present the Brazilian businessman with a very different kind of "game," if we can continue to use our earlier analogy between business and sport, from that in which American businessmen engage.

To examine in detail how little similarity exists between the problems which the Brazilian businessman perceives and the problems U.S. businessmen in comparable-sized companies say that they are facing, we turn now to an analysis of the ten most common problems of the U.S. executives.

The "Game" of Management — Played by Michigan (USA) Ground Rules

The 106 executives who reported the problems they considered most important to Michigan small businessmen, listed a total of 264 different problems.[8] These fell into fourteen major categories. Of the fourteen categories, only ten were reported by 5% or more of the sample. These ten problems are reported here. (See Table 36.2.)

Table 36.2
The Ten Most Common Problems Mentioned
by 106 Michigan (USA) Top Managers in 1962

Rank	Problem	% Mentioning
1	Competition from larger companies	37
2	Taxes	31
3	Getting, keeping and motivating employees	27
4	Difficulties with unions	23
5	Government interference and red tape	19
6	Keeping in control of the business — developing records	17
7	Financial problems	15
8	Sales and marketing problems	11
9	Personal shortcomings and inability to afford staff help	10
10	Finding, training, holding executives and foremen	9

1. Competition — Especially Competition from Larger Companies

As in Brazil, competition was a major problem. Of the 106 Michigan executives who responded to the questionnaire, 39 men (37%) mentioned this problem. However, instead of complaining as the Brazilians did about competition from companies in other states, nearly half (17) of the Michigan executives referred to the problem of competing with *larger* companies. The size, rather than the location of the competition was the critical factor. Here are some representative comments.

> The large operation today is forcing the small businessman out; however, I feel with education and training he can compete.

> The big problem is the constant pressure of big companies to take over small business.

[8] This study has been reported in Winston Oberg, "Some Problems Faced by the Small Businessman in Michigan" *The Michigan Economic Record*, vol. 4, no. 11 (December, 1962) pp. 3, 6.

Our big problem is trying to compete with the larger companies. Whereas we can provide local service, apparently most business is done on price.

Others spoke of their "inability to compete with big business in the realms of labor and executive talent," and the "difficulty of competing against the buying advantages of big business." Eight spoke simply of a "profit squeeze" due to increasing competition. Four mentioned specific kinds of competition which they considered unfair, if not actually unethical.

2. Taxes

31% of the companies mentioned taxes as a problem. More than half of these simply said, "taxes," or "taxation," or "growing taxation" when asked what their major problems were. A few expanded on this theme. One man said,

(A major problem is) the gradual removal of incentive to grow which is necessary if we are to provide jobs and opportunities for the young people coming into the labor market. If a businessman can overcome the hurdles placed in his way by today's unions and make a profit, the government's share payable in cash doesn't leave him with enough reward to make it worthwhile to extend himself beyond the comfortable point.

Another said, "The tax program could be geared to give a little better break to small business." This point of view was expanded on by another who said the problem was "how to encourage Congress to let small business grow before taxing it the same as giant corporations so that small business can accumulate some capital to buy the latest machinery, hire the best engineers." A slightly contrary view was expressed by another man who said both big and little business were taxed "excessively." "Small industry," he said, "generally is faced with many of the same problems as big industry such as excessive workmen's compensation costs due to the leniency of the commission as well as the courts."

3. Getting, Keeping, and Motivating Employees

27% of the companies had problems in this area. Most frequently mentioned (9 times) was the problem of getting and keeping good skilled or technically trained help. As one man said, a major problem is "the inability to attract and retain good personnel. If they do show promise, you lose them to larger concerns." One man criticized most newly-hired employees because "their attitude toward customers is one of antagonism rather than one of service." Another spoke of the "disinclination of employees to give of themselves for the company." A third said his major problem was "building an organization of dedicated loyal people who want to earn what they are paid."

4. Difficulties with Unions

23% of the companies said their labor relations presented major problems. The most representative expression of this problem is probably this one:

> The large corporations set the pattern for wage increases and the unions then expect the same increases and benefits from small business.

Other responses include comments like these:

> The small businessman doesn't stand much of a chance to hold his own if a union decides to make an example of him. In too many cases 'bargaining' should be called 'bludgeoning.'

> We are in a marginal industry — underground mining — but are nevertheless saddled with basically the same labor agreement as the entire steel industry. This presents problems.

> Labor's attitude (is) that the employer should offer security from date of employment until death. This is difficult for a small employer.

5. Government Interference and Red Tape

19% of the men complained about increasing government interference. One cited as a major problem "how to maintain 'ownership' in face of increasing government pressure to obtain control of all business activity." Another said,

> The problem small businessmen face is, in reality, the broad problem facing our country for some 25 years. It is the problem of an imbalance in the eternal struggle between freedom of the individual and statism. And while this problem is a philosophic one, the struggle will have to be won ultimately on the political level.

Several men complained about "too much government" or "too much government interference" or even the "socialization of everything" and "trying to exist in a socialistic economy." At a less emotional level, others spoke of the great difficulty they experienced in "keeping up with complex state and federal laws affecting . . . business."

6. How to Keep on Top of or in Control of the Business — How to Develop Adequate Records

17% of the companies mentioned problems in this area. One man, a partner in an insurance company, spoke not of his problems but of the problems of his clients:

> (The big problem is) accounting! Too many small businessmen are being led astray or allowed to drift into rough financial seas because of insufficient, inaccurate, unrealistic 'accounting' as done by the so-called accounting and bookkeeping services.

Another said the big problem was how to keep books "so as to be able to determine what financial position (you) are in." Several men mentioned problems with accounting controls; a smaller number talked about problems in interpreting the company's financial data; and a few said they had difficulty knowing what price to charge in order adequately to cover their costs.

7. Financial Problems

This was one of the most difficult problems facing the Rio Grande do Sul executive. In Michigan, although the problem was also important, it was slightly different in its nature. In Rio Grande do Sul the banks didn't even have the money, and the problem was one of providing working capital right now. In Michigan the problem was more one of looking to the future, of which source of money it was best to use, or of how one could get money for R & D work or for company expansion. 15% of the men mentioned this problem. One man said his big problem was "lack of capital, insufficient finances to develop new products (R & D) or to outlast prolonged recessions." Another said his problem was "how to go public with a stock issue." The majority simply commented on growth problems and how to raise capital for growth.

8. Sales and Marketing Problems

Where Brazil and most of Latin America is heavily production oriented — sales will pretty much take care of themselves, there's a shortage of everything — the U.S. executive is being forced to become more marketing oriented.[9] The production problems are largely solved; the problem, even for small business, is becoming how to get rid of what comes off the production line. 11% of the companies mentioned this as a problem. As one man said,

> As a small manufacturer in a small town, I think too many of us think of manufacturing as 'making something.' Actually no matter how well a product is made, there is still the big problem of placing it into proper channels.

Another said,

> (Too many) businessmen feel that all they need to do is develop a quality product and it will sell itself. To most management, management means production. Sales management is nil or doesn't exist.

[9] Just how great a cleavage exists between heavily marketing-oriented U. S. Managements and the predominantly production-oriented Brazilian managers was indicated by the different responses U.S. and Brazilian executives made to the "Wickersham Mills Case," a fictional account of a company which had to choose a new president. The Brazilians chose the candidate with a production background. U. S. executives preferred the man with the marketing background and orientation. See Winston Oberg "Re: 'Debate at Wickersham Mills' " Harvard Business Review, vol. 39, no. 5 (September-October, 1961) pp. 42, 44, 48.

Marketing and sales promotion is something they've heard big business speak of but doesn't concern them, and advertising . . . is some kind of magic potion that when sprinkled upon the ground produces a genie which will cure all of their sales problems.

The bulk of the problems in this area had to do with getting and keeping and motivating salesmen.

9. *Personal Shortcomings of the Top Manager Himself and His Inability to Afford Competent Specialists*

10% of the companies commented about such things as "how to keep informed in areas where big business hires specialists," or lack of "time or ability to analyze business progress or retrogress," or "the need for specialist advice and work and the difficulty because of (low) volume of maintaining specialists on the staff," or the "inability to handle administrative problems without being able to afford specialists. . . ."

10. *Finding, Training, Holding Executives and Foremen*

This was the third problem common to the Michigan and Rio Grande do Sul executives. However, here again the similarity was more apparent than real. In the Michigan sample, the problem was not the fact that there was an actual absence of qualified management candidates, it was the competition of other wealthier companies for the available men. 9% of the companies mentioned this as a problem. Here are some typical comments:

Our biggest problem is the very fact that we are small. We find it increasingly harder to compete with larger companies for high caliber personnel as we cannot afford the many fringe benefits nor the opportunities in a large corporation.

Small businessmen do not have the opportunity to hire college trained administrative personnel and usually their administrative heads have come up through the ranks.

(One big problem is the) inability of small corporations to secure high caliber men or men with high potential, due mainly to inability to pay comparable wages due to competition.

This concludes the list of ten most important problems facing these Michigan executives in early 1962. Most of their main problems, for example, competition with large companies both for sales and for people, high taxes, union pressure, government interference, marketing (rather than production) problems, are quite different from those of the Brazilian executives studied.

Table 36.3 shows that there is actual overlap in the case study of only a third of the problems, and the discussion to this point should have made it abundantly clear that much of the overlap is more apparent than real. What these two surveys show is that men can occupy the same position in an organization hierarchy, manage companies of comparable size engaged

Table 36.3
Problems Which Appear to Be Similar for Both Rio Grande
do Sul and Michigan Executives

| | Rank | | % mentioning | |
Problem	in RGS	in Mich.	in RGS	in Mich.
Competition: from other states	2		29	
from larger companies		1		37
Financial problems/shortage of capital	1	7	32	15
Finding and keeping competent executives	3	(10)*	26	(9)
Finding and keeping competent foremen	7	(10)*	18	(9)

* In the Michigan sample, the problem of finding and keeping competent executives was combined with the problem of finding and keeping good foremen. In Brazil, the two problems appeared to be less closely related and were listed separately.

in parallel lines of economic activity and yet, because the milieus in which they operate are highly dissimilar, the two groups of executives concerned can have remarkably few problems in common.

Summary and Conclusions

While two small-scale surveys of the kind reported here cannot be made to bear the weight of a set of formal conclusions, the results can at least have some implications for management theory.

1) The first such implication was suggested in the opening paragraph of this report. There it was reported that management theorists are turning their attention to the wealth of research opportunities being opened by the burgeoning U.S. interest in international trade as well as in international economic development. The findings presented here should emphasize that if universal principles do indeed exist they must stand up to rigorous testing in cross-cultural studies far more sophisticated and more adequately designed and controlled than the surveys described here. If management principles are to be truly universal, it is clear that they must face up to the challenge of other cultures and other business climates. This paper suggests the challenge will be a major one.

2) The second implication of this paper is that facile assumptions like that attributed to the 1962 recipient of the Gantt Medal to the effect that,

. . . management is management wherever practiced, a universal profession whose principles can be applied in every organized form of human activity. . . .[10]

[10] See Harwood F. Merrill, "The Listening Post" *Management News*, vol. 36, No. 1, (January, 1963) p. 4. The words are attributed to Austin Tobin, executive director of the Port of New York Authority. A very similar point of view is found in the introductory management text of Koontz and O'Donnell, *Principles of Management*, (New York, McGraw-Hill Book Company, Inc., 1959).

are hardly warranted by either evidence or intuition at this stage in the development of management science. What may be equally or even more probable is the conclusion reached by two colleagues of mine after they had spent some years as technical consultants to a business school in central Brazil. They studied the applicability of U.S. management experience and know-how to the Brazilian situation and concluded that,

> American management experience abroad provides evidence that our uniquely American philosophy of management is not universally applicable but rather is a special case.[11]

In any event, the assumption that universal principles exist needs to be examined for what it is — a declaration of faith rather than a proposition established by adequate cross-cultural research.

Postscript

The perceptive reader will have seen that the thrust of this paper goes well beyond the comparisons made and the conclusions suggested. If management principles should prove to be limited in their applicability to a particular culture or social climate, as this report suggests, their general applicability within a particular culture will also be open to question. For example, if no principle can be found which applies significantly to both the U.S. and the Brazilian businessman, it may well be questioned whether any principles can be found which apply significantly to such dissimilar U.S. sub-cultures as those of the small rural businessman and the head of a giant corporation. The area of applicability of generalizations, laws, theories or principles of management will thus shrink indefinitely. It is my personal belief that such will be the case and that management theorists and teachers in departments of management who still hold what Dale calls the universalist view should take note of recent developments in both the physical and social science fields.[12] It is already more than ten years since Gouldner, for example, surveyed the social science literature on leadership and found that the age-old quest for universal leader traits or attributes had virtually been abandoned.[13] Instead, social scientists had accepted the view that the qualities necessary for leader success were situationally determined and varied from one situation to another. One situation might call for physical prowess, courage, or superior intelligence while success as a leader in another situation might have no relevance at all to physical attributes or courage. Indeed, in some cases scientists found too high an IQ to be a handicap.

---

[11] Gonzalez and McMillan, *op. cit.*, p. 41.

[12] Ernest Dale, *The Great Organizers*, (McGraw-Hill Book Company Inc., New York, 1960).

[13] Alvin Gouldner (ed.) *Studies in Leadership*, (Harper & Bros., New York, 1950).

Among physical scientists, whose most famous law, $e = mc^2$, has probably served as the model for a generation or more of management scientists showing what a universal principle or law ought to be, some highly significant shifts in orientation are also taking place. In a recent issue of *Science*, Simpson notes that physical scientists are themselves abandoning belief in the existence of absolutes, determinate solutions, or principles that apply to all phenomena.[14]

If the social sciences, in their studies of areas quite closely linked to the theory of management, have adopted a situational point of view, and if the physical sciences are now abandoning faith in the existence of universals, it is hardly likely that those of us operating in such a complex and imprecise field as that of management theory can be justified in continuing to assert our faith in the existence of universal principles, absolutes or determinate solutions. Instead, we might be well-advised to concern ourselves more with a study of variants of what Mary Parker Follett once called the "law of situation."[15] A search for generalizations which are simply situationally valid and admittedly situationally limited in their applicability, although more modest than the quest for universal truth, may well turn out to be a good deal more fruitful and hence, in the long run, more significant.

[14] George G. Simpson, "Biology and the Nature of Science," *Science*, vol. 139, no. 3550 (January 11, 1963) pp. 81–88.

[15] H. C. Metcalf and L. Urwick (eds.) *Dynamic Administration: the Collected Papers of Mary Parker Follett*, (Harper & Brothers, New York, 1940).

37

Managerial Motivation in Soviet and Czechoslovak Industries: A Comparison*

Barry M. Richman

University of California, Los Angeles

Again cultural variations in the rules of the management game are considered, this time in a comparison of managerial performance in Soviet and Czechoslovak enterprise. This research explored the major structural changes introduced as reforms by the Soviets and the Czechs, to determine their impact on managerial behavior. The analysis centers on changing elements of motivation in the two systems. Not only is there considerable diversity in the two systems, but the forces for change are clearly present in both.

During the 1950's, the performance of industrial enterprise managers in the Soviet Union and Czechoslovakia tended to deteriorate steadily. Desired enterprise results in both countries were not being achieved. The basic reason for this ineffective performance at the operating level was that the overall economic, cultural and institutional environment in which these enterprise managers operated was defective. Typically, undesirable managerial behavior was not a question of incompetence, although some inept managers did exist. The basic problem was that even an extremely competent person could not perform effectively within the framework in which he operated.

The response to this type of problem was to make significant changes in the "rules of the game" for enterprise managers in an effort to encourage managerial behavior suited to changing conditions. This proved difficult

* Taken and adapted from *The Journal of the Academy of Management*, vol. 6, no. 2, June, 1963, pp. 107–128. The author wishes to acknowledge the financial assistance provided by the Columbia Business School, and currently by the Division of Research of the UCLA Business School.

in a monolithic society which was convinced of its possession of absolute answers to all questions of economic organization. But in spite of its rigidity, changes were made at a rapid pace.

The purpose of this paper is to examine the major structural changes made by the Soviets and Czechs and to determine what impact these reforms have already had on managerial behavior.[1] Since the Soviet reforms have differed significantly from the Czech, it is interesting to compare how the two industrial states reached substantially different conclusions concerning the same types of problems. It is also useful to examine such reforms to consider how communist states do change through time. Capitalist observers often see only solid unanimity in the communist bloc;[2] in fact, there is considerable diversity between the institutional and economic structures in these two countries. We will also examine critically new reforms contemplated by the Soviets which are intended to further improve managerial and, hence, overall economic performance.

Historical Perspective[3]

In Russia and Czechoslovakia, predetermined production quotas and resource allocations rather than competitive buying and selling regulate the activities of the myriad of interdependent producing enterprises on the basis of one comprehensive national plan. Each enterprise receives an annual plan with quarterly subdivisions. If the plan is sound, and if managers do their jobs properly, the results should be the production of the right amount of goods and services. This production should be of the right assortment and quality, delivered to the right place at the right time. In theory, the proper design and execution of the plan means that resources are efficiently utilized, and that nothing is wasted, since no unneeded excesses or shortages of goods would appear at any point. It is also hoped

---

[1] Much of the information utilized in this paper has been obtained from interviews with Soviet and Czech officials in 1960 and 1961. In total, more than 100 economists, planners, academicians, and industrial officials, including managerial personnel at 16 enterprises, were interviewed by the author. Since space only permits a limited amount of documentation and evidence in connection with the findings presented here, those readers interested in further elaboration and documentation can see the author's recently completed doctoral dissertation: *Informal Managerial Practices and Formal Enterprise Goals in Soviet Industry* (Columbia University, N.Y., 1962).

[2] Yugoslavia with its "market-socialism" may be an exception, since some readers may know that the Yugoslav economy represents a break from Communist orthodoxy.

[3] Joseph Berliner, in his book *Factory and Manager in the U.S.S.R.* (Harvard University Press, Cambridge, 1957) has made perhaps the greatest contribution to understanding Soviet managerial motivation and behavior prior to 1958. Many Czech officials interviewed indicated that the problems of managerial motivation were very similar in Czechoslovakia until 1958. See also for example, R. Lavicka, and J. Toman, *Nova Organizace Planovani Narodnio Hospodarstvi* (Orbis, Prague, 1959). This book is also partially translated into English by the U.S. Joint Publications Research Service (JPRS), Washington, D. C., 1961.

that factory managers would tend to innovate in both the product and process sense.

Although the managers are narrowly confined by the aggregate targets and resource limits prescribed by the plan, their expert knowledge and participation are indispensable to both the formulation and execution of the plan. It is physically impossible for superior authorities to plan in detail without close consultation with plant executives, or to exert instantaneous effective control over the execution of plans at the vast number of enterprises. The men on the spot are in the best position to determine in detail the capabilities and resource needs of their enterprises, and to adapt the plan to unforeseeable changing conditions. In addition, enterprise innovation depends greatly on what managers choose to do or not to do. Those who imagine the communist countries to be pure "totalitarian command economies" in which enterprise managers merely carry out detailed orders have no conception of reality.[4]

Prior to 1958 the key operational goal of enterprise managers was a monthly premium (bonus) whose size depended on the fulfillment and degree of overfulfillment of aggregate production targets. The index of gross output was the key enterprise success indicator. Managers could potentially receive premiums equivalent to 40% or more of their basic salaries, depending on the type of enterprise. The premium was also highly valued because its size has been a measure of managerial skill and of conformity with the state's desires, thus providing a means for attaining other personal goals such as promotions, prestige, power and recognition.

In pursuit of premiums managers strove for gross output targets that could easily be exceeded. They tended to hide resources, conceal production capacity, overstate resource needs, and generally conceal the facts from higher authorities. By doing this, they could often get easy gross production targets, leading to overfulfillment of plans. Unfortunate managers who were either honest or poor bargainers in their dealings with higher authorities were often stuck with impossibly high production goals.

In their efforts to fulfill and exceed gross output targets, managers frequently failed to fulfill other enterprise targets and tasks set down in their plans. This was most pronounced at enterprises that obtained difficult plans, and many did. The fulfillment of cost of production, profit and various other targets was often sacrificed. The emphasis on gross output led to underemphasis on quality and proper product mix. Also relevant was the inability to deliver goods at the proper time. Since one enterprise's output is another enterprise's input, misguided production results tended

---

[4] For a current discussion on managerial authority in the Soviet Union see, B. Richman, "Formulation of Enterprise Operating Plans in Soviet Industry," in *Soviet Studies*, July, 1963.

to percolate through the economy. In the consumer goods sector unwanted and unsaleable inventories began to mount. Plants desiring to meet even modest production targets were forced to hoard raw materials, equipment and components, thus compounding the supply crisis. Product and technological innovation also lagged since there was no incentive to create better products or install new technology and processes. The expenditure of time, effort and resources, as well as the risks and delays inherent in introducing new innovations all made innovation something to be actively avoided. Given the premium-success-indicator system and the uncertainty of supply, it could be expected that managers would do all in their power to get modest production targets, and if necessary to fulfill them in undesirable ways. No manager would willingly expose himself to failure. The distortions and supply problems created and aggravated by imperfect managerial incentives led to poor enterprise results.

It should also be noted that there is no market-price system in either country, and the suppliers and quantities of goods they are to supply a customer enterprise are determined in the plan. If a supplier failed to fulfill his commitments, and an item became in short supply, the price did not increase in order to spur more production of this item. Since there was usually no other source of supply readily available, the manager often was compelled to accept inferior goods not in accordance with stipulated specifications, and to obtain supplies through bribery, personal influence or whatever illegal means he could. The utilization of inferior supplies caused deficient output at a given plant, while illegal procurement activities often deflected supplies earmarked for, and crucially needed by, other enterprises. When shortages existed in only a few lines these were not crucial problems, but when shortages of critical supplies pervaded the entire economy, inability to achieve desired enterprise results became widespread.

When the communist countries were less complex industrially, output without regard to other considerations could be a meaningful goal. Pressure for forced industrialization meant shortages of every type of good; hence anything produced could be used somewhere in the economy. But as the economies grew more complicated, as the interrelationships between steadily expanding industries became more delicate, and as a wider choice of consumer goods created an increase in the standard of living, the aggregate gross output indicators of success became less meaningful. In an earlier period, particularly in Russia, the crudest planning was adequate to insure sufficient supplies of raw materials, components and equipment for the relatively few industrial establishments. Consumers in desperate need of all types of goods were willing to purchase almost anything. By 1957, it was increasingly obvious that poorly designed enterprise plans and even subtle deviations from plan targets was leading to extreme waste and inefficiency.

The general problem of both the Soviet and Czech governments became one of restructuring managerial incentives and certain other "rules of the game" in an effort to improve managerial performance. To these reforms we now turn.

Managerial Motivation in Soviet Enterprise in Current Times

Current System of Success Indicators

The 1959 Soviet success indicator reform[5] shifted primary emphasis from gross output to cost of production results expressed in terms of the cost per one ruble of marketable (saleable) production. Premiums are now awarded quarterly and managers can potentially receive premiums equivalent to 40% to 60% of their basic salaries depending on the type of enterprise. Both gross output and labor productivity targets[6] must be fulfilled for any premiums to be awarded. However, the total amount of premiums awarded for a given quarter depends on the degree of overfulfillment of the cost target (that is, above plan cost savings). In some cases additional premiums may be awarded up to the maximum allowable limit for overfulfilling the gross output target, but more weight is given to above plan cost savings.

The reform stipulates that various other conditions must be fulfilled for management to receive premiums, and these conditions depend on the branch of industry and type of enterprise. These other conditions may include certain physical assortment indices, quality, product delivery schedules to customer enterprises in other regions and major technical and product innovation measures. In reality, these other conditions are apparently enforced at only relatively few enterprises.[7]

It was hoped by the Soviets that the new system of success indicators would prove to be a panacea in terms of the shortcomings of managerial action in the past. By emphasizing cost results it was hoped that enterprises would utilize resources more efficiently.

---

[5] A description of the reform can be found in *Pravda*, October 28, 1959.

[6] Labor productivity is calculated as the ratio of gross output to total number of enterprise industrial personnel.

[7] For an elaborated discussion on this point see author's dissertation, *op. cit.*, chapter 4. Some producers have a rather broad assortment of success indicators expressed in physical terms such as square meters of silk fabric, and pairs of men's and women's shoes without regard to style or variety. Several of the machine tool enterprises have stipulated quantities of certain types of standardized products as a necessary condition for the receipt of premiums. However, many types of producer goods output are expressed in total weight (ton) and the weight index is a necessary condition. Quality represented by allowable proportions of total output in terms of quality grades (1st, 2nd, 3rd, etc.) is a necessary condition for some of the consumer goods producers. The fulfillment of product delivery schedules to other regions was a necessary condition at only one machine tool enterprise surveyed. The fulfillment of innovation tasks is rarely a necessary condition for the receipt of premiums.

The Premium Remains as the Key Managerial Goal

The premium is still the most highly valued managerial goal even in light of the change in the system of success indicators. The premium is not a mere aspiration but often a reality for many managers. At five out of ten Soviet enterprises surveyed by this writer, maximum or near maximum premiums were received for a majority of quarters in 1960.[8]

There are certain other monetary rewards available to enterprise management. Managers may receive bonuses from the Enterprise Fund which is formed from a small portion of the profits earned by the enterprise. There are also bonuses available for fulfilling major technological and product innovation tasks. However, these other forms of incentives currently have little impact on managerial motivation, and the desire for premiums still usually takes precedence in terms of managerial action.[9]

Deficient Provision of Resources Remains as Key Obstacle to Premium Attainment

Although many managers do earn premiums, the deficient provision of resources, particularly supplies, still serves as the key obstacle that many managers must overcome in order to derive premiums.

Evidence clearly indicates that numerous plants are not allocated necessary resources to fulfill production targets. This is true in spite of two major reforms introduced in the Soviet economy since 1957 in an attempt to rectify this situation.[10] In the past the state followed a policy of over-committing national resources when establishing the national economic plan. This resulted in strained (i.e. imbalanced) national plans, and this strain was passed down through the industrial hierarchy directly affecting a great number of enterprises. This was one of the chief causes of resource shortages which in turn led to undesirable managerial behavior in the formulation and execution of plans. Since 1958 the state has attempted to establish more realistic annual national plans by curtailing the policy of substantially overcommitting national resources.[11]

8 *Ibid.*, chapter 4, table I, p. 100.

9 *Ibid.*, chapters 4, 11, 12. In spite of reforms introduced in 1961 to encourage enterprise innovation, managerial opposition to innovation remains a key problem. See also, B. Richman, "Product Innovation in the U.S.S.R.: Causes and Effects of Managerial Opposition," to be published in a forthcoming issue of the *California Management Review*.

10 *Ibid.*, See also a recent doctoral dissertation by H. Levine, A *Study in Economic Planning: The Soviet Industrial Supply System* (Harvard University, 1961); *Pravda*, February 20, 1962, *Izvestia*, July 14, 1962.

11 The sixth Five-Year National Plan began in 1956 and ended in less than two years when it became obvious that the output goals were too ambitious. The average annual projected growth of industrial production for the Seven-Year-Plan, adopted in 1958, was 8.6 percent compared with 10.5 percent for the scrapped sixth Five-Year-Plan, and 11.3 percent for the fifth Five-Year-Plan. See, W. Nutter, *Growth of Industrial Production in the Soviet Union* (Princeton University Press, 1962).

Secondly the industrial hierarchy was reorganized from a highly centralized branch-of-industry ministerial setup to a somewhat more decentralized territorial system of industrial planning and control.[12] This was an attempt to provide for a more efficient communication network, thus leading to a more efficient allocation of resources to enterprises. In this same vein it was also hoped that planning errors that became evident during the operating period would be rectified in a more timely fashion, and that more effective control would be exerted over timely and proper deliveries to customer enterprises. This reform has been only partially effective. The personal status of economic council officials, who are the direct superiors of enterprise managers, hinges on the aggregate results of subordinate enterprises. For this reason they do extend fairly effective control over output destined for plants in the same region. However, most enterprises receive a substantial portion of their supplies from other regions. Control is least effective in connection with consumer goods since they are destined for the trade sector, and the happenings there are of no concern to economic council officials.[13] Such behavior on the part of regional economic councils has been branded as "localism" and "narrow self-interest" by Soviet leaders.

All in all the above two reforms have led to some improvement since a greater proportion of enterprises have been fulfilling their aggregate output targets in recent years. Prior to 1958, generally 25 to 40 per cent of all enterprises failed to fulfill their aggregate output plans.[14] In 1959 this figure was only 11 per cent.[15] However, there are still certain branches of industry, particularly the consumer goods sector, faced with serious resource deficiencies because of their low priority in the eyes of the regime.

Even though aggregate output targets are being fulfilled at more plants than in the past, as will be discussed shortly, the actual assortment produced by a vast number of enterprises often does not conform to specifications stipulated in the plan. Hence even those enterprises that are allocated adequate quantities of supply are still insecure about the timely

[12] For a discussion of the 1957 reorganization see, A. Nove, "The Soviet Industrial Reorganization," *Problems of Communism*, November-December, 1957; O. Hoeffding, "Soviet Industrial Reorganization of 1957," *American Economic Review*, May, 1959.

[13] Richman, dissertation, *op. cit.*, chapters 5, 7, and 9; H. Levine, *op. cit.*, chapter 10; M. Kasar, in *Value and Plan*, ed., G. Grossman (University of California Press, Berkeley, 1962). Control by local Communist Party and trade union officials is also impeded because they, too, are evaluated and rewarded by the same criteria as enterprise management. See also, A. Nove, *The Soviet Economy*, chapters 6 and 7 (Praeger, New York, 1961).

[14] *Pravda*, August 10, 1955; J. Berliner, *op. cit.*, p. 320, and, J. Berliner in *Joint Economic Committee, Comparisons of the United States and Soviet Economics*, Part I, p. 358 (Government Printing Office, Washington, 1960).

[15] A. Vedishev, "Three Years of Work under New Conditions," translated in *Problems of Economics*, p. 53, III:9, 1961.

receipt of supplies according to specifications during the related operating period.

In addition to the supply program, a growing scarcity of manpower is apparently emerging in Soviet industry. The labor force, in terms of total numbers and required skills, is not keeping pace with increasing industrial expansion and complexity. This is evidently most severe in certain outlying areas where living conditions leave much to be desired, as well as in some low priority branches of industry. However, manpower shortages are gradually being felt throughout the economy.[16] Therefore, many managers are concerned that their enterprise will not be allocated or possess adequate manpower to fulfill production plans.

Managerial Behavior

During the Planning Process: Even though the success indicator system linked to the receipt of premiums has been changed, the aggregate success indicator targets are still expressed in terms of 100%. This fact induces even those managers relatively assured of adequate resources to conceal productive capacity, hoard resources, and overstate resource needs in order to derive success indicator targets which can readily be fulfilled and over-fulfilled. In general, the shift of emphasis to cost results has intensified management's efforts to obtain over-abundant supplies and inflated expense budgets in an attempt to derive easy cost of production targets. There is much current evidence suggesting that most managers still understate plant capacity by hoarding equipment and establishing faulty equipment utilization norms. Managements also attempt to overstate supply, working capital and manpower needs by establishing faulty material and labor utilization norms.[17]

The change in the system of success indicators has not made management any more concerned about customer needs or consumer demand. Production quotas are approved, for the most part, in aggregate terms, and the manager plays a major role in negotiating his enterprise's detailed product mix with customers.[18] In many cases, enterprises are allocated

[16] A. Khavin, "Problems of Manpower Distribution," translated in *Current Digest of the Soviet Press* (CDSP), XIII:33, 1961; V. Moskalenko, in *Sotsialisticheskaya Trud,* 1960:5. Even in developed regions with favorable living conditions labor shortages are apparently being felt. Managers interviewed by this writer at two Kharkov machine-tool plants asserted that the non-receipt of premiums in 1960 was due to inadequate manpower.

[17] All of the undesirable managerial practices during the planning process still prevail throughout Soviet industry. For an elaborated discussion see, Richman, dissertation, *op. cit.,* chapter 6; see also, *Pravda,* July 23 and September 9, 1962. *Izvestia,* May 5, and June 6, 1961. *Ekonomicheskaya Gazeta,* January 24, August 13, 1961, and September 21, 1962; A. Nove, 1961, *op. cit.,* chapter 6.

[18] For a discussion on managerial authority and the enterprise's product mix see Richman, in *Soviet Studies, op. cit.*

aggregate quantities of resources, such as so many tons of leather or metal, so many meters of cloth, or so many lathes. The detailed specifications of the product mix are usually worked out between supplier and customer enterprises, and for consumer goods between the producer and wholesale trade officials. The product specifications agreed upon are indicated in supply contracts which are formally approved by higher authorities. Managers tend to act in ways most beneficial to the fulfillment and overfulfillment of key aggregate enterprise targets. There are many examples of supplier enterprises compelling customers to agree to contractual terms in which many of the items are not those most needed by the customer or in demand.[19] This is especially frequent where the customer is not of very high priority in the eyes of the state, and therefore lacks bargaining power.

In the past managers desired to produce high priced items, usually with little concern about unit cost, since this leads to favorable gross output results. Currently, managers are more inclined to try to compel customers to agree to contractual terms where the assortment provides for large price-cost gaps (profit margins), preferably where the actual size of such gaps are not apparent to higher authorities.

The lack of operational long-range enterprise plans in conjunction with the current system of success indicators discourages enterprise product and technological innovation. There is much evidence indicating that the shift to cost results as the key success indicator has further intensified management's efforts to avoid innovation assignment in the enterprise operating plan.[20] Managers rarely initiate or desire innovation tasks unless it is felt that they would have a favorable effect on short-run success indicator results and premium attainment. The major underlying causes of this conflict between premium attainment and innovation are that adequate resources are usually not provided for innovation activities, and unforeseeable costs often arise in connection with such activities.[21]

The planning process in Soviet industry is somewhat like a strategy-style-bargaining-game with enterprises trying to obtain easy plans, while central authorities desiring tight plans try to cut away the "fat" incorporated into enterprise planning proposals.[22] This conflict of interests between the state

[19] A. Nove, 1961, *op. cit.*, chapter 6; *Pravda*, July 14, 1960, June 28, 1961, February 20, 1962.

[20] Richman, dissertation, *op. cit.*, chapters 10 and 11; Richman in *California Management Review*, *op. cit.*, A. Nove, 1961, *op. cit.*, chapter 6; A. Nove, "Revamping the Economy," *Problems of Communism*, January-February, 1963.

[21] *Ibid.*

[22] One enterprise manager gives this vivid description of the planning process in *Pravda*, July 23, 1962, p. 2; he states, "How are plans drafted at present? The planning agencies argue vigorously with the managers of enterprises to induce them to accept a higher plan. The representatives of the enterprises, on the other hand, argue with equal energy that the high assignments are unrealistic." See also, Richman, dissertation, *op. cit.*, chapter 7.

and plant managers breeds a circle of distrust and uncertainty. This results in a kind of arbitrary target planning. Much unproductive time, effort and expense is expended in calculations, information gathering and bargaining since enterprise plans are often established with little regard for data and proposals submitted by the enterprise. This does not imply that the planning process is entirely chaotic.

A major stabilizing factor with respect to enterprise planning over time is the procedure of point of departure planning. It is clearly understood by enterprise managers that higher authorities would usually show great displeasure if they proposed plans which did not show at least some improvement as compared to results achieved to date. However, if easy plans have been approved for enterprises in the past, and the enterprise continues to maintain excess resources and capacity, point of departure does not provide for efficient plans. Some, but not all, excess reserves may be revealed during the course of overfulfilling success indicators, but the system of premiums would serve as an upper limit in this connection. For this reason many enterprises maintain excess reserves, by hoarding and not revealing improvements in operations, over long periods of time. Point of departure planning also does nothing to deter managers from adversely affecting the enterprise assortment plan, or from stifling beneficial innovation assignments.

Evidence indicates that because of the nature of the planning process a majority of enterprises probably obtain plans which are overly strained or too easy. Only relatively few plants obtain tight but realistic plans.[23]

During the Operating Period: During the operating period, in cases where enterprises underfulfill plans, many customer enterprises suffer and this often leads to adverse consequences even at those plants that have obtained realistic plans. In cases where enterprises overfulfill plans, evidence reveals that above-plan output often does not serve to satisfy customer needs or consumer demand.[24]

Managers frequently disregard products and product specifications stipulated in their assortment plans in order to fulfill and overfulfill aggregate success indicators, and often substitute unneeded or unsaleable items in their place. This is most pronounced in the consumer goods sector although probably a major portion of the product mix at a given enterprise conforms to plan, evidence clearly reveals that a substantial portion at numerous enterprises does not.[25] The emphasis on cost results does not insure that the enterprise's product mix will be according to plan, or that delivery schedules will be executed on time. The cost index does not

[23] *Ibid.,* See also, *Pravda,* July 14 and 23, and, September 13, 1962; O. Antonov, in CDSP, XIV:21, 1962.

[24] Cf., *Pravda,* July 20, 1960; J. Berliner, 1960, *op. cit.*

[25] Cf., A. Nove, 1961, *op. cit.,* chapter 6; Richman, dissertation, *op. cit.,* chapter 8; *Pravda,* June 26 and September 9, 1962; *Izvestia,* May 6 and August 28, 1961; *Ekon. Gaz.,* December 25, 1961.

provide a measure of the commercial success of the enterprise. As long as the total cost of producing finished goods does not exceed the plan, the cost target is considered fulfilled even if goods rot in warehouses. Whether the product mix is according to plan is of no significance in computing cost results.

The switch to cost results as the key success indicator has greatly intensified output quality distortions.[26] Although quality of output is a necessary condition for the receipt of premiums at some consumer goods producers, quality distortions are often successfully undertaken in devious ways. Substandard output in the consumer goods sector has become such a severe problem that a state campaign is currently being waged against quality deterioration.[27]

There are certain penalties, such as fines, used by the state to induce producers to fulfill assortment plans in terms of stipulated specifications. However, evidence clearly indicates that these penalties are frequently ineffective and not enforced.[28] Customers often have no choice but to accept substandard goods and items not in accordance with plans. Plan fulfillment would be even more difficult for them if they did not, since there is usually no other source of supply readily available. In addition, they are usually reluctant to alienate suppliers by pressing for penalties for fear of upsetting future relations. In cases where the customer enterprise is of very high priority in the eyes of the state, managers of the supplier enterprises would rarely engage in output distortions since severe penalties may result.

Evidence also reveals that managers, particularly those at enterprises having difficult plans, ignore innovation tasks and various other "planned obligations" such as maintenance, repairs, and labor training in their efforts to fulfill and overfulfill success indicators.[29] Hence many activities which would result in favorable long run benefits to both the enterprise and society are sacrificed.

Managers at enterprises with easy plans rarely overfulfill success indicators beyond the point where allowable quarterly incentive compensation is

[26] Cf., most of the sources cited in footnote 25, above. CDSP, IV:21, 1962, p. 15; G. Dikhtiar, "Soviet Trade in the Period of Full-Scale Building of Communism," Problems of Economics, August, 1962.

[27] It is interesting to note that a director of a shoe factory interviewed by the writer has recently been fined and imprisoned for quality distortions at his enterprise; Izvestia, August 27, 1961.

[28] See most of the sources cited in footnote 13, above. See also, Pravda, July 14, 1962. E. Johnson, "Planning and Contract Law," Soviet Studies, 1961. In addition to the attitudes of customers and those officials responsible for controlling enterprise output distortions, penalties and controls are often ineffective because it is difficult to attribute blame for distortions to a given producer since it, in turn, may have received faulty supplies.

[29] Cf., Richman, in California Management Review, op. cit., Richman, dissertation, op. cit., chapters 10 and 11; A. Nove, 1961, op. cit., chapter 6.

maximized, as this would lead to more difficult plans in the future. Thus many enterprises that overfulfill plans are still in possession of excess capacity and resources.[30] There is no cost or penalty entailed for maintaining excess working capital and equipment. Managers also currently falsify actual operating results in their attempts to obtain premiums. This situation has been so serious recently that a state decree provides for stiff sanctions including imprisonment.[31]

Many managers still engage in illegal procurement activities in their attempts to obtain enough resources to fulfill aggregate output targets.[32] In many instances such activities deflect earmarked resources from other enterprises, thus causing them to underfulfill their plans. This greatly aggravates the supply problem in Soviet industry.

Concluding Remarks on Soviet Industry

It is apparent that the reforms undertaken by the Soviets to eliminate undesirable managerial behavior and improve economic results have not been effective. Undesirable managerial practices and poor results, now as in the past, are not due to mere idiosyncracies or a lack of patriotism. Rather, this is due to certain shortcomings in the rules of the game within which Soviet managers are supposed to operate. The principal shortcomings remain the system of success indicators on the one hand, and the deficient provision of resources to enterprises on the other hand. The two interact causing a vicious circle that greatly hinders managerial performance and economic results.

While aggregate output targets for some industrial sectors are modestly overfulfilled, and barely fulfilled in others, a significant portion of economic growth is not meaningful since it represents unsaleable, unusable and unneeded output.[33] In addition, the rate of Soviet industrial growth is de-

---

[30] Cf., *Pravda*, October 12, 1962, p. 3; *CDSP*, XIV:41, 1962, p. 16; B. Miroshnichenko "Problems of National Economic Planning," *Problems of Economics*, IV:2, 1961.

[31] *Pravda*, May 25, 1961.

[32] Cf., *Pravda*, June 26, 1962; *Izvestia*, July 14, 1962; Richman, dissertation, *op. cit.*, Chapter 5.

[33] Not all of the wasteful output in the consumer goods sector can be attributed to undesirable managerial practices since the trade officials who perform the major tasks of demand analysis are often ineffective in their job. However, most sources attribute a major share of the blame to managerial practices at producing enterprises; cf., the sources cited in footnotes 24, 25 and 26 above. There are literally millions of rubles of unneeded, unsaleable and unusable output produced each year: Cf., *Izvestia*, February 21, 1960, December 21, 1961, April 15, 1962. To cite one concrete example of the extent of waste one source reveals that as of January 1962 there were about 2 billion (new) rubles of unsaleable and unplanned output of consumer goods in the Soviet economy; about ⅓ of all consumer goods produced in the Russian Republic were of substandard quality reflecting much spoilage (G. Dikhtiar, *op. cit.*). See also recent sources on national plan fulfillment, *Pravda*, January 23, and July 21, 1962.

clining.[34] The inefficiencies present in the economy, arising from the inability to properly match productive resources through well designed enterprise plans, greatly impedes meaningful economic growth.[35]

The problems remain critical, perhaps more critical than ever, and the Soviets, once again, are looking to new reforms to improve the situation. Many of these reforms are similar to the Czech reforms of 1958–59, and we will postpone our analysis of them until we have explored the Czech situation.

Managerial Motivation in Czechoslovak Enterprise in Current Times

The Reforms[36]

During 1958–59 there were certain major reforms introduced in Czechoslovak industry dealing with organization, planning and monetary incentives for enterprise managers and employees. These reforms were undertaken to stimulate a more efficient utilization of enterprise resources, the design of sounder operating plans, greater concern for customer needs and consumer demand, and better innovation results.

In 1958, the newly projected annual rate of growth of industrial production until 1965 was somewhat less than preceding years.[37] The Czechs, like the Soviets, had been experiencing much waste and inefficiency because of the establishment of strained national plans. While material resources were overcommitted and the supply situation was quite severe, manpower shortages was the greater problem. The labor force, in terms of quantity and skills, could not keep pace with the growing productive capacity of the country.

[34] Cf., W. Nutter, *op. cit.*, pp. 223–224.

[35] The Soviets are having great trouble in properly matching productive resources primarily as a result of faulty information provided by enterprise managers. To cite a few concrete examples of inefficiency: Checks at 408 enterprises in 33 regions disclosed 4 billion (old) rubles of idle and uninstalled equipment; as of April 30, 1960, there was 18 million rubles worth of idle machinery and equipment at plants in the Russian Republic, CDSP, XIII:43, 1960, pp. 23–24. CDSP, XI:49, 1959, p. 3ff., reveals that checks at a large number of plants in various regions disclosed excess hoarded supplies to the extent of 15 million rubles, while numerous other plants were confronted with supply shortages to the extent of billions of rubles. Because of extreme inefficiency and waste in the economy, and various other reasons, the latest indications are that the Soviets have scrapped the last two years of the current Seven-Year-Plan in favor of a more realistic plan. See, *Los Angeles Times*, Section G, p. 14, March 17, 1963.

[36] In addition to information obtained from personal interviews the following sources discuss the recent reforms. R. Lavicka and J. Toman, *op. cit.* A series of articles in *Organizace a Planovani Socialistichaho Prumysloveho Podniky* (Statni Pedagogicke Nakladateistui, Prague, 1961). Articles in *Patnact let Hospodarskvi Lidove Demokraticheho Ceskoslovenska* (Statni Pedagogicke Nakladateistui, Prague, 1960). See also J. Michal, *Central Planning in Czechoslovakia*, p. 58ff. (Stanford University Press, 1960).

[37] See, J. Michal, *op. cit.*, p. 55.

As of 1958 enterprises were reorganized into multiplant production monopolies, called economic production units, according to branch of industry. Both horizontal and vertical integration took place, and the related units engaged in activities corresponding to the same product line. The reorganization has facilitated the timely receipt of supplies among related plants. The number of independent whole production units has been reduced by two-thirds. The new large enterprises now have considerably more bargaining with other supplier enterprises, thus reducing the uneven market power of suppliers. Enterprise management has been delegated much more authority over the use of funds, the working out of plan indices, and in negotiations with customers and suppliers. The enterprise now partakes in market and demand analysis to a much greater extent. Central authorities still approve enterprise aggregate output and labor productivity targets. They also allocate and approve the output assortment of key commodities, but the total number of commodities subject to central decision has been substantially reduced. Enterprises are now much freer to determine and negotiate their supply needs and product mixes with customers and suppliers. While central authorities still make major investment decisions, enterprise managers have a much greater amount of investment funds at their disposal. Central authorities still issue directives on some major product and technological innovation tasks.

The current system of enterprise success indicators and related incentives has been designed to encourage managers to strive for tight but realistic plans. Monetary gain to personnel is progressively higher where more difficult targets are initiated and fulfilled by the enterprise. There is also an operational five-year plan to which the system of incentives is linked.

There are two major sources of incentive compensation at Czechoslovak enterprises. First, wages of all personnel, including managements, are directly linked to labor productivity targets. The higher the increase in labor productivity planned for and achieved by the enterprise for a given year, the larger the enterprise payroll. This emphasis on labor productivity is chiefly in response to manpower shortages. The formulae linking average wages and payroll to labor productivity differ by branch of industry. They are worked out by central authorities taking into account the availability of adequately skilled labor and technology in a given branch.

The second source of managerial incentives is related to profits. The higher the planned profit target undertaken and achieved by the enterprise, the greater would be the proportion and total amount of profits that could be retained by the enterprise. In addition, at most enterprises, the amount of profits retained is also related to the amount of enterprise fixed and working capital. This essentially represents enterprise rate of return, and managers are rewarded for achieving profit targets with a minimum of fixed and working capital. They can, however, invest retained profits in order to further increase their profits in the future. The proportion of allowable retained profits at Czechoslovak enterprises is many times larger than at Soviet plants. It is much more beneficial for the enterprise to fulfill a fairly ambitious profit target than to overfulfill an easy one, although absolute benefits do vary with total results. In many cases the amount of total retainable profits would be about double if ambitious plans were initiated to begin with.[38] A portion of retained profits is used for the payment of bonuses to management each month, quarter or year. The rate of retained profits as well as the conditions for incentive payments vary somewhat by branch of industry, and in some cases for individual plants. As part of the switch to profit as a key success indicator it was necessary to revise the fixed wholesale prices of most products, and to determine the rates of retained profits in light of a given type of enterprise's ability to make profits.

The maximum allowable bonuses to management for a given period varies from 25% to 50% of basic wages depending on type of enterprise. In order to pay out any bonuses to management from earned profits, certain other plan indices must be fulfilled. The nature of these indices varies in light of the specific conditions deemed most important by the state for a given branch of industry, or large plant. For example, where a major portion of an enterprise's output is for export, quality, and not necessarily cost of production, is often an obligatory condition. At some enterprises where shortages of the commodity exists, aggregate output is an obligatory condition. For some machinery producers certain major product or technological innovation measures are obligatory conditions. Since there are substantially fewer enterprises and obligatory plan indices to be controlled by superior authorities in Czechoslovakia as compared with Russia, such control in the former country is less difficult and more effective.

Incentive compensation is provided for in the enterprise plan. Rates for progressive wages and profit retention, as well as other conditions for incentive payments, are known in advance. The size of the wage fund and the amount of retainable profits are determined on an annual basis in light of the planned obligations undertaken by the enterprise, but the basic rules remain unchanged for the duration of the long-range (five-year) plan.

Product and technological innovation are closely linked to the long range and annual enterprise plans. Even in their five-year plans, enterprises have fairly detailed assignments for significant innovation measures. A serious attempt is made to provide adequate funds and resources for enterprise innovation, and a major portion of financial resources is derived from earned profits. Financial means for innovation can be carried over from year to year. The planned profit performance over time attempts to take into account the short-run handicaps placed on profit performance by innovation activities. Should benefits from innovation be reaped only after

[38] This was the case at the Czechoslovak enterprises visited.

two or three years, an attempt is made to provide for this in the five-year plan. Decentralized investment and the introduction of new technology often enable substantial increases in profit and labor productivity over the five-year period, and the more rapid the introduction and perfection of such measures the greater will be total enterprise benefits over this period. The assortment and quantities of important type of new products, such as machinery, to be produced by a given enterprise are indicated in its long range plans. Contractual obligations between suppliers and customers for such new products must be adhered to lest the profit performance of the supplier suffer.

Analysis of Current Problems and Managerial Behavior

Evidence indicates that while many enterprises undertake fairly ambitious plans on their own initiative, apparently many still try to obtain modest plans.[39] There are a number of reasons for this. No doubt even in cases where adequate resources are assured, some managers, out of habit, still feel more secure with modest plans that can readily be fulfilled. While the reorganization of enterprises and the strengthening of the bargaining position of buyers apparently have improved the supply situation, there are still shortages of some commodities, such as metals.[40] More significant is the problem of inadequate manpower facing many enterprises. In addition to true labor shortages there is much evidence of absenteeism and laziness on the part of some workers, particularly since the shift to incentives based on collective results.[41] The overall manpower situation tends to induce many managers to understate enterprise potential, and to establish loose plant labor norms.[42] Czech authorities interviewed by this writer also attributed foreign trade activities as a factor inducing some managers to seek modest plans. This country engages extensively in foreign trade, and there are frequent changes in export needs. Such changes often result in central directives to enterprises concerning their product mixes. These directives usually take priority, thus upsetting enterprise plans and operations. For this reason managers at some enterprises producing export goods often maintain substantial excess reserves for flexibility purposes.

Managers confronted with supply and/or manpower shortages currently engage in a variety of undesirable practices in their attempts to fulfill both profit and labor productivity targets. Because of manpower problems over-

[39] See *Summary of the Czechoslovak Provincial Press*, translated by U.S. Joint Publications Research Service, (JPRS, Washington, D.C.), February 6, 1962, No. 134; December 29, 1961, No. 128; November 2, 1961, No. 120.

[40] *Ibid.*, November 17, 1961, No. 121; September 12, 1961, No. III. See also Antonin Novotny (First Secretary of the Czechoslovak Communist Party Central Committee), *Current State of the Economy*, translated by JPRS, December 18, 1961.

[41] *Summary of the Czechoslovak Provincial Press*, November 21, 1961, No. 123; October 6, 1961, No. 116; September 15, 1961, No. 112; December 29, 1961, No. 128.

[42] *Ibid.*

time work is sometimes required to fulfill labor productivity targets. This has an adverse impact on cost of production, and hence profit results. In an effort to compensate for overtime labor costs and fulfill the profit target, quantity of production often suffers and violations in the assortment plan occur. Product mix and quality distortions are still most pronounced when the customer is not of very high priority, but the extent of such distortions appears to be less than in the past probably because of the strengthening of all enterprises in their roles as customers. Nevertheless, evidence indicates that many enterprises still produce substandard output, items not according to specification, and unplanned items, in order to fulfill profit targets and derive a favorable rate of return.[43] This aggravates the supply situation, although in many cases the unplanned output produced does often satisfy the needs of society at least to some degree, but forfeited output may be in greater need or demand.[44] Profits do depend on actual sales, and the production of completely useless or unneeded goods, regardless of their profit margins, would generally tend to be discouraged.

The price structure and the lack of alternate sources of supply are at the root of the product mix problem. Wholesale prices of nearly all standardized commodities are fixed by the state, and remain unchanged for the duration of the five-year plan. Because of volume, cost patterns and various other improvements realized, some items became much more profitable to produce than others over time. If shortages arise, there are no price increases to spur increased output of scarce items and there are few, if any, alternative sources of supply. For this reason the allocation of various commodities that become scarce must be decentralized from time to time.[45] In cases where the enterprise can directly influence prices of certain kinds of output, management frequently engages in much cost-price inflation to insure for plan fulfillment.[46] Czech officials interviewed claim that this is one of the most serious undesirable managerial practices, and the most difficult to control.

Innovation tasks as well as other measures beneficial for the long run, such as maintenance and repairs, are often sacrificed in order to fulfill annual profit and labor productivity targets.[47] Evidence also indicates that in many cases long-range plans are not as operational as central authorities

[43] *Ibid.*, November 17, 1961, No. 122; April 8, 1961, No. 93; January 15, 1962, No. 139; A. Novotny, *op. cit.*

[44] *Ibid.*, November 17, 1961, No. 120; January 15, 1962, No. 132.

[45] *Rude Pravo*, Prague, December 1, 1961, translated in *JPRS*, No. 11685, December 28, 1961, p. 73ff; see also A. Nove, 1961, *op. cit.*, 242–246.

[46] *Summary of the Czechoslovak Provincial Press, op. cit.*, October 25, 1961, No. 119; November 2, 1961, No. 120; March 14, 1961, No. 88; April 18, 1961, No. 93. Price inflation is possible with custom-built and unstandardized products, new products, and products where design and specification changes are understaken. This is also true at Soviet plants, see Richman, in *Soviet Studies, op. cit.*

[47] *Ibid.*, September 20, 1961, No. 113; March 7, 1962, No. 141; March 5, 1962, No. 139; A. Novotny, *op. cit.*

would like them to be. Since long range targets and rules of the game remain intact regardless of changing conditions, product mix, quality, innovation and various other results are not those most desired by the state. There are also problems relating to the establishment of effective formulae which link wages to the growth of labor productivity. Evidence reveals that many such formulae are ineffective, and that it is difficult to maintain a proper and efficient relationship between wages and labor productivity.[48]

Concluding Remarks on Czechoslovak Industry

Czech industrial officials and economists interviewed readily admit that a number of problems must still be "ironed out" in Czechoslovak industry. However, they, as well as current sources, assert that recent reforms have had a very favorable impact on managerial behavior. It is claimed that the reforms, in total, have improved the utilization of enterprise resources, the satisfaction of customer needs and consumer demand, and innovation. They have also discouraged many enterprises from striving for deficient easy plans. This in turn has led to a better harmony of interests between the state and managers during the planning process. Thus, unfruitful time and expense which result from arbitrary planning is reduced. Finally, it has made planning more stable and it is now easier to coordinate the economy. There are not nearly as many plants substantially underfulfilling their plans as in the past.

These assertions no doubt suggest a rosier picture than actually exists. There is, however, other evidence that suggests significant improvements have occurred. Following the implementation of the reforms, the national plans for 1958 and 1959 were overfulfilled beyond expectations. The growth in industrial production surpassed the average annual growth as planned for the 1960–65 period. As a result the targets for the 1960–65 five-year plan were revised upwards,[49] and to date evidence indicates that most of these targets are being achieved.[50] While there has been, and still is, considerable evidence of waste and inefficiency in the economy, it is probably less severe than in the past since the planners would otherwise probably not have revised the targets upwards. The recent results of the consumer goods sector — in the past a low priority sector in which much waste occurred — have led to special plaudits from Czech leaders.[51]

More important, perhaps, is the fact that in spite of existing problems, there do not appear to be any major reforms contemplated by the Czechs. This is not true in the Soviet Union where many of the reforms proposed, and being experimented with, are similar to the recent Czech reforms.

---

[48] *Ibid.*, January 12, 1962, No. 131; March 5, 1962, No. 139; March 2, 1962, No. 138.
[49] See J. Michal, *op. cit.*, Appendix.
[50] Cf., *Rude Pravo*, Prague, December 1, 1961, translated in JPRS, No. 11685, December 28, 1961, p. 69ff.
[51] *Ibid.*, p. 77.

This in itself leads us to conclude that the current Czechoslovak system does not have definite advantages over their former system, and over the existing Soviet system. Of course, some of these advantages can be attributed to the much smaller size of the Czechoslovak planned economy.

The Winds of Change in the Soviet Union

Currently, Soviet sources are voicing continuous and widespread criticisms of shortcomings in the economic structure which greatly hinder managerial performance. There are many proposed changes in the rules of the game within which managers must operate. What is most striking is that the reforms under study, and being implemented, are less trammeled by dictates of traditional ideology than ever before.

Many prominent Soviet economists, planners, academicians, and industrial managers are clamoring that profitability should become the key enterprise success indicator.[52] There are indications that this will take place in the foreseeable future. While Mr. Khrushchev has postponed a final decision on this matter he has paved the way by the following statement: "We should remember V. I. Lenin's directive that we be able, if necessary, to learn from the capitalists, to adopt whatever they have that is sensible and advantageous."[53]

Under the proposed system, which is being experimented with at a number of different types of enterprises, each enterprise would measure its rate-of-return on fixed and working capital. The object here is to induce enterprises to utilize more efficiently their fixed assets and inventories, and to be more concerned about customer needs and consumer demand, since the way to derive a higher return would be to produce and sell more with given resources. Managers would be rewarded depending on the rate of return of their enterprise. The size of bonuses would depend on the rate of increase of profitability each year, within the framework of the enterprise's long-range plan. As is the case in Czechoslovakia, the rules would be fixed for the duration of the long-range plan.

A manager would propose his own rate-of-return each year, and at the outset of the long-range plan. The higher the rate-of-return proposed, the bigger the potential rewards he would be paid if he achieves the target

[52] The proposed reforms dealing with profitability are known as the Liberman Plan. These reforms appeared in *Pravda*, September 6, 1962 (translated in CDSP, XIV:36, 1962, p. 13ff.), and they were elaborated in *Ekonomicheskaya Gazeta*, November 10, 1962. The editors of *Pravda* applauded Liberman's proposals asking for comments from the masses. (This procedure usually indicates that Soviet leaders intend to adopt the proposals, perhaps with some modifications.) The responses by industrial officials, planners and economists — some of them very prominent — have given overwhelming support to the Liberman plan, with only a few exceptions. See, for example, *Pravda*, September 13, 21, and 26, 1962. See also translations in CDSP, XIV:37, 38, 39, 45 and 48, 1962; and A. Nove, 1963, *op. cit.*

[53] N. S. Khrushchev, *Pravda*, November 20, 1962. (Translated in CDSP, XIV:47, 1962, p. 3ff.)

figures. Higher authorities would continue to approve only aggregate gross output, major items of the product mix and delivery schedules to be met. The enterprise would retain, and have more control over, a much greater share of profits earned. This provides for much decentralized investment. This system would generally provide for much more autonomy at the enterprise level, and Soviet experts agree that this is necessary in light of the cumbersome bureaucratic apparatus with which the manager must deal. The enterprise would still be assigned, in aggregates, the bulk of the necessary resources to accomplish its job. Depending on type of enterprise, a small number of other indices would also have to be fulfilled for bonuses to be paid, and this again is similar to the Czech system. Absolute monetary rewards would still be greater if targets are overfulfilled, but much more substantial bonuses would be earned for bidding high at the outset and then accomplishing the task. It is also urged that the costs and over-all impact of product and technological innovation be given proper weight when drawing up and approving enterprise plans.

It is anticipated that the above system will motivate managers to initiate sound rather than easy plans, and that adequate attention will be given to innovation. It is also hoped that artificial shortages will disappear. Under present conditions, the enterprise manager has an incentive to maintain excess resources of all types; under the proposed system it is hoped that he will desire to minimize such holdings. The above scheme would not prove effective in practice unless the situation of supply uncertainty confronting enterprises is eliminated. For no manager would initiate ambitious plans as long as this situation persists.

At present, a customer enterprise receiving defective merchandise has no incentive not to accept it, since such merchandise may be better than nothing. The proposed profitability scheme also offers no alternative supplies to hapless customers, except that completely useless supplies would undoubtedly be rejected since enterprise rate-of-return would be lowered. Soviet experts agree that variations in profits in light of the product mix produced can not be avoided. The product mix problem remains critical, and the experts hopefully claim that enterprises would not make profitable but unneeded and unsaleable items since such output would always be refused by customers. Given the inflexibility with respect to alternative sources of supply, and the existing lack of effective controls over product mix distortions, this is a mere aspiration. The problem would be most acute in connection with the delivery of consumer goods to the wholesale trade organizations. For officials at these trade organs are also not evaluated on the basis of sales to ultimate consumers.

In order to grant considerable authority to enterprise managers in a country as vast as the Soviet Union, objective criteria that serve as guidelines to managerial behavior are essential for effective results. In any measure of profitability prices are critical. It is clearly acknowledged by the

Soviets that the bonus system linked to profitability must be established taking fully into account the ability of a given enterprise to make profit in light of the pricing structure. To do this would be a very formidable task in a country having many thousands of enterprises. If prices are too high, enterprises would make profits without effort. Since factories are producing mainly for assigned customers who badly need the items, demand factors are not particularly meaningful in the Soviet Union at present, nor would they be under the proposed profit scheme. Wholesale prices for goods in the Soviet Union, like Czechoslovakia, are quite inflexible, being set at infrequent intervals by the planners on the basis of average costs (plus a small profit margin) for an industrial sector that produces the item in question. For this reason product mix distortions would not be eliminated, as is the case in Czechoslovakia.

The Soviets realize that the effective adoption of the proposed profit motive scheme must be preceded by a major overhauling of the pricing structure. There is currently much discussion about pricing reforms, and some revisions in fixed prices have begun in 1962. In general, however, there is no accord among the experts on how to handle the pricing problem. They all agree that prices are reviewed and revised too late, and that prices must be "simultaneously flexible and stable." Many Soviet economists and planners have their own ideas on how this may best be done. Although an effective solution has not yet evolved it appears that the proposed profitability scheme would be accompanied by some system that enables timely revision of prices on the basis of current rather than historical conditions.[54] Such changes hopefully would prevent easy profits from being made, as well as correcting potential inequities where prices are too low. This type of price fixing would place new responsibilities on the planners, since errors here could easily vitiate the entire plan.

Closely related to profitability is the proposal that interest charges on capital be adopted, and that these charges be included in production costs. In addition, depreciation charges would be made on uninstalled and un-utilized equipment (this is not the case now). These proposals have the support of top-level authorities, and it is hoped that if they are implemented, managers would be more reluctant to maintain idle plant and equipment.[55]

Another proposed reform is that enterprise payroll be linked to labor productivity in a way similar to that existing in Czechoslovakia.[56] This

[54] See especially the discussions on pricing in CDSP, XIV:48, 1962, p. 31; L. Maizenberg, "Revision of Wholesale Prices and Some Problems of Price Formation in the U.S.S.R." (translated in Problems of Economics, June, 1962); Izvestia, November 29, 1962, p. 3; and most of the sources cited in footnote 20 above.

[55] C.f., papers recently presented at a major Soviet economic conference, reported in Ekon. Gaz., October 16, 1961. See also, V. Nemchinov in Pravda, September 21, 1962; and A. Nove, 1963, op. cit., p. 13.

[56] C.f., Z. Atlas, Ekon. Gaz., October 16, 1961.

proposal has not, however, received much support from Soviet leaders. Any attempt to link wages to labor productivity would require a complete overhauling of wage structure. In addition, a thorough study of the different technical conditions existing in the different sectors and myriad of plants would be necessary to establish effective formulae. Because of the size of the country, and the greatly differing technical conditions, this would be an immense problem.

Still another proposed reform, now being implemented, is the establishment of so-called "firms" which are somewhat similar to the Czechoslovak economic production units. This entails both horizontal and vertical mergers among producing enterprises. A chief aim here is to give the much larger amalgamated firm more bargaining power with suppliers. It is hoped that in this way suppliers will pay more attention to the needs of the firm, and that resources will be more efficiently utilized within the firm. In case of vertical integration it is anticipated that greater dependability of supply will also occur. For example, clothing producers merged with cloth producers might well eliminate many of the product mix, quality, and delivery time problems.

This type of merger movement is already underway at several different types of enterprises in various regions, and the trend is growing.[57] Mr. Khrushchev, himself, has endorsed the idea, and it is likely that it will continue.[58] It is also proposed that consumer goods producers be integrated into the trade and retail complex, possibly by opening up their own stores. This type of reorganization in the consumers goods sector is only being tried on a very limited scale; but if it becomes more widespread it could well induce producers to be more concerned about consumer demand. The merger trend in conjunction with a profit motive could probably somewhat reduce product mix distortions and the supply problem.

It has also been proposed that more effective control over enterprise operations, particularly product mix and quality distortions, can be derived by reorganizing economic regions. There are presently 103 economic regions in the Soviet Union, each with its own petty prerogatives, and the resulting "localism" in the industrial sector has not led to good economic results. The proposal, now approved by Khrushchev, calls for an integration of many economic regions along more autarkic lines, making regions as self-sufficient as possible in economic terms.[59]

It is possible that this proposed reorganization is part of a longer range plan which would have enterprises under the jurisdiction of 17 large geographical territories.[60] It is hoped that this will insure uniform territorial

---

[57] For actual examples see *CDSP*; 7, 20, 21, 25, 26 and 48, 1962; *Pravda*, June 19, 20 and 29, 1962; and *Izvestia*, February 18, June 19 and 22, 1962.

[58] N. S. Khrushchev, *op. cit.*, and *Izvestia*, May 18, 1962.

[59] N. S. Khrushchev, *op. cit.*

[60] *Ekonomicheskaya Gazeta*, May 28, 1961; and *Pravda*, February 23, 1962.

growth and development, and the construction of complementary enterprises within each region. It is possible that each territory would become fairly autonomous with central decisions pertaining primarily to strategic considerations such as national defense, transportation and certain highly important commodities.

The nature of the above proposals suggests the difficulty the Soviets have with interregional dealings between widely scattered enterprises with widely differing interests. If an optimum span of control combined with a high degree of self sufficiency can be achieved, this would probably do much to reduce waste and inefficiency in the Soviet economy. It remains to be seen whether this *can* be achieved.

The difficulties many factories have in obtaining the proper type of components and raw materials from designated suppliers have led to suggestions that most trading in commodities of an industrial nature be changed to a type of state trading. Here, firms would be free to buy from any supplier they chose, excepting only certain key commodities in short supply.[61] Prices would be fixed by the state, but the firms would be free to pick and choose. While this proposal has been fairly extensively discussed, it has thus far received little support from top leaders in the Soviet Union. Such a system could perhaps eventually become widespread in conjunction with various types of minor commodities.

The adoption and extensive implementation of the above reforms could probably somewhat improve managerial performance and economic results. The extent of the improvements depend on how effectively the propoals are implemented in practice. The key to substantial improvements may well depend on the effectiveness of the pricing system in conjunction with a meaningful profit motive, and more operational long-range plans. The Soviets will probably have more difficulty in deriving substantial improvements than the Czechs because of the vast size and greater complexity of their planned economy.

Conclusions

It is clear that both the Soviets and Czechs — particularly the former — are encountering severe difficulties in structuring their economies to provide enterprise managers the proper incentives to obtain desired results. Adherence to Communist theology and the difficulties encountered in developing an integrated and workable plan have led to serious operational problems in both countries.

When theology in economics breaks down the dogma has to be discarded. The stakes — in terms of demonstrating the superiority of the

[61] See V. Nemchinov, *Voprosy Ekonomiki*, 1960, No. 12; and *Pravda*, September 21, 1962.

communist system — are too large to allow for failure through blind adherence to faith. Hence, major shifts occur in the rules of the game in these states. Ironically enough, the measures adopted and being considered are converging toward capitalist techniques to a considerable extent.

It is clear that the communist states do not hesitate to modify their system when it proves defective. The alternative systems of profitability, enterprise mergers, decentralization of authority, interest charges on capital, more operational long-range plans, and other reforms may turn out to be more workable in terms of economic results. However, the absence of a market-price mechanism, a capitalistic profit motive, and competition impedes efficient resource utilization, the satisfaction of customer needs and consumer demand, and innovation. As the Czech and Soviet economies become more complex, and as the base level upon which meaningful industrial growth is measured becomes higher, these problems will no doubt become more acute. The communist countries may once again have to undertake major structural reforms. Developments in the communist bloc are worth close observation by Western scholars and businessmen. Perhaps in the long run the communist and capitalist systems may turn out to be much more similar than initially contemplated.

A B C D E F G H I J — R — 7 3 2 1 0 / 6 9 8 7 6